THIS IS POETRY

FORUM PUBLICATIONS LTD.

Published by
Forum Publications Ltd.
23 Washington Street, Cork.
Tel: (021) 4270525 · (021) 4270500
Fax: (01) 6335347

Additional writing and research by Siobhán Collins

Design and layout: Dominic Carroll

ISBN: 978-1-906565-01-5

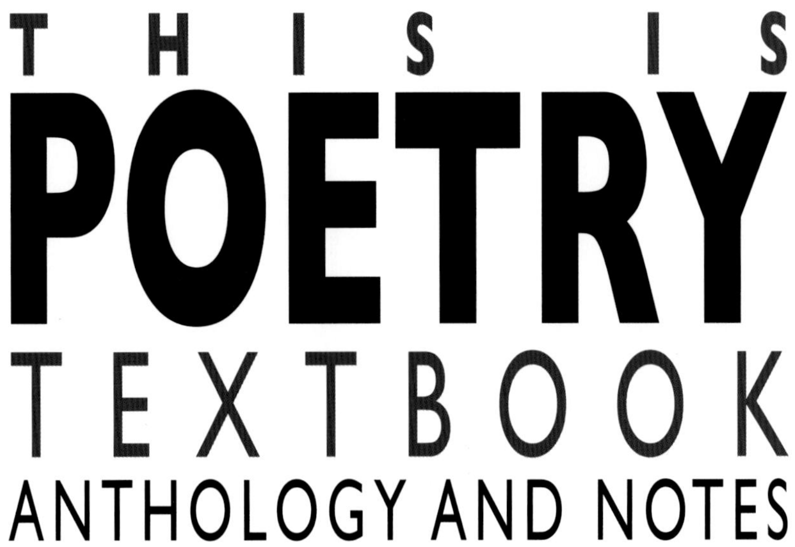

HIGHER LEVEL LEAVING CERT

2010

Brian Forristal & Billy Ramsell

FORUM PUBLICATIONS LTD.

POEMS

NOTES

EAVAN BOLAND

BIOGRAPHY

Eavan Boland was born in Dublin in 1944. Her father was a diplomat and her mother was a well-known painter. At the age of six she and her family moved to London, when her father was posted to the Irish diplomatic service there. Boland seems to have found it somewhat difficult growing up in England, where she experienced some anti-Irish prejudice.

These experiences, expressed in her poem 'An Irish Childhood in England: 1951', made her keenly aware of her Irish heritage.

She later returned to Ireland where she attended Trinity College and began writing poetry. As she puts it in her book *Object Lessons*: 'I began writing poetry in the Dublin of the early Sixties'. She found 1960s' Dublin a supportive and inspirational environment for a budding writer: 'The pubs were crowded. The cafés were full of apprentice writers like myself, some of them talking about literature, a very few talking intensely about poetry'. In this atmosphere of pints, coffee and literary chat Boland's talent began to flourish and she composed the poems that featured in her first book, entitled *New Territory*, which was published when she was only twenty-two.

Her life changed, however, when she married, had her first child, and moved to the suburb of Dundrum. Boland suddenly found herself occupying two very different and opposing roles; as a poet on the one hand, and as wife and mother on the other. Initially, Boland saw no contradiction between her duties as a mother and her aspirations as a poet: 'I wanted there to be no contradiction between the way I made an assonance fit a line and the way I lifted up a child at night'. She quickly discovered, however, that there was no real tradition of poetry about motherhood and the duties of the housewife: 'poetic conventions ... whispered to me that the daily things I did, things which seemed to me important and human, were not fit material for poetry'.

No longer was she a part of Dublin's artistic society, frequenting the city's trendy bars and literary cafés. Instead, she was confined to the comfortable safety of the suburbs. Though living only a few miles from the city centre, Boland felt half a world away from the vibrant artistic scene she had been part of as a student. To her literary friends who haunted the city centre the suburbs might as well not have existed: 'Only a few miles away was the almost invisible world that everyone knew and no one referred to. Of suburbs and housing estates. Of children and women. Of fires lighted for the first winter chill; of food put on the table. The so-called ordinary world ... was not even mentioned'.

Boland's new writing began to explore this 'ordinary world'. She turned away from the romantic and traditional poems she had written in college: 'The poems I had been writing no longer seemed necessary or true'. Her new work would focus on her life as a married mother, dealing with themes such as love and marriage, children and motherhood, and the seemingly ordinary life of the suburbs. She began to write 'On rainy winter afternoons, with the dusk drawn in, the fire lighted and the child asleep upstairs'.

Boland's poetry gradually won her more and more attention. Volumes such as 1975's *The War Horse* (which contains 'The War Horse', 'The Famine Road' and 'Child of Our Time'), *In Her Own Image* and *Night Feed* established Boland as a woman writing about a woman's experiences – something that was extremely rare in Irish poetry: 'I know now that I began writing in a country where the word woman and the word poet were almost magnetically opposed'. These volumes staked out Boland's poetic territory, establishing the concerns that would dominate her poetic career: history and its victims, Ireland and Irishness, myth, and the beauty of the everyday.

From the late Sixties to the late Eighties Boland worked as a freelance journalist and broadcaster, writing articles for the *Irish Times* and producing programmes for RTÉ. Since the mid-Eighties she has taught writing at several American colleges, including the prestigious International Writing Program at the University of Iowa. She is currently a professor of English at Stanford University and divides her time between Ireland and the US.

Yet despite this success, for Boland the contradiction between being a woman and a poet was never completely resolved: 'These, after all, are the two lives – a woman's and a poet's – that I have lived and understood. They are the lives whose aspirations I honour and they remain divided'. Instead of healing this division, Boland uses the tension it creates as the spur for poetic creativity, as the impetus to create a fresh style of writing with a radically different subject matter.

The War Horse

This dry night, nothing unusual
About the clip, clop, casual

Iron of his shoes as he stamps death
Like a mint on the innocent coinage of earth.

I lift the window, watch the ambling feather
Of hock and fetlock, loosed from its daily tether

In the tinker camp on the Enniskerry Road,
Pass, his breath hissing, his snuffling head

Down. He is gone. No great harm is done.
Only a leaf of our laurel hedge is torn –

Of distant interest like a maimed limb,
Only a rose which now will never climb

The stone of our house, expendable, a mere
Line of defence against him, a volunteer

You might say, only a crocus, its bulbous head
Blown from growth, one of the screamless dead.

But we, we are safe, our unformed fear
Of fierce commitment gone; why should we care

If a rose, a hedge, a crocus are uprooted
Like corpses, remote, crushed, mutilated?

He stumbles on like a rumour of war, huge
Threatening. The neighbours use the subterfuge

Of curtains. He stumbles down our short street
Thankfully passing us. I pause, wait,

Then to breathe relief lean on the sill
And for a second only my blood is still

With atavism. That rose he smashed frays
Ribboned across our hedge, recalling days

Of burned countryside, illicit braid:
A cause ruined before, a world betrayed.

[4] **mint:** *place where coins are made.*
[6] **hock:** *joint in the hind leg.*
[6] **fetlock:** *joint of a horse's leg between the knee and the hoof.*
[27] **atavism:** *the return to something ancient or ancestral.*

COMPREHENSION

Some months later I began to write a poem. I called it 'The War Horse'. It's argument was gathered around the opposition of force and formality. Of an intrusion of nature – the horse – menacing the decorous reduction of nature that was the suburban gardens. And of the failure of language to describe such violence and restrict it.

1 Consider the description of the horse in the first eight lines. How would you characterise the animal? Look at how the poet uses language to make the horse as real as possible for the reader. What words and phrases are particularly effective in this regard?
2 The third and fourth lines tells us how the horse 'stamps death/ Like a mint on the innocent coinage of earth'. Yet this is achieved with the 'clip, clop, casual// Iron of his shoes'. Does the description 'clip, clop, casual' render the horse innocent or does it make the violence of his actions out to be all the more sinister?
3 How does the speaker initially respond to the horse? Is she frightened or fascinated by the animal?
4 'No great harm is done'. What damage has the horse caused according to lines 10 to 16? Does the speaker's description of the damage allow us to believe that 'no harm' has really been done here?
5 The similes and metaphors that the speaker uses to describe the damaged flowers and plants are particularly brutal. What might we ordinarily associate these descriptions with?
6 'But we, we are safe'. What sort of attitude does the speaker exhibit here to the incident?
7 The speaker asks 'why should we care// If a rose, a hedge, a crocus are uprooted?' Is she still talking only about the incident in her garden, or has this particular incident become representative of something greater?
8 What does the description of the speaker's neighbours using the 'subterfuge// Of curtains' tell us about them and their attitude to the difficulties that might threaten their world?
9 The speaker introduces a connection with the violent past of Ireland in the last four lines. What are her feelings about this past? Does she sympathise with need for violence or does she see it as a recurring evil in the world?
10 Describe in detail how violence is illustrated and portrayed throughout the whole poem.

PERSONAL RESPONSE

1 The poet takes the fairly innocuous event of a loosed horse passing through her garden and uses it to describe the brutality of war and people's indifference to it. How effectively did you feel the incident functioned as a metaphor in this regard?
2 How did the poem make you feel? Were you shocked at the poet's violent descriptions of damaged flowers and plants?
3 The poem presents a rather damning critique of suburban life. What impression did you get of the sort of people living in such places? Do you sympathise with their attitude?
4 Do you think that the poem presents a fair picture of how people in general respond to acts of great violence in the world today?

IN CONTEXT

Many of Boland's poems reveal an enormous sensitivity towards the victims of violence. She is also very aware of the failures of others to respond and act appropriately.

Discuss this statement with regard to 'The War Horse', 'Child of Our Time' and 'Outside History'.

The Famine Road

'Idle as trout in light Colonel Jones
these Irish, give them no coins at all; their bones
need toil, their characters no less.' Trevelyan's
seal blooded the deal table. The Relief
Committee deliberated: 'Might it be safe,
Colonel, to give them roads, roads to force
from nowhere, going nowhere of course?'

one out of every ten and then
another third of those again
women – in a case like yours.

Sick, directionless they worked; fork, stick
were iron years away; after all could
they not blood their knuckles on rock, suck
April hailstones for water and for food?
Why for that, cunning as housewives, each eyed –
as if at a corner butcher – the other's buttock.

anything may have caused it, spores,
a childhood accident; one sees
day after day these mysteries.

Dusk: they will work tomorrow without him.
They know it and walk clear. He has become
a typhoid pariah, his blood tainted, although
he shares it with some there. No more than snow
attends its own flakes where they settle
and melt, will they pray by his death rattle.

You never will, never you know
but take it well woman, grow
your garden, keep house, good-bye.

'It has gone better than we expected, Lord
Trevelyan, sedition, idleness, cured
in one; from parish to parish, field to field;
the wretches work till they are quite worn,
then fester by their work; we march the corn
to the ships in peace. This Tuesday I saw bones
out of my carriage window. Your servant Jones.'

Barren, never to know the load
of his child in you, what is your body
now if not a famine road?

Famine Road: *during the Famine the British government set up a relief scheme whereby people would be paid for the construction of roads. However, these roads were rarely meant to be used and often went nowhere in particular, frequently ending in a bog or field.*

[1] **Colonel Jones:** *One of the British officers in charge of relief works around Newry.*

[3] **Trevelyan:** *Charles Trevelyan was in charge of the whole relief project, operating out of London.*

[4] **Relief Committee:** *one of the committees that organised local schemes to try and alleviate the starvation.*

[22] **pariah:** *outcast.*

[30] **sedition:** *conduct or speech inciting rebellion against the authority of a state or monarch.*

COMPREHENSION

The questions that follow focus initially on sections 1, 3, 5, and 7 (the non-italicised sections of the poem) before addressing the sections that are in italics. Read the complete poem a few times, however, before answering the questions.

Lines 1-7

1 Who is speaking in the first three lines? Who is he addressing?
2 What sort of tone do you think is being used in the opening lines?
3 What has Trevelyan's letter to Colonel Jones achieved?
4 What agreement results from this piece of correspondence?

Lines 11-16

5 Who is being described in this section of the poem?
6 Whose sentiments are being expressed in lines 12–16?
7 What does the word 'cunning' imply?

Lines 20-25

8 How do the group respond to the death of one of the labourers? Why do they act in this manner?
9 How have the conditions and the treatment of the Irish affected the way people relate to one another?
10 In lines 23 to 25 the poet uses the falling snow to illustrate the terrible loss of humanity and community that has occurred. Explain the simile in your own words. Does it work effectively?

Lines 29-35

11 Colonel Jones evaluates the results of the decision reached in the opening section. What is his overall assessment?
12 What seems to have been the real motivation behind having the Irish work on these roads?

Italicised Sections

1 These sections involve a doctor speaking to a woman. What is the doctor talking about?
2 How would you describe the doctor's treatment of the situation? Is he sympathetic and reasonable? Would you describe his words as condescending?
3 Whose sentiments are expressed in the final three lines of the poem?
4 How are the two aspects of the poem related? How can we consider the woman's plight to be similar to that of the starving Irish of the famine who were forced to work these roads?

PERSONAL RESPONSE

1 The poem brings together two very different incidents in order to draw a parallel between them. Explain in your own words the association that the poet intends.

IN CONTEXT

Boland's poems reveal a great sensitivity for the unnamed victims of history. Would you agree with this assessment? Discuss these points of view in terms of three poems by Boland on the course.

Child of Our Time

for Aengus

Yesterday I knew no lullaby
But you have taught me overnight to order
This song, which takes from your final cry
Its tune, from your unreasoned end its reason;
Its rhythm from the discord of your murder,
Its motive from the fact you cannot listen.

We who should have known how to instruct
With rhymes for your waking, rhythms for your sleep
Names for the animals you took to bed,
Tales to distract, legends to protect,
Later an idiom for you to keep
And living, learn, must learn from you, dead,

To make our broken images rebuild
Themselves around your limbs, your broken
Image, find for your sake whose life our idle
Talk has cost, a new language. Child
Of our time, our times have robbed your cradle.
Sleep in a world your final sleep has woken.

COMPREHENSION

1 Who is the speaker addressing?
2 What prompted her to write this poem?
3 How does the speaker feel about the child's death in the first stanza? What words and phrases describe the killing?
4 According to the second stanza, what should the adult community have been doing when this child was alive? What does this stanza suggest is most important for young children to experience?
5 What must the adult community do now that the child is dead?
6 Our 'idle/ Talk has cost' this child its life. What do understand this 'idle' talk to refer to?
7 What does the speaker mean when she says that we must now find 'a new language' and 'rebuild' 'our broken images' around the limbs of the child?
8 The poem is ultimately part lullaby and part dirge (song of mourning). Which parts of the poem would characterise as lullaby and which parts are more in keeping with a dirge?

PERSONAL RESPONSE

1 What sort of impression of the world are you left with when you read this poem?
2 The speaker is obviously outraged at the murder of this innocent child. But she feels that this death need not be in vain. Is the poem ultimately a poem of hope or of despair?
3 How realistic do you find the actions proposed by the speaker in the third stanza? How would you suggest these be realised?

IN CONTEXT

In 'Outside History' the poet seeks to face up to the violence of the past and attend to the many nameless victims of those caught up in our turbulent and troubled history. In 'Child of Our Time' the poet discovers that the present also needs careful attention and consideration. Discuss Boland's response to the awful need for conflict and violence in the world. What can we learn from her poems in order to improve conditions?

The Black Lace Fan My Mother Gave Me

It was the first gift he ever gave her,
buying it for five francs in the Galeries
in pre-war Paris. It was stifling.
A starless drought made the nights stormy.

They stayed in the city for the summer.
They met in cafés. She was always early.
He was late. That evening he was later.
They wrapped the fan. He looked at his watch.

She looked down the Boulevard des Capucines.
She ordered more coffee. She stood up.
The streets were emptying. The heat was killing.
She thought the distance smelled of rain and lightning.

These are wild roses, appliquéd on silk by hand,
darkly picked, stitched boldly, quickly.
The rest is tortoiseshell and has the reticent,
clear patience of its element. It is

a worn-out, underwater bullion and it keeps,
even now, an inference of its violation.
The lace is overcast as if the weather
it opened for and offset had entered it.

The past is an empty café terrace.
An airless dusk before thunder. A man running.
And no way now to know what happened then –
none at all – unless, of course, you improvise:

The blackbird on this first sultry morning,
in summer, finding buds, worms, fruit,
feels the heat. Suddenly she puts out her wing –
the whole, full, flirtatious span of it.

[13] **pliquéd:** *decorative needlework.*
[17] **bullion:** *a heavy lace trimming made of gold or silver threads.*
appliquéd: *decorative needlework.*

COMPREHENSION

I was aware of my own sense of the traditional erotic object – in this case the black lace fan – as a sign not for triumph and acquisition but for suffering itself ... something which spoke of the violation of love while still showing the old context of its power. In other words a back-to-front love poem.

1 Describe in your own words the weather conditions as presented in the poem's first twelve lines. How does the weather contribute to the poem's atmosphere? What do you think it suggests about the state of the couple's relationship?
2 How does the weather contribute to the poem's atmosphere?
3 What do you think it suggests about the state of the couple's relationship?
4 'She was always early. / He was late'. Why do you think the woman was always early for their meetings while the man was always late? What does this say about their relationship?
5 What is the man doing that makes him particularly late on this occasion?
6 'The rest is tortoise shell and has the reticent, / clear patience of its element'. What do you understand by this phrase? What qualities are being associated with the fan?
7 What do the woman's actions suggest about her mental state as she waits in the café for her boyfriend to arrive?
8 Describe the fan in your own words.
9 *Group discussion:* 'The lace is overcast as if the weather / it opened for and offset had entered it'. What does Boland mean by this? What does it suggest about the couple's relationship?
10 What is the significance of the final image of the blackbird? How does it relate to the rest of the poem?
11 What similarities are there between the blackbird and the fan as depicted in this poem? What differences are there?

PERSONAL RESPONSE

1 Write a few lines describing your impression of the love affair between the couple in this poem.
2 Would you agree that this poem in no way presents an idealistic view of love, that the speaker is fully aware of the stresses, difficulties and pressures that are a part of every relationship? Give reasons for your answer.
3 Both the black lace fan and the blackbird are associated with violence and 'violation'. How? Do you think these two images are effective or appropriate symbols of love and romance? Give reasons for your answer.
4 Would you agree that this poem successfully evokes an atmosphere of drama and tension?
5 This is often considered to be an 'erotic' poem. What elements of the poem might lead people to this conclusion? (Consider the poem's symbolism, its atmosphere, and its description of the weather).

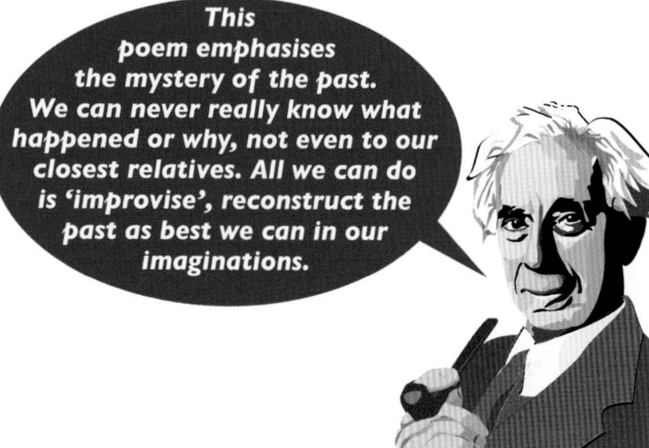

This poem emphasises the mystery of the past. We can never really know what happened or why, not even to our closest relatives. All we can do is 'improvise', reconstruct the past as best we can in our imaginations.

6 Would you agree with this assessment?
7 Taking the above questions into account write a few lines describing your personal reaction to this poem.

IN CONTEXT

Marriage is a theme that preoccupies Boland in much of her work. Compare her depiction of marriage in this poem to that in 'Love' and 'The Shadow Doll'. Which of these poems do you find most realistic in its approach to marriage?

The Shadow Doll

They stitched blooms from the ivory tulle
to hem the oyster gleam of the veil.
They made hoops for the crinoline.

Now, in summary and neatly sewn –
a porcelain bride in an airless glamour –
the shadow doll survives its occasion.

Under glass, under wraps, it stays
even now, after all, discreet about
visits, fevers, quickenings and lusts

and just how, when she looked at
the shell-tone spray of seed pearls,
the bisque features, she could see herself

inside it all, holding less than real
stephanotis, rose petals, never feeling
satin rise and fall with the vows

I kept repeating on the night before –
astray among the cards and wedding gifts –
the coffee pots and the clocks and

the battered tan case full of cotton
lace and tissue-paper, pressing down, then
pressing down again. And then, locks.

[1] **tulle:** *a fine silk netting used in dress-making.*
[2] **oyster:** *an off-white colour.*
[12] **bisque:** *a type of unglazed porcelain.*
[14] **stepahotis:** *a tropical plant.*

COMPREHENSION

1. 'a porcelain bride in an airless glamour / the shadow doll survives its occasion'. *Group discussion:* What is meant by these rather mysterious lines?
2. The doll, we're told, has experienced 'fevers, quickenings and lusts'. Yet how could a porcelain object experience these things? Would you agree that some kind of symbolic or metaphorical meaning is intended here?
3. Why do you think the young bride-to-be could 'see herself / inside' the doll's glass case? Is this a pleasant or unpleasant thought for her?
4. Why do you think the speaker 'kept repeating' her marriage vows on the night before her wedding?
5. The poem's final half line is particularly mysterious and powerful. What is being 'locked' here? Who or what is being locked in?

PERSONAL RESPONSE

1. What, in your opinion, are the two most powerful images in this poem? Give reasons for your answer.
2. 'This poem features some sudden and startling shifts in perspective that lend it a powerful sense of drama'. What shifts in perspective are being referred to here? Would you agree that these shifts add to the power of the poem?
3. What view of marriage is put forward in 'The Shadow Doll'? Do you find it a reasonable or realistic view?

IN CONTEXT

How does the Boland's attitude to marriage in 'The Shadow Doll' compare to her approach to the same topic in 'The Black Lace Fan My Mother Gave Me'? Would you agree that both poems depict marriage in a negative light? Give reasons for your answer.

White Hawthorn in the West of Ireland

I drove West
in the season between seasons.
I left behind suburban gardens.
Lawmowers. Small talk.

Under low skies, past splashes of coltsfoot,
I assumed
the hard shyness of Atlantic light
and the superstitious aura of hawthorn.

All I wanted then was to fill my arms with
sharp flowers,
to seem, from a distance, to be part of
that ivory, downhill rush. But I knew,

I had always known
the custom was
not to touch hawthorn.
Not to bring it indoors for the sake of

the luck
such constraint would forfeit –
a child might die, perhaps, or an unexplained
fever speckle heifers. So I left it

stirring on those hills
with a fluency
only water has. And, like water, able
to re-define land. And free to seem to be –

for anglers,
and for travellers astray in
the unmarked lights of a May dusk –
the only language spoken in those parts.

[5] **coltsfoot:** *a wild plant with yellow flowers.*

NOTE

In Ireland a number of superstitions are traditionally associated with the hawthorn bush, which is sometimes described as a 'fairy tree' and is associated with supernatural forces. It is bad luck to uproot a hawthorn bush and anyone who brought hawthorn flowers into their house risked the possibility of a death in the family. It has been suggested that this superstition arises from the flower's unpleasant smell, which is eerily like that of decaying flesh.

COMPREHENSION

Only a few miles away was the almost invisible world that everyone knew of and no one referred to. Of suburbs and housing estates. Of women and children. Of fires lighted for the first winter chill. Of food put on the table. The so called ordinary world ... which could only dissipate poetry ... a life for which no visionary claim could be made.

1 In this poem the speaker contrasts two very different worlds. An eastern world of tame 'suburban gardens' and a wild western world covered with glorious wild flowers. Would you agree with this analysis? Which of these worlds does the speaker seem to prefer? Why do you think this?

2 'I drove West / in the season between seasons'. *Group discussion:* What does the speaker mean by the season between seasons'? Could this phrase have more than one meaning?

3 Write a couple of lines describing both the landscape the speaker leaves behind and the landscape in the west to which she drives.

4 Having reached the west what does the speaker want to do?

5 What prevents her from doing this?

6 Towards the poem's conclusion the hawthorn is compared to water. What similarities, according to the speaker, exist between these substances? Do you find this comparison reasonable or outlandish? Say why.

7 *Group discussion:* According to the speaker the hawthorn might seem to be 'the only language spoken in these parts'. What do you think Boland has in mind here? How could a lot of bushes on a hill possibly resemble a language?

IN CONTEXT

'Both this poem and 'The Warhorse' contrast the tameness of suburbia with the wildness and energy of nature'. Do you agree with this statement? Give reasons for your answer.

PERSONAL RESPONSE

1 Make a list of five different images in this poem. Which image did you find most effective? Why?

2 In this poem the speaker seems to want to 'disappear', to lose herself in the western landscape. She seems to want to fade into the hills and somehow become a part of the hawthorn that grows on them (line 11 or become a 'traveller astray' among the hills and glens. Bearing this in mind what state of mind do you think the speaker was in when she set out on her journey westward? Do you think she was happy/ sad/ bored/ suicidal? Give reasons for your answer.

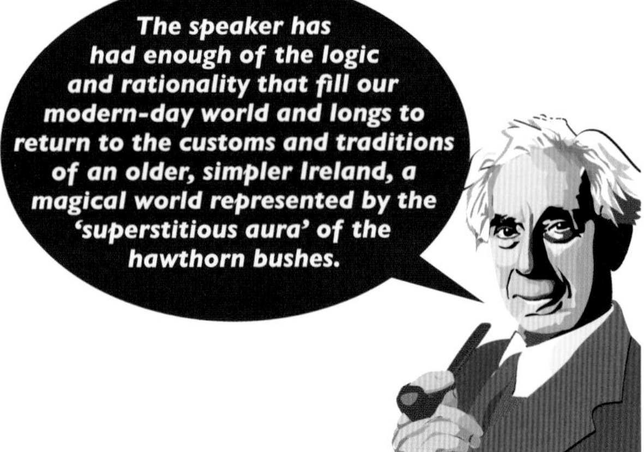

The speaker has had enough of the logic and rationality that fill our modern-day world and longs to return to the customs and traditions of an older, simpler Ireland, a magical world represented by the 'superstitious aura' of the hawthorn bushes.

3 Would you agree with this assessment?

4 Do you think the poem provides a realistic portrayal of the attitudes and customs that prevail today in rural Ireland?

5 Write a few lines describing your reaction to this poem.

Outside History

These are outsiders, always. These stars –
these iron inklings of an Irish January,
whose light happened

thousands of years before
our pain did: they are, they have always been
outside history.

They keep their distance. Under them remains
a place where you found
you were human, and

a landscape in which you know you are mortal.
And a time to choose between them.
I have chosen:

out of myth in history I move to be
part of that ordeal
who darkness is

only now reaching me from those fields,
those rivers, those roads clotted as
firmaments with the dead.

How slowly they die
as we kneel beside them, whisper in their ear.
And we are too late. We are always too late.

COMPREHENSION

1. What do think it means for something to be 'outside history'?
2. How does the poet consider the stars to be 'outside history'?
3. The poet contrasts the stars with 'a place where you found/ you were human'. What place is she referring to? How does she characterise this place?
4. The stars ultimately function as a metaphor for 'myths' and the poet contrasts these myths with actual historical happenings. How do they differ? Why does the poet choose to move 'out of myth into history'?
5. What aspect of history does the poet choose to be 'part of'?
6. To whom do you think the poet refers in the last three lines of the poem?
7. What do you think the poet means when she says that 'We are always too late'?
8. Is this poem specifically about Ireland or do you think it has global significance?

PERSONAL RESPONSE

1. The stars serve as a metaphor for 'myth' and planet earth is considered to be the locale of 'history'. What purpose do myths serve in various cultures? Think of the Irish myths that you know about. Do you think it is a straightforward step to separate myth and history and to choose between the two?
2. Do you think that the metaphor of the 'stars' works effectively?

IN CONTEXT

In 'The Famine Road', 'Child of our Time', and 'Outside History', Boland deals with the sufferings and wrongs of the past. Write an essay discussing the different ways each poem addresses the theme of human suffering.

This Moment

A neighbourhood.
At dusk.

Things are getting ready
to happen
out of sight.

Stars and moths.
And rinds slanting around fruit.

But not yet.

One tree is black.
One window is yellow as butter.

A woman leans down to catch a child
who has run into her arms
this moment.

Stars rise.
Moths flutter.
Apples sweeten in the dark.

COMPREHENSION

1 Where is this poem set?
2 What time of day is it?
3 What is the significance of the window? Why is it described as being yellow as butter? Are we given any clue as to who might live behind this window?
4 Describe this little scene in your own words.
5 What atmosphere is created by the poem? Would you agree there is an element of mystery present in the poem?
6 It has been suggested that this poem is 'a feast for the senses'. Which of our senses are appealed to in this poem and in which lines?

PERSONAL RESPONSE

1 What do you think this poem has to say about motherhood? Would you agree that is in some sense a celebration of the relationship that exists between a mother and her child?

This poem is a celebration of the ordinary and the everyday. It slows time to show us the magic and mystery that occurs out of sight in a single seemingly ordinary moment.

2 Would you agree with this assessment? Give reasons for your answer.

IN CONTEXT

The idea of the suburbs and suburban life is one that occurs again and again in Boland's poetry. Both this poem and 'White Hawthorn in the West of Ireland' touch upon this theme. What differences are there between the speaker's attitude to the suburbs in each of these poems?

'This Moment' can also be usefully compared to 'The Pomegranate'. What similarities are there between these poems' depiction of motherhood? What important differences are there?

The Pomegranate

The only legend I have ever loved is
the story of a daughter lost in hell.
And found and rescued there.
Love and blackmail are the gist of it.
Ceres and Persephone the names.
And the best thing about the legend is
I can enter it anywhere. And have.
As a child in exile in
a city of fogs and strange consonants,
I read it first and at first I was
an exiled child in the crackling dusk of
the underworld, the stars blighted. Later
I walked out in a summer twilight
searching for my daughter at bed-time.
When she came running I was ready
to make any bargain to keep her.
I carried her back past whitebeams
and wasps and honey-scented buddleias.
But I was Ceres then and I knew
winter was in store for every leaf
on every tree on that road.
Was inescapable for each one we passed.
And for me.
            It is winter
and the stars are hidden.
I climb the stairs and stand where I can see
my child asleep beside her teen magazines,
her can of Coke, her plate of uncut fruit.
The pomegranate! How did I forget it?
She could have come home and been safe
and ended the story and all
our heart-broken searching but she reached
out a hand and plucked a pomegranate.
She put out her hand and pulled down
the French sound for apple and
the noise of stone and the proof
that even in the place of death,
at the heart of legend, in the midst
of rocks full of unshed tears
ready to be diamonds by the time
the story was told, a child can be
hungry. I could warn her. There is still a chance.
The rain is cold. The road is flint-coloured.
The suburb has cars and cable television.
The veiled stars are above ground.
It is another world. But what else
can a mother give her daughter but such
beautiful rifts in time?
If I defer the grief I will diminish the gift.

The legend will be hers as well as mine.
She will enter it. As I have.
She will wake up. She will hold
the papery flushed skin in her hand.
And to her lips. I will say nothing.

NOTE

The 'legend' refers to an ancient Greek and Roman myth that tells of the abduction of Persephone by Pluto (also known as Hades), the god of the Underworld. Persephone's mother was Ceres, the goddess of agriculture. When Ceres eventually locates her daughter in the Underworld she calls on Jupiter (the chief god) to grant her daughter's release. Jupiter says that she can go free as long as she has not eaten anything. Discovering that Persephone has indulged in six seeds Jupiter decrees that each year she must spend six months in the Underworld with Pluto. Autumn and winter are said to be the period when Ceres is mourning for her daughter, hence why the plants wither and die.

PRE-READING

Are there any stories, books, or films that you really love and to which you often relate? Do you identify yourself with any particular character? How does identifying with this character influence your life?

COMPREHENSION

Lines 1–23

1 The poem speaks of the poet's love of an ancient myth about a mother and daughter, Ceres and Persephone. Lines 1 to 23 describe two moments in the poet's life when this story became particularly meaningful to her. How did she first identify with the 'legend'? Which character did she relate to this first instance? How did London resemble the underworld of the myth?

2 The second time the myth became relevant to her life was when she was much older. How did it differ to her first identification with the story?

3 Although it was summer the poet says, 'I knew/ winter was in store for every leaf/ on every tree'. What sort of knowledge has the poet gained now that she is older and has a child?

Lines 24–54

4 The poem shifts to the present day. Describe the domestic scene portrayed in this part of the poem. What sort of place does the poet now live in?

5 'The pomegranate!' What part of the myth does the poet suddenly remember? What simple truth does this recollection of Persephone and the pomegranate reveal to the poet?

6 In line 42 the poet begins to get anxious. What do you think is she considering telling her daughter at this point?

7 'It is another world'. This modern world is a strange place compared to the world of the myth. Yet there is sense in which the concerns of Ceres as a mother are no different to the concerns of the poet. Discuss this with regard to the poem.

8 What do you think the 'beautiful rifts in time' refer to?

9 'If I defer the grief I will diminish the gift'. Explain in your own words what you understand the 'grief' and the 'gift' to be in line 49.

10 The poet sees an inevitability to the daughter's engagement with the world beyond her maternal protection. How does the pomegranate serve as a metaphor for necessary life experience in the final lines of the poem?

11 Even though the poet knows that the eating of the pomegranate leads to separation and suffering why does she decide to 'say nothing' in the end?

PERSONAL RESPONSE

1 Do you think that this poem effectively captures the complex emotions, responsibilities, and choices that come with being a parent?

2 How does this poem reveal the personality of the poet?

Love

Dark falls on this mid-western town
where we once lived when myths collided.
Dusk has hidden the bridge in the river
which slides and deepens
to become the water
the hero crossed on his way to hell.

Not far from here is our old apartment.
We had a kitchen and an Amish table.
We had a view. And we discovered there
love had the feather and muscle of wings
and had come to live with us,
a brother of fire and air.

We had two infant children one of whom
was touched by death in this town
and spared: and when the hero
was hailed by his comrades in hell
their mouths opened and their voices failed and
there is no knowing what they would have asked
about a life they had shared and lost.

I am your wife.
It was years ago.
Our child was healed. We love each other still.
Across our day-to-day and ordinary distances
we speak plainly. We hear each other clearly.

And yet I want to return to you
on the bridge of the Iowa river as you were,
with snow on the shoulders of your coat
and a car passing with its headlights on:

I see you as a hero in a text –
the image blazing and the edges gilded –
and I long to cry out the epic question
my dear companion:

Will we ever live so intensely again?
Will love come to us again and be
so formidable at rest it offered us ascension
even to look at him?

But the words are shadows and you cannot hear me.
You walk away and I cannot follow.

[8] **an Amish table:** *A table manufactured in the reclusive Amish communities of North America, who are known for their skill with arts and crafts.*

NOTE

This poem has two distinct strands, which intermingle the speaker's memories of the time she spent in America with imagery borrowed from the Greek myths.

COMPREHENSION

1 What do you understand by the phrase 'when myths collided'?
2 According to the speaker what strange transformation is undergone by the Iowa river?
3 What kind of atmosphere is created by the poem's opening lines?
4 When the couple were in America the love between them was at its height. What image does the speaker use to convey this?
5 What technique is used by the speaker to convey the intensity of this love? Do you think it is successful?
6 The couple also endured a traumatic and frightening event during this period. What was it?
7 How does the speaker describe her present day relationship with her husband?
8 What happened to the hero when he visited hell?
9 Why do you think the speaker wants to return to the past, to see her husband once again as he was on the banks of the Iowa river all those years ago?
10 When the speaker thinks of her husband as he was all those years ago how does she imagine him?
11 Does she believe that such a return is possible?

PERSONAL RESPONSE

1 What emotions, if any, did you feel on reading the poem's conclusion? Do you think the conclusion is an effective summing up of the poem's major themes? Give reasons for your answer.
2 Write a couple of lines describing the story of the mythological 'hero' as it is presented in this poem. How does the speaker relate this story to her own situation?

The traditional love poem carries with it a concealed boast, a hidden brag about the power of poetry itself. That it could turn back time. That it could fend off decay.

3 To what extent is this a poem that attempts to 'turn back time'?
4 Do you think Boland's use of this mythological material is effective in illustrating her theme?
5 Do you think the speaker might be looking at the past through 'rose tinted glasses', that she is neglecting her present happiness by longing for past events to which she can never return?

This is a simple poem of nostalgia, in which the speaker wants to somehow meet again a long ago version of her husband. She wastes her time and ours wishing for something that is simply impossible.

6 Do you agree with this assessment?

IN CONTEXT

Write a few lines comparing the different uses of myth in 'Love' and 'The Pomegranate'. In which poem do you think is myth most effectively deployed? Give reasons for your answer.

T.S. ELIOT

BIOGRAPHY

Thomas Stearns Eliot was born on 26 September 1888 in St Louis. His family were prosperous and socially active Unitarians. In 1905 they left for Massachusetts, where Eliot had holidayed yearly as a boy. It was during these early summer vacations that he developed a love of the sea, and memories of the sea recur in his poetry.

Eliot spent a year at Milton Academy, then entered Harvard, where he was to remain – apart from a year in Paris – until 1914. Here, as an undergraduate, he pursued his studies of Greek and Latin, which he had begun in St Louis. He continued, too, with French and German, and took courses in medieval history and comparative literature. At Harvard there was a well-established tradition of Dante studies, and in 1919 Eliot first read the *Divine Comedy*. This work of Dante's influenced Eliot throughout his life. The epigraph in 'Prufrock' is a quotation from the *Divine Comedy*.

A friend of Eliot's at Harvard, Conrad Aiken, said that Eliot was 'a singularly attractive, tall and rather dapper young man'. In fact, he was terribly shy but made deliberate efforts to overcome his shyness by plunging into college social life and attending dances and parties. He took his BA in 1909 and enrolled for the MA in English Literature. Between 1907 and 1909 he had contributed a few poems to the *Harvard Advocate* which were technically good and exhibited a preoccupation with images of flowers.

However, in 1908 Eliot discovered what was to become an influential book for him in the library of the Harvard Union: Arthur Symons' *The Symbolist Movement in Literature*, an important work of criticism which introduced to the English-speaking world some of the most significant French poets of the age. This book Eliot later described as 'one of those which have affected the course of my life.' Symons introduced him directly to Laforgue, a poet of whom Eliot said 'was the first to teach me how to speak, to teach me the poetic possibilities of my own idiom of speech'.

From Laforgue, the young poet learned the possibility of an ironic, self-deprecating diction that offered him a means of expression that was not available to him in English. 'Prufrock' is a poem that owes much to Laforgue in style, for it was this French poet that showed a shy and sensitive Eliot the means of distancing and presenting for contemplation experiences too painful to deal with more personally. Laforgue was really only a strong influence on the early poems of Eliot, though he seemed to have a longer influence over Eliot's personality.

Symons quotes a description of Laforgue by a friend which refers to his formal demeanour, his top hat, his sober necktie, his English jacket, his clerical overcoat, and the umbrella always under one arm. Apart from the top hat, this would serve as a pretty good description of Eliot even in later years. In 1919 Eliot wrote about a 'feeling of profound kinship, or rather of a peculiar personal intimacy, with another, probably a dead author ... It is a cause of development, like personal relations in life. Like personal intimacies in life, it may and probably will pass, but it will be ineffaceable'.

In 1910 Eliot moved into a new and more mature phase of poetic activity. He wrote, among other pieces, the first two 'Preludes' and the first part of 'Prufrock', which was completed in 1911, when he also wrote the third and fourth 'Preludes'. In the autumn of 1910 Eliot, after taking his MA, went to Paris to spend an academic year studying French literature and philosophy. In the summer of 1911 he travelled in Europe, visiting northern Italy and Munich, where 'Prufrock' was finished. In September he was back at Harvard.

Eliot believed that the twentieth century could be defined in terms of humankind's loss of value and meaning. In the cities he visited and lived in as a young man he witnessed mass numbers of workers who were no better than machines serving the masters of industry and time. He observed the mindless routines that so many adhered to religiously: rising in the morning at the same time and pressing to 'early coffee-stands'. As he writes in 'Preludes', 'One thinks of all the hands/ that are raising dingy shades/ In a thousand furnished rooms.'

With the poems written between 1910 and 1912 Eliot attained an astonishing creative maturity and, in effect, invented modern poetry in English. He had succeeded, almost it seemed without effort, in bringing the achievements of French symbolism into English poetry. Any reader of his poems around this time needed to go no further than the third line of 'Prufrock' to realise that something new was happening in English verse. Eliot likens the evening sky to 'a patient etherised upon a table'.

Furthermore, the work of 1910 to 1912 represents a level of intense creative activity and achievement that did not occur again until Eliot wrote 'The Waste Land' in 1921. The remarkable fact of his achievement with 'Prufrock' and the 'Preludes' is that they were composed independent of any modern group or movement in English literature. It was of his own accord that he ended up realising the possibilities of combining Laforgue with established English writers, particularly dramatists of the late-Elizabethan and Jacobean period. 'I do not know anyone who started from exactly that point,' he said in 1928.

'Prufrock' and 'Preludes' were the first and unmistakable signs of Eliot's genius, and we find aspects of these poems recurring throughout his career. One of them was his use of literary sources, his direct and indirect reference to an eclectic range of classical works. Although accused by some critics of plagiarism, Eliot was not doing anything so different to many great writers, such as Chaucer and Shakepeare, who made free use of foreign sources for their own ends.

Eliot returned to Harvard in the autumn of 1911, 'perceptibly Europeanised,' in Conrad Aiken's words, carrying a cane in a very un-American way'. Although his work for the MA had been mostly in English literature, Eliot's studies for the Ph.D on which he now embarked were in philosophy and Oriental studies. In the spring of 1914 Bertrand Russell, a well-known British philosopher, was a visiting professor at Harvard and Eliot attended his classes. Russell, with whom Eliot would later become good friends when living in England, gave his initial impression of Eliot in a letter written to a friend: 'This morning two of my pupils came together to ask me a question about work – one named Eliot is very well dressed and polished.'

Within a few weeks Russell had formed a high opinion of the student, though he also noticed that Eliot was by no means the life of one party he had attended: 'My pupil Eliot was there – the only one who is civilized, and he is ultra-civilized, knows his classics very well, is familiar with all French literature ... and is altogether impeccable in his taste but has no vigour or life – or enthusiasm. He is going to Oxford where I expect he will be very happy'.

In London Eliot was to meet another American poet called Ezra Pound. Though never as accomplished poetically as Eliot, Pound was a big mover-and-shaker on the English literary scene. He was by nature an entrepreneur and energetic organiser who regarded it as his mission to improve the quality of English culture. After Eliot called around to his place for the first time, Pound remarked: 'An American called Eliot called. I think he has some sense, though he has not yet sent me any verse'.

Pound was London correspondent for the American magazine *Poetry*. On September 30 he wrote enthusiastically to the editor of this magazine: 'I was jolly well right about Eliot. He has sent me in the best poem I have yet had or seen from an American.' Eliot, he acutely remarked, had 'actually trained himself and modernized himself on his own. The rest of the promising young have done one or the other but never both'. The poem Eliot had shown him was 'Prufrock', and Pound had at once sent it to the editor with the urge that she 'get it in soon', though she seems not to have been as enthusiastic.

In October Eliot went to Oxford to embark on his last year as a student of philosophy. He disliked London initially, and told Aiken, 'a people which is satisfied with such disgusting food is not civilized.' Oxford was no better: 'Oxford is very pretty, but I don't like to be dead ... O conversation, the staff of life, shall I get any at Oxford?' During 1914 to 1915 Eliot was energetically cultivated by Pound, and was noticed as an enigmatic new arrival among the visitors to the celebrated triangular sitting-room of Pound's small flat in Kensington. For all his longing for conversation, Eliot was chiefly remarkable for his lack of talk – one member of the group was struck by his ability to sit for a whole afternoon in complete silence – as well as his exotic good looks.

In June 1915 Eliot married Vivien Haighwood, who was the daughter of a painter. The marriage was a crucial event in Eliot's life. It was to cause him much unhappiness and appears to have reinforced rather than lessened the sexual anxieties expressed in his earlier poetry. From the beginning the Eliots struck those who knew them as sharply contrasted temperaments: if T.S. Eliot was quiet and complex and rather difficult socially, Vivien was, in one friend's words, 'gay, talkative, a chatterbox'. Bertrand Russell, with whom Eliot had resumed contact, remarked in a letter of July 1915: 'I dined with my Harvard pupil, Eliot and his bride. I expected her to be terrible, from his mysteriousness; but she was not so bad. She is light, a little vulgar, adventurous, full of life ... she says she married him to stimulate him, but finds she can't do it. Obviously he married in order to be stimulated. I think she will soon be tired of him. She refuses to go to America to see his people, for fear of submarines. He is ashamed of his marriage, and very grateful if one is kind to her.'

Marriage meant that Eliot, who had been a student for nearly ten years, had to take a job. He became a schoolmaster for a few years until he gave it up in 1917 to take a post in the foreign department at Lloyds Bank in London, where he remained for eight years. He later wrote: 'I prefer ... a condition of affairs in which I have a daily routine of work or business, the greater part of which I find boring ... a certain amount of routine, of dullness and of necessity seems inseparable from work; and for myself, I am too skeptical of my own abilities to be able to make a whole-time job of writing poetry, even if I had the means.'

At about this time, Eliot's thoughts turned again to the long poem that had been in his mind since 1919. In May 1921 he wrote to a friend of the pressure of work at the bank; it was his responsibility, he said, to deal with all debts and claims of the bank arising out of the peace treaties after the war. Nevertheless, he added that he had 'a long poem in mind and partly on paper which I am wishful to finish.' In December 1921 Eliot visited Paris and presented Pound with the manuscript draft of 'The Waste Land', which Eliot then regarded, and for some time after, as a series of poems rather than a single unified work. Pound, ever astute, at once recognised it as a work of genius, but decided it needed editing and suggested to Eliot a number of cuts and revisions, most of which were gratefully accepted. On 15 December 15 1922 'The Waste Land' was published in book form. It was to become one of the most important poems of the twentieth century.

It surprised many people when the author of such a poem of spiritual barrenness converted to Christianity. In 1927 he was baptised and confirmed in the Church of England. 'The Journey of the Magi' reflects something of Eliot's spiritual struggle. The Magi's journey to Bethlehem becomes a powerful metaphor for the spiritual voyage undertaken by Eliot as he underwent the processes of conversion to the Anglo-Catholic faith. The religious life, Eliot believed, is trying and difficult. This is reflected in the hardships endured by the Magi.

In 1948 Viviene Eliot died, after years of madness and confinement. Eliot's religious principles had never allowed him to consider divorce, but now he was free to marry again. In November of the same year he was awarded the Nobel Prize for Literature. After several years as his secretary, Valerie Fletcher became Eliot's wife in 1957. All those who knew him have testified to the transformation that his second marriage brought about. It proved to be a happy ending to a rather bleak, though enormously influential and successful life. One friend, Robert Giroux, writes of the change in Eliot in his last years: 'In retrospect, the most striking single aspect of the years during which I was privileged to know him as a friend is the contrast between the rather sad and lonely aura that seemed to hover over him in the early period, and the happiness he radiated in the later one. "Radient" may seem an odd word to apply to T.S. Eliot, yet it is an accurate description of the last eight or so years of his life, and this was due of course to his marriage in 1957 to Valerie Fletcher. More than once in those years I heard him utter the words, "I'm the luckiest man in the world."'

The Love Song of J. Alfred Prufrock

S'io credesse che mia risposta fosse
A persona che mai tornasse al mondo,
Questa fiamma staria senza piu scosse.
Ma perciocche giammai di questo fondo
Non torno vivo alcun, s'i'odo il vero,
Senza tema d'infamia ti rispondo.

Let us go then, you and I,
When the evening is spread out against the sky
Like a patient etherized upon a table;
Let us go, through certain half-deserted streets,
The muttering retreats
Of restless nights in one-night cheap hotels
And sawdust restaurants with oyster-shells:
Streets that follow like a tedious argument
Of insidious intent
To lead you to an overwhelming question ...
Oh, do not ask, 'What is it?'
Let us go and make our visit.

In the room the women come and go
Talking of Michelangelo.

The yellow fog that rubs its back upon the window-panes,
The yellow smoke that rubs its muzzle on the window-panes
Licked its tongue into the corners of the evening,
Lingered upon the pools that stand in drains,
Let fall upon its back the soot that falls from chimneys,
Slipped by the terrace, made a sudden leap,
And seeing that it was a soft October night,
Curled once about the house, and fell asleep.

And indeed there will be time
For the yellow smoke that slides along the street
Rubbing its back upon the window panes;
There will be time, there will be time
To prepare a face to meet the faces that you meet;
There will be time to murder and create,
And time for all the works and days of hands
That lift and drop a question on your plate;
Time for you and time for me,
And time yet for a hundred indecisions,
And for a hundred visions and revisions,
Before the taking of a toast and tea.

continued over

In the room the women come and go
Talking of Michelangelo.

And indeed there will be time
To wonder, 'Do I dare?' and, 'Do I dare?'
Time to turn back and descend the stair,
With a bald spot in the middle of my hair –
(They will say: 'How his hair is growing thin!')
My morning coat, my collar mounting firmly to the chin,
My necktie rich and modest, but asserted by a simple pin –
(They will say: 'But how his arms and legs are thin!')
Do I dare
Disturb the universe?
In a minute there is time
For decisions and revisions which a minute will reverse.

For I have known them all already, known them all –
Have known the evenings, mornings, afternoons,
I have measured out my life with coffee spoons;
I know the voices dying with a dying fall
Beneath the music from a farther room.
So how should I presume?

And I have known the eyes already, known them all –
The eyes that fix you in a formulated phrase,
And when I am formulated, sprawling on a pin,
When I am pinned and wriggling on the wall,
Then how should I begin
To spit out all the butt-ends of my days and ways?
And how should I presume?

And I have known the arms already, known them all –
Arms that are braceleted and white and bare
(But in the lamplight, downed with light brown hair!)
Is it perfume from a dress
That makes me so digress?
Arms that lie along a table, or wrap about a shawl.
And should I then presume?
And how should I begin?

. . . .

Shall I say, I have gone at dusk through narrow streets
And watched the smoke that rises from the pipes
Of lonely men in shirt-sleeves, leaning out of windows? ...

I should have been a pair of ragged claws
Scuttling across the doors of silent seas.

. . . .

And the afternoon, the evening, sleeps so peacefully!
Smoothed by long fingers,
Asleep … tired … or it malingers,
Stretched on the floor, here beside you and me.
Should I, after tea and cakes and ices,
Have the strength to force the moment to its crisis?
But though I have wept and fasted, wept and prayed,
Though I have seen my head (grown slightly bald)
brought in upon a platter,
I am no prophet – and here's no great matter;
I have seen the moment of my greatness flicker,
And I have seen the eternal Footman hold my coat, and
snicker,
And in short, I was afraid.

And would it have been worth it, after all,
After the cups, the marmalade, the tea,
Among the porcelain, among some talk of you and me,
Would it have been worth while,
To have bitten off the matter with a smile,
To have squeezed the universe into a ball
To roll it toward some overwhelming question,
To say: 'I am Lazarus, come from the dead,
Come back to tell you all, I shall tell you all' –
If one, settling a pillow by her head,
Should say: 'That is not what I meant at all.
That is not it, at all.'
And would it have been worth it, after all,
Would it have been worth while,
After the sunsets and the dooryards and the sprinkled
streets,
After the novels, after the teacups, after the skirts
that trail along the floor –
And this, and so much more? –
It is impossible to say just what I mean!
But as if a magic lantern threw the nerves in patterns
on a screen:
Would it have been worth while
If one, settling a pillow or throwing off a shawl,
And turning toward the window, should say:
'That is not it at all,
That is not what I meant, at all.'

. . . .

continued over

No! I am not Prince Hamlet, nor was meant to be;
Am an attendant lord, one that will do
To swell a progress, start a scene or two,
Advise the prince; no doubt, an easy tool,
Deferential, glad to be of use,
Politic, cautious, and meticulous;
Full of high sentence, but a bit obtuse;
At times, indeed, almost ridiculous –
Almost, at times, the Fool.

I grow old ... I grow old ...
I shall wear the bottoms of my trousers rolled.

Shall I part my hair behind? Do I dare to eat a peach?
I shall wear white flannel trousers, and walk upon the beach.
I have heard the mermaids singing, each to each.

I do not think that they will sing to me.

I have seen them riding seaward on the waves
Combing the white hair of the waves blown back
When the wind blows the water white and black.

We have lingered in the chambers of the sea
By sea-girls wreathed with seaweed red and brown
Till human voices wake us, and we drown.

Notes

Epigraph: *These lines are taken from Dante's Inferno, Canto XXVII, and are spoken by the character of Count Guido da Montefelltro. Dante meets the punished Guido in the Eighth chasm of Hell. Guido explains that he is speaking freely to Dante only because he believes Dante is one of the dead who could never return to earth to report what he says. Translated from the original Italian, the lines are as follows: 'If I thought that my reply would be to someone who would ever return to earth, this flame would remain without further movement; but as no one has ever returned alive from this place, if what I hear is true, I can answer you with no fear of infamy.'*

[14] **Michelangelo:** *the Renaissance painter and sculptor, best known for his painting of the ceilings of the Sistine chapel and for his statue of David.*

[52] **a dying fall:** *Duke Orsino describes a piece of melancholic music as such in Shakespeare's* Twelfth Night.

[57] **sprawling on a pin:** *In the study and collection of insects, specimens are pinned into place and kept in cases. Prufrock is perhaps comparing himself to such an insect.*

[63] **Arms that are braceleted white and bare:** *a reference to John Donne's poem, 'The Relic'.*

[82] **Though I have seen my head ... brought in upon a platter:** *reference to the serving of John the Baptist's head on a plate. See Matthew 14:3–11, Mark 6:17–29*

[94] **squeezed ... ball:** *reference to Andrew Marvell's carpe diem poem of seduction, 'To his Coy Mistress'.*

[96] **Lazarus:** *the man who Christ raised from the dead. See St John's Gospel 11: 1–44.*

[116] **Hamlet:** *the main character in Shakespeare's play of the same name, who worries about his own seeming inability to make decisions and take action.*

[118] **To swell a progress:** *'progress' in Elizabethan times referred to a state or royal journey,*

[123] **Fool:** *a character in Elizabethan drama, who entertains the nobility and speaks in apparent nonsense and riddle. His speech, however, is found to contain paradoxical wisdom. Hamlet's court jester was Yorick.*

[126] **Shall I part my hair behind?:** *A fashionable hairstyle at this time, considered to be 'daringly bohemian'.*

[129] **mermaids singing:** *a reference to John Donne's poem, 'Song: Go and Catch a Falling Star'.*

The less we know of a poet before we read him, the better. For the poem is a thing in itself, and should be enjoyed before it is understood.

COMPREHENSION

1 Write a few sentences on your initial response to this poem.

2 The title of the poem says that it is a 'love song'. Does the poem match your expectations of what a love song would be about?

3 Who is the speaker of the poem?

4 Underline all the words and phrases in the poem that indicate Prufrock's physical appearance. Do you think Prufrock's description of his physical appearance allows the reader some insight into his inner self?

5 Why do you think the narrative of the poem proceeds in such a seemingly illogical fashion?

6 Make a list of all the repetitions, and how often they occur, within this poem. Reviewing this list, what do you think the main themes of the poem might be? *Group discussion:* The opening line of the poem suggests that the speaker is about to embark on a journey of sorts.

7 Do you think that this journey involves physical movement for the speaker or do you think it is a journey through the speaker's mind?

8 In line 2–3, What does the speaker's comparison of the evening to an anaesthetised patient lying on a hospital table suggest about his attitude to the evening ahead?

9 Note all the images Prufrock uses to measure time. Do these images allow the reader an insight into his character, and his experience of life?

10 What type of society is depicted in lines 1–12?

11 Critics have suggested that the image of the fog in lines 15–22 is cat-like. Do you agree? Do you think that the use of personification in the portrayal of the movement of the fog serves as an apt metaphor for the speaker's own experience, or life journey?

12 Consider the repetition of 'Do I dare?' in line 38. What do you think it is that Prufrock would dare to do if he had the courage?

13 What is the tone of lines 49–54?

14 Is Prufrock's attitude towards women in lines 55–69 contradictory?

15 Do you think Prufrock identifies with the 'lonely men in shirt-sleeves' that he has seen 'leaning out of windows' (line 72)?

16 In lines 84–7 Prufrock seems to suggest that it was because he was 'afraid' that his life turned out to be 'no great matter'. Do you agree? What do you think Prufrock was afraid of? Do you think that fear is a theme of this poem?

17 *Class discussion:* Consider the refrain: 'In the room the women come and go / Talking of Michelangelo', with the following questions in mind:

18 Do you think that the women are actually discussing the Renaissance artist, Michelangelo, or is the speaker just imagining that they are speaking about such a lofty subject? Does the refrain express Prufrock's sense of inadequacy in your opinion? How does the refrain contribute to the meaning of the poem?

19 Paraphrase lines 89–115. What is the question Prufrock ponders in these lines? Does his deliberation on this question give some insight into his character?

20 Focus on lines 116–24, why do you think Prufrock says that he is no Hamlet? Comment on the speaker's sense of himself as a character within a play. Shakespeare's Hamlet is characterized by indecision. Does Prufrock share this quality?

21 Why do you think that the 'eternal Footman' would 'snicker' at Prufrock?

22 How do the references to the sea and mermaids in the final lines relate to the more concrete city images in the earlier sections of the poem? Is there an incongruity between fantasy and reality in this poem?

PERSONAL RESPONSE

1 Consider the phrase 'To prepare a face to meet the faces that you meet' (line 27). Do you think that the faces that Prufrock meets, or imagines meeting, are also put on? If so, what does this suggest about the society that he lives in?

2 *Class discussion:* Discuss a situation, real or imagined, whereby you would attempt to make your face mask-like in order to disguise your true feelings from the people around you. Do you think that 'wearing a mask' would exacerbate or protect you from ridicule, or from feelings of loneliness and alienation.

IN CONTEXT

[Poetry] may make us from time to time a little more aware of the deeper, unnamed feelings which form the substratum of our being, to which we rarely penetrate; for our lives are mostly a constant evasion of ourselves, and an evasion of the visible and sensible world. But to say all this is only to say what you know already, if you have felt poetry and thought about your feelings.

T.S Eliot states that readers should interpret a poem as a thing that exists apart from the poet's own life and times. Do you agree? Is there a contradiction between Eliot's claim that a poem transcend its historical context and his poetic depiction of modern urban life as degenerate and alienating in 'The Love Song of J. Alfred Prufrock' and 'Preludes'?

Preludes

I

The winter evening settles down
With smell of steaks in passageways.
Six o'clock.
The burnt-out ends of smoky days.
And now a gusty shower wraps
The grimy scraps
Of withered leaves about your feet
And newspapers from vacant lots;
The showers beat
On broken blinds and chimney-pots,
And at the corner of the street
A lonely cab-horse steams and stamps.

And then the lighting of the lamps.

II

The morning comes to consciousness
Of faint stale smells of beer
From the sawdust-trampled street
With all its muddy feet that press
To early coffee-stands.

With the other masquerades
That time resumes,
One thinks of all the hands
That are raising dingy shades
In a thousand furnished rooms.

III

You tossed a blanket from the bed,
You lay upon your back, and waited;
You dozed, and watched the night revealing
The thousand sordid images
Of which your soul was constituted;
They flickered against the ceiling.
And when all the world came back
And the light crept up between the shutters
And you heard the sparrows in the gutters,
You had such a vision of the street
As the street hardly understands;
Sitting along the bed's edge, where
You curled the papers from your hair,
Or clasped the yellow soles of feet
In the palms of both soiled hands.

continued over

IV

His soul stretched tight across the skies
That fade behind a city block,
Or trampled by insistent feet
At four and five and six o'clock;
And short square fingers stuffing pipes,
And evening newspapers, and eyes
Assured of certain certainties,
The conscience of a blackened street
Impatient to assume the world.

I am moved by fancies that are curled
Around these images, and cling:
The notion of some infinitely gentle
Infinitely suffering thing.

Wipe your hand across your mouth, and laugh;
The worlds revolve like ancient women
Gathering fuel in vacant lots.

[22] **shades:** *window blinds*

[36] **curled the papers from your hair:** *paper was wrapped around the hair to make it curl before curlers were manufactured*

COMPREHENSION

1 Read the First Prelude aloud. Describe the setting with as much detail as you can, and in your own words.
2 Read this section of the poem again. How does Eliot's use of alliteration and assonance contribute to the atmosphere of this scene?
3 A 'Prelude' is a musical term. What type of music does it describe?
4 How does the scene and atmosphere change in the Second Prelude? Is it more or less oppressive?
5 What role does smell play in the poem's description of urban life in the first two Preludes?
6 Do you think that the urban landscape described in this poem is dysfunctional and degenerative? What images suggest this?
7 In the Second Prelude, the speaker suggests that time itself puts on various 'masquerades'. What does this say about the speaker's experience of life? Can time be read as a character in this poem?
8 Compare the third Prelude to the first two. How does the scene change, and what is its focus? Support your answer with references to the poem.
9 The speaking voice in this poem is like a silent observer of life, but he very subtly leads the reader into seeing the world through his perspective. Do you agree with this statement? Write a paragraph on the role of the speaker in the first three Preludes.
10 Does the voice of the poem change at any time? Where does the first mention of the lyrical 'I' take place?
11 What is the tone of the poem?
12 Would you agree that characters are depersonalised in this poem? How is this conveyed?
13 Make a list of all the bodily images in the poem. What do these tell us about the poem's characters. Are the characters easily distinguishable from one another, or do they fuse into one? What do you think motivates the characters in the poem?
14 In the Fourth Prelude, the speaker refers to the 'conscience of a blackened street / Impatient to assume the world'. What does this image suggest to you? Can you visualize it? Is it a positive or a negative image?
15 Examine the musical effects of the poem, its use of rhythm, rhyme and repetition. Do these reinforce or contrast with the poem's setting and theme of meaninglessness?
16 What comparison is being made in the final two lines of the poem?
17 Why does the speaker say: 'Wipe your hand across your mouth, and laugh'? Do you think that he is suggesting that laughter is the only appropriate response we can make in the face of the inevitability and purposelessness of infinite suffering?

PERSONAL RESPONSE

1 *Class discussion:* Imagine the poem as a stage play. Comment on the setting, the characters and the point of view of the camera. Are there any dramatic events in this poem?
2 Describe your emotional response to this poem.
3 The reference to 'these images' in line 49 refers to the images of urban life depicted previously in the poem. Read lines 48–51 carefully. What is associated with these images that the speaker finds so moving and poignant?

IN CONTEXT

Compare and contrast the speaker in 'The Love Song of J. Alfred Prufrock' to the speaker in 'Preludes'.

Aunt Helen

Miss Helen Slingsby was my maiden aunt,
And lived in a small house near a fashionable square
Cared for by servants to the number of four.
Now when she died there was silence in heaven
And silence at her end of the street.
The shutters were drawn and the undertaker wiped his feet –
He was aware that this sort of thing had occurred before.
The dogs were handsomely provided for,
But shortly afterwards the parrot died too.
The Dresden clock continued ticking on the mantelpiece,
And the footman sat upon the dining-table
Holding the second housemaid on his knees –
Who had always been so careful while her mistress lived.

[10] **Dresden:** *a town in Germany that manufactures clocks with white porcelain ornaments or figurines*

COMPREHENSION

1. Do you think the speaker of this poem cared for his aunt? Is he criticizing her lifestyle?
2. In the first line the speaker twice stresses that his aunt never married. Do you think that this fact in some way influences the speaker's attitude towards his aunt. Do you think he knew her well?
3. Do you think aunt Helen's servants respected her?
4. Does anybody in this poem mourne the death of aunt Helen?
5. Where is the poem set? List the details of the home of aunt Helen, do they suggest a warm comfortable home?
6. What does the Dresden clock in Helen's home symbolise?
7. Does the poem contain any critique of society? If so, where do you see this?
8. What is the tone of the poem?

PERSONAL RESPONSE

1. How does Eliot present a sense of the class structures that make up society in this poem?
2. Traditionally a sonnet has 14 lines, why do you think that this poem departs from this convention by having only 13 lines? Write a fourteenth line to this sonnet.

IN CONTEXT

Do you think Helen's life was any less pointless and aimless than Eliot's characters in 'The Prelude'? Refer to both poems in detail in your answer.

Quote from T.S. Eliot: 'When a poet's mind is perfectly equipped for its work, it is constantly amalgamating disparate experience; the ordinary man's experience is chaotic, irregular, fragmentary'.

A Game of Chess
from *The Waste Land II*

The Chair she sat in, like a burnished throne,
Glowed on the marble, where the glass
Held up by standards wrought with fruited vines
From which a golden Cupidon peeped out
(Another hid his eyes behind his wing)
Doubled the flames of sevenbranched candelabra
Reflecting light upon the table as
The glitter of her jewels rose to meet it,
From satin cases poured in rich profusion;
In vials of ivory and colored glass
Unstoppered, lurked her strange synthetic perfumes,
Unguent, powdered, or liquid – troubled, confused
And drowned the sense in odors; stirred by the air
That freshened from the window, these ascended
In fattening the prolonged candle-flames,
Flung their smoke into the laquearia,
Stirring the pattern on the coffered ceiling.
Huge sea-wood fed with copper
Burned green and orange, framed by the coloured stone,
In which sad light a carvèd dolphin swam.
Above the antique mantle was displayed
As though a window gave upon the sylvan scene
The change of Philomel, by the barbarous king
So rudely forced; yet there the nightingale
Filled all the desert with inviolable voice
And still she cried, and still the world pursues,
'Jug Jug' to dirty ears.
And other withered stumps of time
Were told upon the walls; staring forms
Leaned out, leaning, hushing the world enclosed.
Footsteps shuffled on the stair.
Under the firelight, under the brush, her hair
Spread out in fiery points
Glowed into words, then would be savagely still.

'My nerves are bad tonight. Yes, bad. Stay with me.
'Speak to me. Why do you never speak. Speak.
  'What are you thinking of? What thinking? What?
'I never know what you are thinking. Think.'

I think we are in rats' alley
Where the dead men lost their bones.

'What is that noise?'
The wind under the door.
'What is that noise now? What is the wind doing?'
Nothing again nothing.

continued over

'Do
'You know nothing? Do you see nothing? Do you remember
'Nothing?'
I remember
Those are pearls that were his eyes.
'Are you alive, or not? Is there nothing in your head?'
But
O O O O that Shakespeherian Rag –
It's so elegant
So intelligent

'What shall I do now? What shall I do?
'I shall rush out as I am, and walk the street
'With my hair down, so. What shall we do tomorrow?
'What shall we ever do?'
The hot water at ten.
And if it rains, a closed car at four.
And we shall play a game of chess,
Pressing lidless eyes and waiting for a knock upon the door.

When Lil's husband got demobbed, I said –
I didn't mince my words, I said to her myself,
HURRY UP PLEASE ITS TIME
Now Albert's coming back, make yourself a bit smart.
He'll want to know what you done with that money he gave you
To get yourself some teeth. He did, I was there.
You have them all out, Lil, and get a nice set,
He said, I swear, I can't bear to look at you.
And no more can't I, I said, and think of poor Albert,
He's been in the army four years, he wants a good time,
And if you don't give it him, there's others will, I said.
Oh is there, she said. Something o' that, I said.
Then I'll know who to thank, she said, and give me a straight look.
HURRY UP PLEASE ITS TIME
If you don't like it you can get on with it, I said.
Others can pick and choose if you can't.
But if Albert makes off, it won't be for lack of telling.
You ought to be ashamed, I said, to look so antique.
(And her only thirty-one.)
I can't help it, she said, pulling a long face,
It's them pills I took, to bring it off, she said.
(She's had five already, and nearly died of young George.)
The chemist said it would be all right, but I've never been the same.
You are a proper fool, I said.
Well, if Albert won't leave you alone, there it is, I said,
What you get married for if you don't want children?
HURRY UP PLEASE IT'S TIME
Well, that Sunday Albert was home, they had a hot gammon,
And they asked me in to dinner, to get the beauty of it hot –
HURRY UP PLEASE ITS TIME
HURRY UP PLEASE ITS TIME
Goonight Bill. Goonight Lou. Goonight May. Goonight.
Ta ta. Goonight. Goonight.
Good night, ladies, good night, sweet ladies, good night, good night

Notes

This poem is section II of T.S. Eliot's famous and highly influential poem, The Waste-Land, published in 1922. The Waste Land expresses the disenchantment, disillusionment, and disgust of the period after World War I. It portrays a barren world of fear and lust, where people are condemned to a living death, while searching for some sign or promise of redemption. The poem's style is complex, scholarly, and allusive, and the notes below explain some of the work's many literary allusions.

A Game of Chess: the title is taken from a satirical play of the same name by Thomas Middleton (1570?–1627), which allegorized English conflict with Spain as a chess match. The title also alludes to Middleton's play, Women Beware Women, in which a young woman is raped while her mother, unsuspectingly, is playing chess downstairs.

[1] **Chair ... throne:** *alludes to Shakespeare's Antony and Cleopatra, Act 2. Scene 2. 190. This scene describes how Cleopatra looked when Mark Antony first met her: 'The barge she sat in, like a burnished throne, / Burned on the water ...'*

[4] **Cupidon:** *a handsome young man / lover (with echoes of Cupid)*

[12] **Unguent:** *ointment*

[16] **laquearia:** *means a panelled ceiling. Eliot cites Virgil's Aeneid, I. 726 as his source for the term. This passage, which describes a banquet given by the Dido, queen of Carthage who subsequently falls in love with Aeneas, may be translated: 'Blazing torches hang from the gold-panelled ceiling [laquearibus aureis] ...'*

[22] **sylvan scene:** *taken from Milton's Paradise Lost, Book 4. line 140, in which Satan approaches Eden describing it as a 'delicious Paradise' and a 'sylvan [mystical woodland]scene'.*

[23] **Philomel:** *reference to the story of Tereus and Philomel as told in Ovid's Metamorphoses, Book V. vi. In this tale of transformation, Philomela is raped by her sister's husband, Tereus, who also cuts off her tongue to prevent her telling. Philomela weaves her story into a garment to inform her sister, Procne, who in revenge kills Tereus' son. Tereus, in turn, pursues the sisters, but the gods change all three into birds. Tereus becomes a hawk, Procne a swallow, and Philomel a nightingale. Poets often use the nightingale as a symbol of the poetic voice.*

[49] **pearls ... eyes:** *a line from Ariel's song in Shakespeare's The Tempest, I. 48, which speaks of drowning.*

[51] **Shakespeherian rag:** *alludes to a popular song, published in 1912, called 'That Shakespearian Rag'.*

[62] **Pressing lidless eyes ... door:** *ref. to the game of chess in Middleton's Women beware Women.*

[63] **demobbed:** *demobilized, or released from the armed service.*

[100] **Good night, ladies ... good night:** *Ophelia's last words in Shakespeare's Hamlet, spoken to King Claudius and Queen Gertrude, before she took her own life by drowning.*

When a poet's mind is perfectly equipped for its work, it is constantly amalgamating disparate experience; the ordinary man's experience is chaotic, irregular, fragmentary.

COMPREHENSION

1 The first scene of the poem is set in a lady's boudoir (lines 1–62), the second scene (lines 63–101) is set in a public house. Look at the first couple of lines in each scene and comment on their different tone and use of language.

2 The first 34 lines describe a lady sitting at a dressing table in her boudoir. Read these lines carefully. What words and phrases convey the woman's wealth?

3 Make a list of all the items that surround the woman. Does the excessive richness and elaborate decoration of the objects suggest a sense of oppresiveness?

4 Describe in your own words, the images that adorn the lady's dressing table. What do these images signify?

5 How are the lady's perfumes personified? Do you think that the speaker creates a vivid and realistic atmosphere in his description of the smells of 'her strange synthetic perfumes'?

6 How do the perfumes affect the smoke from the candles?

7 How would you describe the poet's use of language in the first twenty lines. Is it an everyday language or is it highly poetic?

8 Lines 21–4 refer to the Greek myth of Philomel who was changed into a nightingale after being raped. Do you think that this myth has relevance to the overall theme of the poem?

9 What adjectives are used to describe the lady's hair, which, in the speaker's imagination, transform into words (lines 32–4). What do they suggest about the speaker's attitude towards her, and her way of communicating?

10 Lines 35–62 represent a one-way conversation between the lady and a silent male character. What do you think is the nature of their relationship? Is it a healthy relationship? Give reasons for your answers.

11 Write a paragraph on what you can glean of their

respective characters from this conversation? Do you think she is anxious, irrational, neurotic? Is his state of mind any healthier than hers? Do you find it easy to empathize with either of the characters in the first scene?

12 With what images does the first scene close? Do they contribute to a sense of resolution and closure or does an uneasy sense of purposelessness remain.

13 The second scene (lines 63–100) is set in a pub at closing time, where an unidentified lower-class lady tells a story about Lil and her husband. Rewrite the story in your own words.

14 Do you feel sympathy for any of the characters in this story?

15 Do you see a link, particularly in relation to the themes of hopelessness, waste and lust, between the two scenes?

16 How does this scene interweave the past and the present?

17 Is this a dramatic poem?

18 Describethecharacterofthenarratorinthesecond scene. Do you think she is a good friend to Lil?

PERSONAL RESPONSE

1 A scholar has argued that Eliot's misogyny is revealed in this poem in his depiction of 'the stink of femininity'. Do you agree. Refer to details within the poem in your response.

2 This poem depicts 'people as pawns moving about in two games that end not in checkmate but in stalemate'. Write an essay on why you agree or disagree with this statement.

3 Which of the two scenes in this poem did you prefer? Give reasons for your answer.

IN CONTEXT

Compare the representation of time as 'withered stumps' in this poem to the image of time as cigarette butts in ' The love story of J. Alfred Prufrock'. Is the representation of time personal or objective?

'The lives of Eliot's characters are ultimately sterile'. Discuss this statement with reference to 'A Game of Chess' and 'Aunt Helen'.

Journey of the Magi

'A cold coming we had of it,
Just the worst time of the year
For a journey, and such a long journey:
The ways deep and the weather sharp,
The very dead of winter.'
And the camels galled, sore-footed, refractory,
Lying down in the melting snow.
There were times we regretted
The summer palaces on slopes, the terraces,
And the silken girls bringing sherbet.
Then the camel men cursing and grumbling
And running away, and wanting their liquor and women,
And the night-fires going out, and the lack of shelters,
And the cities hostile and the towns unfriendly
And the villages dirty and charging high prices:
A hard time we had of it.
At the end we preferred to travel all night,
Sleeping in snatches,
With the voices singing in our ears, saying
That this was all folly.

Then at dawn we came down to a temperate valley,
Wet, below the snow line, smelling of vegetation;
With a running stream and a water-mill beating the darkness,
And three trees on the low sky,
And an old white horse galloped away in the meadow.
Then we came to a tavern with vine-leaves over the lintel,
Six hands at an open door dicing for pieces of silver,
And feet kicking the empty wine-skins.
But there was no information, and so we continued
And arrived at evening, not a moment too soon
Finding the place; it was (you may say) satisfactory.

All this was a long time ago, I remember,
And I would do it again, but set down
This set down
This: were we led all that way for
Birth or Death? There was a Birth, certainly,
We had evidence and no doubt. I had seen birth and death,
But had thought they were different; this Birth was
Hard and bitter agony for us, like Death, our death.
We returned to our places, these Kingdoms,
But no longer at ease here, in the old dispensation,
With an alien people clutching their gods.
I should be glad of another death.

Magus: *singular of Magi, the three wise men who brought gifts to the baby Jesus in Bethlehem*
[26] **white horse:** *image of Christ in Revelations 19: 11.*
[42] **the old dispensation:** *old way of life before the birth of Christ, which heralded in a new era of Christianity.*

COMPREHENSION

1 The Magi are the Three Wise Men who visited Jesus at his birth in Bethlehem. What does the title lead you to expect from this poem? Did the poem meet your initial expectations on reading the title?
2 The speaker is an old man remembering his past journey towards Bethlehem. In what way was the journey a difficult one? Is he nostalgic?
3 Line 8 mentions regrets, what did the speaker regret at times during the course of his journey?
4 Why do you think that the cities are described as 'hostile'?
5 The speaker describes how 'voices' sang in their ears, saying that their journey 'was all folly' (lines 19–20). Does it surprise you that the Magi would have experienced doubt on their way to visit the infant Jesus? What do you think compelled them to undertake this arduous journey?
6 *Class discussion:* The dawn arrival to the 'temperate valley' begins the second section of this poem. Read lines 20–32. What do the following images suggest to you: (a) 'a water-mill beating the darkness' (line 23), (b) the 'three trees' (line 25), and (c) 'an old white horse' (26)?
7 Comment on how the imagery in lines 20 to 32 is suggestive of both birth and death.
8 Do you think that the Magi would undertake such a journey a second time?
9 The speaker describes their encounter with the infant Christ as 'Satisfactory'. Why do you think that he chooses this adjective? Is it an understatement, in your opinion?
10 The speaker likens birth to death in lines 36–40. Is this a paradox? How can death be the same as birth?
11 In these lines, is the speaker referring to Christ's death, the death of an old pagan way of life, or both.
12 Why is the Magi no longer at ease in his own kingdom (refer to lines 41–4)?
13 In the final line, why do you think the speaker says that he would be 'glad of another death'? Is the connection between death and birth (or rebirth) relevant here?
14 Describe the tone of the poem?
15 Why do you think that the poet uses both lower and higher case for birth and death in this poem?

PERSONAL RESPONSE

The birth the Magi witnessed began the death of his old way of life, and alienated him from everything 'in the old dispensation, However, it did not, with the same concrete certainty, replace the old world with anything new.

1 Discuss this point of view in an essay on 'Journey of the Magi'.
2 Write a paragraph describing what would motivate you to undertake an extremely difficult task, even though the outcome could not be guaranteed.
3 Would you agree that Eliot depicts the Magis and their emotions in a realistic fashion?

IN CONTEXT

How does Eliot's use of paradox in both 'Journey of the Magi' and 'East Coker IV' contribute to the mood and message of these two poems.

Usk

extract from *Landscapes III*

'Do not suddenly break the branch, or
Hope to find
The white hart behind the white well.
Glance aside, not for lance, do not spell
Old enchantments. Let them sleep.
'Gently dip, but not too deep',
Lift your eyes
Where the roads dip and where the roads rise
Seek only there
Where the grey light meets the green air
The hermit's chapel, the pilgrim's prayer.'

Usk: *an area in Wales. This poem is from a set of poems called 'Landscapes'.*

[3] **hart:** *a male deer, perhaps a pun on heart*

[6] **Gently dip, but not too deep:** *a line from a play by George Peele (1558–96) called The Old Wives' Tale. In this play, the line is spoken by a magical head; the play details incidents and rituals drawn from folk tales.*

[11] **hermit:** *one who chooses to live a life of prayer and isolation.*

[11] **pilgrim:** *one who journeys to a spiritual place*

COMPREHENSION

1. What period of history do you think is evoked in this poem, with its mention of the 'white hart', a 'lance' and 'Old enchantments' ?
2. What is the speaker's attitude to the past?
3. Is there a sense of movement and transition between the past and the future in this poem? Explain your answer with reference to the poem.
4. What kind of journey is being described in the poem?
5. What is the desired end to the journey?
6. How does the poet's use of alliteration and repetition add to the atmosphere of the poem?
7. Is the speaker's presence prominent in this poem?

PERSONAL RESPONSE

1. This poem is from a set of poems called *Landscapes*, and describes a spiritual journey of sorts. Do you think that this poem achieves a balance between an actual and an inner 'landscape'?
2. Describe a place, real or imagined, that reflects an emotion that you've experienced.

IN CONTEXT

Compare and contrast this poem with 'Rannoch, by Glencoe'. Focus especially on the different atmospheres created by each piece.

Rannoch, by Glencoe

extract from *Landscapes IV*

Here the crow starves, here the patient stag
Breeds for the rifle. Between the soft moor
And the soft sky, scarcely room
To leap or soar. Substance crumbles, in the thin air
Moon cold or moon hot. The road winds in
Listlessness of ancient war,
Languor of broken steel,
Clamour of confused wrong, apt
In silence. Memory is strong
Beyond the bone. Pride snapped,
Shadow of pride is long, in the long pass
No concurrence of bone.

Rannoch, by Glencoe: *An area of the Scottish highlands. This poem is from a set of poems called* 'Landscapes'.

The only way of expressing emotion in the form of art is by finding an 'objective correlative'; in other words, a set of objects, a chain of events which shall be the formula of that particular emotion; such that when the external facts, which must terminate in sensory experience, are given, the emotion is immediately evoked.'

COMPREHENSION

1 What mood does the first line and a half of this poem evoke? Mention the specific words and phrases that convey this mood.

2 Is there a contrast between open spaces and a sense of desperation and claustrophobia in the first quatrain?

3 Discuss the impact the poet's use of alliteration has in the second quatrain.

4 Trace the development of the images of violence and death in the first eight lines. Are these images natural or man-made, from the past or from the present?

5 Write a short paragraph describing the landscape you visualise when you read this poem?

6 Do you think that the tone changes in the final four lines?

7 What do you understand by the phrase 'no concurrence of bone'?

8 What role does 'memory' play in this poem? Does it connect the past with the present and future? Discuss the concept of memory in some detail.

9 How does the repetition of 'long' in the second last line contribute to the theme of the poem?

PERSONAL RESPONSE

10 Describe your personal response to this portrait of a landscape.

11 Do you think that this is an effective anti-war poem. Write a detailed answer to this question, referring to images from the poem.

IN CONTEXT

Compare and contrast this poem with 'Usk' under the heading of one of the following themes: 'Life and Death' or 'Movement and Stillness' or 'Time'.

East Coker IV

extract from *The Four Quartets*

The wounded surgeon plies the steel
That questions the distempered part;
Beneath the bleeding hands we feel
The sharp compassion of the healer's art
Resolving the enigma of the fever chart.

Our only health is the disease
If we obey the dying nurse
Whose constant care is not to please
But to remind of our, and Adam's curse,
And that, to be restored, our sickness must grow worse.

The whole earth is our hospital
Endowed by the ruined millionaire,
Wherein, if we do well, we shall
Die of the absolute paternal care
That will not leave us, but prevents us everywhere.

The chill ascends from feet to knees,
The fever sings in mental wires.
If to be warmed, then I must freeze
And quake in frigid purgatorial fires
Of which the flame is rose, and the smoke is briars.

The dripping blood our only drink,
The bloody flesh our only food:
In spite of which we like to think
That we are sound, substantial flesh and blood –
Again, in spite of that, we call this Friday good.

East Coker: *A village in Somerset, England from which Eliot's ancestor, Andrew Eliot, left for America around 1699. T.S. Eliot's ashes are buried there.*

[1] **Steel:** *scalpel*

[15] **Prevents:** *used in the seventeenth-century sense of 'to anticipate'; in the context of this poem it means to go before and guide one to prepare for the Last Judgement.*

[19] **Purgatorial fires:** *In Catholicism, Purgatory is a temporary state or place where the soul goes through a purification by punishment before it can reach heaven.*

COMPREHENSION

1 The first stanza presents a number of oxymorons. Make a list of these and explain how they produce a contradictory effect.
2 Who do you think the 'wounded surgeon' might represent? Why do you think he is described as a 'wounded surgeon'?
3 Why is 'compassion' described as 'sharp'?
4 Do you find the description of the healing process reassuring in the opening stanza, or does the imagery disturb you. Explain your response.
5 In the second stanza, the speaker refers to 'the disease'. Does the poem suggest that this disease is physical or spiritual (or both)? Where is this conveyed?
6 Explain the paradox, 'Our only health is the disease'.
7 Make a list of all the other paradoxes in this poem.
8 What is 'Adam's curse'? Do you think it bears a relation to the 'disease' mentioned in line 6?
9 Trace the conceit of the 'hospital' as it is developed in the first three stanzas.
10 Who do you think is being described as the 'ruined millionaire': Adam or Christ? Explain the reasons behind your answer.
11 Eliot's image of the Eucharist in lines 21–2 is both striking and disturbing. Does this image evoke the concept of sacrifice or salvation, or both?
12 How would you describe the tone of 'East Coker IV'?
13 How does the poet's use of alliteration in stanza 4 contribute to the poem's images and themes.
14 Why do you think that Eliot repeats the phrase 'in spite' twice in the last stanza? Why do you think 'Good Friday' is so called?
15 Personal Response
16 Read lines 14–15 carefully. Do you think that the 'absolute paternal care' is presented as a positive or a negative force?
17 Describe your emotional response to this poem.
18 What do you think is the main theme of this poem?
19 Group work: make up five oxymorons and five paradoxes.
20 This poem suggests that in order to experience eternal joy we must first suffer death. Do you agree with the sentiment that physical suffering is necessary for spiritual healing?

IN CONTEXT

With the themes of suffering, death and rebirth in mind, compare this poem to 'The Journey of the Magi'.

PATRICK KAVANAGH

BIOGRAPHY

In 1904 Patrick Kavanagh was born in Inniskeen, in the townland of Mucker, Co. Monaghan. Kavanagh was one of ten children. His father was a shoemaker by trade and the family also had a small farm. Kavanagh's father worked hard, from six in the morning till nearly midnight each day, his kitchen alive with the talk of customers and journeyman cobblers. Kavanagh left school at thirteen, and it was expected that he would follow in his father's footsteps and become a shoemaker and part-time farmer.

He spent his days working on the family farm or as hired hand on the farms of his neighbours. He would thin turnips, spray potatoes and haul dung in a cart. When the weather was too wet for farming he would spend his time learning his father's trade. There was always a sense, however, in which Kavanagh was not cut out for the life his parents chose for him.

He was always something of a dreamer who tended to have his head in the clouds or stuck in a book. From the age of about twelve he began writing verses of his own. As he grew older he began sending his work to various journals, newspapers and literary magazines. Gradually, he began to see himself as a poet, as someone who was different from the other farmers in his parish.

When his father died in 1929, Patrick became the man of the house, his mother's mainstay and support. Antoinette Quinn describes what was for many years his daily routine: 'Rise at 6 to 7a.m. on weekdays, feed the hens, milk the cows, tend the fire, prepare the breakfast, work all day on the farm except in very wet or wintry weather, home at noon for dinner, finish work at sunset in time for tea. After tea he cycled to the village to buy the paper, practise football, visit a friend, gossip with the neighbourhood lads at the Chunk or play pitch and toss. Invariably, every evening, either before or after these leisure time activities, he would devote a couple of hours to literary pursuits, reading and scribbling by candlelight in an upstairs bedroom'.

Of course there was always the dances which he loved to attend, though he was an awkward and clumsy dancer. Quinn tells us that he 'generally joined a group of male wallflowers, middle-aged spectators who passed the time commenting on the merits and demerits of the dancing couples. One of their staple topics of discussion was the likely number of virgins among the women present. For him, as for most of his acquaintances, the draw of the dance place was the proximity of so many pretty young women; he would select the prettiest and then follow her progress, rarely approaching her but agonising over the possible success of those who did'.

He was better suited to the Gaelic-football field than the dance floor. He was taller than most of his companions and he became the Inniskeen goalkeeper in 1929. He was, however, a rather erratic and unreliable one. Easily bored with standing about when nothing was happening in his vicinity, he had a habit of deserting his goal to run up the field and take close-in frees, hot-footing it back before the action returned to his end of the pitch. On one occasion he left his goal to go and buy ice-cream.

In the late 1930s Kavanagh's life began to change. His first book, *The Ploughman and Other Poems*, was published in 1936, and an autobiography, *The Green Fool*, was published in 1938. In the wake of these publications, Kavanagh left Co. Monaghan and moved to Dublin in order to focus on his writing. In Dublin Kavanagh worked as a journalist, columnist and film reviewer, but often experienced periods of grinding poverty. In 1952 he and his brother Peter founded

Kavanagh's Weekly, a newspaper in which he scrutinised and criticised every aspect of Irish society. The paper folded after only thirteen issues.

During this time Kavanagh wrote 'Advent', 'A Christmas Childhood' and 'On Raglan Road'. Yet his poetry did not win him the fame and fortune he so desired. His two major works of this period, a long poem called 'The Great Hunger' and a novel called *Tarry Flynn*, were banned by the Irish state because of their grimly realistic portrayal of Irish rural life. These works frankly depicted the sexual and social repression common in rural Ireland of the time. This was a message the authorities were not ready or willing for the people of Ireland to hear.

Kavanagh became something of a fixture in the bars frequented by the city's literary community, acquiring a reputation as a wild, eccentric and unpredictable character. He could be gruff, rude and contrary but also kind and generous. Just as in Monaghan, Kavanagh felt like something of an outsider. In Monaghan he felt different to the other farmers because of his poetic leanings. In Dublin he felt different to the other writers because of what they saw as his humble country origins. He could be intensely critical of his fellow Dublin poets and writers, and in his satirical poem 'The Dunciad' portrayed the majority of them as talentless time-wasters.

In 1954 Kavanagh's life changed once again. He sued *The Leader* newspaper for libel but lost, an undertaking that left him in dire financial straits. He was also diagnosed with lung cancer and was admitted to hospital where he had a lung removed. Yet it was in this dark time that Kavanagh felt he was 'reborn' as a poet and a person. He recovered from this operation by relaxing on the banks of the Grand Canal in Dublin, where he wrote 'Canal Bank Walk', 'The Hospital' and 'Lines Written on a Seat on the Grand Canal, Dublin'. The negative experienced of the past year filled him with a new sense of calmness and acceptance, and he vowed to appreciate the beauty in the 'habitual and banal' things that surrounded him.

In his later years Kavanagh's poetry began to receive the acclaim he felt it had always deserved. His reputation began to grow, not only in Ireland but also in the United States and Britain. He won several awards and was invited to give lectures in UCD and in various American colleges. He also became a hero – if not a legend – to the younger generation of Irish writers. He represented Ireland at international literature conferences and became a judge of the Guinness Poetry Awards. Kavanagh died in a Dublin nursing home on 30 November 1967. Shortly before his death he had married Katherine Moloney, his longtime companion.

Inniskeen Road: July Evening

The bicycles go by in twos and threes –
There's a dance in Billy Brennan's barn tonight,
And there's the half-talk code of mysteries
And the wink-and-elbow language of delight.
Half-past eight and there is not a spot
Upon a mile of road, no shadow thrown
That might turn out a man or woman, not
A footfall tapping secrecies of stone.
I have what every poet hates in spite
Of all the solemn talk of contemplation.
Oh, Alexander Selkirk knew the plight
Of being king and government and nation.
A road, a mile of kingdom. I am king
Of banks and stones and every blooming thing.

[1] **Alexander Selkirk:** *(1676–1721), a Scottish sailor who spent four years alone on an uninhabited island. His solitary sojourn provided the inspiration for Daniel Defoe's Robinson Crusoe.*

A man is original when he speaks the truth that has always been known to all good men.

COMPREHENSION

1 The title of this poem is very specific regarding place and time. How important do you think that the setting is to the meaning of this poem?
2 What do you understand by the phrase 'half-talk code'?
3 Where, and in what circumstances, do you think the type of body language that Kavanagh describes as the 'wink-and-elbow language of delight' is most likely to take place?
4 Do you think that the speaker of the poem is privy to the 'mysteries' and 'secrecies' surrounding the dance at Billy Brennan's?
5 Do you think that the assonance and alliteration in line 8, 'A footfall tapping secrecies of stone', is suggestive of the quietness that now surrounds the speaker? Look at other examples of alliteration in the poem and explain their effect.
6 What do you think it is that 'every poet hates'?
7 What is the tone in the second stanza of this poem?
8 What does the speaker have in common with Alexander Selkirk?
9 Do you think the speaker is pleased to be king 'Of banks and stones and every blooming thing'?
10 Compare and contrast the adjectives in the first stanza to those in the second? Write a few lines on how the adjectives contribute to the development of mood and thought in the poem?
11 What are the main contrasts that inform this poem?
12 The word 'blooming' is a pun, in that it has more than one meaning. Write a paragraph on how its different connotations effect how one might interpret the final line of the poem.

PERSONAL RESPONSE

1 *Class discussion:* Do you think that the speaker of the poem fits the stereotypical image of the poet. Give a detailed response.
2 'Would you agree with the view that 'Kavanagh is a whinging self-pitying introvert who wants to have his cake and eat it'?
3 Do you think that the speaker's particular experience of loneliness in this poem expresses a universally known feeling, in Kavanagh's words, a 'truth that has always been known to all'.

IN CONTEXT

What are the similarities and differences between this poem and 'On Raglan Road'? In your answer take into account both the representation of the poet figure, and the poet's seeming alienation from love relationships.

Epic

I have lived in important places, times
When great events were decided, who owned
That half a rood of rock, a no-man's land
Surrounded by our pitchfork-armed claims.
I heard the Duffys shouting 'Damn your soul!'
And old McCabe stripped to the waist, seen
Step the plot defying blue cast-steel –
'Here is the march along these iron stones.'
That was the year of the Munich bother. Which
Was more important? I inclined
To lose my faith in Ballyrush and Gortin
Till Homer's ghost came whispering to my mind.
He said: I made the Iliad from such
A local row. Gods make their own importance.

Epic: *a lengthy poem, centered upon a hero, in which a series of great achievements or important events is narrated in elevated style.*
[8] **march:** *boundary*
[9] **Munich bother:** *1939*
[11] **Ballyrush and Gortin:** *townlands in Co. Monaghan*
[12] **Homer:** *a Greek poet, who wrote the Iliad, an 'epic' poem.*

COMPREHENSION

1 An epic is a literary genre. What poetic conventions and subject matter are associated with this genre. Does the poem fulfil any of the conventions associated with the epic?
2 What are the 'great events' described in the poem? Do you agree that these are important matters, or that they are a suitable subject for a poem that has the grand title of 'Epic'?
3 Describe the setting of the drama that is taking place in the first eight lines.
4 Make a list of all the war imagery in the poem.
5 Consider the verbs used in the second quatrain of the poem. What do these suggest about rural life? How do the verbs relate to the war imagery?
6 What is the 'Munich bother' the poet refers to? What is the poet's attitude to the 'Munich bother'?
7 Do you think that the phrase 'God's make their own importance' is an ironic comment on the 'great events' described in the poem's octave, or does the phrase affirm their importance?
8 Does the poet change his mind over the course of the poem?
9 Discuss the relevance of the line, 'Till Homer's ghost came whispering to my mind' (12) to (a) the development of thought in the poem, and (b) the representation of the speaker's character.
10 How does the tone of the first line compare to that of the final line?

PERSONAL RESPONSE

1 Describe an incident, real or imagined, that at the time it occurred took on major importance, but that on reflection seemed of little significance.
2 Do you think that the phrase 'God's make their own importance' is an ironic comment on the 'great events' described in the poem's octave, or does the phrase affirm their importance?

IN CONTEXT

'Kavanagh represents rural life as full of conflict, violence and frustration'. Discuss this statement with reference to 'Epic' and 'Great Hunger I'

Shancoduff

My black hills have never seen the sun rising,
Eternally they look north towards Armagh.
Lot's wife would not be salt if she had been
Incurious as my black hills that are happy
When dawn whitens Glassdrummond chapel.

My hills hoard the bright shillings of March
While the sun searches in every pocket.
They are my Alps and I have climbed the Matterhorn
With a sheaf of hay for three perishing calves
In the field under the Big Forth of Rocksavage.

The sleety winds fondle the rushy beards of Shancoduff
While the cattle-drovers sheltering in the Featherna Bush
Look up and say: 'Who owns them hungry hills
That the water-hen and snipe must have forsaken?
A poet? Then by heavens he must be poor.'
I hear, and is my heart not badly shaken?

[3] **Lot's wife:** *Genesis 19:23. Lot's wife was turned into a pillar of salt when, fleeing the idolatrous city of Sodom, she looked back with curiosity at its destruction.*

[5] **Glassdrummond chapel:** *this is in Co. Down*

[10] **Rocksavage [11], Shanacoff [12], Featherna Bush:** *all names of places close to the poet's father's farm in Co. Monaghan.*

COMPREHENSION

1 Write a paragraph on the significance of the poet's use of colour imagery.
2 How important are place-names in this poem?
3 Do you think that the poet's identity is rooted in his sense of place?
4 Why do you think that the poet describes the 'black hills' as eternal?
5 Discuss the religious imagery in the first stanza?
6 How does the poet personify the hills in line 4? Where else does the poet use personification, and to what effect?
7 How many times does the possessive pronoun, 'my' occur in this poem? What does this say about the narrator's feelings for nature?
8 What is the tone of the poem?
9 What poetic devices are used in the line, 'The sleety winds fondle the rushy beards of Shancoduff', and to what effect? Try to rephrase this line using ordinary language. Does it lose some of its atmosphere and meaning when translated into prose?
10 Discuss the metaphors in lines 6–7, and the references to money in line 14.
11 Do you think the cattle-drovers and the poet share similar values? Explain your answer with reference to the poem.
12 Do you think that this poem celebrates rural life? Discuss, with reference to the poem.
13 Do you think that the poet consider himself to be poor?

PERSONAL RESPONSE

1 *Class discussion:* the third stanza has 6 lines, one line more than the other two stanzas. Do you think that this structure draws our attention to that extra final line, which ends with a question mark? Is this a rhetorical question, in your opinion? How would you interpret / answer it?
2 What are your feelings about where you live? Write a paragraph in which you describe this place and what it means to you?

IN CONTEXT

'Kavanagh's use of language is both commonplace and poetic'. Discuss this statement with reference to 'Shancoduff' and one other poem by Kavanagh on your course.

The Great Hunger

I

Clay is the word and clay is the flesh
Where the potato-gatherers like mechanised scare-crows move
Along the side-fall of the hill – Maguire and his men.
If we watch them an hour is there anything we can prove
Of life as it is broken-backed over the Book
Of Death? Here crows gabble over worms and frogs
And the gulls like old newspapers are blown clear of the hedges, luckily.
Is there some light of imagination in these wet clods?
Or why do we stand here shivering?
Which of these men
Loved the light and the queen
Too long virgin? Yesterday was summer. Who was it promised marriage to himself
Before apples were hung from the ceilings for Hallowe'en?
We will wait and watch the tragedy to the last curtain,
Till the last soul passively like a bag of wet clay
Rolls down the side of the hill, diverted by the angles
Where the plough missed or a spade stands, straitening the way.

A dog lying on a torn jacket under a heeled-up cart,
A horse nosing along the posied headland, trailing
A rusty plough. Three heads hanging between wide-apart
Legs. October playing a symphony on a slack wire paling.
Maguire watches the drills flattened out
And the flints that lit a candle for him on a June altar
Flameless. The drills slipped by and the days slipped by
And he trembled his head away and ran free from the world's halter,
And thought himself wiser than any man in the townland
When he laughed over pints of porter
Of how he came free from every net spread
In the gaps of experience. He shook a knowing head
And pretended to his soul
That children are tedious in hurrying fields of April
Where men are spanging across wide furrows.
Lost in the passion that never needs a wife –
The pricks that pricked were the pointed pins of harrows.
Children scream so loud that the crows could bring
The seed of an acre away with crow-rude jeers.
Patrick Maguire, he called his dog and he flung a stone in the air
And hallooed the birds away that were the birds of the years.
Turn over the weedy clods and tease out the tangled skeins.
What is he looking for there?

He thinks it is a potato, but we know better
Than his mud-gloved fingers probe in this insensitive hair.

'Move forward the basket and balance it steady
In this hollow. Pull down the shafts of that cart, Joe,
And straddle the horse,' Maguire calls.
'The wind's over Brannagan's, now that means rain.
Graip up some withered stalks and see that no potato falls
Over the tail-board going down the ruckety pass –
And that's a job we'll have to do in December,
Gravel it and build a kerb on the bog-side. Is that Cassidy's ass
Out in my clover? Curse o' God –
Where is that dog?
Never where he's wanted.' Maguire grunts and spits
Through a clay-wattled moustache and stares about him from the
        height.
His dream changes like the cloud-swung wind
And he is not so sure now if his mother was right
When she praised the man who made a field his bride.

Watch him, watch him, that man on a hill whose spirit
Is a wet sack flapping about the knees of time.
He lives that his little fields may stay fertile when his own body
Is spread in the bottom of a ditch under two coulters crossed in
        Christ's Name.

He was suspicious in his youth as a rat near strange bread
When girls laughed; when they screamed he knew that meant
The cry of fillies in season. He could not walk
The easy road to destiny. He dreamt
The innocence of young brambles to hooked treachery.
O the grip, O the grip of irregular fields! No man escapes.
It could not be that back of the hills love was free
And ditches straight.
No monster hand lifted up children and put down apes
As here.
                    'O God if I had been wiser!'
That was his sigh like the brown breeze in the thistles.
He looks, towards his house and haggard. 'O God if I had been
        wiser!'
But now a crumpled leaf from the whitethorn bushes
Darts like a frightened robin, and the fence
Shows the green of after-grass through a little window,
And he knows that his own heart is calling his mother a liar.
God's truth is life – even the grotesque shapes of its
        foulest fire.

The horse lifts its head and cranes
Through the whins and stones
To lip late passion in the crawling clover.

continued over

In the gap there's a bush weighted with boulders like
morality,
The fools of life bleed if they climb over.

The wind leans from Brady's, and the coltsfoot leaves are holed
with rust,
Rain fills the cart-tracks and the sole-plate grooves;
A yellow sun reflects in Donaghmoyne
The poignant light in puddles shaped by hooves.

Come with me, Imagination, into this iron house
And we will watch from the doorway the years run back,
And we will know what a peasant's left hand wrote on the page.
Be easy, October. No cackle hen, horse neigh, tree sough, duck
quack.

[6] **coulter:** *part of a plough*
[81] **whins:** *gorse, furze*
[87] **Donaghmoyne:** *a townland in Co. Monaghan*

COMPREHENSION

1 What does the title lead you to expect from this poem?
2 Discuss Kavanagh's use of metaphor in the opening line of this poem. Does it have religious significance? What tone does it set for the poem?
3 How is rural life represented in this poem? Is it full of mystical wonder or is it one of hardship and frustration?
4 Why do you think the poet described the potato-gatherers as 'mechanized'?
5 What do you think the poet means by the 'Book of death'. Why do you think he uses capital letters for this phrase?
6 What metaphor for marriage is used in lines 25 and 28? What does this suggest about Maguire's attitude to marriage? Are these metaphors still used today?
7 Why do you think that Maguire's mother 'praised the man who made a field his bride' (57). Rephrase this line to make it applicable to modern urban life.
8 How strong an influence did Maguire's mother have on his life?
9 Was Maguire true to his own self?
10 Discuss the irony in the following lines: 'He lives that his little fields may stay fertile when his own body / Is spread in the bottom of a ditch under two coulters crossed in Christ's Name.' (60–1).
11 What does Maguire sacrifice for the sake of his land?
12 Do you think that the speaker feels empathy for Maguire? Write a paragraph explaining your answer with detailed reference to the poem.
13 Kavanagh's use of simile in this poem is extensive. How does his use of simile add to his depiction of Maguire.
14 List all the religious imagery that occurs in this poem. Is religion portrayed in a positive or a negative light? How does the religious imagery contribute to the meaning of the poem?
15 The speaker uses the metaphor of 'a wet sack flapping about the knees of time' to describe Maguire's 'spirit'. Analyse this metaphor. What does it suggest about (a) Maguire's character, and (b) the speaker's attitude towards Maguire.
16 How do the final lines of this poem relate to lines 11–12.
17 Does the time of year have significance in this poem?
18 Do you agree that Maguire's life is a 'tragedy' (14)? What do you understand by the word 'tragedy'?
19 Do you think that Kavanagh, in this poem, has a particular message to impart to the reader? If so, is this message relevant to Irish society today?

PERSONAL RESPONSE

1 *Class discussion:* How do the following themes of the poem relate to each other: marriage, fertility, death, nature and religion.
2 The speaker mentions 'imagination' twice in this poem, first in the opening stanza and again in the last. Why do you think that the imagination is so important to the speaker? Does Maguire have an imaginative outlook on life?
3 Describe the character and physical appearance of Maguire in your own words.
4 *Class discussion:* What does the animal imagery in lines 62–4 suggest to you about Maguire's attitude towards women?

The critic, Antoinette Quinn, writes: 'The poem's title and recurrent motif of potato-harvesting suggest a disturbing analogy between the psycho-sexual deprivation that is de-populating and devitalizing contemporary Ireland and the famine that ravaged the country in the mid-nineteenth century'.

Discuss this statement in an essay on 'The Great Hunger I'.

IN CONTEXT

'In Kavanagh's lyrics 'a world comes to life'. Discuss this statement in relation to 'The Great Hunger I' and 'Epic'.

A Christmas Childhood

I

One side of the potato-pits was white with frost –
How wonderful that was, how wonderful!
And when we put our ears to the paling-post
The music that came out was magical.

The light between the ricks of hay and straw
Was a hole in Heaven's gable. An apple tree
With its December-glinting fruit we saw –
O you, Eve, were the world that tempted me

To eat the knowledge that grew in clay
And death the germ within it! Now and then
I can remember something of the gay
Garden that was childhood's. Again

The tracks of cattle to a drinking-place,
A green stone lying sideways in a ditch
Or any common sight the transfigured face
Of a beauty that the world did not touch.

II

My father played the melodion
Outside at our gate;
There were stars in the morning east
And they danced to his music.

Across the wild bogs his melodion called
To Lennons and Callans.
As I pulled on my trousers in a hurry
I knew some strange thing had happened.

Outside the cow-house my mother
Made the music of milking;
The light of her stable-lamp was a star
And the frost of Bethlehem made it twinkle.

A water-hen screeched in the bog,
Mass-going feet
Crunched the wafer-ice on the pot-holes,
Somebody wistfully twisted the bellows wheel.

My child poet picked out the letters
On the grey stone,
In silver the wonder of a Christmas townland,
The winking glitter of a frosty dawn.

Cassiopeia was over
Cassidy's hanging hill,
I looked and three whin bushes rode across
The horizon – The Three Wise Kings.

An old man passing said:
'Can't he make it talk –
The melodion'. I hid in the doorway
And tightened the belt of my box-pleated coat.

I nicked six nicks on the door-post
With my penknife's big blade –
There was a little one for cutting tobacco,
And I was six Christmases of age.

My father played the melodion,
My mother milked the cows,
And I had a prayer like a white rose pinned
On the Virgin Mary's blouse.

[17] **Melodion:** *a small accordion*
[37] **Cassiopeia:** *a northern constellation of stars*

Advent

We have tested and tasted too much, lover –
Through a chink too wide there comes in no wonder.
But here in the Advent-darkened room
Where the dry black bread and the sugarless tea
Of penance will charm back the luxury
Of a child's soul, we'll return to Doom
The knowledge we stole but could not use.

And the newness that was in every stale thing
When we looked at it as children: the spirit-shocking
Wonder in a black slanting Ulster hill
Or the prophetic astonishment in the tedious talking
Of an old fool will awake for us and bring
You and me to the yard gate to watch the whins
And the bog-holes, cart-tracks, old stables where Time begins.

O after Christmas we'll have no need to go searching
For the difference that sets an old phrase burning –
We'll hear it in the whispered argument of a churning
Or in the streets where the village boys are lurching.
And we'll hear it among decent men too
Who barrow dung in gardens under trees,
Wherever life pours ordinary plenty.
Won't we be rich, my love and I, and
God we shall not ask for reason's payment,
The why of heart-breaking strangeness in dreeping hedges
Nor analyse God's breath in common statement.
We have thrown into the dust-bin the clay-minted wages
Of pleasure, knowledge and the conscious hour –
And Christ comes with a January flower.

Advent: *the coming of Christ on Judgement day; a time of prayer, fasting and atonement*
[13] **Whins:** *gorse or furze.*
[24] **dreeping:** *coined perhaps from the adjectives dripping and creeping, both of which could be applied to the hedges.*

COMPREHENSION

1 What does 'Advent' mean? What does the title of the poem lead you to expect it will be about?
2 Do you agree that the opening lines of the poem suggest that knowledge makes 'wonder' impossible. What is the tone in these lines?
3 Are there connotations of good and evil in the contrast set up in the first stanza between knowledge and wonder; adulthood and childhood?
4 What biblical event do you think the poet is referring to in the line 'The knowledge we stole but could not use'?
5 What is the tone of the second stanza? Is it nostalgic or disdainful?
6 Do you think that the speaker wishes to recapture the 'wonder' and 'astonishment' he once felt for a 'black slanting Ulster hill' or for the 'tedious talking / of an old fool'. Give reasons for your answer.
7 *Class discussion:* Consider the line 'please / God we shall not ask for reason's payment'. What do you think the poet means by this?
8 What is the poet's attitude towards spirituality and sexuality in this poem?

PERSONAL RESPONSE

1 Kavanagh originally gave this poem the title, 'Renewal'. Why do you think he changed the title to 'Advent'? Which title do you think is the more apt?
2 Are you persuaded by the speaker's confidence that he and his beloved will experience 'newness' once more?
3 Do you think that Kavanagh is reflecting on the imagination and on poetic inspiration in this poem. Give details from the poem in support of your answer.

IN CONTEXT

Both 'Advent' and 'A Christmas Childhood' end with an image of a flower. What does the flower represent in each poem? What other similar images are common to both these poems?

My beginnings were so peculiar, humble and illiterate that I have never dared to write about them.

COMPREHENSION

1 Who tempts the speaker away from the innocence of childhood?
2 Why does the speaker link knowledge with death?
3 Discuss the biblical imagery in the lines: 'O you, Eve, were the world that tempted me/To eat the knowledge that grew in clay/And death the germ within it'. What do these lines suggest about the speaker's attitude towards adulthood and experience?
4 How does the speaker recapture a sense of innocence and wonder?
5 Discuss the view that a child's sense of imagination and wonder can transform 'any common sight' into a thing of beauty. Do you think that the poet also has the ability to turn the ordinary and commonplace into something wondrous? Support your answer with reference to the poem.
6 Why do you think that music figures so prominently in this poem.
7 What do children represent for the poet in this poem?
8 What effect does the poet's use of compound words have on the poem's meaning?
9 Where does the poet use the image of light in this poem, and what does it represent?
10 What does the poet's use of the senses – sight, hearing and taste – contribute to the poem's meaning.
11 Do you think that this poem captures the magic of Christmas childhoods?
12 The speaker mentions 'Eve' in the first stanza and 'Virgin Mary' in the final line. How does he relate these religious female figures to his experience of life?
13 Make a list of the many contrasts that inform this poem.
14 Do you think that the speaker of this poem is that of the 'child poet' or the adult poet, or does the voice of the narrator change as the poem progresses?

PERSONAL RESPONSE

1 *Class discussion:* compare the adult's view of religion to the child's.
2 Do you think that this poem presents an overly idealistic view of childhood?
3 'Kavanagh believes that the childhood sense of wonder is essential to adult happiness'. Do you agree with this statement. Discuss this statement with reference to the poem.
4 What does the phrase 'the inner-child' mean to you?

IN CONTEXT

Compare the poet's representation of childhood in this poem with the attitude towards children expressed by Maguire in 'The Great Hunger I'.

On Raglan Road

sung to the air of 'The Dawning of the Day'

On Raglan Road on an autumn day I met her first and
knew
That her dark hair would weave a snare that I might
one day rue;
I saw the danger, yet I walked along the enchanted way,
And I said, let grief be a fallen leaf at the dawning of
the day.

On Grafton Street in November we tripped lightly along
the ledge
Of the deep ravine where can be seen the worth of
passion's pledge,
The Queen of Hearts still making tarts and I not making
hay –
O I loved too much and by such and such is happiness
thrown away.

I gave her gifts of the mind I gave her the secret sign
that's known
To the artists who have known the true gods of sound
and stone
And word and tint. I did not stint for I gave her poems
to say.
With her own name there and her own dark hair like
clouds over fields of May

On a quiet street where old ghosts meet I see her walking
now
Away from me so hurriedly my reason must allow
That I had wooed not as I should a creature made of
clay –
When the angel woos the clay he'd lose his wings at the
dawn of day.

Raglan Road: *a street off Pembroke Road in Ballsbridge, Dublin, where Kavanagh lived for a time.*

COMPREHENSION

1. Write a paragraph on the poet's use of personification and simile in his depiction of the woman's dark hair.
2. What is the 'snare' that the poet fears?
3. What do you think the poet means by the phrase 'enchanted way'?
4. Discuss the imagery and internal rhyme in the line 'let grief be a fallen leaf at the dawning of the day' (4) and line 11, 'And word and tint. I did not stint for I gave her poems to say'.
5. Comment on the speaker's attitude to love as expressed in his idea that 'the worth of passion's pledge' can be seen in 'the deep ravine'.
6. In your own words, describe the 'gifts' the poet gives to his beloved.
7. Does the poet's evocation of 'old ghosts' in line 12 hint that his relationship with the woman with dark hair is in some way dead?
8. In the final lines the speaker describes how he wooed 'a creature made of clay', and sets up a contrast between an 'angel' and clay. Do you think that the speaker sees himself as an angel?
10. *Class discussion:* What does the dawn symbolize in the poem?

The Hospital

A year ago I fell in love with the functional ward
Of a chest hospital: square cubicles in a row
Plain concrete, wash basins – an art lover's woe,
Not counting how the fellow in the next bed snored.
But nothing whatever is by love debarred,
The common and banal her heat can know.
The corridor led to a stairway and below
Was the inexhaustible adventure of a gravelled yard.
This is what love does to things: the Rialto Bridge,
The main gate that was bent by a heavy lorry,
The seat at the back of a shed that was a suntrap.
Naming these things is the love-act and its pledge;
For we must record love's mystery without claptrap,
Snatch out of time the passionate transitory.

[2] **Hospital:** *the Rialto Hospital, Dublin, where Kavanagh, suffering from lung cancer, spent some time in the mid 1950s.*

COMPREHENSION

1. Who or what does the speaker fall in love with?
2. What response does the poet's feelings towards 'the functional ward' elicit in you? Do you think that the adjective the poet uses to describe the ward is deliberately at odds with the emotion of falling in love?
3. What is the tone of the poem?
4. The poet states that 'we must record love's mystery without claptrap'. Do you think that he achieves this?
5. Do you agree that love's mysteries may be found in the 'common' and 'banal'?
6. The poet begins this poem with 'A year ago I fell in love ...' Do you think that this love lasted.
7. What significance does the poet place on 'Naming'?
8. *Class discussion:* What do you think the poet means by, 'Snatch out of time the passionate transitory'. Do you think this is paradoxical?

PERSONAL RESPONSE

1. What does this poem say about Kavanagh's attitude to (a) love and (b) poetic creation?
2. *Class discussion:* Do you agree with the statement in this poem that 'nothing whatever is by love debarred'?
3. Do you think that there is a fear of mortality at the core of this poem?

IN CONTEXT

'The Hospital' and 'Advent' are both poems about poetry, about the best poetic themes and the emotional states conducive to the creative act.

Discuss this statement, comparing and contrasting the two poems.

Canal Bank Walk

Leafy-with-love banks and the green waters of the canal
Pouring redemption for me, that I do
The will of God, wallow in the habitual, the banal,
Grow with nature again as before I grew.
The bright stick trapped, the breeze adding a third
Party to the couple kissing on an old seat,
And a bird gathering materials for the nest for the Word
Eloquently new and abandoned to its delirious beat.
O unworn world enrapture me, encapture me in a web
Of fabulous grass and eternal voices by a beech,
Feed the gaping need of my senses, give me ad lib
To pray unselfconsciously with overflowing speech
For this soul needs to be honoured with a new dress woven
From green and blue things and arguments that cannot be proven.

Canal Bank: *near Baggot Street Bridge, Dublin*

COMPREHENSION

1 Describe, in your own words, the relation between nature and God in the first two and a half lines?
2 The speaker mentions doing the 'will of God'. What does he think the 'will of God' is for him?
3 What is the tense of the poem?
4 What do you understand by the line: 'And a bird gathering materials for the nest for the Word'? Do you think that this phrase is suggestive of the art of poetic creation?
5 Read the poem aloud. How do the 'run-on' lines contribute to the poem's meaning and atmosphere?
6 Trace the poet's use of the image of water in the poem. What does water symbolise for the poet?
7 Is there a change in tone between the octave and the sestet of this sonnet?
8 What is the speaker's state of mind?
9 What do you think that the poet is seeking when he prays for his soul to be clothed in 'green and blue things and arguments that cannot be proven'?
10 How does the sestet achieve its hymn-like quality?

PERSONAL RESPONSE

1 How close do you think is the connection between God, nature and poetry for Kavanagh?
2 How important is colour imagery in this poem?.

IN CONTEXT

'This poem represents the rebirth of Kavanagh as a poet, he has achieved 'the luxury of a child's soul', which he sought for in Advent'. Discuss.

Lines Written on a Seat on the Grand Canal, Dublin

'Erected to the memory of Mrs. Dermot O'Brien'
O commemorate me where there is water,
Canal water, preferably, so stilly
Greeny at the heart of summer. Brother
Commemorate me thus beautifully
Where by a lock niagarously roars
The falls for those who sit in the tremendous silence
Of mid-July. No one will speak in prose
Who finds his way to these Parnassian islands.
A swan goes by head low with many apologies,
Fantastic light looks through the eyes of bridges –
And look! a barge comes bringing from Athy
And other far-flung towns mythologies.
O commemorate me with no hero-courageous
Tomb – just a canal-bank seat for the passer-by.

[5] **niagarously:** *after Niagera Falls, suggesting the noise of the torrent of water*
[8] **Parnassian:** *of Parnassus, a Greek mountain sacred to Apollo and the poetic muses.*
[11] **Athy:** *a town in the Midlands*

COMPREHENSION

1 Describe, in your own words, the relation between nature and God in the first two and a half lines?
2 The speaker mentions doing the 'will of God'. What does he think the 'will of God' is for him?
3 What is the tense of the poem?
4 What do you understand by the line: 'And a bird gathering materials for the nest for the Word'? Do you think that this phrase is suggestive of the art of poetic creation?
5 Read the poem aloud. How do the 'run-on' lines contribute to the poem's meaning and atmosphere?
6 Trace the poet's use of the image of water in the poem. What does water symbolise for the poet?
7 Is there a change in tone between the octave and the sestet of this sonnet?
8 What is the speaker's state of mind?
9 What do you think that the poet is seeking when he prays for his soul to be clothed in 'green and blue things and arguments that cannot be proven'?
10 How does the sestet achieve its hymn-like quality?

PERSONAL RESPONSE

1 How close do you think is the connection between God, nature and poetry for Kavanagh?
2 How important is colour imagery in this poem?.

IN CONTEXT

This poem represents the rebirth of Kavanagh as a poet. He has achieved 'the luxury of a child's soul', which he sought for in 'Advent.'

Discuss this statement.

JOHN KEATS

BIOGRAPHY

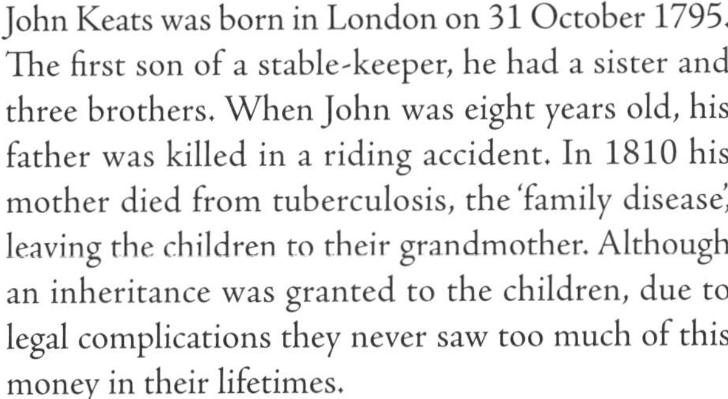

John Keats was born in London on 31 October 1795. The first son of a stable-keeper, he had a sister and three brothers. When John was eight years old, his father was killed in a riding accident. In 1810 his mother died from tuberculosis, the 'family disease', leaving the children to their grandmother. Although an inheritance was granted to the children, due to legal complications they never saw too much of this money in their lifetimes.

Though of small stature, as a young boy Keats was fond of cricket and fighting. He was a diligent student. According to a friend, 'He was at work before the first school hour began, and that was at seven'. He was not university educated. Upon leaving school he began a five-year apothecary's apprenticeship. He was, at least at the start, a good student, and his commitment to his career in medicine was such that in 1816 he began to study further to qualify as a surgeon. However, his interest in poetry was always there and it vied constantly with his career.

In 1817 he chose not to sit his surgical examinations in order to be present whilst his first collection of poems was being printed. He finally abandoned his studies, sacrificing his medical ambitions to a literary life. According to his friend Charles Brown 'he ascribed his inability [to be a surgeon] to an overwrought apprehension of every possible chance of doing evil in the wrong direction of the instrument. "My last operation," he told me, "was the opening of a man's temporal artery. I did it with the utmost nicety; but, reflecting on what passed through my mind at the time, my dexterity seemed a miracle, and I never took up the lancet again."'

Keats, like many of his contemporaries, felt that he couldn't really be a poet unless he composed a long poem, and so set about writing the 4,000-line 'Endymion'. Though it deals with many of the themes that occur throughout the later writings, such as the imagination, love and beauty, the poem lacked cohesion. The poet Shelley, a friend of Keats, wrote that 'no person should possibly get to the end of it'.

Around this time his younger brother Tom had just started showing signs of consumption and needed Keats to look after him. The poet had also just fallen in love with a young woman named Frances (Fanny) Brawne. Following the death of his brother in December 1818 Fanny became an important element in Keats' life. He would interrupt his serious poetry to write quick sonnets to Fanny, including the famous 'Bright Star'. Most of these works dwell upon her physical charms, but they also celebrate the enjoyment and pleasure he found in her company.

In late April 1919, Keats began composing one of his best-loved works, 'La Belle Dame Sans Merci'. But even it gives no hint of the great works to come; Keats himself considered it mere light verse and, in a letter to his brother George, dismissed it with a joke. Then, in the space of a few weeks, he composed three of the most beautiful works of poetry ever written – 'Ode on a Grecian Urn', 'Ode to a Nightingale' and 'Ode on Melancholy'. Later that August he wrote 'To Autumn'. Keats was only twenty-three at this time.

The prospect of marriage brought fresh worry regarding his already difficult financial situation. He met with his publishers in November and plans were made for another book of poems. In January, his brother George returned from America to borrow more money from Keats, who could ill-afford it. He came to an agreement with their guardian over the final settlement of his grandmother's estate. It was a small sum of money in the end, and Keats decided to give most of it to George. Though younger, George was married and settling into his own business while Keats could not afford to marry Fanny. 'George out not to have done this,' Keats remarked to Fanny about the loan, 'he should have reflected that I wish to marry myself – but I suppose having a family to provide for makes a man selfish.' His letters to George and Georgiana, both before and after George's January 1820 visit to England, are wonderful documents – engaging, witty, profound, but rarely does Keats admit to any depression and worry. His protective instinct towards his siblings would never disappear.

On 3 February 1920 Keats began to cough blood. This frightening event was later described by his friend Brown, whom Keats was visiting at the time. He arrived at Brown's house in a sort of fever. His friend immediately realised Keats was ill and sent him upstairs to bed. Brown then brought him a glass of spirits. As he entered the room, he heard Keats cough. It was just a slight cough, but Keats said: 'That is blood from my mouth.' There was a drop of blood upon his bed sheet. He said to Brown, 'Bring me the candle and let me see this blood.' Both men looked upon it for a moment; then Keats looked up at his friend calmly and said, 'I know the colour of that blood; it is arterial blood. I cannot be deceived in that colour. That drop of blood is my death warrant. I must die.'

Over subsequent months Keats' health grew worse. Though he was not immediately diagnosed with tuberculosis it soon became clear that this was the cause of his ill health. Though his spirits were often low he managed to make the final corrections to his latest manuscript of poems and these were submitted for publication in June. The good reviews the book garnered lifted Keats' mood, but his ill health prevented any real celebration. His friends suggested a trip to Italy to recover his health, a trip he undertook with his friend, the artist Joseph Severn, in August. Such trips to warmer climates were common for tubercular patients. However, no recovery was to take place. Keats dies in Rome the following February. Upon his tombstone, by request, was inscribed: 'Here lies one whose life was written in water'.

To One Who Has Been Long in City Pent

To one who has been long in city pent,
'Tis very sweet to look into the fair
And open face of heaven,– to breathe a prayer
Full in the smile of the blue firmament.
Who is more happy, when, with heart's content,
Fatigued he sinks into some pleasant lair
Of wavy grass, and reads a debonair
And gentle tale of love and languishment?
Returning home at evening, with an ear
Catching the notes of Philomel, – an eye
Watching the sailing cloudlet's bright career,
He mourns that day so soon has glided by:
E'en like the passage of an angel's tear
That falls through the clear ether silently.

[1] **pent:** *confined, shut up in a small place.*
[8] **Philomel:** *daughter of the king of Athens whom the gods turned into a nightingale for her own protection; a nightingale.*

I scarcely remember counting upon happiness – I look not for it if it be not in the present hour – nothing startles me beyond the moment.

COMPREHENSION

1. What does it mean to be 'in city pent'? Have you ever felt this way about being in a city?
2. What does Keats suggest as a remedy for someone who has 'been long in city pent'?
3. The poet describes his ideal way to relax. Describe in your own words what this entails.
4. What could this person expect to hear and see on the way home after such a relaxing day?
5. In the last three lines of the poem Keats compares the silent passing of the day to the fall of an angel's tear. How are the two similar? Why do you think Keats chose to use such a comparison?

PERSONAL RESPONSE

1. Did you enjoy reading this sonnet? Do you think that Keats' advice is still as apt today as it was when the poem was written?
2. Once again we are presented with exquisite lines of poetry. Say which lines you found most impressive and discuss their poetic qualities.

IN CONTEXT

Like many of Keats' poems 'To One Who Has Been Long in City Pent' acknowledges the pains of living without lapsing into despair. At the heart of the poem is a realisation of the beauty that the natural world holds and the joy it can bring. Compare three poems by Keats in light of these comments.

On First Looking into Chapman's Homer

Much have I travell'd in the realms of gold,
And many goodly states and kingdoms seen;
Round many western islands have I been
Which bards in fealty to Apollo hold.
Oft of one wide expanse had I been told
That deep-brow'd Homer ruled as his demesne;
Yet did I never breathe its pure serene
Till I heard Chapman speak out loud and bold:
Then felt I like some watcher of the skies
When a new planet swims into his ken;
Or like stout Cortez when with eagle eyes
He star'd at the Pacific – and all his men
Look'd at each other with a wild surmise –
Silent, upon a peak in Darien.

Chapman: *George Chapman (1559–1634, writer who translated works by Homer.*
Homer: *Ancient Greek poet, author of The Iliad and The Odyssey.*
[1] **realms of gold:** *the world of the imagination. Apollo, who as the sun god was related to gold, was also the god of poetry.*
[3] **western islands:** *Britain and Ireland.*
[6] **demesne:** *dominion.*
[7] **serene:** *air.*
[10] **ken:** *knowledge, range of vision, sight.*
[11] **Cortez:** *Explorer, one of the first Europeans to see Mexico City. Keats confuses him with another man, Bilboa, who was first European to reach the Pacific.*
[14] **Darien:** *An old name for the Panama isthmus, the neck of land joining North and South America.*

COMPREHENSION

1 What does Keats mean by 'realms of gold'?
2 What do you think he means when he says he has 'travell'd' to these realms?
3 Why do you think Homer is described as being 'deep-brow'd'?
4 List, in your own words, the characteristics of Homer's 'demesne', as Keats describes it.
5 Why has Keats been unable to breathe the 'pure serene' of Homer's realm? Why is he now capable of doing this?
6 What two comparisons does Keats use in order to convey his excited reaction to Chapman's translations?
7 Why do you think Cortez and his men were 'silent' when they stood upon the 'peak in Darien'?

PERSONAL RESPONSE

1 What does this poem reveal about Keats' attitude to poetry? Do you find his feelings about poetry to be reasonable or over-the-top? Give reasons for each of your answers.
2 'This poem skilfully uses images of travel and discovery to convey the pleasure and excitement of reading poetry'. List the different images of travel and discovery used throughout the poem.

When I Have Fears that I May Cease to Be

When I have fears that I may cease to be
  Before my pen has glean'd my teeming brain,
Before high piled books, in charactery,
  Hold like rich garners the full ripen'd grain –
When I behold, upon the night's starr'd face,
  Huge cloudy symbols of a high romance,
And think that I may never live to trace
  Their shadows with the magic hand of Chance:
And when I feel, fair creature of an hour,
  That I shall never look upon thee more,
Never have relish in the faery power
  Of unreflecting Love: then on the Shore
Of the wide world I stand alone, and think
  Till Love and Fame to Nothingness do sink –

[2] **teeming:** *stocked to overflowing, abundant, prolific.*
[3] **charactery:** *print.*
[4] **garners:** *storehouses for corn, granaries.*

If I should die, said I to myself, I have left no immortal work behind me – nothing to make my friends proud of my memory – but I have loved the principle of beauty in all things, and if I had had time I would have made myself remembered.

COMPREHENSION

1 According to poem's first four lines what is Keats desperate to accomplish before he dies?
2 He says that his brain is 'teeming'. What is his mind teeming with?
3 What metaphor does Keats use to describe the creative process in these lines?
4 The poem's opening quatrain contains many phrases and images associated with fertility and abundance. List them.
5 What metaphor does Keats use to describe the night sky?
6 What does he feel when he looks at the 'night's starr'd face' ?
7 What fear is discussed in lines 9 to 12?
8 What is Keats' response to the various fears he outlines in lines 1 to 12?

PERSONAL RESPONSE

1 How would you describe the tone or atmosphere of this poem? Would you say it is solemn, urgent, despairing or hopeful?
2 *Class discussion:* What view of romantic love is suggested by this sonnet? How does it differ from the view of love put forward in other Keats poems?
3 This poem is about fear. Would you agree that it also contains hope? Give reasons for your answer, focusing especially on the poem's conclusion.
4 Based on your reading of this poem what would you say are Keats' hopes, fears, dreams and obsessions? How do his concerns and priorities in life differ from your own?

La Belle Dame Sans Merci

O what can ail thee knight at arms,
   Alone and palely loitering?
The sedge has withered from the Lake
   And no birds sing!

O what can ail thee, knight at arms!
   So haggard and so woe-begone?
The squirrel's granary is full
   And the harvest's done.

I see a lily on thy brow
   With anguish moist and fever dew,
And on thy cheeks a fading rose
   Fast withereth too –

I met a Lady in the Meads,
   Full beautiful a faery's child
Her hair was long, her foot was light
   And her eyes were wild –

I made a Garland for her head,
   And bracelets too, and fragrant Zone;
She look'd at me as she did love,
   And made sweet moan –

I set her on my pacing steed,
   And nothing else saw all day long
For sidelong would she bend and sing
   A faery's song –

She found me roots of relish sweet
  And honey wild, and manna dew
And sure in language strange she said
  'I love thee true' –

She took me to her elfin grot
  And there she wept and sigh'd fill sore
And there I shut her wild wild eyes
  With kisses four.

And there she lulled me asleep,
  And there I dream'd – Ah! Woe betide!
The latest dream I ever dreamt
  On the cold hill side.

I saw pale kings and Princes too,
  Pale warriors, death pale were they all;
They cried – 'La Belle Dame sans Merci
  Hath thee in thrall'

I saw their starv'd lips in the gloam
  With horrid warning gaped wide,
And I awoke and found me here
  On the cold hill's side.

And this is why I sojourn here
  Alone and palely loitering;
Though the sedge is wither'd from the Lake
  And no birds sing –

La Belle Dame Sans Merci: *the title of the poem is borrowed from Alain Chartier's poem of the same name. It means the beautiful lady without mercy.*

[3] **sedge:** *coarse grass.*
[13] **meads:** *meadows.*
[18] **zone:** *girdle or ornate belt.*
[29] **elfin:** *fairy.*
[29] **grot:** *grotto, cave.*
[40] **thrall:** *a state of submission or enslavement.*
[41] **gloam:** *twilight.*

A poet is the most unpoetical of anything in existence; because he has no identity – he is continually informing – and filling some other body.

COMPREHENSION

Stanzas 1 to 3

1 Who is speaking in the poem's first three stanzas?
2 Where is this poem taking place? Describe the scene in your own words.
3 What time of year is it?
4 Describe, in your own words, the knight's appearance.

Stanzas 4 to 7

5 Who is speaking in these stanzas?
6 Who did the knight meet 'in the meads'? What did this person look like?
7 How did the knight and the Lady spend the rest of the day?
8 'And sure in language strange she said / 'I love thee true'.' Why do you think the lady speaks in a 'strange' language?

Stanzas 8 to 12

9 Where do the knight and the lady go that evening?
10 *Class discussion*: 'And there she wep't and sigh'd full sore'. Suggest why the lady might be weeping.
11 Describe the knight's dream in your own words.
12 *Group discussion:* What do you think happened to the 'Pale warriors' that appear in the knight's dream?
13 Where is the knight when he wakes up?
14 'And that is why I sojourn here'. Write a paragraph explaining why the knight is forced to sojourn to the hill side. What do you think will happen to him now?

PERSONAL RESPONSE

1 What kind of mood or atmosphere is created by this poem? Would you agree that the atmosphere changes throughout the poem? Write a short paragraph giving the reasons for your answer.
2 Why do you think Keats uses two different voices in this poem? Would you agree that the knight's tale is actually a story within a story? What effect did this structure have on your reading of the poem?
3 Many female critics have expressed unhappiness with this poem. Could you suggest why this might be the case?
4 Did you like or dislike this poem? Write three paragraphs explaining your response to this question. Each paragraph should focus on a different point.
5 Would you agree that this poem could be described as a 'fairy story'? Give a reason for answer.
6 Write a short paragraph describing the emotions you experienced when you first read this poem.
7 Write a paragraph commenting on Keats' use of repetition in this poem.
8 Identify two images in this poem that you found effective and say why you liked them.

IN CONTEXT

What attitude toward love is expressed in 'La Belle Dame Sans Merci'? How does it compare to the attitude toward love expressed in the other poems by Keats on this course?

Ode to a Nightingale

I

My heart aches, and a drowsy numbness pains
My sense, as though of hemlock I had drunk,
Or emptied some dull opiate to the drains
One minute past, and Lethe-wards had sunk:
'Tis not through envy of thy happy lot,
But being too happy in thine happiness, –
That thou, light-winged Dryad of the trees,
In some melodious plot
Of beechen green, and shadows numberless,
Singest of summer in full-throated ease.

II

O, for a draught of vintage! that hath been
Cool'd a long age in the deep-delved earth,
Tasting of Flora and the country green,
Dance, and Provencal song, and sunburnt mirth!
O for a beaker full of the warm South,
Full of the true, the blushful Hippocrene,
With beaded bubbles winking at the brim,
And purple-stained mouth;
That I might drink, and leave the world unseen,
And with thee fade away into the forest dim:

III

Fade far away, dissolve, and quite forget
What thou among the leaves hast never known,
The weariness, the fever, and the fret
Here, where men sit and hear each other groan;
Where palsy shakes a few, sad, last gray hairs,
Where youth grows pale, and spectre-thin, and dies;
Where but to think is to be full of sorrow
And leaden-eyed despairs,
Where Beauty cannot keep her lustrous eyes,
Or new Love pine at them beyond tomorrow.

IV

Away! away! for I will fly to thee,
Not charioted by Bacchus and his pards,
But on the viewless wings of Poesy,
Though the dull brain perplexes and retards:
Already with thee! tender is the night,
And haply the Queen-Moon is on her throne,
Cluster'd around by all her starry Fays;
But here there is no light,
Save what from heaven is with the breezes blown
Through verdurous glooms and winding mossy ways.

Notes

[2] **hemlock:** *a poison or sedative*

[3] **opiate:** *a drug that makes you sleep.*

[3] **drains:** *dregs*

[4] **Lethe:** *in Greek mythology Lethe was one of the rivers that flowed through the underworld Hades and whose waters had the power to make the souls of the dead forget their life on earth.*

[7] **Dryad:** *wood nymph or spirit of the tree, a poetic reference to the nightingale.*

[13] **Flora:** *the Roman goddess of flowers.*

[14] **Provencal song:** *in the Middle Ages travelling singers, troubadours, from Provence, a region in the south of France, were famous for their music.*

[15] **warm South:** *wine from the South.*

[16] **Hippocrene:** *a spring on Mount Helicon, sacred to the Muses; has connotations of poetic inspiration.*

[32] **Bacchus:** *Roman god of wine.*

[32] **pards:** *leopards.*

[33] **viewless:** *invisible.*

[36] **Queen-Moon:** *Diana, the moon-goddess.*

[37] **Fays:** *fairies.*

[43] **embalmed darkness:** *darkness steeped in scent, but also suggesting the concern with death in the following stanza.*

V
I cannot see what flowers are at my feet,
   Nor what soft incense hangs upon the boughs,
But, in embalmed darkness, guess each sweet
   Wherewith the seasonable month endows
The grass, the thicket, and the fruit-tree wild;
   White hawthorn, and the pastoral eglantine;
Fast fading violets cover'd up in leaves;
   And mid-May's eldest child,
The coming musk-rose, full of dewy wine,
   The murmurous haunt of flies on summer eves.

VI
Darkling I listen; and, for many a time
   I have been half in love with easeful Death,
Call'd him soft names in many a mused rhyme,
   To take into the air my quiet breath;
Now more than ever seems it rich to die,
   To cease upon the midnight with no pain,
While thou art pouring forth thy soul abroad
   In such an ecstasy!
Still wouldst thou sing, and I have ears in vain –
   To thy high requiem become a sod.

VII
Thou wast not born for death, immortal Bird!
   No hungry generations tread thee down;
The voice I hear this passing night was heard
   In ancient days by emperor and clown:
Perhaps the self-same song that found a path
   Through the sad heart of Ruth, when, sick for home,
She stood in tears amid the alien corn;
   The same that oft-times hath
Charm'd magic casements, opening on the foam
   Of perilous seas, in faery lands forlorn.

VIII
Forlorn! the very word is like a bell
   To toil me back from thee to my sole self!
Adieu! the fancy cannot cheat so well
   As she is fam'd to do, deceiving elf.
Adieu! adieu! thy plaintive anthem fades
   Past the near meadows, over the still stream,
Up the hill-side; and now 'tis buried deep
   In the next valley-glades:
Was it a vision, or a waking dream?
   Fled is that music: – Do I wake or sleep?

[46] **eglantine:** *the sweet-briar, a wild rose.*

[51] **Darkling:** *in darkness.*

[60] **requiem:** *funeral music.*

[66] **Ruth:** *In the Bible Ruth is forced by circumstance to work in foreign fields (see Ruth 2:3).*

[69] **casements:** *a type of window.*

[73] **fancy:** *imagination.*

I scarcely remember counting upon happiness – I look not for it if it be not in the present hour – nothing startles me beyond the moment. The setting sun will always set me to rights, or if a sparrow come before my Window I take part in its existence and pick about the gravel.

COMPREHENSION

1 *Class discussion:* How would you describe Keats' reaction to the nightingale's singing?
2 How does Keats describe his emotional state in the first stanza?
3 What does he mean when he declares that he has sunk 'Lethe-wards'
4 Describe, in your own words the nightingale's environment.
5 What does Keats want to drink?
6 How does he convey the fantastic qualities of this liquid?
7 Why does he want to drink this wonderful substance?
8 Why does Keats want to 'Fade far away, dissolve, and quite forget'?
9 Make a list of the different woes Keats mentions in stanza 3.
10 What do you understand by the expression 'where but to think is to be full of sorrow'?
11 What is it that the nightingale 'has never known'?
12 How will the poet 'fly' to the nightingale?
13 What do understand by the reference to 'Bacchus and his pards'?
14 Is the night dark or relatively bright? Give a reason for your answer.
15 Describe the main features of the forest in your own words.
16 What desire does the poet express in stanza 6?
17 *Class discussion:* What literary devices does the poet use to convey this desire?
18 In stanza 7 the speaker mentions a number of places where the nightingale's song has been heard. List them.
19 What does the speaker mean when he declares that the nightingale was not born for death?
20 What happens at the beginning of stanza 8?
21 What is the poet's reaction to this event?

PERSONAL RESPONSE

The critic Brian Stone has suggested this is a poem of 'pervasive darkness and mystery'.

1 Would you agree with this assessment?
2 Write a brief paragraph describing the atmosphere created by this poem. Would you agree that the atmosphere shifts from stanza to stanza?
3 *Class discussion:* Several critics have suggested that the nightingale in this poem functions as a 'symbol'. What might it symbolise?
4 Identify the three images in the poem that most appealed to you and say why you like them.
5 Write a paragraph describing the Keats' use of assonance and alliteration in this poem. How does it contribute to the poem's atmosphere?
6 On balance would you consider this to be a sad or a happy poem? Give reasons for your answer.

IN CONTEXT

Write a brief paragraph comparing and contrasting the depiction of nature in this poem with that in 'To Autumn'.

Ode on a Grecian Urn

I

Thou still unravish'd bride of quietness,
Thou foster-child of silence and slow time,
Sylvan historian, who canst thus express
A flowery tale more sweetly than our rhyme:
What leaf-fring'd legend haunts about thy shape
Of deities or mortals, or of both,
In Tempe or the dales of Arcady?
What men or gods are these? What maidens loth?
What mad pursuit? What struggle to escape?
What pipes and timbrels? What wild ecstasy?

II

Heard melodies are sweet, but those unheard
Are sweeter; therefore, ye soft pipes, play on;
Not to the sensual ear, but, more endear'd,
Pipe to the spirit ditties of no tone:
Fair youth, beneath the trees, thou canst not leave
Thy song, nor ever can those trees be bare;
Bold Lover, never, never canst thou kiss,
Though winning near the goal – yet, do not grieve;
She cannot fade, though thou hast not thy bliss,
For ever wilt thou love, and she be fair!

III

Ah, happy, happy boughs! that cannot shed
Your leaves, nor ever bid the Spring adieu;
And, happy melodist, unwearied,
For ever piping songs for ever new;
More happy love! more happy, happy love!
For ever warm and still to be enjoy'd,
For ever panting, and for ever young;
All breathing human passion far above,
That leaves a heart high-sorrowful and cloy'd,
A burning forehead, and a parching tongue.

IV

Who are these coming to the sacrifice?
   To what green altar, O mysterious priest,
Lead'st thou that heifer lowing at the skies,
   And all her silken flanks with garlands drest?
What little town by river or sea shore,
   Or mountain-built with peaceful citadel,
Is emptied of this folk, this pious morn?
   And, little town, thy streets for evermore
Will silent be; and not a soul to tell
   Why thou art desolate, can e'er return.

V

O Attic shape! Fair attitude! with brede
   Of marble men and maidens overwrought,
With forest branches and the trodden weed;
   Thou, silent form, dost tease us out of thought
As doth eternity: Cold Pastoral!
   When old age shall this generation waste,
Thou shalt remain, in midst of other woe
   Than ours, a friend to man, to whom thou say'st,
'Beauty is truth, truth beauty,' – that is all
   Ye know on earth, and all ye need to know.

[1] **unravish'e:** *untouched, virginal.*
[3] **Sylvan:** *of the woods.*
[7] **Tempe:** *a valley in Ancient Greece, celebrated for its beauty and the happiness of its inhabitants.*
[7] **Arcady:** *a region in southern Greece; the ideal pastoral world.*
[8] **loth:** *unwilling.*
[10] **timbrels:** *percussion instruments, held in the hand like tambourines.*
[13] **sensual:** *physical.*
[29] **cloy'd:** *wearied by excess of sweetness.*
[41] **Attic:** *Grecian.*
[41] **brede:** *an archaic poetic expression referring to a frieze or narrow band of ornamentation; braid.*
[42] **overwrought:** *the design of the artwork on the surface of the urn; to be overcome emotionally.*
[45] **Pastoral:** *art dealing with the countryside.*

COMPREHENSION

I
am certain
of nothing but the
holiness of the heart's
affections and the truth
of imagination – what the
imagination seizes as beauty
must be truth – whether it
existed before or not.

Stanza 1

1 *Group discussion:* The poet uses three metaphors in the opening lines to describe the urn. Identify these and discuss what you think each of them means.

2 The remainder of the stanza asks many questions regarding the detail of the decoration on the urn. What sort of event is shown on the urn?

Stanza 2

3 The poet describes the 'melodies' that the 'soft pipes' play. What is unusual about these melodies? Why does the poet think them 'sweeter' than 'heard melodies'?

4 *Class discussion:* Do you think that the poet pities or envies the 'Fair youth's' predicament?

5 The 'Bold Lover' seems destined to be eternally frustrated. However, the poet urges him to 'not grieve'. How does Keats consider the Lover fortunate?

Stanza 3

6 Keats refers to the trees, the musician, and the lovers depicted on the urn. Why does he consider each of these to be so 'happy'?

7 The last six lines of the stanza compare the love that exists in the static world of the urn with that of real human love. Which does Keats consider more appealing? Why does he think this?

8 Is there irony in the fact that the superior passion depicted on the urn is also incapable of being fulfilled, that satisfaction is impossible?

Stanza 4

9 The poet focuses on another detail of the urn's decorative narrative. Describe what he sees.

10 The last six lines of the stanza involve the poet imagining the 'little town' that has been left behind. Why will this town be forever 'silent'?

Stanza 5

11 How does the focus of this stanza contrast with the previous four?

12 How does the urn 'tease us out of thought'? How is it similar to 'eternity' in this regard?

13 *Group discussion:* What do you think Keats means when he refers to the urn as 'Cold Pastoral'? Is the term paradoxical? Are there other paradoxes evident in the poem?

14 *Class discussion:* What message does the urn convey in the last two lines of the poem?

PERSONAL RESPONSE

1 Were you surprised by the poet's reaction to a piece of sculpture? What did you find most interesting about his thoughts on the urn?

2 Do you envy the situation of the characters he describes? Are they truly better off than we are?

T.S. Eliot
considered the
last lines of the poem a
'serious blemish on a beautiful
poem'. He could not make sense
of the statement and said that the
reason for this 'must be either
that I fail to understand it,
or that it is a statement
which is untrue.'

3 What do the last two lines mean to you?

IN CONTEXT

In the poetry of John Keats the world of the imagination offers a release from the painful world of actuality, yet at the same time it renders the world of actuality more painful by contrast. Compare 'Ode on a Grecian Urn' and 'Ode to a Nightingale' in light of this observation.

To Autumn

Season of mists and mellow fruitfulness,
Close bosom-friend of the maturing sun;
Conspiring with him how to load and bless
With fruit the vines that round the thatch-eves run;
To bend with apples the moss'd cottage-trees,
And fill all fruit with ripeness to the core;
To swell the gourd, and plump the hazel shells
With a sweet kernel; to set budding more,
And still more, later flowers for the bees,
Until they think warm days will never cease,
For Summer has o'er-brimm'd their clammy cells.

Who hath not seen thee oft amid thy store?
Sometimes whoever seeks abroad may find
Thee sitting careless on a granary floor,
Thy hair soft-lifted by the winnowing wind;
Or on a half-reap'd furrow sound asleep,
Drows'd with the fume of poppies, while thy hook
Spares the next swath and all its twined flowers:
And sometimes like a gleaner thou dost keep
Steady thy laden head across a brook;
Or by a cyder-press, with patient look,
Thou watchest the last oozings hours by hours.

Where are the songs of Spring? Ay, where are they?
Think not of them, thou hast thy music too, –
While barred clouds bloom the soft-dying day,
And touch the stubble plains with rosy hue;
Then in a wailful choir the small gnats mourn
Among the river sallows, borne aloft
Or sinking as the light wind lives or dies;
And full-grown lambs loud bleat from hilly bourn;
Hedge-crickets sing; and now with treble soft
The red-breast whistles from a garden-croft;
And gathering swallows twitter in the skies.

[7] **gourd:** *large fleshy fruit.*
[15] **winnowing:** *the process of separating the grain from the chaff (or covering) at harvest time. The beaten corn was thrown in the air and the wind blew off the lighter chaff.*
[18] **swath:** *a row of corn as it falls when reaped.*
[19] **gleaner:** *person gathering ears of corn left by the reapers.*
[25] **barred clouds bloom:** *the clouds suggest both death and the 'bloom' of life. Barred here means of varying colour.*
[28] **sallows:** *low-growing willow trees.*
[30] **bourn:** *stream.*
[32] **croft:** *small agricultural holding.*

BACKGROUND

Keats wrote 'To Autumn' after enjoying an autumn day; he described his experience in a letter to his friend Reynolds:

COMPREHENSION

Stanza 1

1 How is the season characterised in the opening stanza? What activity does the poet focus on here?
2 Why might autumn be considered a time of 'mellow fruitfulness'?
3 Keats vividly describes the incredible growth that occurs during autumn. Identify the words and phrases he uses to convey this growth.
4 Why is autumn considered a perplexing time for the bees?

Stanza 2

5 The poet personifies the season in the second stanza. How does the description of autumn differ from that given in the first stanza?
6 Autumn is placed in four different settings. List these settings and describe what the season is doing in each.
7 The stanza is particularly concerned with the process of harvesting wheat. Based upon a reading of the stanza what is involved in this process? Does the poet deal with the various stages in the right order?
8 Consider Keats' use of language in this stanza. Identify instances of alliteration and assonance and describe the mood and atmosphere that they create.

Stanza 3

9 The third stanza opens with a rhetorical question regarding the whereabouts of the 'songs of Spring'. What do you think he means by these 'songs'?
10 Keats beautifully depicts an autumnal evening in lines 25 to 26. Describe in your own words the scene he relates and say how the sound of the words contributes to the description.
11 The final seven lines of the poem are concerned with the 'music' of autumn. What does this music consist of?
12 How does the final stanza compare with the opening stanza?

PERSONAL RESPONSE

1 Did you find this poem to be an appealing description of autumn? What images did you find most memorable?
2 Why do you think Keats chose to personify the season in the second stanza? Did you find it an effective device?
3 The poem contains many exquisite lines of poetry. Identify the lines you particularly admired and give reasons for your choice.
4 Can you think of any other poems that deal with autumn? How do they compare to this poem?

IN CONTEXT

1 How does this Ode differ to 'Ode on a Grecian Urn' and 'Ode to a Nightingale'?
2 Each of Keats' Odes is a unique experience, but each of them is also, as it were, a facet of a larger experience. This larger experience is an intense awareness of both the joy and the pain, the happiness and the sorrow, of human life. Discuss the Odes of John Keats in light of this statement.

Bright Star

Bright star, would I were stedfast as thou art –
Not in lone splendour hung aloft the night
And watching, with eternal lids apart,
Like nature's patient, sleepless Eremite,
The moving waters at their priestlike task
Of pure ablution round earth's human shores,
Or gazing on the new soft-fallen masque
Of snow upon the mountains and the moors –
No – yet still stedfast, still unchangeable,
Pillowed upon my fair love's ripening breast,
To feel for ever its soft fall and swell,
Awake for ever in a sweet unrest,
Still, still to hear her tender-taken breath,
And so live ever – or else swoon in death –

[1] **stedfast:** *constant, strong in position.*
[4] **Eremite:** *a hermit, recluse.*
[7] **masque:** *mask.*

I have two luxuries to brood over in my walks, your loveliness and the hour of my death. O that I could have possession of them both in the same minute.

COMPREHENSION

1. What does it mean to be 'steadfast'?
2. How does the poet describe the star in the first four lines?
3. What does the poet imagine the star sees on earth?
4. Does the poet want to be in the star's position?
5. What does the poet envy the star? What does he find unenviable about the star's condition?
6. Where would the poet like to be?
7. What does the poet suggest would be a desirable alternative should his wish for immortality not be granted?

PERSONAL RESPONSE

1. What does the poem suggest to you about the poet's views on love? Do you think that Keats is a realist or idealist when it comes to affairs of the heart?
2. What does reading this poem make you think about? Has reading the poetry of John Keats enriched your appreciation of the world and life?

IN CONTEXT

Discuss how Keats links love and death in both 'Bright Star' and 'When I have Fears that I May Cease to Be'. How do the poems compare and differ?

MICHAEL LONGLEY

BIOGRAPHY

Like many writers and artists Longley was something of an outsider. Though he was born in Belfast his parents were English: 'My parents came from London in 1927. I was born there in 1939, two months before the outbreak of war. They never went back to London'. Longley, then, was born an Englishman in a part of Ireland that was strictly divided between two communities, Protestant and Catholic, neither of whom had much time for England. As a young boy he developed two identities – an Ulster Protestant one at school and an English one for his parents' home: 'My twin and I went to a largely working-class primary school where I grew up and became street-wise quickly. I remember my parents, who spoke with English accents, being very alarmed by the broad Belfast accent which my twin and I immediately adopted in order to survive playground politics. I had to adapt myself, modify myself and recreate myself twice a day going into the playground and then coming back home'. Longley, then, was strictly speaking neither an Englishman, nor an Irishman nor an Ulsterman. This lack of a stable identity looms large over his poetic career. A great deal of Longley's work is devoted to creating an identity for himself, to putting down roots and discovering a personal history that he can relate to and a place where he can truly belong. The west of Ireland, in particular, is a location that offers him the possibility of belonging. The Mayo Longley writes about is a largely unpolluted place, free from politics and the ancient conflicts between Ireland and England, where the poet can wander at peace with nature.

Much of Longley's poetry is influenced by the military career of his father, who was a veteran of World War One. His father, who was an Englishman, joined the British army when he was only seventeen. He fought at some of the war's bloodiest battles and rose to he rank of captain, experiences that lie behind poems such as 'Wounds' and 'Last Requests'. As Longley puts it: 'He was a teenage soldier in the trenches in the First World War. By the time he was twenty he was a captain in charge of a company and won a medal for knocking out a machine-gun post more or less single-handed. After weeks and weeks of sitting in the rain and being heavily bombarded, he lost his temper and went over the top. He said that in the Second World War he would have been court-martialled for reckless behaviour but in the first world war he got a medal'.

Yet Longley's father was forever haunted by his experiences at the front: 'There was a thin wall between his bedroom and my twin's and my bedroom, and we were aware of the fact that occasionally he would wake himself up with nightmares. In one he relived chasing this tubby German, and eventually catching up on this unfortunate, overweight enemy and bayoneting him ... You could say he was bayoneting someone he didn't hate at all, in fact whom he felt sorry for'. The lasting effect of these haunting experiences on Longley's father is evidenced in 'Wounds', where he is described wandering a 'landscape of dead buttocks' for fifty years.

Unusually for a successful artist, Longley seems to have had a fairly untroubled adolescence: 'I went to the Royal Belfast Academical Institution, which is a wonderful title for a school, and it's mercifully abbreviated to "Inst". I was happy there. I played games. I was quite a good rugby player. I was interested in girls. I had a perfectly normal and really rather square teenage life'. It was only when he went to study at Trinity College in Dublin that his interest in poetry began to flourish. Longley was officially at college to study classics. It seems, however; that much of his time was spent drinking and smoking, listening to music in various bars, and reading and writing poetry.

At this time he shared an apartment with his fellow poet Derek Mahon, who became a close friend and important influence on his work. Their apartment in Merrion Square has been described as an 'embodiment of squalor'. Hygiene, apparently, was not very high on their agenda. It was in this 'slum', however, that Longley's talent grew. Mahon introduced him to a great deal of modern poetry that would have a profound influence on his work. As he puts it: 'There were many influences. We were hoovering up poetry at a fierce rate'.

Eventually, poetry became more important to Longley than classics. He gave up plans to become a teacher and decided to chance his arm at being a poet. Longley is respected by many people in Belfast because he stayed in that city all through the years of bombs and bitterness, while many of Northern Ireland's other writers and artists left it behind for more peaceful shores. For many years he worked in the Arts Council there, and is proud of the efforts he made to bring about a greater understanding between the two communities. The Northern conflict occupies a central place in his poetry, and he unflinchingly examines the despair and destruction caused by that thirty-year-long tragedy.

Longley, however, remains committed to understanding the psychology that could make people commit such barbarous acts. The terrorists, he claims, are not complete strangers. They were 'just as much products of our society as we were'. As we see in a poem like 'Ceasefire', he believes forgiveness to be a possibility. It is for this reason that he has the 'shivering boy' apologise at the end of 'Wounds': 'I do believe in redemption, eventually we're going to have to forgive these people, and that young murderer's redemption is anticipated in that phrase "Sorry Missus"'.

Badger

For Raymond Piper

I

Pushing the wedge of his body
Between cromlech and stone circle,
He excavates down mine shafts
And back into the depths of the hill.

His path straight and narrow
And not like the fox's zig-zags,
The arc of the hare who leaves
A silhouette on the sky line.

Night's silence around his shoulders,
His face lit by the moon, he
Manages the earth with his paws,
Returns underground to die.

II

An intestine taking in
patches of dog's-mercury,
brambles, the bluebell wood;
a heel revolving acorns;
a head with a price on it
brushing cuckoo-spit, goose-grass;
a name that parishes borrow.

III

For the digger, the earth-dog
It is a difficult delivery
Once the tongs take hold,

Vulnerable his pig's snout
That lifted cow-pats for beetles,
Hedgehogs for the soft meat,

His limbs dragging after them
So many stones turned over,
The trees they tilted.

[2] **cromlech:** *A cromlech is also known as a dolmen. It is a prehistoric structure consisting of a large flat stone that rests horizontally on three or more stones set upright.*

[14] **dog's mercury:** *a herbaceous woodland plant, usually regarded as toxic.*

[18] **cuckoo-spit:** *a frothy substance on plants made by an insect.*

[18] **goose-grass:** *type of weed-like grass that has curved prickles on the stems. Goose grass spreads its seeds by sticking to things, e.g. animals.*

COMPREHENSION

Section 1

1 The first four lines describe the movements of the badger. What is the significance of locating the badger 'Between cromlech and stone circle'? What does it suggest about the badger's activities?

2 Longley describes the 'path' of the badger and contrasts it with the path of the fox and hare. What might the path of each animal tell us about their character?

3 The badger appears very comfortable with the night. How is this conveyed?

4 *Group discussion:* Having read the first section of the poem, choose four adjectives that best describe the badger.

Section 2

5 In this section the poet refers to aspects of the badger, its intestine, its heel, and its head. What is effect of isolating parts of the animal in this manner?

6 Consider the verbs that Longley uses when describing the activity of the badger's intestine and heel. Why do you think he chose these verbs? Is it of significance that the present continuous is used in both instances?

7 In the space of seven short lines the poet mentions five plants that feature in the badger's environment, carefully registering their names. Why do you think he does this?

8 What does it mean that the badger has a head with 'a price on it'? How does the positioning of this information in the middle of the section affect the way we comprehend it?

9 Why is the badger's name one that 'parishes borrow'?

Section 3

10 What would you normally associate the word 'delivery' with?

11 Why does Longley refer to the badger as 'the digger, the earth-dog'?

12 What are the 'tongs' that the poet mentions in line 22? Who is using these tongs?

13 How does the depiction of the badger in this section differ from the previous two sections?

14 Does the final section bemoan or lament the badger's death?

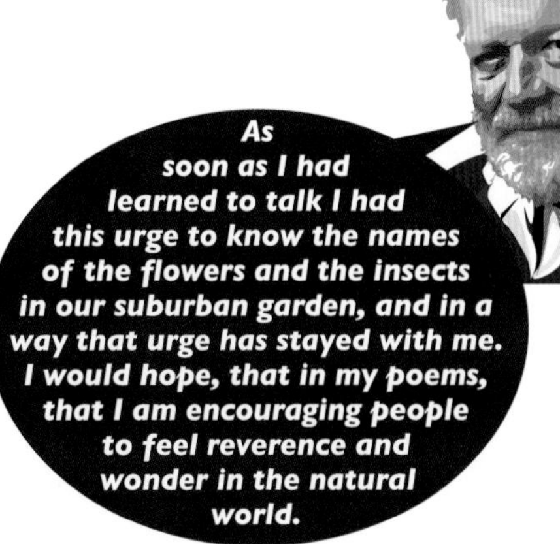

As soon as I had learned to talk I had this urge to know the names of the flowers and the insects in our suburban garden, and in a way that urge has stayed with me. I would hope, that in my poems, that I am encouraging people to feel reverence and wonder in the natural world.

PERSONAL RESPONSE

1 Do you think that this poem is a sympathetic account of the badger? Do you find the poem emotive or is it more matter-of-fact? What is your abiding impression of the badger having read the poem?

2 Can the poem be considered critical of human behaviour with regard to animals like the badger?

IN CONTEXT

In a recent interview Michael Longley said: 'I feel offended, I must say, by Damien Hirst's cut-up cow, the cow halves in formaldehyde and his shark. That is, to me, a desecration. So, I would hope, that in my poems, that I am encouraging people to feel reverence and wonder in the natural world.' Based on your reading of 'The Badger' and 'Carrigskeewaun' discuss how Longley reveals both reverence for and wonder in the natural world.

Wounds

Here are two pictures from my father's head –
I have kept them like secrets until now:
First, the Ulster Division at the Somme
Going over the top with 'Fuck the Pope!'
'No Surrender!': a boy about to die,
Screaming 'Give 'em one for the Shankill!'
Wilder than Gurkhas' were my father's words
Of admiration and bewilderment.
Next comes the London-Scottish padre
Resettling kilts with his swagger-stick,
With a stylish backhand and a prayer.
Over a landscape of dead buttocks
My father followed him for fifty years.
At last, a belated casualty,
He said-lead traces flaring till they hurt –
'I am dying for King and Country, slowly.'
I touched his hand, his thin head I touched.

Now, with military honours of a kind,
With his badges, his medals like rainbows,
His spinning compass, I bury beside him
Three teenage soldiers, bellies full of
Bullets and Irish beer, their flies undone.
A packet of Woodbines I throw in,
A lucifer, the Sacred Heart of Jesus
Paralysed as heavy guns put out
The night-light in a nursery for ever;
Also a bus-conductor's uniform –
He collapsed beside his carpet-slippers
Without a murmur, shot through the head
By a shivering boy who wandered in
Before they could turn the television down
Or tidy away the supper dishes.
To the children, to a bewildered wife,
I think 'Sorry Missus' was what he said.

[3] **Ulster Division:** *a division of the British army in the First World War*
[3] **Somme:** *river in the north of France. Was the scene of some of the bloodiest fighting in the First World War, particularly in 1916.*
[6] **Shankill:** *area in the west of Belfast, one of the main traditionally Protestant areas of the city.*
[7] **Gurkhas:** *an elite fighting force from Asia, who had the reputation of being the fiercest and most determined soldiers in the British Army.*
[9] **padre:** *priest*
[10] **swagger-stick:** *an ornamental cane popular with some soldiers in the war. It was also used as a fashion accessory before and after the war.*
[24] **lucifer:** *an old slang term for a match.*

COMPREHENSION

Stanza 1

1 'Here are two pictures from my father's head'. What do you understand by this?

2 What are the battle cries of the Ulster division? Why do you think they shout these things?

3 How did Longley's father react to their behaviour?

4 What does the 'London-Scottish padre' do following the battle?

5 Why do you think he does this?

6 What does Longley mean when he says that his father followed the 'padre' for fifty years?

7 In what sense was his father a 'belated casualty' of the Somme?

8 What do you understand by the expression 'lead-traces flaring till they hurt'?

Stanza 2

9 What kind of ceremony is described in this stanza? Do you think this ceremony is actually happening or that Longley is merely imagining it?

10 Why do you think Longley chooses to bury the three teenage soldiers beside his father?

11 What significance is there in the fact that he places his father's belongings in the graves of these teenage boys?

12 Why do you think the 'Sacred Heart of Jesus' is described as being 'paralysed'?

13 Describe, in your own words, what happens to the bus-conductor. Why do you think Longley decides to place his uniform in the young soldiers' graves?

14 This poem revolves around three separate incidents of violence. What are they? Make a list of the similarities and differences between these incidents.

PERSONAL RESPONSE

1 What emotions did you experience when you first read this poem?

2 Would you find it easy to forgive the 'shivering boy' for what he did? Would you agree that he could also be considered a victim of the conflict that has engulfed his homeland?

3 Comment on the way the poem is divided into two sections. Would you agree that the stanzas 'mirror' each other? What point do you think Longley is trying to make by using this structure?

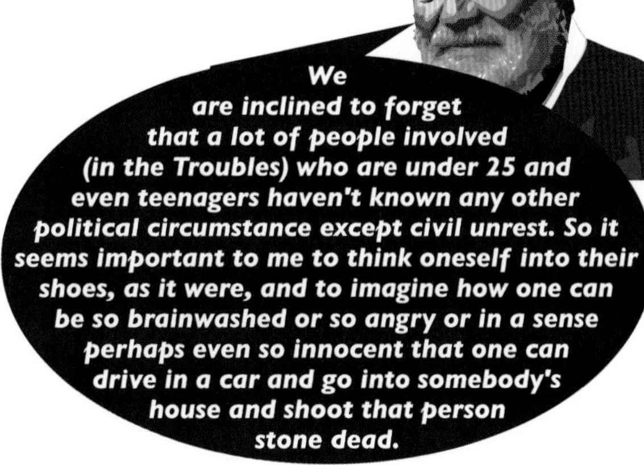

We are inclined to forget that a lot of people involved (in the Troubles) who are under 25 and even teenagers haven't known any other political circumstance except civil unrest. So it seems important to me to think oneself into their shoes, as it were, and to imagine how one can be so brainwashed or so angry or in a sense perhaps even so innocent that one can drive in a car and go into somebody's house and shoot that person stone dead.

4 Would you agree that the poem presents a bleak view of life? Do you think it contains any hope?

IN CONTEXT

Father and son relationships are an important feature of Longley's work. What impression does this poem give us of the relationship between Longley and his father? Compare and contrast the father–son relationship portrayed in this poem with that depicted in 'Laertes' or 'Last Requests'.

This violent, disturbing poem demonstrates how hate breeds hate, and violence begets more violence. The sectarian attitudes expressed by the Ulster Division at the Somme lead directly to the modern day violence described in stanza 2. 'Wounds' presents a world where people are helpless in the face of unstoppable cycles of evil and hatred, a world where young men, in particular, always seem to be the victims.

Poteen

Enough running water
To cool the copper worm,
The veins at the wrist,
Vitriol to scorch the throat –

And the brimming hogshead,
Reduced by one noggin-full
Sprinkled on the ground,
Becomes an affair of

Remembered souterrains,
Sunk workshops, out-backs,
The back of the mind –
The whole bog an outhouse

Where, alongside cudgels,
Guns, the informer's ear
We have buried it –
Blood-money, treasure trove.

[2] **copper worm:** *the metal piping used in the making of poteen. It is called a worm because of the way in which it spirals.*
[4] **vitriol:** *sulphuric acid; something caustic corrosive.*
[5] **hogshead:** *a large cask for holding liquid. Usually made of wood, held together by metal rings.*
[6] **noggin:** *a measure of spirits.*
[9] **souterrains:** *underground caves or chambers.*

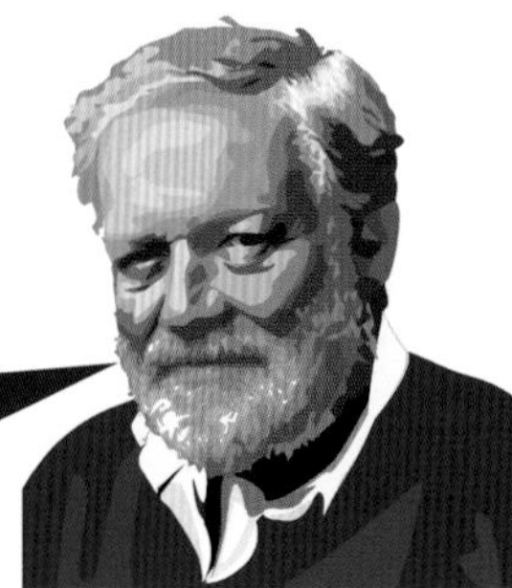

'Poteen' speaks of the violence which lurks under the apparently peaceful surface of our civilisation.

COMPREHENSION

1 Describe the process involved in making poteen. Is there a certain irony in the fact that so much cold water is needed to make 'Vitriol to scorch the throat'?
2 Why do you think 'one noggin-full' of poteen is 'sprinkled on the ground'?
3 How does the speaker's mind get drawn back to the past? What sort of activities does he recall?
4 The illegal process of making poteen is rapidly associated with a dark underworld of violence and secrecy. How is the violence of the past suggested in the poem?
5 In the second last line the speaker says that 'We have buried it'. What has been 'buried'?
6 How might the poem be considered to be about Ireland and the Irish identity?

IN CONTEXT

1 'Longley has the ability to boil poems down till they become just a few lines or sometimes only one line, which results in an extraordinary intensity'. Discuss the poetry of Michael Longley based on this observation.

Carrigskeewaun

For Penny and David Cabot

The Mountain
This is ravens' territory, skulls, bones,
The marrow of these boulders supervised
From the upper air: I stand alone here
And seem to gather children about me,
A collection of picnic things, my voice
Filling the district as I call their names.

The Path
With my first step I dislodge the mallards
Whose necks strain over the bog to where
Kittiwakes scrape the waves: then, the circle
Widening, lapwings, curlews, snipe until

I am left with only one swan to nudge
To the far side of its gradual disdain.

The Strand
I discover, remaindered from yesterday,
Cattle tracks, a sanderling's tiny trail,
The footprints of the children and my own
Linking the dunes to the water's edge,
Reducing to sand the dry shells, the toe
And fingernail parings of the sea.

The Wall
I join all the men who have squatted here
This lichened side of the dry-stone wall
And notice how smoke from our turf fire
Recalls in the cool air above the lake
Steam from a kettle, a tablecloth and
A table she might have already set.

The Lake
Though it will duplicate at any time
The sheep and cattle that wander there,
For a few minutes every evening
Its surface seems tilted to receive
The sun perfectly, the mare and her foal,
The heron, all such special visitors.

Carrigskeewaun: *a townland in Co. Mayo.*
[7] **mallard:** *a wild duck.*
[9] **Kittiwake:** *a small marine gull.*

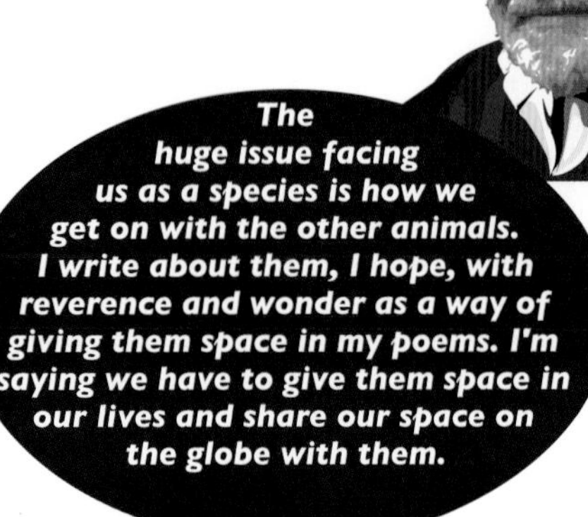

The huge issue facing us as a species is how we get on with the other animals. I write about them, I hope, with reverence and wonder as a way of giving them space in my poems. I'm saying we have to give them space in our lives and share our space on the globe with them.

COMPREHENSION

The Mountain

1 What three adjectives might best describe the landscape of the mountain? Does the poet feel comfortable here?

2 What is the poet doing in the mountain?

3 Why does Longley say that he seems to gather children about him? Are his children with him or is he actually alone?

4 How is a sense of vulnerability apparent in this stanza? Consider how the stanza deals with space and perspective when answering.

The Path

5 How is the poet's sense of awkwardness evident in this stanza?

6 Is the path a more hospitable place than the mountain?

7 Discuss how the stanza offers us a humorous yet deeply respectful picture of the many birds that inhabit the environs of Carrigskeewaun.

The Strand

8 The third stanza, unlike the previous two stanzas, contains neither a sense of dread nor discomfort. How would you describe the poet's response to the strand?

9 Is there any significance to the order of the tracks that the poet identifies?

10 The last two lines of the stanza describe how the shells are broken down to sand. Discuss the metaphor that Longley uses to describe the debris that gathers on the beach. Is it significant that the metaphor links human activity with the activity of the sea?

The Wall

11 How does this stanza differ to the first three stanzas?

12 Who are the men that the poet joins with here?

13 Consider the word 'squatted'. What does it suggest about the shelter that the wall offers?

14 What does smoke rising from the fire remind the poet of?

15 Discuss how the fourth stanza offers us an account of human needs.

The Lake

15 How does the lake 'duplicate' the 'sheep and cattle'?

16 Discuss how the final stanza conveys a wonderful image of harmony and peace.

PERSONAL RESPONSE

1 What is your impression of Carrigskeewaun after reading the poem?

2 Which of the five sections did you enjoy most? Discuss the reasons for your answer.

3 Based upon your reading of this poem, what sort of person do you imagine the poet to be? What is his attitude to the natural world? Do we get a sense of his values from the poem?

4 Did the poem suggest anything to you about the importance of family and the need for shelter?

5 Do you think that the poet considers himself one of the 'special visitors' that come to Carrigskeewaun?

IN CONTEXT

'While Longley clearly loves the Mayo countryside and the west of Ireland he does not depict it in a romanticised way. His poems deal with the harsh and the tender in nature, acknowledging both the bleak and the beautiful that the west has to offer the attentive traveller'. Discuss three of Longley's poems based on these observations.

Wreaths

The Civil Servant
He was preparing an Ulster fry for breakfast
When someone walked into the kitchen and shot him:
A bullet entered his mouth and pierced his skull,
The books he had read, the music he could play.

He lay in his dressing gown and pyjamas
While they dusted the dresser for fingerprints
And then shuffled backwards across the garden
With notebooks, cameras and measuring tapes.

They rolled him up like a red carpet and left
Only a bullet hole in the cutlery drawer:
Later his widow took a hammer and chisel
And removed the black keys from his piano.

The Greengrocer
He ran a good shop, and he died
Serving even the death-dealers
Who found him busy as usual
Behind the counter, organised
With holly wreaths for Christmas,
Fir trees on the pavement outside.

Astrologers or three wise men
Who may shortly be setting out
For a small house up the Shankill
Or the Falls, should pause on their way
To buy gifts at Jim Gibson's shop,
Dates and chestnuts and tangerines.

The Linen Workers
Christ's teeth ascended with him into heaven:
Through a cavity in one of his molars
The wind whistles: he is fastened for ever
By his exposed canines to a wintry sky.

I am blinded by the blaze of that smile
And by the memory of my father's false teeth
Brimming in their tumbler: they wore bubbles
And, outside of his body, a deadly grin.

When they massacred the ten linen workers
There fell on the road beside them spectacles,
Wallets, small change, and a set of dentures:
Blood, food particles, the bread, the wine.

Before I can bury my father once again
I must polish the spectacles, balance them
Upon his nose, fill his pockets with money
And into his dead mouth slip the set of teeth.

COMPREHENSION

The Civil Servant

1 *Class discussion:* How would you describe the tone of 'The Civil Servant'?

2 'A bullet entered his mouth and pierced his skull, / The books he had read, the music he could play'. What do you understand by these lines?

3 'Later his widow took a hammer and chisel / And removed the black keys from his piano'. How would you explain the widow's rather strange behaviour?

The Greengrocer

4 Imagine you were an eye witness to the greengrocer's murder. Describe in your own words what you saw.

5 What clues about the greengrocer's personality are provided by the poem?

6 What do you know about the Shankill Road and the Falls Road? Why is it significant that Longley mentions both of these places?

7 *Class discussion:* Why does Longley mention Astrologers or three wise men'? What significance is there in the fact that the poem is set at Christmas time?

The Linen Workers

8 *Class discussion:* Each of the three stanzas in 'The Linen Workers' focuses on a different image: Jesus Christ, the murder of the linen workers and the poet's father. What are the links between these seemingly very different and unconnected images?

9 What is your reaction to the image of Christ portrayed in lines 25 to 28? Do you find this image weird, disturbing or silly?

10 How does the description of the linen workers' murder differ from Longley's other descriptions of violence in this poem?

11 What do you understand by Longley's claim that he must bury his father 'once again'? Do you think this is an actual burial or merely something that will take place in his imagination?

12 What significance is there in the fact that Longley places the linen workers' possessions on his father's body before burying him? What connection is there between the murdered workers and the poet's father?

PERSONAL RESPONSE

1 Write a paragraph describing the emotions you experienced when you first read 'Wreaths'.

2 Which of these three poems did you like most? Which did you like least? Which did you find hardest to understand? Give reasons for each of your answers.

3 *Class discussion:* What attitude toward religion is conveyed by 'Wreaths'? Based on your reading of these three short pieces would you suspect that Longley is a religious man?

I have written a few inadequate elegies out of my bewilderment and despair. I offer them as wreaths. That is all.

4 Would you agree that 'Wreaths' is an appropriate title for this series of poems? Give a reason for your answer.

5 Would you agree that 'Wreaths' contains some very powerful images? Which image did you find most memorable or effective? Would you agree that the images become less realistic as the poem goes on?

IN CONTEXT

Longley's poetry mixes a keen awareness of violence with a faint but unquenchable hope for a more peaceful future.

Write a short essay comparing 'Wreaths' to at least two other Longley poems in light of this statement.

Last Requests

I

Your batman thought you were buried alive,
Left you for dead and stole your pocket watch
And cigarette case, all he could salvage
From the grave you so nearly had to share
With an unexploded shell. But your lungs
Surfaced to take a long remembered drag,
Heart contradicting as an epitaph
The two initials you had scratched on gold.

II

I thought you blew a kiss before you died,
But the bony fingers that waved to and fro
Were asking for a Woodbine, the last request
Of many soldiers in your company,
The brand you chose to smoke for forty years
Thoughtfully, each one like a sacrament.
I who brought peppermints and grapes only
Couldn't reach you through the oxygen tent.

[1] **batman:** *orderly assigned to serve a British military officer.*
[11] **Woodbine:** *brand of cigarette*

COMPREHENSION

1 Describe what happened to the father in the first stanza. What does this stanza suggest to you about the father and his character?
2 How does the father's 'batman' respond to the event?
3 The poet describes how the father's lungs 'Surfaced to take a long remembered drag'. In what way is the description knowingly ambiguous?
4 In the last two lines of the first stanza the poet tells how the father's heart contradicted an 'epitaph' inscribed 'on gold'. What did this epitaph comprise of? Where was it written?
5 Where are the poet and his father located in the second part of the poem?
6 How does the poet mistake the father's gesture?
7 The central image in the poem is the cigarette. Discuss its significance in both sections of the poem.
8 How does the title of the poem relate to the events described in the poem?

PERSONAL RESPONSE

1 What does the poem suggest to you about Longley's view of his father and the relationship they shared?
2 How might 'Last Requests' be considered a poem about alienation?

IN CONTEXT

What do the poems 'Wounds' and 'Last Requests' reveal to us about the experiences of soldiers in war?

Self-heal

from *Mayo Monologues*

I wanted to teach him the names of flowers,
Self-heal and centaury; on the long acre
Where cattle never graze, bog asphodel.
Could I love someone so gone in the head
And, as they say, was I leading him on?
He'd slept in the cot until he was twelve
Because of his babyish ways, I suppose,
Or the lack of a bed: hadn't his father
Gambled away all but rushy pasture?
His skull seemed to be hammered like a wedge
Into his shoulders, and his back was hunched,
Which gave him an almost scholarly air.
But he couldn't remember the things I taught:
Each name would hover above its flower
Like a butterfly unable to alight.
That day I pulled a cuckoo-pint apart
To release the giddy insects from their cell.
Gently he slipped his hand between my thighs.
I wasn't frightened; and still I don't know why,
But I ran from him in tears to tell them.
I heard how every day for one whole week
He was flogged with a blackthorn, then tethered
In the hayfield. I might have been the cow
Whose tail he would later dock with shears,
And he the ram tangled in barbed wire
That he stoned to death when they set him free.

[2] **Self-heal:** *plant believed to have healing properties.*
[2] **centaury:** *plant found in grassy areas; is said to have been discovered by Chiron the centaur, hence its name.*
[3] **bog asphodel:** *plant commonly found on moors; considered an immortal flower in Greek mythology and, according to Homer's Odyssey, is said to cover the Elysian fields.*
[16] **cuckoo-pint:** *plant sometimes nicknamed 'lords and ladies'. Has sexual connotations because of its appearance.*

COMPREHENSION

1 Read the poem carefully. Who is speaking?
2 How old do you think the speaker was when the incident described in the poem takes place? Give a reason for your answer.
3 Describe the boy's appearance in your own words.
4 What do we learn about his family circumstances?
5 Can you detect any irony in the speaker's comments about the boy?
6 Why, according to the speaker, does she take the boy out walking?
7 Is she successful in this endeavour?
8 'The speaker clearly has an ulterior motive when she invites the boy to walk with her. She is attracted to him but is unable to admit this – not even to herself'. Would you agree with this statement? Give a reason for your answer.
9 *Group discussion:* It has been suggested by several critics that lines 16 and 17 are 'symbolic'. What do you think the 'giddy insects' crawling from the cuckoo-pint might symbolise?
10 What incident takes place during their walk?
11 How does the speaker react to this incident?
12 Would you agree that she seems puzzled or troubled by her own reaction?
13 What punishment is meted out to the boy for his behaviour?
14 How does he respond to this punishment?
15 At the end of the poem the speaker compares herself to a cow whose tail the boy cut off. She also compares the boy himself to a ram. Why do you think she makes these comparisons?

PERSONAL RESPONSE

1 What emotions did you experience when you first read this poem?
2 For whom did you feel most sympathy, the speaker or the boy?

This poem focuses on violence, which is one of the most important themes in Longley's work. It demonstrates how violence inevitably begets more violence, creating vicious cycles of wickedness and terror.

3 Write a paragraph saying whether or not you agree with this statement. Give reasons for your answer.
4 Longley has said that many of his poems explore 'the violence which lurks under the apparently peaceful surface of our civilisation'. Would you agree that this poem presents a negative view of society?
5 Do you think this poem presents an accurate portrayal of rural Ireland? Do you think it is offers a positive or negative image of Co. Mayo?
6 *Group discussion:* 'This poem must be set in the past. Such violence could never happen in the hi-tech modern Ireland of today'. Discuss this statement in small groups and decide whether or not you agree with it.

IN CONTEXT

My poems about the west of Ireland are meant to refract my concern for what's happening at the other end of my island – that is, in Ulster.

What similarities are there between the situation depicted in this poem and that depicted in poems about Northern Ireland such as 'Wreaths' and 'Wounds'?

An Amish Rug

As if a one-room schoolhouse were all we knew
And our clothes were black, our underclothes black,
Marriage a horse and buggy going to church
And the children silhouettes in a snowy field,

I bring you this patchwork like a smallholding
Where I served as the hired boy behind the harrow,
Its threads the colour of cantaloupe and cherry
Securing hay bales, corn cobs, tobacco leaves.

You may hang it on the wall, a cathedral window,
Or lay it out on the floor beside our bed
So that whenever we undress for sleep or love
We shall step over it as over a flowerbed.

Amish: *an Anabaptist Christian denomination found in the United States and Ontario, Canada, that are known for their restrictions on the use of modern devices such as cars and electricity, and for their plain dress.*

[6] **harrow:** *agricultural implement used for smoothing and levelling the soil after ploughing.*

[7] **cantaloupe:** *type of melon.*

COMPREHENSION

1 What impression of the Amish lifestyle is conveyed by this poem?
2 What do you think is the poet's attitude to this way of life? Do you think he envies the Amish the simplicity of their lifestyle?
3 Based on the clues provided in the second stanza write a few lines describing your impression of what the rug might look like.
4 What does the poet want his wife to do with the rug?
5 Identify three metaphors or similes in this poem.
6 Write a brief paragraph describing Longley's use of colour in 'An Amish Rug', focusing especially on how the poem moves from images of black and white to images of colour.

PERSONAL RESPONSE

This is an unusual love poem in that it celebrates the marriage between a middle-aged couple rather than the heady passions of young lovers. It celebrates domesticity, security and family life rather than the razzle-dazzle of a new relationship.

1 Do you think 'An Amish Rug' is a good love poem? How would you feel if your boyfriend or girlfriend wrote a poem like this for you?
2 What did you find to be the most vivid or memorable image in this poem? Give reasons for your answer.
3 What, in your opinion, is the main theme of 'An Amish Rug'?

Laertes

When he found Laertes alone on the tidy terrace, hoeing
Around a vine, disreputable in his garden duds,
Patched and grubby, leather gaiters protecting his shins
Against brambles, gloves as well, and, to cap it all,
Sure sign of his deep depression, a gostskin duncher.
Odysseus sobbed in the shade of a pear-tree for his father
So old and pathetic that all he wanted then and there
Was to kiss him and hug him and blurt out the whole story,
But the whole story is one catalogue and then another,
So he waited for images from that formal garden,
Evidence of a childhood spent traipsing after his father
And asking for everything he saw, the thirteen pear-trees,
Ten apple-trees, forty fig-trees, the fifty rows of vines
Ripening at different times for a continuous supply,
Until Laertes recognised his son and, weak at the knees,
Dizzy, flung his arms around the neck of great Odysseus
Who drew the old man fainting to his breast and held him there
And cradled like driftwood the bones of his dwindling father

Laertes: *Father of Odysseus, the hero of the epic poem the Odyssey. This epic poem describes Odysseus' return from that war and the many adventures he had on the way. Longley's poem is what he called a 'free translation' from one episode in Book 24 of the Odyssey describing the meeting between the hero and his father who has retired to the countryside.*

[2] **duds:** *colloquial word for his gardening clothes.*

[5] **duncher:** *the word used in Belfast for a flat cap.*

I was in Italy in about 1989 and I had a view from the bathroom window of this little villa ... and there was this octogenarian tending his flowers. I had a volume of Homer with me and I wrote the Laertes poem which is also a lament for my father. And that was extraordinary. I really felt as if I had gone back into Homeric times, and I was part of a timeless Mediterranean scene.

COMPREHENSION

1. Where does Odysseus find his father?
2. What is the father doing?
3. How does he appear to his son?
4. Why does Odysseus hesitate before revealing himself to his father?
5. How does Laertes react to seeing his son after all this time?
6. What is the effect of the poem being composed in a single sentence?

IN CONTEXT

Longley has written often and poignantly about his memories of and his relationship with his father. How does the poem 'Laertes' compare with poems such as 'Wounds' and 'Last Requests' as lament for this key person in the poet's life?

Ceasefire

I

Put in mind of his own father and moved to tears
Achilles took him by the hand and pushed the old king
Gently away, but Priam curled up at his feet and
Wept with him until their sadness filled the building.

II

Taking Hector's corpse into his own hands Achilles
Made sure it was washed and, for the old king's sake,
Laid out in uniform, ready for Priam to carry
Wrapped like a present home to Troy at daybreak.

III

When they had eaten together, it pleased them both
To stare at each other's beauty as lovers might,
Achilles built like a god, Priam good-looking still
And full of conversation, who earlier had sighed:

IV

'I get down on my knees and do what must be done
And kiss Achilles' hand, the killer of my son.'

[2] **Achilles:** *legendary young Greek hero and commander of the Greek armies.*

[3] **Priam:** *King of Troy and the father of Hector and Paris. It was Paris who brought about the Trojan War by abducting Helen from Sparta in Greece.*

[5] **Hector:** *The son of Priam and a commander of Trojan armies. He was killed by Achilles and his body was refused burial.*

COMPREHENSION

1 Where is this poem taking place? Describe the scene in your own words.

2 What does Priam want Achilles to do? How does he approach Achilles? Why does Achilles agree to Priam's request?

3 Achilles and Priam are enemies. Are you surprised, therefore, that they weep together 'until their sadness filled the building'? Why do you think Achilles is weeping?

4 Hector's body is described as being 'Wrapped like a present'. Is this a metaphor or a simile? Do you think this is an effective image? Give a reason for your answer.

5 Are you surprised that Priam and Achilles stare at each other and admire each other's good looks? What impression of Classical Greece is given by this stanza? What attitudes and characteristics seem to be valued by this society?

6 What clues does the poem give us about the personalities of these two men?

PERSONAL RESPONSE

1 *Group discussion:* 'This poem demonstrates the universal significance of Homer's *Iliad*. When it was published at the time of the IRA ceasefire in 1994 it was widely considered to be a powerful statement of the difficult acts of forgiveness that are necessary for bitter conflicts to be resolved'. Discuss this statement in small groups. Do you think it is an accurate statement of the poem's themes?

ADRIENNE RICH

Aunt Jennifer's Tigers

Aunt Jennifer's tigers prance across a screen,
Bright topaz denizens of a world of green.
They do not fear the men beneath the tree;
They pace in sleek chivalric certainty.

Aunt Jennifer's fingers fluttering through her wool
Find even the ivory needle hard to pull.
The massive weight of Uncle's wedding band
Sits heavily upon Aunt Jennifer's hand.

When Aunt is dead, her terrified hands will lie
Still ringed with ordeals she was mastered by.
The tigers in the panel that she made
Will go on prancing, proud and unafraid.

The Uncle Speaks in the Drawing Room

I have seen the mob of late
Standing sullen in the square,
Gazing with a sullen stare
At window, balcony, and gate.
Some have talked in bitter tones,
Some have held and fingered stones.

These are follies that subside.
Let us consider, none the less,
Certain frailties of glass
Which, it cannot be denied,
Lead in times like these to fear
For crystal vase and chandelier.

Not that missiles will be cast;
None as yet dare life an arm.
But the scene recalls a storm
When our grandsire stood aghast
To see his antique ruby bowl
Shivered in a thunder-roll.

Let us only bear in mind
How these treasures handed down
From a calmer age passed on
Are in the keeping of our kind.
We stand between the dead glass-blowers
And murmurings of missile-throwers.

Storm Warnings

The glass has been falling all the afternoon,
And knowing better than the instrument
What winds are walking overhead, what zone
Of gray unrest is moving across the land,
I leave the book upon a pillowed chair
And walk from window to closed window, watching
Boughs strain against the sky

And think again, as often when the air
Moves inward toward a silent core of waiting,
How with a single purpose time has traveled
By secret currents of the undiscerned
Into this polar realm. Weather abroad
And weather in the heart alike come on
Regardless of prediction.

Between foreseeing and averting change
Lies all the mastery of elements
Which clocks and weatherglasses cannot alter.
Time in the hand is not control of time,
Nor shattered fragments of an instrument
A proof against the wind; the wind will rise,
We can only close the shutters.

I draw the curtains as the sky goes black
And set a match to candles sheathed in glass
Against the keyhole draught, the insistent whine
Of weather through the unsealed aperture.
This is our sole defense against the season;
These are the things that we have learned to do
Who live in troubled regions.

Living in Sin

She had thought the studio would keep itself;
no dust upon the furniture of love.
Half heresy, to wish the taps less vocal,
the panes relieved of grime. A plate of pears,
a piano with a Persian shawl, a cat
stalking the picturesque amusing mouse
had risen at his urging.
Not that at five each separate stair would writhe
under the milkman's tramp; that morning light
so coldly would delineate the scraps
of last night's cheese and three sepulchral bottles;
that on the kitchen shelf among the saucers
a pair of beetle-eyes would fix her own –
envoy from some village in the moldings ...
Meanwhile, he, with a yawn,
sounded a dozen notes upon the keyboard,
declared it out of tune, shrugged at the mirror,
rubbed at his beard, went out for cigarettes;
while she, jeered by the minor demons,
pulled back the sheets and made the bed and found
a towel to dust the table-top,
and let the coffee-pot boil over on the stove.
By evening she was back in love again,
though not so wholly but throughout the night
she woke sometimes to feel the daylight coming
like a relentless milkman up the stairs.

The Roofwalker

for Denise Levertov

Over the half-finished houses
night comes. The builders
stand on the roof. It is
quiet after the hammers,
the pulleys hang slack.
Giants, the roofwalkers,
on a listing deck, the wave
of darkness about to break
on their heads. The sky
is a torn sail where figures
pass magnified, shadows
on a burning deck.

I feel like them up there:
exposed, larger than life,
and due to break my neck.

Was it worth while to lay –
with infinite exertion –
a roof I can't live under?
– All those blueprints,
closings of gaps,
measurings, calculations?
A life I didn't choose
chose me: even
my tools are the wrong ones
for what I have to do.
I'm naked, ignorant,
a naked man fleeing
across the roofs
who could with a shade of difference
be sitting in the lamplight
against the cream wallpaper
reading – not with indifference –
about a naked man
fleeing across the roofs.

Our Whole Life

Our whole life a translation
the permissible fibs

and now a knot of lies
eating at itself to get undone

Words bitten thru words

meanings burnt-off like paint
under the blowtorch

All those dead letters
rendered into the oppressor's language

Trying to tell the doctor where it hurts
like the Algerian
who walked from his village, burning

his whole body a cloud of pain
and there are no words for this

except himself

Trying to Talk with a Man

Out in this desert we are testing bombs,
that's why we came here.

Sometimes I feel an underground river
forcing its way between deformed cliffs
an acute angle of understanding
moving itself like a locus of the sun
into this condemned scenery.

What we've had to give up to get here –
whole LP collections, films we starred in
playing in the neighbourhoods, bakery windows
full of dry, chocolate-filled Jewish cookies,
the language of love-letters, of suicide notes,
afternoons on the riverbank
pretending to be children

Coming out to this desert
we meant to change the face of
driving among dull green succulents
walking at noon in the ghost town
surrounded by a silence

that sounds like the silence of the place
except that it came with us
and is familiar
and everything we were saying until now
was an effort to blot it out –
coming out here we are up against it

Out here I feel more helpless
with you than without you
You mention the danger
and list the equipment
we talk of caring for each other
in emergencies – laceration, thirst –
but you look at me like an emergency

Your dry heat feels like power
your eyes are stars of a different magnitude
they reflect lights that spell out: EXIT
when you get up and pace the floor

talking of the danger
as if it were not ourselves
as if we were testing anything else.

Diving into the Wreck

First having read the book of myths,
and loaded the camera,
and checked the edge of the knife-blade,
I put on
the body-armor of black rubber
the absurd flippers
the grave and awkward mask.
I am having to do this
not like Cousteau with his
assiduous team
aboard the sun-flooded schooner
but here alone.

There is a ladder.
The ladder is always there
hanging innocently
close to the side of the schooner.
We know what it is for,
we who have used it.
Otherwise
it's a piece of maritime floss
some sundry equipment.

I go down.
Rung after rung and still
the oxygen immerses me
the blue light
the clear atoms
of our human air.
I go down.
My flippers cripple me,
I crawl like an insect down the ladder
and there is no one
to tell me when the ocean
will begin.

First the air is blue and then
it is bluer and then green and then
black I am blacking out and yet
my mask is powerful
it pumps my blood with power
the sea is another story
the sea is not a question of power
I have to learn alone
to turn my body without force
in the deep element.

And now: it is easy to forget
what I came for
among so many who have always
lived here
swaying their crenellated fans
between the reefs
and besides
you breathe differently down here.

continued over

I came to explore the wreck.
The words are purposes.
The words are maps.
I came to see the damage that was done
and the treasures that prevail.
I stroke the beam of my lamp
slowly along the flank
of something more permanent
than fish or weed

the thing I came for:
the wreck and not the story of the wreck
the thing itself and not the myth
the drowned face always staring
toward the sun
the evidence of damage
worn by salt and sway into this threadbare beauty
the ribs of the disaster
curving their assertion
among the tentative haunters.

This is the place.
And I am here, the mermaid whose dark hair
streams black, the merman in his armored body
We circle silently
about the wreck
we dive into the hold.
I am she: I am he

whose drowned face sleeps with open eyes
whose breasts still bear the stress
whose silver, copper, vermeil cargo lies
obscurely inside barrels
half-wedged and left to rot
we are the half-destroyed instruments
that once held to a course
the water-eaten log
the fouled compass

We are, I am, you are
by cowardice or courage
the one who find our way
back to this scene
carrying a knife, a camera
a book of myths
in which
our names do not appear.

From a Survivor

The pact that we made was the ordinary pact
of men & women in those days

I don't know who we thought we were
that our personalities
could resist the failures of the race

Lucky or unlucky, we didn't know
the race had failures of that order
and that we were going to share them

Like everybody else, we thought of ourselves as special

Your body is as vivid to me
as it ever was: even more

since my feeling for it is clearer:
I know what it could and could not do

it is no longer
the body of a god
or anything with power over my life

Next year it would have been 20 years
and you are wastefully dead
who might have made the leap
we talked, too late, of making

which I live now
not as a leap
but a succession of brief, amazing movements

each one making possible the next

Power

Living in the earth-deposits of our history

Today a backhoe divulged out of a crumbling flank of earth
one bottle amber perfect a hundred-year-old
cure for fever or melancholy a tonic
for living on this earth in the winters of this climate.

Today I was reading about Marie Curie:
she must have known she suffered from radiation sickness
her body bombarded for years by the element
she had purified
It seems she denied to the end
the source of the cataracts on her eyes
the cracked and suppurating skin of her finger-ends
till she could no longer hold a test-tube or a pencil

She died a famous woman denying
her wounds
denying
her wounds came from the same source as her power.

DEREK WALCOTT

BIOGRAPHY

Derek Walcott was born in 1930 in the town of Castries on the beautiful island of Saint Lucia. (Saint Lucia is one of the Windward Islands in the Lesser Antilles). The experience of growing up upon this rugged, isolated island runs through all of Walcott's work, casting a large Caribbean shadow over his poems, plays and paintings. Walcott, of course, was greatly influenced by the incomparable beauty of his native island, and in poem after poem he celebrates its colours, sounds and textures. Yet he has also been influenced by the darker aspects of Saint Lucia. For the island is an ex-British colony, and Walcott was all too aware of the great damage European settlers had wreaked upon Caribbean society.

Walcott's keen awareness of colonial history is rooted in his own family background, for both his grandmothers were descended from slaves. Walcott's artistic tendencies have often been said to originate from his father, who was a skilled painter (the father and his paintbrush make an appearance in 'A Letter from Brooklyn'). His interest in religion, meanwhile, is said to have come from his mother, who ran the town's Methodist school. Unfortunately, Walcott's father died when he and his twin brother Roderick were only a few years old, leaving his mother to raise the boys alone.

Walcott was educated at St Mary's College in Saint Lucia, which had been founded by the Presentation Brothers from Cork. Walcott was academically quite gifted, though he also displayed a healthy interest in sport and girls. Like most people from the Caribbean, cricket was his game of choice. Walcott has often credited the Presentation Brothers with encouraging his interest in literature and writing, and his first poem was published in a local newspaper when he was only fourteen. On finishing school Walcott was lucky enough to earn a scholarship to the University of the West Indies in Jamaica. Here – when only eighteen years old – he published his first volume of poetry, *25 Poems*.

After graduating, Walcott moved to Trinidad, where he worked as theatre and art critic. In 1959 he founded the Trinidad Theatre Workshop, which produced many of his early plays. Poetic fame came Walcott's way in 1962 when he published *In a Green Night*, a collection of poems that won him admirers not only in the Caribbean but also in Britain, Ireland and the United States. Over the following thirty years Walcott added to his reputation with many more fine poetry collections and plays. The long poem 'Omeros', published in 1990, is often considered to be his masterpiece, being a perfect summation of the themes that had preoccupied him over three decades. In 1992 Walcott's achievement was acknowledged when he was awarded the Nobel Prize for Literature. He is an immensely popular figure in the Caribbean, and a street and a square have been named after him in his native town of Castries. Despite his fame and the political nature of much of his writing, Walcott is intensely reluctant to take on the role of some kind of 'spokesman' for his people, saying: 'I'm not even interested in sharing feelings of the people, because those who have been asked to share the feelings of the people are the ones who get shot first'.

From quite an early stage in his career Walcott's talents as a teacher and speaker have been in demand at several American and European universities. During these trips to the United States and Europe, Walcott befriended many of the leading writers of the day. Yet despite the acclaim his work has received, and despite being a member of the 'international community' of well-known writers, Walcott still feels that his work is somewhat out of place in the European tradition In an interview, Walcott said: 'But there is still an isolation in the sense that, as West Indian writers, whether we live in London or the West Indies, we are both cut off from and are a part of a tradition'.

Walcott has often declared that his style of writing is 'schizophrenic', or that he is a 'mulatto' of style. (A 'mulatto' is someone who has one black and one white parent). On one hand, Walcott is influenced by what he describes as the 'white' style – the great writers of the Western tradition that he studied at college, such as Shakespeare, Marvell, Eliot and Keats. Yet he is also influenced by what he describes as the 'black' style – the vibrant rhythms, slang and dialects of his native Caribbean. This combination of styles, according to many commentators, is what makes Walcott's writings so unique and memorable. Yet in interviews, Walcott often gives the impression that he is somewhat uneasy or uncomfortable with this 'dual heritage', as if he suspects that his work belongs properly in neither the 'white' nor 'black' traditions.

Since winning the Nobel Prize, Walcott has not slowed down. In recent years he has published several highly praised volumes of poetry as well as an important book of essays that explore West Indian heritage and language. He has produced a major cycle of plays called the 'Haitian Trilogy', which was published as a book in 2001. In 1998 Walcott used his various talents to collaborate with musician Paul Simon on a Broadway musical called *The Capeman*. Although the musical bombed on Broadway, it attempted to do what no other musical had done in the past: focus on the real fears of New York's poor. For many years Walcott has taught at Boston University, spending part of each year in the United States and part in Saint Lucia. As he himself put it, 'nobody wishes to escape the geography that forms you. In my case it is the sea, it is islands, I cannot stay too long away from the sea'.

A Letter from Brooklyn

An old lady writes me in a spidery style,
Each character trembling, and I see a veined hand
Pellucid as paper, travelling on a skein
Of such frail thoughts its thread is often broken;
Or else the filament from which a phrase is hung
Dims to my sense, but caught, it shines like steel,
As touch a line and the whole web will feel.
She describes my father, yet I forget her face
More easily than my father's yearly dying;
Of her I remember small, buttoned boots and the place
She kept in our wooden church on those Sundays
Whenever her strength allowed;
Grey-haired, thin-voiced, perpetually bowed.

'I am Mable Rawlins,' she writes, 'and know both your parents';
He is dead, Miss Rawlins, but God bless your tense:
'Your father was a dutiful, honest,
Faithful, and useful person.'
For such plain praise what fame is recompense?
'A horn-painter, he painted delicately on horn,
He used to sit around the table and paint pictures.'
The peace of God needs nothing to adorn
It, nor glory nor ambition.
'He is twenty-eight years buried,' she writes, 'he was called home,
And is, I am sure, doing greater work.'

The strength of one frail hand in a dim room
Somewhere in Brooklyn, patient and assured,
Restores my sacred duty to the Word.
'Home, home,' she can write, with such short time to live,
Alone as she spins the blessings of her years;
Not withered of beauty if she can bring such tears,
Nor withdrawn from the world that breaks its lovers so;
Heaven is to her the place where painters go,
All who bring beauty on frail shell or horn,
There was all made, thence their *lux-mundi* drawn,
Drawn, drawn, till the thread is resilient steel,
Lost though it seems in darkening periods,
And there they return to do work that is God's.

So this old lady writes, and again I believe.
I believe it all, and for no man's death I grieve.

[3] **pellucid:** *allowing the maximum passage of light, as glass; translucent.*
[3] **skein:** *a length of thread or yarn wound in a loose long coil.*
[5] **filament:** *a very fine thread or threadlike structure.*
[18] **recompense:** *to repay; remunerate; reward, as for service, aid, etc.*
[34] ***lux-mundi:*** *the light of the world, associated with Christ.*

I will never lay claim to hearing my own voice in my work. If I knew what that was, what infinite boredom and repetition would lie ahead, I would fall asleep at its sound. What keeps me awake is tribute – to the dead, who to me are not dead, but are at my elbow.

COMPREHENSION

1 The speaker describes the old lady's handwriting as 'spidery'. How do you imagine her writing based on this description?
2 How does the speaker convey the fact that the old lady's thoughts sometimes appear disjointed to him?
3 Lines 4 to 6 describe the structure of the letter in terms of a spider's web. How does the speaker suggest that the two correspond?
4 What do you think the speaker means when he refers to his 'father's yearly dying'?
5 What does the speaker remember of the old lady from his childhood? Was she somebody who made a big impression on him back then?
6 Why does the speaker say 'God bless your tense'? Why did the old lady use this tense?
7 How does the speaker respond to the old lady's description of his father?
8 What sort of life did the father lead?
9 How does the old lady describe the father's death in terms of her religious beliefs?
10 Line 25 is paradoxical. The speaker describes the 'strength of one frail hand'. How does the old lady's frail hand have strength?
11 What does line 27 suggest about the speaker's faith prior to receiving the old lady's letter?
12 In lines 30 to 31 the speaker tells us that the old lady is still beautiful and engaged with the world. Why does he say this? How does he reach this conclusion?
13 Lines 32 to 37 describe the old lady's faith and her conception of heaven. What sort of place does she imagine heaven to be?
14 According to line 34, heaven is a place where all was 'made' and it is to there that people like his father's '*lux-mundi*' gets drawn. To what is the speaker referring when he speaks of '*lux-mundi*'?
15 What do you think the 'thread' in line 35 symbolises?
16 How has the speaker's attitude to his father's death changed by the end of the poem?

PERSONAL RESPONSE

1 Did you find this an inspiring poem?
2 The poet uses the image of a spider's web repeatedly throughout the poem to metaphorically represent the old lady's thoughts. How effective did you find the poet's use of this metaphor?
3 Would you agree that this poem is less about the poet's father than about the old lady?

IN CONTEXT

1 In a number of poems on the Leaving Cert course Walcott deals with the process of grief and how people cope with bereavement. Compare and contrast the different ways in which the poems 'For Adrian' and 'A Letter from Brooklyn' deal with these issues.

The poetry of Derek Walcott often deals with and documents the terrible sadness and the pain that accompanies loss. However, time and time again Walcott reveals great strength of character in his expressions of hope and his unshakable belief that life is ultimately good.

2 Discuss three poems by Derek Walcott based on the professor's opinion of the poet's work.

Endings

Things do not explode,
they fail, they fade,

as sunlight fades from the flesh,
as the foam drains quick in the sand,

even love's lightning flash
has no thunderous end,

it dies with the sound
of flowers fading like the flesh

from sweating pumice stone,
everything shapes this

till we are left
with the silence that surrounds Beethoven's head.

[9] **pumice stone:** *a porous or spongy form of volcanic glass, used as an abrasive*

COMPREHENSION

1 How do the poem's opening two lines relate to its title?
2 According to these lines how do things generally end?
3 What do you think Walcott means by 'love's lightning flash'?
4 According to Walcott love 'has no thunderous end'. What kind of ending does love actually have?
5 'it dies with the sound / of flowers fading'. What sound do flowers make when they are fading or withering? What point do you think Walcott is trying to make with this rather peculiar comparison?
6 'everything shapes this'. What does Walcott mean by this? Would you agree that he seems to suggest that everything in life leads to one particular conclusion? What conclusion is this?
7 Read an article about Beethoven online or in an encyclopaedia. What does Walcott mean by the 'silence that surrounds Beethoven's head'?
8 How would you describe the tone of this poem? If you were to read it aloud what tone of voice would you use?

PERSONAL RESPONSE

1 'Endings' has been described as 'a poem of intense and memorable images'. List the different images that feature in the poem, describing each in your own words. Which images do you feel are most effective? Give reasons for your answer.
2 In this poem Walcott puts forward a particular view of 'how things end'. Write a few lines describing this view in your own words. Based on your own experiences in life do you think Walcott's view of endings is realistic? Give reasons for your answer.
3 What view of love and relationships does 'Endings' articulate? Do you think it is a realistic view?
4 'The conclusion of this poem perfectly fits its main theme. Its last lines have a deliberately limp and anti-climactic rhythm. The poem ends with a whimper rather than a bang' Do you think the poem's conclusion is effective? Do the last two lines fit well with the rest of the poem?

The Sailor Sings Back to the Casuarinas
from *The Schooner Flight*

You see them on the low hills of Barbados
bracing like windbreaks, needles for hurricanes,
trailing, like masts, the cirrus of torn sails;
when I was green like them, I used to think
those cypresses, leaning against the sea,
that take the sea-noise up into their branches,
are not real cypresses but casuarinas.
Now captain just call them Canadian cedars.
But cedars, cypresses, or casuarinas,
whoever called them so had a good cause,
watching their bending bodies wail like women
after a storm, when some schooner came home
with news of one more sailor drowned again.
Once the sound 'cypress' used to make more sense
than the green 'casuarinas', though, to the wind
whatever grief bent them was all the same
since they were trees with nothing else in mind
but heavenly leaping or to guard a grave;
but we live like our names and you would have
to be colonial to know the difference,
to know the pain of history words contain,
to love those trees with an inferior love,
and to believe: 'Those casuarinas bend
like cypresses, their hair hangs down in rain
like sailors' wives. They're classic trees, and we,
if we live like the names our masters please,
by careful mimicry might become men.'

This is an extract from 'The Schooner 'Flight',' a poem about a sailor named Shabine who takes to the sea aboard a ship called 'Flight'. On the voyage he gets to thinking about his life and his identity. The route the schooner takes is similar to the route taken by slave ships that would have carried his African ancestors to the islands.

Casuarinas: *tropical tree with long feathery branches.*

[3] **cirrus:** *a high-altitude cloud composed of narrow bands or patches of thin, generally white, fleecy parts.*

[20] **colonial:** *of, concerning, or pertaining to a colony or colonies.*

[27] **mimicry:** *the act, practice, or art of mimicking*

Deprived of their original language, the captured and indentured tribes create their own, accreting and secreting fragments of an old, an epic vocabulary, from Asia and from Africa, but to an ancestral, an ecstatic rhythm in the blood that cannot be subdued by slavery or indenture.

COMPREHENSION

1 The speaker uses two similes to describe the trees in the opening lines. Identify these similes and discuss the comparisons that the speaker makes.
2 The speaker refers to a time when he was 'green'? What does it mean to be 'green'?
3 Lines 4 to 7 describe an issue regarding the identity of the trees that arose when the speaker was younger. How do you suppose the confusion regarding the proper naming of the trees arose?
4 How does the captain of the ship add to the complexity of the situation?
5 Is the speaker annoyed that such differences arise over the naming of the trees?
6 How are the trees linked with lives and emotions of the inhabitants of the island?
7 In line 14 the speaker tells us that there was a time when the 'sound cypress' used to make more sense'. When and why do you think this was?
8 What does the speaker suggest about the wind's attitude to the trees? Do you think he envies the wind's attitude?
9 The trees are said to have 'nothing else in mind/ but heavenly leaping or to guard a grave'. Explain how you understand the trees' sense of purpose.
10 What does it mean to say that 'we live like our names'?
11 *Class discussion*: The poem finishes with a list of things that being 'colonial' teaches you. What does it mean to 'be colonial'?
12 *Group discussion*: The speaker says that you would have to 'be colonial to know the difference'. What is this 'difference' of which he speaks? You would also, according to the speaker, have to be colonial to 'know the pain of history words contain'. How can words be said to contain the 'pain of history'?
13 Who do you reckon the speaker is quoting in the last five lines?
14 What do the last two lines suggest about the lives that slaves had to live?

PERSONAL RESPONSE

1 The poem is very visual. List the similes and metaphors that the speaker utilises to convey an impression of these trees. Which ones do you think work most effectively?
2 Did you find the poem confusing? Do you think that the poem has a clear message to impart to the reader?
3 What did you make of the speaker's language? Did you find lines such as 'trailing, like masts, the cirrus of torn sails' to be inconsistent with the more ordinary lines of dialect such as 'Now captain just call them Canadian cedars'? Did you get a sense of what kind of person the speaker might be?
4 What issues does the poem raise? Based on your own sense of identity, can you identify with any of these issues?
5 Would reading this extract make you want to read the entire poem?

IN CONTEXT

1 Discuss how the notion of colonialism is dealt with in both 'Omeros' and 'The Sailor Sings Back to the Casuarinas'?

The rich imagery associated with everyday life and the complex psychology of colonial heritage that we find in Walcott's poems allows the uninitiated reader a rare and special insight into life in the Caribbean.

2 Discuss the poetry of Derek Walcott based on the professor's statement.

To Norline

This beach will remain empty
for more slate-coloured dawns
of lines the surf continually
eases with its sponge,

and someone else will come
from the still-sleeping house,
a coffee mug warming his palm
as my body once cupped yours,

to memorize this passage
of a salt-sipping tern,
like when some line on a page
is loved, and its hard to turn.

Memory that yearns to join the centre, a limb remembering the body from which it has been severed, like those bamboo thighs of the god.

COMPREHENSION

1 Where is this poem set? What time of day is it?
2 Describe, in your own words, the scene that confronts the speaker.
3 What is his reaction to this scene?
4 In line 5 the speaker talks about 'someone else'. Who do you think he has in mind here?
5 Identify one metaphor and two similes in this poem.
6 Write a few lines describing Walcott's use of rhyme in 'To Norline'.
7 Consider the poem's title. Having read the poem several times what relationship do you think Norline has with the poet? Do you think that the relationship between Norline and the poet is over or still continuing?

PERSONAL RESPONSE

1 Do you think 'To Norline' could be described as a love poem? Give reasons for your answer.
2 Walcott has been described as 'the ultimate poet of memory'. In what sense is that comment true of this poem?

IN CONTEXT

1 'To Norline', like many of Walcott's poems, demonstrates his fascination with the passage of time. Identify two other poems where Walcott deals with this subject. Compare or contrast their treatment of this theme with that to be found in 'To Norline'.

Summer Elegies

I

Cynthia, the things we did,
our hands growing more bold as
the unhooked halter slithered
from sunburnt shoulders!

Trembling I unfixed it
and two white quarter-moons
unpeeled there like a frisket,
and burnt for afternoons.

We made one shape in the water
while in sea grapes a dove
gurgled astonished 'Ooos' at
the changing shapes of love.

Time lent us the whole island,
now heat and image fade
like foam lace, like the tan
on a striped shoulder blade.

Salt dried in every fissure,
and, from each sun-struck day,
I peeled the papery tissue
of my dead flesh away;

It feathered as I blew it
from reanointed skin,
feeling love could renew it –
self, and a new life begin.

A halcyon day. No sail.
The sea like a cigarette paper
smoothed by a red thumbnail,
then creased to a small square.

The bay shines like tinfoil,
crimps like excelsior;
All the beach chairs are full,
but the beach is emptier.

The snake hangs its old question
on almond or apple tree;
I had her breast to rest on,
the rest is History.

[7] **frisket:** *a mask of thin paper laid over an illustration to shield certain areas when using an airbrush.*

[10] **sea grapes:** *a tropical American tree, Coccoloba uvifera, of the buckwheat family, bearing grape-like clusters of edible purple berries.*

[17] **fissure:** *a narrow opening produced by cleavage or separation of parts.*

[25] **halcyon:** *happy; joyful; carefree.*

[30] **crimps:** *to press into small regular folds; make wavy.*

[30] **excelsior:** *fine wood shavings, used for stuffing, packing, etc.*

Visual surprise is natural in the Caribbean; it comes with the landscape, and faced with its beauty, the sigh of History dissolves.

COMPREHENSION

1 What is an elegy? What sort subject would an elegy normally deal with?
2 How would you characterise the atmosphere of the first three stanzas?
3 The poem is addressed to Cynthia. What do we learn about Cynthia as the poem progresses?
4 How is the speaker's sense of excitement conveyed in the first two stanzas?
5 The removal of Cynthia's bikini top is compared to the unpeeling of 'a frisket'. How are the two acts similar?
6 In the fourth stanza the speaker says that 'heat and image fade/ like foam lace'. What does he mean by this? What 'image' do you think he is referring to?
7 The days were 'sun-struck' and 'salt dried in every fissure'. What impression are we given of how the summer was spent?
8 Twice in the poem the speaker mentions peeling layers away, once in relation to Cynthia's bikini and then again when speaking about his own skin. What significance is attached to this act of peeling?
9 The speaker says that when on the island he had a 'feeling love could renew it-/ self, and a new life begin'. What does this sentiment suggest about the speaker's experience before spending the summer with Cynthia? Was he right in this instance to think that 'love could renew itself'?
10 Do you think that the speaker is referring to a day from that summer from he says a 'halcyon day', or is he referring to the present day?
11 Lines 26 to 28 compare the sea to 'cigarette paper'. How are the two similar? In what way could the sea be 'creased to a small square'?
12 The eight stanza is set in the present. Where is the speaker now? Is Cynthia with him?
13 Lines 31 to 32 involve a paradox. How could the beach be 'emptier' when the 'beach chairs are full'?
14 The final stanza is somewhat cryptic. Is the speak referring to an actual snake or do you think that it is a metaphor? What is the 'old question' that the snake 'hangs'?
15 What is the speaker's attitude to the whole affair at the end of the poem?

PERSONAL RESPONSE

1 Did you find this poem sad? What is the poet lamenting?

The poem opens with the name 'Cynthia' and the speaker hints at the many good times they had together. Yet, apart from the opening description of them making love, perhaps for the first time, the poet does not mention her again until the second last line of the poem.

2 What, if anything, does this suggest to you about the speaker and the way he views the time spent on the island with Cynthia?
3 The first three stanzas deal happily and humorously with the early passion of the relationship. How do the second three stanzas of the poem compare? Did you find the poem got more interesting as it progressed?

IN CONTEXT

1 'Summer Elegies' closes with the word 'History', spelt with a capital *H*. Pentecost ends with the word 'Soul', again given a capital letter. 'The Young Wife' has 'Love' as the last word. Why do you think Walcott repeatedly finishes his poems with such capitalised words?

For Adrian

April 14, 1986
To Grace, Ben, Judy, Junior, Norline, Katryn, Gem, Stanley and Diana

Look, and you will see that the furniture is fading,
that a wardrobe is as unsubstantial as a sunset,

that I can see through you, the tissue of your leaves,
the light behind your veins; why do you keep sobbing?

The days run through the light's fingers like dust
or a child's in a sandpit. When you see the stars

do you burst into tears? When you look at the sea
isn't your heart full? Do you think your shadow

can be as long as the desert? I am a child, listen,
I did not invite or invent angels. It is easy

to be an angel, to speak now beyond my eight years,
to have more vestal authority, and to know,

because I have now entered a wisdom, not a silence.
Why do you miss me? I am not missing you, sisters,

neither Judith, whose hair will banner like the leopard's
in the pride of her young bearing, nor Katryn, not Gem

sitting in a corner of her pain, nor my aunt, the one
with the soft eyes that have soothed the one who writes this,

I would not break your heart, and you should know it;
I would not make you suffer, and you should know it;

and I am not suffering, but it is hard to know it.
I am wiser, I share the secret that is only a silence,

with the tyrants of the earth, the man who piles rags
in a creaking cart, and goes around a corner

of a square at dusk. You measure my age wrongly,
I am not young now, nor old, not a child, nor a bud

snipped before it flowered, I am part of the muscle
of a galloping lion, or a bird keeping low over

dark canes; and what, in your sorrow, in our faces
howling like statues, you call a goodbye

is – I wish you would listen to me – a different welcome,
which you will share with me, and see that it is true.

All this the child spoke inside me, so I wrote it down.
As if his closing grave were the smile of the earth.

[2] **vestal:** *chaste, pure.*

COMPREHENSION

1. Read the poem carefully. Who is speaking?
2. What event has just taken place?
3. Where do you think this poem is set? Give a reason for your answer.
4. 'Look and you will see that the furniture is fading'. What do you understand by this rather peculiar opening line? In what sense might the furniture be described as 'fading'?
5. Adrian seems to find it strange that his family are upset, asking them 'why do you keep sobbing?'. Why do you think he is surprised at their emotional reaction?
6. Group Discussion: In lines 5–10 Adrian makes a number of mysterious and mystical statements. Discuss each of these pronouncements in turn and say what each of them might mean.
7. 'It is easy / to be an angel'. In what sense does Adrian now resemble an angel?
8. Adrian says that he is 'not missing' his relatives. Why do you think this is so?
9. In lines 15 to 19 Adrian mentions a number of different individuals. What do we learn about the relationships between these people? How are each of them related to Adrian himself?
10. Adrian declares that he is now 'wiser'? Why do you think he makes this claim?
11. What does Adrian have in common with the 'tyrants of the earth' and 'the man who piles rags / in a creaking cart'?
12. Adrian claims that he is now 'part of the muscle / of a galloping lion, or a bird keeping low over / dark canes'. What do you understand by this pronouncement?
13. In lines 29 to 31 Adrian maintains that his family are mistaken about something. What, according to him, have they failed to understand?
14. What is the 'different welcome' referred to in line 31?
15. Who is speaking in the poem's final two lines?
16. *Group discussion*: Repetition is an important feature of this poem. Identify the different examples of repetition in this poem. How does this use of repetition contribute to the tone of the poem? What is Adrian's attitude to his family members?

PERSONAL RESPONSE

1. What emotions did you experience when you first read this poem?
2. Make a list of the different images in this poem. Which two images did you find most effective? Give reasons for your answer.
3. Would you describe 'To Adrian' as a sad poem, or do you feel that it could be better described as a positive, hopeful piece of writing?
4. In what sense is 'For Adrian' a religious poem? What aspects of the piece are not conventionally religious? Would you agree that the view of life after death presented in this poem is not a typically Christian view?

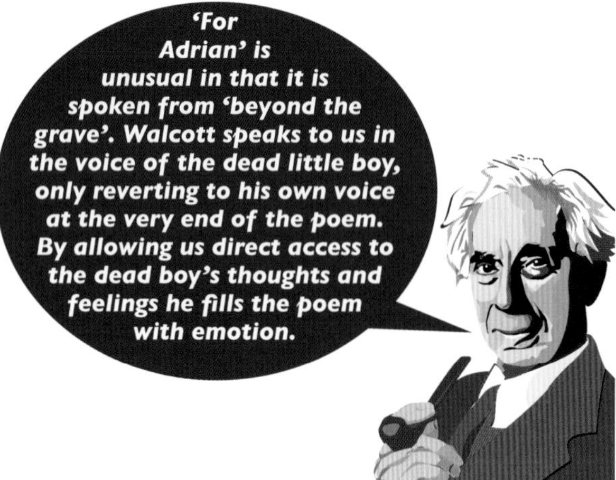

'For Adrian' is unusual in that it is spoken from 'beyond the grave'. Walcott speaks to us in the voice of the dead little boy, only reverting to his own voice at the very end of the poem. By allowing us direct access to the dead boy's thoughts and feelings he fills the poem with emotion.

5. Would you agree that this technique is an effective means of increasing the poem's emotional impact?
6. Do you think 'For Adrian' is a suitable poem for reading at a funeral? Give reasons for your answer.

IN CONTEXT

1. The struggle between faith and doubt is a theme that recurs throughout Walcott's poetry. Identify two other poems where Walcott addresses this subject and say which provides the most optimistic view of life and death. Which poem do you think is most pessimistic?

The Young Wife

For Nigel

Make all your sorrow neat.
Plump the pillows, soothe the corners
of her favourite coverlet.
Write to her mourners.

At dusk, after the office,
travel an armchair's ridge,
the valley of the shadow in the sofas,
the drapes' dead foliage.

Ah, but the mirror – the mirror
which you believe has seen
the traitor you feel you are –
clouds, though you wipe it clean!

The buds on the wallpaper
do not shake at the muffled sobbing
the children must not hear,
or the drawers you dare not open.

She has gone with that visitor
that sat beside her, like wind
clicking shut the bedroom door;
arm in arm they went,

leaving her wedding photograph in
its lace frame, a face smiling at
itself. And the telephone
without a voice. The weight

we bear on this heavier side
of the grave brings no comfort.
But the vow that was said
in white lace has brought

you now to the very edge
of that promise; now, for some,
the hooks in the hawthorn hedge
break happily into blossom

and the heart into grief.
The sun slants on kitchen floor.
You keep setting a fork and knife
at her place for supper.

The children close in space
made by a chair removed,
and nothing takes her place,
loved and now deeper loved.

The children accept your answer.
They startle you when they laugh.
She sits there smiling that cancer
kills everything but Love.

COMPREHENSION

Stanzas 1 to 3

1 Who is speaking in this poem?
2 Is it possible to make 'sorrow neat'? Why do you think the husband attempts to do this?
3 What does the opening stanza suggest to you about how the husband is coping with the death of his wife?
4 Discuss the images that the poet uses in the second stanza. What sort of atmosphere do they create? What do they reveal about the husband's life now that his wife is gone?
5 The 'mirror' is said to 'cloud' though the husband wipes 'it clean'? Do you think that the speaker of the poem intends this to have metaphorical significance?
6 Why do you think the husband feels he is a 'traitor'?

Stanzas 4 to 9

1 How do the objects in the house, the furniture and decorations, appear now that the wife has died?
2 In the fifth stanza the speaker describes the wife's death in terms of leaving the house with a stranger. Discuss the metaphorical description of death used here. Is the wife's death seen in some manner to have been a betrayal of the marriage?
3 The wife is still very much a presence in the house though she is dead. What has the wife left for the husband?
4 The speaker says that 'The weight// we bear on this heavier side/ of the grave brings no comfort'. What is this 'weight' that we bear? Why is life considered to be 'heavier' than death?
5 The husband has been brought to 'the very edge/ of that promise' he made when he got married. What is this promise and why is he now said to be at the edge of it?
6 For 'some/ the 'hooks in the hawthorn hedge/ break happily into bloom// and the heart into grief'. What does this line suggest about the greater world and the husband's grief? How do the real flowers differ from the representations of flowers on the curtains and wallpaper within the house.

Stanzas 9 to 11

1 How does suppertime reveal the wife's absence?
2 How do the children respond to the fact that their mother is no longer there with them at the table?
3 'The children accept your answer'. What question do you think they have asked the father? What do imagine his answer to be?
4 Why is their laughter startling for the father?
5 The poem closes with a suggestion that the wife is still their with them 'smiling'. Why does she smile?

PERSONAL RESPONSE

1 Did you think the poem vividly described the terrible grief that accompanies the loss of a loved one? What lines and imagines best convey the husband's grief?
2 Did you find the poem uplifting or depressing?
3 What does the poem suggest about love and family?

IN CONTEXT

1 In 'For Adrian' Walcott deals with death and the grief that those who continue to live must feel. How do the two poems compare in terms of their under standing of death and grief? What similarities exist between the poems?

Though a number of Walcott's poems deal with death and loss they are never bleak. In 'A Letter From Brooklyn' the poet writes of the death of his father and the comfort a letter from an old lady brings him. In 'The Young Wife' it is the husband's children who offer him hope.

2 Discuss the two poems and say how each of them acknowledge the pain that comes with loss yet ultimately offer the reader great hope.

Saint Lucia's First Communion

At dusk, on the edge of the asphalt's worn-out ribbon,
in white cotton frock, cotton stockings, a black child stands.
First her, then a small field of her. Ah, it's First Communion!
They hold pink ribboned missals in their hands,

the stiff plaits pinned with their white satin moths.
The caterpillar's accordion, still pumping out the myth
along twigs of cotton from whose parted mouths
the wafer pods in belief without an 'if'!

So, all across Saint Lucia thousands of innocents
were arranged on church steps, facing the sun's lens,
erect as candles between squinting parents,
before darkness came on like their blinded saint's.

But if it were possible to pull up on the verge
of the dimming asphalt, before its headlights lance
their eyes, to house each child in my hands,
to lower the window a crack, and delicately urge

the last moth delicately in, I'd let the dark car
enclose their blizzard, and on some black hill,
their pulsing wings undusted, loose them in thousands to stagger
heavenward before it came on: the prejudice, the evil!

Saint Lucia: *an island in the eastern Caribbean Sea where the poet was born. Named after St Lucy of Syracuse, the patron saint of blindness.*

[1] **asphalt:** *brownish-black solid or semisolid mixture of bitumens obtained from native deposits or as a petroleum by-product, used in paving, roofing, and waterproofing.*

[4] **missals:** *books containing all the prayers and responses necessary for celebrating the Mass throughout the year.*

COMPREHENSION

1 Describe, in your own words, the scene depicted in the poem's first five lines.
2 What does Walcott have in mind when he refers to the 'caterpillar's accordion'?
3 What do you understand by the expression 'belief without an 'if'!'?
4 What is the speaker's response to the sight of the communion girls?
5 What are the 'moths' that appear in lines 13–20?
6 Identify four metaphors or similes in this poem.
7 Group Discussion: What mood or atmosphere does Walcott create in this piece?

PERSONAL RESPONSE

1 Group Discussion: Images of light and darkness are an important feature of this poem. Identify these images as they occur throughout the poem and say how each contributes to its meaning.
2 Do you think this poem is optimistic or pessimistic or a mixture of both? Write a short paragraph outlining the reasons for your answer.

IN CONTEXT

1 The struggle between faith and doubt is an important theme in Walcott's poetry. Compare Walcott's treatment of this subject in 'Saint Lucia's First Communion' to that in 'For Adrian' or 'A Letter from Brooklyn'.

Pentecost

Better a jungle in the head
than rootless concrete.
Better to stand bewildered
by the fireflies' crooked street;

winter lamps do not show
where the sidewalk is lost,
nor can these tongues of snow
speak for the Holy Ghost;

the self-increasing silence
of words dropped from a roof
points along iron railings,
direction, if not proof.

But best is this night surf
with slow scriptures of sand,
that sends, not quite a seraph,
but a late cormorant,

whose fading cry propels
through phosphorescent shoal
what, in my childhood gospels,
used to be called the Soul.

Pentecost: *a Christian festival celebrated on the seventh Sunday after Easter, commemorating the descent of the Holy Ghost upon the apostles.*

[15] **seraph:** *an angel.*

[16] **cormorant:** *marine diving bird of the genus Phalacrocorax, having dark plumage, webbed feet, a slender hooked bill, and a distensible pouch.*

[18] **phosphorescent:** *emission of light without burning.*

In serious cities, in grey, militant winter with its short afternoons, the days seem to pass by in buttoned overcoats, every building appears as a barracks with lights on in its windows.

COMPREHENSION

1. The speaker establishes two preferences in the first six lines. What does he compare in these lines? What option does he prefer?
2. In the second stanza the speaker mentions 'winter lamps' and 'tongues of snow'. Where do you think the speaker is? What does he mean by 'tongues of snow'?
3. *Group discussion*: Stanza 3 is quite cryptic. What do you think the speaker means here? Is there any religious significance to these lines?
4. In the fourth stanza the speaker tells us what he thinks is 'best'. What is his ultimate preference?
5. The 'night surf' does not send the poet a 'seraph', but a 'late cormorant'. What does this bird reveal to the speaker?
6. *Class discussion*: Why do you think the poem is called 'Pentecost'?

PERSONAL RESPONSE

1. Did you find this poem had something interesting to say about modern life and modern values? Discuss what you think the poet's outlook on life is based on a reading of this poem.

from Omeros

Chapter XXX, I, lines 1–65

He yawned and watched the lilac horns of his island
lift the horizon.
'I know you ain't like to talk,'
the mate said, 'but this morning I could use a hand'
Where your mind was the whole night?'
'Africa.'
'Oh? You walk?'
The mate held up his T-shirt, mainly a red hole,
and wriggled it on. He tested the bamboo pole

that trawled the skipping lure from the fast-shearing hull
with the Trade behind them.
'Mackerel running,' he said.
'Africa, right! You get sunstroke chief. That is all.

You best put that damn captain-cap back on your head.'
All night he had worked the rods without any sleep,
watching Achille cradled in the bow; he had read

the stars and known how far out they were and how deep
the black troughs were and how long it took them to lift,
but he owed it to his captain, who took him on

when he was stale-drunk. He has not noticed the swift.
'You know what we ketch last night? One mako size 'ton,'
using the patois for kingfish, blue albacore.

'Look by your foot.'
The kingfish, steel-blue and silver,
lay fresh at his feet, its eye like a globed window
ringing with cold, its rim the circular river

of the current that had carried him back, with the spoon
bait in its jaw, the ton was his deliverer,
now its cold eye in sunlight was blind as the moon.

A grey lens clouded the gaze of the albacore
that the mate had gaffed and clubbed. It lay there, gaping,
its blue flakes yielding the oceanic colour

of the steel-cold depth from which it had shot, leaping,
stronger than a stallion's neck tugging at is stake,
sounding, then bursting its trough, yawning at the lure

of a fishhook moon that was reeled in at daybreak
round the horizon's wrist. Tired of slapping water,
the tail's wedge had drifted into docility.

Achille had slept through the fight. Cradled at the bow
like a foetus, like a sea-horse, his memory
dimmed in the sun with the scales of the albacore.

'Look, land!' the mate said. Achille altered the rudder
to keep sideways in the deep troughs without riding
the crests, then he looked up at an old man-o'-war

tracing the herring-gulls with that endless gliding
that made it the sea-king.
'Them stupid gulls does fish
for him every morning. He himself don't catch none,

white slaves for a black king.'
'When?' the mate said. 'You wish.'
'Look at him dropping.' Achille pointed. 'Look at that son-
of-a-bitch stealing his fish for the whole fucking week!'

A herring-gull climbed with silver bent in its beak
and the black magnificent frigate met the gull
halfway with the tribute; the gull dropped the mackerel

but the frigate-bird caught it before it could break
the water and soared.
'The black bugger beautiful,
though!' The mate nodded, and Achille felt the phrase lift

his heart as high as the bird whose wings wrote the word
'Afolabe,' in the letters of the sea-swift.
'The king going home,' he said as he and the mate

watched the frigate steer into that immensity
of seraphic space whose cumuli were a gate
dividing for a monarch entering his city.

Notes

This extract comes from the 325-page poem 'Omeros'. Many consider it Walcott's finest work. It is, in part, a retelling of the story of the Odyssey, set on the Caribbean island of Saint Lucia. The narrative of 'Omeros' is multi-layered. Walcott focuses on no single character as does Homer with Achilles in the Iliad or Odysseus in the Odyssey. Rather, many critics have taken the 'hero' of Omeros to be the island of Saint Lucia itself.

[10] **lure:** *a decoy; live or esp. artificial bait used in fishing or trapping.*

[10] **shearing:** *cutting.*

[11] **Trade:** *the Trade Winds blow continually towards the equator.*

[21] **mako:** *a large bluish-coloured shark.*

[21–2] **ton/ kingfish/ albacore:** *a long-finned tuna.*

[22] **patois:** *a regional form of a language, esp. of French, differing from the standard, literary form of the language.*

[31] **gaffed:** *to hook or land (a fish) using a gaff (a long stick with a hook).*

[44] **man-o'-war:** *also called the frigate-bird.*

[55] **tribute:** *a payment made to a ruler as a mark of respect.*

[61] **Afolabe:** *Achille's African ancestor.*

[64] **seraphic:** *of, like, or befitting a seraph (an angel).*

[64] **cumuli:** *dense, white, fluffy, flat-based clouds with multiple rounded tops and well-defined outlines.*

COMPREHENSION

1 Where is this extract set?

2 What time of day is it?

3 Briefly describe the two characters who feature in this extract. What is the relationship between them? Lines 1 to 20

4 What do Achille and the mate talk about?

5 Why does the mate suggest that Achille might have sunstroke?

6 How did the mate spend the night? How did Achille spend it?

7 How did the mate navigate the boat? How can he tell if fish are in the area?

8 Why is he grateful to Achille? Lines 21 to 41

9 What kind of fish did the mate catch the night before?

10 Describe in your own words the process by which this fish was caught.

11 Write a few lines describing the fish's physical appearance.

12 Identify three similes in this passage. Say whether you think each simile is effective. Give reasons for your answer. Lines 42 to 65

13 How does Achille steer the boat? How does he navigate the boat over the water in this fashion?

14 What tactic does the man-o-war use in order to provide itself with food?

15 Why does Achille describe the herring-gulls as 'white slaves for a black king'?

16 What is the mate's reaction to this comment?

17 Why do you think that the fish the herring-gull drops from its beak is described as a 'tribute'?

18 Write a few lines describing Achille's reaction to the man-o-war.

19 Why do you think the man-o-war reminds Achille of Afolabe, his African ancestor?

PERSONAL RESPONSE

1 Identify the different uses of Caribbean dialect in this poem. In your opinion does this use of dialect words and phrases detract from or add

The dialects of my archipelago seem as fresh to me as those raindrops on the statue's forehead, not the sweat made from the classic exertion of frowning marble, but the condensations of a refreshing element, rain and salt.

to the poem? Give reasons for your answer.

2 Like so much of Walcott's poetry this extract from Omeros is filled with images of the natural world. Make a list of the various nature-images that feature in the poem. Say which image you think is most vivid or memorable. Give reasons for your choice.

3 What kind of person do you think Achille is? What clues about his personality are to be found in the extract?

4 'The notion of Africa haunts the whole of Omeros. The poem presents a terrible contrast between the present and the past. In the past Achille's ancestors were black kings of Africa but in the present Achille is a poor fisherman struggling to make ends meet.' In small groups discuss the role that Africa plays in this extract. Do you agree with the statement that the notion of Africa 'haunts' the extract?

IN CONTEXT

1 Omeros is often compared to Walcott's earlier long poem The Schooner Flight. Write a few paragraphs outlining the main similarities and differences between this extract from Omeros and 'The Sailor Sings Back to the Casuarinas', which is an extract from The Schooner Flight.

W.B. YEATS

BIOGRAPHY

William Butler Yeats was born in Dublin on 13 June 1865. His father John Butler Yeats was an interesting character. He gave up a career in law to pursue his passion for painting, and when Yeats was only a child he moved the entire family to London to become a painter. However, though quite talented, his father was never able to make painting pay, and though he maintained a very positive attitude, the family were soon reduced to begging the local grocer for credit. In 1872, when William was seven, the family travelled to Sligo for a summer holiday, staying with the mother's family. The holiday lasted the best part of two-and-a-half years. However, it proved a vital experience for Yeats' consciousness. He fell in love with the landscape and listened intently to the servants' stories of fairies. The memory and attraction of Sligo was to remain with the poet for the rest of his life.

Back in England Yeats attended school, though his record was not great. In English he was considered 'very poor in spelling', a weakness that actually persisted throughout his great poetic career. In fact, it was in science that he excelled. His father, when reading William's report card – upon which 'of exceptional ability' was written alongside science – exclaimed that his son would be 'a man of science; it is great to be a man of science'.

In 1881 the family moved back to Dublin, living for a period of time in Howth. Every morning William travelled by train to Dublin to attend the Erasmus Smith High School on Harcourt Street. However, he found it hard to 'attend to anything less interesting than [his] thoughts'. Of his education, he remarked: 'I had begun to think of my school work as an interruption of my natural history studies [Yeats had developed a particular interest in the rock formations and the flora and fauna around Howth] ... and what could I, who had never worked when I was not interested, do with a history lesson that was but a column of seventy dates? I was worst of all at literature, for we read Shakespeare for his grammar exclusively'. In later life he regretted that his father had not taken him away from school and educated him personally.

In terms of academic success Yeats was a relative failure. He declined to sit the Intermediate Examination or the scholarship examinations to the university. Therefore, unlike his father and grandfather, he did not go to Trinity. This was primarily due to his uneven academic record and partly, perhaps, to his developing sense of a different destiny. However, his father was always encouraging of his son, and Yeats grew up with a healthy attitude toward discovering his own path and individual talent. John B. Yeats provided him with a world of ideas and stressed the importance of art. He even told his son that regular employment would be a barrier to creativity and is best avoided. In contrast with his wife, John Butler Yeats was an atheist whose political interests were nationalist. William soon became passionate about the Irish cause when he met an ex-Fenian named John O'Leary.

O'Leary was striking in his appearance, and his twenty years of imprisonment and exile, his dignified sense of patriotism, his devotion to cultural nationality rather than militant nationalism, all held an attraction for the young Yeats. John O'Leary embodied a sense of the older Ireland. He stood for 'Romantic Ireland', ancient and mysterious – what Yeats later termed the 'indomitable Irishry'.

Yeats began to translate Irish writings into English, and he became fascinated by the ancient Irish legends. He concentrated upon trying to draw attention to the cultural heritage which was to be found in the ancient stories of heroes and magic. Yeats was later to express the opinion that his work in reviving an Irish heritage was as important for Ireland as the work of those involved in nationalist politics.

Yeats was also very interested in the occult, attending séances and reading widely the mystical literature of other cultures or belief systems, such as Buddhism and Judaism. In 1890 he joined the Order of the Golden Dawn, a secret society with initiation rites and magical practices. The society believed that through ritual and ceremony, understanding of the universe could be achieved. The sense of ritual and symbolic importance in the revelation of truth was never to leave Yeats.

It was around this time that the poet met Maud Gonne. Of their first meeting, Yeats wrote: 'I had never thought to see in a living woman so great beauty. It belonged to famous pictures, to poetry, to some legendary past. A complexion like the blossom of apples ... and a stature so great that it seemed of a divine race'. Maud Gonne inspired him through a lifetime of great love poetry and unrequited passion. She refused all his marriage proposals (he proposed to her three times, and once to her daughter), suggesting that the pain of his longing would convert itself into poetry. In 1903 she married the soldier and republican John MacBride, whom Yeats mentions in 'Easter 1916'.

In 1894, Yeats met Augusta Gregory, the widow of a colonial governor, and her estate at Coole Park in Galway was to be a summer retreat for Yeats for many years. They shared an interest in Irish heritage and she was instrumental in the forming of the Irish National Theatre. Their relationship was characterised by great respect and affection. She listened to him and encouraged him, supported him and gave him a place to retreat to at Coole when it was needed. At Coole Park, Yeats found links to a different past – stately, noble and representing connections to a continuous artistic and cultural tradition.

Yeats married Bertha Georgie Hyde-Lees, a friend of a friend, in 1917. Georgie, as she was known, shared an interest in the occult with her husband, and after they were married took up automatic writing, feeling her hand, as it held a pencil over paper, moved by an external force as if something were using her as a medium to write. Yeats was tremendously excited by this, and it gave his writing a new life and energy – a new system of metaphors, images and symbols. In 1915 the couple bought a Norman castle, Thoor Ballylee. In the last phase of his life, the poet sought to turn it into a symbol, to invest it with deeper significance. The tower became central to his thought, and it was from the tower, at times, that he observed the strife that was raging through Ireland. By now, Yeats was a celebrated man. He was awarded the Nobel Prize for Literature in 1923 and became a respected senator of the Irish Free State, formed after the War of Independence.

The Lake Isle of Innisfree

I will arise and go now, and go to Innisfree,
And a small cabin build there, of clay and wattles made:
Nine bean-rows will I have there, a hive for the honey-bee,
And live alone in the bee-loud glade.

And I shall have some peace there, for peace comes dropping slow,
Dropping from the veils of the morning to where the cricket sings;
There midnight's all a glimmer, and noon a purple glow,
And evening full of the linnet's wings.

I will arise and go now, for always night and day
I hear lake water lapping with low sounds by the shore;
While I stand on the roadway, or on the pavements grey,
I hear it in the deep heart's core.

[1] **Innisfree:** *a rocky island on Lough Gill, Co. Sligo*
[2] **Wattles:** *rods interlaced with twigs or branches*

COMPREHENSION

1 Why do you think that he wants to go to Innisfree?
2 Why do you think that the poet wishes to 'live alone'?
3 Discuss the use of alliteration in this poem—does it contribute to the poem's meaning?
4 Do you think that the poet wants to shun society?
5 Comment on the idea that the poet will find 'peace' in a 'bee-loud glade', where the evenings are 'full of the linnet's wings'. Does peace equate to quietness in this poem?
6 How does the poet's use of colour and imagery contribute to meaning in this poem?
7 Do you think that the poet's attitude towards nature is realistic?
8 What view of city life is presented in this poem?
9 What does this poem suggest about the speaker's state of mind and about his values?
10 How does the poet's use of repetition contribute to the mood of the poem?
11 What tense is used in the phrase, 'I will arise and go now ...' Do you think that he will actually go to Innisfree? Support your answer with references to the poem.

PERSONAL RESPONSE

1 When you read this poem for the first time how did it make you feel? Write a few lines detailing your response to the poem.
2 Have you ever wished to escape from your current surroundings and move to a far away place? Describe in some detail a place, real or imagined, that you would consider to be an ideal haven.
3 Group discussion: How does the poem appeal to the senses? List all the words and images associated with sight and sound.

IN CONTEXT

1 What similarities are there, if any, between the ideal place depicted in this poem and the ideal portrayed in 'Sailing to Byzantium'. What major differences are there?

September 1913

What need you, being come to sense,
But fumble in a greasy till
And add the halfpence to the pence
And prayer to shivering prayer, until
You have dried the marrow from the bone?
For men were born to pray and save:
Romantic Ireland's dead and gone,
It's with O'Leary in the grave.

Yet they were of a different kind,
The names that stilled your childish play,
They have gone about the world like wind,
But little time had they to pray
For whom the hangman's rope was spun,
And what, God help us, could they save?
Romantic Ireland's dead and gone,
It's with O'Leary in the grave.

Was it for this the wild geese spread
The grey wing upon every tide;
For this that all that blood was shed,
For this Edward Fitzgerald died,
And Robert Emmet and Wolfe Tone,
All that delirium of the brave?
Romantic Ireland's dead and gone,
It's with O'Leary in the grave.

Yet could we turn the years again,
And call those exiles as they were
In all their loneliness and pain,
You'd cry, 'Some woman's yellow hair
Has maddened every mother's son':
They weighed so lightly what they gave.
But let them be, they're dead and gone,
They're with O'Leary in the grave.

[8] **O'Leary:** *John O'Leary (1830–1907) A Fenian arrested and sentenced to twenty year's imprisonment in 1865. He was released early on condition of exile, and did not return to Ireland until 1885.*

[17] **The wild geese:** *Irish soldiers forced into exile after the Williamite victory of the 1690s.*

[20] **Edward Fitzgerald:** *Lord Edward Fitzgerald (1763–98), one of the leaders of the United Irishmen. He died of wounds received while being arrested.*

[21] **Robert Emmet:** *leader of the rebellion of 1803.*

[21] **Wolfe Tone:** *(1793–98) Leader of the United Irishmen. He committed suicide in jail after being sentenced to death.*

COMPREHENSION

1 Who do you think the 'you' of the first line refers to?
2 Read the first five lines aloud. What is the tone of these lines?
3 Discuss the sound of, and the connotations associated with, the words 'fumble' and 'greasy'. How do these words contribute to the poet's portrayal of the new Irish middle classes?
4 Why do you think the poet links 'pence' and 'prayer' so closely together in his description of the middle classes?
5 What do you understand by the phrase, 'You have dried the marrow from the bone'?
6 Do you think that the poet is being sarcastic when he says that 'men were born to pray and save'? Support your answer with references to the poem.
7 What do you think the poet means by 'Romantic Ireland'?
8 Why does Yeats describe the Irish nationalists as a 'different kind'? Who do they differ from?
9 What is the poet's attitude towards (a) materialism and (b) idealism?
10 What effect does the poet's use of repetition have on the poem's meaning?
11 What does Yeats mean by 'a terrible beauty'?
12 How do you think the speaker feels about heroism? Consider, in particular, the phrases: 'All that delirium of the brave' and 'They weighed so lightly what they gave'.
13 What emotional response is suggested by line 25, 'Yet could we turn the years again'.
14 'Some woman's yellow hair / Has maddened every mother's son'. What does this 'cry' tell us about the poet's attitude to the passion that inspired the heroes of the past?
15 How, and why, is the refrain 'Romantic Ireland's dead and gone, / It's with O'Leary in the grave' altered in the final stanza?

PERSONAL RESPONSE

1 Class discussion: Do you think that the poem presents an optimistic or pessimistic view of human nature?
2 What do you think is the main message of this poem?
3 In your opinion, is it possible to find a balance between materialism and idealism?

IN CONTEXT

1 In 'The Second Coming' Yeats writes that 'The best lack all conviction, while the worst are full of passionate intensity'. Does this statement have relevance to the poet's views in 'September 1913?

The Wild Swans at Coole

The Trees are in their autumn beauty,
The woodland paths are dry,
Under the October twilight the water
Mirrors a still sky;
Upon the brimming water among the stones
Are nine-and-fifty swans.

The nineteenth Autumn has come upon me
Since I first made my count;
I saw, before I had well finished,
All suddenly mount
And scatter wheeling in great broken rings
Upon their clamorous wings.

I have looked upon those brilliant creatures,
And now my heart is sore.
All's changed since I, hearing at twilight,
The first time on this shore,
The bell-beat of their wings above my head,
Trod with a lighter tread.

Unwearied still, lover by lover,
They paddle in the cold
Companionable streams or climb the air;
Their hearts have not grown old;
Passion or conquest, wander where they will,
Attend upon them still.

But now they drift on the still water,
Mysterious, beautiful;
Among what rushes will they build,
By what lake's edge or pool
Delight men's eyes when I awake some day
To find they have flown away?

Coole: *Coole Park, Gort, Co. Galway and home of Yeats' friend, Lady Augusta Gregory, whom he visited often.*
[7] **the nineteenth autumn:** *reference to the summer and autumn of 1897 when Yeats stayed at Coole; at that time he was passionately involved with Maud Gonne and in a state of nervous exhaustion.*

COMPREHENSION

1 Why do you think that the opening stanza has been described as having a 'painterly quality'?
2 What is the speaker counting in the second stanza?
3 What words and phrases used in the second stanza help you to visualize the swans?
4 In the third stanza the speaker's heart is 'sore' when he now looks 'upon those brilliant creatures'? Why do you think this is?
5 Where does the poet use alliteration, and what is its effect?
6 The speaker describes the swans as 'unwearied' in the third stanza. What is the tone of this stanza? What does the speaker reveal about himself in these lines?
7 What characteristics does the poet attribute to the swans in stanza 4?
8 What personal issues are raised during the course of the poem?
9 How does the poet relate his own experience of love to the swans'?
10 List the contrasts that structure the narrative's development in this poem.
11 What is the tone of the final stanza?
12 Does the poem have a sense of resolution or closure?
13 How important is the season to the theme of ageing and loss in the poem?

PERSONAL RESPONSE

2 In his Sonnet 64, Shakespeare wrote, 'This thought is as a death, which cannot choose / But weep to have that which it fears to lose'. How well, in your opinion, do Shakespeare's lines express the theme of Yeats' poem, 'The Wild Swans at Coole'?
3 Do you find it easy to empathise with the speaker of Yeats' poem? Explain why.
4 At the very centre of this poem is the phrase, 'All's changed since I . . .' How important is this phrase to our understanding of the poem? Is it the scene, or the poet's attitude towards the scene, that has changed?

IN CONTEXT

2 Discuss how the representation of nature in this poem compares and contrasts with the representation of nature in 'The Lake Isle of Innisfree'.

An Irish Airman Forsees His Death

I know that I shall meet my fate
Somewhere among the clouds above;
Those that I fight I do not hate,
Those that I guard I do not love;
My county is Kiltartan Cross,
My countrymen Kiltartan's poor,
No likely end could bring them loss
Or leave them happier than before.
Nor law, nor duty bade me fight,
Nor public men, nor cheering crowds,
A lonely impulse of delight
Drove to this tumult in the clouds;
I balanced all, brought all to mind,
The years to come seemed waste of breath,
A waste of breath the years behind
In balance with this life, this death.

The speaker in this poem is Major Robert Gregory, the only son of Yeats' friend Lady Augusta Gregory of Coole Park, near Gort, Co. Galway. He was a pilot in the Royal Flying Corps in the First World War and at the time of his death, on 23rd January 1918, was on service in Italy. It emerged later that he had been accidentally shot down by the Italian allies.

[3] **Those that I fight:** *the Germans*
[4] **Those that I guard:** *the English or possibly the Italians*
[5] **Kiltartan Cross:** *a crossroads near Robert Gregory's home at Coole Park.*

COMPREHENSION

1 Consider the title alone before you read the poem. How do you imagine the pilot? What do you think his feelings and thoughts might be?
2 Who is the speaker of this poem?
3 In the first two lines the speaker announces that he knows that he will die in combat. Do you find this disturbing? What do these lines suggest about the speaker's own feelings about dying? Read these lines aloud to determine their tone.
4 What do you think motivates the speaker to fight those he does not hate and guard those he does not love?
5 What country is the speaker fighting for? Who is he fighting against?
6 What effect does this war have on the speaker's country and people?
7 The speaker mentions things that didn't motivate him to fight. What are they?
8 Do you think that the speaker likes his life as a fighter pilot?
9 The last quatrain begins with 'I balanced all'. How is this balance reflected in the formal structuring of the final four lines?
10 Why do you think that 'the years to come seemed waste of breath' for the speaker before he decided to become a fighter pilot?
11 Do you think that there is a contradiction within the phrase 'A lonely impulse of delight' (line 11)?
12 Why do you think the poet chose to use the word 'tumult' in line 12? Can you think of any other word he might have used in its place?
13 Do you think that the speaker regrets his decision to become a fighter pilot?
14 Who do you think is the addressee of this poem? Give reasons for your answer.
15 Do you think that the speaker's decision to become a pilot was impulsive?
16 Is the speaker's nationality relevant to the poem, in your opinion?
17 What are the main themes of the poem?

PERSONAL RESPONSE

1 *Class Discussion:* Do you think that the speaker's family would support his decision to become a pilot if they read this poem?
2 Write a paragraph on what the word 'fate' means to you. Do you think that this word has more than one meaning as it is used in the poem?
3 Write a paragraph on how the style of language used in this poem contributes to its mood. Is the language plain, simple and logical or is it intricate and figurative, or a combination of both?
4 Is it easy or difficult to identify with the speaker in this poem? Give reasons for your answer.

IN CONTEXT

1 What other poem(s) by Yeats on your course shares similar thematic concerns with this one?

Easter 1916

I have met them at close of day
Coming with vivid faces
From counter or desk among grey
Eighteenth-century houses.
I have passed with a nod of the head
Or polite meaningless words,
Or have lingered awhile and said
Polite meaningless words,
And thought before I had done
Of a mocking tale or a gibe
To please a companion
Around the fire at the club,
Being certain that they and I
But lived where motley is worn:
All changed, changed utterly:
A terrible beauty is born.

That woman's days were spent
In ignorant good-will,
Her nights in argument
Until her voice grew shrill.
What voice more sweet than hers
When, young and beautiful,
She rode to harriers?
This man had kept a school
And rode our wingèd horse;
This other his helper and friend
Was coming into his force;
He might have won fame in the end,
So sensitive his nature seemed,
So daring and sweet his thought.
This other man I had dreamed
A drunken, vainglorious lout.
He had done most bitter wrong
To some who are near my heart,
Yet I number him in the song;
He, too, has resigned his part
In the casual comedy;
He, too, has been changed in his turn,
Transformed utterly:
A terrible beauty is born.

continued over

Hearts with one purpose alone
Through summer and winter seem
Enchanted to a stone
To trouble the living stream.
The horse that comes from the road,
The rider, the birds that range
From cloud to tumbling cloud,
Minute by minute they change;
A shadow of cloud on the stream
Changes minute by minute;
A horse-hoof slides on the brim,
And a horse plashes within it;
The long-legged moor-hens dive,
And hens to moor-cocks call;
Minute by minute they live:
The stone's in the midst of all.

Too long a sacrifice
Can make a stone of the heart.
O when may it suffice?
That is Heaven's part, our part
To murmur name upon name,
As a mother names her child
When sleep at last has come
On limbs that had run wild.
What is it but nightfall?
No, no, not night but death;
Was it needless death after all?
For England may keep faith
For all that is done and said.
We know their dream; enough
To know they dreamed and are dead;
And what if excess of love
Bewildered them till they died?
I write it out in a verse –
MacDonagh and MacBride
And Connolly and Pearse
Now and in time to be,
Wherever green is worn,
Are changed, changed utterly:
A terrible beauty is born.

Notes

Easter 1916: *On Easter Monday, 24 April 1916, about 700 Irish volunteers, led by members of the Irish Republican Brotherhood, seized key buildings in Dublin city centre and proclaimed an Irish Republic independent of England. The uprising lasted six days, until April 30. Fifteen of the leaders were executed between 3 and 12 May.*

[1] **them:** *those republicans*

[17] **That woman:** *Countess Markievicz, formerly Constance Gore-Booth (1867–1927) of Lissadell, Co. Sligo. She was sentenced to death for her part in the rebellion; her death sentence was commuted to penal servitude for life from which she was eventually released in 1917.*

[24] **This man:** *Pádraig Pearse (1879–1916). teacher and poet, he founded St Enda's College, placing Irish language and culture at the centre of the curriculum. He believed that a blood sacrifice was necessary to redeem Ireland and the Irish people. He was commandant General and President of the Provisional Government during the Easter rising.*

[25] **wingèd horse:** *Pegasus, a mythological winged horse and symbol of poetic vision.*

[26] **This other:** *This other: Thomas MacDonagh (1878–1916), a poet and lecturer in English at University College Dublin, who was executed for his role in the rebellion.*

[31] **This other man:** *Major John MacBride, who had fought with the Boers against the British in South Africa. In 1903 he married Maude Gonne, the woman Yeats was in love with. He was executed for his part in the rising.*

[68] **England … faith:** *The Bill for Irish Home Rule had been past in the Westminister Parliament, but suspended in 1914 because of the outbreak of World War I. England gave assurances that it would be put into effect after the war.*

[76] **Connolly:** *James Connolly (1870–1916). Trade Union organiser and founder of the Citizen Army, which fought alongside the Volunteers under his military command at the GPO the Easter rising. He was wounded in the fighting and subsequently executed.*

PRE-READING

1. Write a paragraph on the social and political significance of the date 'Easter 1916' in Irish history. Discuss, in class, what you expect this poem to be about, based on its title alone.

COMPREHENSION

1. What do you think of the opening line of this poem? Do you think that it successfully engages the reader's attention? Look at each word in this line carefully and specify how the poet's use of language is designed to appeal to the reader's curiosity.
2. Who does the pronoun 'them' refer to?
3. Make a list of synonyms for the word 'vivid'. Use this list to describe in more detail the people the speaker meets. Why do you think the faces of the people the speaker meets were 'vivid'?
4. What does the contrast between the people's 'vivid' faces and the 'grey Eighteenth-century houses' suggest about the poet's attitude to the times he was living in?
5. Note each mention of time in this poem. What is its significance?
6. Where does the poet use past tense, and where does he use present tense?
7. What does 'motley' mean?
8. Read lines 5–14. What is the effect of the poet's use of run-on lines and repetition in this section? Do you think that the speaker's attitude to 'them' is dismissive? If so, how is this suggested?
9. Lines 11–14 contains two reasons why the speaker felt comfortable 'mocking' 'them'. What are they? Which reason more strongly motivated him, in your opinion?
10. Explain why the phrase 'terrible beauty' is an oxymoron.
11. What is the tone of the last two lines of the first stanza?
12. Who is 'the woman' the poet refers to in stanza 2?
13. Consider the connotations associated with the word 'shrill'. What do you think the poet's attitude is towards this woman. Does it indicate his attitude towards women generally?
14. What does the phrase 'she rode to harriers' mean?
15. Lines 24–40 paint a picture of two men. Who are they? In your own words, describe these two men as the poet represents them. What particular

words and images most strikingly indicate their respective characters?

16 Why does Yeats include in his 'song' a man who has 'done most terrible wrong'?
17 What does the phrase 'casual comedy' signify?
18 Does the refrain, 'A terrible beauty is born' change in tone between the first and second stanza? If so, explain why you think it does.
19 Change and transformation is emphasised in the refrain of the first two stanzas. What line reintroduces this theme into the third stanza. How does this stanza develop the theme of transformation. Is the theme of transformation portrayed positively or negatively?
20 Comment on the effect of the poet's use of repetition and animal imagery in the third stanza.
21 What, in the poet's opinion, makes a 'stone of the heart'?
22 What does this poem say about the role of the poet?
23 Does the question, 'What is it but nightfall?' reinforce or problematise the analogy between sleep and death in lines 62–6?
24 Referring to MacDonagh, MacBride, Connolly and Pearse, the poet asks: 'Was it needless death after all?'. Do you think that the poet answers this question in this poem? Give a detailed response.
25 How does the poet's statement that it is 'enough / To know they dreamed and are dead' relate to his view of the poet's role?
26 What is striking and significant about the poet's use of punctuation and conditional phrases in the final stanza?

PERSONAL RESPONSE

1 *Class discussion:* notice Yeats comparison of a poet to a mother. Do you think this is an apt simile? Explain your answer.
2 Write a few lines on how you think the following phrases from the poem: 'Too long a sacrifice', 'heart of stone' and 'excess of love', may be linked. Do they give an insight into the poet's view of the people his poem commemorates?
3 Discuss the importance of the images of birth and death, and their relation to one another, in this poem.
4 Do you think Yeats fulfils the role of the poet, as he defines it in this poem?

IN CONTEXT

1 Compare and contrast this poem to 'September 1913', particularly in relation to their respective portrayals of revolutionary politics.

The Second Coming

Turning and turning in the widening gyre
The falcon cannot hear the falconer;
Things fall apart; the centre cannot hold;
Mere anarchy is loosed upon the world,
The blood-dimmed tide is loosed, and everywhere
The ceremony of innocence is drowned;
The best lack all conviction, while the worst
Are full of passionate intensity.

Surely some revelation is at hand;
Surely the Second Coming is at hand.
The Second Coming! Hardly are those words out
When a vast image out of Spiritus Mundi
Troubles my sight: somewhere in sands of the desert
A shape with lion body and the head of a man,
A gaze blank and pitiless as the sun,
Is moving its slow thighs, while all about it
Reel shadows of the indignant desert birds.
The darkness drops again; but now I know
That twenty centuries of stony sleep
Were vexed to nightmare by a rocking cradle,
And what rough beast, its hour come round at last,
Slouches towards Bethlehem to be born?

The Second Coming: *See Matthew 24; Yeats adapts the biblical account of Christ's second coming to foreshadow the advent of a new, brutal deity as the second Christian millennium expires.*
Gyre: *the gyre is a very important symbol for Yeats …*
Spiritus Mundi: *'The spirit of the world', described by Yeats as a 'storehouse of images which have ceased to be a property of any personality or spirit'.*

PRE-READING

1 Whose return does the biblical concept of 'The Second Coming' anticipate, and what, according to the New Testament, will this return bring about? From the title of this poem alone, write a few lines on what you think this poem might be about.
2 Read and discuss the following passages from the Bible:
3 'For there shall arise false Christs, and false prophets, and shall shew great signs and wonders; insomuch that, if it were possible, they shall deceive the very elect' (Matthew 24: 24).
4 'And I stood upon the sand of the sea, and saw a beast rise up out of the sea, having seven heads and ten horns, and upon his horns ten crowns, and upon his heads the name of blasphemy' (Revelation 13).

COMPREHENSION

1 Read the first two lines, and explain (a) what the word 'gyre' means, and (b) its relationship to the movement of the falcon.
2 What do you think might happen to the falcon once he can no longer hear the falconer.
3 The phrase 'Things fall apart' has been borrowed and used by another author, Achebe, as the title of a book. What do you think it is about this phrase that makes is so effective as a book title?
4 What does 'anarchy' mean? Why do you think that the speaker uses the adjective 'mere' to describe anarchy?
5 Try to visualize the image of the 'blood-dimmed tide'. What, in one word, is your reaction to this image. Where else is water imagery used in this stanza? Traditionally, water is a symbol of cleansing, purification, new life and baptism. Write a paragraph about Yeats use of water imagery in the first stanza of this poem.
6 What do you think the 'ceremony of innocence' refers to?
7 lines 7 and 8 are extreme and absolute in their claim that 'The best lack all conviction, while the worst / Are full of passionate intensity'. Do you think that these lines may be read as an explanation for the death of innocence as suggested in line 5?
8 What elemental (earth, air, fire and water) imagery is used in the second stanza?
9 What is the tone of the first stanza?
10 Is there a change of tone in the opening lines of the second stanza?
11 How does the adjective 'vast', used to describe the 'image out of Spiritus Mundi', contribute to the developing atmosphere of the poem?
12 Why do you think that the 'desert birds' are 'indignant' (line 17)? Support your answer with references to the poem.
13 Within the context of the poem, explain the phrase 'The darkness drops again'.
14 How many years is 'twenty centuries'? What is the biblical relevance of this time span?
15 What is the significance of the symbol of the 'rocking cradle'?
16 What is the sound effect of the word 'Slouches'. Say the word aloud a couple of times and describe the type of gait, posture or movement it implies.
17 Describe your reaction to the association of the 'rough beast' with Bethlehem, the place of Jesus' birth.
18 Is there a change of tone as the second stanza progresses?

PERSONAL RESPONSE

1 Have a class discussion on the topic of nightmares, listing their common traits. How nightmarish is the vision presented in the second stanza of this poem? Does the ambiguity of the imagery contribute to its nightmare effect, in your opinion?
2 Class Discussion: divide into small groups and note all uses of alliteration and assonance that you notice in the second section of this poem. Write a few lines on their effect, on how these poetic devices contribute to the poem's atmosphere. Share your ideas.
3 'The Second Coming', which offers a disturbing image of an inhuman world about to be born, was written in the aftermath of World War I, at a time when communism and fascism were on the rise. Do you think that this historical background is relevant to the poem? Give a detailed response.
4 Discuss the symbolism at the beginning of the poem, focussing particularly on the gyre, the falcon and the falconer.

IN CONTEXT

1 'The best lack all conviction, while the worst / Are full of passionate intensity'. How does this statement from 'The Second Coming' relate to Yeats' view of self, society and politics in 'September 1913' and 'In Memory of Eva Gore-Booth and Con Markiewicz'?

Sailing to Byzantium

I

That is no country for old men. The young
In one another's arms, birds in the trees
– Those dying generations – at their song,
The salmon-falls, the mackerel-crowded seas,
Fish, flesh, or fowl, commend all summer long
Whatever is begotten, born, and dies.
Caught in that sensual music all neglect
Monuments of unageing intellect.

II

An aged man is but a paltry thing,
A tattered coat upon a stick, unless
Soul clap its hands and sing, and louder sing
For every tatter in its mortal dress,
Nor is there singing school but studying
Monuments of its own magnificence;
And therefore I have sailed the seas and come
To the holy city of Byzantium.

III

O sages standing in God's holy fire
As in the gold mosaic of a wall,
Come from the holy fire, perne in a gyre,
And be the singing-masters of my soul.
Consume my heart away; sick with desire
And fastened to a dying animal
It knows not what it is; and gather me
Into the artifice of eternity.

IV

Once out of nature I shall never take
My bodily form from any natural thing,
But such a form as Grecian goldsmiths make
Of hammered gold and gold enamelling
To keep a drowsy Emperor awake;
Or set upon a golden bough to sing
To lords and ladies of Byzantium
Of what is past, or passing, or to come.

Byzantium: *The Roman emperor Constantine, who became a Christian in AD 312, chose Byzantium as his capital city, renaming it Constantinople in 330. For Yeats, the Byzantium Empire is representative of the highest culture and civilisation. He believed that in Byzantium 'religious, aesthetic and practical life were one, that architect and artificers ... spoke to the multitude and to the few alike'.*

[1] **That:** *usually taken to refer to Ireland*

[17] **O sages ... mosaic:** *probably refers to the depiction of the martyrs being burned alive in a fire in a mosaic at the church of San Apollinare Nuovo in Ravenna, which Yeats saw in 1907.*

[19] **perne:** *another name for a cone shaped spool or bobbin used in weaving; Yeats uses the word as a verb to indicate the idea of circular movement.*

[19] **gyre:** *a cone shape that expands as it spins outwards from the apex, or contracts as it spins inwards from the base. In Yeats' cosmology, he imagines two cones (or gyres) interpenetrating one another—the base of one intersecting the apex of the other. The base of one represents the dominance of objective, rational values; the base of the other represents the dominance of subjective, imaginative values. The gyres can symbolise conditions of the human personality and / or phases of history. In other words, a gyre is a spiraling cone of time.*

[19] **perne in a gyre:** *unweave yourself through time*

[24] **artifice:** *something constructed, outside of nature*

[27] **such a form ... golden bough:** *Yeats writes that in the Emperors' Palace in Byzantium there was 'a tree made of gold and silver, and artifical birds that sang'.*

COMPREHENSION

1 The poem's theme centres on the contrast between that which decays and ultimately perishes (the human body) and that which is unchangeable and permanent (aesthetic artefacts).
2 What effect does the pronoun 'that' have in the opening phrase 'That is no country for old men'. What does this phrase tell us about the speaker's age, sex, attitude towards Ireland?
3 Is there a difference of tone between the first and second line of the poem. Give reasons for your answer.
4 Who are 'Those dying generations'? Does this phrase include the speaker?
5 Tension between youth and age is one of the contrasts set up in stanza 1. Name two more.
6 Where does the poet use alliteration in the first stanza, and to what effect?
7 What type of objects could be described as 'Monuments of unageing intellect' in your opinion?
8 What does the speaker compare the decrepitude of old age to in lines 9 and 10? What is your reaction to this comparison?
9 Read the first four lines of stanza 2 carefully, and answer the following questions. What is the significance of the imagery of clothing in these lines? What do these lines suggest about the relationship between the body and the soul? Does the poet consider the body or the soul to be superior? Why do you think the soul might celebrate 'every tatter in its mortal dress'?
10 Considering the christian conception of the soul as both immortal and immaterial, do you think Yeats' image of the soul clapping its hands and singing is unusual?
11 Why has the speaker chosen to live in Byzantium. What does Byzantium represent for the speaker?
12 What is a 'sage'?
13 Explain the phrases: 'perne in a gyre', 'sick with desire'.
14 In stanza 3 the speaker asks for his heart (or soul) to be untied from his body.
15 What form does the speaker wish his soul to take in stanza 4?
16 What does the golden bird symbolize?
17 Write a paragraph on the conflict in the last stanza between the speaker's desire to be removed from the natural cycle of time and his wish to sing 'Of what is past, or passing, or to come'?
18 What, in your opinion, is the central symbolic contrast in this poem?
19 Do you find it shocking that the speaker wishes to be taken out of the processes of nature?
20 Do you think it is ironic that, although the speaker wanted to escape out of time into the eternity of art, the golden bird's song is about time. Write a detailed response, referring to other relevant details in the poem.

PERSONAL RESPONSE

1 Quotation from a critic: 'Yeats could never sponsor one term of an antithesis for long without moving to embrace its opposite; and, even as he sidled away from the original term, he would cast longing glances back in its direction'.
2 Write an essay relating this statement to the poet's representation of the body and the soul in 'Sailing to Byzantium'.
3 What do you understand by the phrase, 'artifice of eternity'? Would you agree that art has a timeless quality about it?
4 Do you think that the 'sensual music' celebrated by the 'young' in stanza 1 differ from the song the poet wishes to 'sing' in stanza 4? Write a detailed answer to this question.
5 A critic writes that: 'God in the poem stands less in the position of the Christian God than in that of supreme artist, artificer of eternity and the holy fire; he is thus also the poet and the human imagination' Discuss.
6 Do you think that the phrase 'hammered gold' is an apt metaphor for the art of poetic creation? Write a detailed answer to this question.
7 Do you think that Yeats has immortalized himself in this poem?

IN CONTEXT

1 Write an essay discussing the central importance of bird imagery in two or more of Yeats poems.

The Stare's Nest by My Window

Section VI, from 'Meditations in Time of Civil War'

The bees build in the crevices
Of loosening masonry, and there
The mother birds bring grubs and flies.
My wall is loosening; honey-bees,
Come build in the empty house of the stare.

We are closed in, and the key is turned
On our uncertainty; somewhere
A man is killed, or a house burned,
Yet no clear fact to be discerned:
Come build in he empty house of the stare.

A barricade of stone or of wood;
Some fourteen days of civil war;
Last night they trundled down the road
That dead young soldier in his blood:
Come build in the empty house of the stare.

We had fed the heart on fantasies,
The heart's grown brutal from the fare;
More Substance in our enmities
Than in our love; O honey-bees,
Come build in the empty house of the stare.

Stare: *starling*
[13–14] trundled ... That dead young soldier: *this apparently took place beside Yeats' Galway house, Thoor Ballylee.*

COMPREHENSION

1. Describe the scene portrayed in the first three lines of the poem. Does the scene have warmth in your opinion? Is it a particular or general situation that is depicted?
2. What change takes place between line 3 and 4 of the first stanza?
3. Discuss the refrain 'Come build in the empty house of the stare'.
4. What do the 'honey-bees' represent for the speaker of this poem? In what other Yeats' poem is the honey-bee mentioned?
5. Read this poem aloud. What is its tone?
6. Does this poem have a message?
7. *Class discussion:* Discuss the phrase, 'More substance in our enmities / Than in our love'. Think of any situation, real or imagined, where this statement may ring true.
8. Is there any sense of hope in this poem?
9. What is the effect of 'uncertainty' on the speaker's thoughts and emotions in stanza 2?
10. The poet gives emphasis to the verb 'loosening' through repetition. What connotations does this word have for the speaker ?
11. The language used in this poem is less metaphoric and more direct. Do you agree? Write a paragraph on why you agree or disagree with this statement.

PERSONAL RESPONSE

1. This poem is a section from Yeats' larger work, 'Meditations in Time of Civil War'. Having read this section, would you be interested in reading the complete work?
2. What does the word 'meditation' mean to you? Do you think it is important in a time of war and chaos to be able to reflect on life?
3. Describe your personal response to this poem. Do you think it has relevance for our lives today?

IN CONTEXT

1. 'We had fed the heart on fantasies,/ The heart's grown brutal from the fare' (lines 16–17). Analyse this sentiment, and consider how it compares and develops the view expressed in 'Easter 1916', that 'Too long a sacrifice / Can make a stone of the heart' (lines 57–8).

In Memory of Eva Gore-Booth and Con Markiewicz

The light of evening, Lissadell,
Great windows open to the south,
Two girls in silk kimonos, both
Beautiful, one a gazelle.
But a raving autumn shears
Blossom from the summer's wreath;
The older is condemned to death,
Pardoned, drags out lonely years
Conspiring among the ignorant.
I know not what the younger dreams –
Some vague Utopia – and she seems,
When withered old and skeleton-gaunt,
An image of such politics.
Many a time I think to seek
One or the other out and speak
Of that old Georgian mansion, mix
pictures of the mind, recall
That table and the talk of youth,
Two girls in silk kimonos, both
Beautiful, one a gazelle.

Dear shadows, now you know it all,
All the folly of a fight
With a common wrong or right.
The innocent and the beautiful.
Have no enemy but time;
Arise and bid me strike a match
And strike another till time catch;
Should the conflagration climb,
Run till all the sages know.
We the great gazebo built,
They convicted us of guilt;
Bid me strike a match and blow.

October 1927

Notes
Eva Gore-Booth: *(1870–1926) She was actively involved in social causes, including the women's suffrage movement. She is the 'gazelle' of the poem.*
Con Markievicz: *Formerly Constance Gore-Booth (1867–1927). She was sentenced to death for her part in the 1916 rebellion; her death sentence was commuted to penal servitude for life from which she was released in 1917. She became the first Irish woman government minister in the Dáil Éireann of 1919.*

[1] **Lissadell:** *Georgian mansion in Co. Sligo where the Gore-Booth family lived.*
[7] **The older:** *Constance.*
[8] **lonely years:** *her Polish husband returned to his homeland and she was separated from her children.*
[9] **Ignorant:** *Yeats uses this adjective in another poem, 'No Second Troy', to describe Maud Gonne's revolutionary colleagues.*
[21] **Dear shadows:** *reference to the sisters both of whom were dead at the time Yeats wrote this poem.*
[30] **gazebo:** *may possibly refer to the Anglo-Irish contribution to Irish life, which was considered to be merely conspicuous and of no use. Because of this, a number of mansions – not Lissadell – were burnt.*

PRE-READING

1 Find out as much information as you can about Eve Gore-Booth (1870–1926) and Constance Markiewicz (1868–1927). What do you think are the most memorable details and remarkable achievements of their lives? What aspects of their lives do you think the poet will celebrate in this poetic remembrance of the two sisters?

COMPREHENSION

1 Discuss the scene depicted in the first four lines of the poem. Describe in your own words how you visualize 'Lissadell' and the 'two girls' from these opening lines.
2 Do you think that this scene is a memory that is treasured by the poet.
3 How would describe the change of tone and atmosphere in line 5?
4 How is autumn personified in line 5? How effective is the poet's word choice in this line?
5 How do the rhymes 'shears / years' and 'wreath / death' contribute to the poem's meaning and atmosphere?
6 Who is the poet referring to as 'the ignorant' (line 9). What do you think he's attitude is towards these people?
7 The poet suggests that Eva in her old age is an image of her political beliefs. Look at lines 10–14. What does the image and word-choice presented in these lines say about the poet's attitude to (a) old age, and (b) Eva's political outlook.
8 Who are what are the 'Dear shadows' addressed in line 21?
9 What knowledge does the speaker expect the 'two girls' gained through their life experience?
10 What is the tone of the second stanza?
11 How does the speaker portray time, and what is his own attitude towards it, in the second stanza?
12 What do you think 'the great gazebo' refers to?

PERSONAL RESPONSE

1 Do you think that Eva Gore-Booth and Constance Markiewicz would be pleased with Yeats' representation of then in this poem, in other words, is this how they would have liked to be remembered, do you think? Give detailed references to the poem in your answer to this question.
2 Declan Kiberd points out that: 'The 1922 constitution gave women full voting rights, seven years before their sisters in Britain and Northern Ireland: but the inveterate opposition of women deputies to the Treaty had deeper long-term consequences. It prompted the governments' propagandists to caricature political women as 'hysterical', a term used by W.B. Yeats'
3 What does this poem suggest about Yeats' attitude to women who become actively involved in politics? Do you agree with Yeats' views?

IN CONTEXT

1 Compare and contrast the representation of women and politics in this poem and in 'Politics'.

Swift's Epitaph

Swift has sailed into his rest;
Savage indignation there
Cannot lacerate his breast.
Imitate him if you dare,
World-besotted traveller; he
Served human liberty.

Jonathan Swift: *Admired by Yeats, Jonathan Swift (1667–1745) was the most famous Dean of St Patrick's, Dublin. He wrote satires, essays and political pamphlets, and is considered one of the greatest masters of English prose and one of the most zealous satirists of human folly; he is less well-known for his poetry. His works include:* Gulliver's Travels, A Modest Proposal, The Drapier's Letters, *and* A Tale of a Tub.
Yeats' poem is a translation, with some alterations, of the Latin epigraph on Swift's gravestone in St Patrick's. This is a translation of the original Latin epitaph:

Here is laid the Body of
JONATHAN SWIFT
Doctor of Divinity,
Dean of this Cathedral Church,
Where savage indignation
Can no longer
Rend his heart,
Go traveller, and imitate,
If you can,
This ernest and dedicated
Champion of liberty.
He died on the 19th day of Oct.,
1745 A.D. aged 78 years.

Swift sleeps under the greatest epitaph in history.

PRE-READING

1 Find out some information on Jonathan Swift.

COMPREHENSION

1 What does the verb sailed suggest about Swift's death?
2 What do the terms 'Savage indignation' and 'lacerate' suggest about the type of man Swift was, and about the type of life he led?
3 Do you think Yeats admires Swift? Give reasons for your answer.
4 What challenge is presented to the reader in line 4?
5 Compare and contrast the translation into English of Swift's original epitaph with Yeats' reworking of it:
'Here is laid the Body of
JONATHAN SWIFT
Doctor of Divinity,
Dean of this Cathedral Church,
Where savage indignation
Can no longer
Rend his heart,
Go traveller, and imitate,
If you can,
This ernest and dedicated
Champion of liberty.
He died on the 19th day of Oct.,
1745 A.D. aged 78 years.'

PERSONAL RESPONSE

1 Write an epitaph for a public figure that attempts to capture his or her essence.

IN CONTEXT

1 Compare and contrast 'Swift's Epitaph' with Yeats' epitaph, which is taken from the last lines of one of his final poems, 'Under Ben Bulben':
'Cast a clod eye
on life, on death.
Horseman, pass by!'

An Acre of Grass

Picture and book remain,
An acre of green grass
For air and exercise,
Now strength of body goes;
Midnight, an old house
Where nothing stirs but a mouse.

My temptation is quiet.
Here at life's end
Neither loose imagination,
Nor the mill of the mind
Consuming its rag and bone,
Can make the truth known.

Grant me an old man's frenzy,
Myself must I remake
Till I am Timon and Lear
Or that William Blake
Who beat upon the wall
Till Truth obeyed his call;

A mind Michael Angelo knew
That can pierce the clouds,
Or inspired by frenzy
Shake the dead in their shrouds;
Forgotten else by mankind,
An old man's eagle mind.

Notes

[2–5] **acre … house:** *reference to the farmhouse, Riversdale, in Rathfarnham that Yeats leased in 1932 for thirteen years.*

[15] **Timon:** *legendary Athenian who died in 399 BC Shakespeare, in his play* Timon of Athens, *presents him as a person who suffers deep disillusionment, becomes a misanthrope, and prefers to live in the wilderness rather than within any human community.*

[15] **Lear:** *from Shakespeare's play,* King Lear, *about the ageing king of Britain, who, having given up his throne to his daughters, went mad on the wild heath where he also learns from his mistakes and becomes more self-aware.*

[16] **William Blake:** *[1757–1827] engraver and writer of mystic, apocalyptic visionary poems, he was an independent thinker who challenged the conventional values of his day*

[19] **Michael Angelo:** *Michelangelo Buonarroti (1475–1564), Renaissance sculptor, architect, painter and poet, perhaps best remembered for his painting of the ceiling of the Sistine Chapel, and the statue of David.*

COMPREHENSION

1 Do you think that 'house' is a metaphor for the speaker's body in line 5? If so, explore this metaphor, and its development in line 6.
2 What is the symbolic relevance of the time, 'Midnight' (5).
3 What is your understanding of the phrase, 'My temptation is quiet'?
4 Can you imagine what it must feel like to be old and at 'life's end'? Do you think the speaker has accepted his ageing?
5 Why do you think the poet describes his imagination as 'loose'?
6 What metaphors does the poet use for the mind in lines 10 and 11.
7 The second stanza suggests that neither the speaker's imagination nor his mind can serve to 'make the truth known'. How important is the quest for truth to the poet?
8 What is the tone in the first two stanzas?
9 Discuss the use of the word 'frenzy' in stanza 3 and stanza 4. Does it have the same connotations in both stanzas?
10 Stanza 3 consists of a series of run-on lines following on from the word 'frenzy', which gives to this stanza a new energy. Is this energy reflected in the focus of this stanza?
11 What characteristics are associated with Timon, Lear and William Blake that would make the speaker want to transform himself into them?
12 What does the phrase 'an eagle mind' suggest to you?
13 What are the central themes of this poem?

PERSONAL RESPONSE

1 *Class Discussion:* Compare the imagery in stanza 1 to that used in stanza 4. Which stanza uses the more striking images?
2 In your opinion, has the speaker undergone a transformation by the time we reach the final line, 'An old man's eagle mind'? Consider the development of the tone, imagery and word choice over the four stanzas when answering this question.

IN CONTEXT

1 Discuss the theme of transformation in Yeats poetry, focusing on this poem and two other poems of your choice.

from Under Ben Bulben

V

Irish poets, learn your trade,
Sing whatever is well made,
Scorn the sort now growing up
All out of shape from toe to top,
Their unremembering hearts and heads
Base-born products of base beds.
Sing the peasantry, and then
Hard-riding country gentlemen,
The holiness of monks, and after
Porter-drinkers' randy laughter;
Sing the lords and ladies gay
That were beaten into the clay
Through seven heroic centuries;
Cast your mind on other days
That we in coming days may be
Still the indomitable Irishry.

VI

Under bare Ben Bulben's head
In Drumcliff churchyard Yeats is laid.
An ancestor was rector there
Long years ago, a church stands near,
By the road an ancient cross.
No marble, no conventional phrase;
On limestone quarried near the spot
By his command these words are cut:

Cast a cold eye
On life, on death.
Horseman, pass by!

The final draft of this poem was completed on 4th September 1935, about five months before the poet's death.
Under Ben Bulben: a renowned mountain in Co. Sligo, under which the fairy host—the Tuatha De Danann—were thought to live.

[11–12] **Sing the Lords ... beaten into the clay:** *refers to the Cromwellian settlement of 1652 which evicted the majority of native Irish landowners to Clare and Connaught to make room for new English settlers. Unlike the Gaelic Lords, the new English landlords offered no patronage to poets, who had previously enjoyed a high standing in the social hierarchy.*

[13] **centuries:** *since the Norman invasion of Ireland in the twelfth century*

[18] **Drumcliff churchyard:** *the site of a sixth century monastery at the foot of Ben Bulben*

[19] **ancestor ... rector:** *John Yeats (1774–1848)*

[27] **horseman:** *has echoes of the fairy horseman of folk belief, but might also have associations with the Irish Ascendancy class, with the 'Hard-riding country gentleman' of line 8.*

COMPREHENSION

1 Who is this poem addressed to?
2 Does the second line suggest that Yeats conceived of poetry as inspiration or as craft, or both?
3 Who or what is the speaker referring to when he advices poets to 'scorn the sort now growing up'?
4 What is your reaction to Yeats description of those 'now growing up' as 'base-born products of base born beds'?
5 Do you think the speaker is impressed by the art that is being produced by the new era of poets? How does he describe this art?
6 What does the word 'heroic' convey in this poem?
7 What type of people do lines 7–10 suggest are the proper subject matter for poetry?
8 What is the speaker's attitude to the past, present and future? Explain your answer with references to the poem.
9 What is the poet's public role according to this poem? Is it an important role in your opinion?
10 How does the rhyming scheme contribute to the chant-like effect of this poem?
11 How would you describe the speaker's state of mind in this poem?
12 How do you think the poet wishes to be remembered?
13 What does the poets' description of his burial place say about the values that are important to him?
14 What is the tone of the poem?
15 Do you find this poem appealing? Give reasons for your answer.
16 Do you think Yeats' epitaph captures his essence as man and poet?

PERSONAL RESPONSE

1 Do you find the tone of this poem disturbing in any way. Give reasons for your answer.
2 Class Discussion: why do you think it is important to Yeats to have 'no conventional phrase' carved on his tombstone? Do you think that he was an elitist? Support your opinion with references from the poem.

IN CONTEXT

1 Compare and contrast this poem with Yeats''Sailing to Byzantium' for their respective treatment of the themes of life, death and art. Which poem do you prefer? Explain your preference with detailed reference to both poems.

Politics

'In our time the destiny of man presents its meanings in political terms.'
Thomas Mann

How can I, that girl standing there,
My attention fix
On Roman or on Russian
Or on Spanish politics?
Yet here's a travelled man that knows
What he talks about,
And there's a politician
That has read and thought,
And maybe what they say is true
Of war and war's alarms,
But O that I were young again
And held her in my arms!

Thomas Mann (1875–1955): *German novelist. The epigraph was quoted in an article written by Archibald MacLeish and published in the Yale Review, Spring 1938, which praised Yeats' public voice but suggested that he should use it on political subjects. This poem is a rejoinder.*

COMPREHENSION

1 Read the poem aloud. How is the tone of the first four lines effected by the run-on lines?
2 Why can't the speaker concentrate his attention on politics?
3 Is there a tension between love and politics in this poem?
4 Is the speaker a young or old man?
5 Would you rather here more about what the 'travelled man' and the 'politician' may have to say about politics and war or more about the speaker's feelings for 'that girl'?
6 The phrase 'that girl standing there' is very specific, at the same time it gives no details about the girl. Does the phrase encourage you to imagine a particular person? Do you think that the poet may have deliberately avoided describing the girl in order to allow the reader to form their own mental picture of what she looks like?
7 Do you think that the poet regrets his inability to fix his attention on politics?
8 How many times, and in which lines, does the poet mention the girl? What does this suggest about the importance of the girl to the speaker?
9 Does the poet deliberately diminish the importance of politics in your opinion?
10 Do you think that the speaker will ever get to hold the girl in his arms?
11 Do you think that the poet is successful in getting his point across about the relative importance of love and politics in such a short poem?
12 Is the poem's brevity part of its charm?
13 Yeats includes Thomas Mann's epigraph as part of his poem. Do you think that Yeats agrees with Mann's point of view? Refer to the poem in your answer.
14 The poem ends with the word 'arms'. Do you think that this is a deliberate pun playfully pointing to both the lover's arms and arms associated with war? Support your opinion with references to the poem.

PERSONAL RESPONSE

1 What are the central conflicts set up in this poem
2 How would you describe the style of language used in this poem?
3 Class Discussion: Symbol and metaphor are very important to Yeats, as can be seen in his poems 'Sailing to Byzantium and 'The Second Coming'. This poem, in contrast, uses a simplicity of language. Share your ideas on how you think this simplicity of language contributes to the poem's meaning.

IN CONTEXT

Compare and contrast Yeats' style of language in this poem to that used in 'Sailing to Byzantium'.

NOTES

POETIC LANGUAGE

The language of poetry is derived from the same language that is used in everyday communication – letter writing, speech, etc. – and poets ultimately have to avail of the same lexicon of words as you and I do when we seek to express ourselves. It is how they *use* this language that makes it poetic. We might say that poetry de-familiarises the ordinary – that is, it does something unusual with ordinary words, something special that grabs our attention, stimulates our imagination, and allows us to see the world afresh.

Poets are very careful about the specific words that they choose to use. In a perfect poem there should be nothing superfluous, every syllable ought to have its place and purpose. In response to a young poet looking for advice, Philip Larkin once wrote: 'A poem is usually a highly professional artificial thing, a verbal device designed to reproduce a thought or emotion indefinitely: it should have no dead parts, and every word should be completely unchangeable and unmovable ... Someone once defined poetry as "heightened speech" – does that suggest my meaning? Features such as metre and rhyme help this heightening: they aren't just put in to make it more difficult to do'.

Take, for example, these lines by Hopkins describing the inspiring flight of a falcon:

striding
High there, how he rung upon the reign of a wimpling wing
In his ecstasy! then off, off forth on swing,
As a skate's heel sweeps smooth on a bow-bend

We would have to say that this is an extraordinary use of language, far removed from everyday conversational speech. Even if you do not initially understand exactly what is happening you will instantly appreciate the pleasant sound of the lines. Hopkins consciously brings together words that sound similar, and uses both assonance and alliteration to achieve a lyrical beauty that corresponds with the smooth, yet vigorous, flight of the falcon. He also uses a wonderful simile, comparing the bird's movement to that of a skate on ice.

PUNCTUATION

Punctuation establishes the pace of the poem. Depending on whether they are included or not, punctuation marks determine where we pause when reading, and for how long. Consider these lines from Philip Larkin's poem 'At Grass':

then the long cry
Hanging unhushed till it subside
To stop-press columns on the street.

The lines run on in a fluid manner, mirroring the breathless excitement that occurs when a horse race has just being won. And just as the cry of the crowd is said to not 'subside' until the news of the victory is broadcast in the streets, so the reading of the lines remains uninterrupted by any punctuating marks. In contrast, the lines that follow are very different.

Do memories plague their ears like flies?
They shake their heads. Dusk brims the shadows.

Moving away from the excited world of the races, the poem considers the horses as they are now, grazing peacefully in a field at dusk. Look particularly at the last line quoted above. The two short sentences, divided by a full-stop, slow our pace of reading and alter the mood of the poem considerably. The quick tempo of the first three lines quoted is broken, and the poem becomes more serene and melancholic.

If we look at the opening lines of Yeats' 'In Memory of Eva Gore-Booth and Con Markiewicz', we will see how the poet uses commas in the first four lines to create a tempered, peaceful tone and atmosphere that corresponds with his recollection of the stately Lissadell and its beautiful inhabitants. This atmosphere is then shattered in the fifth and six lines with the introduction of a wonderful metaphor for the destructive passage of time, where no commas occur.

The light of evening, Lissadell,
Great windows open to the south,
Two girls in silk kimonos, both
Beautiful, one a gazelle.
But a raving autumn shears
Blossom from the summer's wreath

The use of punctuation in poetry often functions in a manner much the same as in prose – it orders the words into coherent units. However, sometimes poets use punctuation in more unusual ways. Consider these lines from a poem by Emily Dickinson:

This is the Hour of Lead –
Remembered, if outlived,
As Freezing persons, recollect the Snow –
First – Chill – then Stupor – then the letting go –

The last line in particular uses unusual punctuation. Dickinson uses dashes where commas and full-stops might ordinarily feature. But the line also involves a dash where we might expect no punctuation, before the word 'Chill'. This has a number of effects. Just like any punctuating mark, it introduces a pause. However, here it also sections off the word 'Chill' so that visually it is isolated within the line. This serves to emphasise the word, giving it greater presence and significance. Ending the poem with a dash also creates an unusual effect. In contrast with a full-stop, the dash seems to indicate incompletion. Its use is disconcerting and introduces an intriguing element to the line, something that would not have existed had a full-stop been used.

LINE LENGTH AND LINE BREAK

Unlike prose, where the length of the line is generally determined by the width of the page, breaks in the lines of poems are either consciously established by the poet or by the form of poem that is being written. A sonnet, for example, is traditionally composed of sixteen lines, each line having ten beats. In such a poem the form dictates when each line will end. Look at the opening of 'No Worst, There is None' by Hopkins. Each line has ten beats and so a new line commences when this metre has been satisfied. (Of course, it is important to note how Hopkins skilfully crafts each line to suit the metre).

No worst, there is none. Pitched past pitch of grief,
More pangs will, schooled at forepangs, wilder wring.
Comforter, where, where is your comforting?

In much modern poetry, however, no official form is adhered to. As such, the poet determines when a line break will occur. Consider these lines in 'Elm' by Sylvia Plath:

The moon, also, is merciless: she would drag me
Cruelly, being barren.
Her radiance scathes me. Or perhaps I have caught her.

Here the line break is determined not by form but by the will of the poet. The lengths of the lines vary, allowing for different effect. Although Plath has made a conscious decision to introduce a break in the first line after the word 'me', it is open to interpretation why the break occurs here. Perhaps it allows for greater emphasis to be placed upon the word 'Cruelly'.

METAPHOR AND SIMILE

Metaphors and similes are incredibly common in poetry, and many poems owe their most vivid and memorable moments to these techniques. The ability to correctly identify similes and metaphors is very important when it comes to dealing with the unseen poem.

- A metaphor is when one thing is compared to something else.
- A simile is very similar to a metaphor in that it also compares one thing to something else. The big difference is that it uses the words 'like' or 'as'.

Each of the following phrases compares the hurler DJ Carey to a lion:

- 'DJ was like a lion in attack.'
- 'DJ played as if he was a lion in attack.'
- 'DJ was a lion in attack.'

The first two comparisons are similes because they use the words 'like' or 'as'. The third comparison is a metaphor because it does not feature the words 'like' or 'as'. Very often a metaphor is referred to as a 'strong' or 'direct' comparison, while a simile is referred to as a 'weak' or 'indirect' comparison As a general rule, similes tend to occur more often than metaphors, especially in modern poetry.

Consider the following phrases and in the case of each say whether it is a metaphor or a simile:

- 'The words are shadows' – *Eavan Boland*
- 'One tree is yellow as butter'– *Eavan Boland*
- 'Suspicion climbed all over her face, like a kitten, but not so playfully' – *Raymond Chandler*
- 'A leaping tongue of bloom' – *Robert Frost*
- 'Love set you going like a fat gold watch' – *Sylvia Plath*
- 'a dump of rocks / Leftover soldiers from old, messy wars' – *Sylvia Plath*
- 'The mists are … Souls' – *Sylvia Plath*
- 'He stumbles on like a rumour of war'– *Eavan Boland*
- 'My red filaments burn and stand, a hand of wires' – *Sylvia Plath*
- 'I thought of London spread out in the sun / Its postal districts packed like squares of wheat' – *Philip Larkin*
- 'The sky is a torn sail' – *Adrienne Rich*

PERSONIFICATION

This is a technique whereby an inanimate object is described as if it had the qualities of a living thing.

- In 'Out, Out –', for example, Frost suggests that a buzz saw was 'snarling', making it seem like a hungry and dangerous animal.
- Personification also occurs in 'Rathlin' where Derek Mahon describes the 'bombs' that 'doze in the housing estates' of Belfast. Here, the bombs are made to seem more menacing because they are presented as living creatures, dozing for a brief spell before they awake to wreak their havoc.

Personification can also involve speaking of plants and animals as if they had human attributes:

- Mahon uses this technique in 'A Disused Shed in Co. Wexford' where a group of mushrooms are described as if they had human feelings and emotions, and are presented as experiencing fear, hope, despair and insomnia.

HYPERBOLE

This is where we deliberately exaggerate to make a point.

- In 'After Apple-Picking', for instance, Frost refers to the fact that there were 'ten thousand thousand' (i.e. a million) apples in his orchard. Of course he doesn't mean that there were literally a million apples. Rather, he exaggerates deliberately in order to convey the vastness of his harvest.
- Hyperbole also occurs in 'Finisterre' where Plath claims that the sea has 'no bottom' and that there is nothing 'on the other side of it'. Of course, Plath is not really suggesting that the ocean is bottomless or endless – rather she exaggerates for effect, to convey the incredible vastness of the Atlantic as she looks down on it from the cliffs of Finisterre.

METONYMY

This is a technique whereby we describe something without mentioning the thing itself; instead, we mention something closely associated with it.

- For example, we use the phrase 'White House', to refer to the President of the United States and his advisors, or 'Hollywood' to refer to the film industry.

SYNECDOCHE

In this technique we identify something by referring to a part of the thing instead of naming the thing itself.

- A good example is the phrase 'All hands on deck'. In this instance, the sailors are identified by a part of their bodies, i.e. their hands. Similarly, we might use the word 'wheels' to refer to a car or 'head' to refer to cattle.
- We see synecdoche in 'The Whitsun Weddings' where Larkin refers to a street full of cars as a street of 'blinding windscreens'. Here, the cars are identified by a part of the whole, i.e. their windscreens.

SOUND EFFECTS

One of the features that most distinguishes poetry from ordinary language is its 'musical' quality. Much of this 'word music' is generated by assonance, alliteration and onomatopoeia.

Alliteration

Alliteration occurs when a number of words in close proximity start with the same sound.

- For example, the repeated '*s*' sound in 'In the sun the slagheap slept', or the repeated '*i*' sound in 'Iron inklings of an Irish January', or the '*f*' sound in 'fingers fluttering'.

Assonance

Assonance occurs when a number of words in close proximity have similar vowel sounds.

- For example, the repeated '*i*' sound in 'bright litter of birdcalls' or the '*u*' sound in 'fluid sensual dream'.

Onomatopoeia

Onomatopoeia occurs when a word or group of words sounds like the noise it describes. Examples of onomatopoeic words include buzz, murmur and clang.

- In 'All Legendary Obstacles', when Montague refers to the 'hissing drift of winter rain', we can almost hear the rain hissing off the station platform.
- Similarly, when Mahon's description of the sea in 'Day Trip to Donegal' mimics the sound of the tide washing against the land: 'That night the slow sea washed against my head ... Spilling into the skull, marbling the stones / That spine the very harbour wall'.

Euphony and cacophony

Euphony and cacophony are also important concepts. Euphony can be defined as any pleasing or agreeable combination of sounds. Cacophony, meanwhile, is a harsh, jarring or discordant combination of sounds.

- We see euphony in 'Rathlin', where Mahon uses a pleasant, lulling combination of sounds in his depiction of the beautiful bird sanctuary he has come to visit: 'Cerulean distance, an oceanic haze – / Nothing but sea smoke to the ice-cap'.
- Cacophony, meanwhile, can be seen in Eavan Boland's 'The War Horse', where the harsh, jarring nature of the word-music reflects the damage caused by the rampaging horse: 'If a rose, a hedge a crocus are uprooted / Like corpses, remote, crushed, mutilated?'

RHYME

Rhyme schemes

Since time immemorial rhyme has been deeply associated with poetry. The poem's rhyme scheme describes how its rhymes are arranged in each stanza. When we describe a rhyme scheme, we refer to lines that rhyme with one another by the same letter.

- In a 'A Valediction: Forbidding Mourning', for example, the first line of each stanza rhymes with the third line while the second line rhymes with the fourth. We say, therefore, that the poem has an ABAB rhyme scheme:

As virtuous men pass mildly away, A
And whisper to their souls to go, B
Whilst some of their sad friends do say, A
"Now his breath goes," and some say, "No." B

- In 'The Flea', meanwhile, each stanza rhymes AABBCCDDD:

Mark but this flea, and mark in this, A
How little that which thou deniest me is; A
It suck'd me first, and now sucks thee, B
And in this flea our two bloods mingled be. B
Thou know'st that this cannot be said C
A sin, nor shame, nor loss of maidenhead; C
Yet this enjoys before it woo, D
And pamper'd swells with one blood made of two; D
And this, alas! is more than we would do. D

In previous centuries strict rhyme schemes were extremely common, as can be deduced from the work of John Donne. In modern poetry this kind of strict rhyme scheme is less common. However, it can still be seen from time to time. 'Aunt Jennifer's Tigers' by Adrienne Rich, for example, features a strict AABB rhyme scheme, while in 'Cut Grass' by Philip Larkin each stanza rhymes ABAB.

Run-on lines

It can be harder to identify a poem's rhyme scheme when sentences continues over more than one line. This is known as a 'run-on line'.

- In Larkin's 'An Arundel Tomb', for instance, the sentence 'A bright litter of birdcalls strewed the same bone-riddled ground' stretches over lines 27, 28 and 29. In 'Day Trip to Donegal', the poem's final sentence occupies the entire final stanza.

Half-rhyme

An important technique to watch out for is half-rhyme. This is where two lines end in words that almost rhyme.

- Mahon makes extensive use of half-rhyme in 'A Disused Shed in Co. Wexford'. In the poem's second stanza, for instance, there are half-rhymes between 'hotel' and 'keyhole', between 'star' and 'desire', between 'silence' and 'rhododendrons' and between 'clouds' and 'wood'.

Internal rhyme

This occurs when there is rhyme or half-rhyme between two words in a given line.

- In line 19 of 'Finisterre', for instance, there is a half-rhyme between 'striding' and 'horizon'.

Hotel Room 12th Floor

by Norman MacCaig

This morning I watched from here
a helicopter skirting like a damaged insect
the Empire State Building, that
jumbo size dentist's drill, and landing
on the roof of the PanAm skyscraper.
But now midnight has come in
from foreign places. Its uncivilised darkness
is shot at by millions of lit windows, all
ups and acrosses.

But midnight is not
so easily defeated. I lie in bed, between
a radio and a television set, and hear
the wildest of warhoops continually ululating through
the glittering canyons and gulches –
police cars and ambulances racing
to broken bones, the harsh screaming
from frozen coldwater flats, the blood
glazed on sidewalks.

The frontier is never
somewhere else. And no stockades
can keep the midnight out.

SAMPLE ANSWER

1 What does this poem say to you about the city? Point out the words or phrases that especially convey its message to you.

The poem depicts the city as a rather wild and hostile place, a modern Wild West, full of danger and noise. The city's ready hostility is suggested by the metaphorical description of light coming from the many windows as bullets being wildly fired at the 'midnight' darkness: 'Its uncivilised darkness/ is shot at by a million lit windows, all/ ups and acrosses'. Though the darkness is described as 'uncivilised' the city, in turn, is hardly civilised.

The noises heard by the speaker are like those from a primitive society in the wilds of America. He tells us that he hears 'the wildest of warwhoops continually ululating through/ the glittering canyons and gulches'. We might normally associate the term 'warwhoops' with Indian tribes and their 'ululating' cries, and the metaphorical description of the voids between the enormous buildings as 'glittering canyon and gulches', and the mentioning of 'The frontier' in line 19 also evoke the old American Wild West.

The city is a violent place, as primitive and dangerous as any pre 'civilised' world, and the descriptions of the 'ambulances racing/ to broken bones, the harsh screaming/ from cold-water flats, the blood/ glazed on sidewalks' all testify to this.

2 What impresses you about this poem? Quote from or refer to the text in support of your opinion.

What struck me initially about this poem were its many vivid images. The image of the 'blood glazed on the sidewalks' was particularly graphic, and filled me with horror as much as it impressed me. Perhaps this is because of the word 'glazed', which I associate with baking and cooking. The notion of the blood being smeared on the footpath like icing on a cake was something that really impressed me.

What I found almost equally impressive was the poet's use of metaphor and simile. The metaphor comparing the Empire State Building to a 'jumbo size dentist's drill' was both humorous and strangely accurate.

Another brilliant metaphor was the description of the city streets as 'glittering canyons and gulches' surrounded on each side by overbearing buildings. The simile comparing the helicopter to a 'damaged insect' was even more vivid. I could almost 'see' the helicopter fluttering through the sky in my mind's eye.

Another feature of this poem that impressed me was the poet's use of sound effects. We see alliteration, for instance, in 'wildest of warhoops' with its repeated '*w*' sound and in 'broken bones' with its repeated '*b*' sound.

Onomatopoeia, meanwhile, features in line 13. In the word 'ululating' we can almost hear the sound made by the sirens of the police cars and ambulances as they race through the streets. These rich sound effects brilliantly convey the tapestry of noise that the poet experiences as he lies in his hotel bed, and summon up the alien, adrenaline-charged atmosphere of New York City.

EAVAN BOLAND

THEMES

HISTORY

Boland, perhaps above all, is a poet of compassion. Again and again her work pays tribute to history's victims, to those who have lost their lives over centuries of struggle, bloodshed and mankind's inhumanity to his fellow man. Boland's sympathies lie in particular with the victims who lie 'outside history', whose suffering and deaths the history books and official records have forgotten. This compassion is evident in 'The Famine Road' where she remembers some victims of the great hunger of the 1840's. The poem is fuelled by Boland's feeling for these wretches forced to construct a road with their bare hands in order to survive, dying of typhoid and having only 'April hailstones' to relieve their hunger. These 'Sick, directionless' individuals are not presidents or princes whose failings enter the history books, they are not great warriors whose decline and fall will echo through the ages. They are ordinary people whose trials and tribulations are largely unremembered. Boland, however, offers her poem as a memorial to their ordeal, in the hope that their sufferings will not be forgotten. A similar compassion is evident in 'Child of Our Time' where she offers a tender lament for the young victim of a terrorist attack.

This victim, too, is no one special, just another casualty of this island's bloody history. Yet Boland seems determined that his death will be remembered. Out of his suffering she crafts a poem, a 'song' that takes its tune from his final cry. This song, she hopes, will cause the tragedy of the child's needless death to linger in our consciousness.

Anger, too, is a feature of Boland's response to the bloody tide of historical events. 'The Famine Road' is marked by real bitterness toward Ireland's English overlords at the time of the famine who stood by and let the starving Irish suffer. Her quotes from Charles Trevelyan and Colonel Jones condemn these British aristocrats as cruel racists who considered the Irish 'Idle as trout' and were content to let them labour 'till they are quite worn/ then fester by their work'. There is anger too in her depiction of the young boy's needless death in 'Child of Our Time': 'for your sake whose life our idle/Talk has cost'. Here, however, the anger seems mixed with guilt that as a race we have made such a mess of the world, turning it into a place unsafe for children to be born into: 'our times have robbed your cradle'.

Fear, then, also forms part of Boland's response to history. In poem after poem she is profoundly aware of the risks 'our times' pose to us, to our children and to the children of others. 'The War Horse', for instance, is haunted by this dread of violence. The stray horse that passes through the speaker's housing estate is 'like a rumour of war'; an embodiment of the terrible conflict that had erupted in the Northern Ireland and that threatened to spread south. The speaker's terror stems from her knowledge that nowhere, not even a comfortable suburban housing estate, is ever truly safe from violence. (The Dublin and Monaghan bombings in the 1970s, which 'Child of Our Time' laments, brought this fact home to Boland).

In 'The War Horse' Boland seems to regard history as a vicious cycle. The speaker's 'blood is still/with atavism', with ancestral memory. The wrongs done to Ireland in the past still lurk in her consciousness. (This is evident in the scathing portrayal of the British in 'The Famine Road'). It is the memory of these wrongs, however, that leads (indirectly) to the contemporary violence in Northern Ireland, to the rumours of war represented by the horse marauding through the housing estate. History, therefore, is presented as endlessly repeating cycle of bitterness and revenge, as the wrongs of the past give birth to the violence of the present and future. It is a nightmare from which, it seems, there can be no escape.

In 'Outside History', too, history is presented as a dark and terrible force. It is the 'ordeal/ whose darkness/is only now reaching me'. The speaker seems to dread what history represents; its endless tale of pain, suffering and exclusion. In the poem the speaker is faced with a choice between myth and history; between the unchanging beauty of the stars on one hand and the darkness of the human condition on the other. Perhaps surprisingly the speaker chooses history: 'out of myth into history I move'. Her goal is to rediscover the lost histories of those who have suffered but are not remembered, those whose pain has been forgotten. If their stories are told, she feels, perhaps the suffering these people endured will not have been for nothing. No matter how well we remember the tales of history's victims, however, we cannot change or reverse the evil, misery and distress that was visited upon them. In this respect 'We are always too late'.

'Child of Our Time', meanwhile, offers a more optimistic perspective on history. The poem seems to hold out the possibility that mankind might mend its ways, might somehow make revenge and violence a thing of the past. The poem longs for a 'new language', a new way of being, in which peace will be a real possibility.

SUBURBAN WOMAN

Suburban life, it is important to note, has not traditionally been considered 'appropriate' subject matter for poets, who have generally taken inspiration from the buzz city or the beauty of the countryside rather than from the leafy comfort of suburbia. Boland, however, sets out to write poems that explore suburban life and reveal it as a source of poetic inspiration. (This ambition is particularly evident in her second book of poems, entitled The War Horse, which features poems such as 'Ode to Suburbia' and 'Suburban Woman'). 'This Moment', for instance, celebrates the magic in an apparently ordinary evening in suburbia, in a moment that all too often would pass without notice: 'A neighbourhood/ At dusk. / Things are getting ready/to happen/ out of sight'. 'The War Horse', too, finds inspiration in what might be considered ordinary, in the intrusion of horse into a housing estate on the city's edge: 'nothing unusual/About the clip, clop, casual//Iron of his shoes'. 'The Pomegranate' is another poem that finds inspiration in seemingly everyday suburban life. The poet's daughter lies sleeping beside her 'can of Coke/her plate of uncut fruit' in the centre of a safe suburban world: 'The suburb has cars and cable television'. In this banal scene, however, the poet discovers haunting and powerful parallels with the great myth of Ceres and Persephone.

An interesting feature of the 'The War Horse' is that it reveals the ease and safety of suburbia to be distinctly fragile. The escaped horse marauds through the housing estate like a spirit of war, indicating that even the comfortable lives of the suburbanites who live there could be touched by war and violence. (At the time of the poem's composition this seemed like a real possibility. Many people were concerned that the violence that had recently flared in Northern Ireland would spread south to the Republic). The fragility of this seemingly secure suburban lifestyle is suggested by the wild horse tramping through the houses' front gardens: 'a rose, a hedge, a crocus are uprooted'.

Boland's attitude to suburbia, then, is a generally positive one as she sets out to reclaim the suburbs as 'poetic territory', places worthy of being explored and celebrated in art and poetry. There is also a sense, however, in which Boland can't resist regarding the suburbs a somewhat boring or limiting place. This is evident in 'The War Horse' where the wild animal is depicted almost as a force of nature, the source of an energy and wildness that contrasts with the rigid, stable suburbs. As Boland puts it, the poem tells of 'an intrusion of nature – the horse – menacing the decorous reductions of nature which were the gardens'. Do we detect here a lingering dissatisfaction with the tameness and comfort of suburban life?

Such a dissatisfaction is certainly evident in 'White Hawthorn in the West of Ireland'. In this poem suburbia is dismissed as a place of dullness and monotony where little of consequence occurs. The speaker seems glad to leave behind its gossip and pointless banter 'I drove West/in the season between seasons. /I left behind ... Small talk'. The negative aspects of suburbia are symbolised by gardens and especially by lawnmowers: 'I left behind suburban gardens. / Lawnmowers'. To Boland, as we have seen, the suburban gardens are tame 'reductions' of nature that are kept neat and tidy by lawnmowers. The speaker longs to leave behind the dullness of these square gardens and escape to the wildness of the West with its 'ivory, downhill rush' of hawthorn. (The contrast between the orderliness of the suburbs and the wildness of the West is emphasised by Boland's use of language. The vibrant word music line 12 with its repeated broad vowels, 'ivory downhill rush', contrasts with the flat, conversational language used to describe the suburban gardens). A similar approach is evident in 'The Warhorse' where the unexciting comfort of the suburbs is also represented by neat gardens with their hedges and flowerbeds. Boland's attitude to the suburbs, then, is a complex one. On one hand, as we have seen, she is keen to reclaim the suburbs as a place of inspiration, where poetry and creativity can flourish. On the other hand, however, she seems to recognise suburbia's limitations and longs for the power and energy of real nature as represented by the West with its fluidity and wildness, and by the tinker horse that menaces and mutilates the square suburban gardens.

LOVE AND MARRIAGE

As with most poets, love and relationships are recurring themes in Boland's work. Her poems, however, do not present an overly romantic view of love. Instead, they offer a balanced account, focusing both on the joys of romance and on the difficulties and disappointments that accompany any serious relationship. This is particularly evident in 'Love' where she compares two different phases in a relationship. On one hand the speaker tells us about the 'golden period' she spent with her husband in Iowa many years ago. This was the time when the affection between them was at its strongest. It was the time when love 'had come to live with us' and was an extraordinary and 'formidable' presence in their lives. In their present day relationship, however, the love between them is less intense. Over years of marriage the affection between them has grown 'day-to-day and ordinary'. The speaker longs for the powerful emotions they experienced in Iowa but knows, deep down, that they can never 'live so intensely again.' 'The Black Lace Fan My Mother Gave Me' presents a similarly realistic view of marriage. In the fan, the speaker sees an honest and unflinching account of her parents' relationship. The fan represents both the joyous and peaceful times in their marriage as well as the more turbulent periods when they were beset by emotional storms. On the whole then, Boland provides a refreshingly balanced account of love and marriage. While she celebrates the joys of romance, she acknowledges that every relationship has its difficulties and is conscious of the disappointment caused when love diminishes in intensity over time.

In 'The Shadow Doll', however, Boland presents an altogether darker view of marriage. Matrimony is presented as a sinister force that imprisons women, sealing them in its 'airless glamour'. Perhaps the most disturbing consequence of marriage is that it silences women, forcing them to remain discreet about their inner lives. It is important, however, to consider this point in the context of Boland's career as a poet. Perhaps the silence she has in mind here is an artistic or literary 'silence'. It was difficult for women writers to explore marriage and motherhood in their work, as there was a lack of literary examples for them to follow. Such things had never traditionally been considered suitable subject matter for poetry and art. There is a hint also in 'The Black Lace Fan My Mother Gave Me' of marriage's darker side. The speaker refers to the 'violation' associated with the tortoise shell that decorates the black lace fan. This mention of violation, it has been suggested, suggests the constrictions and limitations that marriage will place upon the speaker's mother. By entering into wedlock her freedom, perhaps her very personality, will be 'violated'.

MOTHERHOOD AND CHILDREN

Perhaps the most dominant theme in this selection, and in Boland's poetic output as a whole, is that of motherhood. Again and again her poems return to the image of a mother and a child (especially a daughter). 'This Moment' is a particularly powerful celebration of motherhood. A mother and her child hold centre stage, dominating this atmospheric suburban scene. The evening seems to hold its breath, waiting for them to embrace before the 'Stars rise' and the 'Moths flutter'. 'The Pomegranate', too, centres on a mother's love for her daughter. It skilfully conveys the speaker's affection for her child and her terrible fear, common to most parents, that she might lose her: 'When she came running I was ready/To make any bargain to keep her'. A similar mix of fear and tenderness is evident in 'Love', where the speaker tells us of her child who 'was touched by death in this town.' 'Child of Our Time', too, is awash with maternal feeling, the speaker longing to soothe or reverse the great wrong done to the poor boy who was killed in the explosion. The dark side of maternity is presented in 'The Famine Road' where the tragedy of a woman unable to bear children is compared to Great Famine of the 1840s, one of the greatest catastrophes in Irish history.

The War Horse

LINE BY LINE

The poem describes a loosed horse passing through a suburban neighbourhood on a 'dry night'. The opening line expresses no surprise at this event. There is 'nothing unusual' about the appearance of the horse in the area. The horse seems innocent and harmless – 'clip, clop, casual'. But his shoes are made of 'iron' and as he makes his way through the garden he destroys some of the plants and flowers. We are told that he 'stamps death' on the ground. The poet compares the imprint of the horse's hooves on the garden to the minting of a coin: 'Like a mint on the innocent coinage of earth'.

The poet watches the horse through her window, which she opens to get a better view. She recognizes the horse. It belongs to the tinkers on the 'Enniskerry Road'. The poet describes the horse's leisurely movements as it saunters past her window. She observes the 'ambling feather/ of hock and fetlock'. The 'hock' is the joint on the lower part of a horse's leg and the 'fetlock' is the tuft of hair around this area. She describes the sounds he makes as he passes: 'his breath hissing, his snuffling head'.

In a moment the horse 'is gone'. And the poet tells us that 'No great harm is done'. The horse has damaged some of the plants and flowers in the garden: 'a leaf of our laurel hedge is torn'. A 'rose' and 'crocus' have been destroyed. But the poet tells us that the loss of these flowers and the damage to the leaf is of little consequence. This torn leaf is 'Of distant interest', the rose 'expendable', and the crocus 'only a crocus'.

However, Boland wishes to use the damage inflicted upon her garden as a metaphor for the violence and devastation of war. She, therefore, compares each of the damaged plants to victims of war. The rose is 'a volunteer', a 'mere/ Line of defence' whose life has cruelly been cut short. The damaged leaf is compared to a 'maimed limb'. The crocus is likened to a bomb victim: 'its bulbous head/ Blown from growth'.

The poet suggests that the lack of concern that she and her neighbours exhibit for the damage inflicted by the horse is somehow akin to the apathy they feel when it comes to war and violence: 'why, should we care// If a rose, a hedge, a crocus are uprooted/ Like corpses, remote, crushed, mutilated'. Their nonchalance in the face of a loosed horse is, according to the poet, indicative of their cowardly, selfish natures. What is important to these people is that *they* are safe. What happens to others is of little importance, of 'distance interest'. Snug in their suburban homes people no longer feel moved to act or respond to violence: 'But we, we are safe, our unformed fear/ Of fierce commitment gone'.

Boland compares the horse to a 'rumour of war'. His brief presence gives the poet an intimation of the greater violence that exists in the world. All the time the neighbours hide behind their curtains – 'Neighbours use the subterfuge/ Of curtains'. The poet expresses thanks that the horse has once again passed them by. She pauses to 'breathe relief' while leaning 'on the sill'.

As the poet leans on her window sill and breathes a sigh of relief, she is suddenly struck by the 'rose the horse 'smashed'. The frayed rose, torn and 'Ribboned across' the hedge, serves as a brief, chilling reminder of the past. Boland gets an intimation of a time when the country was at war. She says that her 'blood' is briefly stilled with 'atavism', with the resemblance that the rose bears to distant times. The damaged rose recalls a time when the countryside was destroyed by conflict: 'days// Of burned countryside'.

The torn rose also resembles a ribbon and this makes the poet think of the 'illicit braid', the badge, perhaps, worn by Nationalists to signal their allegiance to their 'illicit', or illegal, fight for independence. Boland says that this 'cause' was 'ruined before' and, in the process, 'a world betrayed'. Perhaps Boland means that those who fought for independence were betrayed by the English government, that promises and commitments were not honoured. There is also a suggestion that we are betraying the people who fought for the freedoms we now have by forgetting the hardships they suffered.

THEMES

Violence

The horse that wanders through the poet's garden serves as a reminder of the fact that the world is not perfect, orderly and safe. There are brute forces in existence that we cannot hope to control. The horse functions as a symbol of destruction, of the fact that war and violence are an ever-present part of the world.

The damage that the horse does to the poet's garden represents the horrors of war. Boland likens the damaged plants and flowers to the victims of war, to the young soldiers who lose their lives and are horribly mutilated in battle. Once again Boland displays sympathy for the faceless victims of history and conflict, the countless individuals who suffer and die because of war. She suggests that such people are too easily forgotten and ignored.

Suburban complacency

'The War Horse' was one of the first poems that Boland wrote when she moved to the suburbs of Dublin. She is critical of the what she perceives to be complacency amongst her neighbours. Boland suggests that people living in cosy, well-kept areas are somehow looking to hide away from the realities of the world. The poem suggests that such a lifestyle is one of 'subterfuge', dishonest and cowardly. People use the anonymity of suburbia to avoid having to face up to the harsh realities of life.

The poem is critical of such people's reaction to war and suffering. Boland suggests that war is 'Of distant interest' to people who live in peaceful areas like the Dublin suburbs. As long as they are not troubled by events they care little for the suffering of others: 'But we are safe ... why should we care'.

However, the poem reminds us of the fact that violence was part of this country not so long ago. The frayed rose in the poet's garden reminds her of a time when the countryside was devastated by conflict. It also resembles a 'braid' that was worn by some involved in Ireland's fight for independence. The rose therefore serves to recall how people once devoted themselves to a cause, gave their lives for something they believed in. 'The War Horse' seems to be critical of the fact that people no longer feel a sense of commitment and responsibility. Boland says that our sense of 'fierce commitment' is 'gone'. We choose to ignore the troubles in the world and dismiss the sufferings and plights of others as of no real interest. There is a sense at the end of the poem that we are dishonouring those had no choice but to fight and die for their country.

The Famine Road

INTRODUCTION

The Irish Famine

In 1845 a potato blight hit Ireland with devastating consequences. For the Irish people the potato had become the basis of their diet. Many labourers received, as payment for their work, a small patch of ground on which to grow potatoes instead of a monetary wage. These people worked the land of wealthy landowners who made money by producing grain which was a very successful cash crop.

The Irish labourers were poor people who worked just to survive. And the survival of this vast impoverished population depended on the recurring fruitfulness of the potato. In September of 1945 potato blight came to Ireland and destroyed the crop. The English authorities took prompt but ineffective action. A relief commission was established. Relief works were set up to provide employment. It was proposed to sell food rather than give it away. Among the relief works organised to allow the hungry to earn money was road construction. However, many of these roads were never really intended for use and often ended redundantly in a bog or field.

Sir Charles Trevelyan was in control of relief. In the middle of the crisis Trevelyan published his views on the matter. He saw the Famine as a 'mechanism for reducing surplus population'. He described the famine as 'The judgement of God sent ... to teach the Irish a lesson ... that calamity must not be too much mitigated ... The real evil with which we have to contend is not the physical evil of the Famine, but the moral evil of the selfish, perverse and turbulent character of the people'. Though the Irish population were starving food was still exported from the country for profit.

LINE BY LINE

STANZA 1

Colonel Jones was one of the officers in charge of relief works around Newry. In the opening stanza of the poem Trevelyan instructs him as to what is to be done about the starving people of Ireland. He is told not to give them any financial aid: 'give them no coins at all'. According to Trevelyan the Irish are a lazy bunch, 'Idle as trout'. What they need is not aid but honest hard work: 'their bones/ need toil, their characters no less'. Trevelyan adds his seal to his instructions. These instructions sealed the fate of millions of lives. The red wax splattered on the table is likened to blood: 'Trevelyan's/ seal blooded the deal table'.

A Relief Committee chaired by Colonel Jones consider how best to follow Trevelyan's instructions. They consider how the Irish might be best put to work. One of their chief aims is to keep the Irish busy so that the cash crops might still be safely exported from the country. One of those at the table proposes a solution. He suggests that the Irish be kept busy building useless roads: 'Might it be safe,/ Colonel, to give them roads, roads to force/ From nowhere, going nowhere of course?'

STANZA 2

The second stanza describes the starving Irish working on the roads. They are 'sick' and the work they are doing is without reason or purpose: 'directionless they worked'. They have not even been given basic tools for the work they must do. They work as though back in prehistoric times before such tools were invented: 'Fork, stick/ were iron years away'.

The appalling attitude of such men as Trevelyan towards the helpless Irish is once again made evident in the second stanza. Perfectly aware of the terrible conditions that those working on the roads must endure, the freezing temperatures and punitive labour, the attitude of those in power is pitiless. Knowing that the Irish are without food and water, the suggestion is made that they 'suck, April hailstones' and drink their own blood 'for food and water'. Once again the Irish are described as vile and devious creatures who need to be disciplined. They are said to be 'cunning as housewives', ready to eat each other given half the chance:

Why for that, cunning as housewives, each eyed –
as if at a corner butcher – the other's buttock.

The purpose of such appalling suggestions is to dehumanise and vilify the Irish, to make it seem as though they deserve their cruel fate.

STANZA 3

The evening falls and one of the men working on the roads is too sick to continue. He has typhus and those who work with him are scared of contamination and 'walk clear'. Though he is related to some present, he is treated as an outcast. He 'has become a typhoid pariah, his blood tainted'. The poet compares the sick man's lonely fate to that of the snow flake. She says that he will be given no more regard than the snow gives the individual flakes that fall and melt. Those working with the sick man do not even pause to pray over his dying body. In the final throes of death he is abandoned.

STANZA 4

The final stanza brings us back to the perverse world of those in charge of the relief works. Colonel Jones writes to Trevelyan to inform him of progress. Though the Irish are sick and dying, the plan to have them needlessly build roads is said to have 'gone better than' expected. The goal of the relief works was never to save the Irish but to distract and destroy them so that corn could still be exported from the country with ease: 'We march the corn/ to the ships in peace'.

Jones reflects his master's view that the Irish are a beastly lot in need of harsh treatment and punishment. He tells Trevelyan that throughout the country the 'wretches work till they are quite worn,/ then fester by their work'. The road works were never set up to address the population's hunger, but rather to cure disobedience and laziness. Jones is pleased to report to Trevelyan that both vices have been 'cured/ in one'. He closes his letter with a vulgar note of excitement. As he travelled through the country during the week he 'saw bones' out of the carriage window.

A woman's plight

In between the stanzas of 'The Famine Road' Boland has broken up a shorter poem. Only when we have read the complete text can we understand the significance of these fragmented parts. This poem is about a woman being informed by a doctor that she is infertile.

The doctor begins by quoting statistics. 'One out of every ten' couples are affected by infertility and in a third of these cases it is the woman who is unable to conceive. The woman that the doctor addresses is unable to conceive, but he is not able to say exactly why she is unable to do so: 'in a case like yours/ anything may have caused it, spores,/ a childhood accident'. No empathy shown to the woman, just a cold, professional prognosis – 'one sees/ day after day these mysteries'. For the doctor this is just another case.

The third fragment is particularly insensitive. The doctor tells the woman in no uncertain terms that '[She] never will' be able to have a child. He follows this with a remark of great condescension, arrogance and insensitivity: 'but take it well woman, grow/ your garden, keep house, good-bye'.

The final fragment is very different in tone. It begins, just as the second and third stanzas of 'The Famine Road', with a single unsettling word. In this instance it is 'Barren', a bleak and hopeless word. She will never 'know the load' of husband's child in her. Her body is as redundant as 'a famine road'.

THEMES

History and suffering

In 'Outside History' the poet spoke of the need to move out of myth and into history in order that the victims of the past might be properly acknowledged. In 'The Famine Road' Boland focuses on the suffering masses of Irish who were treated appallingly throughout the Famine by the ruling British forces. Her account of their efforts to construct roads that often went nowhere is a chilling reminder of the human suffering of the past. Boland is conscious of the need to remember the victims of the past. History is not something that we can confine to the chapters of a book. It is populated by countless individuals who endured real hardships and trials.

Man's inhumanity to man

'The Famine Road' describes the despicable response of the British government to the Irish Famine. Their plan to have the starving masses work on redundant roads as a means of addressing the devastating effects of the potato blight is shown not merely to be a failure, but an evil and inhuman act. The helpless, hungry workers are depicted as lazy and problematic by those in charge of the relief works. Their cruel fate is viewed as just punishment by Trevelyan and his servile representative, Colonel Jones. Neither man feels an ounce of human sympathy for the thousands of men, women and children sent to their deaths, starving, while food is carefully shipped out of the country. The fact that they suffer and die is considered a success by Colonel Jones, who writes to his master, Trevelyan, that everything is going 'better than' expected.

Women and motherhood

The poem also focuses on the plight of women who are unable to bear children. This plight is compared with that of the workers who were forced to build the roads during the Famine. The doctor in the poem displays absolutely no sympathy for the woman who has just been told that she is infertile. As such, his actions mirror those of the callous British who oversaw the construction of the roads.

Child of Our Time

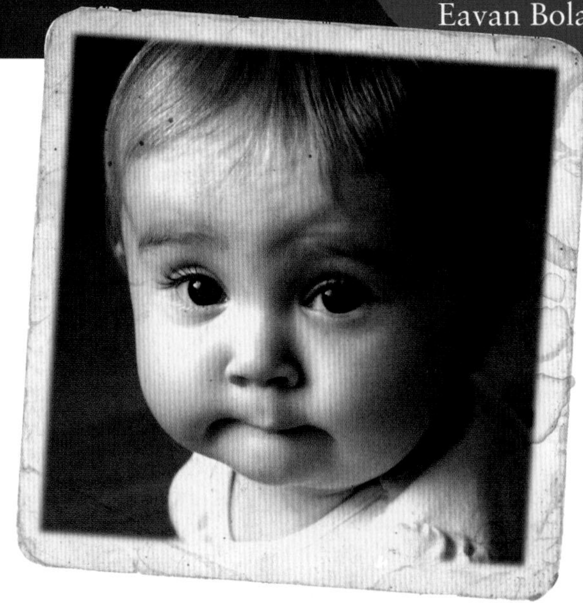

LINE BY LINE

LINES 1 TO 6

This poem was written in response to the death of a child in the Dublin bombings of May 1974. Boland begins by addressing the child. She tells the child that before this tragic event she 'knew no lullaby'. She had no poems or songs designed to soothe children. However, the death of the child has moved her to compose 'This song'. It is a terrible lullaby to have to write, taking its 'tune' from the 'final cry' of the child. Lines 3 to 6 outline the difficulty involved in seeking order in 'discord' and unreason. Yet this is what she is seeking to do in writing this poem. She sees the need to take something from this terrible event, to respond to it and, ultimately, to 'learn'.

The whole poem is constructed around the child's death. The reason that the poet is writing the poem is because something wholly unreasonable has occurred. The poem's 'rhythm' must be found in the 'discord' of the child's 'murder'. The poet is faced with an almost impossible task, because what 'reason' can be discovered in unreason, what 'rhythm' in 'discord'. She is seeking certain values in the very antitheses of these values. But that is the reality of the situation. Because of the terrible tragedy that has taken place the poet finds herself writing a 'lullaby' for a child who 'cannot listen'.

LINES 7 TO 12

The second line involves a bitter irony. The adults who should be teaching the child now need to be 'taught' by the child. 'We who should have known how to instruct/... must learn from you dead'. The poet implies collective responsibility for what has gone wrong in this instance. There is a sense that every grown-up has failed the child. The first line of the second stanza suggests that adults did not know 'how to instruct' prior to this event.

The poet lists the kind of instructions that the child ought to have received. They are not the terrible truths of war or the lessons that must be learned from tragedy. Instead, they are the things that every innocent child should have. Nursery 'rhymes' for when the child wakes, songs when it needs to sleep, 'Names for the animals you took to bed'. The poet suggests that children should be protected from the violence of the world. The stories that a child hears should be ones 'to distract', to fuel the child's imagination and wonder.

The poet also speaks of 'legends to protect'. Perhaps these are stories with morals, instructions about avoiding the wrong paths in life. Out of careful instruction the child eventually receives 'an idiom', a way to express its own thoughts and views as it goes through life. However, education is not something that is ever completed. The poet stresses the need to live in order to 'learn'. But this child is dead. The last word of the second stanza is a solemn reminder of the act of violence that gave rise to the poem. So, instead of doing what ought to be done for every child, in this instance we 'must learn' from a child.

LINES 13–18

In the final stanza the poet outlines the lessons that we need to learn from this tragic event. We must learn from the dead child to 'make our broken images'. It is not clear what the poet means by this. What 'images' is she referring to? Are these images the impressions that we have of ourselves? Or is the poet referring to some other representations? It is difficult to know what Boland means by making these images, whatever they are. How do you 'make' a broken image? Surely only by breaking an image. Whichever way we interpret the word 'images', it is hard to know how they should be rebuilt around the limbs of a dead child. Does Boland just mean that we need to rethink ourselves, and our values, holding the death of this child in mind?

It is also the 'broken/ Image' of the child that we need to take into consideration. Again, what this 'Image' might be is unclear. Is it the shattered image of innocence, of what a child's life ought to be? On top of all this we must learn to 'find for [the child's] sake whose life our idle/ Talk has cost, a new language'. There is a collective responsibility for the child's death. It is the fault of our 'idle' talk. Presumably Boland means the sort of political and ethical talk that never converts itself into action. However, it is not the task of converting talk into action that the poet proposes we must undertake. Instead, we must find 'a new language'. But what does it mean that we find a 'new language'? Perhaps it is a new form of discourse that the poet is looking for, a new way of approaching the problems that give rise to these terrible acts of violence.

The poem closes with the poet addressing the child. In a way it is an apology for what has happened, an admission of guilt. The poet finishes with a soothing line, a prayer that the child will find peace in another place. The soft sounds of the 's' that the poet uses are tender and soothing. However, the greater part of the poem is like an elegy, a poem of serious reflection for someone who has died.

THEMES

History and the cost of conflict

The poem is ultimately an emotional response to an innocent victim of violence. That a child should have its life taken because of the political squabbles of the community into which it is born is a travesty and an outrage. 'Child of Our Time' focuses on a single casualty of this island's bloody history and asks what sort of reason lies behind these terrible acts. How can a supposedly 'adult' community allow such needless bloodshed to occur? The poem looks at the 'idle talk' of politics and says that there is grave need for new approaches that take real account of the victims of militant behaviour.

The Black Lace Fan My Mother Gave Me

INTRODUCTION

In this poem the speaker envisages the early days of the romance between her parents, which took place long before she was born. The poem centres on a lace fan, which was the first gift the speaker's father gave her mother: 'It was the first gift he ever gave her, / buying it for five francs in the Galeries / in pre-war Paris'. The mother in turn has passed the fan on to the speaker, and it is this object that triggers her imagination. It is important to note that fans such as the one discussed in this poem have traditionally been regarded as 'erotic' objects. Often exchanged between lovers, they served as tokens of passion, love and romance. (The fan is also decorated with roses, which are, of course, the traditional flowers of romance). For the speaker, the fan's link with romantic love is strengthened by the fact that it is associated with the earliest days of her parents' relationship. It inspires in her a moving meditation on the strengths and difficulties of her parent's enduring love.

LINE BY LINE

SECTION 1: LINES 1–12

The poem's opening section attempts to imaginatively recreate the evening on which her father gave her mother this beautiful but haunting gift. The poem is set in Paris, that most romantic of cities, during a summer in the 1930's ('pre-war'): 'They stayed in the city for the summer'. It seems to be an early stage in the couple's relationship, for they meet only in cafés: 'They met in cafés. She was always early. / He was late'. On the evening he gives his lover the black lace fan the father is even later than usual: 'That evening he was later. / They wrapped the fan. He looked at his watch.' It is unclear, however, whether the father is particularly late on this occasion because he stopped off to buy the fan or if he is late anyway and decides to purchase the fan as an apology for his tardiness. Meanwhile his waiting lover seems to be growing impatient. Her first cup of coffee has been drunk and there is still no sign of her boyfriend: 'She ordered more coffee'. She stares down the street, hoping, presumably, that he will appear at any moment: 'She looked down the Boulevard des Capucines'. Eventually, she appears to be on the verge of leaving: 'She stood up'. The poor girl, evidently, has had enough of waiting and wrongly assumes that she has been stood up.

Most readers of 'The Black Lace Fan' identify an atmosphere of tension in the poem's first twelve lines, lurking beneath the few straightforward details we are given about this Parisian summer night. To a large extent this sense of tension is due to Boland's extensive use of short, clipped sentences, that shift focus rapidly from one subject matter to the next. This rapid-fire burst of short sentences conveys the agitation of the late young man as he hurries to keep his appointment: 'They wrapped the fan. He looked at his watch.' It also puts across the nervous tension of the young woman, anxiously waiting for her lover to appear: 'She ordered more coffee. She stood up'. This tension reaches its climax as the woman stands up to leave, while her lover, a few streets away, rushes to meet her with his gift of the black lace fan. These lines, in their own way, are dramatic and suspenseful. Will the young man get there before his lover leaves, annoyed, it seems, at his lack of punctuality?

The speaker's description of the weather also contributes to the poem's atmosphere of tension. An oppressive heat dominates the city: 'It was stifling ... The heat was killing'. (The heat is also reflected in the father's choice of gift. The fan he purchases for his lover will be used to relieve the discomfort of this overwhelming heat). Though the weather is hot and dry it is also cloudy and overcast, suggesting that a storm is about to break: 'A starless drought made the weather stormy'. (The nights are 'starless' because the overcast clouds conceal the stars). As the young woman waits for her lover she can almost sense the coming storm: 'She thought the distance smelled of rain and lightning'. The humid, muggy weather conditions, with their implication of a storm about to break, greatly add to the air of barely suppressed tension that dominates the poem's first twelve lines.

It has been suggested by several critics that this oppressive weather serves a symbolic function. The stormy weather that lies in wait represents the difficulties and tribulations that will occur during the long years of the couple's relationship. On this reading the distance that 'smelled of rain and lightning' refers not only to physical distance but also to the lovers' future. The overcast skies and stifling heat suggest the 'emotional storms' they will have to endure throughout their years of love and marriage. (This technique, where the weather reflects human emotions, is known as the 'pathetic fallacy').

There is a sense, in fact, that the first of these 'emotional storms' may be about to break on the very night the mother gets the black lace fan. The fact that the young woman always turns up early for their meetings while the young man is always late suggest that the lovers are not quite on the same wavelength. Of course this could merely reflect the fact that the speaker's father was a poor timekeeper. Yet given the air of doom-laden tension that overshadows the poem it is difficult not to see this persistent lateness as a symptom of some deeper problem with the relationship. The fact that the couple never arrive for their meetings at even roughly the same time suggests that they are somehow out of synch. Furthermore both lovers' appear tense on this occasion, the evening of the black lace fan. Does the father purchase the fan as an apology for some wrong he has committed, or for his persistent lateness? Perhaps the first storm is brewing in their relationship.

SECTION 2: LINES 13–20

In line 13 the poem's focus shifts abruptly from pre-war Paris to the present day. The speaker contemplates the black lace fan, given to her mother on that long-ago evening and which, as we have seen, was passed on to her. It is made of tortoise shell and silk, onto which wild roses have been stitched. The speaker seems highly conscious of the skill and craft involved in its construction: 'There are wild roses, appliquéd on silk by hand, / darkly picked, stitched boldly, quickly'. She also praises the beauty of the tortoise shell material: 'The rest is tortoise shell and has the reticent, / clear patience of its element'. The gentle, soothing quality of this material is suggested by the repeated 'e' and 'a' sounds in the phrase 'clear patience of its element' which generates a pleasant and euphonious musical effect.

Despite her awareness of the fan's beauty the speaker does not regard this inherited object in an entirely positive light. To her, it seems, the fan is a somewhat sinister item, associated with the dark stormy weather that held sway on the night it was presented to her mother as a gift. The roses that decorate it may be beautiful, but they also (to the speaker at least) possess a somewhat menacing quality, having been stitched 'darkly' into the fabric. There is a restless, jerky quality to the lines depicting the appliquéd roses, generated by a rapid-fire burst of short phrases separated by commas: 'There are wild roses, appliquéd on silk by hand, /darkly picked, stitched boldly, quickly'. The verse here has an edgy, restless quality, reflecting the almost palpable tension that clogs the air during the hours before a storm.

Even the attractive tortoise shell material has a sinister association, bringing with it a suggestion (or 'inference') of the poor tortoise that was made to suffer and die in order to provide this glamorous substance: 'it keeps, / even now, an inference of its violation'. The speaker describes the removal of this poor creature's shell and its use in the manufacture of the fan as a 'violation'. To her it is a violent intrusive act, like theft or rape. Using a wonderful metaphor she describes the fan's black lace as 'overcast', as if the dark storm clouds that threatened on that evening have somehow entered the fabric: 'The lace is overcast as if the weather/ it opened for and offset had entered it'. (The fan was designed to be 'opened' or unfurled in humid, stormy weather in order to 'offset' the heat).

However, the 'weather/it opened for and offset' could also refer to the stormy emotional climate that dominated the lovers' relationship on that long ago evening in Paris. On this reading, 'weather' serves as a metaphor for the difficulties that existed in the young couple's relationship around this time. The young man hoped to 'offset' these relationship difficulties by impressing and delighting his future wife with the gift of the black lace fan.

On one hand, then, the speaker regards the fan as thing of beauty, as a skilfully constructed and gorgeous object. On the other hand, however, she associates it with storms, with overcast weather and darkness, and, most disturbingly of all, with violation. How do we explain the speaker's seemingly ambiguous and confusing attitude toward the black lace fan? To the speaker this pre-war antique seems to function as a symbol of her parent's relationship. (This is in keeping with Boland's strategy throughout her 'Object Lessons' series of poems, where objects are used to embody and explore various ideas and institutions). The history of her parent's marriage seems to be almost written into the fan and it represents both the good and bad aspects of their relationship.

Like the fan their love is 'worn-out, underwater bullion'. It is precious and rare as gold ('bullion' is name for gold bars). Yet their relationship is also 'worn-out', they are weary, presumably, from years of being together, from the rigours of child rearing and from the conflicts and difficulties that feature in any long-term relationship. The 'reticent, / clear patience' of the fan's transparent tortoise shell material represents the quiet and peaceful periods in the relationship when things were clear and straightforward between them. The 'overcast' black lace, meanwhile, which seems to have been 'entered' by stormy weather, represents the more turbulent times in their marriage. It symbolises the conflicts and arguments that flared up between them over the years, the periods in their relationship when the future seemed murky and uncertain rather than transparent and straightforward. (The threat of these 'emotional storms' is present even at the beginning of their relationship, as we see in the poem's opening section). The roses, those ancient symbols of eroticism, which have been stitched into the fan's fabric can be taken to symbolise the physical passion that existed between the speaker's parents over the years of their marriage. As we have seen, however, the 'darkly picked' roses also have sinister connotations, being associated with storms and darkness, with the difficult and turbulent periods of her parent's relationship. On the whole, then, the black lace fan provides the speaker with a potted history of her parents' marriage. In its surface she sees an account of the ups and downs they enjoyed and endured, of the good and bad times they went through together.

SECTION 1: LINES 21–8

In this section the action of the poem shifts once more, back to that long ago Parisian evening. The father rushes to meet his lover at the café as the storm prepares to break: 'The past is an empty café terrace. / An airless dusk before thunder. A man running'. (The assonance in line 22 with its repeated 'u' sound generates a powerful verbal music in which we can almost hear the storm that is about to break). There is an air of sorrow in these lines as the speaker laments the fact that the past can never be rediscovered. How successfully will the lovers overcome the tension that seems to exist between them on this humid Paris night? More importantly, how will they weather the ups and downs, the trials and tribulations, which will emerge over their years of marriage? We can never know. The past is a closed book: 'And no way to know what happened then-/none at all'.

According to the speaker the only way to answer these questions is to 'improvise', to imagine how the lovers got on over their years of marriage. The speaker does this by means of another symbol. She decides to represent her parents' marriage not by the fan but by a blackbird: 'The blackbird on this first sultry morning, /in summer'. (Birds, of course, are a traditional symbol of love). The unfurled fan and the blackbird's outstretched wing have a similar physical appearance. Yet there are important differences between these two symbols. The fan, though beautiful, is associated with storms and darkness while the blackbird is associated with summer and with pleasant 'sultry' weather. It is a 'worn-out' antique while the blackbird is full of life and energy. The fan is an inert object while the bird is a living, breathing part of nature: 'finding buds, worms, fruit'.

As we have seen the fan represents both the good and bad aspects of the parents' marriage, symbolising both the clear and cloudy periods of their relationship. The blackbird, on the other hand, is a more straightforwardly positive symbol of their love. By choosing the blackbird as the final symbol of her parents' marriage the speaker signals her determination to view their relationship as something glorious and successful, to dwell on the positive rather than the negative aspects of their marriage. As we have seen lines 21–4 leave us with questions as to how the parents overcame both the long and short-term difficulties in their relationship. The speaker's 'improvised' answer to these questions takes the form of the blackbird extending its wing: 'Suddenly she puts out her wing-/the whole full flirtatious span of it'. (Presumably the bird's wing is described as flirtatious because she extends it as part of a mating ritual). The poem's final lines sound a triumphant note. What matters is not the detailed story of the parent's love, with it ups and downs and weathered storms, but the fact that their relationship survived so many years. The duration or time span of their relationship is represented by the 'span' of the bird's extended wing: 'the whole, full, flirtatious span of it'. The poem's final line has a pleasant euphonious effect, generated by its repeated broad vowel sounds: 'the whole, full, flirtatious span of it'. This sweet word music reflects both the beauty of the bird's wing, and of the marriage it represents. It has been suggested that the use of the words 'whole' and 'full' suggests the wholesome nature of the parents' marriage and the abundance of love that existed between them. The word 'flirtatious', meanwhile, suggests the physical passion that was a feature of their marriage.

THEMES

The tensions and uncertainties of early love

This poem provides a wonderful depiction of the doubts and uncertainties that often hold sway at the beginning of a relationship. Both the speaker's mother and her father appear tense and agitated around the time of their date in Paris. Both, it seems, are not quite certain of the other's affections. There is a real possibility that their relationship will not survive beyond its early stages.

The impossibility of rediscovering the past

The poem movingly depicts how difficult it is to recreate the past. The things that happened long ago are lost to us. In this instance the speaker is unable to tell the full story of her parents' love. She simply does not have the facts. At the same time, however, the poem celebrates the artist's ability to recreate the past, to improvise or imagine what might have happened. The speaker, therefore, chooses to represent her parent's love by means of the triumphant symbol of the blackbird with its extended wing. It is not clear, however, how much this glorious symbol reflects the actual facts of the parents' life together and how much reflects the speaker's artistic imaginings.

The ups and downs of marriage

The marriage is represented by two symbols: the black lace fan and the blackbird. In the black lace fan the speaker sees an honest and unflinching symbol of her parents' marriage, one that represents both their good and bad times together. The fan, therefore, represents their love with balance and realism rather than in a purely romantic light. The blackbird, however, serves as a more straightforwardly positive symbol of their marriage. It celebrates the survival and endurance of their love, its lavish and beautiful 'span', rather than dwelling in detail on the difficulties they experienced over the years.

The Shadow Doll

INTRODUCTION

This poem is a meditation on marriage, which occupies a complex and ambiguous place in Boland's work. On one hand she is anxious to commemorate the married lifestyle in her work, to demonstrate that the everyday life of the modern mother is a worthy subject for great poetry. In this poem, however, marriage is presented in a particularly negative light. 'Wedlock' depicted as a trap that constrains and confines women, suffocating their personalities.

The poem was inspired by a porcelain doll from the nineteenth century that the poet encountered in a museum. Such dolls were used by brides in the process of choosing a wedding dress. Dressmakers would garb them in miniature versions of wedding dresses, allowing brides to get a clearer sense of the gowns' design without the expense and hassle of having a full-sized dress manufactured. Using these tiny 'models' as a guide the bride and her family could accept or reject the dress on offer, or suggest alterations.

The poem can be divided into three sections. In the first the stanzas the speaker describes the doll on display in its museum case. In stanzas four and five she imagines the thoughts of the young nineteenth woman who used the doll to choose her wedding dress. The final two stanzas, meanwhile, find the speaker remembering the night before her own wedding.

LINE BY LINE

STANZAS 1–3: *The doll*

The poem begins by describing the tiny dress worn by the model in the museum. Its veil is decorated with flowers stitched from 'ivory tulle'. ('Tulle' is a soft silky material used for veils and netting). The brightness and clarity of the veil is emphasised by its 'oyster gleam'. The fact that it is described in terms of ivory and oysters captures its intense, virginal whiteness. The little dress seems to be incredibly detailed, right down to the 'hoops' that were a feature of many nineteenth century gowns: 'They made hoops for the crinoline'. The doll's little dress, then, is clearly a thing of beauty, given the lavish material involved in its production, its rich detail and its blazing whiteness.

Yet the speaker feels nothing but pity for this 'glamorous' doll. For its glamour is an 'airless glamour' as it remains contained in the unventilated atmosphere beneath its dome of glass. The speaker laments the fact that the doll is imprisoned 'Under glass, under wraps'. She is particularly conscious of the fact that the doll is doomed to silence. As a prisoner behind glass it can never talk about or express the things it has experienced. It is forced to remain forever 'discreet': 'it stays/even now, after all, discreet about/ visits, fevers, quickenings and lusts'.

In these lines Boland uses a poetic technique called personification, whereby an inanimate object is presented as if it had human qualities. In this instance the doll is depicted as being capable of human experiences such as 'fevers' and 'lusts' and as being capable of expressing these experiences if it hadn't been silenced in its prison of glass). Yet perhaps the most tragic aspect of the doll's predicament is that it has outlived its usefulness. It has survived long past the 'occasion' when it served a purpose. Now it is just a toy, a trinket in a museum to be admired by visitors.

STANZAS 4–5: *The young bride-to-be*

Stanzas 4 and 5 present the young nineteenth-century woman for whom the doll was manufactured as an aid in choosing her wedding dress. When she examines the doll this young bride-to-be has a nightmarish vision, imagining herself trapped beneath its ceiling of glass, clutching fake flowers: 'she could see herself // inside it all holding less than real/stephanotis, rose petals'. She imagines being transformed into a ceramic doll, turning from a creature of flesh and blood into a 'porcelain bride' who will no longer experience bodily processes such as breathing: 'never feeling/satin rise and fall with the vows'.

This nineteenth-century girl seems to suspect, therefore, that getting married will rob her of her individuality. She will be imprisoned by the institutions of marriage just as the doll is by its dome of glass. As a married woman she will be kept 'under wraps', and will be forbidden to explain or express certain aspects of her existence. Like the porcelain doll she will have 'survived her occasion'. She will have outlived her usefulness as a bargaining chip in the affairs of men. She will survive only as a possession of her husband, a living doll to be admired and adorned.

STANZAS 6–7: *The night before the speaker's wedding*

The poem's concluding stanzas present us with an abrupt shift from the thoughts of this young nineteenth century woman to the speaker's worries on the night before her own wedding. The speaker, like the nineteenth century girl, seems to regard her upcoming marriage with trepidation. She mutters her wedding vows again and again: 'the vows/ I kept repeating on the night before'. The speaker's incessant repetition of her marriage vows stems from the nervous tension she feels on the night before her big day. She repeats these oaths over and over as if she is testing their meaning, wondering about the restrictions they will place upon her life. Is she prepared to embrace these vows and surrender herself to the institution of marriage? Is she ready to obey her husband, to embrace his name and be guided by him in all things?

Our sense of the speaker's agitated mental state on the night before her wedding is reinforced by her description of herself as being 'astray among the cards and wedding gifts'. The fact that the speaker is 'astray' indicates that she feels lost, confused, and perhaps even desperate at the looming prospect of her marriage. There is a powerful sense of claustrophobia in these concluding lines, as if the speaker is trapped and overwhelmed by the clutter of the wedding preparations: 'the coffee pots and the clocks and/the battered tan case full of cotton/ lace and tissue-paper'. She seems trapped and hemmed in by the chaos of the wedding preparations: just as the porcelain doll is trapped in the 'airless glamour' of its glass case.

This atmosphere of claustrophobia is reinforced by the poem's final lines, in which the speaker describes her attempts to close the bulging tan suitcase that contains her wedding dress. She depicts herself 'pressing down, then/ pressing down again' on the case's lid.

This 'pressing down' motion reflects the confines and constraints of marriage that are closing in her. (The intensity of this pressure is emphasised by the repetition of the phrase 'pressing down').

The poem's final isolated three words also strike an ominous note. On one hand of course the item that 'locks' here is the bulging tan suitcase, having finally been closed by the pressure the speaker exerts on it. On another level, however, the 'locks' referred to here are the vows of marriage, which are reinforced and policed by tradition and society. These 'locks' will soon click into place behind the speaker, trapping her in the marriage's 'airless glamour'.

LANGUAGE

Symbolism

'The Shadow Doll', as we have seen, is a highly symbolic poem. The doll in its glass display case functions as a symbol for the negative effects marriage has on a woman. The institution of marriage, the poem suggests; limits and confines women just as the glass case imprisons the shadow doll. According to the speaker, then, when a woman marries she surrenders certain important freedoms and allows herself to be placed 'under wraps' by the restrictions of her role as wife and mother. According to several critics the wedding dress being forcibly pressed into the suitcase also serves as a symbol of marriage. Marriage will press down upon the speaker and 'lock' her in place just as the wedding dress is confined by the suitcase.

Sound effects

In this poem Boland's use of sound effects is typically effective. The splendour of the doll's miniature dress is suggested by the repeated broad vowel sounds in 'oyster gleam of the veil', which generate a pleasant musical effect. A similarly pleasant word music is generated by the alliteration in line 11 with its repeated sibilant 's' sounds: 'shell tone spray of seed pearls'. Meanwhile there is a harsh, almost cacophonous, quality to the phrase 'airless glamour' generated in part by the clashing repetition of its 'l' sounds.

Another interesting feature of the poem is the way the speaker's troubled mental state on the eve of her wedding is suggested by the technique of listing a variety of nouns linked by the conjunction 'and': 'the cards and wedding gifts-/the coffee pot sand the clocks'. This technique lends the verse a breathless hurried quality, reflecting the agitated and panicky mental state of the speaker.

THEMES

A negative view of marriage

'The Shadow Doll' presents an extremely negative view of marriage. Many women find the notion of marriage glamorous or attractive and from an early age dream about their wedding day. The poem suggests, however, that the glamour of marriage is an 'airless' glamour. Women are as confined by the vows and institutions of marriage as the doll is within the confines of its glass case. Like the doll they will have 'survived their occasion'. They will have outlived their usefulness as productive members of society, continuing to exist only as the possessions and playthings of their husbands.

The poem also suggests that married women are placed 'under wraps', that they sacrifice the ability to speak about important aspects of their existences. Brides, like dolls and children, are to be seen rather than heard. They are to be admired for their beauty, for the 'oyster gleam' of their pretty dresses, rather than for their experiences and their ability to express themselves. In particular they are forced to remain 'discreet' about their bodies and the sexual side of their beings, about 'visits, fevers, quickenings and lusts'. 'Quickenings' and 'fevers' suggest the heat and excitement of sexual arousal, the accelerated heartbeat and the quickening of the pulse. (The word 'visits', too, has sexual connotations, suggesting experiences of intense pleasure and almost spiritual ecstasy).

Too harsh a view of marriage?

Yet surely the view of marriage in this poem is outdated or too harsh? Today we think of marriage as a loving partnership in which both partners share life's burdens and protect one another. Why then does Boland present marriage as something that suffocates women's personalities, that degrades their humanity and silences them? Boland is partly referring to the history of marriage here. In the nineteenth century when the doll was manufactured, for example, a woman was generally expected to obey her husband. It would also have been unthinkable for her to discuss sexual desires and bodily processes. Even in the last century women were regarded as subservient to their husbands and were restricted in various ways by marriage. (In Ireland it was only in the mid-1970's that a married woman was allowed to work outside the home). To the feminists of Boland's generation, then, marriage was regarded as a symbol of oppression, of the tyranny women had been subjected to in the past. It is in this context, therefore, that we should consider the poem's devastating critique of marriage and its institutions.

White Hawthorn in the West of Ireland

INTRODUCTION

This poem describes a trip made by the speaker from her home in a Dublin suburb to the West of Ireland: 'I drove West ... I left behind suburban gardens'.

LINE BY LINE

The magic of the West

The speaker, then, abandons the comfortable dullness of the suburbia with its 'Lawnmowers' and 'Small talk'. She drives into the untamed beauty of the Irish west with its 'low skies' and 'splashes of coltsfoot'. ('Coltsfoot' is a wild yellow flower).

The complexity and beauty of the western light is emphasised. At any given moment the light seems to be both hard and soft ('shy'): 'The hard shyness of Atlantic light'. Boland uses an oxymoron, 'hard shyness'; to capture the shifting quality of this Western light. (An oxymoron is when a noun is described by a seemingly contradictory or unexpected adjective. In this case we don't usually associate the quality of 'hardness' with the idea of 'shyness')

The west, in this poem, is presented as an almost magical place, a kind of never-land where the ordinary rules of nature have been suspended. Importantly, the speaker travels there in 'the season between seasons', a phrase reminiscent of something we might find in a fairy tale. This 'season between seasons' seems to be a brief, enchanted moment, neither Winter, Spring, Summer nor Autumn, in which the ordinary rules of the rational world no longer apply. At this haunted moment everything in the West seems shifting and uncertain.

Given the west's haunting mystical atmosphere it is unsurprising that he speaker finds herself thinking of superstition, of the 'superstitious aura of hawthorn'. The speaker is filled with the desire to pick some of the hawthorn's flowers. She is aware, however, that according to superstition the hawthorn was never to be touched: 'I had always known/the custom was/not to touch Hawthorn'. In Irish myths and legends the hawthorn tree was associated with fairies and magic. Farmers and other country folk, therefore, were always careful not to cut it down or disturb it. To bring hawthorn into the home was to hawthorn was to invite misfortune into the household: 'Not to bring it indoors/For the sake of// the luck/such constraint would forfeit'. To 'constrain' this wild, almost sacred plant by bringing it indoors was to risk a terrible punishment from the supernatural forces associated with it. As the speaker puts it 'a child might die' or farm animals might suddenly become sick: 'an unexpected fever [might] speckle heifers'. (Here the speaker imagines heifers 'speckled' with sores and rashes as a result of illness). In keeping with this 'custom', therefore, the speaker decides not to pick the flowers of the hawthorn tree: 'So I left it / stirring on those hills'.

The hawthorn on the hill

In the poem's final lines the hawthorn on the hill is presented as something less than solid. It is shifting and fluid in a way we associate more with a liquid than with solid matter: 'So I left it/sitting on those hills/with a fluency/only water has'. It seems to be capable of shaping and moulding the earth in which it grows: it is 'like water, able/ To re-define land'. In this western landscape, the speaker claims, the hawthorn seems to have taken over almost entirely. When we travel through such a place, especially at dusk, the evidence of human habitation is minimal, limited to a few uncertain blobs of light among the flowing hawthorn: 'the unmarked lights of a May dusk'. It is as if the hawthorn has somehow choked or overgrown the surrounding rural communities with their human language. It is 'free to seem to be the only language spoken in these parts'.

There is an undoubted atmosphere of peacefulness and comfort in these last lines with their gentle cadences, as the speaker celebrates the beauty of the hawthorn. Yet there is also, surely, a sense of unease before the very wildness and isolation of the West, where the human presence is at times barely noticeable among the flourishing growth of untamed nature.

THEMES

Different Worlds

This is a poem that contrasts two very different worlds: the suburbs of Dublin on one hand and the West of Ireland on the other. The notion of 'suburbia', and of suburban living, is a recurring theme in Boland's work. The tame, ordinary lifestyle of those who inhabit comfortable suburbs is not typically regarded as a suitable subject matter for great poetry. Throughout her career, however, Boland has consistently sought to write poetry that responds in various ways to the life of the suburbs (especially to the life of the suburban woman and mother). Many of her poems celebrate suburbia as an unexpected source of beauty and inspiration (for example 'This Moment'). 'White Hawthorn in the West of Ireland', however, presents the suburbs in a distinctly negative light. The suburb where the speaker lives is depicted as a place of little significance or importance. To her it is associated with inconsequential chatter and mundane household tasks: 'Lawnmowers. Small talk'.

The west is presented as a place of beauty and wildness. Suburbia, on the other hand, is a place of neatly tended gardens with their lawnmowers. The west is fluid and shifting, a place where things seem constantly on the verge of blending into something else. The light there is complex and ever changing, the hawthorn seems to flow, and even the earth itself is fluid and malleable, capable of being 'redefined' by the plants that grown in it.

The suburbs, in contrast, are rigidly ordered. They are a place of houses and gardens, where the borders between different peoples' property are always clearly laid down.

The west is depicted as an almost magical place, basking in 'the superstitious aura of hawthorn'. It is a place where magic and superstition survive and, to the speaker at least, seem very real. Suburbia, in contrast, is associated with ordinariness and boredom, with mundane things such as 'Small talk'. The poem, then, celebrates the wild magical West as a refuge from the choking boredom of suburban living. As we have seen, however, the portrayal of the west is not quite entirely positive. The poem's last lines sound a note of unease, as if the speaker is overwhelmed by the very wildness she celebrates. This place of superstition, where nature is dominant, is also one of a potentially frightening isolation. It is a place where humans with their values and understanding (represented by 'language') are in constant danger of being overwhelmed by nature's abundance.

Connecting with roots

Several critics have suggested that 'Wild Hawthorn in the West of Ireland' is a poem in which Boland describes her attempt to 'return to her roots', to connect with her heritage as an Irish woman and rediscover the countryside and its traditions. To this end she abandons the suburbs and makes a pilgrimage to the wildness of the West with its 'aura of superstition'. Her desire to return to her roots is represented by her longing to touch the hawthorns: 'All I wanted then was to fill my arms with/Sharp flowers'. She imagines that by doing so she will melt into the hawthorn bushes, becoming part of the Irish landscape: 'All I wanted then was to seem, from a distance, to be part of/ that ivory downhill rush'. Yet the speaker knows she must never touch the bushes. To do so is to go against superstition and turn her back on the very traditions she longs to rediscover.

By touching the hawthorn, then, the speaker thinks she might magically become part of the landscape, returning, literally, to her roots. Yet this is an option she can never exercise. This dilemma, it has been suggested, represents the speaker's status as an outsider in the world of the countryside. Her desire to touch and blend into the hawthorn bushes serves as a metaphor for her longing to belong in the West with its wildness and traditions. Yet as a city dweller and a suburbanite she will never truly be part of this world. She will only ever experience it second-hand, from a distance, as a traveller or a holidaymaker. The ban on interfering with hawthorn bushes serves as a metaphor for these obstacles to belonging. No matter how hard the speaker tries she will always remain a tourist or a blow-in. She will never, metaphorically speaking, touch the hawthorn.

Outside History

Note

When we look at stars in the sky we are not looking at the stars themselves, as they exist right now. Rather, stars are so far away from us that it takes of years for their light to reach earth. So what we are seeing in the night sky is an image of the star as it was a long, long time ago.

LINE BY LINE

LINES 1 TO 11

An 'outsider' can be someone who is isolated or detached from the activities or concerns of his or her own community. The poet tells us that there are 'always' people like this.

Boland looks at the stars in the January sky and thinks of them as 'outsiders'. They exist at such distance from the earth that they are constantly remote from what is happening here. Their light, she says, 'happened // thousands of years before / our pain did'.

The poet is likely referring to the pain of the Irish, especially those who suffered throughout the long and troubled course of Irish history. Because the stars are so far removed from us Boland says that 'they have always been/ outside history'. Line 7 suggests that the stars willingly remain detached from our sufferings: 'They keep their distance'.

Boland contrasts the distant stars with 'a place where you found/ you were human'. This is planet Earth, where we are born, live, and die. It is 'a landscape in which you know you are mortal'. The poet says that the time has come for her to choose between this place and the stars: 'a time to choose between them'.

LINES 12 TO 21

The poet has made her choice between the stars and the earth: 'I have chosen'. In so doing she is choosing to move 'out of myth into history'. The poet links the stars with 'myth'. Myths are stories and are often about divine beings. Though they aim to explain events and phenomena, they are generally fantastical and implausible. History, on the other hand, seeks to tell what actually happened in the past. Its aim is to relate the facts of the past and give an honest account of what happened. As such, myth and history are fundamentally different.

So the poet feels that a time has come to disregard myths and consider the facts of the past. She wants to engage with the past, with the suffering of those who came before her: 'I move to be/ part of that ordeal/ whose darkness is // only now reaching me'. To account for the past through myth, it seems, is to distance ourselves from the actual suffering and pain that occurred. The poet wants to bring herself in as close as she can to the reality of the past. She can do this only by focusing on 'history'.

The 'ordeal' that she seeks to be part of is the troubled past of Ireland with its famines and wars. The reality of the individual suffering that occurred over the last few centuries is 'only now reaching' the poet. It is only now, it seems, that she is getting a real sense of the pain that people suffered. And it is only now that she has chosen to consider 'history' rather than 'myth'. For the first time she sees the 'darkness' of the past.

This 'darkness', this painful understanding of the suffering of individuals throughout the course of Irish history, is clearly seen by the poet in the land that surrounds her: 'those fields,/ those rivers,/ those roads clotted as/ firmaments with the dead'. The image that the poet conjures up is grotesque and disturbing. It is as though the dead have come back to life and are clogging the landscape with their bodies.

The final lines of the poem gather us in close to the many victims of history, the multitudes of people whose lives were sacrificed and forgotten. Boland has us 'kneel beside' the many suffering bodies. Finally, it seems, we are acknowledging the people who suffered throughout the course of our history, all those victims that time forgot.

However, though we seek to acknowledge them now, to comfort them with our understanding, we are 'too late'. In the end, having taken the noble decision to re-engage with 'real' history, the poet has to admit that

'We are always too late'. The final line suggests that it always takes too long for us to properly understand and respond to the suffering of others.

THEMES

The nightmare of history

In 'Outside History' Boland again confronts the horrors of the past. Consciously avoiding the myths that seek to tell the tale of the past in romantic and heroic terms, the poet decides to deal with the human reality of history. The myths might speak about the indomitable Irish who heroically fought off their oppressors, but the reality is much more complex and involves the lives of hundreds of thousands of people who each endured hardship and suffering.

Boland suggests that we do these individuals an injustice when we wrap their lives up in a grand narrative that never acknowledges their human plight. And so she seeks to deal with the reality of the past: 'out of myth into history I move to be/ part of that ordeal/ whose darkness is// only now reaching me'. It is only 'now' that the poet is beginning to realise how much human suffering took place in this country over the past few centuries. All around her she begins to see the victims of the past, all those who endured the hardships of war and famine.

A response to suffering

Boland is not just content to describe the sufferings of the past; she sees the need for action, for a proper response. This was also apparent in 'Child of Our Time' where the poet spoke of the need to 'learn' from the terrible tragedy of the child's death. In 'Outside History' the poet makes a deliberate 'choice', she chooses to disregard the myths and focus on the personal sufferings of real people. We cannot allow these countless victims to be forgotten, as though their sufferings were of no consequence. It is a grave injustice to their lives and ordeals if we do so.

And so Boland brings us in close to them, using the powerful image of the victims taking form again in the fields, rivers, and roads that surround us. The poet wishes to do something to let these 'dead' know that they will not be forgotten, that someone is willing to acknowledge their 'ordeal'. But Boland is aware that the past cannot be changed and that she is ultimately powerless to act upon it – 'we are too late. We are always too late'.

This Moment

LINE BY LINE

The poem describes a street or neighbourhood 'At Dusk'. On the street there is a tree. Because it is nearly night-time the tree looks black: 'One tree is black'. A light is on in one of the houses. The light makes the window of the house seem 'yellow as butter'. The street seems calm and peaceful but Boland tells us that 'Things are getting ready / to happen / out of sight' These things that are about to happen involve nature; specifically stars, moths and an apple tree: 'Stars and moths. /And rinds slanting around fruit'.

Line 8 brings a sense of suspense and tension to the poem. The stars, the moths and the apple tree are about to spring into action. But this line represents a kind of pause, a moment of calm before the action commences. Then somewhere in the neighbourhood a child runs into a woman runs into a woman's arms. (It is generally presumed that the woman is the child's mother). As if triggered by this event the moths, stars and flowers finally do their stuff. Stars rise through the evening sky, moths take flight and the apples on the apple tree begin to ripen: 'Stars rise. /Moths flutter./Apples sweeten in the dark'.

LANGUAGE

Mysterious atmosphere

'This Moment' is a wonderfully atmospheric poem. Using only a few words Boland conjures an atmospheric portrait of a street at dusk with its black tree and the lights coming on in its houses. There is an air of suspense and mystery about the poem. This is partly due to the minimal amount of information the speaker gives us. We are told merely that this is 'A neighbourhood'. No specific details are provided. It is also due to the poem's dark and atmospheric twilight setting, This air of suspense is heightened when the speaker declares that 'Things are getting ready/to happen/out of sight'. What are these mysterious events, we wonder, that are about to take place under cover of dusk?

THEMES

The everyday

'This Moment' is a celebration of the ordinary and everyday. It highlights the mystery and beauty that can be found in simple things such as apples on an apple tree, moths swooping through the dark and stars appearing in the evening sky. The poem suggests that even a window with its light on can seem beautiful: 'One window is yellow as butter'. It maintains that these everyday happenings could be a source of wonder and delight if only we took the time to appreciate them.

Motherhood

Mothers play a vitally important role in most of our lives, raising us from helpless children to responsible adults. All too often, however, the work of mothers goes unappreciated and uncelebrated. Their efforts all too often take place 'out of sight'. Yet in this poem nature itself celebrates the role of mothers.

The stars moths and fruit pay their respects to motherhood by waiting until the mother takes the child in her arms. Until that moment things have been 'getting ready / to happen'. Only when the mother picks up the child do they actually start happening. Only then do the stars, moths and apples rise, flutter and sweeten. The poem, then, presents a world where nature celebrates motherhood and the work that mothers do. When the mother does her duty, taking her child in her arms, nature responds by swinging into action.

Suburbia

The poem's suburban setting is important in the context of Boland's philosophy of writing. Suburbs have seldom been regarded as offering much in the way of inspiration to the writer or artist. Suburbia is generally regarded as a place of humdrum family life, lacking both the energy and excitement of the city and the natural beauty of the countryside. In her prose work Object Lessons Boland describes her initial disappointment on moving to the suburb of Dundrum as a newly married mother. She felt cut off from the ideas and inspiration that flowed through Dublin's literary scene. That artistic lifestyle seemed a million miles away from her new role as a housewife and mother of young children. ('White Hawthorn in the West of Ireland' also depicts the suburbs as a dull, uninteresting environment).

In poems such as 'This Moment' and 'The Warhorse', however, Boland attempts to rediscover the suburbs as a site of artistic inspiration. These poems demonstrates that even the most comfortable and humdrum housing estate can provide the impetus for great writing. In 'This Moment' image of the woman lifting up her child might almost be regarded as an emblem of the quiet family living associated with suburbia. Yet the poem shows that this normal, everyday lifestyle can offer the basis for atmospheric and moving poetry.

The Pomegranate

INTRODUCTION

The poem is based around an ancient myth which tells of Persophone's abduction by Pluto. Persophone's mother was Ceres, the goddess of agriculture. Persophone was the goddess of vegetation, but like any girl she loved to travel off with her friends and hang out. One day when she was playing with her friend's in a field she attracted the attentions of Pluto, the god of the underworld. He instantly fell in love with her and decided to kidnap her and bring her back to his subterranean home.

When Ceres got home that evening she looked for Persophone but could not find her. As time passed, and still Persophone did not appear, Ceres' heart beat fast with apprehension and she rushed from place to place calling for her daughter. Days went by and she grew weary with grief. Famine threatened the people and so they prayed for her help. In despair, they eventually turned to Jupiter and begged him to pity them and allow Persophone to return to the upper world once more. Jupiter consented to Persophone's return, upon the condition that she had not touched any food during the time of her stay in the underworld.

Unfortunately Persophone had eaten some pomegranate seeds that very day. Jupiter decided that for every seed she had eaten she would spend one month of every year in her husband's gloomy kingdom. She had eaten six seeds and so was condemned to spend six months in the underworld. And so it came about that whenever Persophone was above ground, her mother was happy and the harvest good. However, once Persophone returned to Pluto, the leaves fell from the trees and plants withered.

LINE BY LINE

LINES 1 TO 12

The opening two lines are meant to surprise us somewhat. For it is strange to hear of someone, particularly a mother, state that she loves 'the story of a daughter lost in hell'. Sounds twisted and nasty. But the third line elaborates the basic details of this particular story or 'legend'. The daughter is 'found and rescued there', a nice Hollywood ending. Indeed, the story contains two great box-office themes, 'Love and blackmail'. Sounds like the perfect pitch to some movie producer. And Boland lists the names of the two leading characters as though she is pitching. We could imagine a meaty producer slouched back in his leather chair chewing a fat cigar exclaiming 'Marvellous, marvellous, Kirsten Dunst and Diane Keaton will love it Dahling!'

Boland places a full-stop at the end of the second line to deliberately break the story into two parts. Part one is the story of a young girl taken to a dark and dreadful place without her consent. The other is the search for, and discovery of, a daughter by her mother.

The poet divides the myth in this manner because it corresponds with the way she has related to the story on two separate occasions. As a young girl she sympathised with Persephone, the abducted daughter. Boland moved to London when she was a child, something she found strange and difficult. She likens the experience to being 'in exile'. The city she was brought to was alien and murky, 'a city of fogs and strange consonants'. She found the pronunciation of familiar words 'strange'.

However, it was whilst living in London that the poet first read the story of Ceres and Persephone. She immediately related to the poor figure of Persephone dragged against her will into the dark underworld.

I read it first and at first I was
an exiled child in the crackling dusk of
the underworld, the stars blighted.

This myth permitted her to see her own situation in the light of a great and fantastic narrative, full of gods and strange happenings. It, perhaps, diminished her isolation and allowed her to feel part of something greater. She saw herself as the tragic figure of Persephone. She now moved within the 'crackling dusk' where the stars are 'blighted'. Such descriptions tell of the heightened imaginative space the myth brought her to.

LINES 12 TO 23

The second time that the myth corresponded with the poet's life was on a summer's eve when out looking for her own daughter. When eventually the daughter came the poet 'was ready/ to make any bargain to keep her'. Suddenly she could empathise strongly with the anguish of Ceres. The fear of ever losing her daughter made her think that she would do anything to prevent this from happening. She carried her daughter home 'past whitebeams/ and wasps and honey-scented buddleias', all symbolic of summer.

Being a mother, like Ceres, the poet understood that 'winter was in store for every leaf'. Her daughter's departure is inevitable, just as Persophone's departure must come with the start of winter. Perhaps Boland is thinking of a time when her daughter must leave the home and start her own life.

LINES 24 TO 54

Line 25 brings us up to the present moment. 'It is winter', the poet tells us, the time when Persophone would no longer be with her mother. The poet climbs the stairs and looks in on her sleeping daughter. The items that are next to the daughter are typical of many young teenage girls, 'her teen magazines,/ her can of Coke, her plate of uncut fruit'. Suddenly the poet remembers the myth: 'The pomegranate! How did I forget it?' If Persophone had not partaken of a few seeds, she could have come home for good. She could, the poet says, have ended 'our heart-broken searching'. However, she was hungry and tempted by the fruit. In her innocence she could never realise the consequences of eating such innocuous seeds.

Lines 35 to 36 dissect the word 'pomegranate' into the 'French sound for apple' ('pomme' means apple in French) and 'the noise of stone' ('granite' sounds similar to 'granate'). Perhaps Boland introduces this to bring the notion of temptation into the poem. The apple was the fruit that Adam was tempted to eat in the Garden of Eden. He lost his innocence because of this act and was damned to mortal life on earth, 'the place of death'.

In a similar manner the young Persophone was punished for her appetite. Yet her act was of the greatest innocence. She was merely a child who was 'hungry'. Even in such a dark place as the underworld, there amidst the harsh environment of 'rocks full of unshed tears', the simple truths of life occur. Yet the price for poor Persophone's action of satisfying her hunger was a terrible one. Should the poet warn her daughter about the consequences of some actions in life? 'There is still a chance'. We must suppose here that Boland is referring to the consequences that come with life experience, with temptation and hunger.

The modern, suburban world is a world far removed from that of the Greek legend. This is 'another world', a world of 'cars and cable television'. And yet the concerns of a mother are no different. Boland asks 'what else/ can a mother give her daughter but such/ beautiful rifts in time?' A 'rift' is a crack, a split in something. So all a mother can do is offer her daughter beautiful experiences over the course of her childhood and then allow her to experience the world for herself.

If the poet holds out on allowing her daughter to grow up she will 'diminish the gift' of life experience. Her daughter must be allowed to grow up and discover all the things that the poet now knows. 'The legend will be hers as well as mine./ She will enter it. As I have.' In the end her daughter will have to grow up and discover the pains and the joys of life. When she wakes in the morning she will reach the pomegranate and put it 'to her lips'. The poet has resolved to 'say nothing'.

THEMES

Myths

'The Pomegranate' emphasises the importance of myths and stories. They often imaginatively describe the difficulties that we must encounter in our lives, the hardships, heartaches and tragedies. In the process they equip us with an understanding of the world and allow us to know that our experiences are universal.

As a child the story of Persephone gave an imaginative twist to the poet's lonely experience in a strange city. Identifying with the character in the myth made her feel part of something greater than herself. Later on in her life the character of Ceres becomes more pertinent. Having a daughter of her own permits the poet to understand the heartache of Ceres. It seems that the poet's acknowledgement of the fact that her daughter must grow up and leave the home is made just a little more bearable because she realises that this is a difficulty that mothers have had to deal with since ancient times.

Motherhood

'The Pomegranate' reveals the difficulties and worries that come with being a mother. The poem describes how a mother's natural impulse is often to protect her daughter from the unpleasant realities of life. However, the poet understands that it would be ultimately wrong to deny or delay her daughter's exposure to the greater experiences of life. Knowing how difficult the world can be and being aware of the pitfalls and temptations that exist beyond the secure bounds of the home makes the poet want to protect and prolong her daughter's innocence. Yet, she is aware of the need for personal experience in life, for each individual to learn their own lessons, even if this means suffering and being hurt along the way.

BACKGROUND

This poem refers to Greek mythology. In a number of Greek legends the hero was required to venture into the land of the dead, here described as 'hell', which was reached by crossing the mythical River Styx. Boland seems to be thinking especially of Aeneas, who adventures were described by the Roman poet Virgil. Virgil tells how Aeneas met his dead friends and comrades in the underworld: 'the hero/ was hailed by his comrades in hell'.

However, according to Greek mythology the living were unable to communicate with those who had passed on. The dead comrades, therefore, were unable to speak to the living hero who had ventured among them: 'their mouths opened and their voices failed and/there is no knowing what they would have asked'. Aeneas' dead comrades found that 'their voices failed' and they were unable to ask the hero about life in the land of the living, about 'the life they had shared and lost'.

Love

LINE BY LINE

Then and Now

The poem is set in a town in Iowa, where many years ago the speaker lived with her husband and children. The speaker has returned to visit this town. It is dusk as she crosses a bridge in the area of town where she and her husband used to live:' Dark falls on this mid-western town ... Dusk has hidden the bridge'. As she crosses the bridge her memories come flooding back:

She thinks of the apartment she used to share with her husband: 'Not far from here is our old apartment. / We had a kitchen and an Amish table. / We had a view'.

The time the couple spent in this town seems to have been a golden period in their relationship. She declares the love between them was so strong that it was almost like a physical presence in their apartment. Love, she says, 'had come to live with us'.

During their stay in Iowa one of their two young children became seriously ill. Their child, we are told, 'was touched by death in this town'. Thankfully, however, the infant survived the illness (was 'spared').

Over the years the speaker's marriage seems to have changed. She and her husband still love each other: 'I am your wife ... We love each other still'. They still communicate with one another: 'Across our day-to-day and ordinary distances/ we speak plainly. We hear each other clearly'. Yet their relationship has lost the some of the intensity it had back when they lived in Iowa. The speaker wonders if she and her husband 'will ever live so intensely again?'.

Their current 'day-to-day and ordinary' relationship is fine but it cannot compare to the magic that flourished between them all those years ago, when their love was almost like a physical presence in the room with them. She longs to somehow return to those glory days and experience her husband as he was all those years ago: 'And yet I want to return to you ... as you were'. Yet she knows that our past glories are over and done with. We cannot return to the golden periods of our lives, no matter how much we might like to.

No going back

As the speaker crosses the bridge she has a strange experience. She is struck by an exceptionally vivid memory of her husband as he was when they lived in this town. She remembers him walking across this very same bridge with 'snow on the shoulders' of his coat. This memory seems to be so incredibly vivid that the speaker can almost see her young husband on the bridge in front of her.

She imagines her young husband as the great hero Aeneas: 'I see you as a hero in a text'. She imagines her present day self as one of Aeneas' companions in the underworld. She imagines the river beneath her not as the Iowa but as the mythical Styx: 'the river/which slides and deepens/to become the water the hero crossed on his way to hell'. (The fact that the river 'slides and deepens' indicates the slick and treacherous depths of this fabled stream).

She longs to reach out to or communicate with this memory of her young husband. Yet she can no more talk to this memory than the souls of the dead could talk to Aeneas when he visited the underworld. Her 'words are shadows', pathetic, insubstantial things, which he cannot understand or even hear: 'you cannot hear me'. After all, we cannot communicate with a memory, no matter how vivid it may be. She wants to be with this memory of her husband as he was all those years ago, to follow him through the darkening streets. Yet she knows that this is impossible: 'You walk away and I cannot follow'.

LANGUAGE

Personification

Personification occurs when an idea or emotion is presented as a living being. In this poem Boland personifies the emotion of love, depicting it as a winged cupid-like creature that came to live in her home: 'And we discovered there/love had the feather and muscle

of wings'. She describes this creature as formidable and powerful force of nature, a brother of 'fire and air'. Whenever they looked at this God-like presence they experienced 'ascension', a type of spiritual ecstasy: 'Will love ever come to us again and be/ so formidable at rest that it offered us ascension / even to look at him?'

Myth

In this poem, as in 'The Pomegranate', Boland makes use of classical mythology. Her personification of love as a winged male creature is influenced by the depiction of Cupid or Eros, the god of love in classical myths and legends. The myth of the hero visiting the underworld is used to explore the speaker's desperate longing for a time that has past.

THEMES

Nostalgia and memory

Perhaps the dominant emotion in 'Love' is that of nostalgia. The speaker is filled with longing for a golden period in her life, for the time when her relationship with her husband was at its most intense. She would love to somehow reverse into the past, to live those days all over again and experience her husband as he was during that special time: 'I want to return to you ... as you were'. The poem also deals with the power of memory, demonstrating how sometimes a memory can be so vivid and powerful that it seems real to us. As the speaker crosses the bridge see can almost her husband as he was all those years ago.

Yet the speaker knows that what's past is past. We are condemned to live in the present and cannot experience our glory days all over again. No matter how vivid a particular memory may be we cannot touch it or communicate with it. The 'ordinary distances' between the speaker and her present day husband can be crossed easily, but the distance separating her from her past life never can. There can be no going back.

An interesting feature of this poem is that the past is associated with the living while the present is associated with the dead. (Usually it is the other way around). The speaker depicts her long-gone youthful husband as a living hero and her present-day self as a ghostly dead companion, whose words are shadows. The past, then, is depicted as being more intense, real and vivid than the present. The speaker, it seems, feels that she was more truly alive in the past than she is now. As she puts it: 'Will we ever live so intensely again?'

Love and marriage

'Love' depicts a relationship at its most intense. When the speaker and her husband lived in Iowa the love between them was so intense that it seemed almost like a physical presence in their home: 'love ... had come to live with us'. It was so strong and 'formidable' that it filled them with ecstasy: 'it offered us ascension'.

The poem could also be regarded as the story of is in one how even the most intense emotions fade over time. For the couple's relationship no longer reach the heights of epic intensity it did in Iowa all those years ago. The speaker wonders: The poem, then, reflects the fact that In a marriage it is difficult to maintain the same level of passion year after year.

Yet the poem also celebrates marriage and the fact that the couple's relationship has survived for so long. Their passion may not be as intense as it used to be but they 'love each other still' and are raising children together. Their lives may be more 'day-to-day and ordinary' than they used to be, but they still communicate well: 'we speak plainly. We hear each other clearly'. The depiction of marriage in this poem, then, is far more positive than that in 'The Shadow Doll'.

BOLAND AT A GLANCE

WAR AND HUMAN SUFFERING

'The Famine Road' highlights the appalling plight of the starving Irish during the Famine and documents the heartless response of the English government to the situation.

In 'The War Horse' the poet shows how people living in the comfort of their suburban homes can turn a 'blind eye' to war and the distant suffering of others.

'Child of Our Time' deals with the tragic loss of life caused by war and conflict, showing how, all too often, it is innocent children who suffer.

'Outside History' also deals with the nameless victims of war and conflict that have suffered throughout the ages. The poet longs to give a voice to these voiceless millions.

MOTHERHOOD

'This Moment' celebrates motherhood. In the poem nature itself seems to respond to the love between a mother and her child.

'The Pomegranate' describes the concerns that a mother feels as she watches her teenage daughter grow up and venture out into the world. The poem suggests that, though the world is full of uncertainties and dangers, it is necessary to allow a child the freedom they need to grow up and learn.

A mix of fear and tenderness is also evident in 'Love' where the poet describes how her child was touched by death but survived.

'The Famine Road' describes the tragedy of a woman being told that she will never bear a child. The poem compares the woman's plight to that suffered by the Irish nation in the Famine of the 1840's.

LOVE AND MARRIAGE

'The Black Lace Fan My Mother Gave Me' presents a complex and realistic view of marriage. The fan comes to represent not only the joyous times in a relationship, but also the troubled, darker periods.

A similar viewpoint is evident in 'Love'. This poem highlights a golden period in the poet's marriage, where the love between her and her husband was at its most intense. However, it also suggests the difficulty of maintaining a relationship during the day to day and ordinary.

'The Shadow Doll' presents a negative view of marriage, suggesting that women are trapped and constrained by its conventions.

SUBURBIA

'White Hawthorn in the West of Ireland' presents suburbia as a place of small talk and lawnmowers, a place where there is little poetic inspiration to be found.

'This Moment', on the other hand, shows how even in the most ordinary suburb moments of magic and inspiration can be found.

'The War Horse' presents a critical view of suburbia, suggesting that the people who live there can remain insulated from the harsh political realities of the world. The poem, however, suggests that the security and comfort is fragile and can easily be disturbed.

T.S. ELIOT
THEMES

RELIGION

In many of his poem's Eliot presents a rather bleak view of Christianity. He tends to emphasise the suffering, effort and sacrifice involved in attaining salvation rather than the joys and comfort of faith. We see this in 'Journey of the Magi', a poem that is haunted by the pain and horror of the Crucifixion. The sights and sounds encountered by the Magi on their journey symbolise aspects of the infant Jesus' eventual and terrible destiny. When they reach the place of Christ's 'Birth' the Magi are filled with premonitions of his suffering and 'Death' at Calvary: 'this Birth / Was hard and bitter agony for us, like Death'.

The extract from 'East Coker' also emphasises the suffering that Christianity entails. Eliot again focuses on the Crucifixion of Christ and seeks to remind us of the fact that we are diseased with Original sin. The poem suggests that if we are to live 'well' we must be prepared to endure physical and mental anguish. 'East Coker' is entirely bleak. Eliot likens Earth to a hospital and suggests that Christ is a 'wounded surgeon' who operates with 'bleeding hands'.

In 'Usk' Christianity is associated with sacrifice, with the hermit's life of self-denial and the pilgrim's arduous journey to a holy well. Eliot implies that we must be like the hermit and deny ourselves certain worldly pleasures if are to become closer to God. We must follow the example of the pilgrims who followed Usk's dipping and rising roads on their way to the holy well. We, too, must make a pilgrimage of our own.

ALIENATION AND PSYCHOLOGICAL SUFFERING

Like many of Eliot's poems 'Journey of the Magi' deals with a depressed and alienated figure. The magus is fundamentally changed by his visit to Bethlehem and feels out of place in his own kingdom after his return. He can no longer feel 'at peace' in his own country and his own people have become 'alien' to him. The world weary tone in the poem's final lines suggest the depression this has caused the magus. He seems tired of life and wishes to leave this troubled world behind.

This kind of alienation is also evident in 'Prufrock' where the speaker presents himself as a troubled figure who feels at home neither in the upper nor the lower class echelons of society. Prufrock seems to frequently pass through the poorer parts of the city and is fascinated by the squalor and rawness of life on show there. He observes the 'lonely men in shirtsleeves, leaning out of windows', but he not a part of this society.

Prufrock is a member of the upper class, the wealthy and privileged people who spend their days uselessly sipping tea and eating 'cakes and ices'. But he feels no more at home in their company. His fascination with squalor and his lonely rambles through the poorer parts of town make him feel wretched and out of place in such refined company. He believes that he would be better off confined to the seabed, away from any form of human company: 'I should have been a pair of ragged claws/ Scuttling across the floors of silent seas'.

Alienation is also expressed by the speaker of 'Preludes', with its imagery of squalor and despair. The poem suggests that modern city life dehumanises people. The inhabitants of the city are reduced to 'hands' and 'feet' that seem to mechanically go through the motions and routines of the day. Though the city is crowded with people, there is a terrible sense of loneliness evident in the poem. Eliot's description of the woman 'Sitting along the bed's edge' clasping 'the yellow soles of feet/ In the palms of both soiled hands' is a devastating image of hopelessness and despair. In the final part of the poem Eliot dismisses the notion that some benevolent, loving God watches over the wretched inhabitants of the city. He laughs off such a notion and implies that man is trapped and alone in the midst of an indifferent universe.

'A Game of Chess', too, depicts psychological distress, with the woman declaring that 'My nerves are bad tonight' and her partner declaring that 'we are in rats' alley / Where the dead men lost their bones'. The woman is portrayed as a troubled soul. She seems trapped or confined in her claustrophobic room, hemmed in by the jewels that spill from their silk boxes, by the strange figures that seem to lean from her paintings and by the sinister scents of the perfumes that 'trouble' and 'confuse' her.

ARTIFICIALITY AND SQUALOR

'A Game of Chess' suggests that modern man has become detached from nature. We are cut off from the natural world by the urban living and the material possessions that surround us. We no longer live as nature intended. This point is made particularly strongly in the poem's opening twenty lines, where we see the lady almost swamped and suffocated by the material goods that surround her.

A similar claustrophobia is evident when the man describes himself and his lady pressing their eyes against the windows of the 'closed car'. There is also something unnatural about the way Lil takes pills to bring her pregnancy to an premature conclusion. The poem also suggests that we are cut off from nature by the ugliness, decay and squalor that characterises much of modern city life. We see this when the lady's partner declares that 'we are in rats' alley', a place of rats and corpses where even the bones of the dead decay.

The filth and rot suggested by the image of 'rats' alley' recalls similar images of urban squalor in 'Prufrock'. At the start of the poem, Prufrock suggests that a journey be undertaken through the 'half-deserted streets', past the 'one-night cheap hotels/ And sawdust restaurants'. In 'Preludes' too we are shown the filth and wretchedness of a modern industrial city. The buildings seem to be decaying. The place is 'burnt out' and everything is 'broken' and 'dingy'. Eliot suggests that the natural world is no longer a thing of beauty and wonder. He describes how 'grimy scraps/ Of withered leaves' are blown through the filthy streets. Man is out of harmony with nature. In 'Preludes' the wind and rain are oppressive forces that 'beat' upon the houses of the city's inhabitants.

THE FAILURE OF LOVE AND SEXUALITY

There are two failed relationships in 'A Game of Chess'. The relationship between the wealthy lady and her partner seems on the verge of collapse. The emotional distance separating the couple has grown so large that the lady has no idea what's going on in her partner's head: 'I never know what you are thinking'. Communication between the two seems to have broken down completely. As the lady puts it: 'Why do you never speak to me?'

In this poem, as in much of Eliot's writing sexuality is presented as something base and animalistic rather than as a gentle celebration of mutual affection. In 'Prufrock' the character seems both attracted to and repelled by the women that he sees. Prufrock is fascinated by women's arms, describing them as 'braceleted and white and bare'. But he seems repulsed by the fact that they are 'downed with light brown hair!' The poorer parts of the city also seem to attract and repel the Prufrock. The 'one night cheap hotels' and the restaurants with 'oyster shells' strewn on the floor would appear to be the haunts of those who are conducting illicit affairs. There is a suggestion of eroticism in these lines, of base sexual desire.

The relationship between the lady and her partner in 'A Game of Chess' seems sexually barren. We get the impression that the lady's partner never speaks to her or stays with her much less sleeps with her. Eliot's negative view of sexuality is also evident in the gossiping woman's description of Lil and Albert's sex life: 'well if Albert won't leave you alone, there it is, I said'. The idea of Lil wanting Albert to 'leave her alone' presents sex almost as a kind of assault, as an act of war rather than an act of love.

Sexuality is depicted as having damaged Lil's health. Though she is only thirty one she has already been pregnant six times. She has nearly died in childbirth and has had an abortion that left her prematurely aged. This echoes the debased and perverted version of sexuality suggested by the painting of Philomel, who was brutally raped by her brother-in-law. The world of 'A Game of Chess', then, is one where all relationships have grown twisted and sour, where normal romance and healthy sexuality is impossible.

LANDSCAPE AND HISTORY

Eliot's series of landscape poems often show how historical events can haunt the landscape they occurred in. In 'Rannoch, by Glencoe' the speaker sees this Scottish highland valley as being haunted by a terrible massacre that took place there in 1692. These 'landscape' poems also show how a landscape's past influences the way we see it in the present. In 'Usk', for example, the speaker says that our perception of the Welsh landscape can be effected by both its ancient association with King Arthur and by its history as a mediaeval place of pilgrimage.

THE DECLINE OF ART AND CULTURE

Eliot was greatly concerned about the decline of art and culture. The modern world, he believed, had lost interest in the great art of the past. We see this in 'A Game of Chess' when he refers to the paintings on the lady's walls as 'withered stumps of time'. These works, he says, are part of great artistic tradition that has 'withered'. People like the lady collect paintings the same way they collect jewellery and perfumes. They value the paintings as status symbols and decorations but not for their artistic merit.

The Love Song of J. Alfred Prufrock

LINE BY LINE

An evening's journey through the city

The poem opens with Prufrock asking someone to accompany him on an evening's journey through the city.

Let us go then, you and I
When the evening is spread out against the sky

He likens the evening to a patient lying unconscious upon an operating table: 'Like a patient etherized upon a table'. The fact that Prufrock compares the evening to something so lifeless and numb suggests that he is less than enthusiastic about the journey he is about to take. The image of the evening as an 'etherised patient' is somewhat disturbing and it seems to deliberately subvert the traditional notion of the evening as something tranquil and peaceful.

It is through the 'half-deserted streets' of the seedier part of town that Prufrock wishes to travel, past the 'one-night cheap hotels/ And sawdust restaurants'. These cheap hotels and restaurants are places visited on 'restless nights'. They are, perhaps, places where dubious, illicit affairs are conducted. This is a part of town that Prufrock seems to escape to, albeit somewhat reluctantly and uneasily, on sleepless nights: 'The muttering retreats/ Of restless nights'.

These streets bother Prufrock; they linger with him and trouble him. As he passes through them he feels ill at ease and threatened. The streets seem to 'follow'

him, forcing him to consider some 'overwhelming question' that he would prefer to avoid: 'Streets that follow like a tedious argument/ Of insidious intent'. He does not want to say what this 'question' might be and wishes only to get to where he is going: 'Oh, do not ask, 'What is it?'/ Let us go and make our visit'.

The scene shifts briefly to a room where 'women come and go/ Talking of Michelangelo'. After the descriptions of the 'sawdust restaurants' and 'cheap hotels', this room seems part of a more sophisticated, upper-class world.

Fog and smoke

Prufrock describes the 'fog' and 'smoke' that moves through the city. He personifies the fog and smoke, comparing its movements to an animal, perhaps a cat. It seductively 'rubs its back' and 'muzzle on the window panes' and intimately explores the 'corners' of the city, no matter how dirty:

Licked its tongue into the corners of the evening,
Lingered upon the pools that stand in drains,
Let fall upon its back the soot that falls from chimneys

The movements of this catlike smog climaxes in 'a sudden leap', after which it settles down to sleep.

Visions and revisions

Prufrock suggests that there is plenty of time for endless things to happen. There will be time for the 'yellow smoke' that languorously 'slides along the street'. There will also be time to put on a face in preparation for those that have to be met: 'time/ To prepare a face to meet the faces that you meet'. There will be time to do such disparate things as 'murder and create'.

These lines suggest a sense of tedium, of boredom and frustration with life's routines and possibilities. Prufrock appears to be frustrated with his own lack of conviction, his constant indecision and revision of plans.

Lines 35 and 36 bring us back to the room where the women 'talk of Michelangelo'. Prufrock tries to imagine whether or not he will have the nerve to enter this room when he comes to it. Perhaps he will turn back at the last moment and 'descend the stair'. He self-consciously thinks about how everybody will react to his appearance when he enters. First he thinks about the 'bald spot' in the 'middle' of his hair and how everybody will remark that his hair is 'growing thin'. He then thinks about how, despite the fact that he will be dressed fastidiously, everybody will comment on how frail he looks.

Prufrock wonders whether he will be bold enough to enter this place. He seems to think that his appearance there will somehow upset the carefully balanced order of things: 'Do I dare/ Disturb the universe?'

A measured life

Wherever it is that he is thinking of going, it seems that Prufrock has been there countless times before. Wearily he recounts how he has 'known them all already, known them all', the 'evenings, mornings, afternoons'. He thinks about how dull, 'measured' and repetitious his life has been: 'I have measured out my life with coffee spoons'.

Prufrock spends his days in the company of people that cause him incredible boredom. But these same people also have the ability to make him very nervous and self-conscious. Their eyes intimidate him. He feels that he is being judged and this makes him terribly uncomfortable.

The people who observe him have their own particular way of judging others, their 'formulated' phrases: 'eyes that fix you in a formulated phrase'. When they fix their eyes on him, Prufrock feels he is being scrutinised like some insect, trapped and utterly helpless: 'when I am formulated, sprawling on a pin,/ When I am pinned and wriggling on the wall'.

In these situations Prufrock is left feeling disgusted with himself and his life. He feels that his 'days' are worthless and wonders how he should begin to speak of how he spends his time: 'how should I begin/ To spit out the butt-ends of my days and ways'.

The women that he sees are so familiar to him. They all seem to be alike. Prufrock speaks of their arms, elegantly 'braceleted and white and bare', lying 'along a table' or wrapping 'about a shawl'. He seems fascinated by these arms, attracted to them maybe, but also slightly repulsed. He mentions how in the 'lamplight' it is possible to see the light brown hair upon the arm.

Prufrock wonders why he was suddenly occupied by such. Perhaps, he surmises, it was the whiff of perfume from a nearby dress that distracted him: 'Is it perfume from a dress/ That makes me so digress'.

He returns to what he was speaking about moments before, namely, how he should respond to the judgemental looks of those in the room he visits. Prufrock wonders whether he should just tell them exactly what he has been doing with his evenings:

Shall I say, I have gone at dusk through narrow streets
And watched the smoke that rises from the pipes
Of lonely men in shirt-sleeves, leaning out of windows?

Thinking about how he spends his time appals and disgusts Prufrock. He feels useless and worthless and thinks he would have been better off a crab 'Scuttling across the floors of silent seas'.

Prufrock thinks about the languid afternoons and evenings spent in the company of these women, drinking tea and eating 'cakes and ices'. He personifies the day, likening it to some lethargic animal that has been caressed to sleep on the floor 'by long fingers'. Prufrock says that the day 'malingers', or pretends to be ill to avoid its duties. The description suggests time uselessly spent, the idle, trivial days of the rich who have nothing much to do.

A moment of crisis

Prufrock wonders whether on such torpid occasions as this he would have the nerve to 'force the moment to its crisis'. It seems that he wants to say something to someone or, perhaps, to everyone present, but lacks the 'strength' and courage to do so. That he has 'wept and fasted, wept and prayed' suggests that he has suffered over the matter for some time. He compares himself to John the Baptist, saying that he has had visions of his head been 'brought in upon a platter' (in the Bible, John the Baptist's head was presented to King Herod in this manner). Prufrock's vision possibly highlights his fear of saying what he believes.

However, Prufrock feels ridiculous comparing himself to such a figure as John the Baptist. He knows that he is 'no prophet' and doubts the importance of what he has to say: 'and here's no great matter'. Even in his vision of himself as John the Baptist he remains self-conscious of his thinning hair. He admits that he is cowardly and imagines that even death, 'the eternal Footman', is snickering at his preposterous life.

But he continues to imagine whether or not it 'would have been worth it' to say what he wanted to say. He positions himself in the room again, where tea is been drunk from 'porcelain' cups and polite conversation taking place, 'some talk of you and me'. Would it have been worth his while, he wonders, to have taken this opportunity and, with a smile upon his face, made his announcement: 'Would it have been worth while,/ To have bitten off the matter with a smile'.

Whereas before Prufrock thought of disturbing the 'universe', here he imagines squeezing it 'into a ball' and rolling it 'towards some overwhelming question'. Again the notion is that what he has to say will greatly disturb and shock the room. And again he imagines himself as some Biblical figure who has something vital to say. He imagines saying that he is 'Lazarus, come from the dead' and ready to tell them 'all'.

However, the response he imagines to his startling news is underwhelming. He imagines a lady 'settling a pillow by her head' and claiming that he misunderstood her intentions: 'If one, settling a pillow by her head,/ Should say: 'That is not what I meant at all./ That is not it, at all.'

Frustration

Prufrock is terribly unsure of the wisdom of making his announcement. But he can't help playing out the scenarios in which he might possibly say what he wants so desperately to say. He imagines details from all the moments that would have to occur before the perfect opportunity would arise: 'the sunsets and the dooryards and the sprinkled streets'.

And again and again he asks himself, 'would it have been worth it'.

Prufrock drives himself to the point of despair imagining all that he would have to do: 'And this, and so much more'. But even worse is the fact that he cannot even express what it is that he wants to say: 'It is impossible to say just what I mean'. However, if he could overcome this difficulty, if some 'magic lantern' could reveal his message to his desired audience, would it then have 'been worth while' if he was casually misunderstood.

Resignation

Finally, with an emphatic 'No!', Prufrock resigns himself to failure. He is not capable of greatness and was never 'meant to be'. Rather than being a heroic, tragic character like the 'Prince Hamlet', Prufrock thinks himself an 'attendant lord', a lesser player who starts 'a scene or two' but is of no real significance to the overall drama. He is too servile and 'cautious', too concerned about not offending others and maintaining face to achieve greatness: 'Deferential, glad to be of use;/ Politic, cautious, and meticulous'. Prufrock gradually chips away at himself, scrutinising and criticising himself, until he has reduced himself to 'the Fool'.

In the end he is resigned to the fact that he will never amount to much. He will 'grow old' and 'wear the bottoms of [his] trousers rolled'. He moves from considering disturbing the 'universe' with 'overwhelming' questions to contemplating parting his 'hair behind'. Prufrock decides that he will 'wear white flannel trousers, and walk upon the beach'.

The mermaids

The poem finishes with Prufrock speaking of some kind of dream or fantasy involving beautiful mermaids. He says that he has heard them 'singing, each to each'. Mermaids are traditional depicted as temptresses who lure men to their doom. But Prufrock does not imagine that they would be interested in him and that their song is meant for others.

Prufrock says that he has seen these seductive women 'riding seaward on the waves'. He speaks of the wind blowing the white tops of the waves back, like hair: 'Combing the white hair of the waves blown back'. The final lines suggest that Prufrock is describing a world of fantasy, a dream world, far removed from the troubles and challenges of the real world. He likens such a fantasy world to the 'chambers of the sea', far removed from the shores of reality. However, his revery is easily disturbed and he is brought back to the real world by the sounds of 'human voices'. The final line suggests that the real world is an unpleasant place where individuals are subsumed and destroyed: 'Till human voices wake us, and we drown'.

THEMES

Who does Prufrock address in the poem?

Prufrock addresses somebody at the start of the poem, but we never find out who that person is. Could it be the woman that he loves? The poem is, after all, a 'Love Song'. Perhaps, however, it is us, the reader of the poem, that he invites to accompany him through what follows.

However, it is entirely possible that Prufrock is addressing himself, or, at least, one aspect of himself. Prufrock is a divided person. He has a social persona, the outer 'face' that he presents to those that he meets. This is the well-dressed Prufrock, 'cautious' and 'meticulous', constantly concerned with his appearance. Then there is Prufrock's inner self, the seething, instinctive, troubled self that knows his public persona is a sham. This inner self is constantly troubling Prufrock, forcing him to question his actions, and giving rise to urges and thoughts which unsettle him.

Prufrock cannot reconcile the two aspects of his personality. His inner self is constantly at odds with his outer persona, the 'self' he presents in public, and this makes it impossible for him to relax and settle upon one course of action. Prufrock is constantly making plans and then revising them. He must allow time for both aspects of himself: 'Time for you and time for me'. The outcome of all this is 'a hundred indecisions'.

Self-loathing

Unable to make clear decisions and act with conviction, Prufrock constantly feels frustrated with himself. He works hard to give an outer appearance of confidence and self-assuredness, but inside he is a mess of insecurity and indecision. He is constantly checking himself, imagining what others are thinking about him: 'They will say: 'How his hair is growing thin!' When he enters the room where the women are drinking tea and discussing Michelangelo, Prufrock feels like an insect, pinned helplessly to the wall by their eyes and scrutinised.

He is disgusted by the fact he spends his evenings walking through the poorer parts of town, fascinated by the 'lonely men in shirt-sleeves, leaning out of windows'. His fascination with the poorer, sleazier parts of the city, and the fact that he is incapable of acting on his convictions, makes him feel tawdry and base. He thinks that he ought to have been a 'pair of ragged claws' confined to the seabed. He compares his 'days and ways' to 'butt-ends'.

Prufrock compares himself to great men and ends up feeling terribly ridiculous. He imagines himself as John the Baptist but quickly concedes that he is 'no prophet'. The fact that the women he meets 'talk of Michelangelo' can only make Prufrock feel inadequate. He admits that he is 'not Prince Hamlet, nor was meant to be'. And yet, Prufrock's monologue calls to mind Hamlet's famous 'To be, or not to be' speech. Like Hamlet, Prufrock carefully ponders the wisdom of acting, of trying to be brave and resolute or just simply giving up. Unlike Hamlet, however, Prufrock seems preoccupied with trivial matters and worries. He is not a great tragic character. At best he is 'an attendant lord', a bit player, someone of no real consequence.

Lack of courage and experience

Prufrock is a cowardly individual, constantly unsure and afraid. He tells us that he has lived a very careful, measured life, one designed to cause the least amount of trouble: 'I have measured out my life with coffee spoons'. He is full of self-doubt, constantly asking himself, 'Do I dare?' He admits that when it comes to acting with conviction he is 'afraid'. He is forever worrying about the consequence of his actions and, therefore, fails to act: 'would it have been worth while, after all,/ Would it have been worth while'. He admits that he is servile, 'Deferential', and 'cautious'.

It seems that Prufrock has not had too much worldly experience. He lacks confidence and assuredness when it comes to dealing with women. The women that he meets in the tearooms intrigue him, but he also experiences a slight revulsion and is uncertain of himself in their presence. He does not know how to speak to them and is worried that when he does he will be misunderstood.

Two worlds

In keeping with his divided self, Prufrock moves between two worlds. There is the poorer part of the city with its 'one-night cheap hotels/ And sawdust restaurants with oyster shells'. It is a world inhabited by, amongst others, 'lonely men in shirtsleeves, leaning out of windows'. Prufrock seems to be fascinated by this world. Here, it seems, there are no pretences. People are not afraid to reveal their desires and emotions. There are sexual overtones to 'one-night cheap hotels' and the 'oyster-shells' that are strewn on the sawdust floors of the restaurants (oysters are considered an aphrodisiac). The men who lean out of the windows are not trying to conceal their loneliness like Prufrock seems to be doing. They are not dressing in fancy clothes to disguise who they really are. Life, in this part of the city, though perhaps dingy and sleazy, is exposed and honest.

This world can be contrasted with the more privileged world where Prufrock wastes his time drinking tea and trying to appear self-assured and important. It is the tedious, dull world of the upper-classes, a world of propriety and pretence. Here people like to talk of 'Michelangelo' and appear intellectual and sophisticated. The streets are sanitised, 'sprinkled' with water. Prufrock seems well aware that this is an artificial world, where people hide their feelings and dare not speak their true desires. He says that it is necessary to 'prepare a face' when going to meet these people.

Overwhelming questions

Around the time of the composition of this poem Eliot endured what one biographer describes as a 'period of intellectual stress'. Eliot felt an overwhelming need to question a drably abhorrent world based on attrition, but did not know in what direction to carry his question. The poem is littered with so many questions. Prufrock longs to reveal what is on his mind to those he visits. But Prufrock is deeply unsure and afraid. 'Do I dare?', he asks. 'So how should I presume?'. 'And how should I begin?'. 'Should I … Have the strength to force the moment to its crisis?'. 'Would it have been worth while…'? However, it is never clear what it is that Prufrock wants to ask.

Is Prufrock just trying to muster the courage to propose marriage? It seems that he wishes to ask some woman a question. The imagined responses in the poem are all made by a woman who seems indifferent to Prufrock. She is described 'settling a pillow by her head' and 'throwing off a shawl'. Prufrock speaks of 'sunsets and the doorways and the sprinkled streets', and we might assume that he is thinking of romantic evening strolls with this woman. But if it is just a simple proposal of marriage or some other romantic overture that Prufrock is considering, why is it so 'impossible' for him to say just what he means?

There is a possibility that Prufrock wishes to say something more profound. The fact that he compares himself to John the Baptist and Lazarus and he has been spending nights fasting and praying, suggests that Prufrock might have arrived at some conclusion about the meaning of life. He speaks of disturbing the 'universe' and talks of 'visions' as though he has something mysterious and wise to reveal. However, it seems likely that Prufrock is just confused and tortured by his thought and does not have anything definite to say. At one point in the poem he blurts out, 'It is impossible to say just what I mean!'

LANGUAGE

The poem is a form of dramatic monologue. A dramatic monologue is a poetic form in which a single character, addressing a silent auditor at a critical moment, reveals himself or herself and the dramatic situation. In contrast with many traditional dramatic monologues, Prufrock reveals little solid information about himself. The poem is fragmented and often confusing and uses language to reflect the stream of consciousness.

Yet, it is highly poetic at times. Eliot incorporates plenty of rhyme and the poem is rich with imagery and sound. The description of the fog moving like a cat through the streets is wonderfully poetic. The language is lush and sensual: 'The yellow smoke that rubs its muzzle on the window-panes/ Licked its tongue into the corners of the evening'. The description of the mermaids riding the waves at the end of the poem is also beautifully achieved, using assonance and alliteration to great effect: 'I have seen them riding seaward on the waves/ Combing the white hair of the waves blown back'.

Preludes

BACKGROUND

The four parts of this poem were not originally intended to comprise a single poem. In its final form, 'Preludes' includes various pieces that Eliot wrote over a couple of years, from 1910 to 1911. He wrote the various sections whilst living in different cities. Two Preludes were set in Dorchester and Roxbury, composed in October 1910; another Roxbury Prelude was written in July 1911, and a final one was written after Eliot returned to America. Eliot gradually saw possibilities for relating the four. He eventually created this four-part sequence called 'Preludes'

LINE BY LINE

I

The first 'Prelude' begins just as the day is ending. It is winter and we are in the city, in an urban back street. The lines create a setting, an atmosphere, almost like the opening scene in a movie. Eliot puts us in the position of some solitary wanderer through this gloomy scene. The smell of cooking spills out from cramped living quarters into the smoky twilight where gusts of wind stir up 'withered leaves' and old newspapers, and the rain beats down on buildings. The tone is explicitly set with adjectives such as 'burnt-out', 'grimy', 'withered' and 'broken'. Just as in 'Prufrock', Eliot opens the poem with a reference to 'evening' in an urban setting. And again we are quickly brought into a frustrated and tarnished world. The third line is abrupt and punctures, as does the third line of 'Prufrock', the rhythm of the opening two lines.

Six o'clock.
The burnt-out ends of smoky days.

The fourth line describes an exhausted world. No energy or vitality remains. The days are compared to cigarettes that have been stubbed out and discarded. And, like the days, we imagine that the inhabitants of the city are 'burnt-out' too, wrecked from their day of toil, ready to sink into the oblivion of the evening. The day itself is described as 'smoky', the city being an unhealthy furnace of industry, factories clogging the air with smoke. And even nature itself appears to be against the desperate inhabitants of this morbid metropolis. It does not allow them to escape their squalor but, rather, 'wraps/ The grimy scraps/ Of withered leaves about your feet'. Time is another important factor in the poem. It dictates peoples' lives. The inhabitants of the city march wearily, but obediently, to its beat.

There is no relief from the sordidness of the industrial city with its grime and smoke. Showers 'beat/ On broken blinds', adding further misery to these already broken inhabitants. The blinds are pulled down to shelter them from the reality outside, but they are 'broken' and offer little relief. The city, which should be the crowning glory, the apotheosis of man's civilisation and progress, has become a recurring nightmare, a purgatorial sentence. The evening described is a prelude to all evenings, since the cycle of city life goes on endlessly, and all days lead back to the same evenings.

And at the corner of the street
A lonely cab-horse steams and stamps.

Nobody is visible in this opening Prelude. It is as though everyone is hiding themselves away, retreating from the world. The city is described by way of certain physical objects and sensations – the smell of steaks cooking, the sound of rain on broken blinds, the sight of newspapers in vacant lots. It is the streets and buildings, the houses, that feature strongly here. We get a real feeling for the place, the city itself, as an entity, soiled, worn-out, beaten down. All we have by way of life is a solitary work-horse. The camera pans down from the stormy sky over the buildings to this 'lonely' creature that possesses significant presence. He exhibits great, impatient energy, the brute qualities of a steam-driven machine, as his shod foot thunders on the cobble. The horse appears to represent the frustrations of the solitary inhabitants, the workers, of the city.

The 'lighting of the lamps' rounds off the 'Prelude', closes the scene. It is the final act of the day. Yet, the positioning of the line and the way it reads, particularly in contrast to the line that immediately precedes it, gives it a special quality. The line reads more quickly than its rhyming companion 'A lonely cab-horse steams and stamps', despite the fact that both lines have eight syllables. The words in the second-last line, especially 'steams' and 'stamps', slow the line, whereas the word 'lighting' in the last line quickens the pace by removing a stress from the line. The images in the two lines also serve as contrasting symbols. The horse is heavy, burdened and earthbound, whereas the lamps cause us to look upward, they light the air and suggest that something positive is about to happen. The lamps represent the possibility of enlightenment, the hope of transcending the grimy city of routine. The horse represents the great body of workers who live in the city, people who have been reduced to machines and are sunk blindly in the routines of their labour. Eliot returns to this notion in the third and fourth 'Preludes' as certain inhabitants try to gain a vision of something beyond the streets.

II

Like the first 'Prelude', the second opens with a line personifying a section of the day. In the first 'Prelude' it is the 'evening' that 'settles down', as though it is someone relaxing after a long day of work. Here in the second 'Prelude' 'The morning comes to consciousness'. Somehow we are given the impression that it is time and not individuals who have autonomy in the poem. In contrast most of the people are described as fragments of bodies, parts of some greater faceless process.

Often morning is depicted as a something fresh, a new awakening, the hope of possibilities. Here Eliot describes the dawning of a new day with words such as 'stale' and 'muddy'. The morning is something tedious and old. It 'comes to consciousness' as though struggling once again to locate itself within the world. And instead of bringing birdsong and slanting rays of brilliant sunshine it carries the 'faint smell of beer/ From the sawdust-trampled streets'. The mention of 'beer' tells of the previous nights efforts to escape, to embrace oblivion and forget the tedium of existence. The new morning is simply just a sour extension of the night before. Anyone who has woken on the floor in the morning after a party, where countless empty and half-empty cans of beer surround you, along with the butts of a hundred cigarettes, must understand something of what Eliot is trying to convey here. Yet, this is not an isolated morning that Eliot describes for the inhabitants of the city. He is conveying a world of the greatest tedium, where day follows night and night follows days of toil and filth. Nothing new enters this terrible cycle of existence. Eliot does not permit the morning to be the bearer of anything like hope. It is 'stale' from the beginning. It is like it was yesterday and like it will be again tomorrow. For there will be no great change. And those described in this section are almost automata, simply continuing the 'masquerades/ That time resumes'.

It is 'time' that provides the impetus here, it is 'time' that seems to possess the will, not people. Time 'resumes' these activities and the drone-like populace falls into line. Urban life has broken the collective will of the people. They serve industry and forego innovation and spontaneity. Life has become an unimaginative cycle of work and escape, the city having become a purgatorial place where time is served and endured. Industrialisation has reduced them to parts, to hands and feet. People are now the sum of their parts and no greater. They are possessed by the city, instruments to a will that is no longer their own, and they tramp the endless treadmill of the daily round. They 'press/ To early morning coffee-stands', herd-like, to rouse their dulled minds and alert themselves to the tedious tasks of the day. The observer of the poem imagines disgustedly 'all the hands/ That are raising dingy shades/ In a thousand furnished rooms'. There is no allowance here for individualism. Everybody does the same thing. Their personalities mesh into one, no matter which way they arrange their furniture.

III

The third 'Prelude' describes the restless night of some woman in one of the 'thousand furnished rooms'. The description is given by the unseen observer who recounts the nights events.

You tossed a blanket from the bed,
You lay upon your back, and waited

What does she wait for? Sleep? Some insight into the meaning behind the 'masquerades' of life? The third 'Prelude' gives us the first inkling that some speak of sensitivity persists in the inhabitants of the city. The night is often a time for introspection, a time when distractions have vanished and you are left alone with nothing more than the darkness and the thoughts in your head. There is a hint of agitation in the fact that the blanket is 'tossed' from the bed. The waiting implies some sort of expectation, as though the woman has a notion that something will arrive if she gives it time. Yet we can imagine that she is frustrated and nothing is revealed to her. We might recall the lines in Prufrock where he laments: But though I have wept and fasted, wept and prayed ... I am no prophet. And so she drifts into sleep, no longer able to maintain her vigil.

You dozed, and watched the night revealing
The thousand sordid images
Of which your soul was constituted

All she gets from the night is a little sleep and the uncomfortable details of herself, the 'sordid images' that define her meaningless life. She is unable to avoid these 'sordid images' because the distractions, the 'masquerades' of the day, are no longer there to keep her mind away from the terrible truths of her existence. These come to her now in the darkness like some horror movie projected on to the ceiling above her ('They flickered against the ceiling'). The description of the woman's soul allows for no redemption. She views a 'thousand sordid images' and seems to have no recourse to beauty or love. It is a pretty bleak account of a life. It seems that her enlightenment, her insight into the meaning of her life, only serves to disturb her rather than fulfil. There is the notion here that a 'vision' or insight is only achieved through suffering and anguish. Yet, perhaps those who suffer, like this particular woman, have at least gained some meaning, displaced themselves somewhat from the unthinking, herd-like masses. The first three lines of the third 'Prelude' begin with the word 'You', establishing the woman as a person and not just a part.

The dawn shatters the lonely isolation of this woman by bringing sounds and light to her room. Yet, the fact that the light has to creep 'between the shutters' suggests that this might be an intrusion rather than a saving grace. She hears 'sparrows', but these birds do not represent any form of beauty as they are 'in the gutters'. Even those with wings are bogged down in this grimy town. She has not gained the transcendence that she possibly desired. Perhaps she longed for something that would grant her relief, reveal something spiritual, something 'infinitely gentle'. But all she gets is 'a vision of the street/ As the street hardly understands'. We are not told what this 'vision' is. Perhaps has had an insight into the terrible 'masquerades' that constitute modern life, into the meaningless cycle that so many endure. Her 'vision' as such is not fulfilling. But it seems to be all that she can hope for. God has not spoken to her. She has not been granted any notions that something good might rest behind this hellish life. And so she is left alone with herself, alone in her grimy little world.

Sitting along the bed's edge, where
You curled the papers from your hair,
Or clasped the yellow soles of feet
In the palms of both soiled hands.

IV

It is not clear whose soul is referred to in this last Prelude. At least in the third Prelude we got some insight into the woman's life. We can say that she is one of the many who occupy the 'thousand furnished rooms' in the city. However, we are given nothing but the word 'His' in the fourth Prelude to allow us characterise this individual. Some critics suggest that this is the person who observes in the first three Preludes. They describe him as a 'seeker', someone who has spent time watching the life of the city and seeking some kind of meaning behind it all. However, there is no real basis for assuming that the person mentioned in the final Prelude has any particular role in the first three.

The final Prelude conveys the mindset of someone who experiences the drudgery and the inanity of city life and yet holds aspirations beyond the 'masquerades'.

His soul stretched tight across the skies
That fade behind a city block

That this 'soul' is 'stretched tight' implies strain and discomfort, the endurance of some form of crucifixion. It also suggests a desire for transcendence, a yearning to get beyond the dreadful city. But the countless inhabitants mill across it, beating it back down with their 'insistent feet' (An interesting comparison could be drawn between these lines and the opening lines of Emily Dickinson's poem 'I felt a Funeral, in my Brain', which describes boots of lead 'treading' across her mind until she eventually breaks down). These are the same feet that 'press/ To early coffee-stands' in the second Prelude. There is a terrible rhythm to these feet, a mind-numbing robotic aspect to their movements. Line 42 drills this home to us – 'At four and five and six o'clock'. It is all horribly monotonous and the lack of spontaneity and imagination is ultimately soul-destroying. Once again it is the clock that controls people. The day is defined by work and eating patterns. The masses are little more than machines that need to be refuelled regularly.

The 'fingers stuffing pipes', the 'evening newspapers' and the 'eyes/ Assured of certain certainties' seem to have the same effect on this 'soul' as the trampling of feet. There is no reason why a man stuffing his pipe should be indicative of a tedious and mindless existence. However, Eliot never speaks of anyone, but only of 'short square fingers'. This removes any notion of autonomy, of personhood. People are broken down into components that seem to operate mechanically together. Pipes and newspapers are all part of the endless cycle of a meaningless existence that Eliot is trying to describe, an existence in which people seek oblivion, escape and distraction from the dreadful reality of their lives. The newspapers provide a moments entertainment in the evening and are then discarded in the street, ending up with the 'withered leaves' in 'vacant lots'. This is all routine. People know what they are getting and they expect nothing more. Their 'eyes' are 'Assured of certain certainties'. Perhaps if it were referring to today this line might be about the soap-operas that fill the evening television schedule and define so many people's evenings.

Does the 'soul' of line 39 belong to the 'blackened street' of line 46? It would make certain sense considering that this soul is described as being 'trampled by insistent feet' in line 41. We should recall that in the third Prelude the woman had a 'vision of the street/ As the street hardly understand', implying that the street does understand something. Perhaps, however, there is a person in the fourth Prelude who serves as the 'conscience of a blackened street'. The alternative is that the street is being personified here. Either way the final Prelude gives us the impression of someone, or something, who sees beyond the common knowledge of the evening rush-hour crowd who guards its oblivion with newspapers and stuffed pipes. This being is 'Impatient to assume the world'. To 'assume' here most likely means to seize or take control. The 'conscience' of the 'street' is eager to take control of this mess, possibly to make sense of the world.

Lines 48 to 51 are in the first person. It could be the poet himself or some implied observer throughout the poem that speaks here. Though there is so much bleakness and hopelessness in the poem, the speaker is 'moved' to think of 'some infinitely gentle/ Infinitely suffering thing' that embraces everything. It is remarkable to find some emotion of hope and tenderness after all that has been recorded so far in the poem. However, the language used to express this emotion is vague and the speaker is ultimately not able to truly express himself. The word 'fancies' suggests nothing solid or definite. These are whims, capricious imaginings. The word 'thing' implies that it is ultimately beyond the speaker's grasp to put it in any solid words, but we can possibly understand it as some greater Being, a God-like entity. These lines introduce a sympathetic and tender aspect to the poem, but are ultimately only someone's 'fancies' and provide no counter-balance of real hope for the inhabitants of the city.

Even the speaker is somewhat embarrassed by this brief 'notion'. The last three lines self-consciously ridicule any idea that the world is embraced by some gentle Being with a plan. It now seems like a momentary lapse of judgement by the speaker. And so he ends on a mocking and cynical note, telling himself to 'wipe' his mouth of such ridiculous words.

Wipe your hand across your mouth, and laugh:
The worlds revolve like ancient women
Gathering fuel in vacant lots.

The world is nothing more than a meaningless struggle to exist. The laugh contains no genuine mirth. It is the laugh of cynicism and bitterness, destroying any ideas of pity and tenderness that came before. There is no divine plan behind this city mess, just various 'worlds' that 'revolve'. The fact that 'worlds' is plural suggests, perhaps, that the world might change throughout time, different historical epochs constitute different worlds. In spite of this the same things seem to recur. Perhaps the 'ancient women' are in touch with the only truths in life. Whereas the speaker can only see garbage in the 'vacant lots' of the first Prelude, these women find 'fuel'. There may be an implied message here that what you find ultimately depends on what you look for.

THEMES

In 'Preludes', just as in both 'Prufrock' and 'The Waste Land', Eliot describes a world that is quite ugly and apparently without meaning. This is the world of the great industrial cities where people have become cogs in the machine of industry. The dulled inhabitants go through the motions of living, but don't really seem to be alive. Just as in his later poem 'The Waste Land', Eliot portrays a terrible sense of death-in-life. The people of the city lack any substantial emotional or spiritual centre. They are like robots, programmed or conditioned to carry out their daily tasks and just accept it. In fact, Eliot does not even refer to people most of the time in 'Preludes'. Just as in 'Prufrock' we are presented with parts of people rather than complete persons. The device of using a part to represent the whole is known as 'synecdoche'. In 'Preludes' it is 'hands', 'feet', 'fingers' and 'eyes' that represent the inhabitants. This dismemberment of the body suggests that in modern times people are no longer whole, autonomous beings with souls. Instead, they are just a variety of parts that are either useful or not.

These people don't seem to be in control of their own lives. On a number of occasions throughout the poem we get the impression that time is the master of man. Periods of time are personified and given wills. The first line has the 'evening settling down'. The beginning of the second Prelude tells us that it is the 'morning' that 'comes to consciousness'. Time 'resumes' the activities of the people, not their own wills. Instead, they just fall into line and obey. People serve time like slaves and prisoners.

The city is a dingy and charmless place. The streets are littered with 'grimy scraps/ Of withered leaves'. This is the only impression of Nature we get in the poem. In 'The Waste Land' Eliot expresses his belief that modern man has lost touch with nature. Here the natural world has 'withered' along with the inhabitant's sense of identity and meaning in life. And the buildings in which these people live are in similarly bad condition. The blinds are 'broken' and the shades 'dingy'. Even if someone possesses a soul in this city it is constituted of a 'thousand sordid images'. The days are 'burnt-out' and 'smoky', the feet 'yellow' and the hands 'soiled'. Ultimately the city and its inhabitants reflect one another. It seems that the dilapidation of the buildings and streets is seeping into the souls of those who dwell within its walls.

The poem does suggest that within this mindless and numb environment certain flickers of life and hope exist. First of all we have the woman in her dingy room waiting for some form of vision. Though she ends up frustrated, we are at least made aware that not everybody in this place is happy to get on with the routine, that there is a belief in the fact that something greater might exist. Secondly, there is the 'soul' of one who is 'Impatient to assume the world'. Again there is a suggestion that not all drive and ambition has been extinguished from the city. Eventually the speaker of the poem is moved to say that 'some infinitely gentle/ Infinitely suffering thing' might embrace these wretched people. But this is vague and momentary hope. In the midst of torment it is regarded as sentimental by the rational mind. Immediately reason undercuts it and the poem closes with the depressing belief that life is really just an aimless, Godless affair.

Aunt Helen

LINE BY LINE

The opening line, like most of the lines in the poem, is a statement of fact and tells us that the poet's aunt was never married. We are also given the mundane fact that she is the poet's aunt through the mother's side of the family. It is a line without sentiment. The second line is equally matter-of-fact. The language is formal and the tone is dry. It is similar to something written by a detached journalist, though the third line is a little too awkward even for that. It is a rather rigid line, lacking any element of informality and represents the impersonal relationship that existed with the aunt. The impression the poem gives us is that the aunt shared no intimate relationship with anyone. Nobody cared for her except those she paid.

The fourth line hurries on to the most interesting event in the aunt's life – her death. We realise that the poet has nothing more to say about the woman when she lived. Her life is quickly summed up with the briefest description of her house and her servants. A meagre three lines are devoted to her life and these are the most uninteresting and banal lines of the poem. It is as though the poet finds it hard, given the awkwardness of the third line, to recount even as much as this. The word 'now' in the fourth line signals the fact that the poet was only mentioning what he did in those lines so that he could get on to more interesting details. It is remarkable that more lines are devoted to the aunt's death than to her life.

When the aunt died 'there was silence in heaven/ And silence at her end of the street'. The impression is that her death is of no consequence to anyone. A life ended but no one cared much. The 'shutters were drawn and the undertaker wiped his feet'. Appropriate behaviour and conduct is maintained, but this is the smallest of events. There are no descriptions of sadness or mourning. Nobody sheds a tear. Instead, we are only told of a lone undertaker going about his job. The undertaker 'was aware that this sort of thing had occurred before'. The death is reduced to a level of farce. It is almost as if the aunt's death is brief inconvenience, a mess that will be quickly tidied up.

The ridiculousness of the aunt's values are perfectly illustrated in line 8. She was a person who obviously had more time for dogs than people and they, not her human relations, gain her considerable wealth. This fact alone shows what a small and detached world the aunt existed in. The only exotic element in this world was the aunt's parrot which died 'shortly afterwards'. We sometimes hear of husbands and wives dying shortly after their spouse has died. This is put down to heartache, an inability to live when their life's companion has departed. In this poem it is a parrot rather than a husband that follows her, a comical rather than tragic occurrence.

But life went on in spite of the two deaths. Her fancy clock continued to tick in her absence. And her servants take the opportunity to do something they would not have done had she been alive. The footman 'sat upon the dining-table/ Holding the second housemaid on his knees'. The behaviour is explicitly at odds with the mannered and lifeless existence of the aunt. These people only behaved themselves around the aunt because it was their job to do so. But there was no deeper respect or bond between them. Now that she's gone they have no difficulty in mocking and disrespecting the kind of behaviour the aunt would have expected. The servants represent a different set of values. Their bawdy behaviour mocks the aunt, bringing an element of sexuality into her polished and lifeless world. The close intimacy of their action shows up the distance that the aunt kept with the human world. No doubt she would have considered the servants' actions obscene and base. Her world denied the existence of desire and emotion.

Ultimately the poem mocks the aunt and the way she lived. It was a life that denied life. The aunt defined herself according to her possessions and not her relationships and emotional connections with others. Similar to the world of 'toast and tea' in 'Prufrock', this is a world of the masquerade, the artificial masking the true nature of life. The servants mock the aunt's world and reveal what she always tried to deny. The last two words state that the aunt 'lived'. The poem shows that it was of little consequence that she did. Eliot uses little by way of poetic language. It is a rather stiff and lifeless piece of writing, in keeping with the aunt's style of living. The rhythm of the poem is awkward, the lines do not flow sweetly and the rhymes are rather trite. The poem is almost a sonnet, but falls one line short of this classic form. It seems almost deliberate on Eliot's part. In the end such a life did not warrant a form mastered by the great Shakespeare, often used to celebrate passionate themes.

A Game of Chess

'A Game of Chess' is the second part of *The Waste Land*, a hugely influential poem which was originally published in 1922. 'A Game of Chess' can be divided into three sections. Section One (lines 1–34) describes a rich woman's bedroom. The second section (lines 35–62) consists of a conversation between this lady and an unidentified man who enters her boudoir. The poem's final section consists of lines 63–101 is set in a pub where a woman is gossiping about the marriage difficulties of two people called Lil and Albert.

LINE BY LINE

LINES 1–20: *A luxurious boudoir?*

This section depicts a wealthy lady sitting in her bedroom. The room is filled with riches and luxury:

- The lady's chair resembles a throne: 'The Chair she sat in, like a burnished throne'.
- The room has a marble floor and a 'laquearia' or panelled ceiling.
- There is a 'glass' or mirror which is kept upright by an engraved and golden frame: 'the glass/Held up by standards wrought with fruited vines'. Carved into this frame are tiny angels: 'From which a golden Cupidon peeped out /(Another hid his eyes behind his wing)'
- There is an ornamental fireplace made of 'coloured stone' into which a dolphin has been carved (Lines 18–20).
- There are a number of paintings on the walls, which Eliot describes as 'withered stumps of time': 'and other withered stumps of time / Were told upon the walls'. (The paintings will be discussed in more detail below).
- The lady has so many jewels (such a 'rich profusion') that they spill out of her satin jewellery boxes: 'From satin cases poured in rich profusion'.
- The lady also a great many perfumes, which she keeps in 'vials' or bottles made of 'ivory and coloured glass'. Some of these products are powders, others are liquids while others are ointments ('unguents').

It would be wrong, however, to state that this luxurious room is a pleasant place. There is something sinister and threatening about this environment. The perfumes, for instance, are depicted as strange, unnatural and overpowering:' In vials of ivory and coloured glass / unstoppered, lurked her strange synthetic perfumes'. The use of the verb 'Lurk', which implies threat and menace, suggests that there is something unpleasant about these products. They are described as being almost choking in their intensity: 'they drowned the sense in odours'. They make anyone who inhales them 'troubled' and 'confused'.

The paintings, too, are presented as sinister and threatening. There is something eerie and about the way the people in the paintings stare out of the canvases. These 'staring forms', are described as 'leaning' out of the pictures: 'staring forms/ Leaned out, leaning'. Even the room's artificial light is peculiar and oddly unpleasant. The fire, in which 'huge sea-wood' burns, gives a weirdly artificial 'green and orange' glimmer: 'Huge sea-wood fed with copper/Burned green and orange'. The light from the fireplace is described as 'sad'. It seems to be depressing and melancholic rather that bright and cheery: 'In which sad light a carvèd dolphin swam'.

The room's atmosphere could also be described as cramped and claustrophobic. The lady seems swamped and hemmed in by her possessions, by the jewellery that pours from its cases, by her perfumes with their overpowering odours, by the paintings that seem to 'lean' from the walls to confine and 'enclose' the room in which she sits: 'leaning, hushing the room enclosed'. The lady seems on the verge of being overwhelmed by the cluttered 'profusion' of material goods that surround her.

LINES 21–30: THE CHANGE OF PHILOMEL

One of the lady's paintings depicts 'the change of Philomel'. It hangs above the mantelpiece: 'Above the antique mantel was displayed'. It is 'sylvan' (set in a woodland) and is so realistic that it seems we are looking at the woodland through a window: 'As though the window gave upon the sylvan scene'.

According to Greek legend, Philomel was a princess who was raped by her brother in law, King Tereus of Thrace:' by the barbarous king / So rudely forced'. Tereus cut her tongue out so she could tell no one of his crime. The gods took pity on Philomel and turned her into the first nightingale. The painting depicts the 'change of Philomel', her metamorphosis from a princess to a bird.

Philomel herself has been 'violated' or raped. Yet as a nightingale her song will be 'inviolable'. Nothing can damage, destroy or violate her music. It will go on forever. Philomel, and the nightingales that have come after her, have 'Filled all the desert' with same beautiful tune for century after century.

'Withered stumps of time'

The paintings on the lady's wall are described as 'withered stumps of time': 'And other withered stumps of time/Were told upon the walls'. This raises another of the poem's important themes. Eliot believed that in the modern world most people had simply lost faith and interest in the great tradition of western art. To people like the lady in the poem paintings are things to be collected like jewellery rather than a source of inspiration and creativity. They are mere decorations rather than works of art to be appreciated and understood. The paintings, therefore, are presented as 'stumps of time', the decayed and wasted remains of a once-great tradition.

LINES 35–62: *A disturbed conversation*

This section has been described as a conversation between the lady and the man who has 'shuffled' up the stairs and entered her bedroom; an individual most critics believe to be her husband or lover. Yet strictly speaking it may not be a conversation at all. The woman's words are enclosed in quotation marks ('...'), which indicate that she is speaking aloud. The man's words, however, lack quotation marks, suggesting that he keeps his thoughts to himself, only answering the woman inside his head. In fact, it seems that the man 'never' speaks to the woman: 'Speak to me. Why do you never speak?'

The woman declares herself to be psychological distressed: 'My nerves are bad tonight'. (For someone's 'nerves to be bad' is to be in a tense or agitated mental state). Her mental agitation is evident in her jerky, repetitive speech: 'Yes, bad. Stay with me ... What are you thinking of? What thinking? What?' She speaks in fragments rather than fully formed sentences, with words such as 'Think', 'What' and 'Speak' repeated almost obsessively. Her speech has been described as the agitated babble of a woman on the edge of a nervous breakdown.

Her mental agitation is also evident in her desperate pleas not be left alone: 'Stay with me. / Speak to me'.

It is also evident in her paranoid questions about the sound of the wind: 'What is that noise? … What is that noise now? What is the wind doing?' Even something as innocent as the sound of the 'wind under the door' is enough to upset and frighten this disturbed individual.

Her threat to 'rush out as I am, and walk the street', perhaps in a state of undress ('With my hair down, so'), suggests that her psychological difficulties are on the verge of overpowering her, that she may actually be on the point of losing it completely. There is a real sense of despair in her repeated questions: 'What shall I do now? What shall I do?' The woman, it appears, feels lost and abandoned, with no idea of how to live, or how to relieve her psychological unease.

Her partner, too, seems to be in a state of psychological distress. The woman's questions suggests that while he is physically living he is spiritually and psychologically dead: 'Are you alive or not?' Her partner, she suspects, is experiencing and spiritual and mentally emptiness, the kind of 'hollow feeling' often associated with extreme depression: 'Is there nothing in your head?' This inner emptiness is suggested by the bizarre questions she asks him: 'Do/you know nothing? Do you see nothing? Do you remember/ 'Nothing?

The man's declaration that 'we are in rats' alley/where the dead men lost their bones' also suggests his psychological distress. His mind is in a bad place, a place of rot, decay and emptiness. His bleak view of life is also evident in lines 59–62 when he tells the lady what they will do tomorrow: 'The hot water at ten. /And if it rains, a closed car at four'. We get a sense here that the man regards life as a pointless routine. To him each day is the same. Life is full of deadening monotony.

His despair is evident when he describes the couple in the 'closed car' pressing their open eyes against its windows as they wait desperately for a 'knock upon the door': 'Pressing lidless eyes and waiting for a knock upon the door'. This is nightmarish image of confinement. It suggests that the man views himself trapped in a bleak life of monotony and despair from which their can be no escape.

LINES 63–101: *Barroom Gossip*

With line 63 the poem radically shifts location, from a wealthy woman's bedroom to a working-class pub. We listen to a woman from the 'lower classes', who is gossiping with her companions about a married couple called Albert and Lil. The woman tells us that Albert has recently returned to Lil after four years in the army. (He has been 'demobbed' or demobilised). Their relationship, however, seems to be in difficulty. According to the woman, Albert no longer finds his wife attractive: 'He said, I swear, I can't bear to look at you'. While on leave from the army he gave her money to purchase false teeth, presumably being unimpressed by the state of her dental health:

He'll want to know what you did with that money he gave you
To get yourself some teeth. He did, I was there.
You have them all out Lil and get a nice set.

The woman seems to share Albert's low opinion of Lil's looks (lines 71–2). She told Lil that she needs to smarten up her physical appearance: 'I didn't mince my words, I said to her myself ... Now Albert's coming back, make yourself a bit smart'. Lil, she claims, is only thirty-one but looks much older: 'You ought to be ashamed, I said, to look so antique. / (And her only thirty-one)'. ('Antique', in this context, can be taken as another word for old).

Lil, according to the woman, nearly died while giving birth to her fifth child George: 'She's had five already, and nearly died of young George'. She decided, therefore, to not to give birth to her sixth child, taking pills to terminate the pregnancy: 'It's them pills I took, to bring it off, she said'. The pills, however, have had unwanted side effects, damaging Lil's health and making her look 'antique': 'The chemist said it would be all right but I've never been the same'.

According to the woman the relationship between Albert and Lil has deteriorated to such an extent that Albert may actually leave her for another woman: 'He's been in the army four years, he wants a good time, /And if you don't give it him, there's others will, I said'. The woman suggests that if Albert does 'make off' it will be Lil's own fault for neglecting her physical appearance: 'But if Albert makes off, it won't be for lack of telling'.

There is also a sense that the woman might actually welcome the break-up of Lil and Albert's marriage. Perhaps she has developed feelings for Albert herself? She appears, after all, to be a close friend of the couple; a fact indicated by her invitation to Sunday dinner: 'Well that Sunday Albert was home, they had a hot gammon, / and they asked me in to dinner, to get the beauty of it hot'. In any case Lil seems suspicious that the woman might encourage Albert to leave her: 'Then I'll know who to thank, she said, and gave me a straight look'.

An interesting feature of this section is the way the woman's gossiping speech is occasionally interrupted by the barman's cry of 'HURRY UP PLEASE ITS TIME'. On one level, of course, this is simply the barman shouting last orders, anxious for his customers to drink up and leave the premises. Yet there is also something unsettlingly apocalyptic about this repeated phrase as if time is running out for the characters in the poem and the society they inhabit.

LANGUAGE

Quotations and references

One of the most prominent stylistic features of 'A Game of Chess' is the number of allusions to the work of other writers it contains. The poem's title, for instance, refers to Women Beware Women a work by the seventeenth century playwright Thomas Middleton. In that play a young girl is raped while her mother is in the room downstairs, distracted by playing a game of chess. There are several references to Shakespeare's plays. The poem's opening line is a almost a direct quote form Antony and Cleopatra while its closing line comes from Hamlet.

Line 49, meanwhile, comes from *The Tempest.*

The poem also contains several references to ancient literature. One of the lady's paintings depicts the legend of Philomel while the word laquearia in line 16 recalls the mythical Queen Dido who featured in Virgil's epic poem, the *Aeneid*. Yet the poem also features a reference to popular song. The lines 'It's so elegant / So intelligent' come from 'That Shakespeherian Rag', a hit tune of 1912.

Sound effects

In lines 1–30 Eliot uses lavish and opulent language to capture the sumptuous decor of the lady's boudoir.

- Assonance is used to create a pleasant musical effect. We see this in line 9 with its repeated broad vowel sounds: 'From satin cases poured in rich profusion'. In this line, it has been suggested, we can almost 'hear' the richness of the jewellery.
- A similar effect is created by the repeated 'o', 'u' and 'i' sounds in line 'wrought by fruited vines' and the repeated 'i' sound in 'vials' of ivory'.
- The repeated 'a' sound in line 20, meanwhile, creates an undoubtedly pleasant yet strangely melancholic music: 'in which sad light a carvèd dolphin swam'.
- The repeated 'i' sound in 'inviolable voice' creates a pleasant musical effect suggesting the beauty of the nightingale's song
- Alliteration, too, features prominently throughout this section of the poem. We are presented with the repeated 's' sound in 'strange synthetic perfumes' and in 'sylvan scene'. Again this repetition generates a euphonious musical effect.
- He deploys an abundance of unusual polysyllabic words such as 'candelabra', unguent', 'laquearia', 'coffered' and 'sylvan'.

Eliot's extensive use of assonance and alliteration, combined with the profusion of rare and unusual words, gives the language in this section a rich, abundant quality in keeping with the luxurious sleeping quarters it describes. Yet there is something almost excessive about the use of language in this section. The writing seems cluttered with strange words and musical effects just as the lady's boudoir is cluttered with material goods. The richness of the language tends to leave the reader almost overwhelmed, just as the lady seems swamped by the perfumes and precious things that surround her.

A harsher more cacophonous verbal music is evident in lines 39–40. The phrase 'rats' alley' creates an unpleasant and cacophonous musical effect, generated by its repeated 'a' sound and the harshness of the 'ts' sound in 'rats'. The repeated broad vowel sounds in 'Where the dead men lost their bones', meanwhile, slow the pace of the verse, creating a sad and haunting musical effect.

Stylistic shifts

Another important feature of 'A Game of Chess' is the variety of styles it employs. As we have seen, the poem's opening section is extremely poetic, featuring a great deal of assonance, alliteration and rich, sumptuous imagery. The 'conversation' between the lady and her partner employs a more fragmentary and repetitive style. The jumpy, jagged sentences suggest the couples' disturbed and agitated mental states. The poem's conclusion involves another stylistic shift. The last forty lines are spoken by a woman who uses the everyday speech of the working classes complete with grammatical errors. (in line 85 she says 'them pills' instead of 'those pills'). Her words come across as genuinely conversational, as if we were overhearing her talking to her friends in the pub

THEMES

The failure of love and sexuality

There are two failed relationships in 'A Game of Chess'. The relationship between the wealthy lady and her partner seems on the verge of collapse. The emotional distance separating the couple has grown so large that the lady has no idea what's going on in her partner's head: 'I never know what you are thinking'. Communication between the two seems to have broken down completely. As the lady puts it: 'Why do you never speak to me?'

The man barely responds to his partner's anguished questions and cries for help. He makes no effort to comfort her, replying to her only in short harsh phrases ('Nothing again nothing') or in cryptic allusions to Shakespeare ('Those are pearls that were his eyes'). In fact, it has been suggested that the man is not speaking to his lover at all, that he responds to her only inside in his own head. (This is suggested by the fact that his words are not in quotation marks). What we are confronted with, then, is a portrayal of a failed relationship, one where the connections between the lovers have been completely severed.

Another relationship on the verge of collapse is that between Albert and Lil. Their marriage has come under strain because Albert no longer finds her attractive. Lil is only thirty one but has been prematurely aged by pills she took to terminate a pregnancy. No she has an aged or 'antique' appearance and Albert 'can't bear to look' at her. The woman in the bar suggests that Albert may leave Lil for someone more attractive: he wants a good time, /And if you don't give it him, there's others will'. The relationship between Albert and Lil, then, echoes that between the wealthy lady and her partner. Both are on the verge of falling apart. The poem seems to suggest that love and romance cannot survive in the modern world, irrespective of whether the lovers are from the higher social classes (the lady and her partner) or from the lower (Albert and Lil).

Several literary allusions echo this theme of failed love, referring to women who died after disastrous relationships:

- The opening line, for instance, is a slightly altered quotation from Shakespeare's Antony and Cleopatra. In that play Cleopatra ends up taking her own life after a disastrous affair with the Roman leader Mark Antony.
- The word 'laquearia' in line 16 recalls the story of Dido in The Aeneid, an epic poem by the Roman poet Virgil. Dido was the queen of Carthage who fell in love with the traveller Aeneas and took her own life when he abandoned her.
- The poem's last lines, in which the woman bids goodnight to her drinking companions, are also the last words spoken by Ophelia in Shakespeare's Hamlet, before she drowns herself in despair, driven mad by a failed romance.

In this poem, as in much of Eliot's writing sexuality is presented as something base and animalistic rather than as a gentle celebration of mutual affection. The relationship between the lady and her partner seems sexually barren. We get the impression that the lady's partner never speaks to her or stays with her much less sleeps with her. Eliot's negative view of sexuality is also evident in the gossiping woman's description of Lil and Albert's sex life: 'well if Albert won't leave you alone, there it is, I said'. The idea of Lil wanting Albert to 'leave her alone' presents sex almost as a kind of assault, as an act of war rather than an act of love.

Sexuality is depicted as having damaged Lil's health. Though she is only thirty one she has already been pregnant six times. She has nearly died in childbirth and has had an abortion that left her prematurely aged. This echoes the debased and perverted version of sexuality suggested by the painting of Philomel, who was brutally raped by her brother-in-law. The world of 'A Game of Chess', then, is one where all relationships have grown twisted and sour, where normal romance and healthy sexuality is impossible.

Mental suffering

The lady in' A Game of Chess' contains much mental suffering. The wealthy lady, in particular, is portrayed as a troubled soul. She seems trapped or confined in her claustrophobic room, hemmed in by the jewels that spill from their silk boxes, by the strange figures that seem to lean from her paintings and by the sinister scents of the perfumes that 'trouble' and 'confuse' her.

Her highly agitated mental state is evident in her jerky repetitive speech, in her paranoid reaction to the noise of the wind, and in her desire not be left alone. She seems on the verge of complete breakdown, threatening to run into the streets in what seems to be a state of undress. There is something despairing about her anguished question: 'What shall we do tomorrow? / What shall we ever do?'

We get the impression that the woman has driven to this almost frenzied state by the breakdown of her relationship with her partner. She seems desperate to connect with him, asking him to speak to he and stay with her. We get the impression that her partner's inability to connect with her has driven her to the edge of psychological destruction. She is associated with Dido, Cleopatra and Philomel, other women who were destroyed by the men closest to them.

Her partner is also in a distressed psychological state.

Like someone suffering from severe depression he is emotionally empty and spiritually hollow. The lady makes several references to this, asking him is 'Is there nothing in your head?' He is unable to respond in any meaningful way to his wife's emotional needs. All that remains in his barren, empty mind are scraps of plays that he has read ('Those are pearls that were his eyes') and of a popular song that he has heard ('It's so elegant / so intelligent').

The man's inner emotional life has been extinguished. He is 'dead on the inside', declaring he is in 'rats' alley where the dead men lost their bones'. The lady even asks him 'Are you alive or not?' It is unsurprising, therefore, that this man has bleak view of life, seemingly regarding it as an endless monotonous and deadening routine. We get the impression that he feels trapped and confined in this existence just as in lines 60–2 the couple are confined in a 'closed car'.

In many respects the lady's partner resembles Prufrock. Like Prufrock he is a psychologically troubled and emotionally stunted person who has difficulty communicating and connecting with other people. He shares Prufrock's tendency to respond to emotion with quotes from Shakespeare and literary references. Both he and Prufrock tend to view the world and their relationships through literature rather than in directly emotional terms.

Artificiality

'A Game of Chess' suggests that modern man has become detached from nature. We are cut off from the natural world by the urban living and the material possessions that surround us. We no longer live as nature intended. This point is made particularly strongly in the poem's opening twenty lines, where we see the lady almost swamped and suffocated by the material goods that surround her. A similar claustrophobia is evident when the man describes himself and his lady pressing their eyes against the windows of the 'closed car'. There is also something unnatural about the way Lil takes pills to bring her pregnancy to an premature conclusion.

The poem also suggests that we are cut from nature by the brings to ugliness, decay and squalor that characterises much of modern city life. We see this when the lady's partner declares that 'we are in rats' alley', a place of rats and corpses where even the bones of the dead decay. The filth and rot suggested by the image of 'rats' alley' recalls similar images of urban squalor in 'Prufrock' ('half-deserted streets,/The muttering retreats') and 'Preludes' ('The burnt out ends of smoky days'). The working class pub in section three could also be taken as an example of urban squalor. It resembles the 'muttering retreats' and 'sawdust restaurants' described in 'Prufrock'. In these locations nature seems a great distance away.

The decline of art and culture

Eliot was greatly concerned about the decline of art and culture. We see this when he refers to the paintings on the lady's walls as 'withered stumps of time'. These works, he says, are part of great artistic tradition that has 'withered'. The modern world, he believed, had lost interest in the great art of the past. People like the lady collect paintings the same way they collect jewellery and perfumes. They value the paintings as status symbols and decorations but not for their artistic merit.

The decline of civilisation is also suggested by the mention of the word 'Jug Jug' in lines 26–7. Once the expression 'Jug Jug' was associated with the beautiful song of the nightingale. (The seventeenth century poets, who Eliot loved, would represent the nightingale's song with this phrase). By Eliot's time, however, people were more likely to associate this expression with vulgar sexual connotations than with great poetry and the nightingale's sweet music. Our ears, Eliot suggests, have become 'dirty'. Where once we heard beauty now we hear vulgarity: 'Jug Jug' to dirty ears'.

A similar point is made in lines 49–54 where the man quotes both Shakespeare ('Those are pearls that were his eyes') and the chorus of a hit song called That Shakespeherian Rag'.

This hit of 1912 parodied several of Shakespeare's plays. Culture, the poem suggests, has fallen a long way. Where once we produced Shakespeare now we produce mindless popular songs like 'That Shakespeherian Rag'.

Journey of the Magi

BACKGROUND & INTRODUCTION

This poem is inspired by story of the Magi or 'three wise kings'. According to the Gospel of Matthew the Magi travelled to Bethlehem from their exotic eastern kingdoms to attend the Birth of Christ. In the poem one of the Magi speaks to us, telling the story of his trip to Bethlehem.

LINE BY LINE

LINES 1–20: *A difficult journey*

In the poem's first section the magus describes the various trials and tribulations he and his companions encountered as they travelled from their eastern homelands to the site of Christ's birth:

- The first difficulty described by the magus is that of the terrible weather. Jesus, of course, was born in the middle of December, the 'very dead of winter' as the magus puts it. According to the magus this is no time to set out on a long expedition to foreign lands. It is 'Just the worst time of year/For a journey, and such a long journey'. As the Magi travelled, then, they were forced to endure 'sharp' and bitter weather conditions: 'A cold coming we had of it'.
- The Magi's path was made harder still by the fact that they came across little friendliness or hospitality as they travelled. The towns they stayed in were 'unfriendly', the cities were downright 'hostile' and the villages were 'dirty' and charged too much for food and accommodation.
- Their journey was also made difficult by problems they experienced with their camels. The long trip took quite a toll on these beasts of burden, leaving them 'sore-footed' and disobedient ('refractory'). Eventually the camels became so stubborn that they would prefer to 'lie down in the melting snow' rather than carry their masters in the direction of Bethlehem.

The Magi also ran into problems with their servants, whose task it was to tend to and control the camels. These servants, it seems, became increasingly disenchanted with the difficult journey through cold, foreign lands: 'Then the camel men cursing and grumbling'. They were upset in particular by the lack of alcohol and women available on the long road to Bethlehem: 'and wanting their liquor and women'. Unsurprisingly, then, at least some of the servants ended up abandoning their masters' quest and 'running away'.

However, perhaps the greatest obstacle encountered by the Magi (greater even than refractory camels, grumbling servants and unfriendly foreigners) was that of their own doubts and uncertainties about the journey they were undertaking. There were occasions during their ordeal when these wise kings regretted leaving behind the luxury of their homes in the east, where, it seems, their every whim was catered to by beautiful women: 'There were times we regretted/ The summer palaces on slopes, the terraces, /And the silken girls bringing sherbet'.

As they journeyed to Bethlehem the Magi were troubled by the fear that their arduous voyage was a waste of time. Was it simply madness or foolishness ('folly') to abandon their comfortable lives and follow a star all the way to the kingdom of the Jews? What if their study of the stars had led them astray, and the saviour of the world was not, after all, about to be born in Bethlehem? To the Magi these doubts were like voices that sang in their ears as they travelled: 'voices singing in our ears, saying/That this was all folly'. The Magi, it seems, could not shake off the fear that their long, difficult trek might all be for nothing.

LINES 21–32: *Reaching the stable*

Eventually the Magi leave behind the harsh, inhospitable mountains and travel 'below the snow line' into the shelter of a mild or 'temperate'. In lines 23–9 the magus lists some of the sights he and his companions see as they crossed this temperate valley. They see a stream and a water-mill, an old white horse, a few trees, and a tavern with some men gambling outside.

Finally, the Magi find Joseph and Mary in the stable.

They arrive just in time: 'not a moment too soon / Finding the place'. (According to tradition the Magi arrive in the stable either just before the birth of Christ or just before the holy family flee Bethlehem to avoid King Herod's soldiers). The magus declares himself satisfied with his experience in the stable: 'It was, you may say, satisfactory'. Yet many detect a note of disappointment here, as if the magus' encounter with the infant Jesus didn't live up to the expectations he had for it. The magus seems to be suggesting that the nativity was 'fine' or 'okay' but not exactly incredible or overwhelming.

LINES 33–40: *Birth or death?*

The magus, now an old man, looks back on his trip to Bethlehem with decidedly mixed feelings. On one hand he is glad he made the journey and says that he would do it all over again if he had to: 'All this was a long time ago, I remember, /And I would do it again'. Yet on the other hand he seems confused and disturbed by what he witnessed in the stable, being unsure whether he witnessed a birth or a death: 'were we led all that way for/ Birth or Death?'

Prior to visiting Bethlehem the magus believed that death and birth were two separate things: 'I had seen birth and death, / But had thought they were different'. However, Christ's nativity seemed to combine birth and death in a single event:

- It is a birth in the obvious sense that Mary produced a son: 'There was a Birth, certainly,/ We had evidence and no doubt'.
- It is also a birth in that it signals the beginning of a new era for humanity, the 'birth' of a Christian epoch with an entirely new way of life.
- There is also a sense in which the Magi themselves are 'born again' through their encounter with the new-born Christ. They and their most important beliefs will presumably be altered profoundly by their experience in Bethlehem.

Yet according to the magus the nativity is associated with death and suffering as much as it is with the emergence of new life. As they attend the nativity the magus seems to get some sense of the Crucifixion, the 'Death' with a capitol *D* that will change humanity forever. It seems that in Bethlehem the magus had some inkling of the 'hard and bitter agony' Jesus would eventually undergo at Calvary.

The Magi found their experience in the stable somewhat unpleasant. It also signalled the 'death' of the Magi's old selves, for their lives and personalities will be transformed utterly by their experience of the newborn Christ. This transformation, the magus suggests, is frightening, difficult and painful: it was 'Hard and bitter agony for us, like ... our death'.

LINES 41–4: *Out of place in the old world*

The Magi leave Bethlehem and return to live in their own countries: 'We returned to our places, these Kingdoms'. The magus' countrymen are unaware of the great event that has taken place. They do not know that the birth of Jesus has signalled the beginning of a new 'dispensation' or way of life for the entire world. They continue to exist 'in the old dispensation', living a pagan way of life and 'clutching' their various Gods.

For this reason the magus feels like a stranger in his own land. Because of his experience in Bethlehem he no longer feels 'at peace' with this the 'old dispensation', with this old religion and way of life. His own people, their gods and their ways have all become 'alien' to them. In the poem's final line the magus seems to wish for death: 'I should be glad of another death'. Most critics detect a tone of weariness and resignation here, as if the magus is tired of his existence as a kind of misfit among his 'alien' people.

LANGUAGE

Dramatic monologue

Like many of Eliot's poems 'Journey of the Magi' is a dramatic monologue, a speech given by a literary or historical character. The monologue is wonderfully realistic in tone, with the magus describing the difficulties of reaching Bethlehem, such as terrible weather, grumpy camels, and unpleasant locals. The magus' uses phrases that could be form a normal conversation such as 'you may say'. His hesitant repetitions of the words 'birth and death' suggest that he is struggling to find the right language to express himself as we listen to him. A similar hesitancy is evident when he asks us to 'set down / This set down/ This'.

Symbolism

'Journey of the Magi' is rich in symbolism. This is particularly evident in lines 21–9. On one level these lines list random sights and sounds the Magi happened to encounter as they came ever nearer to the famous stable. On another level, however, it is each of the sights mentioned by the magus serves as a symbol for the sacrifice by which Christ redeemed mankind:

- The 'three trees on the low sky', for example, put us in mind of the three crosses at Calvary, where Christ was crucified along with two thieves.
- The mention of 'six hands' reminds of the hands of Christ and the two thieves, into which the Roman executioners drove their nails.
- The men playing dice outside the tavern, meanwhile, recalls the Roman guards who gambled for Christ's clothes after he had perished on the cross.
- The fact that men are gambling for 'pieces of silver' also reminds us of crucifixion, recalling Judas who betrayed Christ for thirty pieces of silver.
- The mention of wine-skins and the stream recalls the water and wine involved in the mystery of the mass.
- he 'old white horse [that] galloped away in the meadow' is associated with Christ. For in chapters six and nineteen of the Book of Revelations Christ the conqueror is depicted as riding to victory on a white horse.

Quotation

Like many of Eliot's poems 'Journey of the Magi' makes extensive use of material originally written by other writers. The poems opening five lines are an almost direct quotation from a sermon given on Christmas day 1622 by a Bishop called Lancelot Andrews. Andrews' sermons were a great source of inspiration for Eliot as he contemplated converting to the Anglo-Catholic faith and here he highlights his admiration for Andrews' words by incorporating some of them into his poem.

THEMES

Alienation and Depression

Like many of Eliot's poems 'Journey of the Magi' deals with a depressed and alienated figure. The magus is fundamentally changed by his visit to Bethlehem the magus feels out of place in his own kingdom after his return. He can no longer feel 'at peace' in his own country and his own people have become 'alien' to him. The world weary tone in the poem's final lines suggest the depression this has caused the magus. He seems tired of life and wishes to leave this troubled world behind.

The difficulty for the magus is that after his experience in Bethlehem he does not 'fit in' anywhere. Having encountered the one through God in Bethlehem the magus cannot continue to follow the pagan religion of his homeland. Yet he cannot really become a Christian either as Jesus has not yet begun to preach his message and Christianity has not yet been founded. His experience in Bethlehem has made the magus an outsider, someone who can find nowhere to properly belong.

This kind of alienation is also evident in 'Prufrock' where the speaker presents himself as a troubled figure who feels at home neither in the upper class not the lower class echelons of society. A alienation is expressed by the speaker of 'Preludes', with its imagery of squalor and despair. 'A Game of Chess', too, depicts psychological distress, with the woman declaring that 'My nerves are bad tonight' and her partner declaring that 'we are in rats' alley / Where the dead men lost their bones'. 'Journey of the Magi', in its own way, is as dark as any of these pieces, depicting as it does the quiet desperation of an alienated and out-of-place old man as he waits impatiently for death.

A bleak view of Christianity

Like many of Eliot's poems 'Journey of the Magi' presents a bleak view of Christianity. Superficially the poem seems to deal with the joyous event of Christ's birth. In reality, however, the poem is haunted by the pain and horror of the Crucifixion. The sights and sounds encountered by the Magi on their way through the temperate valley symbolise aspects of the infant Jesus' eventual and terrible destiny. When they reach the place of Christ's 'Birth' the Magi are filled with premonitions of his suffering and 'Death' at Calvary: 'this Birth / Was hard and bitter agony for us, like Death'.

The magus seems fairly unimpressed by his encounter with the baby Jesus declaring it merely 'satisfactory'.

What really matters is not the birth of this child but the 'hard and bitter agony' that awaits him at the Crucifixion. Like 'East Coker' and many of Eliot's other religious poems 'Journey of the Magi' focuses on the suffering and humiliation undergone by Jesus in order to redeem humanity rather than on more joyous aspects of religious faith.

The poem presents personal salvation as something that involves much sacrifice and suffering. This is symbolised by the hardships endured by the Magi on their journey to Bethlehem

To be saved through Christ each person must undergo a process of transformation that is challenging, difficult and painful, that is 'Hard and bitter agony'. The process is like a 'death' because many aspects of our self must be destroyed or cast aside. Being a Christian can also leave one feeling out of place in the modern world, just as the Magi are left isolated and alienated in their own kingdoms.

An allegory of faith

'Journey of the Magi' operates on what is known as an 'allegorical' level. The poem, it is important to note, was written in 1927, the year Eliot converted to the Anglo-Catholic faith. The Magi's journey to Bethlehem becomes a powerful metaphor for the spiritual voyage undertaken by Eliot, as he underwent the processes of conversion to the Anglo-Catholic faith. The difficulties met by the Magi serve as metaphors for the mental and spiritual obstacles Eliot was forced to overcome as he endeavoured to put his faith in Christianity and the teachings of the church:

- Few of Eliot's friends or acquaintances understood his involvement with Anglo-Catholicism. The negative attitude of Eliot's friends and family toward his conversion is represented by the unfriendly towns and cities the Magi travel through. Just as the Magi encountered hostility on their journey toward Bethlehem so Eliot was forced to contend with the hostile, unsympathetic attitude of those close to him as he made his own journey toward Christ.
- The stubborn, disobedient camels that plagued the Magi on their passage through the mountains can also be interpreted as serving a metaphorical function. These beasts of burden represent the unpleasant, animalistic aspect of the poet's personality, the part of him that would have to be controlled if he was to complete his journey toward Christ.
- The 'camel men' serve as another metaphor for the poet's darker side. With their demands for women and alcohol they represent the sexual side of his nature as well as his interest in physical pleasure and the things of this world. Just as the Magi had to manage and direct their camels and the camel men in order to reach Bethlehem, so Eliot must control and suppress the sinful, animalistic aspect of his nature before he can complete his spiritual journey toward Christ.
- Like the Magi on the road to Bethlehem, Eliot was haunted by doubts and uncertainties as he prepared to embrace the Anglo-Catholic faith. What if God did not really exist? What if the teachings of the Anglo-Catholic Church were nothing but a tapestry of illusions? By converting to this faith was he making a terrible mistake? Like the Magi, then, he heard the voices of doubt 'singing' in his ears, whispering that his decision to put his faith in Christ was nothing more than 'folly'.

It has also been suggested that the magus' mixed feelings about his encounter with Christ reflects Eliot's own mixed feelings about his religious conversion. Perhaps Eliot is suggesting that his acceptance into the Church did not change his life and personality as quickly and as completely as he might have hoped. Perhaps, like the magus' encounter with Jesus, it was only 'satisfactory'. The magus associates Christ's birth with 'death' and 'pain'. It could be argued that this reflects own fear and anxiety at the great change his life was about to undergo. In the process of baptism his old self would 'die' or disappear as he was reborn through Christ.

Usk

LINE BY LINE

History

This poem was inspired by the Usk region in Wales, which Eliot visited in 1935. Eliot describes Usk as a place of gently rolling hills: 'Where the roads dip and the where the roads rise'.

Two features of Usk's past are important to the poem. Firstly, it was associated with the semi-legendary figure of King Arthur. Secondly it was the site of a holy well associated with a saint who lived a hermit like existence nearby. In medieval times people would make pilgrimages to this sacred well.

The absence of enchantment

Eliot mentions three features of Arthurian legend: a white stag or 'hart', lances and enchantments. White stags appear in several of Arthur's adventures, while lances were the long spears used by him and his knights of the round table. Enchantments, too, are a regular feature of these tales, with many spells being cast by the great wizard Merlin and by other mystical types.

Legend has it that these things were once features of the Usk landscape, as the knights of the round table roamed through it on various quests. Nowadays, however, there are no harts to be found in Usk: 'Do not ... Hope to find / The white hart'. Nor should visitors to Usk expect to see knights riding around with lances: 'Glance aside, not for lance'. Usk, Eliot claims, may once have been filled with 'old enchantments' and 'spells' but that magic is 'sleeping' now: 'do not spell /Old enchantments. Let them sleep'. Merlin, Arthur and his knights are long gone, if they ever really existed.

A focus on spirituality

Eliot says we should ignore the Arthurian aspects of Usk's past and instead focus on its history as a place of pilgrimage. We should meditate on the holy 'white well' that was once a sacred site. Our minds should 'seek' thoughts of the hermit who lived in a tiny chapel nearby and the thousands of pilgrims who visited the well in mediaeval times: 'Seek only there ... The hermit's chapel, the pilgrim's prayer'. If we meditate on these aspects of Usk's history the landscape will bring us closer to God. It will 'lift' our mind's eye toward Him.

LANGUAGE

Rhyme

'Usk' does not have a strict thyme scheme but it does feature a number of full end rhymes; for example 'well' with 'spell' and 'there' with 'air' and 'prayer'.

Structure

The structure of 'Usk' is perfectly symmetrical. There are five lines that deal with the landscape's Arthurian past and five that deal with its Christian past. Between these two sets of five lines there is a single line from the sixteenth century poet George Peele: 'Gently dip, but not too deep'.

As we have seen, Eliot wants us to forget about Usk's association with King Arthur and instead and focus on its Christian past. Yet it is impossible to ignore these myths and legends completely. Therefore Eliot urges us to 'Gently dip, but not too deep' into the well of Arthurian tales associated with Usk. We can remain 'Gently' aware of the landscape's associations with the round table but we must not be too deeply influenced by them.

THEMES

Landscape and Memory

'Usk' like 'Rannoch, by Glencoe' comes from a series of short poems that Eliot called 'Landscapes'. An important theme of these poems is the way a landscape's past influences the way we see it in the present. In 'Rannoch, by Glencoe' the speaker sees this Scottish highland valley as being haunted by a terrible massacre that took place there in 1692. In 'Usk' the speaker declares that our perception of this Welsh landscape can be effected by both its ancient association with King Arthur and by its history as a mediaeval place of pilgrimage.

Eliot's view of Christianity

In many of his poem's Eliot presents a rather bleak view of Christianity. He tends to emphasise the suffering, effort and sacrifice involved in attaining salvation rather than the joys and comfort of faith. We see this in 'Journey of the Magi' and especially in the extract from 'East Coker'. In 'Usk', too, Christianity is associated with sacrifice, with the hermit's life of self-denial and the pilgrim's arduous journey to a holy well.

Eliot implies that we must be like the hermit and deny ourselves certain worldly pleasures if are to become closer to God. We must follow the example of the pilgrims who followed Usk's dipping and rising roads on their way to the holy well. We, too, must make a pilgrimage of our own. It is often suggested that what Eliot has in mind here is more an 'inner' spiritual journey than an physical trek. This is stressed by the fact that the goal of our pilgrimage is a place 'Where the grey light meets the green air'. This is not any physical location but an inner state, a state where we have opened ourselves fully to God's love. (One critic has suggested that the 'grey light' represents the holy spirit descending on the 'green air' of the soul).

If we meditate on the Usk landscape it will lift our eyes toward God and remind us of the sacrifices we must make and the inner pilgrimage we must undertake in order to achieve salvation and become closer to Him. It must be said, however, that 'Usk' is distinctly lighter in tone than Eliot's other religious poems. While it emphasises the self sacrifice necessary to achieve salvation it doesn't have the same focus on blood sweat and tears that we see in 'East Coker' or on the 'death' and 'agony' that we see in 'Journey of the Magi'.

Rannoch, by Glencoe

LINE BY LINE

This poem, like 'Usk', comes from a sequence entitled 'Landscapes'. It describes the landscape of Rannoch, which is in the Scottish Highlands. This area of the Highlands has had a dark past. Glencoe, near Rannoch, was the site of a particularly bloody massacre in 1692. Thirty seven members of the Clan MacDonald were surprised and slaughtered in their beds by forces loyal to the new British monarch, William of Orange. (The Catholic Macdonalds were opposed to King William). Dozens of MacDonald women and children died after their homes were burned.

According to Eliot this terrible deed still haunts Rannoch. It seems to him that this 'confused wrong' from the seventeenth century has poisoned the valley where it took place, draining the very energy or life-force from the landscape:

- The road that leads through Rannoch is described in terms of 'listlessness' and 'languor. (To be 'listless' or 'languorous' is to lack all sense of energy or purpose). The road 'winds' aimlessly through the landscape.
- The 'substance' which makes up this landscape (the rocks, stones and trees) is decaying or crumbling into nothingness: 'Substance crumbles'.
- The landscape seems to be collapsing or shrinking before our very eyes, with the earth and sky being squeezed closer and closer together. There is hardly any space for stags to leap in or for crows to fly through: 'Between the soft moor / And the soft sky, scarcely room / To leap or soar'. These lines create an atmosphere of cramped claustrophobia, as the landscape closes in around the creatures that inhabit it.

The 'broken steel' of the 'ancient war' between Campbells and MacDonalds has brought this 'languor' and 'listlessness' to Rannoch: 'The road winds in / Listlessness of ancient war, / languor of broken steel'. It is a place of silence, as if out of respect for those massacred there so long ago. Such silence, Eliot suggests, is entirely 'apt' or appropriate: 'apt in silence'.

Rannoch is described as a rich hunting ground for deer-hunters, where there are many stags to be shot: 'here the patient stag / Breeds for the rifle'. Eliot depicts it as a kind of 'game-reserve', a place where stags seem to be bred specially for the hunting season and wait patiently for humans to come along and shoot them. Crows normally feast on the carcasses of dead stags. This is not possible, however, when the stags are killed by hunters. The hunters take the stags' bodies home with them, leaving the crows to starve: 'Here the crow starves'

Three hundred years ago the Macdonalds were crushed in defeat, their 'Pride' was 'snapped'. Yet Eliot suggests that their spirits have not found peace. Their bones still litter the 'long pass' of the Rannoch valley and their 'memory' haunts the landscape like a ghost: 'Memory is strong / Beyond the bone'. The bones of the Macdonalds cannot 'concur' or accept the fate history chose for them: 'No concurrence of bone'. Their spirits long to restore the pride of their clan, to avenge the humiliating slaughter of 1692: 'Shadow of pride is long'.

LANGUAGE

Cacophony

In this poem Eliot makes extensive use of cacophony to convey the nightmarish quality of the Rannoch landscape and the horror of the massacre that took place there in 1692. We see this in the opening line, for instance, where the combination of hard consonants creates a harsh, almost unpleasant, musical effect. Cacophony is also present in line 8, with its combination of hard 'c' and 't' sounds: 'Clamour of confused wrong, apt'. A similar effect is created by the combination of plosives ('b', 'p', and 'd' sounds) in line 10: 'Beyond the bone. Pride snapped'. This cacophonous music suggests the atmosphere of dread and foreboding that casts its shadow over the Rannoch landscape.

An interesting feature of the poem is the way the sentence describing the road is spread over five lines (lines 5–9). The sentence seems to wind down the page, as if it is mimicking the meandering path of the road it describes. Just as it takes a long time to follow this listlessly winding road out of the valley, so it takes a long time to get through this sentence. Its repeated long vowel sounds and combinations of harsh consonants slow the pace at which we read it.

THEMES

Landscape and Memory

Eliot's series of landscape poems often show how historical events can haunt the landscape they occurred in. In this instance the massacre of 1692 is depicted as having somehow 'poisoned' or 'corrupted' the Rannoch valley. Like the bones of the Macdonalds this ancient 'confused wrong' has permeated the very soil of Rannoch, draining its energy and turning it into a 'listless' landscape of decay.

Eliot seems to imply that the spirits of the Macdonalds, like their bones, still linger in the valley. Their desire to restore their family's shattered pride is a kind of shadow darkening the landscape: 'Shadow of pride is long'. Yet this line also suggests that the dead Macdonalds' desire for vengeance will endure for a for a 'long' time to come. The grievances and anger of these bones will live on forever, haunting the Rannoch landscape.

The horror and confusion of war

The adjective 'confused' and the noun 'clamour' (meaning) bring to mind the chaos and horror of that long ago morning when so many Macdonalds died. The massacre, Eliot claims, was a 'confused wrong'. On one hand this event was clearly a 'wrong', an evil deed carried out against defenceless men. women and children. It is also possible that the word 'confused' illustrates Eliot's awareness of how difficult it is to make sense of the past and to judge the actions of historical characters. It is impossible for us, hundreds of years in the future, to fully grasp the complicated and bitter conflict of which this atrocity was a part. We may condemn the Glencoe massacre as a terrible 'wrong', but our judgement will always remain a little 'confused', clouded and uncertain.

East Coker IV

LINE BY LINE

LINES 1–5

The first stanza describes a surgeon, who is wounded and bleeding, operating on a body. He skilfully uses the scalpel ('plies the steel') to investigate the diseased, or 'distempered', part of the patient. The surgeon's hands are bleeding as he conducts the operation.

The surgeon is described as compassionate and gifted. His work is considered an 'art'. The work that the surgeon must do is complicated. The patient's 'fever chart' is considered an 'enigma' that the surgeon must resolve.

LINES 6–10

In the second stanza that poet presents us with a paradox. He says that the 'only health' we possess is 'the disease'. He does not say what the 'disease' is, only that if we want to be 'restored, our sickness must grow worse'. The poet says that this will happen if we 'obey the dying nurse'.

This 'nurse' is constantly caring for the sick. However, she does not look to mollify them or to make them comfortable. Instead, her role is to remind us of the fact that we are born with original sin and are mortal beings: 'to remind of our, and Adam's curse'. She is also the person who reminds us of our paradoxical situation, that to get better 'our sickness must grow worse'.

LINES 11–15

The poet describes the 'earth' as a 'hospital'. This 'hospital' is provided for by the 'ruined millionaire', another paradox. The unusual thing about this 'hospital' is that it does not look to save the lives of us, its patients. To 'do well' in this 'hospital' is to 'Die' of the care that is provided.

The care in this 'hospital' is fatherly, or 'paternal', and it is 'absolute', meaning that it is complete and unconditional. Again the care is described as being constant – it 'will not leave us'. It does, however, gravely restrict our freedom by hindering us everywhere: 'prevents us everywhere'.

LINES 16–20

In the fourth stanza the poet describes the effects of the disease. He describes how a 'chill' moves upwards from the 'feet' to the 'knees'. The 'fever' brings about some ecstatic feeling in the brain: 'The fever sings in mental wires'.

The poet says that if he is to be 'warmed' he must 'freeze' in 'frigid purgatorial fires'. Yet again the notion is paradoxical:

- The poet says that he can only be 'warmed' by freezing.
- He will 'freeze' as a result of immersing himself in fire.
- The fire is described as 'frigid', or cold.

These 'frigid' fires are rendered stranger still in the last line of the stanza. The flames are 'roses' and the 'smoke is briars'.

LINES 21–5

The final stanza is no more pleasant, comforting, or easily comprehensible than the first four. Eliot tells us that our only source of nourishment in this earthly 'hospital' is 'dripping blood' and 'bloody flesh'. He says that despite this fact we still 'like to think' that we are 'sound, substantial flesh and blood'.

The final line of the poem makes a reference to Good Friday. The poet picks up on the fact that we refer to the day on which Christ was nailed to a cross as 'good'. And we do this, the poet says, 'in spite of' the fact that our only nourishment is 'dripping blood' and 'bloody flesh'.

THEMES

The poem can be read as an extended metaphor, or conceit, in which Eliot takes the idea of a hospital, of illness and treatment, and uses it to express a religious interpretation of what he felt to be the solution to life. In this reading of the poem the 'wounded surgeon' is Christ, the 'dying nurse' is the Church, and the 'ruined millionaire' is Adam.

Christ as surgeon

It is likely that Eliot meant the 'wounded surgeon' to represent Jesus Christ. Christ, the Son of God, was crucified, or nailed to a cross. It is said that he died for our sins in order that our souls might be saved. His hands are 'bleeding' because of the wounds inflicted by the nails. Eliot sees Christ as a compassionate 'healer', someone who cares deeply about us. But the picture we are given of Christ and his work is unsettling. He works with a scalpel and his 'compassion' is said to be 'sharp'. The fact that he operates with 'bleeding hands' is particularly gory.

The Church as 'dying nurse'

Perhaps Eliot meant the 'dying nurse' to represent the Church. It is the Church's role to spread the Word of God and remind us of the fact that we are mortal sinners whose souls need to be saved. Eliot says that the Church is not there to 'please' us and tell us everything is fine and dandy. Rather, its role is to remind us of 'Adam's curse', which is also our 'curse'. Adam, the first man created by God, was originally placed in the Garden of Eden and promised eternal life as long as he obeyed God. When he disobeyed God by eating the fruit of knowledge, he was banished from the Garden and sent to live, labour, and suffer on Earth where he became mortal. We have inherited Adam's curse.

Human imperfection

We need to realise that, for Eliot, the human condition is one of imperfection. According to the poem every human being is sick with the 'disease' of sin. We are born with our souls already tainted by Original Sin. This is something that we have inherited from Adam, the original sinner. When Eliot speaks of the 'distempered part' he is referring to our souls, which are infected with sin.

Earthly suffering

Earth, therefore, ceases to be a place in which we can create perfect happiness and becomes 'our hospital'. We are born sick with sin. Earth is a place of atonement. It is a place where we can allow the love of God to enter our lives, feel the 'sharp compassion of the healer's art'.

The 'hospital' is the place that Adam 'Endowed' to us when he ate the forbidden fruit. He is the 'ruined millionaire'. Perhaps he is this because he had everything and lost it. His actions meant that we are born with a soul tainted with sin. But he also gave us the hospital in which we can achieve atonement for our sins. Life is an opportunity to find our way back to God. But we need to 'do well'. We need to understand our sins and suffer for them in order to become pure. If we do this we will die 'of the absolute paternal care'.

We need to give ourselves over to that which is greater than us. We must put our faith in God, in his 'absolute paternal care'. For this 'will not leave us' if we do so. Rather, it 'prevents us everywhere'. 'Prevents' is used in the seventeenth-century sense that still exists in prayer books. It means to go before with spiritual guidance, or to predispose to repentance, faith, and good works. So God, if we give ourselves over to him, will guide us in life.

A bleak view of Christianity

Ultimately the poem is Eliot's interpretation of Christianity. It is a bleak view. Eliot focuses primarily on the Crucifixion, on the suffering of Christ. He considers that we are all sick with sin and in need of purification. He suggests that we need to suffer in life for our sins. This is the only way that we can hope to be saved.

Eliot is preoccupied with illness and death. Those who feature in the poem are 'wounded', 'ruined' or 'dying'. Earth is considered a 'hospital'. Life is a process of redemption, of painful repentance, in preparation for the afterlife. As such, Eliot suggests that we do not look for pleasure in this world. We should focus on the purification of the soul.

William James pointed out how each temperament makes religion according to its needs. Eliot's temperament craved an exacting moral code. He said that he must have chastity, austerity, humility, and sanctity in his life or he would perish. And so he was drawn by martyrdom and feats of asceticism more than by Christ's message of compassion and neighbourliness. The notion of Original Sin was particularly important to him. He did not agree with the modern attitude that rejects the idea of Original Sin and believes that man is bad only insofar as society makes him that way. For Eliot it was the opposite. He felt the devil not so much in social wrongs, but within, and believed that the chief purpose of civilisation was to cope with the notion of Original Sin.

ELIOT AT A GLANCE

PSYCHOLOGICAL SUFFERING

- 'The Love Song of J. Alfred Prufrock' gives us an insight into the mind of a man who is psychologically vulnerable and has difficulty communicating.
- In 'Preludes' we are presented with an individual who cannot sleep and lies awake thinking about the 'thousand sordid images' that constitute her life.
- In 'A Game of Chess' Eliot describes a set of relationships that are on the verge of collapse. We are presented with a character who is mentally and spiritually 'dead' and a woman who is on the verge of a mental breakdown.
- 'Journey of the Magi' also presents us with an alienated and troubled figure. Once the Magus returns to his own land, he no longer feels at peace and longs to die.

RELIGION

- In 'Preludes' Eliot sets up the possibility of a benevolent God existing behind the grimness of life, but then dismisses this notion as ridiculous.
- 'Journey of the Magi' depicts a spiritual journey in which the poet deals with the doubts and difficulties that each of us must face on our journey towards God.
- 'Usk' also suggests that we must each undertake a pilgrimage to find God, an inner journey that will lead us to God's grace.
- In 'East Coker' Eliot suggests that religious salvation comes through the suffering of Jesus on the cross and though our own suffering during life.

A GRIM VIEW OF THE MODERN WORLD

- 'Aunt Helen' highlights the materialism and the superficiality that occupy many of us in the modern world.
- 'A Game of Chess' presents a similar view, depicting a wealthy woman almost swamped and overwhelmed by the possessions that surround her.
- 'A Game of Chess' also suggests that the modern world has lost faith and interest in art and culture. All that remains of this great tradition are 'withered stumps of time'.
- 'Preludes' depicts the modern urban world as squalid and dirty. The inhabitants of the city go through their daily routines without hope.

PATRICK KAVANAGH

THEMES

BEING A POET

Being a poet is a small rural town where everybody minds everybody else's business was never going to be easy. Any activity that was contrary to what was considered 'normal' was ripe for disparagement and derision by the locals. As a young man Kavanagh was sensitive to this fact and we witness some of this self-consciousness in his early poems. He is quite aware that his writing poetry sets him apart in the community, renders him something of an outsider. In 'Inniskeen Road' the poet tells us that he has 'what every poet hates in spite/ Of all the solemn talk of contemplation'. This is the 'plight' of being a poet, something he half rues in the poem. Being a poet is a solitary and often lonely occupation and means that he is excluded by the 'language of delight' of the other young men as they travel to the dances.

Being a poet is also an unprofitable occupation. In 'Shancoduff' Kavanagh is mocked by the local 'cattle-drovers' who look upon his land with pity and conclude that if the owner is a poet then 'by heavens he must be poor'. Those who surround him are incapable of understanding the point of poetry.

If the locals are incapable of discovering anything worthy in the poet, Kavanagh had no difficulty finding valuable poetic material in their midst. Kavanagh displayed a unique talent for rendering the ordinary and the 'banal' important and fantastic. He never suppressed his rural roots in favour of writing about lofty idealistic matters or by favouring some 'heroic' past over the everyday present. This is particularly evident in 'Epic', where Kavanagh agonises over the suitability of life in rural Monaghan as material for great poetry. He is on the verge of losing his faith in these townlands as a source of inspiration when, encouraged by the whisperings of Homer's ghost, he declares that it is the poet him or her self who decides which experiences provide suitable subject matter for poetry. Kavanagh decides to follow the example of Homer and the other great poets, these 'Gods' of literature who can make any experience important by transforming it in their verse. As he puts it: 'Gods make their own importance'.

CHILDHOOD AND ADULTHOOD

Many of Kavanagh's poems are written in praise of childhood, specifically the sense of wonder we enjoyed as children that could make even the most everyday things seem extraordinary. To a child even a 'green stone lying sideways in a ditch' or 'the tedious talking/ Of an old fool' could be a thing of wonder. As we grow older, however, this sense of wonder tends to disappear. As we age each of us develops a more sophisticated consciousness and greater awareness of the world around us. They more we learn about life and the more we experience of the world, the less likely we are to be mesmerised by the 'spirit-shocking/ Wonder in a black slanting Ulster hill'.

Many of Kavanagh's poems, then, are marked by a deep suspicion of the knowledge and experience that comes with adulthood. Too much of this adult 'knowledge' and experience, he feels, can be a dangerous thing. Kavanagh is suspicious of adulthood because it involves losing the sense of 'newness' the world had for us as children. Everything, as we grow older, becomes 'stale': 'the newness that was in every stale thing/ When we looked at it as children'. In both 'A Christmas Childhood' and 'Advent' the move from childhood to adulthood is presented in terms of the myth of the garden of Eden. In 'A Christmas Childhood' the world's knowledge and experience tempt the speaker just as Eve tempted Adam with the apple: 'O you, Eve, were the world that tempted me'. By 'tasting' this knowledge he has left behind forever 'the gay/ Garden that was childhood's'. He has lost his sense of childlike wonder. In 'Advent', too, the speaker is tempted by experience in terms reminiscent of Adam's theft of the fruit from the tree of knowledge: 'The knowledge we stole but could not use'. Once again, by 'tasting' this knowledge the speaker has lost his sense of wonder: 'We have tested and tasted too much, lover-/ Through a chink too wide there comes in no wonder'.

In both 'Advent' and 'A Christmas Childhood' Kavanagh makes elaborate attempts to regain the childhood innocence we lose when by assuming the mantle of adulthood, to 'charm back the luxury/Of a child's soul'. In 'A Christmas Childhood' the speaker reclaims this innocence by painstakingly recreating his childhood world in the form of a poem. By bringing his sixth Christmas morning vividly to life the speaker can momentarily re-enter childhood's gay garden. In 'Advent' the speaker proposes to regain his childhood innocence by undergoing a process of penance similar to that undertaken by Christians during Lent and Advent: 'the dry black bread and sugarless tea/ Of penance'. Through this program of self-denial he will cast off the knowledge, experience, and sophisticated consciousness that come with adulthood, just as penance purges a Christian's soul of sin, and regain the innocence of childhood.

Both poems, it is important to note, associate the reclaiming of childhood innocence with Christ and Christmas. In 'A Christmas Childhood' the speaker reconstructs a Christmas memory that is explicitly intermingled with Christ's birth two thousand years before. In 'Advent', meanwhile, the program of self-denial that cleanses the speaker of experience takes place in the run-up to Christmas. Christmas itself, then, heralds the speaker's reclamation of childhood innocence. Both poems, then, present the relationship between childhood and adulthood in religious terms. Childhood innocence is associated with Christ, Christmas and, in 'A Christmas Childhood', with the Virgin Mary. Adult knowledge and experience, on the other hand, are associated with sin, theft, and transgression. The process of regaining lost innocence is associated with practices designed to cleanse the soul of sin. We might question, however, Kavanagh's extremely negative attitude toward adult consciousness and awareness. Is he correct to associate the experiences and learning that come from growing up with sin, and in his desire to throw this knowledge 'into the dustbin'? Is it (or is it not) a little peculiar for a grown man to long so much for the carefree wonder of his childhood days?

The final three sonnets on the course provide a different approach to the issue of innocence and wonder. In 'The Hospital', for instance, the speaker responds to the ordinary with wonder yet makes no mention of the evil of experience or of his desire to return to childhood. The hospital is banal, even ugly, 'an art lover's woe'. To the speaker, however, it seems extraordinary. Even its gravel yard is a source of 'inexhaustible adventure'. In this poem, however, it is not childhood innocence but 'love' that makes the everyday seem extraordinary. The speaker feels such an intense uncomplicated love for the world that even its most 'common and banal' features are things of beauty. As Kavanagh memorably puts it: 'nothing whatever is by love debarred'.

A similar 'love' operates in 'Lines Written on a Seat on the Grand Canal, Dublin'. Here, as in 'The Hospital', an ordinary place is transformed. The light becomes 'fantastic', the silence is 'tremendous' and the banks themselves are presented as 'Parnassian Islands'. 'Canal Bank Walk', too, praises 'the habitual, the banal'. The speaker celebrates the ordinary beauty of the canal; the breeze, the kissing couple, the 'bright' stick. (The fact that a mere stick is described as 'bright' indicates that even the most unremarkable things appear marvellous to the speaker).

In these sonnets, then, Kavanagh seems to have finally regained the state of wonder he enjoyed as a child, the passing of which he had lamented so much. The ordinary fills him with joy and awe, just as it did 'before he grew'. It is important to note, however, that in the later sonnets there is no mention of turning his back on adulthood and the experience and knowledge that comes with it. The speaker, it seems, has no desire in these poems to throw into 'the dust-bin the clay-minted wages/ Of pleasure, knowledge and the conscious hour'. In 'The Hospital' and the canal bank sonnets awe and wonder seem compatible with adult consciousness and the speaker expresses no desire to regress to a state of childhood innocence.

BARREN LIVES

Kavanagh was also capable of stepping back from the details, the 'heart-breaking strangeness in dreeping hedges', and witness the heartbreaking social reality of the countryside he was so familiar with. In 'The

Great Hunger' Kavanagh takes a more philosophical and objective look at small-farm life. Whereas in 'Advent' he spoke of the 'wonder' to be found 'among the simple decent men./ Who barrow dung', in 'The Great Hunger' Kavanagh disrupts the idealisation of small-farm labourers. Too often romanticised in literature and by politicians of the time, the Irish farmer is exposed as a man of often spiritual and sexual starvation, someone who must continually defer what he most deeply desires. The farmer is depicted as a victim of the accepted social practice of inheritance where the oldest son must await his mother's death before he can inherit the land and so take a wife. The poem seeks to answer why so many once young and passionate men end up as lonely, frustrated, childless bachelors with 'no hope' left and 'no lust'.

'The Great Hunger' also expresses Kavanagh's belief that sexuality was a natural part of everyday life, and not, as the church would have it something to be associated with sin and shame. To Kavanagh Irish society's denial of sexuality was an 'anti-life heresy', something that caused the unhappiness of thousands of men and women in the Irish countryside. 'The Great Hunger' laments the frustration and misery of the men who were denied any opportunity to explore their sexuality, who were forced, by the Church and by society to deny themselves any expression of their sexual desires and 'make a field their bride'. A more mature society, he felt, would recognise that the 'fire' of sexual longing, however grotesque it might appear to the clergymen, was part of life, a gift given to us by God: 'God's truth his life-even in the grotesque shapes of its foulest fire'.

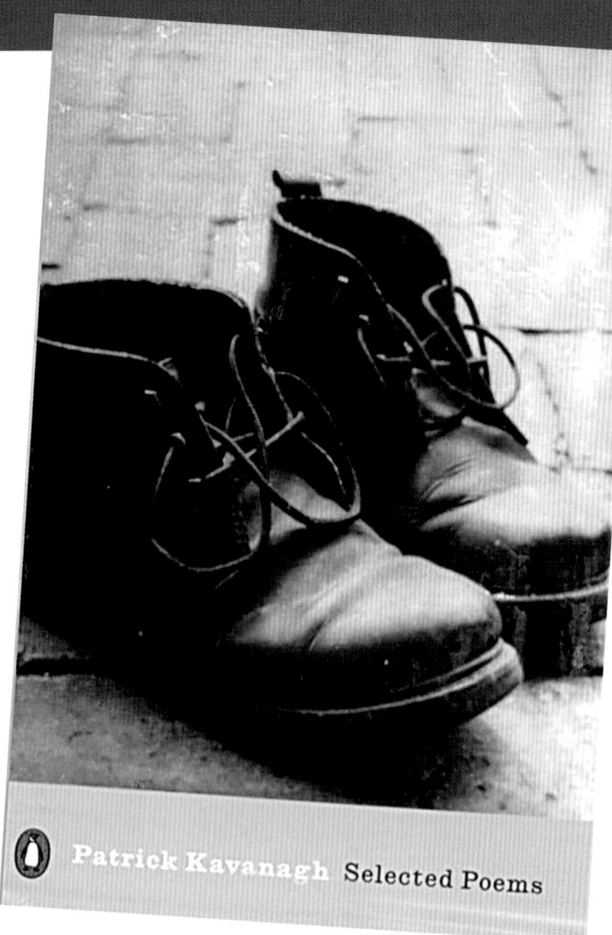

Inniskeen Road: July Evening

LINE BY LINE

LINES 1–4

The first four lines describe groups of people heading to a dance in Inniskeen. The dance is taking place in a local farmer's barn: 'There's a dance in Billy Brennan's barn tonight'. Many people are cycling to the dance and they cycle together is twos and threes: 'The bicycles go by in twos and threes'.

The way that those travelling to the dance interact and speak to one another reflects their excitement. They use words and phrases that hint at the sexual possibilities of the night: 'there's the half-talk code of mysteries'. They nudge one another and wink knowingly as they think about what might take place at the dance: 'the wink-and-elbow language of delight'.

LINES 5–8

The fifth line brings us on to 'Half-past eight' in the evening. Inniskeen road is quiet and deserted now: 'there is not a spot/ Upon a mile of road'. The shadows that appear along the road no longer turn out to be the shadows of people heading to the dance: 'no shadow thrown/ That might turn out a man or woman'. There is only silence now: 'not/ A footfall tapping secrecies of stone'.

LINES 9–14

The poet has not gone to the dance. He stands alone on the deserted road and thinks about his life. He feels different to other people his age because he is a poet. Like every poet he must spend a lot of time by himself in order to write his poems. Kavanagh tells us that he hates having to live this kind of life. Having to be alone and think deeply about things might seem important and serious to others, but Kavanagh says that all poets hate the loneliness that comes with the trade: 'I have what every poet hates in spite/ Of all the solemn talk of contemplation'.

The poet compares his situation to that of Alexander Selkirk, the Scottish sailor who was left alone on an island for four years. He says that Selkirk knew exactly what it's like to stand alone in a deserted landscape and be responsible for all that surrounds: 'Oh, Alexander Selkirk knew the plight/ Of being king, and government, and nation'. Like Selkirk the poet stands alone and isolated in a landscape he considers his own. The deserted road is his 'kingdom' and he is 'king' of all he sees, 'banks and stones and every blooming thing'. The word 'blooming' might refer to everything that grows or blooms, the flowers and plants of the countryside. But it might equally be read as a curse, and thus represent the poet's frustration with his surroundings and his fate.

THEMES

Being a poet

Inniskeen road' is one of Kavanagh's earliest and best known poems. Taking a poetic form he loved, the sonnet, and making it his own, the poem is a prime example of the poet's original voice coming through. Much of Kavanagh's earlier poems were derivative, works that relied too heavily upon the poems he read and admired as he was honing his own particular talent. 'Inniskeen Road' was, therefore, a radical departure for him and an early sign that something novel was happening in Irish poetry. Kavanagh realised that there was poetic material to be discovered in the small rural town in which he lived. He takes the bicycles and the barns and deftly incorporates them into the classical sonnet form.

And yet the poem is one of frustration and loneliness. Being a poet is an isolating and lonely job. Kavanagh suggests that he is not capable of the lightness and the banter that the other people of his age enjoy. They cycle past him and he envies their easy ability to joke and laugh. He feels that it is not his lot to be part of all this, that he is somehow different. Being a poet means having to think deeply about life, to consider the 'secrecies' that are not apparent to the average person. Such a life does not allow, it seems, for frivolity and dancing. The poet curses this fact and says that it is something that every poet 'hates' despite what others might think.

And yet there is a certain sense that the poet feels proud to be different. Though he might curse his fate at the end of the poem, there is a sense in which he feels superior to the rest of the community. He rues his loneliness, but we might guess that he is happy on some level to compare his 'plight' to such famous historical figures as Alexander Selkirk. There is a certain romance to being the outsider, the castaway and having a destiny, no matter how difficult.

LANGUAGE

The alliteration in this first quatrain (Billy Brennan's barn, twos and threes) allows the lines to read quickly and easily. This adds to the liveliness and joy of the occasion. The use of the word 'And' also allows for this easy and fluid movement. There is a change in rhythm in the second quatrain. The long vowel sounds ('Half-past eight', 'no shadow thrown') and the lack of the conjunctive 'And' removes the energetic mood and fun of the first quatrain.

Maintaining a gap between the first eight lines (the octet of the sonnet) and the last six (the sestet) works well with the poems theme of isolation. It reflects the division that the poet feels exists between himself and the rest of those who cycle to the dance. The first eight lines deflate to a very solemn line, 'not/ A footfall tapping secrecies of stone'. After the break the poet starts the sestet with a new surge of energy and speaks to us directly, like an actor delivering a soliloquy on an empty stage.

Epic

'Epic', in many ways, is a poem about poetry itself. It poses a question that concerned Kavanagh for many years: what material is appropriate for poetry? Can poems only be written about beautiful, noble things, like the singing of a nightingale, or the glamour of a beautiful woman? Or could poetry be shaped from material we usually consider mundane, brutal, or even ugly? In particular, Kavanagh pondered the extent to which his background in rural Ireland might provide a legitimate source of poetic inspiration: could great poetry be fashioned from the harsh realities of everyday life in the Monaghan of his youth?

With 'Epic', as with many of Kavanagh's poems, the title is highly significant. An epic is a type of long poem, associated especially with the great poets of ancient Greece and Rome. The great epics, such as Homer's Iliad and Odyssey and Virgil's Aeneid, tell stories of vast scope that deal with great events, and feature a larger-than-life cast of gods, monsters and almost indestructible warriors. The Iliad, for example, deals with the conflict between the Greeks and Trojans that led to the fall of the legendary city of Troy. The poem describes a struggle lasting ten years, a series of glorious battles between the armies of the various Greek and Trojan heroes.

At first glance, the speaker of 'Epic' seems to believe that his Co. Monaghan upbringing has indeed furnished him with experiences that might provide the inspiration for an epic poem: 'I have lived in important places, times/When great events were decided'. However, one of these so-called 'great events' is no more than a disagreement between two local families, the Duffys and the McCabes, over quarter of an acre of farmland: 'who owned/That half a rood of rock'. As material for an epic poem, this hardly compares with the heroic adventures narrated by Homer and Virgil. It becomes apparent, therefore, that the speaker's tone is ironic, that he does not really believe he has lived in important places or witnessed 'great events' of epic proportions.

The remainder of the sonnet's octet describes the feuding families gathered around the disputed piece of ground. They are armed with pitchforks, ready to do battle for its possession: 'a no-man's land/ Surrounded by our pitchfork-armed claims'. From their side of the field, the Duffys curse their opponents: 'I heard the Duffys shouting 'Damn your soul!' Stripped to the waist like a boxer, the leader of the McCabes advances into the disputed plot of ground: 'old McCabe stripped to the waist, seen/Step the plot'. He strides into the no-man's land, seemingly undeterred by the pitchforks of the Duffys: 'defying blue-cast steel'. Old McCabe gestures to the line of stones that, in his opinion, marks the boundary ('march') between the territories of the two families, a boundary, of course, that will leave the disputed quarter acre in the possession of his family: 'Here is the march along these iron stones'.

In the context of epic poetry, this squabble over 'half a rood' of poor farmland hardly compares to the conflict for the legendary city of Troy. As heroes, the McCabes and Duffys with their pitchforks provide no match for Achilles, Hector, and Odysseus, the great warriors of the Iliad. The speaker's ironic tone seems designed to mock the feuding families. By titling his poem about them 'Epic', by describing their little disagreement as a 'great event', he emphasises just how petty and insignificant their quarrel actually is in the greater scheme of things.

The speaker's disdain for the feuding families, and the attitude they represent, continues in the next three lines. The clash between the Duffys and the McCabes, we're told, took place at the same time as the 'Munich bother'. This is a reference to the conference between Hitler, Chamberlain, and the French prime minister Daladier, that took place in Munich, in September 1938. This conference, which discussed the future of Czechoslovakia, was an event of huge importance, when the future of Europe hung in the balance and the Second World War was temporarily postponed.

The speaker compares the events in Munich to those around the 'half a rood of rock', asking 'Which/Was most important?' This is an example of the poetic device known as the rhetorical question, a question to which the answer is so obvious that it is not really a question at all. The answer to this particular question, it might seem, is that the Munich conference is more important. To the Monaghan locals, however, it is only a 'bother', a distant happening of which they know little and care even less. They are more interested; it seems, in the squabble between the Duffys and the McCabes.

At this point, the speaker begins to lose interest in the parishes and townlands of Co. Monaghan: 'I inclined/ To lose my faith in Ballyrush and Gortin'. Perhaps the speaker is annoyed with the people of his home area, disappointed at the attitude of self-involvement that makes them more concerned with their own petty disagreements than with the events in Munich that shaped the fate of nations and prefigured one of the greatest tragedies in history. Or perhaps he feels that the place of his birth cannot provide him with the material necessary for great poetry, that to create work of epic proportions he needs to focus on international events like the Munich conference, and the storm of war that was waiting to break over Europe.

We might expect the poem to end here, with the speaker convinced that the life of his home parish is unable to provide fit subject matter for epic poetry (or perhaps, even, for poetry in general). The poem's conclusion, however, is marked by a surprising intervention. The speaker hears the voice of Homer, the great epic poet himself, echoing in his thoughts: 'Till Homer's ghost came whispering to my mind/He said: I made the Iliad from such/A local row'. Homer's ghost maintains that the monumental siege of Troy was, in its own way, quite similar to the seemingly more mundane conflict between the Duffys and the McCabes. He whispers that both struggles arose from a 'local row', a disagreement between neighbouring tribes over control of a piece of land. The Munich conference, too, might be viewed in similar light, focusing as it did on a territorial dispute between two sides, Germany on the one hand and Britain and France on the other. The difference between the three conflicts, then, is only one of scale. The Duffys and McCabes are involved in a dispute over a plot of ground, the heroes of the Iliad over an ancient city, and the sides involved in the Munich conference over an entire modern country with millions of inhabitants. Yet all three disputes stem from the same war-like impulses of anger, bravado, and the desire for territory that Old McCabe exhibits when we see him 'Step the plot defying blue-cast steel'.

The speaker, inspired by the encouraging words of Homer's ghost, concludes with the haunting, enigmatic statement: 'Gods make their own importance'. Most critics feel that Kavanagh has the 'Gods' of literature in mind here, the great poets and writers like Homer and Shakespeare whose work will live forever. (In 'On Raglan Road' Kavanagh also refers to 'the true gods of sound and stone/and word and tint'). These poet-gods 'make their own importance': through their poetry they can transform even a relatively trivial event into the stuff of epic poetry. Homer, for instance, made the Iliad from a conflict that, compared to the Second World War, seems little more than 'a local row'. The poet, through the transforming power of his verse, can make even the local epic.

'Epic', then, concludes on a note of poetic relativism. The speaker will follow the advice of Homer and attempt to make his 'own importance'. It is the poet him or her self, it seems, who decides what is suitable material for poetry. The speaker's faith in Ballyrush and Gortin, which was slipping away, seems to have been restored. Through the lens of poetry, which makes its own importance, the events in Munich might after all be little more than a 'bother', while the struggle between the Duffys and the McCabes might be a source of 'great events'. The poem's conclusion causes us to re-evaluate its opening lines. Perhaps the speaker was not, after all, being ironic when he declared that he has lived in 'important places'. Great poetry, it seems, can make any place or time important, even Ballyrush and Gortin with their squabbling farmers.

Shancoduff

LINE BY LINE

LINES 1–5

The hills belonging to the poet face north. Because of this they have never 'seen the sun rising'. They are 'black hills', forever in the shade, always looking 'north towards Armagh'.

Kavanagh tells us that his hills are not interested in seeing the sun. They are content to remain as they are, happily facing north when the morning sun shines on 'Glassdrummond chapel': 'happy/ When dawn whitens Glassdrummond chapel'.

The poet contrasts his hills' apparent lack of curiousity regarding the sun with 'Lot's wife'. She was turned into salt by God for looking behind her when she was told not to: 'Lot's wife would not be salt if she had been/ Incurious as my black hills'.

LINES 6–10

Due to the lack of sunshine, patches of snow can still be found on the poet's land in March. Kavanagh compares the white patches of snow to shiny coins and suggests that his hills are saving these coins: 'My hills hoard the bright shillings of March'. The hills keep the patches of snow carefully hidden from the sun, which is described as searching in 'every pocket' of land.

In line 8 the poet refers to his hills as his 'Alps'. Reaching his hungry cattle with hay is like climbing the 'Matterhorn', one of the famous mountains of the Alps: 'They are my Alps and I have climbed the Matterhorn/ With a sheaf of hay for three perishing calves'.

LINES 11–16

The quality of the poet's land is poor. The fields are covered in rushes. Kavanagh compares the growths of rushes to beards: 'the rushy beards of Shancoduff'. The cold 'sleety winds' are to kind the hills, gently stroking the rushes: 'The sleety winds fondle the rushy beards'.

However, the 'cattle-drovers sheltering' from these cold winds are less kind. They wonder who owns such poor land that even the wildlife must have abandoned it: 'Who owns them hungry hills/ That the water-hen and snipe must have forsaken'. When they hear that a poet owns the hills they joke about his prospects: 'A poet? Then by heavens he must be poor.'

In the cattle-drovers' eyes a poet is not good for much, least of all for earning any money. Kavanagh hears what they say and wonders whether he is concerned by their opinion: 'I hear, and is my heart not badly shaken?'

THEMES

The beauty of the ordinary

The poet's hills are not good for farming. They never get any sunshine and exist in constant shade. The poet twice refers to them as 'black hills'. The cattle-drovers describe the hills as 'hungry' and they claim that even the wildlife have deserted them. They see little value in the poet's land. The poet sees the hills differently. He is very proud of them and praises them for never receiving any sunshine. They are magnificent and beautiful. To him they are the 'Alps'.

Kavanagh personifies his hills. He suggests that his hills have consciously turned their backs on the sun. He considers them morally sound for never having been tempted to look around. His hills are confident and 'happy' with what they have. They are also clever. They are able to save the 'bright shillings of March', small patches of snow and frost, and keep them hidden from the sun. To the poet these 'shillings' are more valuable than real money.

The Poet as outsider

The poet must seem an unusual figure to others in the community. He is a farmer but he doesn't seem to care about making money from his land. He takes pride in hills that are 'rushy' and never receive any sunshine.

The poet obviously feels different to the other farmers. He views his land with a poet's eye, perceiving beauty and substance in something that others write off as valueless. Like his hills, perhaps, the poet has turned his back on the community and is proud to be different. He knows that he is mocked and ridiculed for what he does but he is trying to be strong in himself and not care. The last line of the poem does not, however, make it clear if he is yet indifferent to the opinions of others.

LANGUAGE

The poet personifies the hills. This means that he gives them human characteristics and feelings. He describes his hills as 'happy' and 'Incurious' and suggests that they are cunning when they conceal the patches of snow from the sun.

Kavanagh also includes many place names in the poem. He mentions 'Armagh', 'Glassdrummond chapel', 'the Big Forth of Racksavage', 'the Featherna Bush', and 'Shancoduff'. The inclusion of so many place names indicates the poet's great love for the area and his desire to celebrate such ordinary places in poems.

The Great Hunger

INTRODUCTION

The Great Hunger, considered by many to be Kavanagh's masterpiece, is an outpouring of bitter social criticism. In it Kavanagh casts a cold eye on the social conditions that pertained in the rural Ireland of the Twenties, Thirties and Forties. At the time the Irish countryside was bedevilled by the twin evils of poverty and outward migration. Thousands of young men and women were forced to abandon the land for the urban centres, or, more often, for the boat to England or America. The Great Hunger, however, is concerned with the plight of those left behind, rather than the difficulties of those who were compelled to emigrate. The poem describes the life of Patrick Maguire, a farmer who has worked the stony grey soil of Co. Monaghan all his life. When we meet Maguire he is sixty-three years old and filled with bitterness and regret that he has never married. We get the impression, in fact, that he has never experienced a romantic or sexual intimacy with a woman.

Maguire's situation was typical in the Ireland of the day, where country people, especially male farmers, either married very late or remained bachelors all their lives. There were several social and economic factors for this. Firstly, there was the social phenomenon known as 'familism', whereby the eldest male child would inherit the family farm, but only after both his parents were dead. In many rural communities, only a man with land of his own stood a chance of securing a desirable young woman as his bride. Farmers like Maguire, therefore, were encouraged to wait until their parents had died and the farm passed to their name before going in search of a wife. Maguire, like so many others, spends years living with his widowed mother, waiting for her to die so he could begin to court one of the lovely local girls. (Maguire's mother, we learn elsewhere in the poem, is ninety-one when she dies). The tragedy, as Kavanagh saw it, was that all too often by the time their parents passed away the farmers were practically old men themselves, well past their sexual and romantic peak.

The situation was also exacerbated by the social climate of the time. Ireland was a deeply Catholic country, where matters of sexuality were regarded with great suspicion and were seldom, if ever, discussed openly. Sex was associated with guilt and sin rather than with sensuality and pleasure. Even something as innocent as Irish dancing often took place under the watchful eye of the local priest, to ensure the dancing didn't become too overtly sexual. In this climate, relationships outside marriage were simply not an option. The 'great hunger', of the title then, is in an important sense the sexual hunger of the bachelor farmers who spent years living with their ageing parents, unable to marry or pursue love outside marriage, until they were too old for passion.

However, the title also refers to the desire of Maguire and others like him to escape from their lives of brutal, unremitting toil. Farmers like Maguire, the poem argues, were enslaved by the land they worked on, enduring year after year of backbreaking work in an attempt to coax a living from a few hard acres of Monaghan bog or hillside. Their lives and careers were entirely mapped out for them, depriving them of any scope for personal, emotional or spiritual development. The 'great hunger', therefore, is also the burning desire for a better way of life, to be found in some mythical place 'back of the hills where love was free and ditches straight'.

An important feature of the poem is that Maguire does not tell his own story. His situation is related to us by an impersonal narrator, with his own opinions and prejudices regarding the predicament of Maguire and others like him. Throughout the poem the narrator comments on Maguire's misfortunes. At times he seems quite critical of Maguire, blaming the farmer's stupidity and short-sightedness for the fact that he has wasted his life. There are also moments, however, when the narrator appears sympathetic toward Maguire's plight, regarding him as little more than a victim of the society in which he was raised. The narrator, it seems, takes a dim view of the values of mid-twentieth century rural Ireland, angrily attacking the social system that caused thousands of men to waste their lives 'in the grip of irregular fields', sexually and emotionally unfulfilled for the sake of 'the queen too long virgin'.

LINE BY LINE

SECTION 1: LINES 1–17

The poem opens with an almost Biblical declaration: 'Clay is the word and clay is the flesh'. Maguire and his men live in a world of clay, of muck, dirt and mud. Their 'flesh' is not used for pleasure but in the service of this clay. Even their language and conversation is confined to the soil they work on: 'Clay is the word'. They have been denied any form of spiritual, cultural, or intellectual development. The poem's opening line is also rich with religious connotations. It echoes not only the first sentence of the Bible ('In the beginning was the word') but also a refrain from the Angelus, which at the time was said nightly in many Irish households: 'The word was made flesh and dwelt amongst us'.

The opening line, then, is a parody of two key Christian pronouncements, reflecting the narrator's bitterness toward the Catholicism that dominated the Ireland of the time. He believes that the devotion displayed by Maguire and his men to their religion has not brought them happiness or salvation. Instead, it has helped to keep them unfulfilled and undeveloped, imprisoned in their world of 'irregular fields'. The reference to the soil as 'the Book of Death' over which the men bend also has religious connotations. The bible, of course, is often referred to as a 'book of life'. Irish Catholicism, the narrator implies, is for these men a religion of clay and death rather than of hope and life. It is a creed that keeps these 'broken-backed' men tied to the soil.

Maguire and his men, we're told, move like 'mechanised scare-crows'. Their lives of deprivation and hard labour have made them more like robots or straw-stuffed dummies than flesh and blood human beings with authentic emotions. The landscape in which they work is depicted in a grim, miserable light. It is a place of cold and damp, of 'wet clods' and freezing weather: 'why do we stand here shivering?' Even the birds that float through this scene reinforce our impression of bleakness and despair. The crows squabble over scraps of food, adding to the atmosphere of hunger and desperation: 'Here crows gabble over worms and frogs'. The gulls, meanwhile, by virtue of an excellent simile, are described in terms of waste and rubbish: 'And the gulls like old newspapers are blown clear of the hedges, luckily'. This, then, is the grim wasteland in which Maguire lives out his life.

There is an interesting pun in line 8, when the narrator asks 'Is there some light of imagination in these wet clods?' On one level the narrator is referring to the soil, the wet lumps of clay turned up by the potato gatherers. A 'clod', however, was also a contemporary slang term for a fool or an idiot. Maguire and his men, then, are also 'clods' wet from the October drizzle. Throughout the poem the narrator frequently uses this faintly mocking tone to talk about Maguire, as if the pity he feels for him is mingled with contempt. The use of the word 'clod' to refer simultaneously to the soil and to the farmers reinforces the fact that Maguire and his men have been reduced to the status of muck or dirt, they have become indistinguishable from the clay they work with. Line 8 is also a rhetorical question. The narrator asks if there is 'some light of imagination in these wet clods', but he is not genuinely looking for an answer. He believes, of course, that there is no 'light of imagination' to be found in the damp soil. In fact, it is the enemy of imagination, enslaving the farmers who work it to the extent that they have neither the leisure nor the inclination for something as impractical and fanciful as imagination. The rhetorical question also refers to the farmers themselves. No 'light of imagination' shines from them. They are dull and intellectually crippled, their minds caged by their backbreaking lifestyles and the narrow-minded attitudes of their community.

Rhetorical questions also feature in lines 10–14. The narrator asks 'Which of these men/ Loved the light/ And the queen too long virgin? The phrase 'queen too long virgin' is open to a number of interpretations. The 'queen' could, of course, refer to the land on which the farmers toil, the fields they have made their 'bride'. The land is queen-like because it dominates the farmers' lives. Yet it is also 'virgin', it can offer them potatoes but cannot respond to their sexual and emotional needs. The 'queen too long virgin' also calls to mind the Virgin Mary, queen of heaven. We can read the line, therefore, as an attack on the farmers' devotion to the church, which, as we have seen, played a key role in their sexual frustration. They have spent their lives worshipping the Virgin, when they should, the narrator believes, have been in pursuit of real women. However, we can also interpret the word 'queen' as referring to the various farmers' mothers. Due to marriage customs, as we have seen, many farmers spent years living with their widowed mothers. Very often a mother would be reluctant to see her son marry, afraid that she herself might be ejected from the farmhouse in order to accommodate the new wife. They therefore encouraged their sons to devote themselves to work and religion, rather than to the pursuit of love and romance. Furthermore, in many cases they refused to sign the deeds of the farm over to their sons. (Remember, without land of his own it was difficult for a man to secure a desirable young bride). The 'queen', then, can be taken as a reference to the various farmers' mothers who, to a large extent, ruled their lives, who they lived with, honoured and obeyed. The phrase 'too long virgin', on this reading, refers to the men themselves. They have been kept in a virginal state, have been deprived of sexual release, by this futile devotion to their mothers.

There is an aching sorrow to the simple sentence 'Yesterday was summer'. The time of abundance and fertility has passed. It is now October, a time of mist and rain, and the dead season of winter waits. The poem's October setting reflects the situation of the sixty-three-year-old Maguire. The summer of his youth has passed. He is in the autumn of his life, facing his own mortality. The men, it seems, have been constantly putting off marriage, promising themselves each year

that they will soon find a wife, but never taking action: 'Who was it promised/marriage to himself/Before apples were hung from the ceiling for Hallowe'en?' We suspect, however, that by the time they eventually do get around to seeking a wife it will probably be too late. There is a deliberate air of theatricality about line 14, as the narrator addresses the reader directly, offering to present us with the full sad story of Maguire's life: 'We will wait and watch the tragedy to its last curtain'.

SECTION 2: LINES 18–42

Section two is dominated by Maguire's self-delusion. He attempts to convince himself that he was better off avoiding marriage and children. These commitments, Maguire claims, are a 'net spread/in the gaps of experience' and the 'world's halter' (a 'halter' is a bridle used to control a horse). Maguire congratulates himself on how 'he ran free' from these traps, 'thinking himself wiser than any man in the townland' for not being burdened by the responsibility of a wife and kids. Children, he tells himself, are little more than pests, interfering with the serious work of the land: 'children are tedious in hurrying fields of April/Where men are spanging across wide furrows'. (To 'spang' is to work with long, quick steps). Their crying is irritating and might conceal the noise of crows, allowing them to make off with the precious, freshly sown seed: 'Children scream so loud that the crows could bring/The seed of an acre away with crow-rude jeers'. Deep down, however, it seems that Maguire longs for a family. He is, the narrator maintains, only pretending to himself that children are undesirable: 'He shook a knowing head/And pretended to his soul/That children are tedious'. It is difficult to know which is more tragic, Maguire's loneliness or his feeble attempt to convince himself that he is not lonely at all.

In this section the narrator provides us with a vivid sense of the passage of time. Maguire's days vanish in a blur of work: 'The drills slipped by and the days slipped by'. Maguire, the narrator claims, has chased away 'the birds of years'. He is presented as something of a fool, wasting year after year in his efforts to tease a living from the stony grey soil. The poem's autumnal setting is also emphasised in this section. The sound of the October winds is described as a kind of melancholy symphony: 'October playing a symphony on a slack wire paling'. The autumn setting, as we have seen, reflects the fact that Maguire's youth is gone, that he is in the autumn of his life.

Several of the images in section two are characterised by a raw, crude sexuality, with farm animals and equipment mimicking human sexual activity. We see this in line 20's depiction of 'three heads hanging between wide-apart/Legs', which, of course, puts one in mind of oral sex. The heads are those of a 'dog lying on a torn jacket' and of a 'horse nosing alone the posied headland'. The animals' heads hang low, dangling between their legs in an attitude of deep weariness. The shaft of the horse's plough is presented, in a wonderful metaphor, as the third 'head', jutting down between the plough's 'legs'. The life of the land, in the form of the dog, horse, and plough, seems to mock Maguire's thwarted desire, presenting him with a cruel parody of the sexual activity it deprives him of.

A similar sexual innuendo occurs in line 34 where the narrator declares that 'The pricks that pricked were the pointed pins of harrows'. This is obviously a reference to the male sexual organ, which is often vulgarly referred to as a 'prick'. In Maguire's world, however, the only 'pricks' that find a use are the pins of harrows, tools used for turning over soil. (The 'rusty plough' in line 20 has also been interpreted as referring to the penis, suggesting that the elderly Maguire's sexual powers are past their prime).

Throughout the poem, Maguire's relationship with the land he works is presented as a grim parody of marriage. He has, as line 57 puts it, 'made a field his bride'. Maguire is trapped in a 'passion that never needs a wife'; in a devotion to the soil from which he makes his living but which, ironically, drains him of his life and energy.

SECTION 3

Just as Maguire's relationship with the land mimics a marriage, so his attempts to farm it are presented as a parody of sexual intercourse. The pins of the harrow, as we have seen 'prick' the earth. There is also a distinctly sexual overtone to the image, in line 42, of Maguire groping in the soil for a potato. The narrator claims that Maguire is not actually searching the 'insensitive hair' for a potato at all but for something else: 'What is he looking for there?/ He thinks it is a potato, but we know better'. Maguire, the narrator implies, is desperately probing the earth for a way out of the economically and spiritually deprived life to which he has been condemned. This metaphor of the soil as 'insensitive hair', many critics feel; brings to mind pubic hair. Maguire, on this reading, is groping in the soil for the sexual experiences that have eluded him throughout his life. Once again the narrator regards Maguire with mingled pity and condescension. He emphasises the fact that he is more familiar with Maguire's thoughts and desires than Maguire is himself. As the narrator puts it: 'we know better'.

SECTION 4

In this section we hear Maguire speak for the first time. His utterances, of course, are not concerned with the abstract issues of his cultural and sexual deprivation and what the narrator regards as his wasted life. Instead, Maguire speaks in the practical, down to earth language of a farmer preoccupied with the business of growing and protecting his crops of potatoes. His words give us a sense of day to day life in the fields. There is, it seems, an endless series of tasks to be performed, from the straddling of a horse to the gravelling of the 'ruckety pass'. We are left with the impression that Maguire is a grumpy, irritable old farmer. He gruffly dispenses orders to his men: 'Move forward the basket and balance it steady/In this hollow. Pull down the shafts of the cart, Joe'. He is also quick to complain; irritated by the intrusion onto his land by a neighbour's donkey and by the fact that his dog is not where it should be: 'Is that/ Cassidy's ass/Out in my clover? Curse o' God/where is that dog?/ Never where he's wanted'. The life of the land, then, is portrayed as a hard life, in which only tough, practical men like Maguire can survive.

Beneath his gruff, practical exterior, however, Maguire is beset by doubts. He begins to question the certainties he articulated in section two when he declared himself 'wiser than any man in the townland'. It seems that he is no longer convinced that he was right to avoid family commitments and make a 'field his bride': 'And he is not so sure now if his mother was right/ When she praised the man who made a field his bride'. These lines emphasise the dominant role the farmers' mothers played in their lives. (Many mothers, as we have seen, strongly encouraged their farmer sons to remain celibate). Maguire, as he surveys his fields 'from the height', begins to doubt whether he was right to take his mother's advice and devote himself to the land considering what it has cost him in terms of emotional and spiritual development. Significantly, however, these thoughts are not spoken by Maguire himself but are communicated to us by the narrator. Maguire, it seems, is either unwilling or unable to articulate his doubts about the wisdom of dedicating one's life to the service of the land.

SECTION 5: LINES 58–61

The narrator uses an interesting, if abstract, image to describe the hollow, bedraggled state of Maguire's soul. His 'spirit', the narrator claims, 'is a wet sack flapping about the knees of time'. The years of spiritual deprivation and backbreaking work have left his heart and mind empty and worn-out. Lines 60–1 highlight the grim ironies of Maguire's life. 'He lives', the narrator declares, 'that his little fields may stay fertile'. Maguire's own 'fertility' is sacrificed for that of his fields. Maguire is 'infertile' in two senses. Firstly he gives up his desire to father children and secondly he lives a barren lifestyle, devoid, as we have seen, of spiritual, sexual, and emotional development. These sacrifices, of course, are made just so the land will continue to bear potatoes. This is one of the poem's key ironies: the land thrives, or at least survives, but at the expense of those who work on it. In an attempt to ensure their fields' survival, to stave off a repeat of the great famine of the 1840's, the farmers have allowed another 'Great Hunger' to emerge, a terrible starvation of the emotions and the spirit. The human soul has been neglected in favour of the potato.

There is a further irony, though a perhaps grim one, in the fact that after his death Maguire will be buried in the land he worked, with a cross marking his grave: 'when his own body/Is spread in the bottom of a ditch under two coulters crossed in Christ's name'. Even in death, it seems, Maguire will not be able to escape the forces that have oppressed him throughout his life. He will be buried in the very land that held him in impoverished servitude, his resting-place marked by the symbol of the religion that so impeded his sexual and emotional development.

SECTION 6: LINES 62–79

This section begins with a flashback to Maguire's youth and his sexual awakening. His early interest in the opposite sex was contaminated by suspicion, reflecting the deep mistrust in which sexuality was held in the Catholic Ireland of the time. The narrator uses a wonderful simile to convey the young Maguire's unease around women: 'He was suspicious in his youth as a rat near strange bread/When girls laughed'. Beneath this suspicion, however, Maguire realised there was something deeply natural about human sexuality. Sexual interaction between humans is as natural as that between the animals on the farm where he grew up: 'when they screamed he knew that meant/The cry of fillies in season'. To be a sexual being, to pursue women, to have a wife and children, all of these things were 'his destiny'. According to the narrator, however, Maguire was prevented from walking this 'easy road'. The society he lived in, dominated by the puritanical values of the Church, did not allow nature to take its course. Instead, Maguire has been condemned to the 'hard road' of life-long celibacy. A field, as we have seen, is his only bride.

In his poetry, and especially in his prose, Kavanagh was often critical of the Church's condemnation of sexuality. Such a negative attitude to the sensual life, he felt, though it may have been expressed 'in Christ's name' was not really Christian. He believed that the sexuality considered so 'foul' and sinful by the Church was a natural, God-given aspect of human nature. To respect 'God's truth', then, was to allow this aspect of human life to be expressed: 'God's truth is life-even the grotesque shapes of its foulest fire'. (Kavanagh, of course, does not really believe the metaphorical 'fire' of sexuality that burns in each of us to be 'foul' or 'grotesque'. Here he ironically presents the position of the Church whose values he attacks. What is really 'grotesque', the poem shows, are the consequences of the denial of the natural sexual impulses that exist in each one of us).

In lines 67–71 the narrator reflects on the difficulty of escaping the bleak lifestyle of the rural Ireland of the time. (An escape, of course, that Kavanagh himself managed). He uses an interesting metaphor to describe this, declaring that the fields hold their workers in 'a grip': 'O the grip, O the grip of irregular fields!' The tightness of the fields' grasp is emphasised by the repetition of 'grip'. For Maguire, the narrator maintains, there is no easy release from the life that he has lived. It is not possible to escape by simply moving 'back of the hills' to another parish. Throughout the country, he implies, rural Irish life is dominated by backbreaking toil and a religiously inspired suspicion of sexuality. There is nowhere where young people are free to love one another and the ditches do not require straightening: 'No man escapes. /It could not be that back of the hills love was free/And ditches straight'. The narrator once again emphasises the destructive nature of the culture in which Maguire lives. Using a wonderful metaphor, he describes rural Irish culture as a 'monster hand' that shapes and twists the children born into it so they grow up to be almost sub-human. Those unfortunate to grow up in this society are left resembling 'apes', intellectually underdeveloped, emotionally stunted, and inarticulate: 'No monster hand lifted up children and put down apes/As here'.

Maguire's doubts about the wisdom of his lifestyle continue to grow. For the first time he articulates aloud the suspicion that he might have wasted his life: 'O God if I had been wiser!'/ That was his sigh like the brown breeze in the thistles'. Maguire's sorrow at the realisation of his wasted life is conveyed by the fact that he 'sighs' the words, rather than saying them. It is further reinforced by his repetition of the phrase a second time as 'looks toward his house and haggard'. (A 'haggard' is a farmyard for storing hay). Maguire, the narrator informs us, has finally reached the conclusion that his mother was very wrong when she encouraged him to make 'a field his bride': 'And he knows that his own heart is calling his mother a liar'.

SECTION 7: LINES 80–92

In the wake of Maguire's crushing realisation the poem continues with a series of images from the life of the farm. The first of these depicts a horse leaning over a wall to taste the clover in a neighbouring field. The horse 'crashes through the whins and stones' of the wall' to 'lip late passion in the crawling clover'. The horse's situation mirrors that of Maguire. Just as the horse is kept from the clover, so he is kept from sexual fulfilment. In Maguire's case, though, it is 'boulders like morality' that restrain him. These boulders, most critics believe, represent his society's belief that sexuality was inherently sinful and shameful. The narrator maintains that these boulders of morality represent a formidable obstacle. To cross them is to go against the mores and values of an entire society. In a small rural community like Maguire's, to flout the rules of morality was to risk drawing the anger of the local priest and becoming some kind of social outcast: 'The fools of life bleed if they climb over'.

Lines 84–8 are filled with melancholic autumnal imagery, reflecting, perhaps, the fact that Maguire is in the autumn of his life. A cold wind blows, rain falls, and a 'poignant' (sorrowful) light is reflected in the puddles made by horses' hooves. The first part of the poem concludes with the narrator imaginatively following Maguire into 'the iron house' where he lives. The narrator calls on a personification of the power of imagination to accompany him: 'Come with me, Imagination, into this iron house'. This invocation of an abstract force, many critics believe, is another example of the poem's self-consciousness, like the reference to the 'tragedy' and 'the last curtain' in section one. Throughout The Great Hunger the narrator reminds us that what we are reading, while it might be a realistic account of life in rural Ireland, is not actually a true story. It is a product of his imagination, that he brings before our mind's eye, like a director bringing a play to life on the stage of a theatre.

With the aid of 'Imagination' the narrator will make the 'years run back'. The remaining sections of The Great Hunger are a kind of flashback, describing Maguire's life from his youth to the poem's 'present day', and revealing how he ended up in his present miserable condition. The narrator sets out to interpret the thoughts and feelings of the illiterate peasants who couldn't even sign their names, who could only make a 'mark' on whatever legal documents required their signature: 'And we will know what a peasant's left hand wrote on a page'. The narrator, then, sets out, in the remainder of the poem, to give a voice to these voiceless people, to record the restrictions and misery of their lives, things that they themselves were incapable of expressing. The poem concludes with the narrator addressing the month of October as a farmer might address a horse. He urges October to be quiet, calling on the hens not to cackle, the horses not to neigh, the trees to make no sound as the wind blows through them, and the ducks not to quack. This silence, presumably, is required so that the narrator can concentrate on the work of imagination, allowing Maguire's life story to be told.

CONCLUSION

The Great Hunger was intended in part as an antidote to the common portrayal of the rural Irish as jolly, carefree farmers, living in an unspoiled country paradise. It pulls no punches, then, in its portrayal of Maguire and his men as sexually frustrated, emotionally retarded 'apes'. It is a savage piece of social criticism, bitterly attacking the socio-economic system that turned men like Maguire into sexually and personally frustrated slaves of the land they worked on. The poem is a bleak lament for their wasted lives, lives that achieved only a fraction of their true potential. It is a condemnation of the social and economic values that enslaved Maguire and his men to their 'irregular fields', turning them into little more than monstrous 'mechanized scare-crows'. Rural Ireland, the poem argues, has failed its people to such an extent that it has robbed them of their humanity.

A Christmas Childhood

LINE BY LINE

SECTION 1

This poem deals with the magic and mystery of childhood. It describes how even the most mundane and ordinary things can appear wonderful to a child. Kavanagh recalls everyday sights and sounds from his own childhood that filled him with wonder. He mentions the following things:

- Frost in the potato-pits: 'One side of the potato pits was white with frost-/ How wonderful that was, how wonderful!'
- The sounds of the paling-post: 'And when we put our ears to the paling-post/The music that came out was magical'.
- The light shining between hay stacks ('ricks'), which seemed to come from a window in the walls of paradise: 'The light between the ricks of hay and straw/Was a hole in heaven's gable'. (A 'gable' is the end-wall of a building).
- The tracks made by cows: 'The tracks of cattle to a drinking-place'.
- 'A green stone lying sideways in a ditch'.

Kavanagh declares that to the innocent eyes of a child 'any common sight' can seemed 'transfigured', or filled with mystery and beauty. Yet this childhood innocence cannot last. We are forced to leave innocence behind, just as Adam was forced to leave behind the Garden of Eden. Just as Adam was tempted by Eve to eat the apple, so we are tempted by 'the world' to have experiences and acquire knowledge: 'O you, Eve, were the world that tempted me'.

Yet by gaining knowledge and experience we lose our childhood innocence and no longer see the wonder in the everyday things around us. Occasionally, the adult Kavanagh can remember what it felt like to be a child and see wonder everywhere: 'Now and then/ I can remember something of the gay/ Garden that was childhood's'. Yet he knows that he will never experience such innocence again.

SECTION 2

The poet remembers a Christmas morning when he was only six years old: 'I was six Christmases of age'. Like many children on Christmas morning he young Kavanagh wakes up early and quickly gets dressed. He senses that something very special is happening: 'As I pulled on my trousers in a hurry/ I knew some strange thing had happened'. He seems to have been given a penknife for Christmas. We get a sense that this present, with its 'big blade' and its 'little one for cutting tobacco', makes him feel grown up. He hides in the doorway of the house, fooling around with the penknife and looking out at the scene before him:

I hid in the doorway
And tightened the belt of my box-pleated coat.

I nicked six nicks in the door-post
With my penknife's big blade.

It is so early that the stars are still in the sky: 'There were stars in the morning east ... Cassiopeia was over Cassidy's hanging hill'. His father is playing the melodeon out at the front gate while his mother is milking cows in the cowshed. It is so cold that ice has formed in the potholes in the road. The family's neighbours crush this ice on their way to early morning mass: 'Mass-going feet / Crunched the wafer-ice on the potholes'. One of the neighbours praises the father's playing as he passes by: 'An old man passing said: / 'Can't he make it talk' – / The melodion'.

To the young poet the whole parish seems like a winter wonderland: 'In silver the wonder of a Christmas townland,/ The winking glitter of a frosty dawn'. He sees many aspects of this scene as magical or wonderful:

- His father's melodeon playing seems to have magical qualities, making the stars dance and summoning the neighbours from the surrounding farms: 'Across the wild bogs his melodion called / To Lennons and Callans'.
- The noise of the cows being milked has a wonderful musical quality: 'Outside in the cow-house my mother/ Made the music of milking'.
- The cowshed seems like the stable where Jesus

was born and the light that the mother uses to milk the cows seems like the star of Bethlehem: 'the light of her stable-lamp was a star/ And the frost of Bethlehem made it twinkle'.

- Three bushes moving in the wind remind him of the three wise men on their way to Bethlehem: 'I looked and three whin bushes rode across / The horizon – the three wise kings'.

The young poet is so moved by this Christmas scene that he says a prayer to the Virgin Mary. Using a wonderful simile Kavanagh describes the prayer as a rose that is pinned to the virgin's blouse.

LANGUAGE

Sound

Sound and music play an important role in this poem. The father's melodeon, for instance, is depicted not only as filling the parish but also reaching as far as the 'stars in the morning east'. The skill and beauty of his playing are indicated by the praise he earns from an 'old man passing'. Other sounds are also depicted as musical, such as the noise of the paling post

and the sound of the mother milking the cows.

The sounds of Christmas morning are brought vividly to life in section two. There is an onomatopoeic quality to the phrase 'Mass-going feet/Crunched the wafer ice' in which we can almost hear the ice being broken by the trudging feet of the poet's neighbours. There is an element of cacophony to the description of the water-hen's cries, due partly to the harsh onomatopoeic 'screech'. Onomatopoeia is also present in line 32, with describes the sound of the bellows. The clashing 't' an 'w' sounds mimic the shrill whistle of the bellows wheel being turned: 'Somebody wistfully twisted the bellows wheel'.

The poem is also rich in assonance and alliteration, in phrases such as 'winking glitter' with its repeated 'i' sounds, and 'Cassiopeia was over/ Cassidy's hanging hill' with its repeated 'c' and broad vowel sounds.

THEMES

The wonder of the everyday

Like many of Kavanagh's poems 'A Christmas Childhood' emphasises the beauty and strangeness that exist in common, everyday things. Usually we are too busy and to preoccupied to notice the beauty in the mundane things that surround us. Yet the poem gives many examples of mundane things that can appear beautiful and special if we look at them the right way: frost, a green stone, the sound of cattle being milked and sunlight shining on hay-bales. This theme, the notion of the wonder to be found in the commonplace recurs throughout Kavanagh's poetry and can also be seen in 'Advent', 'The Hospital'. 'Lines written on the grand canal' and 'Canal Bank Walk'.

The innocence of childhood

This poem emphasises how magical the world can seem through the eyes of a child. It provides many examples of everyday sights and sounds that seem wonderful to the young poet. The power of a child's imagination is movingly illustrated when the young poet sees the story of Christmas come alive in the fields surrounding his house. In his imagination bushes turn into the Three Wise Kings and the cowshed becomes the stable where Jesus was born. The young poet has the innocent faith of a child as he offers his simple prayer to the Virgin Mary at the close of the poem.

The poem captures how magical a time Christmas can be for a young child. Like many children the poet describes waking excitedly on Christmas morning. He seems delighted with his gift of a penknife. There's a sense of the community coming together as the neighbours pass the poet's house on their way to mass

The loss of innocence

Yet the poem also laments the fact that childhood innocence cannot last forever. The poet suggests that as we grow older and acquire more knowledge of the world we lose the ability to see the world as a magical and wonderful place. The poet likens the loss of this childhood innocence to the banishment of Adam from the Garden of Eden: 'To eat the knowledge that grew in clay'. Childhood is seen as a lost garden of innocence to which the poet can never return. We can remember what it was like to be a child but we can never experience childhood innocence again.

Advent

LINE BY LINE

The poet addresses his 'lover' and tells her that they have explored and experienced 'too much': 'We have tested and tasted too much, lover'. Life no longer surprises or amazes them: 'Through a chink too wide there comes in no wonder'. It could be that they have exhausted the passion that they once felt for one another and that their relationship has gone stale. But the poem suggests that a greater weariness with life has set in. The poet and his lover have become jaded with the world around them and, perhaps, also with each other.

The poet feels that the 'knowledge' they have gained is of no use to them. He also thinks that the knowledge they have acquired is not rightfully theirs. The poet says that they 'stole' this knowledge from 'Doom'. Describing the acquisition of knowledge in this way suggests that learning is both harmful and hollow

The poet now wishes to 'return' this knowledge 'to Doom' and to start afresh. They will achieve this, the poet believes, by undergoing the 'penance' of Advent. They will sit in a darkened room and dine on 'dry black bread and sugarless tea'. They will restore a state of childhood innocence and wonder by denying themselves sensual pleasure and stimulus: charm back the luxury/ Of a child's soul

Having undergone this period of fasting and penance, the poet and his lover will once again experience the world like children. The people and places that surround them will suddenly seem wonderfully new. The 'black slanting Ulster hill' will bring 'spirit-shocking/ Wonder'. The boring chatter of some 'old fool' will seem astonishing and 'prophetic'. Old 'stables' will be associated with fantastic narratives about the beginning of 'Time'. Their excitement at the 'newness' of the world around them will bring them to the 'yard gate' to witness such ordinary things as 'bog-holes' and 'cart-tracks'.

Having rediscovered a childlike state of innocence, the poet and his lover will find poetry and music in the everyday world around them. They will no longer have to go 'searching' for such experiences: 'O after Christmas we'll have no need to go searching/ For the difference that sets an old phrase burning'. Whereas once they needed to define what sets poetry apart from ordinary language, after Christmas they will find poetry in the ordinary. 'Wherever life pours ordinary plenty'.

The sounds of the 'churning' of butter, for example, will speak to them in a profound manner: 'We'll hear it in the whispered argument of a churning'. The sounds of the streets where the 'village boys' move in an unwieldy manner will sound wonderfully musical. Poetry will be discovered among the hard-working, honest men who engage in menial labour: 'And we'll hear it among decent men too/ Who barrow dung in gardens under trees'. Their newfound ability to experience childhood wonder will enrich their lives: 'Won't we be rich, my love and I'. The ordinary things that surround them will fill them with joy.

The poet wishes, however, that their joy will remain innocent. He does not want to start questioning why things appear or sound so beautiful. He does not want to taint his experience of wonder with knowledge and understanding. If 'dreeping hedges' move him in a profound way or he hears 'God's breath' in the words of the common man, he does not want to analyse or question why this happens: 'and please/ God we shall not ask for reason's payment,/ The why of heart-breaking strangeness in dreeping hedges'.

At the close of the poem the poet says that he and his 'lover' have done away with the pursuit of pleasure and knowledge and no longer care to be conscious of their needs and desires. He likens the benefits of such worldly things to the receipt of money, suggesting that they are corrupt and materialistic. The poet says that they have 'thrown' them into the 'dust-bin'. And having rid themselves of such things they are ready to for innocence to once again enter their lives. The poet envisions such innocence arriving in the shape of Christ holding 'a January flower', the white snowdrop.

THEMES

Worldly experience

The poem suggests that experience and knowledge ultimately lead to the destruction of innocence. The more we know and experience, the less we wonder at the world around us. Having 'tested and tasted' so much of life, the poet has become jaded.

Rather than bringing about a positive sense of enlightenment and maturity, the poet's experiences have left him feeling dissatisfied and disillusioned. The opening line of the poem strongly suggests that the poet's disillusionment with the world has resulted from sexual experience. Having 'tested and tasted' so much with his 'lover' he no longer feels a sense of wonder. He has lost his innocence and feels that something sacred has been spoiled.

Religion

The poet's need to observe the Advent traditions of fasting and penance hints at a strong religious conscience. He associates the pleasures of the body and the acquisition of knowledge with sin and misfortune. He suggests that both are somehow harmful and debased and that we are better off discarding them. They blind us to the greater wonder and mystery of the world. Observing the rituals of the Advent period allows for Christ and innocence to once again enter our lives. Having purified our senses we are better capable of discerning God's presence in the world around us.

The opening stanza draws heavily upon the story of Adam and Eve from the Bible. Adam was tempted by Eve to eat the fruit of knowledge. When he did this he lost his innocence and became ashamed. God punished Adam by banishing him from paradise. Kavanagh's notion of stolen knowledge and his association of knowledge with 'Doom' is based on this biblical event.

Childhood innocence

'Advent' celebrates the innocence of the child and laments the fact that we grow up and seek more sophisticated pleasure. Childhood, the poet suggests, is a wonderful time of wonder and magic. In the eyes of a child the ordinary world appears fresh and new. Everyday things such as 'bog-holes' and 'cart-tracks' seem special to the child. Kavanagh considers such innocence a 'luxury' that is lost and spoilt over time.

The ordinary as beautiful

Once again Kavanagh argues that great beauty exists in the ordinary, banal things that lie all around us. The very things that we take for granted and overlook are, according to Kavanagh, wonderful and special. A dark 'Ulster hill' is capable of shocking us with wonder if we look at it the right way. The speech of the common man is infused with 'God's breath'. However, as we get older the world ceases to amaze us. Time and experience jade our senses. What once sounded astonishing becomes tedious and dull.

LANGUAGE

Like 'Canal Bank Walk' and 'Lines Written', Advent features neologisms. Kavanagh coins the word 'Advent-darkened' to express the drab darkness of the room in which he fasts. Seen through a child's eyes the 'black slanting Ulster hill' in the poem is 'spirit-shocking', and the hedges are 'heart-breaking'. Kavanagh also fuses two words to create the word 'dreeping', which appears to be a combination of the dripping and creeping. The new word that Kavanagh uses reflects the creativity of the child's mind which the poet hopes to bring about by way of the Advent fast.

'Advent' represents Kavanagh's particular use of the sonnet form. The poem is an amalgam of two sonnets. The stanza pattern is neither Patriarchal nor Shakespearean. The opening two stanzas each contain seven lines with the third stanza representing an entire sonnet. The division of the sonnet into two septets is unusual and Kavanagh formulates a rhyme scheme to parallel this-: aabbccbd, aab, aacc. Stanza 3 is again different as Kavanagh reverts to the Shakespearean rhyming technique: abab, cded, fgfg, hh.

The thought pattern of the third stanza follows that set out by the opening two stanzas with a natural pause occurring at the end of the seventeenth line. The reason why Kavanagh does not create a fourth stanza is that the rhythm of the third stanza reflects the excitement that Kavanagh associates with having rediscovered 'the luxury of a child's soul' The three stanzas in the poem reflects the three stages in Kavanagh's bid to regain this position – penance, forgiveness, grace.

On Raglan Road

This poem describes a love affair between the poet and a dark-haired woman. Their relationship plays itself out on the streets of Dublin.

LINE BY LINE

STANZA 1

In stanza 1 the poet tells us how he first meets his lover. They meet in Autumn, on Raglan Road, a leafy street in Dublin 4. From the moment the poet sees this woman he knows that he will fall heavily for her. He knows that her beauty will enslave or 'ensnare' him: '[I] knew/ That her dark hair would weave a snare'.

The poet feels that he will 'rue' or regret falling under this woman's spell. He sees that she will only bring him 'grief' and break his heart: 'I saw the danger'. Yet the poet decides to throw caution to the wind and have a relationship with her: 'I said let grief be a fallen leaf at the dawning of the day'. He will walk with her 'along the enchanted way' of love.

STANZA 2

The poet and his lover walk happily down Grafton Street. They 'trip lightly' along together; sauntering in a casual, carefree manner. Yet they are headed for disaster. Sooner or later their relationship will end and they will be cast into grief and misery. The poet uses a memorable image to describe this impending doom. He says that he and his lover are walking along the 'ledge' of a great ravine or chasm which they will eventually fall into.

In this stanza, then, the poet presents a fairly bleak view of love. He claims that the promises and commitments lovers make to each other ('passion's pledge') are worthless. For relationships always end in bitterness and heartbreak. The 'enchanted way' of romance only leads us into the 'deep ravine' of regret and despair: 'A deep ravine where can be seen the worth of passion's pledge'.

The poet seems to regard love as a waste of time. There are better things to do, he feels, than focus on a love affair: 'The Queen of Hearts still making tarts and I not making hay'. The poet his time would be better spent on some useful occupation – 'making hay' – rather than hanging around with this with this beautiful young woman. The speaker's disregard for love is also shown by his reference to the 'Queen of Hearts'. He associates romance with a character from a nursery rhyme, making it seem silly and childish.

STANZA 3

In this stanza the speaker describes the gifts he gives his lover. Instead of clothes or jewellery he gives her poems, which he describes as 'gifts of the mind' because he creates them out of his own imagination. He writes many poems for his beloved, working on them without any stint or rest: 'I did not stint for I gave her poems to say'. The poems feature her name and celebrate her beauty, especially her hair: 'With her own name there / And her own dark hair like clouds over fields of May'.

The speaker tells his lover secrets that are known only to artists: 'I gave her the secret sign that's known/To the artists'. These secrets are possessed by artists who work in music ('sound'), sculpture ('stone'), literature ('word') and paintings ('tint'). The poet presents the artistic community as a kind of secret club or cult that worships the 'true Gods' of art and creativity.

STANZA 4

This final describes the end of the couple's affair. The speaker watches his lover walk quickly away from him: 'I see her walking now/Away from me so hurriedly'. She leaves him behind on a street haunted by ghosts, which probably represent the speaker's memories of their relationship: 'On a quiet street where old ghosts meet'.

The poet describes his lover as a 'creature made of clay', suggesting that she is false, fake or deceitful. He describes himself as an 'angel', suggesting that he is somehow perfect and can do no wrong. The poet suggests, therefore that 'angelic' people like himself should avoid getting involved with 'clay' people like the woman. By 'wooing' her he has somehow been corrupted or contaminated by her false and deceitful nature. He is no longer the perfect 'angel' he once was: 'When the angel woos the clay he'll lose his wings at the dawn of day'.

LANGUAGE

A song

An important feature of 'On Raglan Road' is that it was written to be sung. The poem, then, has several features common to many Irish ballads. It has an AABB rhyming scheme. It also has many internal rhymes; for example 'hair' and 'snare' in line 2, 'leaf' and 'grief' in line 4, 'ravine' and 'seen' in line 6, 'mind' and 'sign' in line 16, and 'woos' and 'lose' in line 20.

The poem's musical qualities are enhanced by assonance and alliteration. We see assonance in such phrases as 'dark hair' and 'making tarts' with their repeated 'a' sounds, 'old ghosts' with it repeated 'o' sound, and 'tripped lightly' with its repeated 'i' sound. Alliteration, too, is prominent, emphasising the song's key phrases such as 'Raglan Road', 'passion's pledge' and 'creature made of clay'.

Metaphors and Similes

'On Raglan Road' features several memorable metaphors and similes:

- Perhaps the finest metaphor is the description of the woman's hair as a 'snare' that will entrap and mesmerise the poet.
- Travelling 'the enchanted way' is an interesting metaphor for the process of falling in love. It suggests, of course, the magic and mystery of a loving relationship. Yet it also has the slightly sinister implication that by falling in love with the woman the speaker will find himself in her power. He will be 'enchanted' by her, held in her thrall as if he was hypnotised or under a spell.
- A simile occurs in stanza 3, where the speaker compares his lover's hair to dark clouds hovering over a summer field.
- The 'old ghosts' in the final stanza are also often taken to be a metaphor, representing the poet's memories of the failed relationship.

THEMES

A negative view of love?

Many readers of 'Raglan Road' feel that the poet has an extremely negative attitude toward love. From the moment he meets his lover he starts to think about the 'danger' she poses to his happiness and the 'grief' she will bring him. Even at the beginning of the relationship he's thinking about its grim and miserable end. Love may be an 'enchanted way' full of mystery and delight but it leads only to a deep ravine of sorrow and regret. We are wrong to feel confident and happy about our relationships because each one of them will end in tears, leaving us haunted by the 'old ghosts' of the happiness we once possessed.

Falling in love, the speaker feels, is the perfect way to throw away one's happiness: 'Oh I loved too much and by such by such / Is happiness thrown away'. The poet believes that the promises lovers make to each other have little or no 'worth'. He seems to regard relationships as a waste of time. He feels that he would be better off 'making hay' – involved in some useful occupation – than spending time with his lover.

A negative view of women?

The poet depicts his lover in a very negative light. Her beauty, he says, is a trap or 'snare' that will only bring him misery. He depicts her as a kind of enchantress who will enslave him with the magic spell of her beauty and lure him 'along the enchanted way' to his doom in the 'deep ravine'. Many readers feel that this is an unfair and stereotypical portrayal of a woman as an evil temptress, a stereotype that goes back to the Bible when Eve tempted Adam with the apple in the garden of Eden.

Feminist writers have criticised the description of his lover as a 'creature made of clay' who corrupts his the perfect 'angelic' poet. They argue that this description also goes back to ancient stereotypes; to the notion of women as impure and sinful creatures who contaminate the men that get involved with them.

Critics have also expressed their unhappiness with this one-sided presentation of the relationship between the poet and the woman. Why, they ask, is it necessary for the woman to be presented as the villain of the piece? The speaker pays no thought to the fact that she might have her own side of the story, that her interpretation of the relationship and its failure might be significantly different to his own.

Poetry and art

The poet comes across as someone who has a very high regard for poetry and artistic creation. He seems proud of the poems he writes for his beloved.

He works on these 'gifts of the mind' without pause or 'stint'. The poet seems to feel that artistic people possess important secret knowledge the rest of us cannot possibly be aware of. In fact, he seems to regard artistic activity as a kind of cult or religion, in which artists worship the 'true Gods' of creativity.

The Hospital

LINE BY LINE

The poem is surprising because the poet speaks of falling in love with something that we do not associate with love. A hospital is a place we generally wish to avoid, to not even think, unless, perhaps, we happen to work there. Hospitals remind us of our mortality, they are where we go when we are not well and when we are dying. Hospitals are not designed to be loved or even liked. They are exactly as the poet has described, 'functional'. The floors are tiled and reek of disinfectant, nobody makes any effort with their appearance, plastic seats sit along the corridors and the lifts are exceptionally large.

The hospital the poet describes is not any different and he openly admits that this is no special place. It is aesthetically unpleasant: 'an art lover's woe'. Somewhat humorously Kavanagh shares the fact that 'the fellow in the next bed snored'. This detail alone is usually the cause for despair, rarely love. Yet it is love that the poet feels for the place. He loves it for these very details. And, according to the poet, it is possible to love anything:

But nothing whatever is by love debarred.
The common and banal her heat can know.

We have seen this in 'Shancoduff'. The roughest of hills are perceived by the poet in the fondest terms. In 'Advent' the poet speaks of the 'heart-breaking strangeness in dreeping hedges'. Yet, in taking a hospital as his subject-matter Kavanagh is going even further with respect to what love 'can know'. We have moved away from the rural, such a familiar setting for poetic material, and into the urban. And a hospital is probably the least likely aspect of a city to lend itself to aesthetic contemplation.

In the last two lines of the octet we move with the poet down the corridor to a 'stairway' that brings us out into 'the inexhaustible adventure of a gravelled yard'. The fact that 'a gravelled yard' can become an 'inexhaustible adventure' tells us of the plentitude of the poet's imagination, his ability to discover greatness in the smallest things. 'This is what love does to things'. When we love something we bathe it in the most positive and forgiving light. We forget ourselves and open our hearts magnificently to what is other. Just as a lover might fondly mention the idiosyncratic details of their beloved, Kavanagh names the little details of the hospital that make the place special.

the Rialto Bridge,
The main gate that was bent by a heavy lorry,
The seat at the back of a shed that was a suntrap.

There is nothing excessive about the description. Kavanagh does not seek to demonstrate his love with hyperbole or magnificent adjectives. The language used is plain. Line 10 is blunt and unadorned with poetry.

Once again Kavanagh moves from a list of details and images to a more abstract consideration. He tells us that this 'Naming' is 'the love-act and its pledge'. As a poet Kavanagh holds the greatest regard for language. Naming something, evoking its presence through the utterance of a word is an act of love, of creation, of care and consideration. It also involves some form of commitment, some connection or bond. This is all done without spurious sentiment or clichéd phrase. Kavanagh does not believe in using flowery language to enhance what is already extraordinary. It is the poet's job to describe 'love's mystery' honestly and plainly, to take possession of and record the simple, everyday moments and details that make life something special:

For we must record love's mystery without claptrap,
Snatch out of time the passionate transitory.

THEMES

Love

When it comes to love our understanding of its ways is often distorted by countless gushy Hollywood productions, melodramatic soap-operas and trite magazine articles. This is the 'claptrap', the insubstantial and unrealistic portrayal of 'love's mystery'. All too often when we think of love we think only

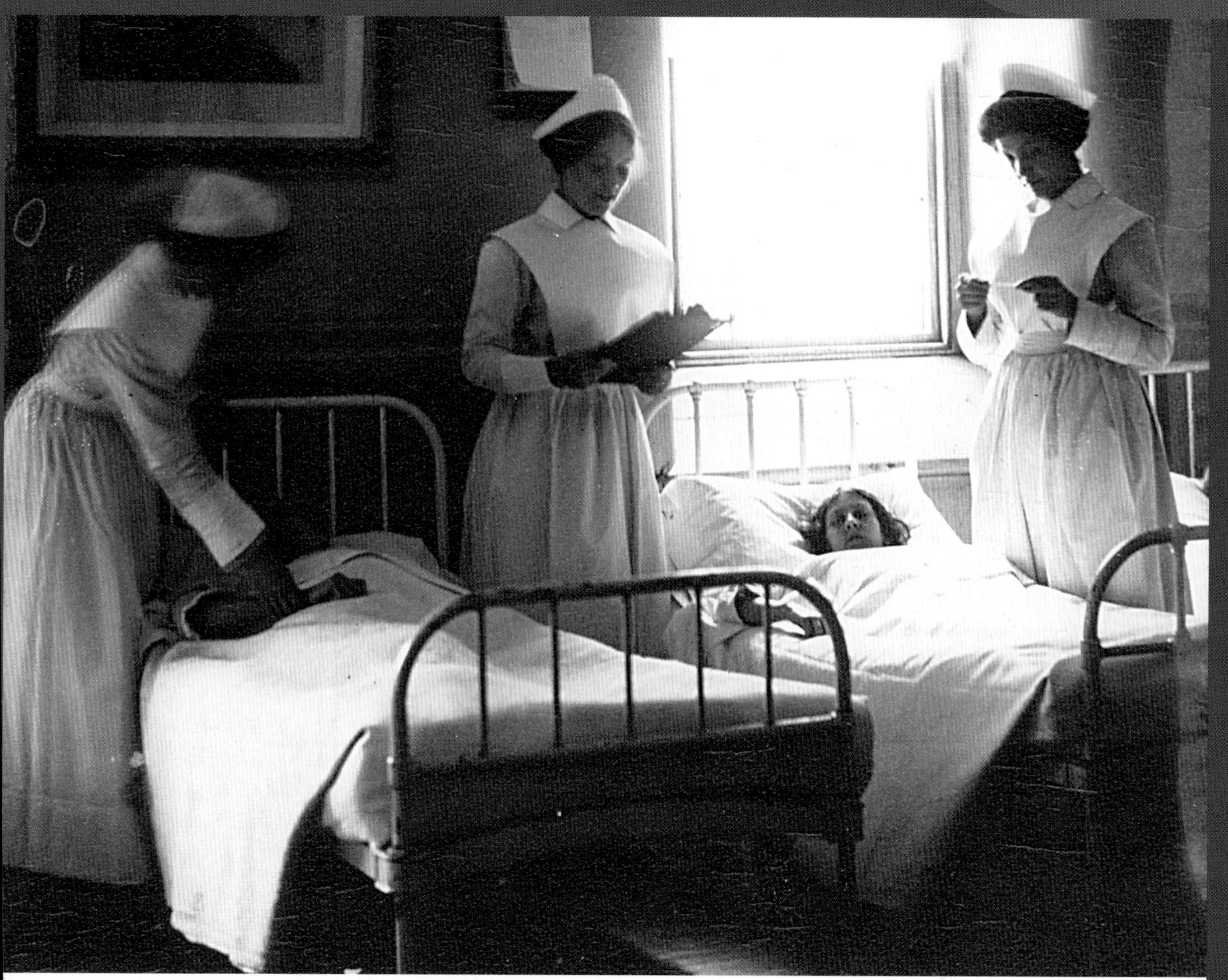

of its romanticised, idealised connotations. But as Kavanagh has shown, love is a bond and 'pledge' that arises between people and the everyday things that they encounter during their lives. It is made up of the small details, the familiar and habitual. It is recorded in his poetry in the most effective way he knows, through the simple evocation, the naming, of things that in time come to hold a place in his heart. By doing this he does not abstract or make statements that hold no solid basis in the real world. Rather, he looks at the real objects and moments that come to occupy an important place in our lives: he takes from this life the 'passionate transitory'.

Celebrating the banal

Kavanagh always had a lot of time for 'Shancoduff' as a poem. He once stated that it was among the favourites of his own compositions. A number of times throughout his career he sought to return to the poetics of 'Shancoduff'. In 'The Hospital' he succeeds in doing just this. He takes as his subject-matter a very ordinary place – a hospital – and sets about illustrating his love for that place. But this is no ordinary place for poetry or, indeed, art of any kind. Yet, Kavanagh incorporates the most unaesthetic subject into the most classic of poetic forms, the Petrarchan sonnet. By so doing he shows perfectly how any place is capable of being embraced by language, how any place is capable of being known by the 'heat' of love. In contrast to 'Shancoduff' Kavanagh does this without a hint of self-doubt. He explicitly states what he only implied in his earlier poem.

Canal Bank Walk

LINE BY LINE

As the poet walks by the canal he gets a wonderful sense that he is in harmony with nature. The natural world, in full bloom and vibrant, seems full of love and life. The banks of the canal are 'Leafy-with-love'. And the 'green waters of the canal' are enriching his soul, healing him and giving him a chance to start again: 'and the green waters of the canal/ Pouring redemption for me'.

The poet suggests that the natural world is doing the 'will of God' by blossoming and thriving. As he takes delight in the common and familiar sights of nature, the poet also feels he that he is doing the 'will of God': 'that I do/ The will of God, wallow in the habitual'. He feels that he is growing 'with nature', coming to life again just as the natural world is flourishing. He says that this is something he used to experience before: 'Grow with nature again as before I grew'.

The poet derives great joy from the simple things that surround him. What he sees represents the glory of life, free from all inhibitions and wonderfully new. There is a rhythm and a purpose to the world and everything that he sees, from the simple detail of a 'stick trapped' to 'a bird gathering materials for the nest'. The 'young couple kissing on an old seat' are part of this world, abandoned to their feelings. The fact that the 'breeze' is said to add a 'third/ Party' to their passion suggests a playful harmony exists the world. Everything that the poet sees is a representation of the 'Word' of God, powerfully 'new', unrestrained and ecstatic: 'Eloquently new and abandoned to its delirious beat'.

The poet calls upon the rejuvenated world to fill him with delight: 'O unworn world enrapture me'. He wishes to immerse himself in the natural world, to be overpowered by the wonderful things that he sees and hears: 'encapture me in a web/ Of fabulous grass and eternal voices by a beech'. His body is hungry for such experiences: 'Feed the gaping need of my senses'. He asks to be given the ability to 'ad lib', to speak without thought, ecstatically and freely, so that he might praise all that he sees: 'give me ad lib/ To pray unselfconsciously with overflowing speech.

The poet feels that his 'soul' has been reborn and that it deserves a 'new dress' to honour the occasion of its renewal. He wishes this 'new dress' to be 'woven' from the 'green and blue things' that fill the rejuvenated world that has enraptured him. He also wishes to be surrounded by arguments that 'cannot be proven'. The poet does not want logic and reason. He wants his soul to be filled with poetry and wonder.

THEMES

The wonder of nature

The natural world is celebrated in 'Canal Bank Walk'. Kavanagh is enriched and inspired by nature's ability to renew itself, to blossom and grow. He feels that the plants and animals are somehow a manifestation of the 'will of God' and as he watches them he comes to believe that he too is part of this special process. Nature is seen as something wonderful and good. The poet senses 'love' in the world that surrounds him. He coins the wonderful adjective 'Leafy-with-love' to describe the banks of the canal and he feels that the waters of the canal are somehow working to cleanse and renew him.

The poet discerns a fantastic rhythm to all that is going on around him. The bird building its nest, the flowing canal waters, and the young couple kissing on the bench are all part of the 'Word', the 'delirious beat' of life. It is as though he has come to see the world through the eyes of a child, something he longed and prayed for in 'Advent'. He is content to 'wallow in the habitual, the banal', to enjoy the simple things in life.

Celebration of life

Kavanagh had just come out of hospital when he wrote this poem. There is great sense in 'Canal Bank Walk' that he is relishing the chance to live again. Having survived a life-threatening illness, the poet suddenly sees life in all its wonder and splendour. He is ecstatic at the beauty of the world and longs to lose himself in the wonderful processes of nature. He is hungry for the pleasures of life and calls upon the world to 'Feed the gaping need of [his] senses.

LANGUAGE

In 'Canal Bank Walk' Kavanagh uses a neologism to start the poem. The term 'leafy-with-love' is his own creation and wonderfully illustrates the lush greenery that features along the banks of the canal. Hyperbole is evident in phrases such as 'delirious beat', 'fabulous grass' and 'gaping need', and it is used to express the poet's excitement and longing. 'Canal Bank Walk' is written in the traditional 14 line sonnet form with no stannic separation. In this poem, Kavanagh combines both the Patriarchal and Shakespearean sonnets using the same methods as in 'Inniskeen Road'.

Lines Written on a Seat on the Grand Canal Dublin

LINE BY LINE

In these lines Kavanagh explains how he would like to be commemorated after his death. He was aware that several benches had been placed on the Grand Canal as memorials to deceased persons. Each of these benches had a plaque with the name of the person it was meant to commemorate. Kavanagh, who loved the Grand Canal area, declares that he would like to be memorialized in this way once he has passed on: 'O commemorate me where there is water/ Canal water preferably'. Such a bench, he feels, would be a beautiful or prefect monument to his life: 'Commemorate me thus beautifully'.

In these lines Kavanagh describes the Canal on a sunny summer afternoon. Its water is green and still. Its banks are incredibly peaceful, filled with 'the tremendous silence / Of mid-July'. This silence is broken only by the water rushing out when one of the canal's locks is opened:

Whereby a lock niagarously roars
The falls for those who sit in the tremendous silence
Of mid-July.

Kavanagh compares this peaceful canal scene to Parnassus, 'these Parnassian islands'. (In Greek mythology Parnassus was a beautiful mountain which was home to the Muses or goddesses of inspiration). Kavanagh declares that anyone who visits the canal will be inspired and find themselves 'speaking poetry'. Every word that comes out of their mouths will be poetic: 'No one will speak in prose/Who finds his way to these Parnassian islands'.

Kavanagh describes a swan gliding along the canal: 'A swan goes by head low with many apologies'. Another example of movement is that of light along the water. In a wonderful metaphor Kavanagh depicts the light looking 'through the eyes of bridges', and we can imagine the circle formed by an arched bridge and its reflection in the water as a kind of 'eye' through which the brightness passes. A final example of movement is that of a barge drifting up the waterway from the direction of Co. Kildare: 'And look! A barge comes bearing from Athy / And other far-flung towns mythologies'.

The poem concludes with Kavanagh once more declaring his desire for a bench to be erected in his memory. He wants no fancy tomb, such as might be built to honour a war hero: 'O commemorate me with no hero-courageous tomb'. The only memorial he desires is a 'canal-bank seat for the passer-by'.

LANGUAGE

Rhyme, neologisms and hyperbole

There is a playful, almost cheeky quality to several of the techniques deployed by Kavanagh in this sonnet, reflecting the lazy, laid back atmosphere of the scene he depicts. The sonnet makes extensive use off half-rhymes and off-rhymes such as 'Brother' and 'water', 'stilly' and 'beautifully', 'silence' and 'islands', 'prose' and 'roars', and, especially, 'bridges' and 'courageous'. These 'almost-rhymes' lend the poem a casual, informal air. A similar playfulness is apparent in the use throughout the poem of 'neologisms', or made-up words. These include 'stilly', 'greeny', 'niagarously', and the adjective 'hero-courageous'. In this poem Kavanagh delights in flouting the formal conventions of language, bending the rules of rhyme and inventing new words as he goes along.

Also playful and humorous is Kavanagh's use of hyperbole, or poetic exaggeration, to convey the splendours of the canal bank. Firstly, he compares one of the locks on the canal to the Niagara Falls: 'Where by a lock niagarously roars / The falls'. A similar exaggeration is evident when Kavanagh declares that those who visit the canal will be so inspired that every line they speak will be poetry: 'No one will speak in prose / who finds his way to these Parnassian islands'.

In an another example of hyperbole the barge carries not just any cargo but 'mythologies'. To Kavanagh, it seems that nothing in the environment of the canal is prosaic or ordinary. Even something as grimly industrial as a barge is presented as a source of poetry and inspiration as it bears its mythological cargo to the capitol. In keeping with the poem's hyperbolic celebration of the canal is the use of superlatives in lines 6 and 10. The silence is 'tremendous' and the light is 'fantastic'. Nothing on its banks, it seems, is anything less extraordinary.

Sound effects

Sound effects play a large part in evoking this poem's relaxed, summery atmosphere. The opening lines feature four words that end in 'y' or 'ly': 'preferably', 'stilly', 'greeny', and 'beautifully'. The repetition of these 'y' and 'ly' sounds creates a pleasant, euphonious music. It also produces an onomatopoeic effect, mimicking the gentle, lulling sound of water lapping the canal banks. Fittingly for such a relaxed scene the movement of the verse is slow, held up by the polysyllabic words 'commemorate', 'preferably' and 'beautifully'. The repetition of whole words, 'water' in lines one and two, and 'commemorate' in lines one and four, adds to the atmosphere of unchanging stillness, to the sense of untroubled relaxation that pervades the opening quatrain.

Kavanagh uses assonance and alliteration throughout the poem to create a pleasant verbal music. We see alliteration in line 1 with its repeated 'w' sound: 'where there is water'. It also occurs in line 11 with its repeated b sound: 'a barge comes bringing' Assonance, meanwhile, features in lines two, three, and four with their repeated broad vowel sounds: 'canal water', 'greeny at the heart of summer', 'thus beautifully'. We also see a profusion of broad vowels in line 13 with its repeated 'o' sounds: 'O commemorate me with no hero-courageous tomb'. These broad vowel sounds contribute to the slow pace of the lines, as broad vowels take longer to read than slender ones. This combination of slow movement and pleasant music is designed to conjure up the laid-back atmosphere of a lazy summer day, a perfect moment when all seems right with the world.

THEMES

A celebration of the everyday

This poem, along with 'The Hospital' and 'Canal Bank Walk', was written during Kavanagh's new lease of life following his recovery from lung cancer in the mid-1950's. His poems of the period express his gratitude at being alive and his new-found desire to celebrate the beauty of the world. Following his brush with death, Kavanagh was determined not to take life for granted, but to be aware of the beauty and mystery that resides even in the most ordinary, everyday sights. The poem celebrates an everyday, urban scene; an industrial canal with barges, locks and swans. Yet Kavanagh demonstrates that even in such an ordinary scene there is beauty mystery to be found.

Memory

The poem is marked by an air of humility. Kavanagh, though considered by many (including himself) to be a great Irish writer, desires no fancy or ostentatious public monument. He has no wish, it seems, to be remembered as a great man or a 'hero'. The only commemoration he desires is a simple canal-bank seat. This, he feels, would be a fitting legacy, allowing passers-by to savour the delights of one of his favourite places. Perhaps, some of these passers-by will be inspired, like him, by the canal's 'fantastic light', finding, as he did, the magic that lurks at the heart of the everyday.

KAVANAGH AT A GLANCE

THE HABITUAL AND THE BANAL

In 'Shancoduff' the poet describes his 'black hills' as a place of mystery and beauty. Despite the critical view of the other farmers, Kavanagh takes great pride and joy in his humble landholding.

'Advent' shows how ordinary, everyday objects and events can seem wonderful.

A similar point is made in 'A Christmas Childhood' where something as simple as a 'green stone lying sideways in a ditch' can seem filled with mystical, 'transfigured' beauty.

The 'Hospital' finds beauty in a most unlikely place, the dreary, functional ward and gravel yard of a community hospital.

In 'Lines Written on a Seat on the Grand Canal', Kavanagh also finds beauty in what we would often consider grim, industrial objects. He seems thrilled by a bridge, a barge and the canals.

'Canal Bank Walk' is probably Kavanagh's most famous celebration of the banal. The everyday sights of the canal and the natural world fill the poet with joy and inspiration.

RURAL LIFE

'A Christmas Childhood' shows how beautiful rural Ireland can be. The 'wonder of a Christmas town land' is described through the eyes of the 'childpoet'.

'Inniskeen Road: July Evening' shows the darker side of rural life, hinting at the loneliness and isolation felt by those who don't properly fit in to rural communities.

'Shancoduff' highlights the poverty that existed in rural Ireland during the mid twentieth century. The poem also describes the narrow-mindedness that can be a feature of rural society. The cattle drovers look upon the poet and his land with disdain.

'The Great Hunger' provides a devastating critique the rural Ireland of the 1930's and 1940's. The poem highlights the psychological and sexual depravation as well as the material poverty suffered by many Irish farmers at that time.

CHILDHOOD INNOCENCE

'A Childhood Christmas' depicts childhood as a magical time. Through the innocent eyes of a child, everything seems wonderful. However, the poem also laments how as we grow older our childhood innocence disappears and the world becomes a duller and less magical place.

A similar point is made in 'Advent' where the poet wishes he could cast off the sophistication and knowledge of adulthood and return to a childlike state of innocence. If he could achieve this, he believes that the world will once again appear wonderful.

In 'Canal Bank Walk' it could be argued that the poet wishes to make a similar return to a childlike state of innocent and wonder. He wants to be as he was before he grew, and see the world once again as a place of magic and wonder.

JOHN KEATS
THEMES

NATURE

For John Keats the natural world was a thing of great beauty and inspiration. The sky, particularly at night, and the ocean were to him sublime entities, capable of inspiring grand thoughts and ideas. He longed to capture as much of their beauty within his poems as he could, harbouring fears that he might not live long enough to record or 'trace' their magnificent forms. Keats was also fascinated by the smaller details of the natural world, the flowers, fruits, trees and animals that he loved to observe in the country. For Keats 'a thing of beauty is a joy forever', and it was the natural world that offered his keen senses the greatest moments of joy. Familiar with the stresses and confined spaces of the city the poet relished the opportunity to spend time in the open spaces of the countryside where he could gaze up at the clear sky above. The natural world provided him consolation for the hardships of life that he was all too familiar with.

In 'To One Who Has Been Long in City Pent' the poet describes the pure joy of escaping the crowded city and spending a day in the country.

In 'Ode to a Nightingale' the beauties of nature again offer the poet consolation for the trials and tribulations of everyday life. Though he cannot see what surrounds him because it is so dark, his senses are filled with the sweet perfumes of the countryside and he imagines each plant and flower that offers it scent on this summer night.

'To Autumn' provides the reader with another wonderfully sensuous account of nature as it appears at a particular time of year. Reading the poem, we can almost taste the fruit the poet describes, feel its plump ripeness, and hear the plaintive choir of insects, birds and animals that play out the final lines.

ART AND IMMORTALITY

The poetry of John Keats very often deals with notions of immortality. His precocious awareness of death led him to explore notions and consider that which never ages and never dies. For Keats it was great works of art in particular that symbolised immortality. In 'On First Looking into Chapman's Homer' the poet speaks of the eternal freshness of Homer's great work. The poem depicts how a work of art is capable of outliving generations of human beings. It abides through the centuries, untouched and untarnished by the years, existing to inspire readers who come to the work long after its creator has turned to dust.

Reading such magnificent, timeless works led Keats to consider his own position as an artist. He fretted that he might not live long enough to create the works that would render him immortal like the great Homer: 'When I have fears that I may cease to be/ Before my pen has gleam'd my teeming brain'. He was conscious of his capabilities as an artist, knew that he was good enough; all he required was sufficient time to write the poems that would last for generations to come.

In both 'Ode to a nightingale' and 'Ode on a Grecian Urn' the poet celebrates the power of art to survive centuries of time. In 'Ode to a Nightingale' the immorality of art is symbolised by the nightingale's song. This song, Keats suggests, has been sung for thousands of years all over the world. Though countless nightingales have died the song has been passed on from generation to generation: 'The voice I hear this night was heard/ In ancient days by emperor and clown'.

In 'Ode on a Grecian Urn' the urn that the poet contemplates is said to be 'unravish'd' by time. After thousands of years it remains to inspire to new generations who come to view it. In the poem Keats considers how the urn will continue to exist, like Yeats' wild swans, after he has died, remaining in the world for generations to come.

To One Who Has Been Long in City Pent

This sonnet offers advice to anyone who has spent too much time closely shut up in the confines of the city.

For someone who has spent too much time in the city it is very pleasant to get gaze up at the open expanse of the sky: ''Tis very sweet to look into the fair/ And open face of heaven'. Keats personifies the sky, comparing it to a benevolent face. In line 4 he mentions the 'smile of the blue firmament'. The image is given a religious significance. In the third line the poet refers to the sky as the 'open face of heaven'. The sky is thus linked with the ideal and the eternal. Before such a scene it is deemed appropriate that a 'prayer' should be said.

The poet then asks a rhetorical question. Who, he wonders, is happier than the person who feeling tired and content lies down in long grass and with a good book? The scenario is one of escape from the hustle and bustle of the city. The poet imagines 'some pleasant lair' where he can momentarily remove himself from the world of fuss and fret. In order to detach himself from reality such a person would immerse himself in a 'gentle tale of love and languishment'. 'Languishment' refers to a state of melancholic weakness, the condition of the lovesick or the broken-hearted.

That same happy person, when hearing the sad song of the nightingale and seeing the clouds sweep across the sky, will mourn the fact that such a day should pass so quickly. The last two lines compare the silent passing of such time to the falling of an angel's tear from heaven to earth.

The last six lines of the poem (the sestet of the sonnet) imagine how this same person would feel when such a fine day had drawn to a close. Listening to the nightingale's song whilst watching the small clouds move rapidly ('career') across the sky, this person would mourn the fact that the day has passed so quickly: 'He mourns that day so soon has glided by'. The last two lines liken the silent, imperceivable passage of time to the 'passage of an angel's tear/ That falls through the clear ether silently'.

LANGUAGE

The form of the sonnet

The sonnet uses the rhyming scheme ABBA ABBA CDCDCD. The first quatrain describes the pleasure found in gazing up at the open sky. The second quatrain considers the joys of retiring to 'some pleasant lair' with a good book. The sestet then involves a turn. The poet moves from considering the joys of a day spent out of the city to the sadness that will accompany the journey home.

Imagery

The poem contains a number of references to classical religion. The sky is referred to as the 'open face of heaven' and the poet suggests that someone gazing up at this sky ought to 'breathe a prayer'. In the last two lines of the poem he compares the passage of the day to 'an angel's tear'. Keats evokes the religious in order to convey the very special nature of the experiences he describes. The sonnet also involves a reference to Greek mythology. In line 10 the poet refers to the song of the nightingale as the 'notes of Philomel'.

Metaphor and similes

Keats' personifies the sky in this sonnet. It is likened to a smiling face. The metaphor thus renders the sky benevolent and sympathetic. The face is said to be 'fair' and 'open', both qualities that we would associate with a decent and honest person. The small clouds also seem to be happily alive.

The final two lines of the poem involve a simile. Keats compares the passage of time to the 'passage of an angel's tear'. The simile suggests the intangibility of time. Like an angel's tear it moves 'silently' and imperceptibly.

THEMES

Escape

'To One Who Has Been Long in City Pent' is a poem about escaping the stressful, confined world of the city for a day. Within the poem Keats conjures up a space cut off from the world of strife where one might curl up with a book. The 'lair/ Of wavy grass' is a private oasis remote from the world of everyday concerns. Like Yeats' lake isle of Innisfree, it functions as tranquil haven where someone can leave behind the clamour of the city and soothe the mind.

Nature

Unlike poems such as 'Ode on a Grecian Urn' and 'Ode to an Nightingale', 'To One Who Has Been Long in City Pent' does not look to escape from the human world into a timeless realm. It is to the real and natural world that Keats looks when considering his escape from the troubles and strife of life. The sonnet seeks no transcendence in its desire to escape the city. Rather it celebrates the beauty of the country and the sublime wonder of the very sky above our heads. The sky features in a number of Keats' poems, representing for him the mystery and the beauty of the world.

Art

Yet, art is considered a part of the escape in the poem. The reading of the 'gentle tale of love and languishment' allows for imaginative escape, a momentary break from the real world into a pleasant world of fiction.

Life

The poem alludes to the stresses of modern city life. The word 'pent' in the title and opening line suggests that the city is a place where people are trapped and confined, almost like a prison. Life is considered exhausting. The imagined person is said to be 'fatigued' as he lays himself down in the long grass. The poem illustrates the importance of taking time to appreciate the beauty of the natural world. The sonnet suggests that it is all too easy to get preoccupied with our everyday worries and stresses. Keats reminds us to look up once in a while, to experience the pleasant open expanse of the sky above our heads.

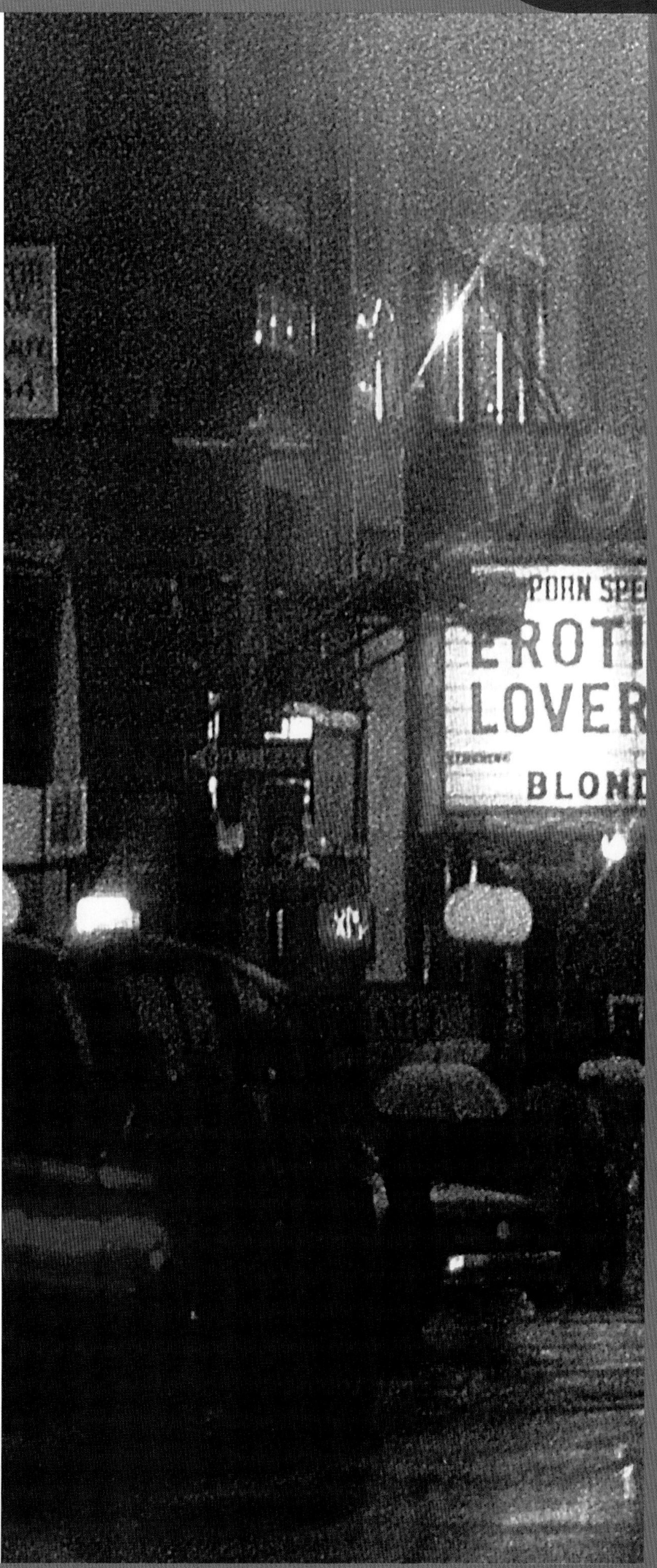

On First Looking into Chapman's Homer

In this sonnet Keats records his pleasure and excitement at discovering George Chapman's translations of the great Greek poet Homer. Homer was famous for his two epic poems The Iliad and The Odyssey. Keats could not read ancient Greek so it was only through Chapman's translations that he could explore these epics, which are often considered to be the foundation of Western poetry.

LINE BY LINE

LINES 1–4: *Reading as travelling*

In these lines Keats uses an interesting metaphor to describe the process of reading poetry. The act of reading, Keats suggests, is like the act of travel. The work of each great poet is like a country or 'realm' waiting to be explored. Each time Keats reads a poet's work he visits his or her 'realm': 'Much have I travelled in the realms of gold'.

Keats has read a great deal of poetry. He claims, therefore, that he has visited the 'realms' of many different poets. Each poet's work is like a different 'state', 'kingdom' or 'island' he has explored: 'many goodly states and kingdoms seen; / Round many western islands have I been'.

LINES 5–8: *Travelling to Homer's realm*

Homer's work, too, is described as realm or 'demesne': 'One wide expanse … That deep brow'd Homer ruled as his demesne'. (The fact that Homer is described as 'deep-brow'd' indicates his enormous intelligence and wisdom). Homer's 'realm' is described as being particularly vast, which reflects his status as arguably the greatest poet who ever lived. Lesser poets are represented by 'goodly' or decent-sized territories on the 'map' of poetry. Homer, however, is represented by an enormous 'wide expanse'.

Keats has often heard about Homer's amazing epics: 'Oft of one wide expanse had I been told'. Yet he has never been able to read them due to his lack of ancient Greek. He has never been able to enter Homer's great realm and breathe the fresh air of that vast domain: 'Yet never did I breathe its pure serene'. ('Serene' is an old-fashioned word for air).

Now, however, Keats has discovered Chapman's translations of Homer's masterpieces: 'I heard Chapman speak out loud and bold'. Chapman's skill as a translator has allowed him to experience Homer's work for the first time. Finally Keats has managed to enter the 'wide expanse' of Homer's realm and breathe its pure clean air.

LINES 9–14: *A great discovery*

Keats is clearly thrilled by his discovery of Chapman's translations. To him the discovery of Chapman's book is as exciting as the discovery a new planet would be to an astronomer or 'watcher of the skies': 'Then I felt as some watcher of the skies / When a new planet swims into his ken'. (Several commentators have suggested that these lines were inspired by the astronomer's Herschel's discovery of the planet Uranus in 1781).

He claims that he is as stunned by his discovery of Chapman's book as the Spanish explorer Cortez was by his discovery of the Pacific Ocean. Keats paints a wonderful picture of the moment Cortez sees the Pacific for the first time from the top of 'a peak in Darien'. ('Darien' is an old name for the South American region of Panama).

Cortez is presented as a powerful soldier and explorer. He is 'stout' or strong and has the 'eagle eyes' of an experienced sailor. Yet even this seasoned campaigner is stunned and moved by the magnificent sight of the sparkling Pacific. He stands 'silent' on the mountain peak, staring down at that seemingly endless body of water. His soldiers, too, are stunned by the discovery.

LANGUAGE

Structure

This poem takes the form of a Petrarchan sonnet, which means that it is divided into an octet (the first eight lines) and a sestet (the final six lines). The octet rhymes ABBA ABBA while the sestet rhymes CDCDCD. As is often the case with Petrarchan sonnets there is a shift in subject matter between the octet and the sestet. The octet centres on the notion of exploration, while the sestet deals with the notion of discovery.

Metaphor

'On First Looking into Chapman's Homer', like so many of Keats' poems, is extremely rich in metaphor. The first eight lines of the poem are dominated by a set of linked metaphors that compare the activity of reading poetry to the activity of going on a journey. The work of each poet is compared to a country or 'realm' to be explored. Homer's work is described as a particularly vast realm renowned for its fresh air ('its pure Serene').

Imagery

Fittingly for a poem that pays tribute to Homer, this sonnet contains a great deal of water imagery. Both of Homer's epics (The Odyssey and The Iliad) contain great sea voyages. The water imagery in 'On First Looking into Chapman's Homer' is evident in line 3 with its reference to western islands, in line 10 with its reference to the planet 'swimming' and in lines 11–14 with their reference to Cortez, who was famous (among other things) for his great sea voyage. Perhaps the most significant instance of water imagery is poem's concluding reference to the Pacific Ocean, which Cortez and his men regard in silent awe from the mountaintop in Darien.

The poem's imagery of exploration and discovery also echoes The Odyssey. In The Odyssey the hero Odysseus explores the Aegean Sea on his way home from the siege of Troy, discovering many weird and wonderful island kingdoms. In the sestet Keats mentions Cortez and an astronomer, who in a sense are modern day versions of Odysseus. explored South America, discovering new lands and new peoples. Astronomers, meanwhile, explores the heavens with their telescopes, discovering new planets. As we have seen, the poem suggests that the activity of reading poetry is also a form of discovery and exploration.

The poem's sestet skilfully combines images of sky, land and sea. There is an image of the sky in lines 9–10, which describes the astronomer discovering a new planet. Land imagery is present in the form of the mountaintop on which Cortez and his men are standing. The sea, meanwhile, is present in the form of the Pacific Ocean. Several critics have suggested that this combination of images is a kind of tribute to Homer, whose poems encompassed every sphere of existence, from the Gods in heaven to the creatures of the sea.

Sound effects

Throughout the poem Keats makes extensive use of assonance to create a pleasant verbal music. We see this in line 4 with its repeated 'o' sound: 'Apollo hold'. A similar repetition of the 'o' sound is evident in line 11: 'stout Cortez'. Line 11 also features a repeated 'e' sound in 'eagle eyes'. Assonance also predominates in lines 6–7. Here we see a repeated 'o' sound in 'deep-brow'd Homer' and a repeated 'e' sound in 'never breathe its pure serene'.

THEMES

The importance and power of poetry

'Chapman's Homer' is a celebration of the power of poetry, suggesting that reading poetry is a thrilling voyage of discovery. This is evident especially in the sestet, where Keats suggests that discovering the work of a new poet is as thrilling as discovering a new planet or a new ocean.

In particular the poem is a tribute to the genius of Homer. Keats indicates Homer's pre-eminent status among poets by referring to his work as a 'vast expanse', which dwarfs the smaller territories represented by the works of other great poets. He suggests the originality and power of Homer's work by referring to the 'pure serene', the fresh clean air, of his realm. Even after thousands of years his poems retain their energy and freshness.

'Chapman's Homer' emphasises the emotional intensity with which Keats responded to works of art. A similar intensity is evident in his response to a decorated vase in 'Ode on a Grecian Urn'. 'Chapman's Homer' reminds us of the keenness and passion with which Keats experienced the world around him. This passion is also evident in 'Ode to a Nightingale', where he describes his rapturous response to a bird's singing, and in 'To Autumn', where he is captivated by the sleepy beauty of the autumn scenery.

When I Have Fears that I May Cease to Be

BACKGROUND AND INTRODUCTION

In this poem Keats confronts the possibility that he might die young, that death might claim him before he has the chance to live life to the full. The poem focuses on three different ways in which he finds the thought of an early death upsetting and disturbing. Firstly, he is worried that death might claim him before he has a chance to realise his potential as a poet (lines 1–4). Secondly, he worries that death might claim him before he is able to write poems that capture the beauty of nature (lines 5–8). Finally, he is worried that death will deprive him of the pleasures of romantic love (lines 9–12).

LINE BY LINE

LINES 1–4

These lines deal with Keats' fear that will die (or 'cease to be') before he has realised his poetic potential. His brain, he says, is overflowing or 'teeming' with ideas for poems. When he puts pen to paper these ideas will be released or 'glean'd' from his brain and will flow on to the page: 'Before my pen has glean'd my teeming brain'. Keats claims to have so much inspiration that he could fill piles of books with his poetry. He could create 'high piled books of charactery'.('Charactery' is another word for writing).

Keats uses the metaphor of the harvest to describe his poetic creativity. His imagination, he says, is like is like a fertile field. There are as many ideas in his imagination as there are ears of corn in a field at harvest time. Just as grain must be harvested and placed in storehouses ('garners'), so must Keats' ideas be transformed into poems and written down in books. Keats must fill his notebooks with poems just as the farmer fills his garners with grain: 'high piled Books … Hold like rich garners the full ripen'd grain'.

Yet Keats is worried that he will 'cease to be' before he has had the chance to 'glean' or release the inspiration that fills his brain and transform it into finished poems. He is terrified by the prospect that he might die before he can 'harvest' the ideas that grow in his imagination and fill notebook after notebook with his words.

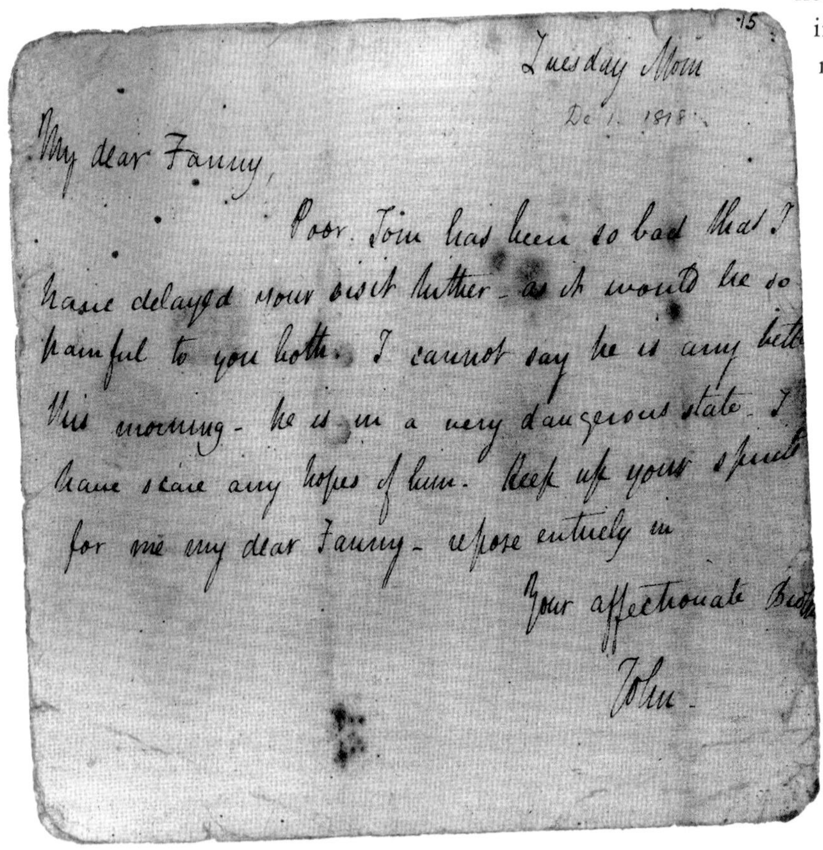
15

Tuesday Morn

Dec 1. 1818

My dear Fanny,

Poor Tom has been so bad that I have delayed your visit hither - as it would be so painful to you both. I cannot say he is any bette[r] this morning - he is in a very dangerous state. I have scarce any hopes of him. Keep up your spirit[s] for me my dear Fanny - repose entirely in

Your affectionate Broth[er]

John -

LINES 5–8

One of Keats' greatest ambitions was to capture the beauty and mystery of nature in his poetry. In these lines he presents us with a powerful image that sums up his sense of nature's majesty. He describes clouds moving across a star-filled night sky: 'When I behold upon the night's starr'd face / Huge cloudy symbols of a high romance'.

He is filled with a burning desire to 'trace' or describe sights like this one in his poetry. Yet he worries that he will 'never live' to achieve this, that he will die before writing poems that adequately express nature's overwhelming beauty.

LINES 9–12

In these line Keats turns his attention to the subject of love. Love, he says, is a kind of magical 'fairy power' in which people take great joy or 'relish'. There is one lady in particular for whom Keats feels great affection, a 'fair creature' he loves more than other.

Yet Keats is gripped by the fear that death will claim before he has the opportunity to properly experience a romantic relationship with this woman. He worries that he will 'Never have relish in the fairy power / Of unreflecting love'. He is terrified that death will put an end to his enjoyment of his beloved's beauty: 'And when I feel, fair creature of an hour, / That I shall never look upon thee more'.

LINES 13–14

Keats, then, is tormented by two different fears, one relating to 'Fame' and the other relating to 'Love'. On one hand he worries that he won't achieve fame as a poet, that death will claim before he has a chance to write the outstanding poems that will ensure his reputation as one England's greatest writers. On the other hand he worries that he will die before properly experiencing love.

Lines 13–14 describe Keats' reaction to these concerns. When he worries that he may never experience love and fame, he responds by convincing himself that love and fame simply don't matter in the first place. When these fears grip him he ventures to the seashore, to the 'Shore of the wide world'. Standing by the ocean, Keats loses himself in meditation: 'I stand alone and think'.

Standing on the sea shore allows him to focus on the 'bigger picture'. He contemplates the wide world that surrounds him and the vast ocean, which seems to go on forever and will still be washing against the shore millennia from now. Perhaps he also considers the night's 'starr'd face', filled with countless points of light that will flicker for millions of years.

When Keats considers this vastness of time and space his own concerns seem petty and unimportant. After all, what significance does any individual person have from the viewpoint of eternity? His hopes and fears regarding romantic love and literary success become 'nothing' in his mind: 'Till Love and Fame to Nothingness do sink'. Keats' response to the fears that grip him has been described as extremely bleak. When he worries about not attaining his goals and fulfilling his ambitions, he convinces himself that those goals and ambitions simply don't matter in the greater scheme of things.

LANGUAGE

Structure

'When I Have Fears' is a Shakespearean sonnet consisting of three quatrains and a concluding rhyming couplet. The poem has the following rhyme scheme: ABAB CDCD EFEF GG. In most Shakespearean sonnets each quatrain deals with a different topic, while the concluding couplet outlines the poet's final response to the issues that have been raised. 'When I Have Fears', however, differs slightly form the typical Shakespearean sonnet:

- The topic of Keat's imagination gets four lines (lines 1–4).
- The topic of Keats' desire to write about nature gets four lines (lines 5–8).
- The topic of love gets three-and-a-half lines (lines 9, 10, 11 and half of line 12).
- The conclusion gets two and a half lines (half of line 12, line 13 and line 14).

In a normal Shakespearean sonnet the topic of love would get four lines and the conclusion only two. According to several critics Keats 'shortens' the third quatrain to reinforces our sense that he is involved in a 'race against time'. It stresses the possibility that death may not grant him the time or space to achieve and experience everything he desires.

Metaphors and similes

Perhaps the most famous metaphor in this poem is that of the harvest. As we have seen, Keats compares his imagination to a fertile field. The ideas that form in his mind are compared to 'full ripen'd grain'. Using a wonderful simile Keats compares the books that will contain those ideas to garners or storehouses: 'high piled Books ... like rich garners'. This extended metaphor or 'conceit' has been praised by many critics and commentators for the skilful manner in which it conveys the fertility of Keats' imagination. Keats also uses a metaphor to describe the night sky, comparing it to a 'face' which is occasionally hidden form view by the cloud formations that blow across it: 'the night's starr'd face'

Imagery

In the opening quatrain Keats presents us with several images of ripeness and plenty. We have the brain 'teeming' with ideas, the piles of books, the 'rich' garners full to bursting with harvested corn and the grain itself which is fully ripened. These images skilfully suggest the fertility of Keats' imagination, which is rich with ideas that are ripe or ready to be transformed into poems.

Another powerful image occurs in lines 5–6, where Keats depicts the star-filled night sky. Yet perhaps the poem's most melancholic and memorable image is that of the poet standing alone on 'the Shore / Of the wide world' as he meditates on the notions of love, death and poetic fame. The imagery in 'When I Have Fears' echoes that in several of Keats' other sonnets. This poem, 'On First Looking into Chapman's Homer' and 'Bright Star' feature images of the night sky and the ocean, two images that for Keats seemed to sum up the awe and mystery of the natural world.

Assonance and alliteration

Like most of Keats' poems 'When I Have Fears' is rich in assonance and alliteration. Alliteration is particularly evident in line 4 with its repeated 'g' and 'r' sounds: 'rich garners the full ripen'd grain'. Assonance, meanwhile, occurs throughout the poem. We see it in line 3 with its repeated 'e' sound: 'pen has gleaned my teeming brain'. It also features in line 3 with its repeated 'i' sound: 'high piled'. Lines 5–8 also feature a pleasant verbal music, generated by the repeated 'a' sound. We see this in the phrase 'starr'd face' and in the phrase 'shadows with the magic hand of chance'.

THEMES

Nature

Keats' almost overwhelming love of nature is evident throughout his poetry. (We see it especially in 'To Autumn' and 'To One Long in City Pent'). In this poem he focuses on his burning ambition to describe the natural world in his poetry. He wants to 'trace' or draw images of nature's beauty with words, just as an artist would with paint and ink. The poem also suggests that Keats somehow 'sees' nature differently than the rest of us. Where the rest of us merely see a 'night sky' he observes a 'starr'd face', where the rest of us see bits of cloud he sees 'symbols of a high romance'. It seems that

Keats' poetic imagination is capable of detecting symbols and meanings in nature that simply elude ordinary people.

Poetry

Keats' almost obsessive concern with the art of poetry is evident everywhere throughout his work. We see it in his intensely emotional response to the work of Homer in 'On First Looking into Chapman's Homer'. It is also evident in 'Ode to a Nightingale' where Keats maintains that the power of the poetic imagination will allow him to 'fade far way' from this troubled world -at least for a brief time.

Yet Keats' feelings about poetry are perhaps nowhere more forcibly expressed than in 'When I Have Fears'. Here we see the obvious pride and delight Keats takes in his own poetic gifts. He seems to relish the richness and variety of the ideas and inspirations and that develop in his imagination. He seems bursting with confidence that he will be able to fulfil his ambition of writing poems that capture nature's beauty, declaring that he is guided by the 'magic hand of Chance'. The only thing that stands between this gifted young poet and his lofty artistic ambitions is the possibility that he will die young, that death will him before he has the chance to make the most of the talent that fills him.

Love

The attitude to love expressed in this poem is rather complex. On one hand Keats clearly regards love as important. People, he says, take great 'relish' or delight in love. He becomes greatly distressed when he thinks that he himself might never experience true love. He clearly enjoys gazing at the beauty of the woman he loves and is terrified that death might snatch him away from her.

Yet the poem also seems to suggest that romantic love is somehow silly or shallow. There is a sense in which Keats suggests that romantic love is a short-lived, transitory emotion. He may feel great affection for the 'fair creature' mentioned in line 9, but he acknowledges that she is merely the fair creature 'of an hour'. In an hour's time, or tomorrow, or next week, his affections could be directed toward someone entirely different. Love, it seems, is a fickle and shallow business.

'When I have Fears' describes love as a 'fairy power'. In Keats' poetry the notion of a 'fairy power' often has negative connotations. (We see this in 'La Belle Dame Sans Merci' where the 'faery child' bewitches the knight and lures him to his doom). Love, then, is presented as a spell or enchantment that bewitches us. It takes over our minds, leaving us 'unreflective' and robbing us of our judgement and good sense. Love, the poem implies, is like some kind of dangerous magic spell that can blind us to reality and bring great suffering into our lives.

Time and human insignificance

Perhaps the most important 'message' put forward by 'When I Have Fears' is that time is of the essence. Each human being has dreams and hopes, goals and ambitions he or she would like to achieve. It is important, however, that we 'seize the day' and begin to realise our potential as soon as possible, for we never know when we might suddenly 'cease to be'.

'When I have Fears' also emphasises the vastness of the universe that surrounds us. The poem's conclusion stresses that we exist in an infinitely huge universe that has existed for millions of years before we were born and will still be around millions of years after our deaths. The life of each human being is tiny and insignificant in the context of this eternal, endless universe. The poem suggests, therefore, that our hopes, dreams and fears simply don't matter in the greater scheme of things. From the viewpoint of eternity our terrors and ambitions sink 'to Nothingness'.

La Belle Dame Sans Merci

THE TITLE

The poem's title, from a 1424 French poem by Alain Chartier, means 'the beautiful woman without mercy'.

LINE BY LINE

STANZAS 1 TO 3: *The knight*

At the beginning of the poem the speaker meets a knight, who seems to be 'loitering' or hanging about aimlessly on the side of a hill. The knight looks terrible. According to the speaker he appears 'pale', 'haggard' and 'woe begone'. ('Woe begone' is another word for sorrowful). He has the appearance of someone who has been struck down by some kind of disease. His brow or forehead is as white as lily: 'I see a lily on thy brow'. His brow is moist with sweat, which the speaker thinks might be caused by fever or anguish: 'with anguish moist or fever dew'. His cheeks, meanwhile, have a worrying red glow. According to the speaker they are the colour of a withering rose: 'And on thy cheeks a fading rose'.

The landscape is barren and wintry. The poem's winter setting is suggested by the fact that the harvest has been completed and the squirrel has finished gathering its supply of nuts for winter: 'The squirrel's granary is full / And the harvest's done'. The speaker conveys the bleakness of the knight's surroundings by declaring that the sedge or grass has withered from the nearby lakeside and that the birds have flown away for winter: 'The sedge has withered from the lake / And no birds sing!' The speaker wonders why the knight is 'loitering', sick and depressed, in such a miserable, wintry landscape. He asks the knight what 'ails' or troubles him: 'O what can ail thee knight at arms / Alone and palely loitering?'

STANZA 4: *Meeting the faery*

In this stanza the knight begins to tell the story of how he came to end up in such a pitiful state. He tells the speaker that he encountered a mysterious lady while he was riding through the 'Meads' or meadows. The knight was struck by this mystery woman's good looks. He claims that she was 'Full beautiful': 'Her hair was long, her foot was light'. Yet this was no ordinary woman, but a strange magical creature. According to the knight she was a 'faery's child' with 'wild' eyes. (Several critics have suggested that the lady's 'wild' eyes suggest the unruly and unpredictable 'faery' magic that dwells within her).

STANZAS 5 TO 7: *The knight and the faery*

In these stanzas the knight recounts how he spent the day with the faery woman. He made little pieces of jewellery for her from the flowers that grow in the meadow, weaving her bracelets, a headband or 'garland', and a belt or 'Zone'. According to the knight, the Lady looked at him as if she were falling in love with him: 'She looked at me as she did love'. Her love for the knight is also indicated by the fact that she made sweet moaning of sighing noises.

The knight placed the lady on his horse and they rode together through the meadows: 'I set her on my pacing steed' While they were riding the lady sang him a 'faery song'. The knight claims that he spent the entire day gazing at the lady. He seems to have been so entranced by her beauty that he could not look away: 'And nothing else saw all day long'.

good as manna from heaven: 'She found me roots of relish sweet / And honey wild, and manna dew'. Then the lady says something in a strange language. The knight, of course, is unable to understand what these strange words mean. He assumes, however, that the lady is telling him she loves him: 'And sure in language strange she said / 'I love thee true'.

STANZA 8 TO 11: *The grotto and the nightmare*

That evening, the lady takes the knight to the mysterious grotto where she lives: 'She took me to her elfin grot'. In the grotto the lady starts weeping and sighing as if she was overcome by a fit of sorrow: 'And there she wept and sigh'd full sore'. The knight attempts to comfort her by kissing her: 'And there I shut her wild eyes / With kisses four'. Finally, the lady 'lulls' the knight to sleep.

While sleeping in the grotto the knight has a terrible nightmare: 'And there I dream'd – Ah woe betide'. In his dream takes it is twilight: 'in the gloam'. Through the dusk comes a procession of ghostly knights: 'I saw pale kings and Princes too / Pale warriors, death pale were they all'. The knights as described as being 'death pale', suggesting they are white as corpses. They also seem to be extremely thin, as indicated by 'their starv'd lips'.

The mouths of these spectral figures open or 'gape' in order to issue the knight a horrid warning: 'I saw their starv'd lips in the gloam / with horrid warning gaped wide'. They warn the knight that he has been enslaved by a beautiful lady without mercy: 'They cried 'La belle dame sans merci / Thee hath in thrall'. ('in thrall' is another expression for 'enslaved to').

Then the knight's dream ends and he wakes up to find himself not in the faery maiden's grotto but on the side of a hill: 'And I awoke and found me here / On the cold hill's side'. The knight, it seems, has remained on the hillside ever since. And he will continue to stay or 'sojourn' there, alone and sick-looking, even though the landscape is turning to winter all around him: 'And this is why I sojourn here / Alone and palely loitering; / Though the sedge is wither'd from the lake'.

AN INTERPRETATION

The traditional interpretation

The standard interpretation of this poem suggests that the Lady is some kind of monster. The Lady, it has been suggested, is a malevolent creature whose purpose in life is to destroy men using her magical powers. The Lady, according to this interpretation, is a kind of predator. She waits in the meadows for men to pass by like a spider waiting for flies to enter her web. When the knight rides past she uses her beautiful appearance to attract him. Then, as they spend the day together, she uses her magical powers to place him under a spell.

Several critics have suggested that the Lady uses her singing to enchant the knight. The Lady's 'faery song', they maintain, is like the song of the sirens in

Greek mythology which bewitched any man unfortunate enough to hear it. The meal the Lady gives the knight could also be part of the spell-casting process. The roots, honey and 'manna dew' that the Lady gives the knight might function as a kind of 'magic potion' that leaves him in her power. Traditionally, of course, spells were cast by speaking 'magic words' and it is possible that this is what the Lady is up to when she speaks to the knight in 'language strange'. The knight assumes that the Lady is telling him she loves him but it is also possible that she is speaking the words of a spell that will destroy him.

Irrespective of how the spell is cast there can be little doubt that by the time they reach the 'fairy grot' the knight is firmly in this malevolent Lady's power. When the knight wakes he has been magically transported from the grotto to the 'cold hill's side'. The Lady, it seems, has placed the knight under an enchantment that prevents him from leaving the hillside. He must remain their, starving, sick and miserable, until he dies.

According to this interpretation, the 'Pale warriors' in the knight's dream are the Lady's previous victims. Not even princes and kings, it seems, could avoid being en snared by the Lady's charms. Like the knight, each of these 'Pale warriors' was entrapped and bewitched by the Lady. Each of them was condemned to remain on the hillside until they were claimed by death. While the knight sleeps their ghosts attempt to warn the knight of the danger he is in. Their warning, however, comes too late. The knight is already 'in thrall' to the Belle Dame Sans Merci.

Power relations

An important aspect of the poem is the shifting nature of the 'power relationship' between the Lady and the knight. Initially, the knight seems to be in control. He places the Lady on his 'steed' and sets off with her across the meadow. Soon, however, the Lady begins to take charge of the situation. This starts to become apparent when the knight declares that he is unable to take his eyes off her: 'And nothing else saw all day long'. It is the Lady, not the knight, who finds food for the couple. Then she takes him to her grotto. Finally, she 'lulls' him into a deep sleep. As the poem progresses, therefore, the knight falls further under the Lady's spell and it is the Lady, not the knight, who is in control.

A Feminist interpretation

A number of feminist critics have taken issue with this 'traditional interpretation' of the poem. They regard as somewhat sexist the depiction of the Lady as a kind of 'femme fatale' who lures men to their doom. The poem, they maintain, stems from a sexist tradition of storytelling whereby the woman is always plays the part of the sinister villain who leads the innocent man astray. According to

The lady found food and drink for him among the meadows. She gives him a meal of wild honey and plant-roots, washed down with dew. Yet this simple fare delights the knight. The roots are 'relish sweet' and the dew tastes as these critics this tradition dates all the way back to the Bible and the story of Adam and Eve. Several feminist critics have suggested that the knight actually rapes the Lady while they are in the grotto. The Lady, they maintain, 'wept and sigh'd full sore' because she was being violated by the knight. The knight is punished for his misdeeds by being condemned to remain forever on the 'cold hill side'.

LANGUAGE

Atmosphere

Perhaps the most memorable feature of 'La Belle Dame Sans Merci' is its alien, otherworldly atmosphere. This peculiar atmosphere is established at the very beginning of the poem with the strange and haunting image of the pale and sick-looking knight 'loitering' aimlessly in a barren wintry landscape. The poem's weird atmosphere also stems from the figure of the Lady, this mysterious stranger with her 'wild eyes', her 'language strange' and her 'faery song'. The references to the 'elfin grot' and to the meal of roots and honey also add to the poem's atmosphere of other-worldliness, as does the knight's terrible dream with its starving, 'death Pale' kings and princes.

Structure

The poem's atmosphere of mystery is greatly increased by the poem's unusual structure. The poem takes the form of a conversation between the knight and an unnamed speaker. In the poem's first three stanzas this speaker asks the knight what's wrong with him. The knight responds by telling the speaker about his encounter with the Lady. All we are given, then, is the knight's own version of events. Yet how do we know

that the knight is telling the truth? Perhaps he is an 'unreliable narrator' who conceals certain aspects of what really happened to him. The fact that the poem takes the form of an 'overheard conversation' greatly increases the poem's sense of strangeness and mystery for we can never be sure if what we're hearing is the truth of these bizarre and alien events.

BALLAD FORM

'La Belle Dame Sans Merci' is a wonderful example of a the poetic form known as a ballad. It has many of the features often associated with the ballad form:

- It is a relatively short poem that tells a story.
- It uses four line stanzas that have an ABCB rhyme scheme.
- In each stanza the second and fourth lines are shorter than the first and third.
- Like many ballads it deals with events of a supernatural nature.
- Like many ballads it features a great deal of repetition. Both of the poem's first two stanzas, for instance, begin with the same line: 'O what can ail thee knight-at-arms'. Furthermore, the last three lines of the first stanza are also almost identical to the last three lines of the final stanza. (According to several critics this gives the poem a 'circular structure'. the poem end precisely where it begun, suggesting that nothing can ever change for the knight. He is trapped on the 'cold hill side' forever).

THEMES

Love

'La Belle Dame Sans Merci' is often regarded as a parable or allegory of love. The poem presents the game of love as a dangerous one. It suggests that when a man falls in love with a woman he risks falling under her spell and becoming 'enslaved' by her beauty, just as the knight becomes 'in thrall' to the Lady. The poem suggests that falling for a beautiful woman can have disastrous consequences. It can fill his mind with emotional torment, leaving his life as bleak as that of the knight who is forced to remain forever on the 'cold hill side'.

The poem draws on the tradition of 'courtly love' poetry, which often depicted the poet's desperate love for a beautiful woman who was unable or unwilling to return his affections. (The title 'La Belle Dame Sans Merci' is borrowed from a 'courtly love poem' written by Alain Chartier in 1424. In Chartier's poem the beautiful woman is 'without mercy' because she refuses to give in to the poet's advances). The poem's wary and negative attitude toward love may also have its roots in Keats own life experiences. For Keats himself was involved in several less-than-entirely-successful relationships that caused him much uncertainty and emotional turmoil. It is perhaps unsurprising, therefore, that in many of his poems Keats describes love as a kind of superficial but dangerous enchantment that brings great misery and suffering into our lives. (This is also evident in 'When I Have Fears', where love is depicted as a 'faery power').

Ode to a Nightingale

LINE BY LINE

STANZA 1: *The nightingale's song*

The poem opens with Keats sitting in his garden on a summer's night, listening to a nightingale sing in a nearby forest. The forest in which the nightingale sings is described as a 'melodious plot / Of beechen green, and shadows numberless'. This plot of woodland is described as 'melodious' because it is filled with the melody of the nightingale's song. It is described as 'beechen' because it contains a lot of beech trees. Because it is night time the forest is filled with thousands of shadows: 'shadows numberless'.

The nightingale is filled with 'ease' as it sings its happy, summery songs: 'Singest of summer in full-throated ease'. The fact that Keats describes the nightingale as 'light-winged' reinforces our impression of its carefree existence: 'Thou light-winged Dryad of the trees'. In one sense this phrase simply describes the bird's tiny, fragile wings. Yet it also suggests that the nightingale is not 'weighed down' by the kinds of cares and worries that trouble human beings. It is unsurprising, therefore, that Keats declares the nightingale's lot in life to be a 'happy' one: 'thy happy lot'.

Yet Keats' reaction to the nightingale's joyous singing is complicated. On one hand its summery songs make him happy. Yet on the other hand he claims they make him too happy. They fill him with sorrow and a feeling of mental 'numbness'. The nightingale's singing, he declares, causes his heart to ache: 'My heart aches'. It causes an unpleasant feeling of numbness to 'pain' his mind (his 'sense') as if he'd drunk poison or taken some kind of sedative drug: 'a drowsy numbness pains / My sense, as though of hemlock I had drunk, / Or emptied some dull opiate to the drains'. ('Hemlock' is a type of poison while an 'opiate' is a sedative drug). The bird's singing makes him feel as if his sinking into forgetfulness. Keats describes this sensation wonderfully, declaring that he feels as if he's sinking into the river Lethe: 'and Lethe-wards had sunk'. (In Greek mythology the Lethe was a river whose waters brought complete forgetfulness to all who drank from them). Keats' response to the nightingale, therefore, is paradoxical. Its singing fills him not only with joy but also with a sorrow that leaves his mind blank, dull and sedated.

Listening to the nightingale's joyous singing and contemplating its carefree existence reminds Keats of the difficulties that fill his own life and the lives of human beings in general. Keats claims, however, that he is not jealous or envious of the bird's existence. In fact, he is happy that the bird has such a beautiful, easeful life: "Tis not through envy of thy happy lot /But being too happy in thine happiness'. What he desires is to somehow join the nightingale in its forest of 'beechen' serenity and share its joyous, carefree existence.

STANZA 2: *Magical wine*

Keats wants to join the nightingale in its dark and peaceful plot of woodland. Human life, as we shall see, is depicted as being full of pain and woe while the nightingale's days are carefree and happy. It makes sense, therefore, that Keats wants to slip quietly away from his present existence, to 'leave the world unseen'. He wants to 'fade away into the forest dim' with the nightingale. In the forest he would be able to share the nightingale's life of serenity and ease.

Keats, obviously, is not a bird but a human being. He cannot simply float away into the woods. It is only in his imagination that he can join the nightingale among the trees and enjoy its life of peace and tranquillity. Keats, it seems, wants to have some kind of 'vision' or intensely vivid daydream in which he wanders with the nightingale through its leafy forest home.

Keats expresses his desire to a drink glass of wine that has come from the Hippocrene, a fountain on Mount Helicon in Greece. According to legend anyone who drank from this fountain would be filled with poetic inspiration. (Whereas earlier poets believed that water flowed from this magical spring, Keats preferred to think of it as a fountain of red wine). He believes that drinking some of the Hippocrene's wine will 'boost' or 'empower' his imagination, allowing him to have a vision of the nightingale's forest.

Keats, then, longs for a 'draught' or 'beaker full' of this enchanted liquid from the 'warm south': 'O for a draught of that vintage!' According to Keats the Hippocrene's magical wine has the following features:

- It is a mixture of red and purple in colour, as suggested by Keats' description of it as 'blushful'. Its colours are so rich that it stains the 'mouth' or rim of any container into which it is poured. Any glass or beaker that contains it will have a 'purple-stained mouth'.
- It is full of bubbles like champagne: 'With beaded bubbles winking at the brim'.
- It matures for centuries in cool, deep caverns beneath the ground before flowing upwards to the earth's surface at Mount Helicon: It has, Keats declares, been 'Cooled a long age in the deep-delved earth'.
- It has an extraordinary taste. According to Keats it tastes of 'Flora and the country green, / Dance, and Provençal song, and sunburnt mirth!' Here Keats uses a poetic device called 'synaesthesia'. Synaesthesia is the technique whereby an experience associated with one sense is described in terms of another sense. In this instance the wine's flavour (associated with the sense of taste) is described in terms of 'Provencal song' (associated with the sense of hearing). Its flavour is also described in terms of 'Flora' or flowers (usually associated with the sense of smell), in terms of sunburn (usually associated with the sense of touch), and in terms of dance and country scenery (usually associated with the sense of sight), The wine's flavour is also described in terms of happiness and laughter ('mirth').

STANZA 3: *This cruel world*

Keats, then, longs for a dose of this miraculous wine, feeling that it would increase the power of his imagination and allow him to experience a 'vision' in which he disappears into the forest with the nightingale. For the duration of this vision he would be able to enjoy the nightingale's serene and peaceful lifestyle. He would be able to 'quite forget' this troubled world and the difficulties that fill our day-to-day lives. In this stanza Keats lists some examples of what he regards as the negative aspects of human existence:

- Our lives are dominated by tiredness ('weariness'), sickness ('fever') and worry ('fret').
- This world is full of moaning and groaning: 'Here, where men sit and hear each other groan' (line 24).
- Every living person is doomed to grow old and die. Youth, unfortunately, cannot last, for each of us is condemned to become pale and thin and as time goes on: 'youth grows pale and spectre thin'. Each of us must face the frailty and indignities of old age when, according to Keats, our bodies will be rocked by 'palsy' or sickness: 'palsy shakes a few, sad, last gray hairs'.
- Keats also laments the fact that physical beauty cannot last. As each of us grows older our good looks diminish until there is nothing for our admirers to 'pine' or long for: 'Where beauty cannot keep her lustrous eyes, / Or new love pine at them beyond tomorrow'.
- Our lives are so terrible that even to consider the reality of human existence is to be filled with despair: 'Where but to think is to be full of sorrow / And leaden-eyed despairs' (lines 27–8).

According to Keats, the nightingale has 'never known' the troubles and torments we human beings must endure as we make our way through life. Instead, it has a life of ease and serenity 'among the leaves' of the forest. It is hardly surprising, therefore, that Keats wishes to leave this cruel world behind, to lose himself in the forest and enjoy the trouble-free existence of the nightingale

STANZAS 4 TO 5: *The vision begins*

As we have seen, Keats believes that poetic inspiration will allow him to have a 'vision' of the forest. Keats is adamant that he does not require alcohol or other drugs to induce this vision. Instead, the vision will come from a pure act of poetic imagination. He will use his artistic imagination to envisage himself travelling through the nightingale's woodland domain.

Keats uses a wonderful metaphor to describe this. He says that he will not be brought into the forest on Bacchus' magical leopard-drawn chariot. (Bacchus is the roman God of wine). Instead, the invisible or 'viewless' wings of poetry will carry him into the forest where he will join the nightingale: 'I will fly to thee ... on the viewless wings of Poesy'. ('Poesy', of course, is an old term for poetry).

Keats worries that his 'dull brain' will not allow this vision to take place. He seems concerned that the everyday, rational part of his mind will 'perplex' and hold back ('retard') his imagination, preventing it from envisaging the forest. In line 35, however, Keats declares that the vision he longs for has commenced. He claims that in his imagination he is 'Already with' the nightingale in its woodland abode. Lines 36–50 describe his 'vision' of the forest:

- The forest is extremely dark: 'I cannot see what flowers are at my feet' (lines 38–41). Keats brilliantly sums up the forest's gloominess by referring to its 'verdurous glooms'. ('Verdurous' is another word for green.)
- The forest is only faintly illuminated by starlight and moonlight. The moon and stars are clearly visible in the night sky. Keats uses a typically vivid metaphor to describe this by saying that the moon is sitting in the sky like some kind of fairy Queen sitting on her throne: 'haply the Queen Moon is on her throne'. The stars, meanwhile, are described as 'Fays' or fairies that surround the Queen, ready to do her bidding. The Queen, according to Keats, is 'Cluster'd around by all her starry fays'. Yet only a little of their radiance makes it through the trees' tangled branches to the forest floor. Keats uses a magnificent metaphor to describe this, saying that the summer breeze carries the moon-light and star-light down from heaven and disperses it among the forest's pathways: 'But there is no light, / Save what from heaven is with the breezes blown / Through verdrous glooms and winding mossy ways'.
- The forest contains many winding paths that are over grown with moss, what Keats describes as 'winding mossy ways'.
- The forest is full of pleasant odours. The 'seasonable month' of May gives (or 'endows') a different scent to each of the trees and plants that grow there: 'each sweet [smell] / Wherewith the seasonable month endows / The grass, the thicket, and the fruit-tree wild'. The woodland air, then, is fragrant or 'embalmed' and the natural perfumes of each flower linger among the trees: 'soft incense hangs upon the boughs' (41–3).
- The forest contains a wide variety of plant-life. In lines 43–7 Keats lists some of the different things that grow there: 'The grass, the thicket, and the fruit-tree wild; / White hawthorn and the pastoral eglantine; / Fast fading violets'. (An 'eglantine' is a type of wild rose often referred to as a 'sweet briar')
- Keats makes a special mention of the 'coming musk rose', which is a type of climbing rose often found near trees. (The rose is described as 'coming' because it is just starting to flower, is just 'coming' into full ripeness). The rose's petals are full of moisture, which, using yet another wonderful metaphor, Keats describes as 'dewy wine'.
- ·The forest contains swarms of flies. On summer evenings the flies cluster around the musk roses and fill the air with the murmur of their buzzing. The roses, Keats declares, become the 'murmurous haunt of flies on summer eves'.

STANZA 6: *A death wish*

In this stanza Keats' vision continues. He still imagines himself among the darkness of the woods, listening to the nightingale's song: 'Darkling, I listen'. (To be 'darkling' is to be in darkness). For a long time, he says, he has been attracted to the notion of dying. Death, he feels, will be 'easeful', a sweet release from the miseries of this life. (Keats has already mentioned some of these horrors of human existence in stanza 3).

Keats uses a typically inventive metaphor to describe his 'death wish', saying that he has been 'half in love' with death. He has 'courted' death with poems ('rhymes') the way other poets might court a beautiful woman: 'Call'd him soft names in many a mused rhyme'. (The description of these poems as 'mused' suggests that they were inspired by the muses, the Greek goddesses of creativity). In these poems Keats has flattered death by calling him 'soft names'. He has implored death to terminate his existence, to gently but firmly put a stop to his breathing: 'To take into the air my quiet breath'.

This night in particular strikes him as a good time to die: 'Now more than ever seems it rich to die'. It would be perfect, he feels, to for his life to 'cease' at midnight: 'To cease upon the midnight with no pain'. He would like to pass away while the nightingale is singing. He wants its joyful, ecstatic music to be the last thing he hears on earth: 'While thou art pouring forth thy soul abroad in such an ecstasy'. (Keats, it is important to note, is only interested in death if there is 'no pain' involved).

If Keats were to die this night the nightingale would continue to sing: 'Still wouldst thou sing'. Its music would become a kind of requiem for the dead poet. (A 'requiem' is the music played at a funeral mass). Keats, of course, would be unable to hear this 'high requiem' because he would be dead. His dead body, he declares, would be a 'sod', little more than a clump of clay or soil. The ears of his corpse would be 'vain' or useless and would be quite unable to hear the nightingale's singing: 'I have ears in vain'.

STANZA 7: *The bird's immortal song*

In this stanza Keats declares that the nightingale will never die. This bird, he claims, is immortal: 'Thou wast not born for death, immortal Bird!' Keats, of course, knows that the particular nightingale he's listening to this summer evening is not really immortal. This particular bird will die like any other. Yet the song it sings is the same song that nightingales have been singing for thousands of years and will continue to sing far into the future. Keats suggests some of the places where the song of the nightingales might have been heard in the past:

- He claims that thousands of years ago nightingales sang in the courts of the great kingdoms of the ancient world. Its song, he claims, entertained both emperors and court jesters: 'The voice I heard this passing night was heard / In ancient days by emperor and clown'.
- Keats suggests that the nightingale's song might also have been heard by Ruth, a character from the Bible who lived thousands of years ago: 'Perhaps the self-same song that found a path through the sad heart of Ruth'. The Bible describes how Ruth was forced to leave her native land and work as a farm girl in a strange, foreign country. Keats, therefore. mentions her 'sad heart' and describes her weeping with home sickness as she works in the fields: 'sick for home / She stood in tears amid the alien corn'.
- Keats claims that nightingale's have also brought their song to mysterious 'faery lands'. Its song has been heard in the 'casements' or windows of magical fairy palaces: 'Charm'd magic casements ... in faery lands forlorn'.

STANZA 8: *The end of the vision*

No sooner has Keats thought of the word 'forlorn' than his vision ends. The word 'forlorn', he says, is like a bell or alarm clock that rouses him from his vivid daydream of the forest. His mind snaps out of its woodland fantasy and returns to the real world 'Forlorn! The very word is like a bell / To toll me back form thee to my sole self'.

The imagination, he says, is like some kind of 'deceiving elf' from a fairy tale. It is famous ('fam'd') for 'cheating' us, by leading us to believe in things that are not real. In this instance Keats' imagination has allowed him to believe he's slipped away into the forest with the nightingale. Yet Keats feels that the imagination's reputation for deluding us is exaggerated: 'the fancy cannot cheat as she is fam'd to do'. (Here Keats uses the word 'fancy', which was a nineteenth century term for the faculty of imagination). He wishes that the imagination's ability to deceive us was actually greater so that reality need never intrude on his vision of the forest. Keats, it seems, would like his mind to remain forever in the forest environment he has so vividly imagined.

The nightingale begins to move away from the piece of woodland near Keats' garden. He listens to its sad singing (its 'plaintive anthem') become fainter as it moves deeper into the countryside: 'Past the near meadows, over the still stream, / Up the hill-side'. Finally Keats can no longer hear its singing at all: 'Fled is that music'. The nightingale is out of earshot, 'deep / In the next valley glades'.

The poem concludes with Keats wondering about the strange mental journey he has just taken through the forest: 'Was it a vision or a waking dream?' The conclusion, then, strikes a note of uncertainty. Keats, it seems, isn't even sure if he's awake or sleeping: 'Do I wake or sleep?' Was his experience of the forest just a particularly vivid daydream? Or was it some kind of mirage or hallucination? Or, like the prophets in the Bible, has he experienced some kind of mystical vision?

LANGUAGE

Metaphors

Entire chapters can and have been written about Keats' use of metaphors in 'Ode to a Nightingale'. In stanza 1, for instance Keats uses a wonderful metaphor to describe the nightingale, comparing it a Dryad. (In Greek mythology 'Dryads' were female spirits that inhabited wooded areas). Another two memorable metaphors are to be found in stanza 4. Keats wittily compares being drunk to being carried off by Bacchus on his magical chariot which was pulled by leopards. (Bacchus was the Roman god of wine). Poetic inspiration, meanwhile, is compared to a set of 'viewless' or invisible wings that take the poet on wonderful imaginary journeys: 'the viewless wings of Poesy'.

Keats also uses metaphors to describe nature. The moon, for instance, is described as the 'Queen' of the night sky, sitting on her throne amid the heavens as she gazes down on humanity. The stars, meanwhile, are described as her fairy servants that 'cluster' around their radiant mistress: 'Haply the Queen-Moon is on her throne / Cluster'd around by all her starry Fays'. In line 49 the moisture in the petals of the musk-rose is compared to 'dewy wine'. Another memorable metaphor is used to describe the emotion and soulfulness of the nightingale's singing. Keats captures the joy and beauty of the nightingale's singing by declaring that the bird's soul is emanating from its mouth: 'thou art pouring forth thy soul abroad / In such an ecstasy'.

Personification

In this poem Keats makes extensive use of the literary device known as 'personification'. Personification is a figure of speech that depicts objects and abstract concepts as if they had human traits and qualities. In stanza 3, for instance, the concepts of love and beauty are presented almost as human beings. 'Beauty', it has been suggested, is presented as a woman with bright 'lustrous' eyes, while 'Love' is presented as a man who 'pines' or longs for her affection.

In stanza 8, the concept of 'fancy' or imagination is personified as a kind of semi-human 'elf'. Keats suggests that the 'fancy' has the all-too-human quality of deceitfulness. Yet perhaps the most memorable 'personification' of an abstract concept is that of death in stanza 6. Death is depicted as a person with who the poet has fallen in love: 'for many a time / I have been half in love with easeful Death'. Keats portrays Death as his lover, as someone he has flattered and courted by writing beautiful poems about him.

The poem also personifies several inanimate objects. In stanza 5, for instance, the 'musk-rose' is depicted as the 'child' of may. (It has also been suggested that this stanza personifies the month of May itself, presenting it as the 'mother' of the different plants and flowers in the forest). There is also an element of personification in Keats' description of the night sky. Both the moon and the stars are depicted as 'people'; the moon as a kind of Queen and the stars as her fairy-like servants.

References and allusions

'Ode to a Nightingale' contains several references to Greek mythology. Keats refers to mythical places such as Lethe and Hippocrene. Lethe, as we have seen, was the river in the land of dead that wiped all memories from the minds of those who drank its waters. The Hippocrene, meanwhile, was the magical fountain of poetic inspiration. The poem also refers to several mythological characters. Alcohol, for instance, is associated with Bacchus, who was the Roman God of wine. Flowers, meanwhile, are associated with Flora, who was the Greek goddess of flowers, plants and gardens. Keats also refers to the nightingale as a 'Dryad'. (The dryads, as we have seen, were magical tree spirits in Greek mythology). The depiction of the moon as a kind of 'Queen' of the night sky also owes something to classical mythology. In Roman legends the Goddess Diana was often associated with the moon.

Stanza 7, meanwhile, contains a reference to the Book of Ruth from the Old Testament, describing Ruth's sorrow and homesickness when she was exiled from her homeland. The poem also contains several references to the world of fairy tale. Stanza 4, for instance, depicts the stars as 'Fays' or fairies. Stanza 7, meanwhile, describes nightingales singing in fairy land, while the description in line 74 of the imagination as a kind of 'deceiving elf' is also reminiscent of something we might find in a fairy story.

THEMES

A world of suffering

'Ode to a Nightingale', it has to be said, presents a fairly negative view of life. The world is depicted as a 'valley of tears', a place full of moaning and groaning: 'here where men sit and hear each other groan'. Our lives, according to Keats, are dominated by worry, sickness and tiredness. The tragedy of existence is the fact that each of us must inevitably grow old and die.

Keats laments the fact that youth cannot last. Each of us, even the strongest and most vibrant, is condemned to grow 'pale' and 'spectre-thin', to be faced with the indignities of old age and finally to die. Worst of all, perhaps, the physical beauty we possess in youth inevitably fades away as we grow older. It can be enjoyed by its possessors and admirers for only the briefest time before disappearing completely.

Keats uses a number of memorable images to reinforce this notion of the world as a bleak an lonely place. Stanza 7, for instance, depicts Ruth working in the fields as she weeps with homesickness. Even the 'faery lands' are described as being 'forlorn' or sorrowful, with their castles that look out over dangerous, lonely oceans. All in all, then, Keats paints a fairly grim portrait of human existence. He suggests that to even think about the human condition is to be filled with sorrow / And leaden-eyed despairs'.

The consolation of nature

Perhaps more than any other poem by Keats, 'Ode to a Nightingale' shows how the poet regards nature as a consolation for the stresses and strains of human existence. (This is also evident in 'To One Long in City Pent'). The depiction of the forest in liens 35 to 40 reveals the great delight the poet takes in the splendours of the natural world. His intensely atmospheric description of the forest's 'embalmed darkness' indicates the relish Keats takes in the sounds, sights and smells of the flowers, trees and insects that surround us. The beauty of the night sky, too, is celebrated in the memorable passage where Keats describes the depicts the moon as the 'Queen' of the night and the stars as her fairy servants. (The splendour of the sky at night is a recurring image in Keats' work. We see it in 'When I Have Feats That I May Cease to Be' and in 'Bright Star'. The night sky also makes an appearance in 'On First looking in to Chapman's Homer' through the figure of the astronomer).

Yet Keats' delight in the natural world is nowhere more evident than in his reaction to the nightingale's singing. The nightingale's song makes Keats overjoyed. He describes himself as being 'too happy', as if he is overcome by emotion at this bird's sweet song 'of summer'. Keats, then, is forced to admit that not every aspect of life is bad. This world may be a place of suffering but the poem suggests that there is ease and pleasure to be found in the beauty of nature.

The consolation of imagination

Perhaps more than anything else 'Ode to a Nightingale' is a celebration of the power of the imagination. Keats, it must be remembered, never actually physically enters the forest. Instead, he simply imagines what the nightingale's leafy abode must be like. Lines 35 to 50 show Keats constructing a little 'imaginary world', creating an intensely detailed and vivid depiction of an environment that exists only in his mind.

The poem, then, shows how Keats retreats from the pain and suffering of the real world into an imaginary haven. 'Fancy', or the power of the imagination, allows him to 'leave the world unseen' and 'quite forget' the trials and tragedies of human existence. Keats' 'fancy' constructs a refuge to which to he can flee in visions, dreams and daydreams, leaving this troubled world behind.

Keats' longing for the poetic inspiration that will make this feat of imagination possible is represented by his desire to drink the wine from the Hippocrene. (Keats, of course, knows that there is no such thing as magical wine. The Hippocrene serves as a metaphor for the sudden burst of inspiration he desires to flash into his brain). In 'Ode to a Nightingale', therefore, poetry and imagination are strongly linked. The powers of imagination that allow him to envisage the forest in such intense detail are the same powers that allow him to write such wonderful poetry.

Yet the poem also acknowledges that there are limits to the imagination's power. According to stanza 8 the Imagination or 'fancy' is famous for its ability to 'deceive' or 'cheat' us into believing in things that are not real. Keats, however, feels that the imagination's powers of deception have been greatly exaggerated. He wishes that it could be even more deceiving, so that his fantasy of the nightingale's forest need never end. Yet the imagination, it seems, will always be 'retarded' or limited by the duller more rational parts of the brain. Keats not remain for long in his imaginary paradise before he must return to his 'sole self' and to reality.

Suicidal tendencies?

'Ode to a Nightingale' displays an unusual attitude toward death, in that the poet actually seems to finds dying a welcome prospect. His mind is filled with sorrow and despair: 'My heart aches'. As we have seen, he regards the world as a place of misery and suffering. It is unsurprising, therefore, that the poet wants to die. For a long time he has found the notion of dying attractive: 'For many a time I have been half in love with easeful death'. Death, he feels, would be 'easeful', a sweet release form this cruel world. He longs to stop breathing, for death to 'snatch' his breath away. He seems specially pleased by the notion of dying on this particular night, with the song of the nightingale ringing in his ears. He longs to 'cease upon the midnight with no pain'.

The attitude toward death expressed in this poem, then, is very different to that presented in 'When I Have Fears that I May Cease to Be'. In 'When I Have Fears' Keats regards the prospect of death with horror, terrified that he might die before he has realised his ambitions in life. 'Ode to a Nightingale', however, reveals a more 'romantic' attitude to death. Death is memorably personified as a kind of friend or lover that the poet 'courts'. The poet flatters death with beautiful words in the hope that death will snatch his breath away and end his troubled existence. Like many romantic poems, 'Ode to a Nightingale' presents the notion of dying, especially of dying young, is regarded as something glamorous and attractive. (Several critics have suggested that a similar attitude to death and dying is evident in 'Bright Star').

Poetry and immortality

The poetry of Keats returns again and again to the notion of immortality, especially the immortality works of art. (We see this in 'On First Looking into Chapman's Homer' and in 'Ode on Grecian Urn'. Both poems celebrate works of art that have lasted for thousands of years). In this poem the immortality of art is symbolised by the nightingale's song. This song, Keats declares, has been sung for thousands of years all over the world. Though millions of individual nightingales have died the song has been passed on from generation to generation. Like Homer's poetry or the Grecian Urn the song of the nightingales' song is eternal and everlasting while all around 'hungry generations' come and go. The nightingale's song, therefore, serves as a powerful symbol for the kind of everlasting art that Keats admires and that he longs desperately to create.

Ode On a Grecian Urn

First published in January 1820, this poem may have been inspired by a visit the poet made to the exhibition of Greek artefacts accompanying the display of the 'Elgin Marbles' at the British Museum.

STANZA 1

In the first stanza Keats addresses the urn directly. He uses three terms for the urn in the opening lines:

'still unravish'd bride of quietness'

The first line offers us a complex metaphorical description of the urn. Keats speaks to the urn, personifying it as the 'still unravish'd bride of quietness'. The urn is closely linked with 'quietness' for obvious reasons – it is a static piece of pottery and incapable of making any sound. This static quality is suggested by the intentionally ambiguous word 'still'. Linked with the word 'unravish'ed' it means 'yet', and it is this meaning that the poet primarily intends. However, because the urn is an inanimate object the word retains its adjectival significance, meaning 'motionless'.

Describing the bride as being 'still unravish'd' means that she has not yet been forcibly sexually violated. There is an implication, due to the word 'still', that ravishment may very well occur, an implicit threat of danger perhaps. If we consider the term 'still unravish'd' in the context of the urn we might understand it to mean that the urn is as yet unsullied or unmarked by the passage of time. It still retains its original beauty, its purity of form. However, there is no guarantee that time will not take its toll – it might yet ravish the urn.

'foster-child of silence and slow time'
The second descriptive phrase for the urn advances the personification of the object. The urn is intimately associated now with two further peaceful terms, 'silence and slow time'. (It is interesting to note how the urn is attached to 'quietness', 'silence', and 'slow time' through familial connections that are legalistic rather than blood in their nature. So the urn has close ties with these things but is not of them; it does not, as it were, share a blood relation with them. This maintains a distance between the urn and these notions. They may have fostered the urn, but they did not create it). The word 'silence' re-emphasises the fact that the urn, being fashioned of clay, makes no noise. However, the term 'slow time' is slightly unusual. Perhaps the poet is suggesting that because the urn is as yet unmarked it is not part of the standard world of time but exists in a special realm, the realm of 'slow time'.

'Sylvan historian'
Keats considers the urn to be a 'historian'. However, it is no ordinary historian, but a 'Sylvan historian'. How are we to understand this phrase? The word sylvan means 'of the woods'. Is the urn, therefore, a historian who dwells in the woods? Or is it a historian who writes histories of the woods? We might consider both meanings relevant to the urn. It is something that tells a 'sylvan' tale of the past whilst also being covered with emblems of the fields and woods (in the fifth stanza the poet tells us that the urn is 'overwrought,/ With forest branches and the trodden weed').

According to the poet the urn is well equipped to tell tales of the woods. In fact, he considers the urn better capable of relating a 'flowery' tale than the poets with their 'rhyme'. The word 'flowery' means decorated with flowers. In relation to speech or writing it can mean 'elaborate'. Both meanings are relevant here. The 'tale' that the urn expresses is elaborate, the design around its body very ornate. And this tale is literally 'flowery' because it is set in the woods and the countryside where flowers abound.

A 'flowery tale'
If the urn is to be considered a 'Sylvan historian', then what story does it tell of the past? What tale is being told in the illustration that circumnavigates its body? We might expect a historian to relate a true story of the past. But this 'sylvan historian' provides no dates or names. Rather than a series of facts the urn offers the poet a 'flowery tale' and a 'leaf-fring'd legend'. The word 'legend' means a traditional story that is properly regarded as historical but is not authenticated. The word 'legend', therefore, calls the reality of its tale into account. Though the urn might be considered a 'historian' the tale it expresses contains more fancy than fact. (The word 'legend', like a number of words in the poem, is ambiguous, for it can also mean 'inscription', and the detail that surrounds the urn can be considered a form of inscription). This particular legend is 'leaf-fring'd', so described because of the leafy decoration that accompanies the story on the urn and also because the story itself is set in the leafy environs of the woods.

Does the story concern gods ('deities') or humans ('mortals')? Perhaps it is 'of both'. Do the characters that feature on the urn appear 'In Tempe or the dales of Arcady'? Tempe, celebrated by the Greek poets as a favourite haunt of Apollo and the Muses, is the ancient name of a gorge in northern Greece. Arcady was home of the temples of Zeus and Hera, and was also the location of the Olympic Stadium, where the Olympic Games were held in classical times.

The men depicted on the urn are in the middle of some 'mad pursuit' of women. These women, whoever they may be, are 'loth' (reluctant) to be caught? They 'struggle to escape' from the hands of the excited men. The chase is accompanied by music played on 'pipes and timbrels'. The whole scene is one of 'wild ecstasy' and Keats is fascinated to know as much as he can about this boisterous woodland frolic.

STANZA 2

The first two lines present us with an unusual paradoxical point of view:

Heard melodies are sweet, but those unheard
Are sweeter

The first half of this proposition is pretty straightforward. Melodies, songs, that we can hear, are pleasant. (Of course Keats was not around to hear the atrocities that pass for melodies in modern day pop. Perhaps he would not have proffered such a generalisation if he had had to sit through an hour of 'You're A Star'). However, the second half of the argument is a little harder to comprehend. Keats claims that 'melodies' never heard are even 'sweeter'. Here the poet is referring to the 'melodies' that the pipers and musicians on the urn are playing. These are imagined tunes for we can never know what melodies they play. Perhaps the poet is suggesting that what we conjure in our minds, with our imaginations, is 'sweeter' than what exits in reality. The notion of 'unheard' melodies is essentially paradoxical because a melody is something that is heard.

Whereas in the opening stanza the poet presented us with a rather chaotic series of questions that gave only a vague sense of what was happening, in the second stanza he begins to focus on more specific details and characters.

The pipes

Keats first focuses on the pipes. He urges the pipes to 'play on' even though they make no audible sound and, therefore, cannot be heard by the 'sensual ear'. The 'soft' music that the pipes play will be for the 'spirit'. These 'ditties of no tone' are considered of greater value than the tunes played for the pleasure of the ear. They appeal to the spiritual, the non-physical, and, therefore, to what is eternal.

The singer

A young man sitting beneath the trees is addressed. In the static world of the illustration this 'youth' will never alter his position; he is frozen in the moment of his performance. If this seems an unpleasant thought then he might comfort himself with the notion that the trees beneath which he sits will never wither.

The lovers

The 'Bold lover' too is frozen in time as he moves to kiss his beloved. Though he is so close to kissing her ('winning near the goal') he will never fulfil his desire. But the poet calls on him not to despair at this because the very thing that prevents him achieving his goal, his inability to move or change, ensures that the object of his affection 'cannot fade'. And though he will never experience the ecstasy of the kiss he might content himself with the knowledge that he will always love this girl and that her beauty and youth will never perish. (The girl can be considered like the urn itself, a 'still unravished bride of quietness'. She has not even been ravished by a kiss and so remains forever 'fair').

STANZA 3: *Happy times*

This stanza goes back over some of the motifs and characters that appeared in the previous stanza: the boughs that cannot shed their leaves, the unwearied melodist, and the ever-ardent lover. However, whereas in the second stanza there was a hint of negativity associated with the condition of those mentioned (The 'fair youth' was construed as being shackled eternally to his 'song'; the 'Bold Lover' condemned to an eternity of frustration and unfulfilled desire), here in the third stanza the trees, the 'melodist', and the lover, are seen in the most positive of lights. Keats uses the word 'happy' six times in the space of five lines, an extraordinary repetition of a single word within so few lines of a poem.

Keats returns to the trees that he mentioned in the second stanza. He once again states that they will forever hold their leaves. The poet considers the branches to be very happy with this state of affairs: 'Ah, happy, happy boughs! That cannot shed/ Your leaves'. For these trees it will always be spring and the winter will never come.

In the second stanza the poet spoke of the 'Fair youth' who could never leave his song. Here he speaks of the 'happy melodist, unwearied,/ For ever piping songs for ever new'. The 'youth' and the 'melodist' might be one and the same person. But whereas the predicament of the 'Fair youth' was presented in a rather negative manner, the poet focusing on what the young man could not do, in the third stanza the situation of the 'melodist' is viewed very positively. He will never tire of the song he plays and the song he plays will be 'for ever new' because it will always be played for the first time.

The sort of love that exists between the 'Bold lover' and his beloved is now termed 'More happy love! More happy, happy love!' Frozen in a moment of longing and desire their love will be 'For ever warm and still to be enjoyed,/ For ever panting, and for ever young'. This form of love is contrasted with the 'All breathing human passion' that we mortals must suffer, a love that climaxes and departs, leaving us heartbroken and sick ('high-sorrowful and cloyed'). The love that is depicted on the urn is considered to be 'far above' any form of 'breathing human' love. The poem rates the idea of consummation above the actuality. The lovers depicted on the urn are considered happy because they are caught in an eternal moment of desire that can never be fulfilled. There is a suggestion here that the act of sex only leads to disappointment.

STANZA 4

In the fourth stanza the poet refers to a procession of people depicted on their way to witness 'the sacrifice' of a cow. We are still in the world depicted on the urn. However, the scene presented here can be contrasted with the earlier stanzas. Whereas the previous two stanzas focused on individuals the fourth stanza is more concerned with a communal form of life. We get a great sense in this stanza of a community together, of shared values and beliefs.

Keats wonders who exactly these people might be ('Who are these coming to the sacrifice?'). In the second line the poet directly addresses the one individual who is set apart from the greater community – the 'mysterious priest' leading the 'heifer'. Where, he asks this priest, is the cow being led ('To what green altar')? The cow is highly decorated with flowers for the ceremony that is about to take place, 'all her silken flanks with garlands drest'.

The poet now shifts his attention from the procession to the imagined town that these people have travelled from. In what some consider the most moving passage of the poem Keats speculates on the strange emptiness of the town which, of course, has not been pictured on the urn at all. What kind of town has been left behind this morning? Is it a small town by a river or by the sea that now stands 'emptied of this folk'? Perhaps the town lies in the mountains. Frozen in time, its streets 'for evermore/ Will silent be'. And no one can ever return to tell the town why this is the case.

STANZA 5

Stepping back from the detail of the decoration, the poet once again addresses the complete urn in a similar fashion to the first stanza. Again he refers to the complete sculpture using a number of phrases. The poet remarks upon its 'Attic shape', a reference to its having been sculpted in ancient Athens. He then comments upon the beautiful configuration of its design, its 'Fair attitude', and in the fourth line of the stanza its 'silent form'.

This wonderfully sculpted piece of Attic art, elaborately decorated with 'marble men and maidens' at various activities amidst 'forest branches and the trodden weed', ultimately teases 'us out of thought/ As doth eternity'. What the urn has to relate to us is as impossible for the mind to comprehend and grasp as the concept of eternity is. The reason for this elusion lies in the fact that the urn offers us a 'flowery tale' of paradox. We can consider the details of the urn, appreciate its form, but it will ultimately elude our understanding – 'tease us out of thought'.

Keats now sums up the tale that the urn relates using two words: 'Cold Pastoral'. The phrase perfectly encapsulates and concludes the many paradoxes that are at the heart of urn represents. A pastoral is a piece of art, often a poem or a piece of music, portraying rural life. The word pastoral generally suggests warmth, the natural, a simple idyll. However, this particular pastoral is 'Cold' because, as Keats clearly acknowledges, it is comprised of 'marble men and maidens'. And this is the central paradox of the poem, that these lifeless, marble figures ultimately convey and represent a tale of great life and warmth.

The abiding message

In the final lines of the poem Keats contrasts the finitude of his generation with the fixity and immortality of the urn. It stands static and unchanging in the midst of life's flux. When one generation has passed away into death the urn will 'remain', in the 'midst of other woe' a 'friend' to those who follow. And just as the urn has revealed something important to the poet so it will continue to relate the very same message to future generations – 'Beauty is truth, truth beauty'. This, according to either the urn or the poet 'is all' that we 'know' and it is all we 'need to know'.

These last lines have preoccupied, baffled, and annoyed readers and critics ever since the poem was first published. There is no authoritative reading or interpretation of them. Taken in isolation the words 'Beauty is truth, truth beauty' are enigmatic. Even if these words make sense to us the fact that this is 'all' we 'know on earth' and, indeed, 'all' we 'need to know' remains controversial. However, these words must be taken in the context of the poem as a whole. They ought to, therefore, reflect back upon the description of the urn given in the preceding stanzas and be a summation of what the urn represents.

The urn is considered a 'sylvan historian'. This historian has a particular 'tale' to tell. It is a tale involving love and music, sacrifice and pious devotion. Yet, unlike a typical historian's tale it involves no dates, no names, and no specific locations. The urn imparts no specifics whatsoever. What it offers us instead is a beautiful representation of what is, perhaps, most vital to human existence – love, music, piety and community. Abstracted from time and place, frozen for all eternity, the sculpture reveals the only 'truth' that we can really 'know' and that we need to know. Because it centres around the abstract quality 'beauty', this 'truth' must be considered utterly different to what we might normally understand truth to be, i.e., scientific truth, comprised of all its facts and data. The 'truth' that the urn relates is something we sense and feel but can never fully understand, like eternity. It is not a fact that we can learn. It is more fundamental.

LANGUAGE

The language of 'Ode on a Grecian Urn' is not as rich and complex as that of 'Ode to a Nightingale'. It lacks, as Cleanth Brooks as said, the adjectival sensuality of that ode. At times it the language used by the poet is quite basic. Consider the third stanza where Keats uses the word 'happy' six times. Yet it also contains lines of high imagination that are rich with meaning. The first four lines, for example, employ metaphors that perhaps nobody but Keats could have created. The poem also relies on repetition to create the appropriate effect. In the second and third stanzas, for example, the poet repeats words for emphasis – 'Bold Lover, never, never canst thou kiss', 'Ah, happy, happy boughs!'

Paradoxes

'Ode on a Grecian Urn' features a number of paradoxical notions. Keats talks of 'unheard' melodies in the second stanza, claiming that these are 'sweeter' than 'heard' melodies. The urn is silent yet it somehow manages to 'express/ A flowery tale'. It is a static piece of art, made of cold 'marble', yet it manages to convey 'wild ecstasy' and depict love that is 'For ever warm' and 'For ever panting'. It is considered a 'silent form' yet it still manages to utter the only 'truth' that we 'need to know'. The beauty of the urn is deathless because it is lifeless.

THEMES

The aesthetic experience

The urn is a piece of sculpture, wrought by man from stone. Yet in its completed form, as a piece of art, it ceases to be just another 'thing' in the world. Keats is especially taken by the representations that adorn the exterior of the urn. These images that circumnavigate the urn constitute a world that is completely other to the everyday world in which the poet exists. The world depicted on the urn is self-contained. The fact that the images circle the body of the urn means that there is no beginning

and no end to this world. The poet enters this world imaginatively and documents his experience. As such, 'Ode on a Grecian Urn' is about the experience of art, the aesthetic experience.

Our initial response to a piece of art is often to question what is happening, what is the piece about. This is exactly how Keats approaches the urn. The first stanza is mainly composed of questions pertaining to what is happening. The poet does not provide answers to these questions. As with most pieces of art such questions are open to interpretation and we should not expect definitive answers. Yet, the characters depicted seem to tell a story and the poet is curious to know exactly what this story is about.

In the second stanza the poet identifies within the frieze certain themes that are common to many artworks – the theme or art itself, as represented by the pipers and their imagined tune; the theme of love, as represented by the 'Bold Lover'; the theme of beauty, as represented by the 'fair' girl that the 'Lover' desires. In this stanza then the poet no longer seeks 'facts' regarding the who, the what, and the wherefore of the artwork. Having identified representations of art, love and beauty, the poet can now sympathise with the piece of art. He can identify with it because it deals with issues that are timeless, relevant to all people at all times. Yet again, however, he does not derive or expect answers or truths to be drawn from what he observes.

Keats' response to the piece of art before him is, perhaps, surprisingly intense. In the first and second stanzas of the poem he rapidly becomes so deeply immersed in the world depicted on the urn as to forget that this world is entirely unreal. What he sees depicted on the urn represents to him the ideal of art, love, and beauty. Art is something that should be ever fresh and new like the piper's songs. Love should be 'For ever warm and still to be enjoy'd'. Beauty should never fade.

The mentioning of 'human passion' in line twenty-eight, however, draws the poet out of the world shown on the urn and reminds him of the fact that what he is viewing is only artifice. The fourth stanza then describes a more sober approach to the representation on the urn. Yet the aesthetic experience that he describes still contains a strong element of fancy. The poet views a processional scene, the community of a small town making its way towards a location where a cow is to be sacrificed. Keats response to this scene represents another typical response to art. A piece of art, whether it is a piece of sculpture or a painting, can only show us so much. We must work with what we are shown and allow our imaginations to do the rest. The artwork, therefore, functions as a prompt that the viewer uses to exercise his own imagination and emotion. In the fourth stanza the poet interacts with the urn, using it as a stimulus for his imagination. Keats gives himself over to the urn and imagines the greater story that the picture proffers. The 'little' town does not, in fact, feature on the urn, its existence is the result of inference on the part of the poet. Through this imagining Keats reveals how the aesthetic experience is one of co-operation between the artwork and the viewer.

Immortality

Those featured on the urn are frozen in a moment of time for all eternity. They will never age or die. The beloved referred to in the second stanza 'cannot fade' and will be forever 'fair'. The urn reveals to the poet an ideal world where the young never age and the trees never shed their leaves. In the third stanza Keats uses the word 'happy' six times to illustrate just how perfect a place he imagines this to be. Here love remains 'For ever warm', 'For ever panting, and for ever young'.

The flux and strife of life

The real world, in contrast, is a place where the heart is left 'high-sorrowful and cloy'd'. It is a place where we grow ill and suffer symptoms such as 'a burning forehead, and a parching tongue'. It is a place where generations are laid to 'waste' and woe follows woe.

Joy and woe

Like so many poems by John Keats, 'Ode on a Grecian Urn' contains moments of great joy and woe. Those that he describes in the first stanza are involved in 'wild ecstasy' whilst the characters he speaks of in the third stanza are repeatedly said to be 'happy'. However, the poet also hints at sadness in his description of the urn. He tells the 'Bold Lover' in the second stanza not to 'grieve'. This suggests that the 'Lover' may in fact be grieving. The 'little' town of the fourth stanza is also described as 'desolate', its loneliness and isolation considered pathetically by the poet.

Love and lust

Those depicted on the urn are said to be involved a 'struggle'. The illustration that the poet considers in the opening stanza is that of a chase. The men pursue the women and the women in turn 'struggle to escape'. It seems a classical depiction of lust. The men are the hot-blooded pursuers whilst the women appear reluctant, trying their best to escape from the excited men. According to the poem the love that is happiest is the love that is never fulfilled. The perfect love remains 'for ever warm and still to be enjoy'd'. Keats suggests that consummated love is undesirable. It leads to heartache and disappointment – 'leaves a heart high-sorrowful and cloy'd'.

To Autumn

LINE BY LINE

STANZA 1

The first stanza describes autumn as a season of great abundance, a time of sumptuous growth. Autumn is depicted collaborating with the sun in a concerted effort to bring about a feast of growth and bloom, where fruits and flowers are fattened and ripened to the point of bursting.

The opening line is beautifully poetic and atmospheric: 'Season of mists and mellow fruitfulness'. The reader gets a sense of the misty days that we might associate with autumn, days when the trees and flowers are moist and alive with colour and blossom. Autumn is also the season when much in nature matures. It is a mild and mellow season, containing neither the burning heat of the summer nor the freezing chill of winter.

In the second line Keats personifies the season. Autumn is seen as the 'Close bosom-friend of the maturing sun'. Together the season and the sun form an elderly alliance and set about the pleasant business of bringing to fruit 'the vines that round the thatch-eves run'. Here Keats refers to the ivies or vines that grow up around the edge of the thatched roofs of houses. Autumn and the sun craftily plan how they will 'load and bless' these plants with fruit. The word 'load' suggests the superabundance of produce that is to be bestowed. The word 'bless' reminds us of pregnancy, how we might refer to someone pregnant as being 'blessed' with a child.

The image of the apple trees bending under the weight of their fruit further illustrates the superabundance of the season. This is a time when the fruits of the countryside will reach their prime, their perfect state of ripeness. Autumn is set to 'fill all fruit with ripeness to the core', to 'swell the gourd, and plump the hazed shells/ With a sweet kernel'. The 'gourd' is a large fruit with a hard shell. The 'kernel' is the edible part of the nut within the shell. Like the apples these too will be brought into the perfect state of ripeness. And the flowers will grow and continue to grow until the bees think that winter will never come. Their hives are already full of honey, their 'clammy cells' already 'o'er-brimmed' from the summer. Everything is at the point of bursting and ripe for harvesting.

The opening stanza depicts autumn as someone or something that brings about an extraordinary amount of growth in the countryside. Keats focuses on the fruits, nuts and flowers that ripen and grow during this time of year. Everything is seen to 'swell' and ripen. It seems a very busy time of year. And yet there is certain mellowness at the heart of autumn. There is a maturity to the growth that occurs, a gradual ripening that might be contrasted with the more youthful budding of spring.

STANZA 2

The second stanza moves on to the harvesting that takes place in autumn. However, rather than describe the farmers at their work, Keats personifies the season (basing the personification most likely on the mythical figure of Ceres, the Roman goddess of agriculture) and places her at the centre of harvesting scenes described. Although autumn plays a very active role in the ripening process that occurs early in the season, the impression we are given of the season in the second stanza is less active.

It would seem that this stanza of the poem is as much inspired by the poet's familiarity with classical descriptions and depictions of autumn, both in paintings and literary works, as it is with any actual experience of the real world of harvesting. The stanza is thus a blending of the fantastical and the real. Keats mentions the actual processes that are involved in the harvesting of wheat but only in the context of locating the imagined personified season. We might discern in this stanza Keats' desire to discover within the real world elements of the fantastical. After all, he does not say that we will find the mythical figure of autumn in these locations, only we 'may' do. The depiction of autumn here is very intimate.

The poet tells us where we might find autumn now that the harvesting has commenced.

1 If we look for autumn we might find her 'sitting

careless on a granary floor'. A granary is a storehouse for threshed grain. To 'winnow' is to blow the chaff (the outer coverings) from grain before it can be used as food The wind that blows through the granary also lifts and separates the hair of Autumn. (Perhaps Keats based these lines around the mythological figure of Psyche. According to the Greek legend of Psyche and Cupid, the beautiful young girl is set many impossible tasks by Aphrodite, mother of Cupid, after she betrays the young man's trust, the first of which is to separate a large pile of different grains. Psyche sits in despair before the task until an ant appears and with his companions achieves the task for her). What is note worthy about the image of autumn 'sitting careless on a granary floor' is the inactivity of the personified season. Perhaps Autumn is worn out from all the work she did earlier or maybe she does not wish to comply in her own destruction.

2 We may find autumn 'sound asleep' on a half-reap'd furrow'. Interestingly Keats does not follow a logical temporal pattern with his images. The image of reaping occurs after the image of winnowing, whereas reaping takes place before winnowing can occur. Again the personified season is most notably inactive. Here she is asleep on the job, 'Drows'd with the fume of poppies'. Poppies are renowned for their opiate properties and are classically associated with sleep. In reality they do not emit any 'fume' that could cause someone to sleep, so again Keats is drawing upon mythical narratives for inspiration. Similar to the first depiction, Autumn does not engage in any work. Her scythe lies idle next to her as she sleeps, thus sparing the next tuft ('swath') of grass and the 'flowers' that are entwined with it.

3 Sometimes autumn can be seen bearing the produce of its harvesting 'across a brook'. In contrast with the first two portrayals of autumn this one has her actually working, bearing a load of produce upon her head as she crosses a stream. Autumn was often depicted in classical paintings with the fruits of the season on her head.

4 Finally autumn is depicted standing by 'a cider-press' watching patiently as 'the last oozings' of juice are pressed from the apples. The final line of the stanza gives us an intimation that the season is drawing to a close. Nature stands by, a patient observer, as the 'last oozings' are squeezed from the apples. The fruits that were ripened in the first stanza have now been harvested and processed by the farmers. And where as in the opening stanza there was a sense given that autumn would never end, here we get the impression that time is running out.

STANZA 3

The final stanza is a celebration of the melancholic 'music' of autumn, a music that plays as the season draws to its close. The poet sets the closing scene with a wonderful description of an autumn evening:

While barred clouds bloom the soft-dying day,
And touch the stubble-plains with rosy hue

While clouds of varied ('barred') colour take shape in the sky, introducing a reddish tint to the fields that have been harvested, and the day draws to its end, it is then that the 'music' of autumn is heard most sonorously and the country is most alive with the plaintive opera of the season.

The 'small gnats' chime in mournfully as a 'wailful choir'. (Gnats are small mosquito-like insects, very similar to 'midges'. These insects thrive over summer, living their short lives by rivers and stagnant pools where they breed and quickly die off). Keats describes this 'choir' of insects rising and sinking among the willow trees by the river as the 'light wind' gusts and 'dies'.

'Full-grown lambs loud bleat' by a stream ('bourn') in the hills. 'Hedge-crickets sing' and then the 'red-breast' enters the chorus 'with treble soft' from a nearby garden. The final component of this seasonal production is the twittering of swallows 'gathering' for their imminent migration south. The last nine lines of the poem are exquisite, aching with a melancholy that is never lapses into depression or melodrama. The language is of the highest poetic order, the images wonderfully plaintive.

THEMES

Autumn

Keats takes an interesting approach to a season that is often associated in literature with demise and death, a melancholic passage of time when leaves fall from the trees and only the cold winter months lie ahead. We might consider these lines from Shelley's poem

'Autumn – A Dirge' in order to appreciate the different approach that Keats takes. The first lines of Shelley's poem are:

The warm sun is failing, the bleak wind is wailing,
The bare boughs are sighing, the pale flowers are dying,
And the Year
On the earth her death-bed, in a shroud of leaves dead,
Is lying.

If we compare these lines with the opening lines of Keats' poem we can see just how differently he views the season. For Shelley Autumn is a cold time of decay and death. For Keats it is a warm time of growth and harvest.

Though 'To Autumn' brings us through the season, from the beginning when the fruits are at their ripest and the flowers still at bloom to the point of late in the season when the fields are reduced to 'stubble-plains' and the swallows are 'gathering' to depart, Keats never descends into morbidity or despair. The final stanza is certainly melancholic, and if we compare it to the opening stanza we can easily perceive a sorrowful cadence at play. Unlike Shelley's poem, however, 'To Autumn' never explicitly identifies the season with decay or death and it is interesting to note how Keats mentions both Summer and Spring in the poem but never Winter.

Three phases of autumn

The season is depicted in the opening stanza as a time of seemingly endless growth when trees and flowers come to bloom and fruit. Autumn is co-conspirator with the sun in bringing about an almost obscene level of growth in the country. The vines are loaded with fruit and the 'moss'd cottage trees' must bend with the weight of apples bestowed upon them. Gourds swell and kernels are plumped and the flowers are 'set budding more,/ And still more' leaving the poor bees with a dilemma regarding what to do with all the nectar they can gather.

After the growth comes the harvesting. Autumn is personified and appears in a number of locations appropriate to the harvest that is now taking place. Perhaps because of all the effort that she had to invest in the growth she is now exhausted and is therefore depicted by the poet at various points of rest and slumber.

In the third stanza we are then presented with the more melancholic final phase of the season. The mood of this stanza is very different to that of the first. Whereas the opening stanza is brimming with life, with productive activity and intensive growth, the final stanza is charged with the melancholy of death. Death has not yet come, only it is near and inevitable. The stanza contains many images activity and of life, only now these images are tinged with a sadness that was nowhere apparent in the first stanza. The third line of the last stanza encapsulates the almost paradoxical quality of autumn in decline. The clouds are said to 'bloom' just as the day is 'soft-dying'. Life and death coexist, the 'light wind lives or dies'. Lambs are now 'full-grown,' implying that it almost time for the slaughter. The 'gnats' provide a plaintive, 'wailful choir' to the whole process. Yet the poem closes on a somewhat subdued and pleasant note, the combined 'treble soft' whistle of the red-breast with the 'twitter' of 'gathering swallows' being decidedly less tragic than the gnats' 'wailful choir'.

LANGUAGE

The poem opens with a wonderfully euphonious line. Using alliteration ('mists and mellow') and sibilance ('Season of mists and mellow fruitfulness') Keats conveys a very pleasant atmosphere. This mellow atmosphere is carried forward through the entire poem and we can locate examples of alliteration and sibilance in almost every line. Consider the lines:

While barred clouds bloom the soft dying day,
And touch the stubble-plains with rosy hue

There is alliteration, the repeated 'b' and 'd' sounds in the first line, and sibilance, 'clouds', 'soft', 'stubble-plains'. Once again these sound effects combine to give a warmth and mellowness to the lines.

Assonance also frequently occurs throughout the poem. There is, for example, the assonance of the 'i's in line 15 ('Thy hair soft-lifted by the winnowing wind') and again in line 29 ('Or sinking as the light wind lives or dies'). The assonance in line 15, combined with the alliteration of the 'w's, beautifully compliments the image that the poet conveys. The words have a soft sound and a lightness to them that effectively serves the image of autumn's hair being

gently lifted by the wind. There is a certain onomatopoeic quality to the line, the words 'winnowing wind' giving us a sense of the sound of the wind itself. Onomatopoeia is also used in line 22 where the poet speaks of the 'last oozings' of the apple juice.

The language of the poem is very sensuous. We can almost taste the 'sweet' fruit that Keats describes, almost feel the 'clammy cells', and hear the lambs bleating in the hills.

IMAGERY AND STRUCTURE

'To Autumn' is rich with autumnal imagery. Set in the country, the poem treats us to a multitude of images that combine to give a detailed picture of the season. Some readers have likened the experience of reading the poem to viewing a painting of an autumnal landscape.

We could imagine that the poem centres round a particular location, a single farm, perhaps, in the English countryside. The poem, therefore, opens close to the farmhouse, focusing on the vines growing up around the 'thatch-eves' and the apple trees that stand close to the house. As the poem progresses we move out into the garden and beyond to the 'granary' and fields where the harvest is taking place. In the final stanza these fields stand bare of their crop and we move to the river that runs by the farm, possibly forming one of its boundaries, to the hills where the lambs 'loud bleat', before returning to the garden where a 'redbreast' is whistling. The final line carries the reader's eyes skywards so that the poem closes with an image of expanse that is in keeping with the positive portrayal of the season.

There is also a structure to the passage of time. The poem brings us through a linear account of the season, opening in early autumn when everything is blossoming and ripening and ending when the harvest has finished and the season is drawing to a close.

We could also imagine that the poem moves through the three phases of the day – morning, afternoon, and evening. The first stanza, therefore, corresponds with the morning when the sun is 'maturing' in the sky. The second stanza centres round the afternoon – we could imagine the character of Autumn is asleep after lunch, having worked the morning. This stanza then closes late in the afternoon. The last stanza is certainly set in the evening. Keats speaks of the 'soft-dying day' as the setting sun casts a warm redness over the harvested fields.

Bright Star

BACKGROUND

The poem was first published in a newspaper in 1838. Keats had previously inscribed it into a friend's copy of Shakespeare's Poems, opposite 'A Lover's Complaint' on September 28, 1820. Although it was long thought to be Keats' last poem, it is now considered to have been written between February and April 1819, around the time of Keats' engagement to Fanny Browne. Addressed to a star, the verse expresses the poet's wish to be as constant as the star while he presses against his sleeping love.

LINE BY LINE

The poet addresses a bright star in the night sky. He tells the star that he would like to be as 'steadfast' as the star is: 'would I were steadfast as thou art'. To be 'steadfast' is to be firmly fixed in place or position. The star never seems to move or change and the poet envies this quality in the star.

However, though he desires to be as steadfast as the star he does not wish to exist as the star does, alone and remote in the night sky: 'not in lone splendour hung aloft the night'. The poet describes how the star watches the Earth, its eyes always open, 'with eternal lids apart'.

Keats compares the star to a religious recluse ('Eremite'). According to the poet this star is like 'nature's patient, sleepless' hermit, steadfastly devoted to watching the movement of the tides. The poet describes the movement of the oceans in terms of a religious cleansing ritual. The oceans have a 'priestlike task/ of pure ablution round earth's human shores'. They act in a religious manner, purifying and cleansing the world.

The poet also thinks of the star 'gazing on the new soft-fallen mask/ Of snow upon the mountains and the moors'. The image is again one of purity, the 'new soft-fallen snow' a clean, white blanket upon the earth's surface.

Yet, though the poet describes two very serene and beautiful pictures of what the star sees with its unblinking eyes, he does not envy the star's position in the sky. What he envies, and what he longs for in the poem, is the quality that the star perfectly represents for him – steadfastness. He does not want to be alone in the night sky but he does wish to be 'still steadfast, still unchangeable' like the star appears to be, only in a different place altogether – 'Pillow'd upon my fair love's ripening breast'.

Here he would like to remain 'Awake for ever in a sweet unrest' feeling the 'soft fall and swell' of his beloved's breast. Like the star he too would like to remain forever awake. But rather than observe the movements of the earth, he wishes to feel the movements of his lover's breast and to 'hear her tender-taken breath'.

THEMES

The eternal

The star in the poem represents that which does not change with time. The poet considers the star 'unchangeable' and eternal. It is immutable. It stands far apart from the world of change, a distant and remote observer. The poem expresses the poet's desire to never change.

The poet envies the star's ability to remain the same. He wishes that he could stay awake forever so that he could watch his beloved sleep. He does not, however, want to distant himself from the world. He wishes that he could be 'steadfast' and 'unchangeable' whilst remaining part of the mortal world where everything changes. Like the star he will never change and never sleep. Frozen in a state of 'sweet unrest' he will happily feel the rise and fall of his beloved's breast and listen to her soft breath. If this is not a possibility then he would rather die – 'or else swoon to death'.

The world of change and motion

Though the poem begins with a wish to be as the star is, 'steadfast' and unchanging, the poem is ultimately a paean to the earth, the human world, and to human love, from which the star remains eternally excluded and remote. It is the earth that the poem ultimately renders attractive, with its constant shifting of the tides and the beautiful 'new soft-fallen mask/ Of snow upon the mountains and the moors'.

The star can only gaze upon this, whereas those who live on earth are part of this beautiful landscape. The star is ultimately rendered unenviable in its role as a distant observer of the human world. For it is within the mortal realm of earth, where things grow and change, that love occurs.

What Keats longs for is unattainable. Essentially he wishes to have his cake and eat it. He wishes to remain untouched and unaffected by time and change whilst still existing within the mortal world. Even if he could become immutable like the star his 'fair love' would have to eventually wake up.

Though the poem renders the earth quite beautiful the poet wishes to only remain a part of it on his own terms. In the final line of the poem he states that if he cannot exist forever with his head resting upon his beloved's breast he would prefer to die: 'And so live ever – or else swoon to death'. There can be no in between

LANGUAGE

The form of the sonnet

The sonnet uses the rhyming scheme ABAB CDCD EFEF GG. Although the quatrains are divided in rhyme they are linked in subject. The poet considers the plight of the star and allows the first quatrain to run into the second. In the first quatrain he describes the star's lonely position in the sky and its remoteness from the world. In the second quatrain he focuses on what the star can see – beauty of the world. As is often the case in a sonnet a 'turn' occurs in the first line of the sestet, signalled here with the blunt word 'No'. The sestet then goes on to describe how the poet would prefer to spend a life of eternal sleeplessness.

Imagery

The central image in the sonnet is that of the star. Keats depicts it as something beautiful yet somewhat tragic. It is isolated from the very beauty that it is destined to observe forever. Keats uses the wonderful description 'lone splendour' to capture the beauty and the tragedy of the star. He then personifies the star, imagining its eyes 'with eternal lids apart'.

The poem, like many of Keats', incorporates images of the sky and the sea in order to covey a sense of majesty and mystery. In this sonnet the poet gazes up at the star in the sky and imagines how it must view the sea below. Keats likens the sea to a cleansing body of water, purifying the world. The image of the snow upon the mountains is also one of purity, its pristine whiteness masking the mountains and the moors.

Assonance and alliteration

The poem contains many wonderful examples of assonance and alliteration. The eight line contains both: 'Of snow upon the mountains and the moors'. The assonance of the 'o's coupled with the alliteration of the 'm's combine to create a very pleasant line. Again in line 11 the poet uses both to fine effect: 'To feel for ever its soft fall and swell'. The soft 's' sounds mix beautifully with the 'f's of 'feel' and 'fall' to give the line a very sweet and dreamy atmosphere.

KEATS AT A GLANCE

NATURE

In 'To One Who Has Been Long in City Pent' nature provides a momentary, peaceful refuge from the stresses and strains of city living.

In 'On First Looking into Chapman's Homer' the Greek poet's great poetic achievement is celebrated using images of land, sea, and sky.

'When I Have Fears that I May Cease to Be' describes the poet's desperate desire to capture the beauties of nature in his poetry.

In 'La Belle Dame Sans Merci' the bleak winter landscape reflects the horror and desolation of the knight's predicament.

In 'Ode to a Nightingale' the nightingale's song becomes a symbol for the immortality of great works of art. The beauties of nature, as represented by Keats' exquisite depiction of the forest, become a consolation for the trials and tribulations of everyday living.

'To Autumn' focuses on the ripening and growth that occurs in the natural world during the early part of the season. The poem contains many beautiful and poignant images pertaining to this time of year.

DEATH

'When I Have Fears that I May Cease to Be' reveals the poet's great terror of death, his desperate fear that death may claim him before he has a chance to realise his artistic and romantic ambitions.

In contrast in 'Ode to a nightingale' the poet claims to be half in love with death. He longs to die in order to escape the evils and hardships of human existence.

'To Autumn' contains a beautifully melancholic description of the demise of the day and the season itself.

In 'Bright Star' death features as something desirable. The poet states that he should rather die if he cannot live forever observing his beloved sleep.

ART AND IMMORTALITY

In 'On First looking into Chapman's Homer' the poet talks of the eternal freshness of Homer's great work. This poem depicts how a work of art can outlive generations of human beings.

'When I Have Fears that I May Cease to Be' describes the poet's terror that he might die before he can create immortal works of art.

'Ode to a Nightingale' celebrates the power of art and imagination as it describes Keats' 'imaginary journey' into the nightingale's forest. The nightingales' song, which has been heard for thousands of years, symbolises how a work of art can last forever.

In 'Ode on a Grecian Urn' the poet speaks of how the urn shall continue to exist though those who appreciate its beauty must die. Those represented on the urn seen to be frozen forever in a moment of time. The poet envies there immortal existence contrasting it with the pains and woes of mortal life.

In 'Bright Star' the star the poet envies the star's apparent ability to exist forever.

MICHAEL LONGLEY

THEMES

WAR

Longley, according to many critics, is one of Ireland's greatest poets of war and violence. The Northern Irish Troubles, in particular, have had a resounding effect on his work. A number of his poems mourn the loss of those who have died in the senseless violence that has dogged that province. 'Wounds', for example, memorialises three teenage soldiers who lost their lives in the conflict, as well as a bus-conductor who was brutally murdered in his own home. 'Wreaths', in a similar fashion, mourns the deaths of a civil servant, a greengrocer, and ten workers in a linen factory, all of whom were murdered in terrorist attacks. An interesting feature of Longley's elegies is his tendency to highlight the victims' occupations. His poems lament the passing of ordinary people with ordinary jobs. To Longley, it seems, a bus-conductor or a civil servant deserves to be remembered in a poem just as much as a great artist or a famous politician.

Longley's poetic career has also been haunted by a number of historical conflicts, especially the First World War. 'Wounds', for instance, provides a moving account of the barbarism involved in that most brutal of conflicts. The poem provides an unflinching portrayal of brutality. We are presented with men going over the top to almost certain death (a 'boy about to die'), and the surreal, haunting image of 'a landscape of dead buttocks'. 'Last Requests', too, details the horrors of World War One with its depiction of the poet's father being almost 'buried alive' on the battlefield. Both 'Wounds' and 'Last Requests' also emphasise the physical and psychological difficulties faced by those who survived the war. The poet's father, a veteran of the conflict, is left mentally scared by the terrible things he witnessed: 'Over a landscape of dead buttocks/My father followed him for fifty years'. The war also scars him physically, however, leaving wounds that Longley believes contributed to the cancer that finally killed him: 'lead traces flaring till they hurt'.

An interesting feature of Longley's work is his tendency to examine the contemporary violence in Northern Ireland in the light of the First World War. This is particularly evident in 'Wounds' where Longley imagines burying victims of the Troubles beside his soldier father, himself a 'belated casualty' of World War One. A similar approach is evident in 'Wreaths' where Longley imagines burying his father 'once again' with items gathered from the corpses of the murdered linen workers. Longley's comparison of the Troubles and World War One presents us with a very bleak view of human nature, throwing up some disturbing parallels between the two conflicts. In each case it is the young, especially young men, who kill and die. (In 1916 we are presented with the dying boy from the Shankill as well as the dead young soldiers from the London-Scottish division. In present day Northern Ireland, meanwhile, we have the three murdered teenage soldiers and the 'shivering boy' who kills the bus conductor). In each generation the young are sacrificed, lead astray by the false dreams of patriotism and glory handed down to them by their elders.

Another parallel between the conflicts is that both rob their victims of any dignity. The dead London-Scottish soldiers with their buttocks on display parallel the murdered British soldiers with their 'flies undone'. The same brutality, it seems, enacts itself in generation after generation. Longley's war poems, then, reveal an extremely bleak view of human nature. Violence, war and revenge, they suggest, are deeply embedded in the human psyche. Man's capacity for inhumanity to his fellow man will unleash mayhem and bloodshed in every generation.

'Wounds' presents Northern Ireland, in particular, as a place that has been cursed with bitterness and hatred. Sectarian hate, the poem suggests, is built into the fabric of that troubled province, what Longley elsewhere described as 'these sick counties we call home'. In 1916 we are presented with 'the Ulster Division at the Somme' shouting anti-Catholic slogans as they charge into battle. The same hatred between Protestant and Catholic exists in Northern Ireland today, giving rise to the cycles of terror and revenge that have marred life there over the past forty years. Hostility and a mutual lack of understanding, it seems, have always existed between the North's two communities and possibly always will. Once again, then, Longley's view of human nature is bleak and uncompromising as he unflinchingly faces up to the darkness at the heart of man.

'Self-heal', though not strictly a war poem, makes a similar point, illustrating how violence inevitably begets more violence. The retarded boy who is abused by his family takes his revenge by stoning a goat to death. Unsurprisingly, therefore, 'Self-heal' has been regarded as a metaphor for the Troubles, as an illustration of how in the North one murder leads inevitably to another, of how vengeance begets more vengeance.

Yet Longley's treatment of war and violence is not entirely without hope. 'Ceasefire', for instance, holds out the possibility that peace can flourish between even the bitterest enemies. (The Trojan War, as recounted in Homer's epic the Iliad, is another conflict that greatly preoccupies Longley, recurring in his poetry almost as much as World War One). 'Ceasefire' demonstrates how in war even mortal enemies are linked by pain and anguish, for both sides suffer in the same way, losing friends, family members and any hope of a normal life. The poem also illustrates, however, the often terrible compromises that must often be made in order for hostilities to be set aside. Priam, in order to regain his son's body must debase himself before Achilles: 'I get down on my knees and do what must be done/And kiss Achilles' hand, the killer of my son'.

'Wounds' and 'Wreaths' also suggest that the cycles of violence and hate may someday be broken. In 'Wounds' the shivering boy's apology, however pathetic it may seem in light of the terrible crime he has just committed, offers at least some hope of reconciliation. It suggests that even the most brutal killers haven't been completely dehumanised, that they are capable of sorrow and remorse for the terrible things they have done: 'I think 'Sorry Missus' was what he said'. 'Wreaths', too, offers some hope that peace and reconciliation may emerge in Northern Ireland. The poet's use of Christian imagery (the Magi travelling to Christ's birth and the Crucifixion) suggests that it is only by embracing the Christian values of understanding and forgiveness that the Troubles' can be ended. (However, It is also possible to interpret this Christian imagery in a more negative light, as suggesting that the divisive effects of religion are at least partly responsible for the Troubles in the first place).

FATHER AND SON

The figure of the father recurs again and again throughout Longley's poetry. His concern with father-son relations permeated his work to such an extent that it might be regarded as a fixation or an obsession. The poet's affection and admiration for his father are evident in several poems. Both 'Wounds' and 'Last Requests' hint at the father's nerve, courage and resilience in the face of battle, suggesting the terrible events he had witnessed and lived through during the First World War. (In 'Last Requests' he is nearly buried alive, while in 'Wounds' he witnesses the slaughter of thousands of his comrades). A number of Longley's poems focus on seemingly insignificant objects associated with the father's life. 'Wounds', for instance, lists several of these: 'His badges, his medals like rainbows, / His spinning compass ... A packet of Woodbines I throw in, / A lucifer'. 'Last Requests', meanwhile, deals with the father's lifelong cigarette addiction while 'Wreaths' focuses on his false teeth. Longley's attention to these little details of his father's life suggests the love he bears him, and provide us with a sense of this formidable man's character and idiosyncrasies.

This love is at its most evident in 'Wounds' and 'Last Requests' where we see the poet tending to his dying father. In 'Wounds' he treats his ailing father with a real tenderness: 'I touched his hand, his thin head I touched'. 'Last Requests', too, provides a glimpse of the intimacy and closeness that exists between them. The poet brings his bed ridden father gifts and longs to reach him 'through the oxygen tent'. The strength and mystery of the father-son bond is also evident in 'Laertes' and 'Ceasefire'. In 'Laertes' the father is 'weak at the knees' upon recognising his son and the deep affection they between them is illustrated by their passionate embrace. 'Ceasefire', too, revolves around a father's affection for his son. Priam illustrates his love for Hector through the extreme measures to which he is willing to go in order to retrieve his dead son's corpse. (Achilles, too, mourns the fact that he is separated from his father, a further illustration of the power of the father-son bond).

An interesting feature of Longley's poetry is that it tends to reverse our usual expectation of the father-son relationship. When we think of fathers and sons we usually imagine the father to be the strong one, taking care of and tending to his child. In these poems, however, it is the father who is weak and requires the care of the younger and stronger son. We see this in 'Wounds' and 'Last Requests' where the father is frail and dying. In 'Wounds' he is presented as a very sick man on the verge of death: 'He said -lead traces flaring till they hurt-/ 'I am dying for King and Country slowly'. In 'Last Requests', meanwhile, the ailing father is a prisoner of the oxygen tent that keeps him alive. 'Laertes', too, presents the father figure as a weak and fragile old man who is almost overpowered by his son 'great Odysseus'. He is depicted as little more than a bag of bones to be 'cradled' by his warrior son: 'And cradled like driftwood the bones of his dwindling father'. In 'Ceasefire', also, the father is presented as a weak and fragile figure, forced to grovel at the feet of his son's killer.

In this selection Longley imagines not one but two funeral services that somehow involve his father. In 'Wounds' he imagines himself burying three murdered soldiers next to his father's grave. In 'Wreaths', meanwhile, he imagines burying his father 'once again' along with items recovered from the scene of a sectarian murder. Several critics have questioned this connection in Longley's poetry between his father and funerals. It is important to note, however, that these imaginary burials make a largely political point, comparing and contrasting the contemporary violence in Northern Ireland with the First World War of which his father was a veteran. As we have seen, these imaginary funeral services illustrate points about human nature as much as they do about the actual relationship between Longley and his father.

THE WEST OF IRELAND

The west of Ireland, specifically Mayo, has loomed large over Longley's poetic career. He has written poem after poem exploring the exquisite bleakness of that landscape and its people. The West has played a complex role in Longley's work and life, and critics disagree as to its precise significance for him. On one hand the beauty and serenity of the west can be identified as a refuge from the war and violence that haunt so much of his work, in particular his poems about Belfast and the Troubles. On the other hand, however, the Mayo landscape is also presented as a place of violence and bleakness.

'Carrigskeewaun', for instance, illustrates the poet's healthy awareness of nature's beauty. This is evident in particular in the poem's haunting description of the lake as 'Its surface seems tilted to receive/ The sun perfectly, the mare and her foal,/.The heron, all such special visitors'. In his Mayo poems Longley comes across as a true naturalist, delighting in the details of the natural world for their own sake. In 'Badger', for instance, he is careful to provide a meticulous sketch of the badger's movements: 'His path straight-and-narrow/And not like the fox's zig-zags'. 'Carrigskeewaun', too, delights in the tiny features of the natural world, all of which Longley, like a naturalist or bird-watcher, carefully records: 'With my first step I dislodge the mallards ... Kittiwakes scrape the waves: then, the circle/Widening, lapwings, curlews, snipe'.

Longley is well known as a poet of lists, especially lists of things associated with the natural world. This tendency is also evident in 'Self-heal' where he mentions some of the flowers growing on the long acre: 'Self-heal and centaury ... bog asphodel'. In 'Carrigskeewaun' the poet experiences a real sense of oneness with this beautiful Western landscape and the people who live there: 'I join all the men who have squatted here/This lichened side of the dry stone wall'

'Carrigskeewaun' presents the West of Ireland as a place of intense isolation where human habitation has had almost no impact on the landscape, being present only as fading footprints or smoke from a turf fire. While this isolation is no doubt attractive to a naturalist and nature-lover such as Longley, there is also something bleak and slightly frightening about it. Human habitation, it seems, is only barely possible in this bleak, rocky landscape. Mayo is presented as a harsh, arid land, a place of death and bones where survival must be eked out: 'This is ravens' territory, skulls, bones, / The marrow of these boulders'.

'Self-heal', too, presents Mayo in a distinctly unflattering light, focusing on the brutality and repression that still exist in rural Ireland. While Longley clearly loves the Mayo countryside and the west of Ireland he does not depict it in a romanticised or uncritical way. Instead, he focuses on what he regards as the negative aspects of rural Ireland as well as the positive. 'Badger', meanwhile, displays another aspect of Longley's nature writing, lamenting the destruction we humans wreak on the landscape that surrounds us. As such 'Badger is a political poem, making a strong and emotional case for conservation and protection of the Irish environment and the animals that inhabit it. (Longley, in fact, has made the point that he is at his most political when writing about nature and the damage 'progress' does to it).

ROMANTIC LOVE

Though Longley is well known as an accomplished writer of love poetry, only one example of this aspect of his work, 'An Amish Rug', has made it into the Leaving Cert selection. This poem can be viewed as an antidote to the turbulence and bloodshed that haunt so many of the other poems on the course. In 'An Amish Rug' Longley yearns for the serenity and simplicity of the Amish way of life to enter his own household. We are provided with a moving portrayal of a mature and loving relationship, centred on the marriage bed, which contrast to the chaos that rages in the outside world. The poet hopes that tranquility, ease, and security will enter his marriage through the agency of the Amish rug, and help to sustain it in the future.

Badger

LINE BY LINE

SECTION 1

Longley begins the poem with the word 'Pushing' and we are instantly made aware of the animal's strength. There is a sense that the badger is constantly labouring, using his time in a productive manner. The word 'wedge' tells of how the animal's body is perfectly suited to forcing itself between objects of resistance. Here the badger is pushing its body 'Between cromlech and stone circle'.

The mentioning of 'cromlech and stone circle' bring a number of things to mind. Firstly these are heavy and imposing obstacles. A 'cromlech' is an ancient tomb consisting of a large flat stone laid on upright ones. A stone circle is an arrangement of stones, large and small, for ancient ritual and astronomical purposes. Thus, the strength of the animal is revealed because of the monumental structures it overcomes.

The reference to 'cromlech and stone circle' also suggest that badgers have been inhabiting the landscape for centuries and continue to do so. The badger carries on the same work he has been doing for centuries, indifferent to the passage of time. The badgers that existed in megalithic times would have worked the earth and area with the same dutiful purpose as contemporary badgers. In contrast the 'cromlech and stone circle' reflect the changes that have come about in the human world, signalling the very different ways that we operate today.

Longley might also be drawing attention to differences between the operations of modern technological man and his megalithic counterpart. The movement of the stones that encompass the cromlech and stone circle would have involved great physical labour thousands of years ago. Perhaps there is a certain analogy in the poem between the way that the ancient peoples would have had to work in order to construct these great monuments and the way the badger works. The modern machines would make short work of such structures. The analogy between the activity of the badger and human activity of old could also be reinforced by the second last line of the poem, 'So many stones turned over'.

But the badger can also utilise the works of man. 'He excavates down mine shafts' and from here 'back into the depths of the hill'. The badger has his own particular way of tunnelling, 'straight and narrow'.

This appears to be its signature. In contrast, the fox 'zig-zags'. There is implication here that the badger is more straightforward creature, hard-working and diligent. In contrast the fox is a sly customer, his movements designed to confuse and deceive. The hare appears lighter, a dancer 'who leaves/ A silhouette on the sky line' as it travels. The badger, by implied contrast, is earth-bound, burdened with the duty of his unending work.

Night is its ally. The badger wears its 'silence' like a cloak 'around his shoulders'. The moon shines upon him in a benevolent fashion. There is an intimacy here, a comfortable harmony. In these conditions the badger can work undisturbed. The poet describes him as '[managing] the earth with his paws'. His work is careful, methodical and purposeful. When digging, a badger appears to be very preoccupied with the process. Digging may continue for hours and huge amounts of soil or sand can be shifted. The close affiliation with the earth is reinforced by the fact that the badger 'Returns underground to die'. The majority of badgers which die naturally, die in their setts.

SECTION 2

In the first section of the poem we are given an impression of the badger's external resilience. The second section paints a similar picture of the badger's internals. Again there is a heavy emphasis on the functionality and practicality of the badger. This is a creature who just gets on with the job. The first three lines of the second section give us an impression of the badger's digestive system. It is, by all accounts, tough as hell.

An intestine taking in
patches of dog's-mercury,
brambles, the bluebell wood

The 'intestine' of the badger is a sturdy organ. Dogs-mercury is known to be poisonous, yet it is digested in 'patches' by the badger and washed down with a few 'brambles'. Line 16 reveals more industrious activity, 'a heel revolving acorns'.

The following line mentions the threat of man to badgers. This is an animal that men like to hunt. Yet there is a sense that this is of no significance to the badger. It is a fact of its life and the badger will just get on with what it must do either way. The fact that this is a hunted animal is no more lingered upon than any other detail in the poem. However, the final line of the second section does set up an interesting disparity. On the one hand man hunts the badger as a prize and a pest. On the other hand he honours the badger by borrowing its name. Places in Ireland, such as Donnybrook, are derived from the badger's name (brook is the anglicised form of '*broc*', the Irish for badger).

SECTION 3

The final section of the poem begins with what seems to be a description of birth. However, we are quickly made aware that this is a 'delivery' of a different kind. The poet describes how a hunted badger is extracted from his sett. This sett is like a womb for the badger, a cosy haven from the world. The section opens with two terms for the badger. It is referred to as 'the digger, the earth-dog'. Once again the badger's industrial strengths are invoked. The term 'earth-dog' tells of how at home the badger is within the earth. However, the badger is forced from his habitat, a 'difficult delivery'.

A pair of 'tongs' are used to grip the head of the badger and pull him out. In the fourth line of the final section we get the first impression of the badger's vulnerability. Up to this point the badger was shown in his natural element to be a resilient and hard worker. Here, finally, he is vulnerable. Without being sentimental the poem tells of how the very snout that is in the grip of the tongs once 'lifted cow-pats for beetles,/ Hedgehogs for the soft meat'. Badgers are known to turn a hedgehog over and access the fleshy part of the animal whilst avoiding the protective spikes.

Once he has been removed from his sett the badger is lifelessly dragged overground. The poem closes with a thought for all the work these limbs achieved in life – 'So many stones turned over,/ The trees they tilted'.

THEMES

Nature

Longley is known for his matter-of-fact approach to descriptions of the natural world. Critics remark upon his naturalist's eye, his keen attention to detail, his avoidance of investing nature with a moral force. Just as in the poem 'Carrigskeewaun', Longley revels in giving a knowledgeable account of the natural world.

The precise naming of plants and animals is important to him. In a way it seems to show great respect for nature, revealing how he has taken the time to understand it and the way it works. Here we have 'patches of dog's-mercury', 'the bluebell wood', 'cuckoo-spit' and 'goose-grass'. In his poem 'The Hospital', Patrick Kavanagh spoke of the importance of 'naming' things in his poetry. He said that 'Naming these things is the love-act and its pledge'. Longley's poetry follows a similar ethos. He refuses to sentimentalise objects or events. Rather, he incorporates things into his poetry in a matter-of-fact way, allowing them to carry their own significance.

Longley does not invest the natural world with explicit metaphorical significance. Neither 'Badger' nor 'Carrigskeewaun' seek to do this. Longley does not look for analogues in nature, does not look to the natural world to illustrate or clarify his own feelings. Instead, he observes the way nature operates, looks at the details of the natural world and builds up a picture without investing it with his own emotions or concerns.

The badger

The poem illustrates what a hardy customer the badger is. There is an implicit respect for the way the badger exists. There are no airs and graces about the animal. He is a private and diligent being, hardworking and not fussy – the badger seems to bear the virtues of a model industrial worker. The badger is defined as an independent and almost conscientious creature throughout the poem. There seems to be such purpose to his work, He is like a caretaker of the earth, managing it with his paws.

Although the poem expresses no explicit sympathy, there is undoubtedly a sadness to the final section of the poem. There is implicit admiration for the character of the badger throughout the poem and it is sad to see such a force removed from his habitat and rendered helpless. The fact that he is forcibly removed from his sett is especially sad given the dignified description of the badger returning 'underground to die' earlier in the poem. The hunters deny him such dignity. Yet, there is also a sense that this is just a fact of life, just part of the nature of things.

Wounds

Longley's father fought with the British army in World War One. Though he was an Englishman he joined the London-Scottish regiment who went into battle wearing kilts. He fought at the Battle of the Somme in 1916, one of the bloodiest battles in the history of modern warfare.

LINE BY LINE

LINES 1–8: *The Ulster Division*

Longley talks about his father's memories of the Battle of the Somme, which he describes 'as pictures from my father's head'. The first memory concerns the Ulster Division. The father remembers these soldiers 'going over the top', leaving behind the safety of their trenches and running at the German lines, in the process exposing themselves to enemy fire. The father remembers the men of the Ulster Division as fierce and courageous fighters. According to the father they were even 'Wilder than Gurkhas'. (The Gurkhas were a Nepalese troop that had the reputation of being the deadliest soldiers in the British army). The father regards the Ulster Division with 'admiration and bewilderment'. He admires their courage and fighting spirit but is bewildered or taken aback at the rage and fury with which they fight.

Many of the Ulster Division came from the Protestant areas of Belfast. This is reflected in the dying boy's cry of 'Give 'em one for the Shankill'. (The Shankill Road, situated in the west of the city, is a traditionally Protestant area). Many of these young Protestants regarded Catholics with hatred and suspicion

– something reflected in their battle cry of 'Fuck the pope!'

Lines 9–12 deal with another of the father's wartime memories. This memory concerns the aftermath of a battle. Many of the father's comrades from the London-Scottish regiment are dead. They lie face down in the mud of battlefield, their kilts unsettled and their buttocks exposed. The father remembers the battlefield as a 'landscape of dead buttocks'. The regiment's 'padre' or chaplain wanders this gruesome landscape, saying prayers over the bodies of the dead. The chaplain 'resettles' the kilts of the dead soldiers with his 'swagger-stick' or cane. He does this so that their buttocks are covered and they have some dignity in death: 'The London-Scottish padre / Resettling kilts with his swagger-stick'.

LINES 14–17: *The war's effect on the father*

These lines describe the long-term effects the war had on the poet's father. Some of these effects were psychological. The father was haunted by the terrible things he'd seen at the front. This is suggested when the poet says his father spent 'fifty years' following the chaplain over a 'landscape of dead buttocks'. The father could never get awful images like this one out of his head.

The war also had long-term physical effects on the father. He was wounded several times, leaving poisonous traces of lead in his body. Many years later these 'Lead traces' were one of the causes of the cancer that killed him. In a sense, then, the father was a 'belated casualty' of the war. Though he did not die in battle his war wounds eventually killed him. This is why he says he is dying 'for King and Country, slowly'.

LINES 18–26: *The three dead soldiers*

These lines deal with three British soldiers who were murdered by the IRA during the Northern Irish Troubles. The soldiers were off-duty and out drinking when they were shot. They die, therefore, with 'bellyfuls of bullets and Irish beer'. While in a bar the soldiers were chatted-up by local women who offered them a sexual encounter. They followed these women to a secluded place only to be shot and killed by the IRA. That is why the soldiers are said to die with their 'flies undone'. (This tactic, using women as 'bait' for off-duty soldiers, was used several times by the IRA during the Troubles).

Longley imagines the funeral of these three dead soldiers. In his imagination these young men are buried beside his father: 'I bury beside him / Three teenage soldiers'. He imagines placing some of his father's personal belongings in the soldiers' graves. These items are associated with the father's military career: his badges, his medals, his compass, a packet of Woodbine cigarettes and a Lucifer or match. ('Woodbines' and 'lucifers' were brands of cigarettes and matches favoured by the father and his comrades in the trenches).

LINES 27–34: *The death of the bus conductor*

These lines describe the death of a bus conductor who was murdered by terrorists during the Northern Ireland Troubles. A young terrorist, who Longley describes as a 'shivering boy', barged into the bus conductor's home. The bus-conductor's family had just finished a meal and were watching television: 'Before they could turn the television down / Or tidy away the supper dishes'. The young terrorist shoots the bus-conductor through the head in front of his wife and children. He then apologises to the bus-conductor's family for this horrific deed: 'To the children, to a bewildered wife, / I think 'Sorry Missus' was what he said'.

THEMES

A tribute to the poet's father

'Wounds' is perhaps first and foremost a tribute to the poet's father. The father is portrayed as a courageous person who has seen warfare at its most terrible, has been wounded in battle and has won medals for bravery. His courage is also evident in the way he deals with his final illness. The father is facing a slow and agonising death from cancer. Yet he still maintains his sense of humour, joking that he is 'dying for King and Country, slowly'.

Like 'Last Requests', 'Wounds' explores the relationship between the poet and this extraordinary man. The poet seems to have a great deal of affection for his father. We see this in the tender way he attempts to comfort him as he lies dying in hospital: 'I touched

his hand, his thin head I touched'. Longley's respect for his father is evident in the way he lists the things associated with him almost as if they were a prayer or a magic spell: 'his badges, his medals like rainbows, his spinning compass'. This respect is also evident in how he responds to the father's memories of war. These traumatic memories are very personal to the father. The poet keeps these memories 'like secrets' and does not share them with a wider public until the father has passed away.

The horrors of war

Like 'Wreaths' and 'Last Requests', 'Wounds' unflinchingly examines the horrors of war. The victims of war crowd the poem: the dying boy who screams 'Give 'em one for the Shankill', the dead men of the London-Scottish division, the three murdered teenage soldiers and the bus-conductor shot dead in his own home. The poet's father, too, is a victim of war having been left mentally and physically scarred by his experiences at the front. The family of the bus-conductor might also be considered victims of the conflict, having been bereaved in violent and horrific circumstances. The poem also emphasises how war strips people of their dignity. The indignity of the dead London-Scottish soldiers with their buttocks bared mirrors that of the murdered soldiers with their flies undone.

The sacrifice of the young

An important theme of 'Wounds' is that in war it is young people, especially young men, who do most of the killing, dying and suffering. In World War One we see the dying boy from the Shankill and the poet's own father, then only seventeen, who endures terrible wounds. From the present Northern Irish conflict we are given the example of the murdered teenage soldiers as well as the children of the bus conductor who witness the execution of their father. The 'shivering boy', too, might be regarded as another young victim of conflict, for his nature has been twisted to the extent that he is capable of this brutal and cold-blooded killing.

Eternal violence?

Perhaps the most interesting feature of 'Wounds' is the way it brings together two different conflicts: World War One and the Northern Ireland Troubles. Longley imagines burying the three teenage soldiers next to his father and placing items associated with his father in the soldiers' graves. By doing so he links two different conflicts: World War One (in which his father served) and the Northern Ireland Troubles (in which the teenage soldiers served).

For this reason 'Wounds' could be considered an extremely pessimistic poem. By linking these two conflicts Longley suggests that not much has changed in the intervening years. Young men are still turned into ruthless killing machines. Hatred still flourishes between different communities. Dead soldiers are still stripped of their dignity. Innocent men still die and innocent families are still bereaved. Violence and war, the poem seems to suggest, are a part of human nature and will occur in generation after generation.

Northern Ireland: hatred and forgiveness

The poem unflinchingly examines the hatred between Catholics and Protestants that was a major cause of the Northern Ireland Troubles. It suggests that this hatred has existed for a very long time and is deeply ingrained in Northern Irish society. At the Somme in 1916 the men of the Ulster Division expressed their hatred of the Catholic community by shouting anti-Catholic slogans like 'Fuck the Pope!'. In the Ireland of the 1980s a young man expresses his hatred of Catholics by murdering a bus conductor. The 'boy about to die/Screaming 'Give 'em one for the Shankill' seems to almost mutate into the 'shivering boy' who fifty or sixty years later ruthlessly guns the bus conductor down.

Throughout the poem this sectarian hatred is met with 'bewilderment'. The poet's father is bewildered by the anti-Catholic cries of the Ulster Division, while the dead man's wife is 'bewildered' by the sudden murder of her husband. The repetition of this key word is significant. Bewilderment, the poem suggests, is the only possible response to such senseless hatred.

The poem's title refers not only to the physical wounds the poet's father suffered at the front but also to the social and psychological wounds inflicted on the people of Northern Ireland as the Catholic and Protestant communities became filled with hatred for one another. The poem suggests that the very soul of the province has been damaged. How else could a society produce men capable of brutal acts like the murder of the off-duty teenage soldiers and the bus-conductor?

'Wounds', however, offers some hope that this bitter conflict might someday be ended, that this hatred and division might be healed. The shivering boy's apology to the dead man's wife, however pathetic it might seem, indicates that not all human feeling has vanished from these sectarian killers, that there is some hope for future reconciliation. As Longley puts it: 'It seems important to me to think oneself into the killers' shoes, as it were, and to imagine how one can be so brainwashed or so angry or in a sense perhaps even so innocent that one can drive in a car and go into somebody's house and shoot that person stone dead ... I do believe in redemption, eventually we're going to have to forgive these people, and that young murderer's redemption is anticipated in that phrase 'Sorry Missus'. This possibility of redemption is also suggested (very tentatively) in 'The Greengrocer' section of 'Wreaths' and, more strongly, in 'Ceasefire'.

Poteen

BACKGROUND

Poteen (*poitín*) is basically any spirit distilled illegally. It could be made from malt, grain, potatoes, sugar or a variety of other basic materials. In Ireland the potato spirit was the most common poteen to be found. Poteen dates from the seventeenth century, when duties were first imposed on the distillation of spirits. But it was really in the following century, as the revenue men got into their stride and laws became tougher and duties higher, that poteen-making really took off. Of course, at the same time revenue officers became more zealous in their hunting down of illicit stills, so that poteen-makers had to head for highlands and boglands, where they set up their primitive apparatus. Any location of difficult access that would give a clear view of approaching officers was suitable.

People were only too happy to outwit the officers of the law and there were plenty of songs and stories about revenue patrols being directed deep into the bogs, sometimes even aided by helpful local 'guides'. However, when local men filled out the ranks of the Royal Irish Constabulary in the nineteenth century and replaced excise officers as the hounds of poteen-makers, the business of concealment became more difficult. Inevitably, the quality of poteen declined as the process of making and ageing it became more risky.

LINE BY LINE

When making poteen it is necessary to have 'Enough running water/ To cool the copper worm'. The 'copper worm' is the coil of metal pipe through which the evaporated alcohol flows and condenses. Longley compares this piping to the veins of the wrist. The veins at the wrist are close to the skin and, therefore, allow the blood to cool, just as the metal pipes allow the alcohol to cool and condense with the aid of the cold flow of water.

Ironically, all this cooling is required to produce a drink that scroches 'the throat'. Poteen, with its high alcohol content, is not pleasant to drink. The poet compares it to sulphuric acid: 'Vitriol to scorch the throat'.

When the poteen has been made and the 'hogshead', or large timber cask, is 'brimming', a single measure, 'one noggin-full', is taken and 'Sprinkled on the ground'. This is possibly a time-honoured ritual, a superstitious act, that lends an importance and sense of occasion to the process.

The poet links the making of poteen to darker events and times. He thinks of 'souterrains', or underground caves. He mentions 'Sunk workshops', places that are deliberately hidden from view beneath the ground, and 'Out-backs', remote and unpopulated places. The 'back of the mind' is where thoughts are often stored or hidden.

The poet thinks of a time when the 'whole bog' functioned as an 'outhouse' for illegal activity. This remote landscape acted as a place where unpleasant things could happen, away from the eyes of the authorities. Out there, the poet says, are weapons that were used to kill and maim, the 'cudgels' and the 'Guns'. Buried in the bog are physical reminders of gruesome acts of violence that were perpetrated in the past. Longley mentions the 'informer's ear', cut off as punishment.

The poet says that in this remote, uninhabited place 'we' have 'buried' the violent affair of our past. The final line mentions money and riches that have illegal and violent associations. 'Blood money' is money paid to an informer in order to cause somebody to be arrested, convicted, or executed. The term 'treasure trove' refers treasure of unknown ownership that is found hidden. Both have dubious connotations and suggest that buried deep beneath the quiet, desolate bog are many valuable reminders of our past that we might just prefer to forget.

THEMES

Violent past

Poteen highlights the violence that happened in the past, violence that often occurred out of sight and is now long forgotten. Longley mentions the 'cudgels' and the 'Guns' that lie buried in the bog, weapons used in a bloody and bitter conflict. The mentioning of the 'informer's ear' is a reminder of the brutal punishments meted out to those who betrayed their own side.

Illegal activity

Poteen was produced illegally and so had to be made away from the eyes of authority. For this reason, makeshift distilleries were set up in remote areas such as bogs. What the poem suggests is that such clandestine activity, though apparently innocuous, was often connected with more sinister events. Out in the remote bogs, in the secret outhouses and sunken workshops where poteen was distilled, men were banding together and orchestrating and conducting violence. The evidence that such activity took place is still out there, buried beneath the bog. But, the poem implies, we would prefer to forget about such things, confine them to the backs of our mind. 'Poteen' suggests that there is a darkness to our country's past that we might not care to acknowledge, a 'violence that lurks beneath the apparently peaceful surface or our civilisation'.

Carrigskeewaun

LINE BY LINE

The mountain

The opening section of the poem describes the bleak terrain of the mountain. It is a place that belongs to the scavengers such as the 'raven': 'This is raven's territory'. Signs of death surround the poet: 'skulls, bones,/ The marrow of these boulders'. He is aware of the presence of the ravens circling above him, supervising 'From the upper air'. The boulders that surround him seem to be stripped bare, liked bones picked of their meat.

The word 'territory' implies that this land is not the poet's, it belongs to the ravens. They control this area. He is not at home here. It is a hostile and unsettling place. It is a wasteland, a boneyard, a chilling reminder of mortality. The poet is aware of his solitary existence. 'I stand alone here'.

But while he stands 'alone' he seems 'to gather children about' himself. Perhaps he has called his children who now come running to his side. They have been picnicking in the mountain. His voice, as he calls out to his children, fills the lonely 'district'.

The path

As the poet walks along the path he disturbs the natural inhabitants of the area: 'With my first step I dislodge the mallards'. The word 'dislodge' suggests that the ducks were nicely settled by the path. We might think of them as lodgers, giving a legitimacy to their dwelling. The poet's presence here is not so natural and there is a sense that he is not in his element here. However, whereas the mountain was unsettling 'ravens' territory', the poet now threads a path, an established piece of land marked out by the movements of man. But there is the definite sense that he is only passing through. And he is confined to his path whereas the mallards take to the air and fly 'over the bog to where/ Kittiwakes scrape the waves'.

The last two lines record his awareness of his position in this environment with some humour. When the birds have taken flight he is 'left with one swan to nudge/ To the far side of its gradual disdain'. Again

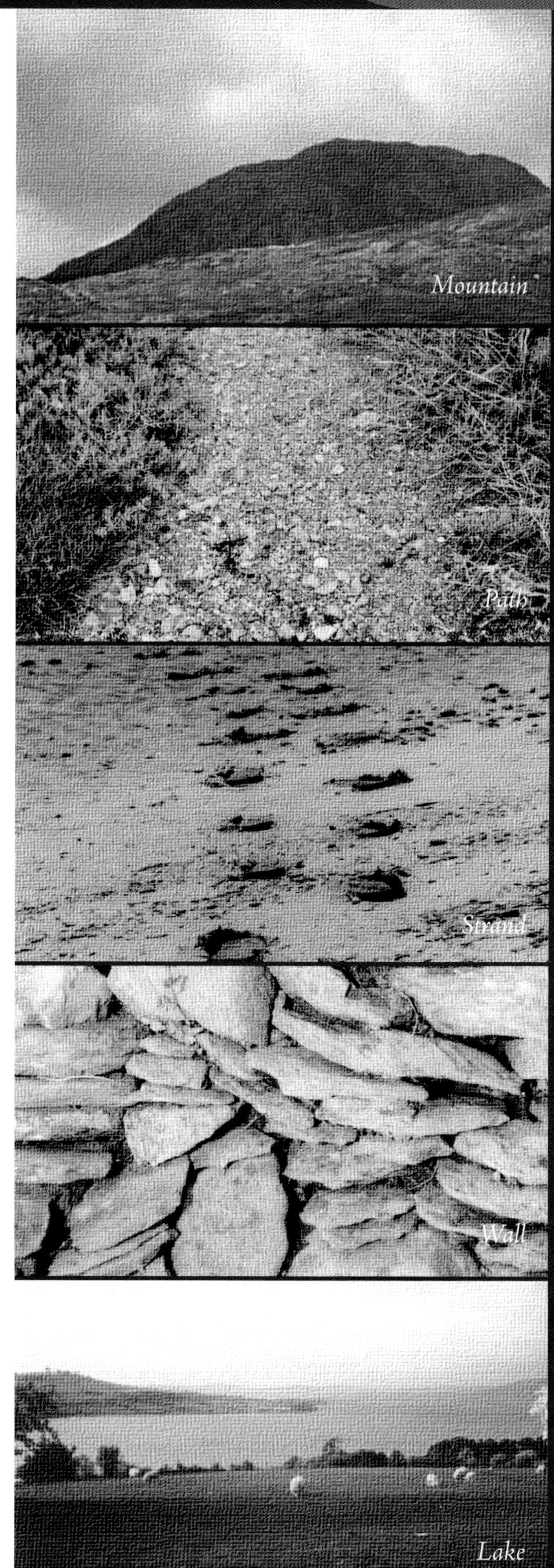
Mountain
Path
Strand
Wall
Lake

the poet is left with a impression of great distance between himself and the natural inhabitants of the area. But this is not something he rues, it is simply part of nature.

The strand

The poet is like an explorer, his eye sensitive to the subtle, delicate details of a seemingly undiscovered landscape. Along the strand, Crusoe-like, he reads the markings in the sand. These are the physical recordings of yesterday's activities, imprints of the past. The poet brings his knowledge of nature to bear upon the scene. There are 'Cattle tracks, a sanderling's tiny trail'. The print of the cumbersome cattle and the fragile sanderling. And there is also 'The footprints of the children and [his] own' remaining from a walk they took the day before.

The tracks of his children and his own link 'the dunes to the water's edge', the land to the sea. There is a sense of being at ease and feeling essentially part of this environment, at least more so than in the first two sections. However, the conquest of time, the inevitability of decay is also apparent here, though in a less dreadful way than the first section. The impact of their feet reduces 'to sand the dry shells'. This debris is considered metaphorically to be the 'toe-/ And fingernail pairings of the sea'. The poet considers the process of erosion that occurs in the sea in a similar light to the pairing of nails. In contrast to the opening stanza the poet seems more at ease with the processes of time and inevitable decay. Perhaps it is because he feels more secure in a place where his children's signatures still remain. This place is not desolate and remote as the mountain. There seems to be multiple claims to this location, whereas the mountain was strictly 'ravens' territory'.

The wall

From the no-mans-land of the mountains the poet arrives at a more secure place. Here is a man-made structure, designed to shelter.

I join all the men who have squatted here
This lichened side of the dry-stone wall

The poet feels a sense of community with all those who have 'squatted here' before him. Yet the very absence (or, perhaps, the ghostly presence) of these men tells of the temporality of life, the idea that man is a transient being, a traveller through life, seeking refuge and shelter along the way. The wall provides a temporary place of shelter. A fire is lit to provide warmth. The temporary dwelling is basic yet the poet uses the location just as someone passing through a thousand years ago might have. The idea that the poet is a squatter shows that he has no legitimate claim to the land. Others have used it before him and it will be used again.

Perhaps it is his thoughts of temporality and need for security that cause the poet to think of home. The smoke that rises from the fire he has lit 'Recalls in the cool air above the lake/ Steam from a kettle, a tablecloth and/ A table she might have already set'. The lines of the section bear out the fundamentals of life – shelter, warmth, sustenance and family. Out here, away from the distractions and commotions of everyday urban life the poet seems to be in tune with what is important. The wall provides a link with the timeless needs and pursuits of man. The bare shelter of the wall allows the poet to think of the greater shelter that his family provides. The poet has moved from the unsettling environment of the mountain where he was out of place to this wall where he feels somewhat at home, though not completely.

The lake

This is the only section in which the poet does not allude to himself. It is a parting snapshot of the beauty and perfection of the area through which he has just travelled. The lake functions in a similar way to the poet. He has reflected the area in his poem. The lake now does this 'perfectly'. Those animals that pass by, the 'sheep and cattle that wander here' are captured by the lake. Each evening the lake seems to consciously tilt toward the setting sun in order to 'receive' it. The poet closes the poem with a perfect image of harmony and feeling that the creatures of this area are 'special'.

THEMES

The west of Ireland

The west of Ireland, especially Mayo, plays an important role in Longley's poetic career. Many of his poems deal with the exquisite bleakness of that landscape and its people. The beauty and the serenity of the west seem to provide a refuge from the war and violence that haunts so much of his work. And yet the Mayo landscape is sometimes presented as a place of violence and bleakness. 'Carrigskeewaun' illustrates the poets awareness of the areas beauty whilst also revealing the intense isolation of a place where human habitation has had almost no impact.

Nature

Longley focuses on different aspects of the Carrigskeewaun landscape and illustrates both the beauty and the bleakness that is to be found there. Nature is seen as something varied and special. The poet focuses on the small details, the flora and the fauna that exist in Carrigskeewaun. The poet takes great interest in the identity and movements of the birds around him. What he observes is a wonderfully diverse community of the air. There is obvious fascination with this, a vast population in its own element. The mention of birds forming a 'circle' suggests completeness and perfection, the circle being a common symbol of both.

The feature of specifically naming and describing the creatures and plants that he sees is something common to much of Longley's many Nature poems. As one critic has put it, 'for him exact naming of species becomes a complex way of Irish belonging, of remembering, of situating himself in a difficult cultural terrain, while remaining true to his sense of a complex inheritance'. Nature, for Longley, is a marvellous miracle, recorded lovingly but without piety or easy sentiment. The characteristic tone of his Nature poetry is that of delight and clear-eyed wonderment before the world's manifold detail.

Wreaths

The poems in wreaths are tributes to the dead, the poetic equivalent of the flowers offered up at funeral services to honour the memory of the deceased. The individuals that 'Wreaths' remembers are all victims of the Northern Irish Troubles. The poems mourn ordinary people with everyday jobs (a civil servant, a grocer and some factory workers) whose lives were brutally cut short by sectarian atrocities.

The civil servant

The first poem of the series remembers Martin McBirney a lawyer and personal friend of Longley who was murdered in his home by the IRA. (The circumstances of his death recall 'Wounds' and the 'shivering boy' who kills the bus conductor in front of his family). One of the most remarkable features of 'The Civil Servant' is the flat, almost conversational language in which it is written. This is particularly evident in the opening lines: 'He was preparing an Ulster fry for breakfast/When someone walked into the kitchen and shot him'. This chatty opening resembles more the beginning of a pub conversation than that of a poetic elegy. The poet's matter-of-fact tone emphasises the extent to which such happenings had become commonplace in the warped moral climate of Northern Ireland. The fact that the murderer isn't even named or described (he is referred to only as 'someone') reinforces our sense that to the poet's community this brutal killing represents nothing particularly out of the ordinary.

One of the most unsettling features of this poor man's death is the unspeakable suddenness with which his life is taken from him. One moment he is cooking breakfast, the next he's yet another terrorist victim. Perhaps even more disturbing is the violation of intimacy his death implies. There is something terrible about the intrusion of the murderer into the very kitchen of his victim – the place that in many homes is the centre of family life. This invasion of privacy is made somehow worse by the fact that the civil servant is not even fully dressed when he's gunned down: 'He lay in his dressing gown and pyjamas'. The intrusion of violence into the everyday life of the family is poignantly symbolised by the 'bullet hole in the cutlery drawer'.

The privacy of his household is violated even further by the detectives who search the premises for clues: 'they dusted the dresser for fingerprints/and then shuffled backwards across the garden/With notebooks, cameras, and measuring tapes'. These lines convey the horribly impersonal nature of the investigators' work. The civil servant's home, the setting for the private life of his family, for their love, difficulties and squabbles, has been transformed into just another crime scene. The intimacy of their household is shattered by the intrusion of the investigators as they record the evidence of this brutal murder.

As we have seen, Longley's tone in 'The Civil Servant' is detached and observational. He simply gives us the facts of this terrible incident and lets them speak for themselves rather than attempting to engage our emotions with highly charged poetic language. Yet we sense the poet's grief for his friend in his description of the bullet passing through the civil servant's brain. He describes the bullet travelling through the dead man's skull, eliminating all the experience and information contained within it: 'A bullet entered his mouth and pierced his skull, / the books he had read, the music he could play'. In their quiet way these lines convey the tragedy of the civil servant's demise. His death means the destruction of a particular set of memories. His knowledge and experience have been lost. Something unique has been snuffed out, an individual personality who had never been before and will never be again. These lines, then, stress Longley's compassion as a poet, his belief in the uniqueness of each individual and the tragedy implied by each and every untimely death.

The poem's conclusion is haunting and enigmatic, describing the aftermath of the civil servant's death: 'Later his widow took a hammer and chisel / And removed the black keys from his piano'. In keeping with the poem's flat, minimal style we are given no explanation of the wife's behaviour. Just as with his depiction of the civil servant's murder, the poet gives us the facts and the facts only, offering no comment on or analysis of the wife's actions. Why then does she forcibly remove the black keys from her husband's piano? There is something unsettling about this act of vandalism. Most commentators agree that it indicates some kind of mental disturbance on the wife's part, suggesting she has been severely traumatised by her husband's violent death. The poet's straightforward, matter-of-fact tone in these lines only reinforces the disturbing oddness of the widow's actions.

The greengrocer

'The Greengrocer' is another tribute to a victim of the Northern Irish conflict. Like the civil servant in the previous poem, the greengrocer of the title has been gunned down mercilessly in a sectarian killing, shot while working behind the counter of his shop. A particularly harrowing feature of his murder is that it takes place in the run-up to Christmas: 'Holly wreaths for Christmas/Fir trees on the pavement outside'. Deaths over the Christmas period, especially violent deaths, are particularly hard on the friends and relatives of the deceased. As in 'The Civil Servant', the brutality of the victim's death is somehow emphasised by the poet's matter-of-fact tone. Once again we are given the bare facts of the murder in plain conversational language: 'He ran a good shop, and he died/ serving even the death-dealers'.

Like 'The Civil Servant', 'The Greengrocer' praises the uniqueness of a seemingly ordinary man. In the previous poem Longley mourns the passing of the knowledge contained in the civil servant's head ('The books he had read, the music he could play'). Here he celebrates the hard work and industry of Jim Gibson the greengrocer. The grocer, we're told, 'ran a good shop'. Unsurprisingly, therefore, he was 'organised' for the Christmas period, having all the right goods in stock. His hardworking attitude to life is indicated by the fact that his murderers find him 'busy as usual/ Behind the counter'. 'The Greengrocer', then, is a poem that mourns the passing of an ordinary working man, while praising his skills and achievements. The ability to run 'a good shop' is by no means undeserving of celebration in a poem.

In the second stanza the speaker's approach strays from the strictly factual. Instead of just simply recording what happened he begins to imagine what 'may' now happen. He pictures a possible aftermath to this tragic event. In describing these imaginings, however, the speaker's tone remains straightforward and conversational rather than flowery or poetic. In keeping with the poem's Christmas setting the speaker envisages the three kings (or 'Magi') who according to the Bible visited the newborn Jesus in Bethlehem. In this poem, however, the 'Astrologers or three wise men' are bound not for a stable in Bethlehem for a 'house up the Shankill / Or the Falls'. (The Shankill is a protestant district of Belfast while the Falls road area is populated mainly by Catholics). The speaker urges these Magi to stop at the murdered grocer's shop, saying they 'should pause on their way/To buy gifts at Jim Gibson's shop'. The speaker imagines the Magi bearing 'Dates and chestnuts and tangerines' instead of their traditional gifts of gold, frankincense and myrrh. (These somewhat exotic fruits would presumably have been stocked by the grocer specifically for the Christmas period).

In his imagination, then, Longley transports these 'three wise men' from the Middle East of Christ's birth to contemporary Belfast. Several critics maintain that this is an ironic or cynical comment by Longley on religion, particularly on Christianity. Is Longley suggesting here that religion is powerless to help us against brutality like that recounted in this series of poems? Does the poem imply that religion encourages bitter conflicts like the one in Northern Ireland rather than helping to resolve them? In his poetry Longley expresses a decidedly mixed attitude to Christianity, describing himself as 'an unbeliever and one of those awkward Protestants'. In 'The Greengrocer' Christmas, the traditional Christian time of forgiveness, becomes a season of death and murder. In a grim irony the holly wreaths in the grocer's shop, intended for the seasonal festivities, become funeral wreaths, marking his untimely passage from this life. The poem suggests that Christ and the religion he founded have divided Belfast, subjecting the city to a vicious cycle of murder and vengeance. This is symbolised by the fact that in the speaker's imagination the Magi, so intimately associated with Christ's birth, carry gifts purchased form a murdered grocers shop. Significantly they venture to a 'house up the Shankill/ Or the Falls'. The religion the Magi represent has split Belfast into two bitterly opposed communities, Protestant and Catholic, giving rise to vicious sectarian murders like that of the greengrocer.

The linen workers

Of the three poems that make up the 'Wreaths' series 'The Linen Workers' is perhaps the most unusual and the most difficult. It is divided into four four-line stanzas each of which deals with a different topic. The first stanza deals with Christ's ascension into heaven. The second, meanwhile, describes one of the speaker's childhood memories, a recollection of his dead father's dentures. The third stanza details the brutal murder of ten linen workers in Belfast. Finally, in the fourth stanza, the speaker imagines himself officiating at a second funeral for his dead father. All four stanzas, however, are linked by the recurring image of teeth.

STANZA 1

Stanza 1 continues the religious line of thought begun at the end of 'The Greengrocer' with its image of the Magi travelling through Belfast. Longley playfully parodies two of the central Christian mysteries: Christ's Crucifixion and his ascent into heaven. Christianity, of course, teaches that forty days after the resurrection Christ ascended body and soul into heaven. Longley, however, strips some of the wonder from this marvel by suggesting that Christ teeth accompanied him on this miraculous journey: 'Christ's teeth ascended with him into heaven'. There is something almost comical in the notion of Christ taking his teeth with him to paradise, complete with a 'cavity in his one of his molars'. Equally silly is the suggestion that the wind whistles through this cavity as it is sent down to us from heaven: 'Through a cavity in one of his molars the wind whistles'. (This image is reminiscent of children's stories that explain the weather by saying that the rain is Jesus' tears). It has been suggested that Longley is poking fun at Christianity in these lines, by pointing out how ridiculous stories such as that of the ascension actually are if looked at in the cold light of day. After all if Christ ascended body and soul into heaven he would have to be accompanied not only by his teeth, but also by his kidneys and his bladder. Surely, however, these organs have no place in paradise? In these lines, then, Longley seems to be playfully attacking Christianity, suggesting, perhaps, that some its central beliefs are little more than superstitions, carrying no more weight than the tall tales told to children.

According to Longley Jesus does not, as the Bible tells us, sit at his father's right hand in heaven. Instead, he has ascended to paradise only to be 'fastened for ever/By his exposed canines to a wintry sky'. There is something gruesome and nightmarish about this image of Christ impaled by his own teeth to the wintry sky. Jesus, it seems, has ascended to paradise only to face a further Crucifixion. Yet this suffering is greater than anything he endured on earth, for not only does he suffer the indignity of being fastened by his teeth, but also his agony will go on 'for ever'. It this stanza, then, Longley attacks religion in two different ways. Firstly, by gently mocking the story of the ascension he suggests that Christianity is a bizarre and outlandish religion, consisting of beliefs that simply don't stand up to scrutiny. Secondly, he condemns religion for its helplessness in the face of violence and mayhem like that which has ruined so many lives in Northern Ireland. Christ is depicted as a forlorn, feeble figure, impaled against the sky. He gazes down on suffering, murder, and violence but is powerless to intervene or help those whose lives have been destroyed. It has been suggested that this image of Christ uselessly fastened to the sky serves as a metaphor for Longley's view of religion as something that is entirely helpless when it comes to eliminating violence and suffering. (In fact, as we have seen at the conclusion of 'The Green Grocer' he seems to suggest that religion actually encourages conflict and aggression rather than resolving it).

STANZA 2

In this stanza the poem's direction changes rapidly as the speaker recounts a childhood memory of his dead father's dentures. The father's false teeth, it seems, are being cleaned. They are left overnight in a glass (a 'tumbler') filled with water and some kind of cleaning solution that bubbles and foams around them: 'the memory of my father's false teeth/Brimming in their tumbler; they wore bubbles'. According to the speaker the dentures in the tumbler seemed to be grinning: 'they wore ... outside of his body, a deadly grin'. The fact that the speaker describes this grin as 'deadly' indicates that he was somewhat upset or frightened by the sight of his father's teeth floating outside the mouth where they belong. There is something amusing about the young speaker's alarm at the sight of his father's dentures. (His shock, however, is understandable, as dentures do indeed look peculiar when removed from their owner's mouth). Yet the tone of the stanza is not entirely playful. There is a note of terrible sadness in the speaker's assertion that he is 'blinded' by this memory of his father's false teeth. Very often when we think of a deceased loved one it is the simple, apparently unimportant memories that cause us the most sorrow. In this instance the speaker's mind is 'blinded' by the seemingly inconsequential memory of an everyday occurrence: the cleaning of his dead father's dentures. Yet this recollection, it seems, is too moving and heart rending for him to dwell on.

STANZA 3

This stanza marks yet another shift in the poem's direction. The speaker describes the brutal murder of ten factory operatives in Belfast. These unfortunate people, who worked Belfast's thriving linen industry, were the victims of a vicious sectarian assault. As in 'The Civil Servant' and 'The Greengrocer' the description of the massacre is flat and conversational in tone. The speaker gives us the information about the bloodbath in a casual, almost off-hand manner: 'When they massacred the ten linen workers'. The stanza's casual tone emphasises the extent to which violence has become part of the fabric of everyday life in Northern Ireland. (The fact that the speaker begins the stanza with the word 'When' suggests that it is taken for granted that such terrible incidents occur in modern-day Belfast. The question is 'when' such things happen rather than 'if').

As in 'The Civil Servant' and 'The Greengrocer', Longley focuses on the victims of violence rather than on the killers, who are referred to merely as 'they'. As in the previous two poems we are given strangely intimate details of the victims' lives. Longley presents us with a list of things the linen workers were wearing or carrying when they were gunned down: 'There fell on the road beside them spectacles, / Wallets, small change, and a set of dentures'. Items like these, wallets, spectacles and dentures, are intimately associated with the everyday lives of the people who own them. There is something deeply moving, therefore, about Longley's description of these personal effects falling on the ground beside their owners. The list of personal items provides us with an impression of the murdered linen workers as a set of individuals rather than as mere statistics, bringing home a sense of the tragedy that each of their deaths implies. It also reinforces our sense that these lives have been suddenly and violently cut short. We are presented with money that will never now be spent, dentures that will never again be cleaned. (This emphasis on the brutal suddenness of the workers' deaths recalls the civil servant who was shot while preparing breakfast and the greengrocer who was killed while busy in his shop. In each instance an ordinary day has been suddenly turned to tragedy). The massacre of the linen workers also involves a violation of privacy, for their most personal and intimate possessions (wallets, dentures, glasses) have become little more than evidence at a crime scene. In death their privacy has been compromised, their personal effects have become public property to be pored over by detectives and curious passers-by. (This violation of intimacy recalls the deaths of the civil servant and of the green grocer, both of whom were gunned down in their personal spaces, and in particular the lines in 'The Civil Servant' which depict the detectives scouring the dead man's house for clues). Each of the murders described in 'Wreaths', therefore, involves some invasion of privacy, an intrusion into the personal lives of the victims.

STANZA 4

The poem's final stanza skilfully combines Longley's memory of his father in stanza 2 with the murder of linen workers as described in stanza 3. He pictures himself preparing his father's body for burial. Before he can dispose of father's body properly he must equip it with items recovered from the murdered linen workers. He places the spectacles from this crime scene upon his father's corpse: 'I must polish the spectacles, balance them/Upon his nose'. He fills his fathers pockets with money from the workers' wallets, with the small change that fell on the ground when they were killed: 'I must … fill his pockets with money'. Finally, he puts the dentures that formerly belonged to one of the linen workers into his father's mouth: 'And into his dead mouth slip the set of teeth'.

Longley's father, it is important to note, was dead at the time he composed this poem. Why, then, does he imagine that he must bury his father 'once again'? Furthermore, why does he picture this bizarre funeral rite that involves items gathered from the murdered linen workers? Longley's father, of course, was a veteran of World War One where he was wounded and decorated for bravery. According to the poet his father's death from cancer, fifty years after the war ended, was partly caused by the wounds he had sustained at the front. (This is dealt with in 'Wounds' where Longley describes his father's wartime injuries contributing to his final illness: the 'lead traces flaring till they hurt'). Longley's imagined funeral ceremony, therefore, identifies his father, a victim of the first world war, with the murdered linen workers who are victims of the contemporary violence in Northern Ireland. By enclosing the linen workers' belongings with his father's corpse Longley suggests a link between these terrible conflicts. The same dark forces in human nature that led to the mayhem and destruction of the First World War are responsible for the current struggle in Northern Ireland. (A similar attitude prevails in 'Wounds', which also features an imaginary funeral service involving the poet's father and victims of the Northern Irish Troubles). 'Wreaths', then, provides an extremely bleak view of human nature. It suggests that violence, cruelty, and aggression are embedded in the heart of man, giving rise to conflict after conflict and murder after murder.

THEMES

A poem of tribute

This series of poems functions as a mark of respect to the victims of the Troubles it remembers. In this sense they are similar to the floral tributes that are presented at a funeral. The poem mourns ordinary people with ordinary jobs, a civil servant, a greengrocer, and a group of factory workers. However, it also celebrates the individuality and achievements of these apparently everyday people. Longley mourns the passing of the knowledge and information that vanished with the civil servant's death: 'The books he had read, the music he could play'. The greengrocer, meanwhile, is praised for running 'a good shop'. Even the ten factory workers are remembered as individuals, their distinctiveness emphasised by the personal items that lie scattered around their corpses: 'Wallets, small change, and a set of dentures'. 'Wreaths', then, presents these twelve murdered people not just as victims of terror but also as individuals in their own right, each of whose lives are worth remembering. The poem is also, of course, a tribute to the poet's father who as we have seen was himself a victim of armed conflict. The father's individuality is emphasised by Longley's memory of his dentures 'Brimming in their tumbler', which gives us an insight into the intimate and private life of this wounded war hero. There is a powerful sense of love and admiration in the poem's concluding lines, as the poet imagines himself tenderly preparing his father's body for burial.

The brutality of the Troubles

'Wreaths' provides an unflinching account of the terrible violence that has marred Northern Ireland, to varying extents, from the 1960's to the present day. As we have already noted Longley's description of the various murders is flat and conversational in tone. Yet his straightforward, almost chatty, description of these incidents brings home their viciousness more effectively than any outpouring of emotional language or burst of carefully constructed metaphors. As we have seen, one of the most appalling aspects of these murders is the abruptness and suddenness with which they are carried out. The victims' lives are ended in an instant, without any sort of warning, allowing them no time to prepare for death or make their peace with God. Almost equally disturbing is the violation of intimacy each of their deaths implies. In the case of each murder the victims' privacy is violated, and their personal lives are (to various extents) exposed to the outside world. (Both the civil servant and the grocer are murdered in their personal spaces, the civil servant's house is invaded by officials, and the linen workers' personal belongings are scattered on the floor). One of the poem's most haunting images is that of the civil servant's wife removing 'the black keys from his piano'. This portrait of an obviously disturbed woman emphasises the mental torture of those bereaved by murders such as those described in 'Wreaths'. In the Troubles it is not only those who are murdered but also their friends and families that can be considered victims.

A bleak view of human nature

'Wreaths', as we have pointed out, offers an extremely pessimistic view of human nature. It presents us with a world where innocent people are killed for absolutely no reason, gunned down without warning in their homes and places of work. Yet this violence is by no means strictly limited to Northern Ireland. By bringing his soldier father into the poem Longley creates a link between the Troubles and the First World War. Human aggression, it seems has held sway throughout history giving rise not only to these two conflicts but also, of course, to many other wars stretching into both the past and future. Cruelty and violence, the poem suggests, are built into the human condition itself. The innocent have always suffered and, unless mankind changes radically, always will.

A pessimistic view of religion

'Wreaths' offers a scathing and sustained attack on Christianity. 'The Greengrocer', by updating the journey of the Magi to present-day Belfast, suggests how religion has bitterly divided Northern Ireland along sectarian lines, leading to bitterness and bloodshed rather than peace and harmony. In 'The Linen Workers' Longley pokes fun at the Christian story of the ascension, suggesting that such miracle stories are beyond credulity, fit to be believed by only by the naïve and gullible. The shocking image of Christ 'fastened for ever/ By his exposed canines to a wintry sky' presents religion as something that is powerless to intervene in or improve the affairs of man. Jesus can only look down powerlessly from his bleak sky as we butcher each other.

'Wreaths' offers a subtle but powerful parody of the last supper. Instead of twelve apostles we have twelve victims of sectarian violence (ten linen workers, a grocer and a civil servant). The bread and wine are provided by the 'food particles' that spill onto the street from the murdered worker's stomachs. Instead of the body and blood of Christ we have the bodies and blood of these murder victims: 'blood, food particles, the bread, the wine'. Christ, on whom the last supper centres, is not a wise and powerful leader but a rather pathetic figure grotesquely impaled by his own teeth. This grim parody of the last supper, one of the central Christian mysteries and the basis for the mass, further emphasises Longley's disillusionment with Christianity as a source of hope or healing. Religion, as we have seen, is at best powerless in the face of man's barbarism and at worst actively encourages it.

However, it is also possible to see in 'The Greengrocer' a somewhat more positive view of religion and Christianity. According to several critics the poem's conclusion implies that it is only through the Christian spirit of forgiveness and turning the other cheek that the divided communities in Northern Ireland can be brought together (a similar point is made in 'Ceasefire' and, more obliquely, in 'Wounds'). Importantly, the 'Astrologers or three wise men', who represent Christian values, seem to be about to visit both communities: 'setting out/ For small house up the Shankill or the Falls'. If these two warring communities embrace the Christian spirit of forgiveness, if they are 'visited' by the values the Magi represent, then perhaps reconciliation of this deeply divided society might be possible, and with it an end to the brutal cycle of murder documented so movingly and unflinchingly in 'Wreaths'.

Last Requests

LINE BY LINE

LINES 1–8

The poet tells of how his father almost died in the first World War. In the midst of battle he was injured, possibly knocked unconscious by an explosion. The father's own batsman thought him as good as dead and abandoned him: 'Your batsman thought you were buried alive,/ Left you for dead'. The batsman stole the father's 'pocket watch/ And cigarette case' and left him lying next to an 'unexploded shell'. This place almost became the father's grave: 'the grave you so nearly had to share/ With an unexploded shell'.

However, the poet's father was a strong man with a serious addiction to nicotine. Defying the odds, he survived. He began breathing again, his lungs expanding in an effort to take a drag of a cigarette: 'But your lungs/ Surfaced to take a long remembered drag'. The father was so close to death that his own cigarette lighter had almost served as a miniature headstone, his epitaph being the initials he had scratched on the gold surface. But his strong heart and will to live prevented his lighter serving this unusual purpose: 'Heart contradicting as an epitaph/ The two initials you had scratched on gold'.

LINES 9–16

In the second stanza the poet recalls being near his father as he lay dying in a hospital bed. Just before he died the father raised his fingers above his lips and waved. The poet initially thought that he was blowing a farewell kiss: 'I thought you blew a kiss before you died'. But he quickly realised that his father was signalling for a cigarette: 'But the bony fingers that waved to and fro/ Were asking for a Woodbine'.

It seems that many soldiers smoked Woodbines during the war. The poet's father continued to smoke this particular brand of cigarette for forty years: The brand you chose to smoke for forty years'. The soldiers who had fought with the poet's father in the war often asked for a cigarette just before they died: 'the last request/ Of many soldiers in your company'.

Because of the cigarettes' association with the war and all the young men who died, the poet's father smoked each cigarette 'Thoughtfully'. They had served as something of a 'sacrament' for many dying men and so the father considers each one sacred.

Realising that his dying father is holding his hand out for a cigarette and understanding the significance of this gesture causes the poet to feel that the 'peppermints and grapes' he brought are ridiculous and meaningless. He stands close to his father but he is cannot make contact with the dying man. The 'oxygen tent' that surrounds the father acts as a barrier. But the poet is also removed from his father because he realises that the dying man is no longer thinking of the hospital and his son but is back with the young men who fought and died with him.

THEMES

War

The poem illustrates the brutal nature of war. The description of the father's near death experience at the start of poem is a snapshot of the sort of horrific experiences soldiers had to endure. The fact that the father is still thinking of these times when he lies dying in hospital many years later shows how mentally wounding the experience of war can be. But it also shows how the experience of enduring such a traumatic event resulted in a life-long bond between those who fought.

Father and son

The poet is obviously very proud of his father. By retelling the war story involving his father he reveals what an extraordinary brave and strong man his father must have been. The poet is also aware of the humour and irony involved in the fact that a need for a cigarette ultimately saved the father's life. Yet he also understands that the war was the defining experience of the father's life, an experience that the poet can only imagine. The poet feels isolated from his father at the end of the poem because of this. He realises that his father has reverted to a time in his life that does not involve him.

Self-heal (from *Mayo Monologues*)

BACKGROUND AND INTRODUCTION

This poem tells the tale of a sexual encounter between the speaker, who is a young woman, and a retarded boy. The incident occurs when the speaker takes the boy for a walk in the countryside. She wants to teach him the names of the various flowers that grow there. Together they walk 'the long acre', the strip of grass found on the sides of country roads: 'I wanted to teach him the names of flowers, /Self-heal and century; on the long acre/Where cattle never graze'.

LINE BY LINE

A grim tale

The boy seems to be a kind of simpleton, little more than an overgrown baby: 'He'd slept in the cot until he was twelve/Because of his babyish ways, I suppose'. He is also, it seems, somewhat physically deformed: 'His skull seemed to be hammered like a wedge/ Into his shoulders, and his back was hunched, / Which gave him an almost scholarly air'.

The boy's misshapen back gives him the appearance of a scholar, of someone whose posture has been ruined from constantly poring over books. This scholarly appearance is ironic given the boy's lack of intellectual capability. There is also a suggestion that the boy comes from an underprivileged background. His father has lost most of the family's land through gambling and has managed to keep only 'rushy pasture', land no good for farming: 'hadn't his father/ Gambled away all but rushy pasture?'

The speaker leads the boy along the 'long acre', telling him the names of the various flowers. The poor boy, however, is unable to remember what the speaker teaches him: 'But he couldn't remember the things I taught'. Longley uses a beautiful simile to describe the boy's frustrating inability to grasp and retain information: 'Each name would hover above its flower/Like a butterfly unable to alight'.

Then, unexpectedly it seems, the boy makes a sexual advance toward the speaker: 'Gently he slipped his hand between my thighs'. There is nothing necessarily threatening or violent about the boy's behaviour. His hand, after all, is placed 'Gently' between the woman's legs. The speaker seems unworried by his advance: 'I wasn't frightened'. Yet she reacts in a way that suggests she is terrified: 'I ran from him in tears to tell them'.

The speaker tells the boy's family of his sexual approach and they punish him brutally, beating him with a stick everyday for a week and tying him up in a field like an animal: 'I heard how every day for one whole week/ He was beaten with a blackthorn, then tethered/ In the hayfield'. When the boy's punishment is over he takes his anger out on two animals, cutting the tail off a cow and stoning a ram to death.

The speaker's attitude to the boy

Perhaps the most interesting aspect of this poem is the speaker's attitude to the boy. She isn't sure if she has feelings for this troubled young man: 'Could I have loved someone so gone in the head?' She is equally uncertain about the motivations that led her to go walking with him. Did she simply want to teach him about flowers or, on some level, was she aiming to tease him and provoke his sexual desire: 'And, as they say, was I leading him on?'

In light of this suggestion the speaker's dissection of the cuckoo-pint plant becomes highly symbolic. (The cuckoo-pint plant, it is important to note, has long been associated with sexuality). The act of tearing the plant apart represents her sexual teasing of the boy while the 'giddy insects' represent his sexual desires; the hidden urges that the speaker's behaviour brings to light: 'That day I pulled a cuckoo-pint apart/To release the giddy insects from their cell'.

Another of the poem's unanswered questions centres on the aftermath of the boy's sexual advance. The speaker states clearly that she was unworried when the boy placed his hand between her thighs: 'Gently he slipped his hand between my thighs/I wasn't frightened.' Why, then, does she burst into tears and run to tell on him? The speaker herself is unable to answer this question: 'I still don't know why'. Did she act this way out of simple mischief and malice, out of a nasty desire to get the boy into trouble? Or did she runaway because she felt that was the way she ought to react to boy's advances? It could also be suggested that she acted the way she did because she was disgusted with herself for being somewhat attracted to this deformed young man?

THEMES

A bleak view of human nature

Like many of Longley's poems 'Self-heal' takes a bleak and pessimistic view of human nature. The poem demonstrates how violence begets violence: the tortured boy takes his revenge by mutilating a cow and stoning a ram to death. Revenge and cruelty, it suggests, are built into the very heart of human nature. Aggression will always give rise to more aggression. ('Wounds' can be read as expressing a similar view of human nature). Unsurprisingly, therefore, several critics have interpreted 'Self-heal' in relation to Longley's poems on the violence in Northern Ireland. In this grim little tale of rural life they see a metaphor for the tit-for-tat nature of the Northern Irish Troubles. The boy's ill-treatment leads to the torture of the ram just as in the North one murder seems to leads inevitably to the next in a vicious cycle of revenge.

A negative view of rural Ireland?

One of the most controversial features of 'Self-heal' is its unflattering depiction of rural society. Rural Ireland, based on the snapshot provided in this poem, exists in a state that could only be described as barbaric. We are presented with poverty and feckless gambling farmers, with a boy forced to sleep in a cot till he is twelve. Perhaps most shocking of all is Longley's description of the awful punishment meted out to the boy. In what civilised country would such mistreatment of a poor retarded young man be allowed to occur? Equally disturbing is the savage nature of the revenge exacted by the boy on his release. His anger and frustration are taken out on a cow and a ram, both of which he tortures: 'the cow/ Whose tail he would later dock with shears/And the ram tangled in barbed wire/That he stoned to death when they set him free'.

The poem, it could be argued, presents rural Ireland as a place a place where sex is regarded as something sinful, dirty and animalistic. This is suggested by the brutal punishment meted out to the boy for a fairly minor sexual indiscretion. The boy has done nothing more than gently touch the girl but he as punishment he is treated literally like an animal, being 'tethered / In the hayfield' for an entire week. This is a world where people keep their sexual desires firmly in the confines of their minds, like the 'giddy beetles' in the cuckoo-pint. Sexuality is something that is never openly acknowledged or discussed.

'Self-heal', then, depicts the dark underbelly of rural Irish life; the aspects of rural living that don't feature in Bord Fáilte tourist guides. Co. Mayo, as he portrays it, is a barbaric, uncivilised territory, a place of tortured animals and mistreated children. This aspect of Longley's work has been praised by several critics, who see in poems like 'Self-heal' an antidote to the traditional image of rural Ireland as an unspoilt, cosy paradise. We might ask, however, whether Longley's account of rural Ireland doesn't stray too far in the other direction. This account of the brutal aspects of rural society needs to be balanced, perhaps, by a portrayal of its more benign, positive features.

An Amish Rug

BACKGROUND AND INTRODUCTION

The Amish are a group of Mennonite Christians who live in isolated farming communities in certain parts rural America, where they make their living from agriculture and traditional crafts. The Amish are forbidden from wearing bright colours and dress exclusively in black. Their religion also forbids the use of modern technologies such as radio, motorised transport, telephones and television. Furthermore, the buildings they live are deliberately plain and simple, lacking the style, sophistication and decoration of much modern architecture. The Amish way of life, then, is a simple and uncluttered one, a far cry from the stress and bustle of modern living.

LINE BY LINE

STANZAS 1 AND 2

The poet brings his wife a gift of a patchwork rug that has been manufactured by Amish people: 'I bring you this patchwork'. The rug is very colourful: 'Its threads the colour of cantaloupe and cherry'. The poet compares it to a tiny field, a 'smallholding', in which lots of different things grow: 'hay bales, corn cobs, tobacco leaves'.

The rug inspires the inspires the poet's imagination. He imagines what life would have been like if he and his wife had been born in the Amish community. As a young man he would have worked the land: 'I served as the hired boy behind the harrow'. He and his wife would get married, travelling to the wedding in a horse-drawn cart: 'Marriage a horse and buggy going to church'. The would live the simple Amish lifestyle, working and living in basic buildings and dressing only in black: 'As if a one-room schoolhouse were all we knew / And our clothes were black, our underclothes black'. Eventually they would have kids. In their black clothes these children would look like 'silhouettes in a snowy field'.

STANZA 3

The poet has given the rug as a gift to his wife. It is her decision, therefore, as to how it is to be displayed: 'You may hang it on the wall ... Or lay it on the bedroom floor'. If she hangs it on the wall it will be as bright and dazzling as a stained glass window on a sunny day. If she places this colourful object on the bedroom floor it will resemble a resemble a flowerbed. The rug would be placed at the centre of their lives, in the marriage bedroom where share their most intimate moments: 'whenever we undress for sleep or love/ We shall step over it'.

LANGUAGE

Metaphor and simile

'An Amish Rug' features several inventive metaphors and similes. The poet uses similes in lines five and twelve when he compares the rug to a tiny field or 'smallholding' and to a flower bed. A metaphor, meanwhile, occurs in line 9, when the poet compares the rug to a stained glass window in a cathedral.

Colour

'An Amish Rug' is a poem that moves from black and white to colour. The poem begins with a depiction of black clothes and black-clad children in a snowy field. The second stanza, however, features more colourful imagery as the poet focuses on the bright, multicoloured rug: 'Its threads the colour of cantaloupe and cherry'. The third stanza also features colourful imagery, as the poet compares the rug to a stained glass window and to a flower bed.

THEMES

A love poem

'An Amish Rug' is a simple and moving poem of love. The poet expresses his love for his wife by giving her a beautiful and unusual gift, a colourful rug manufactured by the Amish people. The poet's description of the rug reveals much about his attitude to his wife:

He associates the rug with natural things such as 'hay

bales, corn cobs, tobacco leaves'. This suggests the ease and naturalness of their relationship.

He also associates the rug with fertility, with plants, a field and a flowerbed. This suggests the fertility of their marriage. Their marriage is fertile because it has produced children. It could also be described as fertile because it has given each of them so much joy and fulfilment over the years.

He also associates the rug with security: 'Its threads ... Securing'. This suggests the secure and comfortable environment their marriage has provided for each other and for their children.

He also describes the rug as a sacred or holy object, comparing it to a stained glass window in a cathedral. This suggests that the poet regards his marriage as something sacred and spiritual.

He also associates the rug with the physical side of his marriage. If the rug is placed on their bedroom floor it will be present whenever the poet and his wife make love. The poem, therefore, also celebrates the erotic dimension of their relationship.

The simple life

Modern life is often described as a 'rat race'. It is complicated, stressful and materialistic. The Amish lifestyle, in contrast, is simple, unhurried and unconcerned with material things.

In 'An Amish Rug' Longley seems to long for the simplicity of this Amish lifestyle. He imagines an 'alternative reality' in which he is not a famous and successful writer but a farmer working on a 'smallholding', in which his wife is not a professor at a major university but a teacher in a 'one-roomed school house'. He imagines his family living without the clutter of the modern world, wearing only black clothes and travelling by 'horse and buggy'. In 'An Amish Rug'. then, the poet expresses a desire many people feel at one time or another, the desire to 'get away from it all' and find a simpler, more fulfilling way of living.

A poem about poetry?

It could also be argued that the 'patchwork' in line 5 is a metaphor for Longley's life's work as a poet. This poem appeared toward the end of Longley's collection Gorse Fires. Just as the Amish craftsman patched together the rug from many different pieces of fabric, so Longley had patched together Gorse Fires from many different poems. He now offers this patched-together book to his wife: 'I bring you this patchwork'. The book is like a 'smallholding' because the poet has worked at it with the tireless dedication of a farmer, tending his imagination in order to make the individual poems flourish.

Laertes

INTRODUCTION

This poem condenses a passage from the Odyssey, an ancient Greek text by Homer. The Odyssey tells of the great warrior Odysseus' difficult journey home after fighting in the Trojan war. One of the last events in the book is the reunion of Odysseus and his father Laertes.

LINE BY LINE

When Odysseus comes across his father, he finds him working alone in his garden, 'hoeing/ Around a vine'. It seems that Laertes has been spending a lot of time working in the garden. The terrace is said to be 'tidy', suggesting that much work has already been done. But in contrast with the tidiness of the terrace, Odysseus' father is a mess. Laertes is dressed in scruffy, 'disreputable', working clothes ('duds'). The ragged gear he wears is 'Patched and grubby', a ridiculous combination of 'leather gaiters', 'gloves' and 'a goatskin dulcher'. The poet says that the last item alone, the 'goatskin' cap, was a sure 'sign' of Laertes' 'deep depression'.

Odysseus is shocked and saddened to see his father looking so 'old and pathetic'. He stands hidden 'in the shade of a pear tree' and weeps. Though his natural impulse is to run to his father and 'kiss him and hug him' and tell him all about the incredible adventures he has had, Odysseus decides not to do this. The tale of what has happened to him since he last saw his father is long and complicated, 'one catalogue and then another'. Seeing his father grown old and frail, Odysseus decides that this would not be appropriate.

Instead, Odysseus chooses to stand back a moment and remember times spent with his father in this garden as a child:

So he waited for images from that formal garden,
Evidence of a childhood spent traipsing after his father

Odysseus remembers following his father through the garden 'asking for everything he saw'. The garden contained a wide variety of fruit trees and vines that would ripen 'at different times for a continuous supply'.

Odysseus waits until his father recognises him. When the old man eventually he sees his son he is overcome with joy. The frail old man passionately embraces his 'great' son. Odysseus cradles his father as though he were a child. As they embrace, Laertes' weakness is made evident. He is described as being 'weak at the knees', 'fainting' and 'Dizzy'. When Odysseus holds his 'dwindling' father he feels how thin and weak he has become. The once rugged man has been reduced to loose collection of bones.

THEMES

Father and son

In 'Laertes' Longley explores the relationship between father and son through the Homeric tale of Odysseus and Laertes. Like a number of Longley poems, 'Laertes' deals with the relationship between an ageing father and his son. The poem describes the return of the 'great' Odysseus to his family home. He is ready to rush to his father, much like he would have done as a child, and tell him all about his adventures. But he does not do this. Shocked to see his father so old and frail, Odysseus, must acknowledge the terrible fact that his father is no longer the strong, towering man that he used to follow through the garden as a child.

'Laertes' thus explores the difficulty of the son having to acknowledge that their father is growing old and weakening. The realisation is all the more upsetting for Odysseus because he has been away for a long time. When he left home his father would still have been a strong man. Since then he has deteriorated rapidly, no doubt in part because of his worry about his son. Odysseus is shocked by the transformation he sees and is unsure about how he should act.

His natural impulse is the child's impulse, to run into his father's arms and look to impress the man with what he has done. But Odysseus quickly realises that things have changed, that he is no longer a child and his father has grown weak and frail. To run to his father and excitedly tell him all that has happened no longer seems appropriate. And so Odysseus stands back and remembers when he was a child, 'traipsing after his father' and waits for his father to see him. In the end it is the father who is 'cradled' by the son. 'Laertes' explores the sad reversal of roles that ageing brings about.

Ceasefire

This sonnet might be described as a 'free translation' from the Iliad, an ancient epic poem by the Greek poet Homer. Longley, who describes himself as a lapsed classicist, studied Greek and Latin at University and his interest in the literature of the ancient world influences many of his poems (for example 'Laertes'). The Iliad is a very long poem that describes episodes from the ten-year siege of the great city Troy by the armies of ancient Greece. The war was sparked when Paris, a prince of Troy, abducted Helen, the wife of a Greek King and according to legend the most beautiful woman in the world. The Greek invasion force was a coalition of many kings under the leadership of their supreme commander Agamemnon. The greatest of the Greek warriors, however, was Achilles, a young hero who was all but unbeatable in combat. The ruler of the Trojans meanwhile was old King Priam whose son Hector led the forces of Troy into battle.

Though greatly outnumbered, Hector held out against the Greek armies for nearly ten years of gruelling siege warfare, at times nearly driving them away from Troy altogether. The Iliad tells how after many bloody battles (and much internal wrangling between the various Greek leaders) Achilles finally killed Hector in single combat. Achilles humiliated the Trojans by desecrating Hector's corpse, tying it behind his chariot dragging it round the walls of Troy and refusing to return it to the Trojans for proper burial. (The idea of proper funeral rites was hugely important to both the Greeks and Trojans. According to their beliefs, if a person's body was not disposed of properly he or she could never enter the afterlife). Finally, greatly distressed by the treatment of his son's corpse, old king Priam went secretly to the Greek camp in order to plead with Achilles for its return. Longley's 'free translation' describes the interaction between Priam and Achilles in the great warrior's tent.

Though 'Ceasefire' is inspired by Homer's ancient epic, it is also a highly contemporary piece of writing. It was composed in the lead up to the IRA ceasefire declared on the first of September 1994. This cessation of hostilities brought with it the first real hope for peace in Northern Ireland for nearly twenty-five years. Longley's poem, which was published on the front page of the Irish Times two days after the ceasefire was declared, celebrates the possibility of peace between bitter enemies. However, it also points out the terrible sacrifices and unpalatable compromises that would have to be made if peace was to become a reality. 'Ceasefire' is written in a variation on the traditional sonnet form. It is divided into three quatrains or four-line sections each rhyming ABCB, and a final rhyming couplet.

The first quatrain tells us of the grief shared by the old king and the young warrior. In the Iliad Priam kneels at Achilles feet and kisses his hands. In order to win his sympathy Priam tells Achilles to think of his own father, hundreds of miles away in Greece who must everyday long for his son's return. (Priam, in contrast, has no hope of being reunited with his own son Hector). Priam's words do the trick and Achilles is 'Put in mind of his own father and moved to the tears'. He helps the old King to his feet: 'Achilles took him by the hand and pushed the old king/Gently away'. Then the two men weep together: 'Priam curled up at his feet and/ Wept with him until their sadness filled the building'. The two men, though mortal enemies, are united in shared grief. Priam, of course, is mourning his dead son. Achilles, meanwhile, is weeping for the homeland and family he realises he will probably never see again, but also for his best friend Patroclus, who had recently been killed in battle by Hector.

The poem's next two quatrains further describe the temporary truce between these foes. Achilles prepares Hector's corpse for Priam, giving the boy of his conquered foe the honour and respect due a great warrior: he 'Made sure it was washed and, for the old king's sake, / Laid out in uniform'. Longley, using an unexpected simile, describes Hector's corpse as a kind of gift: 'ready for Priam to carry/Wrapped like a present back to Troy at daybreak'. There is something grotesque about this comparison of a dead body to a present. Yet there is also something moving about it, for Achilles has indeed given his enemy a 'present' in the form of a dignified and honourable funeral for his son. The temporary closeness between the two men is emphasised by the fact that they eat together, and that during the meal Priam is 'full of conversation'. Our sense of this closeness is reinforced by the almost homoerotic description of the heroes admiring each other's bodies: 'it pleased them both/To stare at each other's beauty as lovers might'.

'Ceasefire' illustrates the suffering and shattered lives left behind by war and conflict, whether it be the Trojan war or the Troubles in contemporary Northern Ireland. Both Priam and Achilles have been bereaved; Priam has lost his son, Achilles his best friend. The poem, then, like 'Wounds' or 'Wreaths', provides an unflinching and moving account of the horrors of war. Yet 'Ceasefire' is perhaps more optimistic than Longley's other war poems, tentatively suggesting that peace may be possible between even the bitterest enemies. It has been described as a poem of forgiveness, for in it Priam forgives the man who killed his son, while Achilles, in releasing Hector's corpse, might be said to forgive the Trojans for killing his best friend Patroclus. The poem shows that friendship is possible between those are on opposing sides, for Hector and Priam eat and talk together and admire each other's physical appearance.

An interesting feature of the truce between Priam and Achilles is that it is born out of shared suffering. In war, it seems; violence unites as well as divides, for both sides suffer in a similar way, enduring bereavements, destruction, and the disruption of normal life. Importantly, it is only when Priam and Achilles weep together for the people that they have loved and lost that the truce between them is solidified. 'Ceasefire', published so prominently and at such a critical moment in the history of Northern Ireland, must be regarded, on some level, as a comment on the peace process in that troubled province. Longley's message to the Unionist and Nationalist communities seems to be that forgiveness and friendship is possible if the two sides could manage to 'weep together', to jointly mourn the suffering each side has endured and inflicted on the other.

Yet his outlook is not straightforwardly soppy or optimistic. Longley accepts that any process of reconciliation will involve terrible compromises. This is indicated in the poem's final couplet: 'I get down on my knees and do what must be done/And kiss Achilles' hand, the killer of my son'. There is something degrading and humiliating in having to kneel before your son's killer and kiss his hand. Yet such an extreme attitude of forgiveness and acceptance toward one's enemies may well be necessary if peace is to be given a chance in Northern Ireland. (An example of this might be the program of prison releases that formed part of the peace process. Many people had to watch convicted terrorists, 'the killers of their sons', walk free from jail. Yet such an unpalatable compromise had to be accepted if the process was to continue).

Like many of Longley's poems 'Ceasefire' centres on the father-son relationship. Priam mourns his dead son Hector, just as Achilles weeps for his absent father. The poem might be said to illustrate the suffering caused when either the father or the son is missing from the equation. Perhaps because of this suffering there is a sense in which the two enemies develop an almost father-son relationship themselves as they sit eating and talking freely. Is it stretching things too much to suggest that Achilles 'built like a god' is temporarily taking the place of Priam's slaughtered son, just as Priam 'good-looking still' is standing in for Achilles' absent father?

Like 'Laertes', then, 'Ceasefire' explores the father-son relationship indirectly, by using episodes from the ancient poetry of Homer. Yet it also recalls poems like 'Wreaths' and 'Wounds', where Longley speaks of burying his father. 'Ceasefire', too, is concerned with the funeral of a dead soldier. In this instance, however, it is the father who must bury the son rather than the other way around. Yet the poem can be regarded a further addition to the series in which Longley is heavily influenced by his soldier-father, celebrating his life and mourning his death.

LONGLEY AT A GLANCE

WAR AND VIOLENCE

- 'Wounds' describes the horrors of war, comparing the violence and loss of life of the First World War with the Northern Irish Troubles. The poem shows how the horrors of war must remain with those who survive.
- 'Wreaths' also mourns the victims of the Northern Irish Troubles, this time focusing on civilians killed in a terrorist attack.
- 'Last requests', in its description of the poet's father, reveals the brutality of war whilst also emphasising the physical and psychological difficulties faced by those who survived the First World War.
- 'Self-heal' illustrates how violence inevitably begets more violence in its depiction of the abused boy taking revenge by stoning a goat to death.
- 'Ceasefire' holds out the possibility that peace can flourish between even the bitterest enemies. It shows how in war even mortal enemies are linked through the pain and anguish they must suffer. The poem demonstrates the very difficult compromises that are required in order that conflict can be resolved.
- 'Poteen' illustrates the violence associated with the recent past of the country and illustrates how people seek to bury knowledge of such violence and attempt to forget it ever happened.

FATHER AND SON

- 'Last Requests' subtly reveal the poet's admiration for his father whilst also disclosing the distance that existed between them, especially at the poignant moment of the father's death.
- 'Wounds' again reveals the poet's understanding of what his father went through in the War. The tenderness with which he treats his dying father reveals the extent of the love he holds for him: 'I touched his hand, his thin head I touched'.
- The strength and mystery of the father-son bond is evident in the poem 'Laertes', where the poet uses a scene from Homer's Odyssey to reveal the deep affection he holds for his father. In a reversal of roles the father now seems as weak and helpless as a small child.
- 'Ceasefire' revolves around the a father's affection for his son. Priam illustrates his love for Hector through the extreme measures he is willing to go in order to retrieve his dead son's corpse.

NATURE AND THE WEST OF IRELAND

- 'Carrigskeewaun' illustrates Longley's awareness of the beauty of nature and reveals the poet's sense of respect for the natural inhabitants of the area.
- 'Badger' shows, through its meticulous description, how the poet takes delight in the small details that define the natural world. The poem reveals the badger to be a fascinating creature and exposes man's contradictory attitude to the animal.
- 'Self-heal' again reveals Longley's love of and attention to the names of things through his mentioning of some of the flowers growing on the long acre.

DEREK WALCOTT

THEMES

GOD AND THE AFTERLIFE, FAITH AND DOUBT

A theme Walcott returns to again and again, in both his poetry and his plays, is that of the struggle between faith and doubt. Walcott is something of a Christian poet and believes that the world is ruled by a benevolent and loving God. He also believes that 'death is not the end', but that when we die our souls continue to live on with God in heaven. Yet Walcott is also tortured by doubts that stem from his experiences of this cruel world with all its trials and tribulations. After all, if this God exists why does evil seem to triumph so often? How can we be sure that our souls survive the extinction of our bodies? This battle between faith and doubt is recorded very movingly in Walcott's poetry.

'Saint Lucia's First Communion', for instance, shows Walcott's desire to experience 'belief without an if', a straightforward and uncomplicated belief in God and in Jesus. He wants a religious faith that is completely untroubled by doubt. This, he suggests, is the kind of faith enjoyed by the communion girls he sees walking in procession on the asphalt road. It is also the kind of faith enjoyed by Saint Lucia of Syracuse in the third century, who died rather than give up her Christian faith. Walcott, however, realises that it is extremely difficult to maintain this kind of simple, uncompromising religious faith in the modern world. This life is so full of 'prejudice' and 'evil' that even the strongest belief in God must eventually be contaminated by doubt. The little first-communion girls may now be lucky enough to experience 'belief with an if', but as they grow older they, like the poet, will have to struggle with doubt.

'A Letter from Brooklyn' also memorably dramatises Walcott's inner conflict between doubt and faith. The poem paints a moving portrait of the simple faith enjoyed by the poet's father and by Mabel Rawlins, a friend of his family. Mabel Rawlins, like the communion girls, is lucky enough to experience 'belief without an if'. She is presented as a devout and religious person with an unswerving faith in the goodness of God. She believes that God has a plan for each of us. According to Mabel, when each of us dies we are brought 'home' to heaven to serve God in a new way: '"He is twenty-eight years buried," she writes, "he was called home, / And is, I am sure, doing greater work"'. The poet's father, too, is presented as a man of faith: '"Your father was a dutiful, honest, / Faithful, and useful person'. The poet, it seems, has been overcome by doubt. He has stopped believing in God and in afterlife. He has abandoned his 'sacred duty' to God. Yet the letter he receives form Mabel Rawlins restores his faith: 'again I believe'. Reading about Mabel and his father encourages Walcott to renew his commitment as a Christian. Mabel's letter 'Restores [his] sacred duty to the word'. His doubts fade away and he once again believes in an that death is not the end: 'I believe it all, and for no man's death I grieve'.

The problems faced by religious belief in the modern world are also powerfully portrayed in 'Pentecost'. Modern cities, according to this Walcott, are soulless, hostile places where it is difficult to have any type of religious experience. The poet longs for God to enter his heart. He wants to have some kind of 'inner experience' that reassures him of God's existence. it seems, however, that in the bleak and barren city landscape such an experience is impossible. The snow that falls on the city streets does nothing to reassure the poet of God's love: 'nor can these tongues of snow / speak for the Holy Ghost'. It is only in a quieter, gentler environment that Walcott can have the type of experience that brings him closer to God. He describes himself on an empty beach at night watching a cormorant dive into the water. The serenity and beauty of this scene fill Walcott with certainty in God, the soul and the afterlife: 'what, in my childhood gospels, used to be called the soul'. He is forced to acknowledge, however, that he has no direct 'proof' of God's existence. All Walcott has to go on is his overwhelming sense that something or someone is out there watching over us.

'For Adrian' is another poem where Walcott deals with the battle between faith and doubt. The poem shows how the family of this dead little boy are convinced that he is gone forever, that they will never see him again. They regard Adrian's death as a 'goodbye'. They are clearly filled with grief at Adrian's passing and stand around his coffin mourning and weeping. (Walcott uses a wonderful simile to describe this, declaring that Adrian's family were 'howling like statues'). The poem, however, attempts to show that it is somehow inappropriate to mourn the deaths of those close to us. Adrian tells his family that 'death is not the end', that in dying his soul has entered not some kind of 'eternal silence' but a 'wisdom'. Adrian claims that in dying he has not 'gone away'. Instead, he has merely been welcomed back into the world in a different form: what 'you call a goodbye is ... a different welcome'. When each member of his family dies their souls will join Adrian in this 'wisdom'. They, like him, will be welcomed back to the world in a different form: 'a different welcome, / which you will share with me'.

An interesting feature of 'For Adrian' is that it does not put forward a conventionally 'Christian' view of the afterlife. As a Christian poet, the majority of Walcott's poems suggest that when we die we ascend to heaven. A Letter from Brooklyn', for instance, suggests that the dead are called 'home' to God's presence where they will continue to serve God. 'Saint Lucia's First Communion', meanwhile, imagines the communion girls ascending 'heavenward' like moths. 'For Adrian', however, suggests that when we die our souls do not go to heaven but become part of the natural world. Adrian declares that his spirit is now 'part of the muscle / of a galloping lion, or a bird keeping low over / dark canes'. Adrian's soul, then has become 'one with the universe' rather than ascending to heaven to sit at God's right hand. 'For Adrian', therefore, has been said to put forward a 'pantheistic' rather than a Christian view of the afterlife. Yet another kind of 'Afterlife' is suggested by 'The Young Wife'. When the bereaved husband sees his children laugh he is reminded of his dead partner: 'They startle you when they laugh'/ In fact, when his children laugh it is like his dead wife is somehow alive again: 'she sits there smiling'. The poem, therefore, shows how we live on after death in the form of our children.

ROMANTIC LOVE

Like most poets Walcott writes a great deal about love and relationships. 'Summer Elegies', for instance, provides an intense celebration of physical and erotic love. The poem lovingly remembers undressing his lover, recalling how 'the unhooked halter slithered / from sunburnt shoulders!'. There is warmth and humour in the way he imagines the passing sea birds being 'astonished' at their love, at the 'changing shapes of love'. 'To Norline', too, celebrates the physical side of love as the poet remembers how he used to lie beside this beautiful woman: 'my body once cupped yours'.

Yet Walcott is all too aware of the negative aspects of romantic love, of the pain and emptiness that comes with the failure of a relationship. 'Endings', in particular, stresses the emotional wreckage that love all too often leaves behind. It suggests that the emotion of love is constantly dying, that it is always quietly but surely fading from our hearts: 'it dies with the sound / of flowers fading'. According to 'Endings', when love disappears we are left with a terrible vacuum. (Walcott memorably describes this emptiness by comparing it to 'the silence that surrounds Beethoven's head'. The loss of love, he suggests, leaves us as frustrated, bitter and miserable as the loss of hearing left Beethoven). 'Summer Elegies' also focuses on the emptiness that love leaves behind. It is a beautiful day but the poet experiences intense feelings of sorrow and emptiness as he remembers his ex-lover and grieves for a love that has been but can never be again: 'All the beach chairs are full / but the beach is emptier'.

It has been suggested that 'To Norline' also focuses on the sorrow that comes after love with its melancholy depiction of the poet walking along an empty beach remembering his lost love. Yet surely Walcott's most moving depiction of the end of a relationship occurs in 'The Young Wife'. This poem shows a loving relationship that has been cruelly ended by death. The man in the poem desperately tries to make sense of his wife's passing. The death of his young partner has left a terrible emptiness in his life: 'You keep setting a fork and knife / at her place for supper'. The house he lives in is haunted by memories of his departed lover. (Walcott wonderfully suggests this with his reference to the 'drawers you dare not open') Yet the bereaved husband has no choice but to go on living for his children. He must continue to carry 'the weight / we bear on this heavier side / of the grave'

COLONIALISM

Walcott is famous for his exploration of his Caribbean history, especially for the way in which he addresses the tragedy of the Caribbean's colonial past. Many of his poems are intensely aware of the way in which the Caribbean islands were exploited by white European settlers. This aspect of Walcott's work is especially evident in the extract form Omeros. In this poem the sailor Achille is the descendant of slaves who were brought to the Caribbean from Africa. Though slavery, of course, is now abolished Achille is forced to live with its legacy. As the descendant of slaves ha occupies what seems to be the lowest rung in society. His life is one of poverty and hardship as he makes a dangerous and meagre living on the treacherous seas. (The poem does an excellent job of describing the appalling working conditions endured by Achille and his mate. The are forced to fish through the night and the only sleeping quarters seem to be out in the open in the bow of the ship).

Achille's terrible situation is made even worse by his memories of his people's glorious past in Africa. His ancestors such as Afolabe were once kings in that great continent before they were enslaved by the white man. The tragedy of the poem lies in our realisation that Achille's people will never be returned to their former glory. Omeros, then, paints a powerful and moving portrait of the damage caused to countless individuals by colonialism. 'The Sailor Sings back to the Casuarinas' explores a different aspect of the legacy of colonialism. The poem shows how those who colonised and exploited the Caribbean islands used language to dominate and control the native population. By forcing the natives to speak French, Dutch or English they could control how they saw the world and thought about their lives. By changing the names for things the colonisers imposed their values on the colonised and changed the way their victims lived. As Walcott so wonderfully puts it: 'we live by our names and you would have / to be colonial to know the difference'.

A Letter from Brooklyn

INTRODUCTION

The poem concerns a letter the poet has received from an elderly lady. The lady, Mable Rawlins, used to live in the same community as the Walcott's when Derek was a child. She now writes to him about his father who died when he was very young. The old lady describes the sort of man the poet's father was and she offers the poet comforting religious counsel regarding his death.

LINE BY LINE

LINES 1–13

The poem opens with a description of the old lady's writing. She writes 'in a spidery style,/ Each character trembling'. The word 'spidery' conjures up the image of a spider and we can imagine the letters on the page being long and frail like spiders' legs. Because the old lady's hand shakes as she writes the characters on the page seem to be 'trembling'.

Looking at the shaky handwriting on the page the poet is able to visualise the old lady's hand: 'I see a veined hand/ Pellucid as paper'. The old lady's skin is as thin and transparent as paper and clearly reveals the veins beneath. The poet describes this hand 'travelling on a skein' of 'thoughts'. A skein is a loose bundle of wool. So the thoughts that the old lady seeks to express in the letter appear to be loosely connected.

In fact, the letter seems composed 'Of such frail thoughts' that the 'thread' that connects them together 'is often broken'. Sometimes, he says, the logic behind what the old lady is saying is not clear to him. It is hard for him to determine how certain phrases tie in with the rest of the letter. Walcott uses the metaphor of a spider's web to illustrate this difficulty. He says that 'the filament from which a phrase is hung/ Dims to my sense'. Just as we might see something suspended from a web without being able to discern the actual thread that holds it, so certain lines in the letter seem to appear to hang independently of the rest of the letter. However, every now and again the 'web' of the letter catches the light and what the old lady is saying becomes crystal clear to him – 'it shines like steel'. At such moments a greater cohesion is glimpsed and it is possible for him to imagine how each phrase is intricately linked. It is like touching a single thread of a web and perceiving how 'the whole web will feel'.

In the letter the old lady describes the poet's father. However, having mentioned this fact in line 8 the poet does not speak much about his father here. He seems more preoccupied with the old woman who is writing the letter. The mentioning of his father's yearly 'dying' suggests perhaps that this subject is too painful for him to speak about. Although she appears to remember his father vividly he does not remember her so well. The ninth line gives us an intimation of the poet's loss, of the pain that is still felt over the death of his father.

The poet says no more about this here and continues instead with his recollection of the old woman. When he thinks of her he remembers her in church 'on those Sundays/ Whenever her strength allowed'. She was obviously a very devout woman and it seems that even when the poet was a child she appeared old and frail. Back then she was 'Grey-haired, thin-voiced, perpetually bowed' and could only attend church 'whenever her strength allowed'.

LINES 14–39

Having given us an impression of the letter and the old lady who wrote it, the poet now brings us through the letter, pausing to reflect on what the old lady writes and how he imagines her writing it. The first line of the letter establishes the writer's connection with the poet: 'I ... know both your parents'. Her use of the present tense (she writes 'I know' rather than 'I knew') touches the poet. His father is long dead yet the old woman speaks of still knowing him. Her turn of phrase, implying as it does a sense of the father continuing to exist, of not having been consigned to the past and forgotten, is appreciated ('God bless your tense'), although for the poet there is no ambiguity regarding his father's status – 'He is dead, Miss Rawlins'.

Using what the poet terms 'plain praise' the old lady

goes on to describe the father. He was, she says, 'a dutiful, honest,/ Faithful, and useful person'. The qualities that she recalls in the father are those simple, selfless qualities of a good and decent man. He may not have been famous but, as the poet acknowledges, when you have the qualities that the old lady describes 'what fame is recompense?'

The old woman goes on to describe what the father did. He was 'A horn-painter, he painted delicately on horn,/ He used to sit around the table and paint pictures'. Like the poet himself the father was a painter. He would decorate pieces of horn and 'paint pictures' at the table. Again we get the impression of a simple life. The father was not pursuing wealth and fame through his art. He required neither 'glory nor ambition' in order to feel satisfied. Obviously a religious man, he had the 'peace of God' with him and was happy with his lot in life.

In line 23 the old lady brings her own faith to bear upon the father's death. Using her 'frail hand' she expresses a religious conviction that is strong. She describes the father's passing away as a calling 'home' to heaven where she is quite 'sure' that he is 'doing greater work'. Her conviction in her belief, her inner strength, restores the poet's 'sacred duty to the Word' of the Bible. It seems that his belief in the teachings of his religion had lapsed. Now 'one frail hand in a dim room/ Somewhere in Brooklyn, patient and assured' manages to 'restore' his faith. It seems ironic, perhaps, that the strength needed to achieve this should come from such a frail source.

The poet is moved by the fact that this frail old woman, so close to death and alone, still has the strength to help him. The writing of the letter is once again likened to the spinning of a web. With her frail hand she weaves together the wisdom of her years: 'she spins the blessings of her years'. Her body might be withered, her 'physical' beauty gone, but she is not without beauty. If she can still move a man to 'tears', the poet says, she must have beauty. And because she is still capable of engaging with someone like the poet and effecting him the way she does it shows that she is still engaged with the real world of human pain, 'the world that breaks its lovers so'. Her thoughts are not just of the afterlife, of the 'home' that she is ever nearing. She might be 'alone' but she has not 'withdrawn' from the world.

But she does believe in 'Heaven' and it is a place that brings comfort to her. It is a place where people like the poet's father go, good, honest people 'who bring beauty on frail shell or horn'. It was in heaven that all was 'made' and it is to there that our spirit is 'drawn'. The old lady suggests that there is a strong tie between our souls and heaven, a bond that, perhaps with faith, can become as strong and 'resilient as 'steel'.

Again the poet draws upon the metaphor of the web to illustrate what the old lady says. The 'thread' of a web is especially resilient considering how thin and frail it appears. And just as the threads of a web can be lost so easily to the eye, so too our faith can seem lost, especially in 'darkening periods'. The poet suggested earlier on in the poem that his own faith had suffered. Now his faith in God, his belief in a destiny and an afterlife for the spirit, is restored. His father has returned to heaven, he now believes, 'to do work that is God's'. This is what 'this old lady writes' to him and he believes her. He believes 'it all' and because he does so he no longer feels that death of any man should be grieved.

LANGUAGE

The metaphor of the web

Throughout the poem the poet uses the notion of the spider's web to convey what the old lady does.

The first line refers to the 'spidery style' of her writing. The word 'spidery' perfectly illustrates the faint, shaky writing that adorns the letter, each being character as frail as a spider's leg or perhaps as faint as a spider's web.

The spider's web then becomes an ideal metaphor for the old lady's 'thoughts.' Initially, her thoughts are seen as 'frail'. The association between her thoughts is often so tenuous that the link gets 'broken' just as link in a web might so easily break.

At times when he is reading the letter the poet fails to perceive or grasp the logic and reasoning behind the old lady's sentiments. Again the idea of the web perfectly illustrates this. Sometimes a 'phrase' appears to just hang there and it is impossible to discern 'the filament' that fastens it to the greater web of thought. Individual phrases sometimes seem to be utterly random that the poet fails to discern any connection to a greater scheme or argument.

But then just as a web might catch the light, suddenly the phrase gains clarity and 'it shines like steel'. What before seemed isolated and random now reveals its attachment to a greater scheme or plan. Everything ties together within the letter just as all the threads of a web are somehow linked so that when you touch one 'the whole web will feel'.

Walcott also uses the metaphor of the web because, though it appears frail, it actually has enormous strength and resilience. The old lady too has great strength though she appears so frail. The poet refers to the 'strength of one frail hand'

The thread she weaves in the letter draws the poet's thoughts to heaven. She re-establishes a link for him between the earthly world and the afterlife and restores his faith. Faith is thus seen as a faint thread that links us to heaven. This thread might seem frail but can be as 'resilient' as 'steel' when we believe.

THEMES

Religious belief

Mable Rawlins is a religiously devout woman. Though she is old and frail she maintains a strong faith in the goodness of God and the notion that he has a plan for each of us. It seems her life has been spent in the service of God. The poet remembers her when he was young as being 'perpetually bowed', a reference perhaps to her posture, yet it also suggests The poet's father also seems to have been a religious man. He is said to have had the 'peace of God' with him and the life he lived seems to have been both humble and devout.

Yet it seems that somewhere along the way the poet's own faith has waned. What restores his 'sacred duty to the Word' surprises him. From a lonely room 'somewhere in Brooklyn' an elderly woman takes the time to write him a letter about his father. In this letter she speaks with great certainty about the father continuing to exist in heaven. According to her he is there doing the work of God. With her 'frail' hand she moves the poet to tears, her steady words of assurance bringing enormous comfort to him. She speaks of heaven being a place 'where painters go' to 'do work that is 'God's'. The poet, moved by the beauty of this notion, believes once again in Word of the bible.

Death and grief

Like both 'For Adrian' and 'The Young Wife,' 'A Letter from Brooklyn documents the pain that comes with bereavement. Though the poet's father has been dead for twenty-eight years it seems that the pain of loss has not diminished. In the ninth line he mentions his 'father's yearly dying', a reference to the annual remembrance of his father's death. Prior to reading the old lady's letter it seems that the poet harboured no notions of his father continuing to exist beyond death. For him death was final. When Mable Rawlins uses the present tense in reference to his father he bluntly replies, 'He is dead, Miss Rawlins'.

However, as the poem progresses his attitude toward the death of his father changes. The words that the old lady writes, her strength of conviction and assurance, makes him think of his father's death in terms of God and the afterlife. He takes great comfort from the notion that his father is doing God's work. He no longer sees death as something final. His father has gone 'home' to heaven. The old lady restores the poet's belief in the existence of the soul, the '*lux-mundi*'. With his faith in the goodness of God and the immortality of the soul restored he no longer grieves for his father, nor for any 'man's death'.

Endings

LINE BY LINE

This poem, as its title suggests, explores the notion of endings. Many of Walcott's poems are concerned with endings of one kind or another, for example the conclusion of a relationship or the passing away of a life.

Walcott suggests that, generally speaking, things do not end in a sudden, dramatic fashion: 'Things do not explode'. Instead, they wither away slowly over time: 'they fail, they fade'. In fact, most things disappear without us even really noticing them. Walcott provides two examples of this. Firstly he mentions the sun going down so that its rays no longer illuminate our skin: 'as sunlight fades from the flesh'. Secondly he mentions sea water draining away into a sandy beach: 'as the foam drains quick in the sand'. Walcott, it seems, believes that most things end in this almost imperceptible fashion, slipping quietly away beneath our notice.

In line 5 Walcott begins to focus on romantic love. Love he says is a 'lightning flash', suggesting that this emotion appears in a person's life as suddenly and dramatically as a bolt of lightning in the night sky. (The comparison of love to lightning also suggests the power of love to 'electrify' those who experience it and to 'light up their worlds'). Love, then, often begins in a sudden and dramatic fashion, transforming a person's life completely in a single instant.

Yet that is not how love usually ends. According to Walcott there is nothing 'thunderous', nothing sudden or explosive, about the way love disappears. Instead, the emotion 'dies' slowly, over a long period of time. Like so much else it slips away without us noticing. Love, Walcott says, 'dies with the sound / of flowers fading'. We are no more capable of perceiving the slow death of love than we are of 'hearing' the flowers wither away. Love disintegrates silently, like pieces of dead skin on a piece of pumice stone: 'It dies ... like the flesh /from sweating pumice stone'. (A pumice stone is often used to scrape away dry skin).

Walcott presents the death of love as a truly distressing thing. When a love affair ends, he suggests, we are left with a terrible vacuum in our lives. Walcott uses a very haunting image to describe this: 'we are left / with the silence that surrounds Beethoven's head'. The great composer Beethoven began to lose his hearing when he was only thirty and ended up completely deaf. For Beethoven, who was blessed with such mastery of music and such an intense relationship with sound, this was an incredible tragedy. Yet, according to Walcott, for a lover the loss of love is as catastrophic as the loss of hearing was for Beethoven. The poem suggests, then, that the loss of love is one of the greatest tragedies that can befall a human being.

THEMES

Love

This poem, it has to be said, presents a fairly bleak view of love and relationships. Walcott accepts that the 'lightning flash' new relationship can dramatically transform a person's life.

Yet the poem also stresses that the emotion of love is always fading away. It disappears as slowly and surely as the sun goes down or flowers wither in a vase. When its finally gone we are left with a terrible vacuum in our lives. The departure of love leaves us with the same kind of bitterness, rage and frustration that Beethoven experienced when he was so cruelly deprived of his greatest gift. The poem leaves us wondering, then, if the fireworks at the beginning of a love affair are worth the misery that, inevitably it seems, accompanies its end.

The nature of endings

'Endings' has been described as a 'philosophical' poem because it makes a general statement about life. As we have seen, in 'Endings' Walcott claims that things generally finish in a quiet, unnoticeable fashion. Walcott probably isn't suggesting that every single thing in the world ends quietly. Instead, he seems to be arguing that many important things in life, such as love, health and youth, disappear slowly and imperceptibly over time rather than vanishing all at once. They end, as T.S. Eliot put it, 'not with a bang but with a whimper'.

The Sailor Sings Back to the Casuarinas (from *The Schooner Flight*)

INTRODUCTION

This is an extract from 'The Schooner 'Flight',' a lengthy poem about a sailor named Shabine who takes to the sea aboard a ship called 'Flight' (A schooner refers to a sailing ship with two or more masts and with its sails parallel to the length of the ship, rather than across it). Shabine is a seasoned, troubled character with complicated colonial heritage. He tells us early in the poem that: 'I have Dutch, nigger, and English in me,/ and either I'm nobody, or I'm a nation'.

Fighting with his woman, having no money ('I was so broke all I needed was shades and a cup') and about to get in trouble for smuggling liquor, Shabine decides that it is best he gets out of Trinidad for a while. On the voyage he gets to thinking about his life and his identity. The route the schooner takes is similar to the route taken by slave ships that would have carried his African ancestors to the islands.

It is the sixth section of the poem that features on the Leaving Cert. course. As the ship sails past the island of Barbados Shabine thinks about the trees that he sees on the 'low hills'.

LINE BY LINE

The speaker points out the trees that he sees growing 'on the low hills of Barbados'. He describes them as follows:

1 First he uses a simile. The trees on the low hills are 'bracing like windbreaks'. The attitude of the trees, the angle at which they stand, makes them appear like windbreaks, rows of trees planted to provide shelter from high winds.
2 Next he uses a metaphor. He considers them 'needles for hurricanes'. Perhaps he says this because they appear so small, little more than needles when confronting the onslaught of a hurricane.
3 The third line involves both a simile and a metaphor. The trees trail 'like masts, the cirrus of torn sails'. The trees are 'like masts' because the material of 'torn sails' has got caught in them. The material itself resembles long wispy clouds ('cirrus' is a type of light feathery cloud that is seen high in the sky).

What sort of trees does he see?

Lines 4 to 8 reveal how complicated the naming of these trees has become for the speaker. The reason for the complication appears to be as follows:

When the speaker was young he was familiar with a certain type of tree called casuarinas. However, trees that he would have once thought were casuarinas came to be called cypresses by others on the island. (Perhaps the people who called the trees cypresses were from another country, such as England. To them the trees looked just like the cypress trees that they were familiar with back home and so they took the trees in the Caribbean to be cypresses too.)

When people would point to cypresses on the island the young speaker would think, 'those cypresses ... are not real cypresses but casuarinas'. To him trees 'leaning against the sea, that take the sea-noise up into their branches' had to be casuarinas. Perhaps someone in his family had told him that trees that make this noise are casuarinas.

Yet, he 'was green' (or naïve) when he thought this. We might guess that others convinced him he was wrong to call them casuarinas and he soon learnt the "correct" name for the trees. So he began to call them cypresses.

And now, to make things even more complicated for him, the captain of the ship has just gone and called them 'Canadian cedars'.

So these trees that stand near the sea and make a distinctive sound are many different things to many different people.

What's in a name?

Though many different terms have been used for these same trees, the speaker does not think that any one term is more correct or better than any other. Because of their differing backgrounds and origins the speaker recognises that people have their own good reasons for calling the trees what they presume to be the correct name – 'cedars, cypresses, or casuarinas, whoever called them so had a good cause'.

Each person presumes to recognise the distinctive shape of the tree. The speaker uses a strong visual image to convey this particular shape. He says: 'their bending bodies wail like women/ after a storm, when some schooner came home/ with news of one more sailor drowned'. The speaker associates both the shape and the sound of the trees with grieving women. This image seems to have been drawn from personal experience on the islands. The trees are linked with the personal experiences of the island's inhabitants.

The speaker reveals how the term 'cypress' eventually became very familiar to him. There was a time, the speaker tells us, when he felt more comfortable calling the trees 'cypress'. The term 'casuarinas' then seemed to him to be 'green' or naïve.

But concern for names and language is ultimately a human concern. To the wind it matters little that the trees might be said to resemble grieving women or that we give them different names. After all the trees themselves have as little concern for the names we call them. According to the speaker they have 'nothing else in mind/ but heavenly leaping or to guard a grave'.

However, names do matter to people: 'but we live like our names'. Perhaps by this the speaker means that we live according to the names we are given and therefore cannot be indifferent to what people call us. Names determine how we come to perceive our selves and our place in society.

Colonial lessons

Living in a place that has been colonised by another country makes you aware of certain things.

- It makes you aware of the differences that can arise when objects are spoken of. The example of the trees seen on the 'low hills of Barbados' testifies to this.
- Being 'colonial' also teaches you about the 'pain of history words contain'. Words are marked by history, they have painful connotations, and those who have experienced colonialism are especially aware of this fact.
- The experience of being 'colonial' has also taught the speaker about loving something with what he terms 'inferior love'. Perhaps this is based upon the experience of witnessing people being treated as inferiors, classed as less worthy of love because of who they are. The speaker suggests that love can be dictated by language and how much we might love something can depend on how we speak of it or classify it.

The poem closes with the speaker stating what, according to him, only a colonial person could think about the trees that he observes. His description of the trees is complicated. Based upon his interaction with a variety of people and cultures he has a complex lexicon of terms and descriptions when he comes to talk of the casuarinas. He tells us that they:

- Bend 'like cypresses'.
- Their 'hair hangs down in rain like sailors' wives'
- They are 'classic trees'.

The suggestion here is that this eclectic mix of terms and descriptions is a direct result of living in a country that has been colonised. In more innocent times he thought the trees simply casuarinas. Now he has a whole range of thoughts on the trees.

The last two lines of the poem recall, perhaps, what some of his ancestors would have been forced to believe: 'if we live like the names our masters please,/ by careful mimicry might become men'. The suggestion here is that the colonised people, along with their language and culture, were seen as inferior. An alien, foreign language was introduced to them and this was deemed the legitimate language. Slaves brought from Africa were given Anglicised names. They were not even considered human. In order to become 'men', they were made to feel that it was necessary to mimic their 'masters'.

The trees that the speaker sees on the hills remind him of this painful fact of history. They too have been renamed so that instead of being called casuarinas it was deemed appropriate to call them cypresses. The suggestion at the end of the poem is that if the trees behave like cypresses, by 'careful mimicry' they might eventually become what the colonisers want them, or presume them, to be.

LANGUAGE

The speaker's description of the trees reveals a poetic imagination. In the opening lines he uses highly visual imagery to describe the trees. Line 3 in particular is very poetic: 'trailing, like masts, the cirrus of torn sails.' The alliteration of the 'i's coupled with the soft 's' sounds makes the line very pleasant to read. A further metaphor is used for the trees in line 11 where the trees are compared to grieving women. In the final lines of the poem the speaker returns to this image and likens the long thin foliage of the trees to hair hanging down in rain.

It is interesting how the poem contains lines that are highly poeticised (line 3, for example) along with lines of very ordinary, everyday dialect ('Now captain just call them Canadian cedars'). Rather than considering this an inconsistency on the poet's part, we might understand the differing lines in terms of the character speaking. 'Shabine', the speaker in 'The Schooner Flight,' is a poet from Trinidad. Lines such as the first and the eight thus carry the cadence of the Caribbean, the vernacular and turn of phrase particular to the islands. Other lines then are more self-consciously poetic. The speaker reveals a talent for lines that are very pleasant to read and visually rich.

THEMES

Colonialism

The poem highlights the impact of colonialism on the inhabitants of the islands. We get a sense that the arrival of other peoples to the islands resulted in confusion regarding the correct and proper use of names for things. The poem suggests that there was a time when the trees speaker sights on the hills of Barbados would simply have been called 'casuarinas'. However, somewhere along the way 'casuarinas' was deemed incorrect and the name 'cypress' considered more appropriate. Someone must have told the speaker that trees that 'take the sea-noise up into their branches' are casuarinas. Perhaps it was someone who was familiar with the older traditional names for the trees. However, the speaker came to consider this name wrong or inappropriate. He tells us that he was 'green' when he thought them casuarinas, a suggestion that he was naïve.

The speaker goes on to say that it hardly matters what the trees are called. He accepts that different people have good reasons for thinking the name that they use correct and he is not upset by the fact that the original island name for the trees has been all but forgotten. However, the speaker cannot be so nonchalant when it comes to names that people possess. Human beings are conscious of the names that others use for them. A person's name is deeply connected with their sense of identity – according to the speaker 'we live like our names'.

The last two lines of the poem conjure up images of the slave trade. Those who were taken from their native countries and sold into slavery were given new names by their 'masters'. Their identity was destroyed and they were forced to adopt new identities, to 'live like the names' their masters gave them. They were not even considered men and were made to feel that only by adopting their new names and living according to the wishes of their master could they 'become men'. So the issue of naming that the sighting of the trees gives rise to takes on a darker significance when applied to the peoples of the island. The poem testifies to the 'pain of history' that 'words contain'.

FOR SALE,
[illegible]tout, likely and very active
Young BLACK WOMAN,
late the property of John H. Carey
She [illegible] offered for any fault, but is
singularly sober and diligent.—
Enquire of JAMES HAYT,
October 3, 1788.

To Norline

LINE BY LINE

Walcott has spent the night in a house beside the sea At dawn he leaves the house while it is 'still-sleeping', while everyone else staying there is still fast asleep. He walks out on the empty beach with a cup of coffee and looks up at the dawn sky. (Walcott memorably describes the dawn sky as being 'slate-coloured', suggesting its dull greyness). He watches waves rolling onto the beach, smoothing away the markings in the sand. Walcott uses a wonderful metaphor to describe this, saying that the surf is a kind of 'sponge' that 'erases' any lines or it comes into contact with.

As the poet walks along the beach he thinks about a woman called Norline. Norline was Walcott's third wife. By the time he wrote this poem, however, their relationship had ended. As he watches dawn break over the bay he thinks about the time he spent with this beautiful woman, remembering how they would lie side by side: 'my body once cupped yours'

He watches a tern fly past, dipping its beak into the salt water. Walcott stares intently at this 'salt-sipping' seabird as it travels over the bay. He wants to memorise precisely how it moves, to 'memorize this passage / of a salt-sipping tern'. He is so taken with the beauty of this beach scene that he finds it difficult to look away. Walcott uses an interesting simile to describe this reluctance. When a lover of poetry comes across a favourite line in a book he or she is reluctant to turn the page. Similarly, Walcott is unwilling to turn away from the placid beauty of this dawn landscape: 'like when some line on a page is loved / and its hard to turn'.

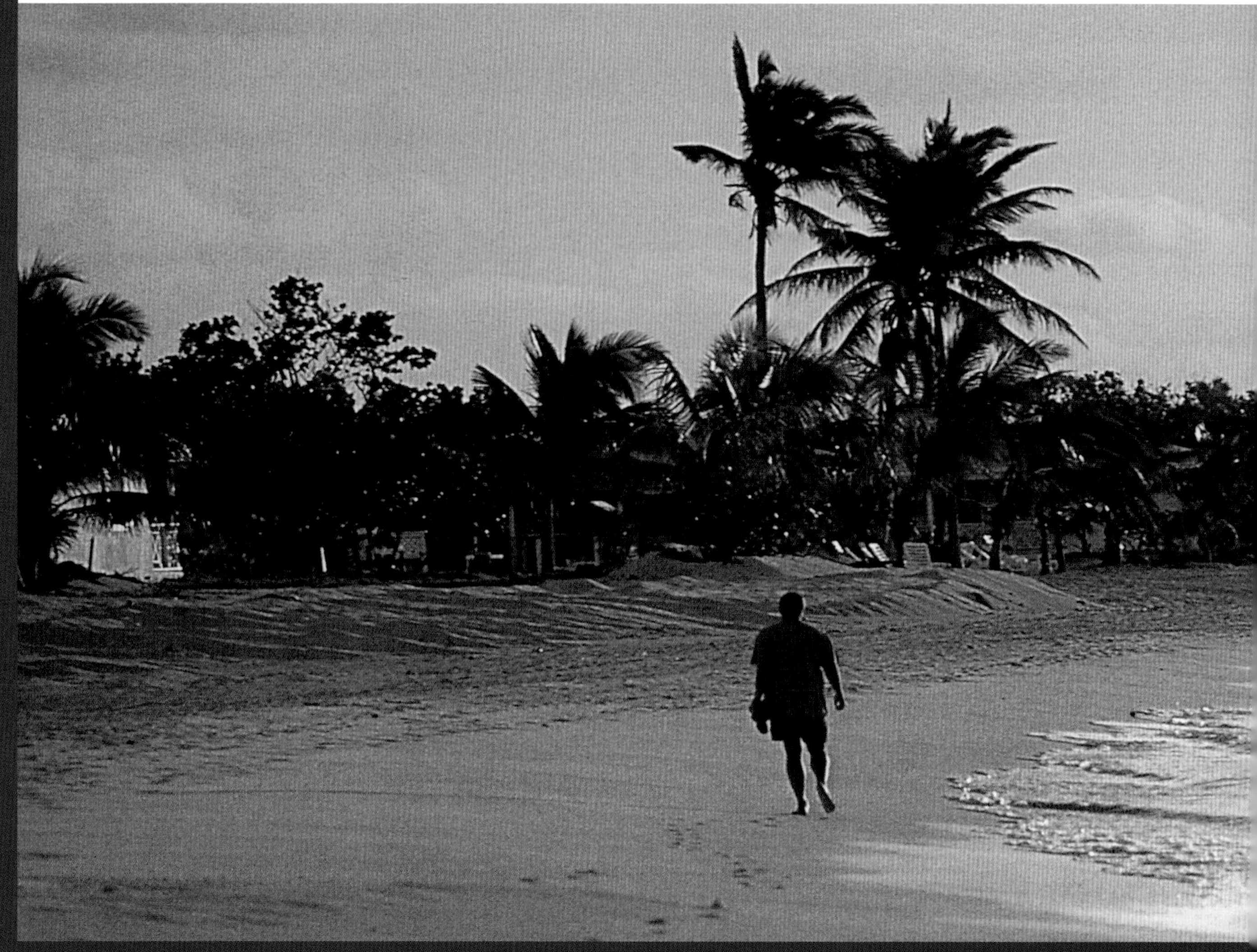

LANGUAGE

Rhyme, assonance and alliteration

'To Norline' consists of three four-line stanzas, each with an ABAB rhyme scheme. Typically, Walcott makes extensive use of half-rhyme, rhyming 'dawns' with 'sponge', 'come' with 'palm' and 'tern' with 'turn'. Assonance occurs in lines 2 and 7 with their repeated 'a' sounds: 'slate-coloured dawn … warming the palm'. We also see it in line 8 with its repeated 'o' and 'u' sounds: 'my body once cupped yours'. Alliteration, meanwhile, occurs in lines 6 and 10 with their repeated 's' sounds: 'still-sleeping … salt-sipping'.

Metaphors and similes

'To Norline' contains a number of memorable similes and metaphors. In a witty and original metaphor, Walcott compares the waves' surf to a sponge that 'erases' the various markings on the sand. There is an equally effective simile in the second stanza, where Walcott describes himself lying beside Norline. His body, he says, was wrapped around Norline's like a hand around a coffee mug. As we have seen, Walcott uses another fine simile at the poem's conclusion, where he compares the sight of the tern flying across the bay to a beloved piece of poetry.

THEMES

The beauty of nature

'To Norline', like many of Walcott's best poems, features beautifully crafted images of nature. The poem rejoices in the natural beauty of the poet's native Caribbean, presenting the vivid images of sea, sand and bird-life that feature in so much of Walcott's work. The poet's intense love and respect for nature is evident in the way he finds difficult to turn away form the beautiful morning scene that has entranced him.

Nature's eternal cycles vs. changing human lives

Walcott knows that there will be many more mornings like this one. Dawn will continue to break each morning over the bay: 'This beach will remain empty / for more slate-coloured dawns'. Terns will continue to glide over the water and the tide will continue to caress the shoreline. People will continue to get up early to enjoy the sunrise, just as Walcott has done on this particular morning: 'someone else will come / from the still-sleeping house … to memorise this passage / of a salt-sipping tern'. 'To Norline', then, contains much hope, suggesting that the beauty of the natural world will continue to flourish well into the future. Even when Walcott himself is no longer around to take pleasure in these sea-side mornings someone else will be. This little scene, then, will be repeated morning after morning for thousands of years to come.

Yet there is sorrow as well as celebration in this carefully crafted piece of writing. As in 'Endings', Walcott demonstrates his intense awareness that little or nothing in our lives can truly last. He cannot bear to turn his back on from the sight of the tern flying over the water. Yet deep down he knows that soon he must leave this beautiful scene behind and get on with his day. Furthermore, there will eventually come a time when he will move away or die and will no longer be able to appreciate mornings such as this one. Someone else will take his place. There is a hint of melancholy in the poet's tone, therefore, when he declares that in the future 'someone else', not him, will emerge from the beach house to enjoy the sunrise.

Lost love

Like 'Summer Elegies', 'To Norline' movingly commemorates a love affair that has ended. There is a real sense of yearning when the poet remembers his body lying next to Norline's, a melancholic sense of longing for a time that has been and can never be again. Someone else, he seems to suspect, will take eventually take his place as Norline's lover, just as in the future 'someone else', not him, will have the privilege of watching the dawn break over this beautiful bay.

Summer Elegies

LINE BY LINE

STANZAS 1 TO 3

The poet recalls a very pleasurable summer spent on an island with a woman named Cynthia. His recollection of that time is addressed to her.

The opening stanza fondly alludes to their lovemaking, the first line intriguingly hinting at many bold, passionate moments Perhaps the first three stanzas refer to the first time they made love. The fact that their 'hands' are said to grow 'more bold' suggests an initial caution, a slight hesitancy that might arise in the first moments of intimacy.

However, as clothes were shed their hands grew bolder. With excited anticipation the speaker's hands 'Tremblingly' undid Cynthia's bikini top: 'Tremblingly I unfixed it'. Her breasts appeared as 'two white quarter-moons' to him as he unpeeled the bikini. Perhaps he describes them as 'quarter-moons' because of the shape of the tan-lines on her breasts – the white, untanned parts being crescent shaped.

The speaker compares the unpeeling of the top to the removal of a 'frisket'. A 'frisket' is a thin frame used in screen-printing to mask any portions not to be printed. The exposed breasts then 'burnt for afternoons'. Perhaps the speaker says they burnt 'for afternoons' because her bikini top remained off for the rest of the afternoons spent on the island.

They made love in the sea, their bodies so closely connected they appeared as 'one shape in the water'. The speaker introduces a whimsical, light-hearted detail to his description of the occasion. From a nearby tree (the sea grape is a small tree that is found near beaches throughout tropical America and the Caribbean) 'a dove/ gurgled astonished 'Ooos' as their bodies writhed in the water, the one 'shape' they made appearing to change as they make love.

STANZAS 4 TO 6

The speaker says that 'Time lent' them the 'whole island'. It is not clear whether they were alone on the island the whole time they were there or just for some moment in between. Since then, however, the passing of time has meant a fading of both 'heat and image'. Perhaps the fading of heat refers to the intensity of their passion – things have cooled off since – whilst also referring to the intensity of the heat of the sun. The 'image' is the speaker's memory of the moments spent on the island.

'Heat and image' are said to 'fade/ Like foam lace'. This is likely a reference to the foam that washes up on the beach (the poet considers the soft, white foam to be like lace). The speaker also compares the vanishing of the 'heat and image' to the fading of 'the tan/ on a striped shoulder blade', an apt comparison for a 'Summer Elegy'.

So time, then, is seen as something that both gives and takes away. It granted them the opportunity to spend many wonderful intimate moments together but now it carries these moments ever further into the past.

The fifth stanza tells of the consequences of spending so many hours swimming in the sea and lying in the sun. 'Salt dried in every fissure'. A 'fissure' is a narrow opening produced by cleavage or separation of parts. The word could, therefore, refer to the fissures of their bodies or the fissures of the island. More than likely it is of their bodies that he speaks.

Every evening the speaker would peel 'the papery tissue/ of [his] dead flesh away'. This activity is considered ceremonial. Beneath the dead skin 'reanointed skin' would appear. Perhaps the skin is considered 'reanointed' because of some cream or lotion that he would apply. To anoint something has obvious religious connotations meaning as it can to consecrate or make sacred in a ceremony.

At the time the speaker felt 'love could renew itself' just as his skin could renew itself. Perhaps he felt that love would develop between himself and Cynthia and that 'a new life' would begin for them. It may be that the speaker had been part of a relationship that ended and he saw his time with Cynthia as an opportunity to find love again.

STANZAS 7 TO 9

These were happy and carefree times for the speaker. A 'halcyon day' is an idyllic day without worry or stress. The island was theirs alone to enjoy, with not even a sail visible on the water. Lines 26 to 28 use an unusual simile to describe the sea, possibly at evening. The flat sea is compared to 'cigarette paper'. Perhaps the 'red thumbnail' that 'smoothed' the paper was the setting sun on the horizon. The sea is then 'creased to a small square'. The final diminishing image might be a metaphor for the collapse of the day into night and the summer into memory.

Stanza 8 shifts to the present. The speaker stands on the island looking out over the bay. The water 'shines like tinfoil' and 'crimps with excelsior'. The word crimp means to press into ridges or waves. So the sea forms waves that appear liked curved wood-shavings (excelsior). Now the beach is very busy, all 'the beach chairs are full'. But for the speaker 'the beach is emptier' for it does not contain Cynthia.

The final stanza is somewhat cryptic. Lines 33 to 34 seem to be a reference to the tale of Adam and Eve in the Garden of Eden. In that story the snake was tempter and the apple the forbidden fruit. Adam and Eve were given a choice. Refrain from eating fruit from the Tree of Knowledge and live in eternal paradise or succumb to temptation and suffer the wrath of God. In the Bible the almond is mentioned also in Genesis, where it is described as "among the best of fruits". It is also mentioned in Numbers. The rod of Aaron is said to have bore an almond tree with sweet almonds on one side and bitter on the other. If the Israelites followed the Lord, the sweet almonds would be ripe and edible, but if they were to forsake the path of the Lord, the bitter almonds would predominate.

So the question that the snake hangs seems to be a question of temptation, a question, perhaps, of choice between what is right and what is wrong. That these lines are in the present tense might suggest that the question does not relate to Cynthia or the time that they spent on the island. Yet, perhaps the speaker is suggesting that this question is a timeless question, posed in every relationship. Perhaps it relates to whether or not he should have stayed with Cynthia, to have tried to see whether that relationship might have worked in the long-term. Did he, perhaps, spoil this relationship by sleeping with another woman. The last two seem to consciously avoid addressing what actually happened. The speaker refers to the pleasurable moment of resting his head on Cynthia's breast. What happened after is 'History'.

LANGUAGE

The poem contains a number of similes and metaphors, some of which are rather complicated and difficult to unravel. In the second stanza the poet compares the parts of Cynthia's breasts that have not been exposed to the sun effectively to 'two white quarter-moons'. The removal of the bikini-top is compared to the removal of 'a frisket' in screen-printing. The comparison is apt, the clear tan lines that separate the tanned parts from the un-tanned parts being very similar to the distinct sections of colour that are created when the frisket is used in the screen-printing process. The comparing of fading of memory to the fading of a tan on a shoulder blade is again apt and easily accessible for the reader. However, Walcott's somewhat complicated simile for the sea in the seventh stanza is less accessible, the link between the folding of a cigarette paper and the sea less obvious than the connection intended in the earlier similes.

THEMES

Love

The poem documents the excitements and pleasures of a new relationship. The opening stanzas describe the wonderful physical and sensual pleasures of sex. The poem reveals what a heady time the beginning of a relationship can be. Being with Cynthia upon the island allowed the poet to think that 'love could renew itself, and a new life begin'. However, the relationship that the poem is based on does not seem to have been very long-term. We might presume that it only lasted as long as the summer. The poem illustrates how fleeting emotions can sometimes be, how love that starts so strong can with time begin to fade and vanish. The poem also reveals how powerful and memorable passionate relationships can be, however short they last. Like 'Endings', 'Summer Elegies' suggests that the loss of love leaves a void or vacuum in our lives. Gazing upon the very beach that he spent such pleasurable and memorable times with Cynthia the poet though the 'beach chairs are full/ the beach is emptier'.

For Adrian

This poem is about the death of Adrian, an eight-year-old boy. It appears to be set in the room where Adrian has died. His family are gathered around his deathbed 'howling like statues'. His sisters Kathryn, Gem and Judith are present, as well as his aunt. Walcott, it seems, is also there. They mourn and weep for the death of their relative. Somehow, however, Adrian manages to communicate with Walcott from beyond the grave. The poet hears the dead boy's voice inside his head: 'The child spoke inside me'. He passes Adrian's words on to us in the form of a poem: 'so I wrote it down'.

LINE BY LINE

The wisdom of the dead

Adrian claims that by dying he has become filled with wisdom: 'I have now entered a wisdom'. The knowledge of the dead has made him wise beyond his years: 'It is easy ... to speak now beyond my eight years'. It is no longer appropriate, therefore, to think of him as a simple eight year old boy: 'You measure my age wrongly. I am not ... a child'. To the spirits of the dead the concept of age has no meaning: 'I am not young now, nor old'.

Death, he claims, has given him access to secret knowledge: 'I am wiser, I share the secret that is only a silence'. These secrets are known to every dead person, from those who in life were rich and powerful ('the tyrants of the earth') to those who were extremely poor ('the man who piles rags / in a creaking cart, and goes around a corner / of a square at dusk'). Now that he has gained this secret knowledge Adrian can speak with a great 'vestal authority' about matters of life and death. ('Vestal' is another word for pure or holy). He compares himself to an angel: 'It is easy / to be an angel'. Just like the angels In the Bible, Adrian wants to bring a message to humanity by sharing with us his new found wisdom.

Wisdom and silence

In line 13 Adrian declares that he has entered 'a wisdom not a silence'. Death, it seems, is not the end but the beginning of a new sort of knowledge. Yet in line 22 he states that the wisdom of the dead is a kind of silence after all: 'I am wiser, i share the secret that is only a silence'. What is meant by this rather mysterious statement? Perhaps Adrian is suggesting that the wisdom of the dead only comes with the peace and silence of the grave. It is also possible, however, that the wisdom of the dead is a type of 'silence' because it cannot be communicated to the living. The dead are forced to remain silent about the knowledge they have gained. In this poem Adrian manages to communicate with the living by using the poet as a 'medium'. It seems, however, that the living are simply incapable of grasping the knowledge Adrian is so desperate to share. The wisdom of the dead, it appears is something when can access only when we too have entered the silence of the grave.

All things move toward their end

In death Adrian seems to have found a new awareness of how everything eventually fades away. He emphasises how quickly time flies by: 'The days run through the light's fingers like dust / Or a child's in a sandpit'. The objects that surround us may appear solid but they are decaying with each passing day: 'Look, and you will see that the furniture is fading'. Even something as sturdy as a wardrobe will disintegrate with the passage of time. Our bodies, too, are decaying more and more with each passing day. Now that Adrian is dead he can see them for the insubstantial things they are: 'I can see through you'. The things of this world may appear solid and stable to us living folk, but to Adrian, with his new-found awareness of the passage of time, it is 'as unsubstantial as a sunset'. Part of Adrian's message, then, is that everything is slowly but surely fading away to nothing. We may not notice these processes of decay but they are occurring relentlessly all around us.

Don't cry for me

Adrian urges his brothers and sisters not to mourn his death. He declares that there is no need for his siblings to feel sad about his passing, asking them 'why do you keep sobbing?' The last thing he wants, it seems; is for his death to cause his family any sorrow or misery: 'I would not break your heart, and you should know it; / I would not make you suffer and you should know it' (lines 19–20). Having passed on, Adrian can no longer be effected by pain, sorrow or loneliness. He does not 'miss' his family in any sense that we could understand: 'I am not missing you sisters' (line 14). In death he is no longer capable of suffering: 'I am not suffering' (line 21). Why, therefore, should his family feel sad for him?

At one with the universe

Adrian claims that death has released his spirit to become one with nature. His soul has been absorbed by the birds and animals of the natural world: 'I am part of the muscle / of a galloping lion, or a bird keeping low over / dark canes'. There is no need, therefore, for his family to miss him: 'Why do you miss me?' His family mourn and weep because they think they are saying good-bye. In reality, however, they are simply welcoming him back to the world in a different form: 'what ... you call a goodbye ... is ... a different welcome'. Eventually, of course, Adrian's loved ones will die themselves. Like him their souls will be welcomed into oneness with nature. They, too, will experience: 'a different welcome, / which you will share with me, and see that it is true'. Their spirits will enter birds, plants, animals and other aspects of the natural world. They will join Adrian in oneness with the universe.

When Adrian's family look at the ocean or the stars they do not mourn. Instead, these wonderful sights fill their hearts with happiness: 'When you see the stars // do you burst into tears? When you look at the sea / isn't your heart full?' Similarly, when they consider Adrian's death they should be filled with happiness not sorrow. Now that he is dead his spirit is part of the very sights that give them such pleasure. He is a part of the sea, the stars, the soil, and the other magnificent phenomena of the natural world. The poem, therefore, ends with a startling image of hope. Walcott, using a wonderful simile, describes Adrian's grave as a gentle, welcoming smile: 'As if his closing grave were the smile of the earth'. (It is easy to imagine how the hole in the ground might resemble a smiling mouth, especially when it is partially filled in). The grave, usually a symbol of fear and finality, becomes a symbol of hope. Death represents not the end of life but a welcome to a new form of existence.

LANGUAGE

Tone

Walcott skilfully captures the tone of the dead Adrian speaking from beyond the grave. There is a sense of mysticism in the dead boy's words, especially when he asks mysterious questions like 'Do you think your shadow can be as long as the desert?', or when he makes mysterious statements like 'I did not invite or invent angels'. There is a real sense of tenderness when he speaks about his family members, such as 'Gem / sitting in a corner of her pain'. Yet there is also a degree of frustration and irritation in Adrian's tone. He seems frustrated that his family continue to mourn his passing, that they are unable to understand that his life has been changed not ended. Adrian seems desperate to get this point across, to communicate his new found wisdom about life and death: 'I wish you would listen to me'. He repeatedly asks his family to 'listen' to his words, and at the beginning of the poem urges them to 'Look', as if he wants his family to perceive the world with the supernatural clarity of the dead. We are left with the impression, however, that Adrian's loved ones will never be able to fully comprehend his message or see things they way he now sees them. The living, it seems, are incapable of fully understanding the wisdom of the dead.

Mysterious statements

'For Adrian' contains a number of mysterious and cryptic statements, In lines 3 and 4, for instance, Adrian refers to his relatives' bodies by mentioning the 'tissue of your leaves, / the light of your veins'. This image, it has to be said, defies straightforward comprehension. Equally incomprehensible are Adrian's comments about shadows and angels: 'Do you think your shadow / can be as long as the desert? I am a child, listen / I did not invite or invent angels'. And what are we to make of his declaration that 'The days run through the light's fingers like dust'? By including these phrases, which are almost impossible to grasp or visualise in any conventional manner, Walcott increases the poem's atmosphere of mystery and strangeness. These mystical images increase our sense that we are being addressed from beyond the grave, by someone who has gained access to the secrets of the dead.

THEMES

Life after Death

'For Adrian' is a poem of hope. It suggests that death is not end, but a 'different welcome', the beginning of a new phase of existence. There is no need, therefore, to mourn the passing of any human being. Like many of Walcott's poems focus on the issue of religious belief. 'Pentecost' and 'A Letter from Brooklyn', for instance, show how an event can renew and strengthen the poet's faith in the existence of the soul and in life after death. 'For Adrian', too, restates Walcott's belief in an afterlife.

'For Adrian', however, it does not put forward a conventional Christian vision of the afterlife, with its notions of heaven and hell. Walcott does not argue that when we die our souls ascend to be judged by God. Instead, the poem seems to be inspired by a philosophy known as 'pantheism', which states that the energy within us does not disappear with our deaths but remains a part of the universe forever. 'For Adrian' suggests that when we die our souls become one with nature. Our spirits will continue to exist forever in the bodies of plants and animals, as well as in the sky, sea and soil.

The beauty of nature

Like so many of Walcott's poems 'For Adrian' reveals the poet's deep love of the nature. Walcott presents several powerful images of the natural world, mentioning the sea, the stars, a lion and a bird swooping over the Caribbean landscape.

The passage of time

'For Adrian', like many of Walcott's poems, stresses how things fade away with the passage of time. The poem emphasises how even the most seemingly solid things, such as pieces of furniture, are all the time fading away. Even though we don't notice it they are worn away slowly and imperceptibly by the passage of time. The poem suggests that eventually, given enough time, every physical thing will disintegrate. (A similar view is put forward in 'Endings'). Yet it also stresses that nothing is ever truly destroyed, only changed from one type of thing to another. Everything, including our souls, decays or is destroyed only to re-emerge as something else. (This is evident in Adrian's declaration that his soul is now a part of birds, animals and other things of the natural world).

The Young Wife

The poem focuses on a husband trying to cope with the recent death of his wife. The speaker of the poem acts like some invisible presence in the house, observing the husband and revealing his thoughts. The husband's world is shown to be a very dark and lonely one now that his wife has died.

LINE BY LINE

STANZAS 1–2

'Make all your sorrow neat', the speaker says at the head of the poem, exposing the husband's efforts to maintain some form of normality and routine, to apply order to his grief. He tries to keep busy by writing to 'her mourners'. But the second stanza exposes the great void that now exists in the husband's life, the terrible absence that the wife's death has brought and which his busying himself cannot conceal.

In the evening when he comes home from the office the fact that he is alone becomes stark. The armchair in which he used to relax with his wife now seems a desolate spot. The speaker describes the husband travelling 'an armchair's ridge' these evenings. The word 'ridge' makes us think of the high edge along a mountain, a dangerous precipice that is far from homely. The once cosy armchair now seems an uninviting and unwelcoming place.

The 'sofas' too appear sinister and foreboding. The speaker describes the place between the arms of the sofa as the 'valley of the shadow', a conscious reference to Psalm 3 in the Bible which is commonly read at funeral services ('... though I walk through the valley of the shadow of death, I will feel no evil: For thou art with me'). The living room has become a shadowy world of death. The speaker refers to the 'drapes' dead foliage', a possible reference to the floral pattern on the curtains now appearing withered.

STANZAS 3–4

In the third stanza the speaker refers to 'the mirror' which he says 'clouds' although the husband wipes 'it clean'. There is a suggestion here that the husband no longer has a clear sense of identity now that his wife is dead. The clouding mirror functions as an effective metaphor for the husband's thwarted efforts to comprehend who he is. He appears lost in a world of shadows and fog. Yet the mirror does remind him of a sense of guilt that he carries. The third stanza tells us how the husband thinks himself a 'traitor'. He believes that the mirror has seen through him and recognises him for what he is. Has the husband been unfaithful to the wife in the past?

The notion that the house has become a lifeless, funereal place is further illustrated in the fourth stanza. The wallpaper remains unmoved by the husband's lonely 'sobbing' which he tries to conceal from the children. Like the 'drapes' dead foliage' the 'buds on the wallpaper/ do not shake'. Not that they ever did, of course, only now their static nature appears deathly whereas before their colour might have added a vibrancy to the house. The speaker also refers to the 'drawers' that the husband 'dare not open'. These are the drawers containing the wife's clothes and possessions, items that painfully recall her presence in the house.

STANZAS 5–11

In the fifth stanza the speaker personifies death. It is seen as 'that visitor/ that sat beside' the wife throughout her illness. She has departed from the house with this figure, silently, invisibly, 'like wind/ clicking shut the bedroom door'. They left 'arm in arm' like a couple in love. It is as though she has been seduced by another man and her death some betrayal of their marriage.

The 'wedding photograph in/ its lace frame' remains as a sad reminder of their former happiness. 'And the telephone' also, another static, silent object like the wallpaper and the furniture, signals the wife's absence – it now represents the lack of her voice. Everything the husband sees in the house somehow signifies the wife's death.

In lines 24 to 26 the speaker says that 'The weight// we bear on this heavier side/ of the grave brings no comfort'. Perhaps the 'weight' is the burden of memory, the pain of loss. The dead take nothing with them, they travel light, as the wife did when she died, departing 'like wind'.

The last two lines of the seventh stanza and the first two of the eight consider how the wedding vows have been brought their conclusion. The final wedding vow has the couple pledge to love one another until death shall part them. So the husband has been brought through the wife's death to 'the very edge/ of that promise', to the final point of the marriage.

The lines that follow show how the flowers in the natural world (unlike the artificial flowers that adorn the curtains and the wallpaper) continue to blossom. There is a suggestion in this image of life continuing as normal. The hawthorn's 'hooks' (thorns) are changing 'happily into blossom' even whilst the hearts of some, like the husband, are breaking 'into grief'. Whereas the husband's heart ought to have been blossoming with the marriage, like the branches of the hawthorn, he has been all too quickly cast into the winter of grief.

In the last eleven lines of the poem the speaker describes the scene in the kitchen at suppertime. The husband sets a place at the table for the wife. Again the wife's death is rendered poignant by the furnishings of the house and the objects she would have used. However, for the first time in the poem others feature. The husband's children sit at the table and their presence alters the gloomy atmosphere that dominated the earlier part of the poem. The children act differently to their father. Rather than maintaining a space that will remain empty they 'close in the space/ made by a chair removed'. This is not to suggest that they have coldly forgotten their mother, for 'nothing takes her place'. She was 'loved' and is 'now deeper loved'.

The implied question in the final stanza probably has to do with where the children's mother is. We get the impression that the father gives them an answer that he might not entirely believe himself. The speaker says that the children 'accept' his answer, implying that his answer does not give the whole truth. But they cope in their own way and the father is startled to hear them laugh. Their laughter seems to have the effect of restoring the mother's presence and she is thought to sit there with them at the table 'smiling' at the fact 'that cancer/ kills everything but Love'.

THEMES

Death and grief

'The Young Wife' is a poem about a husband trying to cope with the death of his wife. The poem reveals the terrible hollow feeling that comes with grief, the great void that appears when someone we dearly love departs. Sorrow is something that takes control of our lives. Though the husband tries to maintain a routine and make his sorrow 'neat', grief is not something he can control or avoid. He is seen plumping the pillows on the bed and soothing the corners of the wife's favourite 'coverlet' but we get the impression that his efforts to act as though everything is normal are in vain. When evening comes the fact of his wife's death haunts the living room where he must alone.

The poem illustrates how the way we feel determines how the world appears to us. The living room is funereal, the flowers on the curtains considered 'dead foliage', the armchair and sofa vast uninviting landscapes. Everything the husband sees reminds him of the fact that his wife is no longer there. The house is filled with memories, the husband's heart heavy with sadness and possibly guilt. Line 11 tells us that the husband perceives himself as a 'traitor'. The first nine stanzas offer a bleak picture of the husband's life. There seems to be no relief from his sorrow, no end to his grief. The wife's death is seen as a form of betrayal. She has left the husband, 'gone with that visitor/ that sat beside her'. Death is personified, likened to another man who has lured her away from her husband.

However, the poem is not entirely bleak. In a similar manner to 'A Letter from Brooklyn', 'The Young Wife' ends with a suggestion of hope. The presence of the children in the last two stanzas lightens the mood of the poem and brings an element of life and vitality to the home. They draw the husband out of himself, 'startle' him with their laughter. Warmth and humour reappear in a house that seemed black with grief in the first nine stanzas. The love that exists in the kitchen evokes the presence of the wife. Just as in 'For Adrian' and 'A Letter from Brooklyn', 'The Young Wife' closes with a suggestion that death is not the end. The wife continues to exist in the love that lives on in the house.

Saint Lucia's First Communion

BACKGROUND AND INTRODUCTION

This poem is set on Walcott's native island of Saint Lucia. The island is named after Saint Lucia (or St Lucy), who lived in Syracuse in the third century. St Lucy was only a young girl when she was put to death by pagans for refusing to renounce her belief in Christ. Lucy suffered agonising tortures at the hands of her pagan tormentors, yet even when they gouged our her eyes she refused to give up her Christian beliefs.

The poem's title, then, has two meanings. On one hand it refers to the day on the island of Saint Lucia when the first communions take place. In the poem the speaker watches a group of girls marching in procession after their first communion ceremony. On the other hand the title refers to the grisly death of Saint Lucia hundreds of years ago in Syracuse. When Lucia was martyred she experienced a type of 'communion' by becoming one with God in heaven. The poem focuses on the contrast between innocence and purity (represented by the modern-day communion girls on Saint Lucia) and cruelty and evil (represented by the horrible death of Saint Lucia herself in the third century).

LINE BY LINE

STANZA 1

The speaker is sitting in his car at evening beside an asphalt road. (Asphalt is tar-like substance used to surface roads). Walcott uses a wonderful metaphor to describe this road, saying that it is like a frayed black ribbon stretched across the island: 'the asphalt's worn-out ribbon'. Suddenly the speaker sees a little black girl in a white dress: 'in white cotton frock, cotton stockings, a black child stands'. Suddenly many more girls in white dresses come into view: 'First her, then a small field of her'. The speaker realises that its First Communion day on the island: 'Ah, it's First Communion!' The girls are carrying prayer books ('missals') that have pink ribbons for bookmarks: 'They hold pink ribboned missals in their hands'. Their hair has been carefully arranged in plaits and they wear satin hair-clips that remind the speaker of moths: 'the stiff plaits pinned with their white cotton moths'.

STANZA 2

In this stanza Walcott focuses on a caterpillar which is moving along a cotton plant. (It has been suggested that this plant is growing on the side of the asphalt road down which the communion girls are walking). Both the caterpillar and the cotton plant are associated with Christ and communion:

- Walcott presents the cotton plant as a symbol of the Eucharist itself. The white buds of cotton that 'pod' or emerge from its twigs are depicted as communion wafers: 'twigs of cotton from whose parted mouths / the wafer pods'.
- The caterpillar, meanwhile, is presented as a symbol of the communion girls. Just as the caterpillar has eaten the wafers of cotton, so the communion girls have 'eaten' wafers of Christ's flesh in the communion ceremony. The caterpillar is about to be transformed. It is 'pumping out' slime for a cocoon which will transform it into from an ugly caterpillar into an elegant moth. Similarly, the girls will be trans formed by their experience of Jesus in the Eucharist. The will be changed from fully fledged followers of Christ.
- Walcott associates both the cotton plant and the caterpillar with faith in Christ. The cotton buds are linked to 'belief without an if!' and the caterpillar is linked to the 'myth' of Christ's death and resurrection. (The use of the word 'myth' here betrays Walcott's own doubts about the truth of Christianity, for a myth is something that may or may not be true).

STANZA 3

As he watches the girls march past him the speaker thinks of the first communion ceremonies that have just taken place 'all across Saint Lucia'. He thinks of the 'thousands of innocents' who have received communion for the first time. He imagines these boys and girls posing for photographs with their families outside the churches where they have just received the sacrament: 'thousands of innocents / were arranged on church steps ... between squinting parents'. He pictures the Caribbean sun setting on these proud, happy families, causing the parents to squint into its brightness. As Walcott puts it, using a typically inventive metaphor, the families were 'facing the sun's lens'. Now, however, the sun has almost completely set. Darkness is filling the island just as it filled the life of Saint Lucia, the girls' patron saint, when she was blinded by the pagans: 'Darkness came on like their blinded saint's'. As the speaker watches the girls parade along the asphalt road, the last traces of light are disappearing.

STANZAS 4–5

As he watches this little procession, the speaker is overcome with concern for the communion girls. This world, he suggests, is an evil place. As they make their journey through life they will face all kinds of threats, dangers and difficulties. Time, the speaker feels, will change the girls for the worst. The innocence that now fills their minds will gradually become tainted by prejudice. The speaker is filled with the desire to somehow 'free' the girls from this existence before they are effected by the prejudice and evil it contains: 'Before it comes on: the prejudice, the evil!' It's as if the speaker considers the girls to be too pure and innocent for this troubled world.

There are several aspects of the girls' appearance which remind the speaker of moths. (This is discussed in more detail below). Now the speaker wishes that the girls would transform into actual moths. If this magical transformation happened the speaker would be able to release the girls from this evil existence with all its trials and tribulations. He would drive his car up close to the swarm of moths, being careful not to disturb them: 'if it were possible to pull up on the verge / of the dimming asphalt, before its headlights lane / their eyes'. Then he would open the car window and attempt to lure them into the car: he would 'lower the window a crack, and delicately urge the last moth delicately in'. (The gentleness with which he would lure the moths into the his car is indicated by the repetition of the word delicately).

As the speaker lured the moths into the car he would

hold each one of them briefly in his hands, indicating the intense love and concern he feels toward these communion girls: 'But if it were possible ... to house each child in my hands'. The speaker's car, then, would be filled with a 'blizzard' of flapping moths: 'I'd let the dark car / enclose their blizzard'. He'd drive it to a hill, where he would open the car windows and release the moths, allowing them to leave this cruel world behind and fly up to heaven: ' on some black hill ... loose them in thousands to stagger / heavenward'.

LANGUAGE

Metaphors and similes

Like many of Walcott's poems, 'Saint Lucia's First Communion' contains a number of extremely inventive metaphors. The asphalt road, for example, is compared to a frayed black ribbon stretched across the island: 'the asphalt's worn-out ribbon'. The communion girls' hair clips are compared to 'white satin moths', and we can imagine how the frilly clips might be said to resemble moths that have alighted on the girls' heads. The communion girls themselves are compared to a field of flowers, the frills on their dresses resembling rose petals. Initially, the speaker sees just a single 'flower' but then a whole field of them come into view: 'First her, then a small field of her'.

Another example of Walcott's keen visual sense can be seen in the metaphor in line 6 where the caterpillar is compared to an accordion: 'The caterpillar's accordion still pumping out the myth'. The caterpillar resembles an accordion because of its 'concertina' style of movement, its body expanding and contracting as it inches along the twig of cotton. Perhaps the poem's most original metaphor occurs in line 18 where the speaker compares the swarm of moths to a blizzard. We can imagine the moths flapping furiously around the car like snowflakes in a blizzard. An example of a simile, meanwhile, occurs in line 11, where the communion girls are compared to candles: 'erect as candles between squinting parents'. This is yet another superb visual comparison. The communion girls resemble candles because of their white clothes and the proud, straight-backed way in which they stand.

Rhyme and assonance

'Saint Lucia's First Communion' does not have a regular rhyme scheme. Instead, the rhyme scheme shifts from stanza to stanza. Stanzas one, two and five have an ABAB rhyme scheme, while stanza 3 rhymes AABB and stanza 4 rhymes ABBA. As is so often the case with Walcott's poems it contains many half rhymes. We see this in the rhymes between 'mouths' and 'moths' for example, as well as in rhymes between 'lance' and 'hands' and 'car' and 'stagger'. Like many Walcott poems 'Saint Lucia's First Communion' is rich in assonance. The repeated 'i' sound in 'pink ribboned missals', for instance, creates a pleasant musical effect. The repeated 'a' and 'i' sounds in 'caterpillar's accordion' also generate a verbal music, as do the repeated broad vowel sounds in 'loose them in thousands to stagger / heavenward'.

THEMES

Innocence and evil

Perhaps the central theme of this poem is the contrast between purity and innocence on one hand and evil and cruelty on the other. To the speaker the communion girls seem the ultimate embodiment of innocence. As he speaker puts it: 'thousands of innocents / were arranged on church steps'. The speaker, however, is all too aware that this world is a cruel and nasty place. As the girls make their journey through life they will encounter a great deal of 'evil' and 'prejudice'. The terrible death of Saint Lucia in the third century serves as a symbol and reminder of the evil the world contains. The speaker knows that the girls' lives will be filled with dangers that threaten their physical and mental well-being. The business of living will strip away their innocence and purity.

The speaker responds to this grim reality by wishing he could transport the girls out of this cruel world to the sanctuary of heaven, where they would be safe and where their innocence would be preserved forever. He fantasises about the girls transforming into moths, which he would drive to a hill from where they would be able to fly directly up to heaven. Yet the speaker, of course, knows that this is only a fantasy. The girls must live their lives like everybody else. They cannot simply float up to the sanctuary of heaven. There is nothing the speaker or anyone else can do to save them from the world's evil and prejudice. The poem, then, presents quite a negative view of life. The world is portrayed as a place of threats and dangers, where evil and prejudice will always triumph over innocence and good. Innocence, it seems, can only survive in Heaven.

Darkness and light

Walcott skilfully uses imagery of darkness and light to convey this theme of innocence and evil. Throughout the poem the innocent communion girls are associated with light and brightness. Their white dresses represent the simplicity and purity of their young minds. They are described as 'candles' in line 11, reinforcing their association with brightness. They are also depicted as moths, which are well known for their attraction to light. The reference to the story of Saint Lucia reinforces the association between brightness and innocence, for the name of this innocent young Saint comes form 'Lux', the Latin word for light.

Evil and prejudice, meanwhile, are associated with darkness. In line 12 we are told that darkness 'came on' just as we are told in line 20 that evil and prejudice 'came on'. The evil and prejudice of Saint Lucia's pagan tormentors filled her world with darkness when they gouged out her eyes. Perhaps the poem's most powerful and haunting image, therefore, is that of the communion girls walking away into the darkness along the 'dimming asphalt'. This image seems to suggest how their purity and innocence will be consumed by the evil and prejudice of this of cruel world.

Religious faith: belief without an 'if'

Many of Walcott's poems address the thorny question of religious faith. His work is haunted by the struggle between faith and doubt, depicting how different experiences threaten and renew Walcott's own belief in Christ. (We see this in 'Pentecost' and 'A Letter from Brooklyn'). In this poem Walcott's doubts are suggested by his use of the word 'myth' in line 6. A 'myth' is defined as ' a foundational or important story which may or may not be based in historical fact'. By referring to the story of Christ's death and resurrection as a 'myth' Walcott suggests his doubts about whether these incredible events ever actually took place.

Walcott seems to long for a simple and unquestioning belief in Christ, a powerful and unwavering faith he describes as 'belief without an if'. This is the kind of faith enjoyed by Saint Lucia, who went to her grave rather than renounce her Christian convictions. It is also the kind of faith enjoyed by the communion girls, whose innocent young minds are untroubled by doubts about God's existence.

The poem, however, suggests that is difficult to maintain such an unquestioning faith in this troubled world. Walcott seems to suspect that the evil and prejudice the girls will encounter on their journeys through life will cause them to question their faith, just as Walcott, on the evidence of poems such as 'Pentecost', has questioned his. He is filled with the desire, therefore, to somehow transport the communion girls directly to heaven before their simple faith can be corroded by life's negative experiences.

The transforming power of Christ

'Saint Lucia's First Communion' also focuses on the transforming power of Christ. Throughout the poem the communion girls are associated with moths. In the second stanza their hair clips are compared to 'white satin moths'. Their white dresses At the poem's conclusion the speaker imagines them as moths flying up to heaven. This comparison of the communion girls as moths suggests how radically Christ has and will transform their lives. Moths evolve from caterpillars like the one on the cotton plant in stanza 2. Similarly, the communion girls have evolved from little children to fully-fledged Christians. The presence of Christ through the Eucharist has transformed them utterly.

Pentecost

The word 'Pentecost' comes from a Jewish harvest festival called Shavuot. The apostles were celebrating this festival when the Holy Spirit descended on them. It sounded like a very strong wind, and it looked like tongues of fire. The apostles then found themselves speaking in foreign languages, inspired by the Holy Spirit. People passing by at first thought that they must be drunk, but the apostle Peter told the crowd that the apostles were full of the Holy Spirit.

LINE BY LINE

Two preferences

1 *Better a jungle in the head*
than rootless concrete

The first two lines establish a preference regarding the state of mind someone might have. The poet says that it is better to have a mind comparable to a jungle than one comparable to 'concrete'.

A jungle is a dense, entangled area of vegetation. It is an organic environment, typically associated with the tropics. Therefore, to have a 'jungle in the head' suggests having a mind that is cluttered and complex, composed of many elements that are entangled. Yet such a mind might be organic, open to growth and change.

The jungle is also a place that contains both ancient, deep-rooted trees and younger plants and seedlings. A corresponding mind might, therefore, be considered to have ideas and values that are deeply rooted in tradition whilst also containing newer values and influences.

The poet contrasts this jungle environment with a place of 'concrete', which he identifies as 'rootless'. The word 'concrete' suggests a fabricated environment. In contrast with the jungle, concrete is inorganic. A mind comparable to 'concrete' is incapable of growing or changing.

So perhaps the poet is saying that it is better to have a mind that is somewhat confused and complicated but deeply rooted in tradition than one that is rigid and shallow.

2 *Better to stand bewildered*
by the fireflies' crooked street ...

Lines 3 to 6 establish another preference that resembles the first preference. It is 'better to stand bewildered/ by the fireflies' crooked street' than to stand upon the sidewalk beneath the 'winter lamps'.

The 'Crooked streets' that the fireflies illuminate must be rural pathways, or, indeed, the paths through jungles (perhaps the poet refers to them in the poem as streets in order to get the necessary rhyme with 'concrete'. Although we might be 'bewildered' here it is preferable to standing beneath the light of 'winter lamps'. One of the reasons for this is because such 'lamps' do not 'show/ where the sidewalk is lost'.

Perhaps what the poet is saying here is that electric lights only ever feature along sidewalks. Once we leave the 'concrete' environment of the towns and cities they cease to exist and can offer no assistance. They are only there to light the concrete paths and cannot guide you out in the wilderness where the 'sidewalk is lost'. Where the 'sidewalk is lost' is the territory of the fireflies, the 'crooked', haphazard paths of the jungle. Unlike the lights of cities the fireflies are not stuck in one place.

LINES 7–12: *Winter in the city*

In the seventh line the poet refers to 'these tongues of snow'. The immediacy of the word 'these' forces us to wonder where the poet is. Is he, perhaps, in a city where snow is falling? This presumes that 'tongues of snow' is a metaphorical description of snow falling. If this is correct then the poet is likening the fall of snowflakes to the tongues of flame that fell upon the heads of the disciples at Pentecost. But whereas the tongues of fire that came down upon the disciples' heads did in fact 'speak for the Holy Ghost' the 'tongues of snow' cannot.

The flakes of snow are then likened to 'words dropped from a roof'. Perhaps these flakes seem to fall from the roofs because they only appear in the lights of the buildings and are impossible to perceive in the black night that hangs above the city. These 'words' are said to be getting quieter of their own accord – 'the self-increasing silence/ of words'. It seems to be getting harder to hear them. Yet, even if they are not heard they gather in such a manner upon the 'iron railings' to offer 'direction, if not proof'.

This stanza in particular is very cryptic. But it seems that the poet is likening the fall of snow to some sort of heavenly message that is getting ever more silent in the modern world. Yet the snow is still falling and gathering in such a way that offers us direction, even if it does not testify to the 'proof' of God.

Night surf

The fourth stanza appears to shift location from the city to the beach. Here the poet observes the 'night surf' and concludes that this is 'best'. He does not state what it is best at, but me might understand it to be 'best' at suggesting a religious presence in the world. As the surf washes up on the shore it makes 'slow scriptures of sand'. The markings on the sand are perceived as some form of religious message akin to the writings contained in the Bible.

Just as the 'words' dropping in the third stanza offer 'direction' towards God but no actual 'proof' of his existence, so the 'night surf' sends 'not quite a seraph,/ but a late cormorant'.

So the poet seems to be saying that on the occasion of this modern-day Pentecost he must make do with the appearance of a bird rather than an actual angel as intimation of God in the world. The cry of this cormorant late at night transmits to the poet, across the glowing fish in the sea, an intimation of what in his 'childhood gospels,/ used to be called Soul'.

THEMES

The jungle and the city

The poem contrasts two different environments, associating each with the different mentalities or states of mind people can have. The first world is the world of the jungle. It is better, according to the poet, to live with a mind that is comparable to a jungle than to have 'rootless concrete' in your head. It is also better to stand beneath the light of fireflies on crooked paths than it is to stand beneath the streetlights on the city sidewalks. Best of all, though, is to stand upon the shore at night watching the tide leave its mark in the sand whilst a cormorant cries over the glowing water.

Perhaps the poet is comparing the sort of life that he has upon the Caribbean island of Saint Lucia with that of life in some of the big American cities he has visited. The island may contain jungle, and indeed the inhabitants may be considered to have 'jungles' in their heads but at least this form of existence has roots. The island also allows the poet such moments of beauty as that of the 'night surf' when the water glows with fish and cormorant's cry suggests the existence of 'Soul' in the world.

God and the modern world

Cities are seen in 'Pentecost' as godless environments. The streetlights are only good for lighting the concrete sidewalks but are useless to show 'where the sidewalk is lost'. Where the sidewalk is lost is the jungle, the natural world that has not been crushed and controlled by man. The poem suggests that it is better to exist in an environment like the jungle where there is bewilderment and mystery rather than in the fabricated environment of the city, with its concrete and electric lights. The light that the fireflies provide in the jungle might also be linked with the manifestation of the Holy Spirit on Pentecost. The Holy Spirit appeared in the form of flames in order to give the apostles the ability to guide people with the Word of God. The fireflies have the obvious association with fire and their light is considered bewildering just as the presence of the Holy Spirit must have been bewildering for the disciples and those to whom they subsequently spoke to. We might also get a glimpse of what 'used to be called Soul' in the natural world. The city, in contrast, is a place where the divine is no longer visible. The word of God seems to be growing ever more silent.

from Omeros

This poem is set on a fishing boat out at sea. It describes a conversation between Achille, who is the ship's captain, and his first mate. The poem takes place early in the morning.

LINE BY LINE

The mate's night

The mate has been up all night fishing: 'All night he had worked the rods without any sleep' (15). He has navigated their position by the stars, measuring how far they are away from land: 'he had read / the stars and known how far out they were' (16–17). By looking at the stars the mate was able to determine the depth of the water around them. As Walcott puts it, he has been able to measure 'how deep / the black troughs were and how long it took them to lift'. While the mate was working Achille was 'lying cradled in the bow' of the boat (16). Achille has slept the whole night through: 'Achille had slept through the night. Cradled at the bow / like a foetus' (39–40). The mate, however, doesn't seem to mind working while his boss relaxes. He feels indebted to his captain. The mate, it seems, had a drink problem and Achille hired him when no-one else would: 'but he owed it to his captain, who took him on / when he was stale-drunk.

Now it is morning and Achille has woken up. The boat is moving quickly, driven by the trade winds: 'with the trade behind them' (11). Walcott refers to the boat's 'fast-shearing hull', suggesting that it shears or cuts its way through the water like a knife. The mate sets about his morning chores, checking the lure that trails along behind the boat: 'He tested the bamboo pole / that trawled the skipping lure from the fast-shearing hull'. By doing this he can tell that a shoal of mackerel are in the area: 'Mackerel running', he said' (12). The mate asks Achille to help him with the morning's tasks, declaring 'this morning I could use a hand' (4).

The conversation

Achille has been generally unhelpful over the past night. Even before he fell asleep in the boat's bow he was silent and withdrawn. His mind, it seems, was somewhere else. In line 5 the mate asks him: 'Where your mind was the whole night?' Achille replies by saying that his mind was in Africa. The mate finds this answer bizarre and ridiculous. He inquires sarcastically if Achille somehow walked to Africa during the night: 'You Walk?"(7). He suggests, again sarcastically, that Achille has been driven crazy by sunstroke and urges him to keep his hat on: 'You get sunstroke chief. That is all. // You best put that damn captain-cap back on your head'.

The albacore

The mate shows Achille an albacore that he caught the previous night. An albacore is a species that has several different names. In English it is often known as a kingfish. In the Caribbean dialect or patois it is known as a 'ton'. According to the mate, this particular albacore is the size of a mako, a small Caribbean shark: 'You know what we ketch last night? One mako size "ton"' (21).

In lines 24 to 38 provide an intense and poetic description of the dead albacore lying 'fresh at the feet' of the mate. According to Walcott, its flaky skin is 'steel-blue and silver', the colour of the ocean where it lived: 'its blue flakes yielding the oceanic colour // of the steel-cold depth from which it had shot'. The albacore lies on the deck of the ship with its mouth open: 'It lay there, gaping'. The albacore, it seems, has bulging globe-shaped eyes. As Walcott puts it, using a wonderful metaphor, its eye was a 'globed window'. In death, of course, the albacore can see nothing. Its dead eyes have become covered in some kind of grey film: 'A grey lens covered the gaze of the albacore'. The globes of the albacore's eyes are now as blind as the globe of the moon: 'its cold eye in sunlight was blind as the moon'. Walcott provides a wonderful description of the albacore's struggle to survive. The albacore was hooked when it bit down on a spoon lure. (A spoon lure is a spoon-shaped piece of metal that reflects the light of the moon and attracts fish with its brightness). According to Walcott, the albacore made a yawning motion in an attempt to extract the hook from its mouth: 'yawning at the lure // of a fishhook moon'. It 'had shot, leaping' from the water in an attempt to break the fishing line to which it was attached. This powerful fish 'burst' through the troughs or waves, straining for freedom with the strength of a stallion tethered to a stake: 'stronger than a stallion's neck tugging its stake'.

Finally, around daybreak, the albacore became too tired too struggle. Gradually it became still or docile and its huge 'wedge' of a tail stopped slapping and thrashing the water: 'Tired of slapping water, / the tail's wedge had drifted into docility'. Once the albacore stopped struggling the mate reeled in the hook to which it was attached: 'the fishhook moon that was reeled in at daybreak'. Once the albacore was reeled close to the ship the mate 'gaffed' it, or pierced it with a kind of spear, lifted it on the deck and clubbed it to death.

The man-o'-war

Achille begins to steer the ship toward land: 'Look, land! the mate said. Achille altered the rudder' (42). He manoeuvres the boat through the water, carefully avoiding being swept upwards on the crest of the huge waves (or 'troughs') that surround them: 'to keep sideways in the deep troughs without riding / the crests' (43–4). As Achille steers he looks up and sees a man-o-war overhead, following a flock of gulls: 'then he looked up at an old man-o'-war // tracing the herring-gulls' (44–5). (A 'man-o'-war' is large black Caribbean sea-bird).

The man-o-war is an unusual species of bird in that it does not catch its own fish. Instead, it follows flocks of sea gulls, which give the man-o'-war some of the herring or mackerel that they catch. As Achille puts it: 'Them stupid gulls does fish / for him every morning. He himself don't catch none'. Achille and the mate watch a gull catch a mackerel and rise up from the water: 'A herring gull climbed with silver bent in its beak'. The man-o'-war flies down toward it: 'the black magnificent frigate met the gull halfway' (54–5). (A 'frigate bird' is another name for a man-o'-war). The gull drops the mackerel for the man-o'-war to collect: 'the gull dropped the mackerel // but the frigate bird caught it before it could break / the water'.

The black king

The man-o'-war is often referred to as the 'sea-king' because of its huge size and the magnificent way in which it glides over the water: 'that endless gliding / that made it the sea-king' (45–6). This notion of the man-o'-war as 'king of the skies' is reinforced throughout the poem. The mackerel it gets form the gulls is referred to as 'tribute'. ('Tribute' is the payment given to a king by his subjects). As Achille puts it, the gulls are 'white slaves for a black king'. The poem's conclusion likens the sight of the man-o'-war soaring into the earth's upper atmosphere to that of a king entering his capitol city: 'The king going home', Achille declares, when the man-o'-war flies away into the sky (62).

Achille takes great pleasure in the sight of the man-o'-war. He seems thrilled to see this powerful bird in action: 'Look at him dropping.' Achille pointed. 'look at that son- / of-a-bitch stealing his fish for the whole focking week!' To him the man-o'-war seems very beautiful: 'The black bugger beautiful, / though!' As he watches it fly away his heart seems to soar in a kind of ecstasy: 'Achille felt the phrase lift // his heart as high as the bird'.

Achille reacts so strongly to the sight of the man-o'-war because it reminds him of his African ancestry. He regards the man-o'-war as a 'black king' of the sky, just as his people were once 'black kings' of Africa. The sight of the man-o'-war reminds him of Afolabe, his African ancestor who was a great tribal leader. To Achille, the flight path of the man-o'-war seems to spell out the name of his illustrious forefather in the sky: 'the bird whose wings wrote the word 'Afolabe'. Walcott suggests that the man-o'-war is somehow writing Afolabe's name in the language of birds: 'in the letters of the sea-swift'.

The poem concludes with a wonderful depiction of the huge sky into which the man-o'-war disappears: 'he and the mate // watched the frigate steer into that immensity / of seraphic space'. This passage is an example of Walcott's writing at its most descriptive. The word 'immensity' conveys the vastness of the sky into which the man-o'-war soars. The description of man-o'-war's domain as 'seraphic space' suggests the intense purity of the air through which it glides. ('Seraphic' means having to do with seraphs, which were a kind of angel). The man-o'-war, Walcott suggests, is flying into some kind of heaven.

LANGUAGE

Metaphors and similes

Like many of Walcott's poems this extract from Omeros contains several inventive similes and metaphors. In a wonderful simile the eye of the dead albacore is compared to the moon: 'Now its cold eye in sunlight was blind as the moon'. Two clever similes are used to describe the sleeping Achille. According to Walcott he is 'like a foetus, like a sea-horse'. We can imagine Achille's body curled up like a sea-horse or a foetus as he sleeps. The poem's conclusion contains an interesting metaphor, which compares the clouds or 'cumuli' above Achille's ship to the gates of a city. These clouds part to let the man-o'-war soar up into the heavens, just as the gates of a city would open to let the city's ruler enter.

Caribbean dialogue

One of the most striking features of this extract is Walcott's use of the Caribbean dialect or 'patois'. The use of dialect expressions such as 'I know you ain't like to talk' instead of 'I know you don't like to talk' and 'You know what we ketch last night' instead of 'You know what we caught last night' lend the poem a sense of immediacy and realism. There is a wit and humour in the mate's sarcastic responses to Achille that would be lost or diminished if this banter were written in conventional English. Yet by writing in the Caribbean dialect Walcott also makes a political point. Poetry, he suggests, can be made from the type of English spoken by Achille and the mate just as much as it can be made from 'proper' or 'standard' English. This Caribbean patois, according to Walcott, is every bit as meaningful and valid as the English spoken in Oxford or Cambridge.

THEMES

Nature

Like so many of Walcott's poems this extract from Omeros is rich in the nature imagery of Walcott's beloved Caribbean. Walcott presents wonderfully vivid descriptions of the sea with its 'deep troughs'. of the island with its 'lilac horns' and of the sky with its 'immensity / of seraphic space'. He also provides incredibly detailed descriptions of the albacore with its eyes that are 'blind as the moon' and of the man-o'-war soaring and diving through the Caribbean sky.

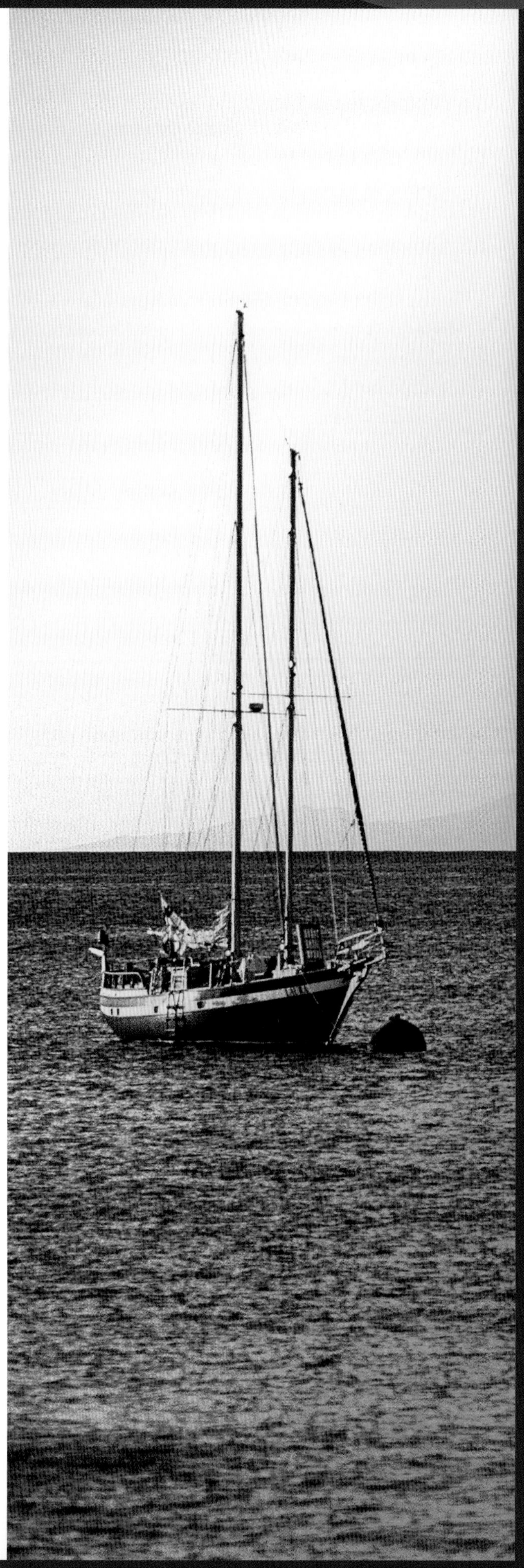

Like 'To Norline' and 'Summer Elegies' this extract mixes weighty concerns with an exuberant celebration of the Caribbean's natural wonders.

Poverty and hardship

One of the stand-out features of this extract from 'Omeros' is its gritty and realistic portrayal of the life of Caribbean fishermen. Achille and his mate survive terrible working conditions in order to make a paltry living. Everyday they endure the dangers of the open sea, struggling to stay alive and afloat on its huge 'black troughs'. (A 'trough', as we have seen, is another word for wave). The harshness of their working life is indicated by the fact that they must work through the night. Even their sleeping quarters seem inadequate. Achille, it appears, does not have any cabin. Instead, he is forced to sleep 'cradled in the bow' of the ship. (Perhaps another indication of their poverty is the fact that the mate's t-shirt has been worn down until it is little more than a 'red hole'). Furthermore, it has been suggested that Achille and the mate have been denied a proper education. This indicated by the fact that they speak in the Caribbean patois rather than in 'proper' English. The poem, then, offers no romantic images of Caribbean life, such as those we might find on a postcard or in a holiday brochure. Instead, it presents us with an unflinching portrayal of the difficulties Achille must confront everyday as he attempts to make a living from the sea.

Africa

Perhaps the dominant theme in this extract is the almost unbearable contrast between Achille's grim present and the glorious past enjoyed by his ancestors in Africa. Once his forefathers such as Afolabe were great tribal kings. But that was a long time ago, before Achille's people were stolen away from Africa and brought to the Caribbean as slaves. As the descendant of slaves Achille still occupies the bottom rung of society. He is poor and uneducated and has no choice but to eke out a paltry living in terrible conditions on the treacherous seas.

Achille seems to be obsessed with the contrast between his ancestors' past glories and his present wretched condition. As line 5 suggests, his thoughts often turn to his ancestral homeland, as he dreams or daydreams about Africa. The sight of the man-o'-war also reminds him of his people's lost glory. The man-o'-war, as we have seen, is depicted as a 'black king' of the sky just as Achille's ancestors were 'black kings' of Africa. Achille's comment about 'white slaves for a black king' is intriguing. He seems to be suggesting that if history had developed a little differently his people might have been the masters rather than the slaves. The extract, then, demonstrates Achille's bitterness and regret at the tragedies of slavery and colonialism, tragedies that deprived his people of their illustrious African heritage and left him in his present miserable state. It also movingly depicts his longing to return to his people's glorious African past.

WALCOTT AT A GLANCE

FAITH AND DOUBT

In 'A Letter from Brooklyn' the poet's faith in God and in an afterlife is restored by a letter about his father that he receives from Mabel Rawlins, a friend of the family. mabel is convinced that the poet's father is with God in heaven and her simple faith helps Walcott overcome his own doubts about religion.

In 'For Adrian' the dead boys spirit attempts to convince his family to have faith in an afterlife. He tries to convince them that death is not the end. After they die they, like him, will become one with the universe.

In 'Saint Lucia's First Communion' the poet longs for the simple faith, the 'belief without an if' enjoyed by the procession of communion girls but also by Saint Lucia who was martyred in the third century. Yet he is all too aware that such faith is difficult to maintain in this modern world with all its prejudice and evil.

'Pentecost' demonstrates how difficult it is to sense God's presence in the environment of the modern city. Cities, the poem suggests, are soulless environments where it is almost impossible to get a sense of the divine. Walcott finds it much easier to be receptive to God's presence when he has by the seashore in his native Caribbean.

LOVE

'Endings' stresses how love and relationships tend to wither and die without us noticing.

'Summer Elegies' provides a memorable portrayal of a love affair and of the emptiness the poet feels when his this affair is over.

'To Norline', also, finds the poet remembering a love affair that is no more.

'The Young Wife' shows the terrible vacuum that remains when a young woman dies of cancer. The young woman's husband must live on in a house where every room reminds of his departed partner.

DEATH AND HOPE

'A Letter form Brooklyn' offers the consolation of religious belief in the face of death. The poet's father may be dead but Mabel is convinced that he has been lives on in heaven as a servant of God.

'For Adrian' shows the devastation wreaked by the death of a young boy whose family are left inconsolable by their loss. Yet it also offers hope for Adrian claims that death is merely a 'welcome' to a different form of existence.

'The Young Wife' shows not only the horror of bereavement but also offers the hope that a dead person somehow might live on in his or her children.

COLONIALISM

'The Sailor Sings Back to the Casuarinas' shows how colonisers have controlled their subject people through language. By imposing their languages on the Caribbean the European conquerors also imposed their values. By controlling how people spoke it was also possible to control how they thought and acted.

The extract from Omeros shows the devastating legacy of the slave trade. In Africa Achille's ancestors were kings and rulers before they were brought to the Caribbean as slaves. Far from being a king their descendant Achille is forced to eke out a meagre living on the treacherous waves as he dreams of his people's former glories.

W.B. YEATS
THEMES

IRELAND

Throughout his life and his poetic career, Yeats enjoyed and endured an abiding obsession with the fortunes of Ireland. His complex and shifting relationship with his homeland provides the focus for many of his most famous works. Yeats' attitude to Ireland is frequently one of disappointment, all too often he is disgusted by what he regards as contemporary Ireland's betrayal of its heroic legacy, the tradition of mythical heroes such as Cuchulain, and fearless revolutionaries such as Emmet and Wolfe Tone. 'September 1913' is probably the most famous articulation of this disgust, the most devastating contrast between past glory and present shame. The Catholic middles classes are presented as penny-pinching fools, completely dominated by the Church, interested only in praying and saving. Yeats contrasts this with the selfless devotion of Ireland's previous heroes, those 'for whom the hangman's rope was spun' yet still gave their lives for the cause. Section five of 'Under Ben Bulben' also derides the contemporary middle-classes, those 'Base-born products of base beds', whose 'unremembering hearts' have forgotten the legacy of Ireland's past. Many of Yeats' poems, therefore, desire a return of the glorious tradition of heroic self-sacrifice that dominated Irish folklore and revolutionary tradition.

Yeats, however, was less enthusiastic about heroic self-sacrifice when he got a chance to witness it up close. 'Easter 1916' is, at best, a highly qualified celebration of the rebels' bravery. Its dominant emotion is one of amazement, as if Yeats cannot quite believe that the very Catholic population he had criticised in 'September 1913' could produce people capable of such selfless courage. In 'The Stare's Nest By My Window', Yeats witnesses the destruction and violence of war in the countryside around his home, the brutality of which is represented by the young soldier 'trundled' down the road 'in his blood'. This bloody conflict, he says, is a product of hearts that heave been brutalised by a diet of fantasies, by a belief in heroism, martyrdom, and self-sacrifice in the name of a cause. These were 'fantasies', however, that Yeats himself had approved of, in 'September 1913' with its 'delirium of the brave' and 'Under Ben Bulben' with its 'seven heroic centuries' of resistance to British rule. Perhaps, therefore, Yeats is happier singing the praises of violence, self-sacrifice and heroism when it is safely in the past.

'NO ENEMY BUT TIME'

Yeats was heavily involved in many of the political controversies of his day and served for a time as senator in the newly independent Irish state. Many of his poems, however, display a suspicion of politics. This is evident in 'An Irish Airman Foresees his Death', where the airman dismisses the influence of the 'public man' and the 'cheering crowds'. Yeats, like the airman, is more interested in exploring a 'lonely impulse of delight' than he is in responding to the wishes of the masses. The same prizing of the private above the public is evident in 'In Memory of Eva Gore-Booth and Constance Markiewicz'. Women like these, he says, have no business becoming involved in public life, in the struggle 'With a common wrong or right'. They have their work cut out for them in the private struggle against time, maintaining their beauty and innocence against the passing years.

Yeats has been accused of sexism in this poem, for suggesting that politics is an inappropriate activity for beautiful young women, and should be left to men. 'Politics', too, values the private world of love, romance and the struggle against old age above the public world of political affairs. In 'Swift's Epitaph', Yeats urges us to imitate Swift by serving 'human liberty'. The liberty Yeats has in mind, however, is more the personal, private liberty of art and expression, the freedom to follow 'the lonely impulse of delight', that it is the public, social liberty of the masses.

ESCAPE FROM REALITY

There is a clear contrast in much of Yeats' poetry between the mortal world of time in which all is 'begotten, born and dies', and the idea of an eternal and unchanging realm the poet often associates with art. The former was often a source of frustration for the poet. This is especially evident in his later poems, when Yeats is an old man and his body has become more of a hindrance than a help.

Yeats was an idealistic poet. Politically and socially he always desired a greatness for Ireland based on the heroic myths and legends he celebrated in his plays. He consistently considered modern times to be mediocre and unexceptional, and he constantly looked to the past for inspiration, shunning the potentialities of the existing society around him. The need to escape from unappealing circumstances and conditions, restricting conditions that frustrate the poet in his quest for perfection and greatness, is a central theme in Yeats' poetry.

This need to escape is evident in his earliest work, in poems such as 'The Lake Isle of Innisfree'. Here the poet desires an escape from the uninspiring 'grey' city of London. The poem details the home he will build in the midst of the peaceful island. However, the poem is more of a romantic dream than an actual plan. It permits the young and despondent Yeats to imaginatively escape the unappealing city streets.

As the poet grew older he increasingly despaired at the consequences of the passing years. The loss of beauty and vitality and the subsequent exclusion from the sensuous activities permitted the young, feature in the poet's later work. In 'The Wild Swans at Coole', a melancholic Yeats walks through the grounds of Coole Park enviously considering the apparently immutable beauty of the swans. The ageing poet uses the swans as a symbol of eternal beauty and contrasts them with the mortal world in which he must grow old and ultimately die.

Poems such as 'Sailing to Byzantium' and 'An Acre of Grass' are more urgent in tone. Registering the unattractiveness and redundancy of the aged body, Yeats desires an escape to a place devoid of change and decay. In 'Sailing to Byzantium' this place is the ancient city of Byzantium where the poet wishes to be immortalised in a gold mosaic. He prays that his 'useless' body be consumed away so that his 'soul', trapped and frustrated in an old man's body, can make the desired journey to the immortal city. The natural environment of the 'Lake Isle' with its bees and linnets is no longer the preferred destination of the older poet. It is the colder and less romantic form of impersonal art that appeals to him.

In 'An Acre of Grass' the poet asks that he be granted 'an old man's frenzy' so that his ever sharper mind can transcend the barren world of his day-to-day existence and access some greater truth. Yeats again wants to escape his circumstances and ultimately 'remake' himself. He wants to be like the poet William Blake and possess the genius of the great Michelangelo. In such a form he feels he can achieve what eludes him in his present state.

POETIC STYLE

It must be remembered that Yeats lived and wrote through a period of history that involved much change, both in poetry and society at large. He began writing at the end of the Victorian era when Tennyson was still alive. The influence of the Romantic movement is very apparent in the early poems. Only one of the poems selected for the course represents what we could refer to as Yeats' 'early' style. 'The Lake Isle of Innisfree' is the work of a young and idealistic poet. Its language and content is romantic.

As Yeats grew older and began to form more cohesive political and cultural ideas, his poetry became more intense and he began to register his reactions to current events. He brooded upon the nature of love (especially his unrequited love for Maud Gonne), and let known his disillusionment felt at the inability of modern Ireland to live up to the Yeatsian ideal. As such, the tone and style of his poems changes. The language and content becomes less idealistic. The romantic wistfulness, the dreamy, decorative quality of much of his earlier verse gives way to a more terse and muscular style. 'September 1913', for example, is an uncompromising assessment of a country and its people, devoid of the images and influences of his earlier work.

The poems written around this time are invested with a specific purpose and Yeats brings a unique and broad range of learning to bear upon themes of modern significance and relevance. From an early stage, and throughout the remainder of his life, Yeats distinguished himself from others by maintaining an interest in the occult, mystical thought and the practice of magic. There is the eclectic range of imagery drawn from Irish myth, Eastern religions, classical legend and Christianity. Using a broad range of images and symbols, Yeats allows the spiritual to shed light on the physical, the past inform the present and continuously attempts to launch upon the world a vision of reality based upon his own imagining. His poems have the ring of conviction, and the energy and urgency of a language held tight within the parameters of expertly contrived metre, rhyme and syntax.

The later poems record much of the poet's bitterness at old age, loss and the mortality of man. But the energy and passion remain, though the hopes and dreams of youth have all but disappeared. The voice of 'Under Ben Bulben' is as antagonistic as ever. The sentiments of 'An Acre of Grass' are full of passionate intensity and express the poet's unceasing desire to delve beneath the façade of the everyday and reach the immortal truth. Ultimately, his unfailing ability to constantly reinvent himself and astonish with the unfaltering standard of his verse, along with the complexity and growth of his maturing vision and concern, makes Yeats' collection of work an uncompromising example of excellence. To read Yeats is to encounter a force, to witness the power and range of a mind expertly articulated and refined throughout a lengthy and productive lifetime.

The Lake Isle of Innisfree

LINE BY LINE

STANZA 1

Yeats wants to go and live on the island of Innisfree. He would like to live there by himself and lead a simple life. He would like to build a small cabin for himself in the middle of a glade. He also wants to grow his own food. He will grow rows of beans and keep bees for their honey.

STANZA 2

Yeats describes the tranquillity of the island. The mornings are very peaceful and filled with the sounds of crickets chirping: 'for peace comes dropping slow,/ Dropping from the veils of morning to where the cricket sings'. At noon the heather glows purple in the sunlight. In the evening you can hear the flapping of linnets wings as they fly around the island. At night the glittering stars are reflected in the water.

STANZA 3

The thought of Innisfree is always in the poet's mind and in his heart: 'I hear it in the deep heart's core'. He is always imagining the pleasant sounds of its waters: 'for always night and day/ I hear lake water lapping with low sounds by the shore'. The thought of Innisfree is especially important to the poet when he is in the city. The cold grey concrete makes him long for the island's tranquillity.

THEMES

Escape

The speaker of the poem is someone who longs for a simple uncluttered way of living. He wishes to live a peaceful life away from the hustle and bustle of the city. The idea of being a self-sufficient and independent person is very attractive to him. He wants to grow his own food and build his own house.

A love of nature

The speaker of the poem is someone who appreciates the sights and sounds of nature.

He longs for the tranquillity and peace of the countryside. He is a daydreamer, someone whose mind is filled with thoughts of Innisfree throughout his daily life in the city.

The poem celebrates the beauty of Innisfree. The island is alive with the sounds of nature. The poet mentions the chirping of the crickets, the buzzing of the bees, the flapping of the linnet's wings, and the peaceful lapping of the water by the shore.

It also celebrates the visual aspect of the island. The poet describes the glitter of starlight reflected in the water and the purple glow of the heather in the noonday sun.

September 1913

BACKGROUND AND INTRODUCTION

In this poem Yeats attacks what was known as the Catholic middle-classes; the industrialists, business-men and wealthy landlords of Dublin. This 'merchant class' of Catholic businessman had replaced the old Protestant landowners as a dominant force in Irish society. In the poem Yeats accuses the Catholic middle-classes of being greedy, mean and materialistic. He also criticises the superficial nature of their religious devotion. He says they have betrayed the legacy of the great heroes of Irish history by making ireland a materialistic and un-Romantic country.

The poem was inspired by the Hugh Lane controversy of 1912–13. Hugh Lane was a nephew of Yeats' great friend Lady Gregory. He had accumulated an important collection of priceless French paintings, which he was prepared to give to the city of Dublin on condition that the Dublin Corporation provided a suitable gallery. The Catholic businessman who ran the Corporation were reluctant to provide public money for the gallery. They were also unwilling to contribute to a private fund set up to cover the gallery's cost.

An important presence in 'September 1913' is that of John O'Leary, an Irish Patriot who had been one of the mentors of Yeats' youth. He had died shortly before the poem's composition. O'Leary had been involved in the Fenian revolt against British rule in 1865. As a result, he had served five years in prison, and fifteen in exile in Paris. He placed great importance on the cultural life of the nation, and introduced Yeats to the work of many Irish poets of the day. To Yeats, therefore, O'Leary symbolized all that was greatest about the Irish nationalist tradition. He represented a perfect blend of courage and learning, of physical daring and a love of culture.

LINE BY LINE

STANZA 1

The poem's opening stanza is very sarcastic. Yeats addresses the Catholic middle classes, telling them they have achieved wisdom or 'come to sense'. They have realised that life is all about praying and saving: 'For men were born to pray and save'. All they need to do is save money to make sure they're all right in this world say a few prayers to make sure their souls will be all right in the next:

What need you being come to sense
But fumble in a greasy till
And add the half-pence to the pence
And prayer to shivering prayer

It's important to be aware of Yeats' sarcasm in this stanza. He doesn't really think the middle classes have 'come to sense'. In fact, he thinks just the opposite. He regards their values and their view of life as being very much mistaken. Similarly, he doesn't really think that 'praying' and 'saving' are the only important things in life. Yeats thinks that the middle class approach to living is much too limited, that it's emphasis on praying and saving doesn't leave space for art and heroism, beauty and love, things Yeats regarded as the highest aspects of human existence.

Yeats has nothing but contempt for the outlook of these middle classes:

He feels that they have dried 'the marrow from the bone'. Their mean-spirited philosophy, in Yeats' opinion, sucks the goodness out of life and disregards everything that make life worth living.

His contempt is evident in the image of the shop-keeper fumbling in a 'greasy till' for a few pennies, which powerfully suggests their meanness and materialism.

His contempt is also evident when he claims that they add prayer to prayer in the same way they add penny to penny. It's as if they're mechanically 'saving up' prayers to secure them against damnation when they die.

Yeats describes their prayers as 'shivering', suggesting that the motivation behind all this praying is fear rather than true spirituality. The middle-classes' prayers are motivated more by fear, either of priests in this life, or of hell in the next, than they are by a genuine desire to communicate with God.

Yeats concludes the stanza by declaring that 'Romantic Ireland is dead and gone'. The crass materialism of 1913 has replaced the romantic heroism of Ireland's history. 'Romantic Ireland' is as dead and buried as John O'Leary himself.

STANZAS 2–3

Yeats contrasts the greedy middle-classes with these selfless heroes of Ireland's past. These heroes, Yeats argues, have little or nothing in common with the penny-pinching merchants of Ireland in 1913: 'Yet they were of a different kind'. They heroes had no interest in praying and saving: 'But little time had they to pray ... And what, God help us, could they save?' Instead, their minds lay on higher things: heroism, honour and freedom.

When the middle-class Catholics were young they looked up to these great heroes from Irish history. Yeats imagines them as children, halting their games whenever their parents mentioned Robert Emmet or Wolfe Tone, eager to hear tales of heroism and courage: 'The names that stilled your childish play'. Yeats mentions specific examples of this heroism:

He mentions the 'wild geese', Irish soldiers who were forced into exile after being defeated in the 1690's, and went on to serve with great distinction in various European armies.

He mentions Edward Fizgerald and Wolfe Tone, who led a rebellion against British rule in 1798. Both were executed after the rebellion failed.

He mentions Robert Emmet who was executed after his own uprising failed in 1803.

Yeats suggests that the middle classes have betrayed the legacy of the heroes they worshipped when they were children. The heroes dreamed of a better Ireland but the middle classes, through their focus on praying and saving, have turned the country into a mean and materialistic place. This un-Romantic Ireland is not the Ireland the heroes fought and died to create: 'Was it ... For this that all that blood was shed?'

STANZA 4

Yeats wonders what would happen if we could turn back the clock ('turn the years again') and bring the suffering heroes back to life:

Yet could we turn the years again
And call those exiles as they were
In all their loneliness and pain

The middle-classes, he believes, would regard the heroes as insane, claiming they'd been driven mad by their love of Ireland: 'You'd cry some woman's yellow hair/ Has maddened every mother's son'. (In songs and stories Ireland was often personified as a beautiful woman with yellow hair). The hero's don't belong in this un-Romantic Ireland. If they were to somehow return to life they would be mocked and ridiculed by the middle-classes who now dominate the country and who are incapable of understanding the heroes' Romantic idealism and self-sacrifice. Yeats concludes, therefore, that it's better to let the heroes rest in peace: 'But let them be they're dead and gone / They're with O'Leary in the grave'.

LANGUAGE

A satirical ballad

'September 1913' has many features associated with political ballads, poems that were written to make a publicise a political or social point:

It has ABABCDCD rhyming scheme, which is often associated with the ballad tradition.

Like many ballads it makes use of a refrain to drum its main point home: 'Romantic Ireland is dead and gone/It's with O'Leary in the grave'. The fact that these lines conclude each stanza reinforces the disparity between the nobility of Ireland's past and the squalid pettiness of its present, and the sense of loss the poet feels at the disappearance of Ireland's romantic, heroic legacy.

Like many ballads it uses repetition to emphasise its message. We see this in stanza 3 with its repetition of the phrase 'Was it for this'. The repetition emphasises

Yeats' contempt for the state of contemporary Irish society, contrasting it each time with an aspect of the country's glorious past.

Like many Irish political ballads it personifies Ireland as a female figure, in this case as a beautiful woman with 'yellow hair'.

Metaphor and simile

Yeats uses a simile in line 11, depicting the heroes' names as gusts of wind that have blown around the world as they became famous internationally for their courage: 'they have gone about the world like wind'. Line 11 can also be interpreted as an example of metonymy, where something associated with an object stands for the object itself.

Here the heroes' names travelling around the world stands for the travels of the heroes themselves, many of whom travelled the world when they were exiled form Ireland after their various rebellions failed. In line 17 a metaphor is used to describe this flight of the patriots into exile, depicting them as geese flying over the sea away from Ireland: 'Was it for this the wild geese spread/ The grey wing upon every tide'. (Here Yeats is playing on the fact that some exiled Irish patriots were nicknamed the 'wild geese').

THEMES

The 'terrible beauty' of patriotism

Like many of Yeats' poems 'September 1913' takes a complex view of patriotism and of those who fight and die for Ireland. On one hand he celebrates the nobility and bravery of these men, stressing that they were a 'different kind' of person to the penny-pinching merchants that dominate Ireland in 1913. The deeds of these 'brave' men have rightly been celebrated. They have been regarded as heroes by generations of Irish children. Stories of their courage have spread all over the world. Their names, he says, have 'gone about the world like wind'. He seems to admire the huge sacrifices made by men like Emmet and O'Leary for their dream of a free Ireland.

Yet there is also a sense in which Yeats seems to regard the heroes as figures to be pitied as much as celebrated. He seems to pity for these men who suffered the 'loneliness and pain' of defeat exile and execution. (His sympathy for them is perhaps suggested by his use of the expression 'God help us' in line 14). He declares that the 'hang man's rope was spun' for these rebels, suggesting that their revolts against the British Empire were doomed to failure before they even begun, that their heroic efforts would only ever lead them to the hangman's scaffold.

There is a sense, then, in which Yeats suspects there was something irrational, or even a little mad, about the heroes' behaviour. He refers to the heroes' 'delirium', suggesting he felt there was an element of madness in their bravery: 'All that delirium of the brave'. The kind of bravery displayed by them required a frenzy of emotion and instinct. How else would they have been spurred to take on the might of the British Crown and face almost certain death?

The middle-classes are criticised for failing to understand the patriots' bravery, for regarding them as simply insane. Yet perhaps Yeats, too, shares a little of this attitude. Perhaps he, too, believes that the heroes had been 'maddened' by their love for Ireland, as a man might be driven mad by his love for a beautiful yellow-haired woman. Yeats says that the heroes 'weighed so lightly what they gave', referring to their patriotic willingness to lay down their lives for their cause. But is there a sense in which he believes that the heroes were a little too willing to die, that they weighed their lives too lightly?

A similar view of patriotic heroism is evident in 'Easter 1916' where Yeats refers to the 'terrible beauty' of the Easter Rising. There is beautiful and noble, he suggests about the bravery and self-sacrifice of patriotic heroes like Pearse and MacDonagh in 1916 or Wolfe Tone and FitzGerald in earlier times. Yet there is also craziness or 'delirium' about their behaviour. There is something 'terrible' or terrifying about their willingness to die – and to kill other people – in the name of Irish freedom. A similar suspicion of patriotism is evident in 'The Stare's Nest By My Window' where these notions of patriotism and sacrifice are dismissed as dangerous 'fantasies' that cause violence and destruction.

A scathing attack

'September 1913' is a devastating piece of satire in which Yeats takes the well-of Catholics of Ireland to task for not only their meanness and materialism but also for the shallow nature of their religious devotion. The image of the shopkeeper fumbling in the 'greasy till' captures their penny pinching greed while the image of them adding 'prayer to shivering prayer' wonderfully sums up their terrified devotion to the Catholic Bishops who were enormously influential in the country at the time.

Yeats declares that through their greed the middle-classes have made Ireland a materialistic and un-Romantic place: 'Romantic Ireland is dead and gone'. By doing so they have betrayed the legacy of the heroes they used to worship when they were children. Wolfe Tone and FitzGerald fought for a noble and Romantic vision of Ireland, not the mean-spirited land the middle-classes have created. The middle-classes, Yeats declares, are incapable of understanding the heroes' courage and self-sacrifice. If they were to somehow meet these heroes now they would simply call them mad.

While undoubtedly a powerful piece of satire, some critics have wondered whether Yeats isn't a little too hard on middle-class Dublin. He never stops to consider the good features this group might have possessed. As we have seen Yeats was motivated to write the poem because Dublin Corporation and various wealthy businessmen failed to come up with the money for an art gallery. Is Yeats guilty of releasing his anger with a few individuals in a vicious verbal assault against a whole social class?

Lament for a vanishing past

Like many of Yeats' poems 'September 1913' laments a vanishing Ireland. It mourns the disappearance of Ireland's 'Romantic', noble and heroic past and its replacement with the greed and materialism of 1913. Yeats believed that a noble society had to be organised in the traditional way, with the wealthy aristocrats in their mansions ruling over the peasants that worked happily in the fields. The rise of the Catholic middle-classes with their businesses and factories meant Ireland no longer had this old-fashioned structure. Yeats' 'Romantic Ireland' was dead and gone.

Yeats, it could be argued, also mourns the disappearance of this old Ireland in 'Under Ben Bulben', where he refers to hard-working peasants, monks, and 'hard-riding country gentlemen', all of which are a far cry from the businessmen who dominated Ireland in 1913. A similar lament for a vanishing Ireland is evident in 'In Memory of Eva Gore-Booth and Con Markiewicz', the last lines of which mourn the decline and disappearance of the Protestant aristocracy.

The Wild Swans at Coole

BACKGROUND AND INTRODUCTION

This poem is set in Coole Park, Co. Galway, a place Yeats visited frequently throughout his life. He is wandering through the grounds of the park when he sees a flock of swans floating on a lake. The sight of the swans reminds Yeats of his first visit to the park nineteen years earlier. All of a sudden he feels very old. He thinks about how much his life has changed in the nineteen years since he first visited the park and saw the swans.

LINE BY LINE

STANZA 1

The poem begins by setting an autumn scene. Yeats describes his surroundings and the time of year. It is a dry October day and the trees in Coole Park are covered with multicoloured leaves. The water is still and reflects a likewise still sky, signifying that this is a beautiful, calm, peaceful place. The last two lines of the stanza introduce the swans that are sitting upon the water.

STANZA 2

It is nineteen years since Yeats first visited the park and saw the swans upon the lake. On that first visit he attempted to count the number of swans: 'The nineteenth autumn has come upon me / Since I first made my count'. He remembers how the swans flew into the air before he could finish counting them: 'I saw, before I had well finished, / All suddenly mount'. The strength and power of the swans is suggested by the poet's description of them flying away. Their wings flapped so powerfully that they made a 'clamourous' or noisy sound.

STANZA 3

The poet admires the swans, calling them 'brilliant creatures'. But the sight of their beauty makes him feel sad: 'I have looked upon these brilliant creatures, / And now my heart is sore'. He is sad because his life has changed so much since he first saw the swans nineteen years ago, when a much younger man. Back then he 'Trod with a lighter tread'. His body was youthful and his life was more carefree.

STANZA 4

Yeats speaks further about the swans:

- They are 'Unwearied still'. The swans still have the strength to 'climb' powerfully into the air like they did when the poet first saw them nineteen years ago.
- Yeats says that the swans' hearts 'have not grown old'. Their lives are still full of passion and adventure: 'Passion or conquest ... Attend upon them still'.
- The swans are not alone. They travel in pairs: 'lover by lover'. The streams they paddle in are companionable because they are so full with other swans.
- The swans are free to fly anywhere they please. As Yeats puts it they can 'wander where they will'.

STANZA 5

For the moment the swans are swimming peacefully on the lake in Coole Park. Yeats admires the mystery and beauty of these creatures. But he knows that sooner or later they will fly away. He will wake up one morning and they will be gone. He wonders where the swans will build their nests once they leave Coole Park: 'Among what rushes will they build / By what lake's edge or pool'. Wherever they go they will bring pleasure to those who see them. They will 'Delight men's eyes'.

THEMES

Growing older

In this poem Yeats is preoccupied with growing older. He is struck by the fact that nineteen years of his life have rushed by since he first saw the swans. He is no longer as youthful and carefree as he used to be. He is weighed down by the cares of middle age and no longer walks with the 'lighter tread' of youth. The setting of the poem in autumn is significant, as the poet is in the 'autumn' stage of his life. In the nineteen years since Yeats first saw the swans he has grown older while they seem not to have changed at all. Their bodies are 'Unwearied', and their hearts 'have not grown cold'. They are still filled with 'Passion' and a longing for adventure. As a middle-aged man Yeats feels passion and adventure are no longer a big part of his life. Soon passion and adventure will leave his life completely, just as the swans will fly away from the lake at Coole.

The beauty and mystery of nature

The poet describes the peaceful, still atmosphere of Coole Park, with its trees and tranquil lakes. He also praises the majestic and inspirational beauty of the swans. He regards them as graceful and elegant, but also powerful and strong as they suddenly take to the air.

The swans as symbols of the eternal

Thought it is obvious that the swans that Yeats observes in the first stanza are not the swans counted nineteen years previous, they come to be one and the same for the poet. They are indistinguishable from each other because Yeats observes something timeless in them, the permanent presence of beauty. The swans, therefore, come to symbolise that which is eternal. In contrast, the autumnal surroundings symbolise the temporal – that which is prone to decay. The poet is very much part of this world.

The swans offer him a glimpse of that which lies beyond the world of mortality. Yeats is both fascinated and envious of what he sees within the swans. Though they are beautiful and 'brilliant', their unchanging form can only remind him of what he is losing and has already lost. It is interesting to compare this poem with 'Sailing to Byzantium' in which the

An Irish Airman Forsees His Death

poet once again deals with the issues of growing old and change. However, in place of the swans the poet uses the colder, lifeless gold mosaics of Byzantium to symbolise perfection and immutability.

BACKGROUND AND INTRODUCTION

This poem was inspired by Major Robert Gregory, an Irish friend of Yeats who fought with the British Royal Flying Corps in World War One. In the war he flew on many missions against the Germans. He was shot down and killed in 1918.

LINE BY LINE

The airman knows he will die in battle: ' I know that I will meet my fate'. He knows that his plane will be shot down 'somewhere among the clouds above'. Though the airman has a premonition he will die in combat he still volunteers to fight. Why does he make this seemingly suicidal choice?

The airman did not volunteer because he hates the Germans: 'Those that I fight I do not hate'.

He did not volunteer because he loves the British people and wants to protect them from their enemies: 'Those that I guard I do not love'.

He did not volunteer in order to help his own people, the poor folk of Kiltartan in Co. Galway. He knows that the result of the war will make no difference to them and to the rest of the Irish nation.

He did not volunteer out of a sense of 'duty'. As an Irish person he did not feel he it was his moral duty to fight for England.

He did not volunteer because he was required to do so by 'law'. As an Irish person the airman was not legally obliged to join the British army.

He was not motivated to volunteer by the speeches of politicians ('public men') nor by the patriotic cheering of the crowds that listened to them.

Instead, the airman was driven to volunteer by an 'impulse of delight'. He takes great pleasure and 'delight' from going on missions, from soaring above the clouds and risking his life in the chaotic 'tumult' of battles with the enemy. The airman, it seems, joined the Flying Corps simply in order to experience the thrill of flying and the excitement of aerial combat.

The airman, then, comes across as what today we would call a 'thrill-seeker' or an 'adrenaline-junkie'.

The airman says it was a 'lonely impulse' that drove him to join the Flying Corps. It has been argued that this relates to the act of flying itself, that the airman feels a strange kind of 'lonely delight' when he's isolated in the cockpit of his plane with the world and its troubles hundreds of feet below him. This phrase also suggests that the 'impulse' driving the airman to volunteer is different from those that motivate his fellow soldiers. They fight for the reasons mentioned above while he fights for the thrill of it.

This 'lonely' impulse may also refer to the airman's bleak and depressing view of life. The airman says he has rationally and logically examined every aspect of his life, weighing up the pros and cons of living: 'I balanced all / brought all to mind'. He concludes that life is meaningless and futile, that both his past and future years are no more than a pointless 'waste of breath':

The years to come seem waste of breath,
A waste of breath the years behind

This sad or 'lonely' conclusion impels into the air where he will meet his death. Despite his premonition that he will die he ventures into battle, as if he longs to terminate this meaningless existence: 'In balance with this life, this death'.

THEMES

A bleak view of life

The airman has a very negative view of life. He has carefully weighed up or 'balanced' every aspect of his existence and decided that the whole thing is a pointless 'waste of breath'. It is unsurprising that he describes himself being driven by a 'lonely impulse', given his depressing outlook on life. The airman knows that he will 'meet his fate' in battle but continues to fly, as if he longs to die and leave this dreary and pointless life behind. The airman, then, could be described as having 'suicidal tendencies' or a 'death wish'.

The airman takes 'delight' in the thrill and 'tumult' of aerial combat but finds the rest of life a 'waste of breath'. Like participants in various 'extreme sports' he takes 'delight' and pleasure in risking his life. It's as if he only feels alive when he is involved in the chaos and 'tumult' of battle above the clouds. He would rather die, therefore, than stop flying into combat. He will fly to meet his fate rather than remain on the ground.

The airman seems to view death in aerial combat as a fitting or appropriate end to the life he has lived: 'In balance with this life / This death'. This line is open to a number of interpretations. Perhaps the airman feels that going down in a blaze of glory will 'balance out' or make up for the pointless waste of breath that was his life. It is also possible that the airman wants to die in aerial combat because that was the only place he truly felt alive. Such a death, therefore, would be a 'balanced' or appropriate conclusion to his life.

Many readers have taken issue with the poems contemptuous disdain for everyday life. To the airman life is only worth living when it's at its most intense. Ordinary life seems to him a stale, pointless routine. The things that dominate the average existence, working, falling in love, rearing children, seem to have no appeal for him. Can we endorse the airman's verdict that these things represent no more than 'waste of breath'? Can we agree with this out-of-hand dismissal of the trials and joys of everyday existence? Or can we reject his view of life as that of a 'lonely' individual whose only relief from depression comes in the thick of aerial combat?

A lonely impulse: Yeats and men of action

In many of his poems Yeats reveals a complex attitude to those who risked their lives in combat or sacrificed themselves for a cause. On one hand he clearly admired these 'men of action'. It is tempting to suggest that he also admires or approves of the attitude articulated by the airman. The airman is a man of action who takes 'delight' in braving the tumult of aerial combat. His 'lonely impulse of delight' separates him from the average soldier, making him superior to those who volunteer because of laws, public men or cheering crowds. His suicidal insistence on fighting despite his premonition of death is presented as something rational. The airman has assessed his life and found it pointless. Therefore despite his premonition of his death he ventures into battle.

Yet it would be wrong to say that Yeats presents the airman's actions as completely logical or rational. There is also a sense in which the airman is depicted as a kind of addict whose craving for the thrill of aerial combat forces him into the clouds, despite his knowledge that he 'will meet his fate' among them. It could be argued that he is 'driven' to keep flying by this 'impulse' as much as he is by rational decisions. His almost suicidal behaviour is as reckless and impulsive as it is logical.

Yeats, then, depicts the airman not only as brave and admirable but also as reckless, impulsive and perhaps even a little crazy. This echoes his presentation of 'men of action' in 'September 1913' and 'Easter 1916'. 'September 1913', while it praises the courage of past Irish leaders, suggests there was an element of 'delirium', of delusion or madness, in their extreme willingness to lay down their lives for their cause. Similarly, 'Easter 1916' praises the bravery of Pearse and MacDonagh but acknowledges that there was something 'terrible' about their self-sacrifice. Yeats, it could be said, regards the airman's decision to fly to his death as an act of a similar 'terrible beauty'.

Easter 1916

INTRODUCTION

The Rising

On 24 April 1916 a group of about 700 republicans began a rebellion. England had gone to war with Germany and the republicans felt that this would be a good time to strike. Wolfe Tone had once stated that 'England's difficulty is Ireland's opportunity', and those involved in the rebellion thought that England would be unable to deal with an Irish uprising whilst fighting the Germans.

It was decided that a number of strategic points would be occupied in Dublin. The General Post Office was seen as a valuable post and so a squad of republican soldiers took over the building. They held on amidst heavy gunfire for a number of days before finally surrendering. Those not killed were taken prisoner. Fifteen rebel leaders were later executed for their involvement. The rebellion became known as the 'Easter Rising'.

Yeats' response

Yeats, who was in London at the time, suffered a mixture of emotions when he heard of the happenings. Initially, he was a little put out that he had not been consulted before the event. He said that when he heard the news of the Rising he 'fretted somewhat that [he] had not been consulted, had been left in ignorance of what was afoot'.

However, the greatest difficulty for the poet lay in understanding the event in terms of his own beliefs and convictions. The very people he had derided in 'September 1913' for their lack of passion had just died for a cause. But Yeats could not simply condone and celebrate armed nationalism. Though he celebrated the actions of the heroic figures of the past, he did not advocate violence as a solution to Ireland's difficulties in his own time. His personal devotion was to the resurgence and regeneration of cultural nationality. 'Easter 1916', therefore, documents Yeats' difficulty in appropriating and understanding the heroic deeds and terrible deaths of men and women he knew.

LINE BY LINE

SECTION 1

The poem begins with Yeats recounting how he used to meet those involved in the Rising before it took place. He would meet them as they came from their various places of work in the evening. Their faces are described as 'vivid', in stark contrast to the 'grey/ Eighteenth-century houses'. Perhaps the contrast is intended to highlight the difference between the reserved, dignified aristocratic world that Yeats so admired and the modern, brash group of political activists that he despised.

It is clear from the first section of the poem how little the poet thought of these people. He knew some of them, and we can be sure that many knew him. But his attitude towards them is one of polite tolerance. As he passed them he would 'nod' his head or say something polite and meaningless. Sometimes they would stop and a conversation would take place. Even as he would be speaking to them he would be thinking about a 'mocking tale or a gibe' to tell his friends 'at the club'.

Yeats justifies his attitude at the time by saying that he was sure Ireland was a place of farce, a place 'where motley' was worn. Motley means a varied mixture of colour and traditionally refers to the style of clothes worn by jesters. So Yeats considered Ireland to be a ridiculous place at the time, much in keeping with the description he gives in 'September 1913'.

The final two lines of the opening section recur throughout the poem as a refrain. The events of Easter 1916 changed everything: 'All changed, changed utterly:/ A terrible beauty is born'. Out of the blue, the very people he had mocked and thought ridiculous have undertaken to rise up in arms against the British occupiers. Not only that but many have been shot for their part in the Rising. Having disregarded the Ireland of his times as unheroic, more concerned with materialism and blind adherence to the teachings of the Catholic Church than with greatness and individual exception, Yeats is forced to acknowledge that something of the bravery that he saw existing only in the legends of the past, resting in the graves of Wolfe Tone and John O'Leary, was all the while present in some of his contemporaries. The very men he used to pass every day in the street have resurrected the 'Romantic Ireland' that he spoke of in 'September 1913'.

But the 'beauty' of this re-emergence of heroism is tempered by the 'terrible' reality of blood-loss and death. Some of those who rose up so magnanimously to fight for Ireland's freedom have been executed. The principle of the Rising is beautiful – it is a tale of heroism and Romanticism. However, it is much easier to celebrate such activity when the characters involved are far removed from you in time. Having to face the fact that men that you passed in the street only weeks before have been brutally executed is much harder to idealise. The oxymoron 'terrible beauty' is Yeats' effort to personally reconcile these two factors of the Rising.

SECTION 2

In the second section of the poem Yeats describes some of those that took part in the Rising, people that he would have known. He begins with a woman who was a close acquaintance of his:

That woman's days were spent
In ignorant good-will

The first person that Yeats mentions is Constance Gore-Booth (or Constance Markiewicz after she married the Polish Count Casimir Markiewicz in 1900). Yeats' description of Constance is not flattering, at least not initially so (for a broader analysis of Yeats' view of Constance and her sister Eva read 'In Memory of Eva Gore-Booth and Con Markiewicz'). He believes that her intentions were good, if misguided. The word 'ignorant' is a harsh appraisal of her understanding of the political issues to which she devoted her life. Her defence of these issues, experienced by the poet no doubt on many an evening spent in her company at Lissadell, is also belittled. Her 'nights', he says, were spent 'in argument/ Until her voce grew shrill'. It is the word 'shrill' that is particularly unflattering, suggesting as it does that Constance had little self-possession in argument, being reduced to hysteria in an attempt to get her views across. Yeats does not pull punches in his appraisal of the 'woman's' role in Irish political affairs.

But on the other hand 'What voice more sweet than hers', he muses, 'When young and beautiful/ She road to harriers?' Yeats was much taken by both Lissadell, the Gore-Booth's impressive family estate in Sligo, and the two 'beautiful' daughters who resided there when he first visited. Lissadell offered him a wonderful example of the aristocratic lifestyle that he so admired, with its social stability, style and elegance. However, Constance's active role in the mire of

militant Irish nationalism did not sit well with the ideal picture that Yeats carried in his mind. Had she stayed riding horses on her estate he would, no doubt, have been more pleased. He would have preferred her to remain a symbol of beauty, like the swans who settled in the waters of the estate year after year.

This man had kept a school
And rode our winged horse

This man was Pádraig Pearse. Yeats refers to the fact that Pearse had run a school and also wrote poetry: 'And rode our winged horse'. The 'winged horse' is Pegasus, a mythical figure that represents poetry.

This other his helper and friend
Was coming into his force;
He might have won fame in the end,
So sensitive his nature seemed

Yeats is referring to Thomas MacDonagh, who was also a poet and dramatist. He taught English Literature in University College Dublin. Yeats obviously felt that MacDonagh was on the verge of becoming a significant writer. He was 'coming into his force'. Yeats reckons 'He might have won fame in the end' for his writing. He is described as 'sensitive' and his thought as 'so daring and sweet'. These may be the qualities of good writer. They are not the qualities of man suited to bloody conflict.

This other man I had dreamed
A drunken, vainglorious lout

The final person that Yeats describes is John MacBride. Yeats, who was infatuated with Maud Gonne, never liked John MacBride. Terming him a 'drunken, vainglorious lout' he alludes to MacBride's mistreatment of Maud Gonne and her daughter in lines 33 and 34 where he says that the man did 'most bitter wrong/ To some who are near my heart'. But the key word in Yeats' description of MacBride is the word 'dreamed'. What the poet used to think of the man is irrelevant now. It is as if the poet had 'dreamed' that MacBride was a drunk and a 'lout' because, following his participation in such a momentous event, he, along with all the rest, has 'resigned his part/ In the casual comedy' and been 'changed', 'Transformed utterly' into something else.

The poet's description of life in Ireland as 'the casual comedy' takes us back to the first section of the poem where Yeats says that he was once sure that Ireland was a place where 'motley is worn'. What line 37 suggests however is that Ireland is still such a place. It is only that these people can no longer be considered a part of it. Ireland has not 'Transformed utterly' because of the Rising, only the individuals who sacrificed their lives for Ireland's freedom. In a country that he otherwise considered ridiculous these individuals have produced something amazing and terrible.

SECTION 3

In the third section of the poem Yeats analyses the mentality of those who are willing to lay down their lives for a single cause. Those who commit their lives to 'one purpose alone' are like stones that 'trouble the living stream'. Such people stand in opposition to one of the principle facts of life, the fact that everything changes. The hearts of such people, he feels, have been 'Enchanted to a stone', remaining unchanged 'Through summer and winter'. To be devoted exclusively to 'one purpose alone', Yeats suggests, is to be bewitched by something.

The 'living stream' metaphorically represents the flux of life. Its flowing waters mean that it is impossible for the stream to ever remain the same. If life is a process of continual change then the stone stands in conflict with it.

Lines 45 to 54 are dynamic and full of constant movement and change. The poet considers the horse and rider 'that [come] from the road' at the same time as 'birds' fly between clouds that are themselves 'tumbling' and changing 'Minute by minute'. Interlinking the elements of the scene, Yeats considers the cloud's shadow 'on the stream' and how it too 'Changes minute by minute'. Further extending the dynamism of the whole scene the poet considers the horses movement from the road to the stream describing the 'horse-hoof' as it 'slides on the brim' before the horse is immersed and splashing the water.

This image of the horse as its hoofs 'plashes within' the stream illustrates the turbulent nature of life. Adding to the great drama of the scene Yeats describes the 'long-legged moor-hens' diving toward the stream and their 'call' to their partners the 'moor-cocks'. The final description of the 'hens' calling out to the 'moor-cocks' introduces the fundamental need in life for re-generation, the life-continuing act of reproduction. The whole dramatic scene presents us with a spirited and vigorous picture of life. And in the 'midst of all' this lies the stone, immutable and static, stubbornly opposing the natural flow of life.

SECTION 4

Those who devote themselves to one cause seem incapable of engaging with the varied, colourful life described in the third section of the poem. Those who 'sacrifice' the other elements of their lives to some cause will in time 'make a stone of the heart'. Such a heart is closed to the minutiae of life.

Whilst the poet's surprise and shock at the events that have unfolded are apparent in the first three sections of the poem, it is only in the final section that we really get a sense of how this has personally affected him. The third line – 'O when may it suffice?' – is a heartfelt exclamation of sorrow and despair for the blood that has been spilt in the name of Irish freedom. Having celebrated self-sacrifice in the past as something wonderfully heroic, Yeats is suddenly confronted with the stark reality of what this entails. Men he knew have been shot dead. One of those executed for his involvement, James Connolly, had to be shot whilst sitting tied to a chair because a wound in his leg was so badly infected he was unable to stand. When will the sacrifice be deemed sufficient, Yeats asks, for what Ireland desires?

Such a question, the poet feels, is not ours to answer. It is 'Heaven's part' to know when all the sacrifice will 'suffice'. The implication here is that such matters are ultimately out of our hands. Is Yeats saying that human action alone is incapable of bringing about such significant change, that some divinity ultimately dictates when significant social transformations occur? Perhaps he is only saying that it is not our part to know the future, only 'Heaven's'. All we can do is respond to events as they unfold. It is 'our part/ To murmur name upon name'.

The act of murmuring 'name upon name' probably refers to the way those who live keep alive the spirit of the dead by speaking of them. The simile that Yeats uses to illustrate the naming of the dead is particularly tender. Likening those who have died to a child upon whose tired bodies sleep now falls introduces an element of innocence and beauty into the poem.

Yeats appears conscious of the problem of appropriating the deaths of these men in such a manner. Having likened their death to sleep he further considers this comparison, seeks to better understand the true nature of this tragedy. 'What is it but nightfall?' Is it just a case that night has fallen upon these men as sleep falls upon a tired child? 'No, no', the poet says quickly. That is not the case. It seems that Yeats is struggling to comprehend the meaning of their deaths in his own mind, to appropriate them adequately. To say that it is 'but nightfall' would be to soften the cold fact of this tragedy. These men do not sleep. Yeats is unable and unwilling to coat the stark facts of this incident in poetic metaphor. He has to acknowledge the reality.

Having done so the poet considers briefly the possibility that their deaths were in vain. England had, after all, promised to give Home Rule to Ireland once the war (the First World War) was over. Many believed that this was sure to happen though there were also many who remained highly sceptical about England's ability to keep such promises. But this, line 70 suggests, is of minor consideration. These people shared a dream and they died for that dream. We know that much and that is 'enough'. It might have been the great 'love' they held for their cause that 'bewildered them'. It may be that their actions were foolhardy and unnecessary. It may have been that their hearts were 'Enchanted to a stone' by their obsessive, inhuman commitment to a single idea. At this moment in time, the poet acknowledges, all this is possibly irrelevant and speculative.

The only thing the poet knows with any certainty is that these people have left behind their place in the mortal world where such considerations take place and moved into the realm of myth and legend. Yeats names them as he named the great figures in 'September 1913', preserving their names in 'verse', the first time actual names are used in the poem:

MacDonagh and MacBride
And Connolly and Pearse

They have 'resigned' their parts in the 'casual comedy', shrugged off their suits of 'motley', and in so doing have restored the possibility of greatness in Ireland. But they have also exposed the unpleasant reality of heroic violence. However, by the close of the poem, it seems possible for 'green' to be 'worn' again. The country is not entirely kitted out in 'motley'. But the wearing of such 'green' has come at a great and shocking price, a price that is 'terrible'.

THEMES

A change of opinion

In 'Easter 1916' Yeats has to admit that he was wrong to presume that no great acts of selfless heroism were possible in his time because the Irish population in the twentieth century did not have it within them to produce anything great. We can only imagine what a shock it must have been to Yeats when he heard men and women he knew well had just sacrificed themselves for their country and their beliefs. All the more so since he thought them a joke before their involvement in the Rising.

Yeats had observed them in the years prior to the event and thought that there was little substance behind their rhetoric. He had celebrated heroic figures in the past and deemed the contemporary population of Ireland incapable of ever matching the achievements of such people as Wolfe Tone. In 'September 1913' he lamented the fact that Ireland had become a petty bourgeois country more concerned with making money than ever doing anything great. So the first thing that Yeats sets out to do in 'Easter 1916' is to expose how wrong he was to deride these people and expect so little from them. Heroism has come to exist in his own time and he is forced to reassess the very people he once belittled.

Transformation through death

Yeats is quick to realise how those who were involved in the Rising, especially those who lost their lives, can never be thought of in the same way again. They have transformed themselves into legends, heroic figures that will be forever remembered. But only days before the rising, Yeats points out, these were relatively ordinary people with ordinary jobs and ordinary human failings. Con Markiewicz was a fine horse rider but did not impress the poet with her politics. Pearse was a schoolteacher who liked to write poetry. MacBride was, according to the poet, a despicable person who drank too much and mistreated his wife and daughter.

But Yeats might have well have 'dreamed' all this because these details are now somehow insignificant. Each of those named has 'resigned' their 'part/ In the casual comedy' of everyday life. It doesn't matter if they spent the great majority of their lives doing mundane, mediocre, or even despicable things. The final moments of their lives have transfigured each and every one of them. They have left the mortal world and entered the immortal pantheon of legend, taken their places alongside Wolfe Tone and Robert Emmet.

A terrible sacrifice

Yeats understands that this is something significant, even beautiful. But the rising has revealed in stark detail the 'terrible' price that has to be paid for legendary status. And it is not only the price of death. 'Easter 1916' looks closely at the price that such people paid in life. A significant part of the poem considers how those who commit themselves totally to 'one purpose alone' become incapable of appreciating the way in which life is a thing of perpetual change. So even those who have not lost their lives in the rising have still sacrificed an essential part of themselves. They may have written their names into history but they paid a substantial price. Yeats can acknowledge this but he cannot say whether this price was worth paying.

Who were the people Yeats includes in the poem?

Constance Markievicz

Though she was born to and then married into wealth and privilege, Constance was not content to lead an insulated life of luxury. From an early age she had a deep concern for the poor, an attitude probably influenced by her father who was known for his decency as a landlord. Following her marriage Constance settled in Dublin where she developed a reputation as a talented landscape artist and also acted in several plays at the Abbey. Her interest in the struggle for women's rights led to her join Maud Gonne as a member of the revolutionary group, the 'Daughters of Erin'. In 1908 she joined Sinn Féin and the following year she founded Fianna Éireann, the youth movement of the IRB, which was like the boys scouts but with firearms.

Most of the women who took part in the Rising participated as nurses or as messengers between groups. But Countess Markiewicz was second in command at the St Stephen's Green holding. Here she was right in the middle of the fighting and lent her fair share to the resistance, holding out for six days before finally giving up when the British brought a copy of Pearse's surrender order. Following her arrest she was taken to Kilmainham jail where she was placed in solitary confinement. Here she sat in her cell listening to the explosion of the guns as her fellow insurgents were executed. She expected to die herself but her sentence was commuted to life in prison on account of her sex. When told of this she is reported to have said, "I do wish you lot had the decency to shoot me".

Pádraig Pearse

Born in Dublin in 1879, from an early age Pearse was passionate about the Irish language that was in steady decline since the early nineteenth century. In 1898 he joined the Gaelic League, an organisation established in 1893 to encourage Irish people to take pride in their language and culture, and in 1903 he became editor of *An Claidheamh Soluis*, the League's weekly newspaper. He was an avid writer and wrote many articles on politics, education, history, literature and religion. However, he soon began to feel that the League was limited in its ability to influence the Irish population. In 1905 he made a tour of Belgium, studying its systems of education. He was very impressed by the fact that the students were taught to speak both French and Flemish and decided upon his return to open his own bilingual school. This school was called St Enda's and Pearse proved himself to be a gifted teacher, full of passion and zeal, outspoken in his belief that the exam-orientated educational system was a sham. His school was renowned for its informal approach and classes were often held out of doors when the weather allowed, generally with the minimum of supervision. However, the school was never a financial success and though he struggled to keep it in existence, in the years before the Rising Pearse became increasingly more absorbed by the political scene in Ireland.

Similar to Yeats, Pearse was someone who steeped himself in Irish mythology and folklore. His great Irish hero was Cuchulain and he was obsessed by the deeds of the Fianna, leading him to believe, like Yeats, in the existence of an ancient Irish nation, peopled by heroes and warriors. Pearse was known from his college years to be a loner and a bad mixer. He disapproved of alcohol, tobacco and swearing. In the years preceding the Rising he became increasingly convinced that there was no peaceful solution to the Irish problem. Though he was a shy man with a slight stammer, Pearse forced himself to be an effective public speaker. His speeches contained some of the most aggressive sentiments expressed at the time. "Give me a hundred men and I will free Ireland", he claimed. He warned Britain that should its promises not be kept the Irish would 'answer them with violence and the edge of the sword".

Pearse also wrote poetry (it is to this that Yeats refers to when he says that Pearse 'rode our winged horse'. The 'winged horse' is Pegasus, a Greek symbol of poetic vision). In some of these poems he declared his willingness to lay down his life for Ireland's cause. His poem Renunciation composed well before the Rising was planned contains the following lines:

I have turned my face
To this road before me
To the deed that I see
And the death I shall die

Pearse was influenced by many of the people who inspired Yeats, people such as Robert Emmet and Wolfe Tone. But whereas Yeats was only moved to write about them Pearse was moved to exemplify them. Looking to the deeds of Tone and Emmet, Pearse began to glorify militarism and saw bloodshed as a reviving and restoring force. He joined the Irish Volunteers, a militant organisation established in 1913 in response to the establishment in the North of the UVF, a group determined to fight for continued union with Britain at a time when Home Rule for Ireland seemed a strong possibility.

When the Rising was eventually planned Pearse was a key figure, one of five members of the Military Council, the most aggressive faction of the Volunteers. When the supreme leader of the Volunteers, Eoin MacNeill, who was not privy to the Military Council's plans, declared at the last minute his disapproval of the Rising, Pearse was chosen to assume the role of commander-in-chief. It was Pearse who stood on the steps of the GPO after it was successfully occupied and proclaimed the Irish Republic to the small and puzzled crowd that stood before him. It was also Pearse who had to make the final decision to surrender five days later. On the afternoon of Saturday 29 April, knowing that any further resistance would be futile and only result in the loss of more lives, Pearse handed over his sword to General Lowe. Four days later he was sentenced to death and shot.

Thomas MacDonagh

Thomas MacDonagh was born in 1878 in Tipperary. He studied to be a priest at Rockwell College but soon realized that it was not for him and left for France where he began teaching. Like Pearse he was passionate about the Irish language and joined the Gaelic League in 1901. He became a close friend of Pearse around this time, meeting him for the first time in the Aran Islands where both frequently liked to travel. In 1908 he assisted Pearse in the setting up of St Enda's school and taught there when it opened. He was also a poet and a playwright and was beginning to achieve some success in the years before the Rising (his play When the Dawn is Come was produced by the Abbey in 1908 and Metempsychosis by the Theatre of Ireland in 1912). Yeats obviously felt that MacDonagh had potential, describing his 'thought' as 'So daring and sweet'. It is the highest praise given to anyone mentioned in the poem for what they did before the Rising. MacDonagh was executed for his role in the Rising on the same day as Pearse. In a final letter written to his wife a few hours before his death he wrote: 'I am ready to die, and thank God that I am to die for so holy a cause. My country will reward my deed richly. I counted the cost of this, and I am ready to pay it'.

Major John MacBride

John MacBride was born in 1865 in Westport, Co. Mayo. He studied medicine, but gave it up and began working with a chemist firm instead. He joined the IRB and became friends with Michael Cusack, who founded the GAA. In 1896 he travelled to the United States to raise support for IRB and upon his return he emigrated to South Africa. Here he took part in the Boer war (a colonial war in which the Boer's fought the British) where he was commissioned with the rank of major in the Boer army. After the war he travelled to France where he married Maud Gonne. However the marriage soon failed amid accusations of domestic violence and he returned to Dublin. Unlike the other Rising leaders, MacBride was not a member of the Irish Volunteers. Instead, he offered his services to Thomas MacDonagh on the day and was appointed second in command at the Jacob's factory. He was executed in Kilmainham Jail on 5 May 1916.

The Second Coming

LINE BY LINE

LINES 1–8

Yeats wrote 'The Second Coming' in 1919, which was a time of chaos and uncertainty across Europe. The Great War had just ended, leaving devastation in its wake. Many countries were gripped by revolution, economic turmoil and political instability. A vicious flu epidemic was raging across the continent, taking millions of lives. To Yeats it seems like the whole world is falling to pieces: 'Things fall apart, the centre cannot hold'. He claims that anarchy or political chaos is everywhere: 'Mere anarchy is loosed upon the world'.

1919 was also a time of violence. The great slaughter of World War One was barely over when terrible civil wars broke out in Russia and in other eastern countries. Ireland, too, was gripped by war as the IRA fought for independence from British rule. Looking at these events Yeats felt that violence and revolution were about to spread from country to country until the whole of Europe was at war. He uses a wonderful metaphor to describe this, saying that a tide of water reddened by blood is on the rise and will engulf the entire world:

The blood-dimmed tide is loosed, and everywhere
The ceremony of innocence is drowned

This bloody tide, he says, drowns the 'ceremony of innocence'. Here Yeats is not referring not to a specific ceremony (for example marriage or baptism). Instead, he has in mind a ceremonial, orderly, perhaps even aristocratic, life-style. According to the poet, this was the type of life-style that produced innocence, nobility and dignity. However, the chaos and violence that are 'everywhere' make this way of life impossible. Yeats' final complaint is that evil men seem to be full of strength, energy, and a sense of purpose. Good men, on the other hand, lack these qualities: 'The best lack all conviction, while the worst / are full of passionate intensity'.

The poem's opening lines are a metaphor for this chaos that has gripped the world. Yeats depicts a falcon is soaring into the air, spiralling upwards and outwards away from the falconer's hand. Its flight path forms the shape of a 'gyre', or upside down cone: 'Turning and turning in the widening gyre'. As the falcon wheels further away from the falconer it can no hear longer his commands: 'The falcon cannot hear the falconer'. Yeats believes that world events, like the falcon, are spinning out of control.

LINES 9–22

Yeats suggests that these outbreaks of violence and chaos are omens of an impending apocalypse: 'Surely some revelation is at hand / Surely the Second Coming is at hand'. (In the Bible the Book of Revelation and the second Coming are associated with the end oft eh world|). No sooner has Yeats considered the notion of the second coming, than he experiences a supernatural vision:

The Second Coming! Hardly are these words out
When a vast image out of Spiritus Mundi
Troubles my sight

Yeats says his vision comes from Spiritus Mundi, which he believed was a set of mystical mental images experienced by prophets when they went into a trance-like state. The vision is quite disturbing. He sees a monster that lives in the desert and is part lion and part human: 'somewhere in sands of the desert/A shape with lion body and the head of a man'. This beast's eyes are terrifying. Yeats uses a wonderful simile to describe them, declaring it has a 'gaze blank and pitiless as the sun' and we can imagine the monster's gaze being as cruel and unforgiving as scorching sun of the desert.

According to Yeats this monster has been sleeping for 'twenty centuries'. or two thousand years. Now, however, this vast creature has woken up and is on the move. Yeats describes it 'moving its slow thighs', moving off slowly but steadily toward its ultimate destination. The monster is surrounded by birds of prey: 'all about it / Reel shadows of the indignant desert birds'. They birds 'reel', suggesting that there is something violent and frenzied about their motion. The birds, it seems, are 'indignant' because they have been disturbed by the monster waking up We can imagine the din of their angry cawing, as they lurch through the air.

Yeats' supernatural vision ends abruptly. The image of the monster is replaced by darkness, like a curtain falling before a stage: 'The darkness drops again'. Yeats, however, has seen enough. He knows the beast's time is coming. Its two thousand year long slumber is at end and it moves toward Bethlehem, where it will enter the world: 'what rough beast, it's hour come round at last / Slouches towards Bethlehem to be born?'

The beast seems to be a 'moving statue' made of stone. It has been dormant and motionless for two thousand years of 'stony sleep'. But now that its time is coming it begins to move, startling the desert birds that have perched on it. The depiction of the beast seems inspired by the statue of the sphinx at Giza in Egypt. Like the sphinx, it exists in the 'sands of the desert' and is part lion, part human.

THEMES

A time of violence

'The Second Coming' is a powerful response to a time of violence and chaos. Everything seems to be falling apart and a the world is drowning in a tide of violence. The poem predicts that even greater destruction is on its way, represented by the pitiless beat that 'slouches toward Bethlehem to be born'. In 1919 Yeats predicts that apocalyptic events are coming and the course of European history in the years afterwards was certainly proved him correct.

In this poem Yeats responds to the dark events of his day, to the tide of violence that seems to be sweeping over the world. A similar response to war and violence is evident 'Politics' and 'The Stare's Nest By Window'. 'The Second Coming' depicts a world where bad men pursue their goals with energy while good men lack the 'conviction' to act. It could be argued that 'September 1913' and 'The Stare's Nest By Window' also depict a situation where 'the worst' are in the ascendant.

'The Second Coming' is also a poem for our times. In our age two it seems that 'things fall apart', that chaos and anarchy are everywhere. Each day the newspapers are so full of reports from 'small wars' around the world that its easy to think we're drowning in a 'blood-dimmed tide'. Watch 'Sky News' for even an hour and it's quite clear that evil is triumphing while good men do nothing. The worst are still 'full of passionate intensity', while the best, unfortunately, still lack all conviction. Given the state of the world today it's easy to think, sometimes, that beast is still out there waiting to be born, and even now it's hour is coming around.

Order and aristocracy

Yeats, it is important to note, was a great believer in the aristocracy. He believed that society should be organised in the traditional way, with the wealthy aristocrats in their mansions ruling over the peasants that worked happily in the fields. We see this in 'Under Ben Bulben' with its peasantry and 'hard-riding country gentlemen'. Yeats valued the aristocratic lifestyle because it was highly civilised, ceremonial and orderly. The mansions of the aristocracy, he believed,

produced goodness, innocence and dignity. His high regard for this lifestyle is evident in 'In Memory of Eva Gore-Booth and Con Markievicz', which praises the aristocratic Gore-Booth sisters and their mansion Lissadell.

However, when he wrote 'The Second Coming' Yeats believed that the aristocratic way of life he loved so much was under threat. Upheavals across Europe, especially the growth of communism, threatened to radically change the structure of society and make the aristocracy a thing of the past. In Ireland, too, the aristocracy were facing extinction. The old Protestant land-owning class, of which Yeats was a part, had seen its power slowly evaporate. The War of Independence against British rule that broke out in 1919 threatened to erode their influence still further. Everywhere Yeats looked he saw the 'ceremony' of the aristocratic lifestyle being swept away: 'Everywhere the ceremony of innocence is drowned'.

The occult

Throughout his life Yeats was intensely interested in the occult and the supernatural. These interests are reflected in 'The Second Coming'. Yeats believed in the occult notion that human history was divided into eras, each lasting roughly two thousand years. Each era ends in great violence, destruction and general mayhem. Our present era is the Christian era, which began with the birth of Christ. Because this about two thousand years old, will soon be extinguished. Like all the other eras it will vanish in a cataclysm of terrible apocalyptic events and be replaced by a new form of civilization. This cataclysm is represented by the beast with its 'slow thighs' and its terrible 'pitiless' gaze.

Yeats' choice of Bethlehem as the beast's birthplace is highly symbolic. Just as Bethlehem was the place where the Christian era began with the birth of Christ, so it is the place where that era will end, with the coming of the beast. This almost blasphemous inversion of the Christmas nativity tale gives the conclusion of the poem real power, real shock value. Many early readers of the poem were horrified at the image of this rough, slouching monstrosity defiling the holy place of Christ's birth.

Yeats, of course, didn't believe that an actual lion with the head of a man was going to suddenly appear in Bethlehem. To him, the beast is a symbol, representing 'laughing, ecstatic destruction'. Its 'birth' can be regarded as a metaphor; symbolising the cataclysmic wave of violence and devastation Yeats believed was due to engulf the world. As we have seen, this apocalyptic series of events would mark the end of the two thousand year old Christian era, and the beginning of a new type of civilization.

In this poem Yeats uses several Biblical references: the second coming, Bethlehem, and revelation. It is important to note, however, that his outlook is not Christian. The apocalyptic event he predicts is not the end of the world as described in the Bible, when Jesus will return to defeat Satan (the beast or antichrist) and judge the living and the dead. Yeats has in mind not the end of the world but the end of a particular phase of human history and the beginning of another.

Yeats' attitude to the beast

Yeats' attitude to the impending catastrophe is somewhat unclear. He certainly presents the beast as being very unpleasant. Yet many readers feel there's a sense in which he actually seems to welcome its approach. Yeats was very unhappy with the current state of what he described as our 'scientific, democratic, fact-accumulating civilization'. Yeats said that the beast represented 'laughing, ecstatic' destruction that would sweep away our tired, worn-out civilisation. He looked forward to the new era the this destruction would usher in. This new era, he felt, would be more in keeping with his own values, being spiritual rather than scientific and aristocratic rather than democratic.

In this poem, as throughout his work, Yeats displays a complex attitude toward violence. On one level he seems to dread the beast and the destruction it represents. A similar dread of war and violence is also evident in 'Politics' and 'The Stare's Nest By My Window'. Yet, as we have seen, there is also a sense in which Yeats seems to welcome the beast's 'ecstatic destruction'. A similar attitude is perhaps evident in 'Easter 1916' and 'An Irish Airman Foresees his Death, where war and violence are depicted as dignified and noble and possess a 'terrible beauty' all of their own.

Sailing to Byzantium

LINE BY LINE

STANZA 1

The poet looks at the country in which he is living and thinks that it is no place for an old man to be. Ireland, he says, is 'no country for old men'. When he thinks of Ireland all he sees are young people enjoying life. Not only that, but it is summer and the natural world that surrounds him is in its prime, full of vitality and life. Everything seems to be at odds with how he feels. There are the young lovers enjoying the pleasures of love for the first time. In the trees the birds are 'at their song'. The rivers are full of salmon, the seas crowded with 'mackerel'. Everywhere he looks, youth abounds.

But the poet, in his old age, is astutely aware of the arc of life. In every living thing, in every generation, there is the seed of death, the inevitability of decline. The young that he sees, the fish and birds, are all mortal beings, moving towards their death.

Of course neither the birds nor the lovers are thinking of death. They are 'Caught in that sensual music' that their healthy condition permits them to enjoy. Their healthy bodies enable them to enjoy the moment in which they are living, undisturbed by thoughts or considerations of mortality. The poet appreciates this and possibly envies this display of sensuality. He acknowledges the vitality of those who 'commend' or endorse the cycle of life.

However, the poet thinks that the young are missing out on something important. Absorbed in their sensual pleasures, they 'neglect/ Monuments of unageing intellect'. These 'Monuments' are works of art. Yeats is fascinated by such works and considers how those in their younger years give no thought to them.

STANZA 2

Yeats thinks about what it is like to be an old man. He says that physically an old man is frail and insubstantial: 'An aged man is but a paltry thing'. Yeats compares such a being to a scarecrow. The flesh of an old man hangs upon his skeleton like the 'tattered coat' of a scarecrow 'upon a stick'.

But an old man does not necessarily need to feel so inconsequential. He is only a paltry thing if he thinks of himself in terms of physical flesh and bone. Yeats thinks instead of the soul, which never ages and weakens. If he uses his 'soul' effectively he need not feel so decrepit and old. As the body ages and withers, Yeats, suggests, the soul ought to celebrate and 'sing': 'Soul clap its hands and sing'.

The 'soul' is the non-physical element of a person that remains untouched and untarnished by the passage of time. Yeats suggests that an old man should allow his soul to 'sing' and express itself. The closer the body comes to death the closer the soul comes to being free.

While the 'soul' is still confined within the body it is possible to enrich it by 'studying/ Monuments of its own magnificence'. These are the works of timeless art alluded to in the opening stanza. Yeats is suggesting that these great works of art are the products of the 'soul', physical examples of 'its own magnificence'.

Because Ireland is 'no country for old men' and because the soul of man needs great attention and instruction, Yeats states that he has 'sailed the seas and come/ To the holy city of Byzantium'. He has left Ireland and all its youthful sensuality and natural vibrancy and travelled to a place where the soul is given more consideration – the ancient city of Byzantium.

STANZA 3

Having moved away from Ireland to the 'holy city of Byzantium', Yeats asks that his physical body be destroyed so that his 'soul' can gain the complete freedom it needs. He contemplates particular piece of Byzantine art, a mosaic depicting a number of 'sages' being burned to death, and prays for assistance. He appeals directly to these wise figures and asks them to come and help him with his plight.

O sages standing in God's holy fire
As in the gold mosaic of a wall,
Come from the holy fire, perne in a gyre,
And be the singing-masters of my soul.

The sages that he sees in the mosaic are concerned only with their souls. They are resigned to having their bodies destroyed because they have a greater belief in the eternal existence of the soul. He, therefore, calls on them to come from the work of art, to travel through time and help him with this matter: 'Come from the holy fire, perne in a gyre,/ And be the singing masters of my soul'. A 'gyre' is spiral or vortex. Yeats uses the word to refer to the distance in time that exists between him and Byzantine sages. To 'perne' means to revolve. He therefore wants the sages to come spinning across this distance in time and save help him.

The poet is no longer interested in the body. He tells us that his heart is 'sick with desire'. He still has the same longings that the young have but he is unable to fulfil them because his heart is 'fastened to a dying animal'. Though he may long for love and love's pleasures, his heart is now trapped within the body of old man and can no longer be fulfilled: 'it knows not what it is'.

Seeing the wise men whose bodies are being burnt away and who are now preserved for eternity in a gold mosaic, Yeats calls on them to travel through time and destroy his 'sick' heart: 'Consume my heart away'. Once this has been achieved the poet will be ready to change form. No longer confined within an ageing body, he will be ready to become part of something artificial and timeless.

STANZA 4

Yeats wishes for his soul to take 'such a form as Grecian goldsmiths make'. Here the poet refers to the goldsmiths of another civilisation renowned for its intellectual and artistic excellence – ancient Greece. Yeats would like his soul to be embodied in some piece of art that is made of 'hammered gold and gold enamelling'. Perhaps the form he takes will be that of a sculpted bird.

In such a form he would continue his role as artist, unaffected by age and the concerns of bodily decrepitude. He would pass his days singing to the 'lords and ladies of Byzantium'. Ironically, having escaped time he will sing to them of just this: 'Of what is past, or passing, or to come'.

THEMES

Youth and old age

The description of Ireland in the first five lines is of a vibrant country, full of life and regeneration. It is, however, 'no country for old men'. The young lovers, in the prime of their lives, cruelly reveal to the poet the shortcomings of his aged body. His body is 'a paltry thing'. Withered with age, his flesh hangs like a 'tattered coat' upon his bones. Whereas the young endorse the mortal body by revealing the pleasures that it can permit the poet reveals the unpleasant fact of the body's decline, the fact that everything that lives must ultimately wither and die.

The 'young' are preoccupied by the 'sensual music' of youth. They are distracted by the temporary physical pleasures of the body and ignore the intellectual pleasures of the mind. The old, in contrast, are excluded from the sensual games of the young and are, therefore, free to enrich their minds with great works of art.

Eternal life

The notion of 'eternity' that Yeats presents in 'Sailing to Byzantium' is not the heavenly, paradisiacal eternity commonly associated with Christianity. Whilst presenting a similar notion of duality as Christianity, Yeats does not believe that the soul returns to heaven when the body dies. Instead, the poem seems to describe something more akin to reincarnation. The poem suggests a belief in some fundamental spirit that will continue to exist after the body has died. However, this spirit or 'soul' never exists as an independent entity, as some spirit that rises to heaven but, rather, moves from one host to another.

The first two lines of the final stanza suggest that Yeats believes he has the power to determine what his next host will be. Once he has been released from the body in which he now finds himself, he 'shall never take' his 'form from any natural thing'. The commendations that the 'young' and the 'birds' provide in the opening stanza for such existence are not enough to entice the poet back into such a form. He would prefer to be part of an eternal piece of art and remain forever free of the ageing process.

The need to tend to the soul

Yeats believed in the necessity of preparing the 'soul' for its existence after death. In 'Sailing to Byzantium' the poet speaks of a 'singing school' for the 'soul' and the 'studying' of 'Monuments of its own magnificence'. Death, he believed, was something to be approached with dignity and it was necessary to be prepared for what comes after. It is the soul that will abide and it is this that requires attention. The body is only a temporary thing that will eventually wither. An old man should not pay much attention to his body and ficus instead on that which is eternal, his soul. He can enrich his soul by considering great works of art. These, Yeats, believes are the product of the soul.

In order for the poet to best enrich his soul, he tells us that he has left Ireland behind and 'come/ To the holy city of Byzantium'. The city of Byzantium represents a place where art is given the consideration and respect it deserves. As such, it is a place for the soul, just as Ireland seems to be a place ideally suited to the youthful. Here Yeats can happily exist for all eternity in the form of a piece of art that never ages.

The Stare's Nest by My Window

BACKGROUND AND INTRODUCTION

This poem was written during the Irish Civil War of 1922–23. The civil war was fought between the 'anti-treaty' side, which was lead by de Valera, and the 'pro-treaty' side, which was lead by Michael Collins. This was a time of great hatred and turmoil in Ireland as former comrades turned against one another other, some opting to follow de Valera while others sticking with Michael Collins. Men who had fought the British side by side now fought and killed each other. Towns, villages and even families were split down the middle as brother turned against brother.

When the Civil War broke out Yeats was staying at his Galway home, Thoor Ballylee, an ancient tower that he and his wife had recently renovated and moved into. For a time Yeats was isolated by the guerrilla warfare that raged in the countryside around him and made travel impossible. This isolation was made worse when the anti-Treaty forces blew up the bridges and blocked the roads in the surrounding area. This cut off the supply of newspapers and the post meaning that Yeats was essentially ignorant of how the war was progressing around the country.

STANZA 1

The opening stanza focuses on Yeats' home of Thoor Ballylee. The tower, it seems, is crumbling a little. Its stonework ('masonry') is 'loosening' and breaking up, leaving gaps or crevices. These holes in the wall have become homes for creatures of the wild. Swarms of bees have chosen some of the crevices as a location for their hives, as a place in which to construct their honeycombs: 'The bees build in the crevices / Of loosening masonry'. Other gaps in the tower's walls have been colonised by birds. The birds have nested in these crevices and their chicks have hatched there. Each day the 'mother birds' bring food back to the tower for their young: 'and there/ The mother birds bring grubs and flies'.

Yet one of the nests in the tower wall has been abandoned. Once a starling (a 'stare') had raised its young there. Now, however, it seems that this family of birds have moved on. The starling's 'house', its nest, is empty. Yeats, it seems, wants a swarm of bees to inhabit this gap in his tower wall. He wants them to construct their honeycombs in the empty crevice where the stare once nested: 'honey bees, / Come build in the empty house of the stare'.

An important feature of this fist stanza is the repetition of the word 'loosening'. We see this in line 2 with its mention of 'loosening masonry' and again in line 3 where Yeats tells us that 'My wall is loosening'. This repetition emphasises the fact that the tower is crumbling somewhat. The poet's home, the walls that protect him from the outside world, aren't as stable or secure as they once were. Surprisingly, however, Yeats seems to welcome this 'loosening' of his defences. He seems happy that nature's creatures have made their homes among the walls' gaps and instead of filling in the crevice where the stare's nest was he calls on the bees to build in it.

STANZAS 2–3

These stanzas create a claustrophobic sense of isolation. The people of the Galway countryside were essentially trapped in their homes by the guerrilla warfare that raged throughout the land: 'We are closed in, and the key is turned'. As we have seen this feeling of being trapped was made worse by the fact that anti-treaty forces barricaded the roads, making travel even more of an impossibility: 'A barricade of stone or wood'. The civil war, then, effectively made Yeats and his neighbours prisoners in their own homes.

They are filled with uncertainty, left unaware of the war's latest developments because of the lack of newspapers and the closing of the roads: 'the key is turned / On our uncertainty'. All they have to go on is vague rumours about the terrible events that are taking place throughout the country: 'somewhere / A man is killed, or a house burned'. Yet they cannot determine with certainty what is going on: 'no clear fact to be discerned'.

These stanzas also provide a moving description of the horrors of war. Death and destruction are everywhere throughout the land: 'A man is killed, or a house burned'.

The brutality of the civil war is indicated by the image of the young soldier's body being dragged down a country road: 'Last night they trundled down the road / The dead young soldier is his blood'. This young man has been stripped of all dignity, his corpse 'trundled' down the road like a sack of grain. (These lines were inspired by an actual incident that took place near Yeats' home in Galway where a young soldier was beaten so badly that his mother could only recover his disembodied head for burial).

In a few short lines, then, Yeats brilliantly captures the brutality and inhumanity of war. Of course the real tragedy in the Civil War is that Irish men were committing these barbarous acts against other Irish men, against people who had been their friends, neighbours and comrades in the struggle against British rule. Stanzas two and three, then, outline 3 negative consequences of the 'fourteen days of civil war'. Firstly it has created a claustrophobic sense of isolation, preventing travel and trapping people in their homes. Secondly, it has created a great sense of dread and uncertainty about present events and about what the future holds. Thirdly (and most importantly) the Civil War has produced terrible acts of violence and inhumanity.

STANZA 4

In this stanza Yeats points out what he sees as the key cause of the Civil War. The Irish people, he believes, have filled their minds with dreams of Irish freedom, with notions of revolution and martyrdom. Yeats uses a wonderful metaphor to describe this, saying that the Irish have fed 'the heart on fantasies'. Overindulging in these notions, he maintains, has poisoned the minds of the Irish people. This 'diet of fantasies' has caused their hearts to become 'brutal', making them bloodthirsty, savage and inhuman: 'the heart's grown brutal from the fare'.

Their brutal hearts cause the soldiers in on both sides of the Civil War to commit terrible acts against their fellow countrymen. Yet is not just the hearts of the soldiers that have become brutal. For during the Civil War years the whole population of Ireland was filled with incredible hostility and anger. Communities and families became bitterly divided, some people pledging allegiance to de Valera and the anti-Treaty forces and others supporting Collins and the pro-Treaty faction. Whereas once the Irish people thrived on friendship, family, and community now they are driven by conflict, bitterness and hatred. Once again the metaphor of 'feeding the heart' is used to describe this. Now that they've become brutal the hearts of the Irish people get their nourishment (their 'substance') from 'enmity' and conflict rather than from love and friendship: 'More substance in our enmities than in our love'.

THEMES

The Horrors of war

'The Stare's Nest By My Window' presents a community and a country that has been shattered by the horrors of war. Barricades and the threat of violence disrupt travel and communication. Death and destruction stalk the country as men are killed and peoples' homes are burned to the ground. The image of the soldier's corpse being dragged down the road provides a haunting insight into the violence that has gripped the land. Importantly he is described as a 'young soldier' for it is one of the greatest horrors of war that it is the young who do most of the killing and dying.

The atmosphere, especially in stanzas two and three, is haunted by the terror and uncertainty that come with war. Caught up in the midst of the conflict the poet and others who live around him have no clear idea of what is going or what the future holds for them and for their country. There is 'no clear fact to be discerned'.

A Diet of fantasies

As we have seen the Irish race have grown addicted to dreams of nationhood, patriotism and martyrdom. Yet these ideas, Yeats claims, are mere 'fantasies'. Irish freedom, he suggests, don't really matter in the greater scheme of things compared to friendship, love and family. The idea that independence is worth killing or dying for is no more than a fantasy or an illusion. The Irish people, however, have fallen under the spell of this illusion and it has made them 'brutal'. Now the notion of freedom means more to them that family, friendship or life itself. Many Irish people are willing to die to defend a particular concept of Irish freedom and are willing to kill those, including their former friends and comrades, who believe in a different concept. Now enmity and conflict nourish their souls rather than love, community and friendship.

The birds and the bees

As we have seen stanzas two, three and four describe the bitterness that has taken root in the Irish heart and the violence and chaos that rage throughout the country. Each stanza, however, concludes with Yeats' plea to the honeybees to 'Come build in the empty house of the stare'. It's as if he is offering the work of the bees could as a cure or antidote to the chaos and violence that each of these stanzas describes so well. We must look to nature, Yeats believes, if we are to reverse the damage that has been done to the soul of the Irish nation.

Whereas the Irish people have become dedicated to destruction, the birds and bees that dwell in the tower walls are dedicated to building and creation. Whereas the Irish people have taken to burning homes down, the birds and bees create them, the birds assembling their nests in the tower's crevices and the bees patiently constructing their honeycombs. The Irish people willfully destroy life. The birds and bees, on the other hand, are dedicated to bringing new life into the world. They create nests and hives for their young to be born into and the mother birds bring food to keep their chicks alive. The challenge for the Irish nation, then, is to follow nature's example. They must turn away from the path of destruction and must begin to rebuild their homes, their shattered country and their trust in one another.

Loosening walls

A new mental attitude is needed if the brutality that has become rooted in the Irish heart is to be removed. The bees building their honeycomb in the tower wall is a symbol for the change of heart that is necessary if the bitterness of the civil war years is to be left behind. The tower, on this reading, serves as a metaphor for the Irish psyche itself.

The honeybees, meanwhile, are a symbol of forgiveness. Just as the tower walls must loosen in order to create the crevices in which the bees can build their honeycomb, so must the Irish psyche 'loosen' in order to create the space for forgiveness to take root.

The Irish people must relax their attitudes of hatred and intolerance, they must re-examine their prejudices and certainties. If they do so there is the possibility that a new attitude of forgiveness will slip into the national psyche just as the bees slip into the tower wall. Forgiveness, the poem suggests, is as sweet as the honeycomb the bees construct and will serve as an antidote to the sour attitudes of hatred that have so gripped the national psyche.

In Memory of Eva Gore-Booth and Con Markiewicz

BACKGROUND AND INTRODUCTION

In 1894 Yeats stayed at Lissadell, the beautiful mansion of the aristocratic Gore-Booth family in Sligo. During his visits, Yeats became friendly with the daughters of the house, Constance and Eva. Yeats was greatly taken with these two fine looking young women, especially Eva. For a while he even considered asking for her hand in marriage.

Yeats was also taken with the aristocratic life-style Lissadell embodied. It was an environment of style and elegance, where art, learning, and new ideas were greatly appreciated. Yeats always looked back on his time at Lissadell with great affection. In 1916, twenty years after his visit, he wrote to Eva: 'Your sister and yourself, two beautiful girls among the great trees of Lissadell, are among the dear memories of my youth'. This poem was written in 1927, just months after the death of Constance. Eva had died the previous year.

LINE BY LINE

LINES 1–20

The opening four lines present us with a golden memory from the poet's youth: a summer evening spent with two beautiful young women in the surroundings of a beautiful house. Evening light was shining through the mansion's 'Great' windows. The elegant sisters were wearing Japanese dresses: 'two girls in silk kimonos'. Though Yeats recognised the beauty of both girls he admired Eva in particular. He describes her as 'a gazelle', a type of small antelope famous for the graceful way it moves.

However the girls' youthful beauty could not last. Just as autumn strips away the foliage of summer, so the passage of time stripped away the sisters' beauty. Yeats argues that their involvement with politics contributed to the decline of their good looks.

Constance fought in the 1916 rising and was 'condemned to death' by the British but was 'pardoned' and eventually released. She remained active in the fight for Irish freedom, taking the losing Anti-Treaty side in the civil war and afterwards serving in the Sinn Féin party. Yeats regarded these later stages of Constance's career as a complete waste of time, believing that she wasted her youth and energy 'Conspiring' with people who were misguided and 'ignorant'. These, he felt, were 'lonely years' because her involvement in revolutionary politics led to the breakdown of her marriage and her separation from her children:

The older is condemned to death,
Pardoned, drags out lonely years
Conspiring among the ignorant.

Eva also became involved in the politics of her day. She eventually moved to London and joined the women's suffrage movement, which campaigned for women's right to vote. She was also committed to social work, and spent much of her time voluntarily helping the poor of London, and campaigning for the rights of trade unions. Yeats attacks what he regards as the vagueness and unrealistic idealism of her goals: 'I know not what the younger dreams – / – Some vague Utopia'. He believes that Eva's political struggles have 'withered' her gazelle-like beauty, leaving her 'old and skeleton-gaunt'.

Lines 14–20 are full of regret. Yeats says he often thought of 'seeking out' the sisters to talk about old times: 'and speak/ Of that old Georgian mansion'. He uses a wonderful metaphor to describe the activity of sharing memories with old friends. To do this, he says, is to mix/Pictures of the mind'. However, we get the impression that he never quite got around to having this wonderful nostalgic conversation with the Gore-Booth sisters. Now they're dead and his chance is gone. Yeats returns to the image of the beautiful girls in their silk kimonos. Though the same words are used, the image now seems tainted with regret and muted sadness at the sisters' decline and death.

LINES 21–30

Yeats speaks to the dead sisters, calling them 'shadows' because they are now only ghosts or memories. He accuses them of 'folly' (silliness, stupidity) for becoming involved in political life, claiming they had no business involving themselves in political 'fights' about right and wrong:

Dear Shadows, now you know it all,
All the folly of a fight
With a common wrong or right.

Yeats seems to be playing on three separate meanings of the word 'common' here. He may be suggesting that political battles are 'common' because they effect the entire community. The sisters, however, should have ignored these communal struggles and focused on their personal battle to retain their innocence and beauty. He may also be suggesting that the world of politics is 'common' in the sense that it is coarse and vulgar and quite unsuited to these beautiful aristocratic women. Finally, he may be suggesting that political struggles are common because they are everyday, endless and gruelling campaigns that wore away their beauty.

By joining these 'common' struggles the girls have made the destructive work of time easier and aided the erosion of their own beauty. Eva's efforts leave her worn out and exhausted; withered like a skeleton. Constance, meanwhile, is reduced to a lonely, ignorant conspirator. Yeats, then, claims that people who are

innocent and beautiful should avoid the common world of politics, suggesting that political struggle will only rob them of these fine qualities. Instead, they should focus on protecting their beauty and their innocence against the ravages of time: 'The innocent and the beautiful / Have no enemy but time'.

Yeats expresses his desire to overcome time itself. He wants to destroy time by setting it on fire with a match: 'Arise and bid me strike a match/And strike another till time catch'. If he's successful, if the blaze (the conflagration) 'climbs' or gets going, he wants the dead girls to tell all the wise men in the afterlife: 'Should the conflagration climb/Run till all the sages know.'

The poem's conclusion deals with the decline of the Irish Protestant landowners, the so-called 'ascendancy' class from which Yeats and the Gore-Booth girls were descended. Yeats believed that this Protestant aristocracy had created a civilisation and culture all of its own. Yet this civilisation was as flimsy and fragile as a gazebo, a small roofed structure that is used for outdoor entertaining and dining. When the Catholic middle-classes came to power after independence from Britain in the 1920s they 'convicted' the ascendancy of guilt, regarding them as little more than collaborators with British oppression. They tore down the ascendancy civilisation as easily as one might a gazebo. (In fact, during the struggle for independence many of their mansions were burned down by the IRA).

LANGUAGE

Sound effects

The music of the poem's opening lines reflects the serenity and grandeur of that long ago evening in Lissadell. Yeats uses assonance to achieve this. In lines one and three, for example, the repetition of the 'i' sound creates a pleasant, euphonious effect: 'The light of evening Lissadell ... two girls in silk kimonos'. A similar word-music is generated by line 2, with its repeated broad vowel sounds: 'Great windows open to the south'. Alliteration also contributes to the harmony of the lines, through the repeated 'l' sound in 'light' and 'Lissadell', and the 'b' sound that's repeated in 'both / Beautiful'.

The slow, stately pace of line 2, courtesy of the proliferation of broad vowel sounds, suggests the majesty and dignity of the Georgian mansion. Lines 5–6, however, shatter this pleasant music. Just as summer gives way to autumn so the soothing music of lines 1–4 gives way to the harsh, cacophonous combination of sounds in lines 5–6. The words 'raving' and 'shears', in particular, contribute to this jarring effect.

Personification

There is an element of personification in lines 5–6: 'But a raving autumn shears/Blossom from the summer's wreath'. Here autumn is depicted almost as a human being, a wild or 'raving' gardener equipped with shears. We can imagine autumn as a violent reaper, stripping away the beautiful flowers and green leaves of summertime.

THEMES

Looking back with nostalgia

'In Memory' is a masterpiece of nostalgia in which Yeats deftly recreates a golden memory from his youth. (It is similar in this regard to 'The Wild Swans at Coole', another poem in which the poet finds himself looking back at an earlier stage in his life). There is something very moving about the poet's declaration that he often thought about 'seeking out' the sisters to reminisce with them about the summer evenings they spent together at Lissadell. Sadly, however, its seems that Yeats left it too late to meet up with the sisters and 'recall / That table and the talk of youth'. Like many of us he was simply too busy to find the time for chatting with old friends.

Old age and time

Like many of Yeats' poems 'In Memory' deals with the theme of old age. It laments how Eva is transformed from a creature of gazelle-like beauty and elegance into a 'withered', 'skeleton-like' old woman. The ravages of old age are also referred to in 'Sailing to Byzantium', which describes an old man as 'tattered coat upon a stick', and in 'An Acre of Grass', which laments how 'the strength of body goes' from the elderly.

Time, Yeats declares, is the enemy of not only of physical beauty but also of innocence. Time's relentless march destroys the innocence and beauty in each of us: 'The innocent and the beautiful / Have no enemy but time'. Yeats, therefore, imagines himself protecting innocence and beauty by destroying time itself. He longs to somehow put a match to time and consume it in a great and climbing 'conflagration'.

The notion of overcoming time, or making it run backwards is one that occurs again and again in Yeats' poetry. We see it in 'Politics', where the poet wishes he could somehow be young again and win the favour of the beautiful girl 'standing there'. It is also evident in 'September 1913' where he imagines the years turning backwards and the heroes of Irish history rising from their graves. In 'The Wild Swans at Coole' time is defeated by the 'unwearied' swans that are depicted as impervious to its effects.

Yeats, of course, doesn't think he can literally set time on fire. The act of putting a match to time is a metaphor for overcoming time's destruction through the power of art. The artist, he believes, can defeat time by recovering an event or person lost in the past – an evening in Lissadell and two girls in silk kimonos, for instance – and preserving it in a piece of art to be enjoyed by future generations. As a poet Yeats can undo the action of time by immortalising, in poetry, the beauty and innocence of the girls. (A similar notion of the 'immortality of art' is explored in 'Sailing to Byzantium').

Women and politics

Yeats decrees that the 'innocent and the beautiful' have no business with the 'common' world of politics. Beautiful aristocratic women like the Gore-Booths have no business intervening in social and political matters. They have their work cut out as it is, guarding their good looks and their innocence against the march of time, a decline involvement in the common world of politics can only accelerate. Political campaigning, the 'fight/With a common wrong or right', can be left to the men and, presumably, to women from a lower social background.

Unsurprisingly many critics find this attitude sexist. Yeats values women like the Gore-Booths for their physical appearance and their 'innocence' rather than for their abilities and achievements. He celebrates Constance's prettiness as a young girl rather than her courage in the 1916 rising or her achievement in becoming one of Europe's first female government ministers. He celebrates Eva's gazelle-like beauty but not the selfless work she did on behalf of London's poor.

Critics argue that not only does Yeats make the sexist claim that beautiful, aristocratic women have no business in politics but that he also unfairly devalues the sisters' social and political energy. He dismisses their political beliefs as the striving for 'Some vague Utopia' and an 'ignorant conspiracy'. By doing so he shows his own ignorance of the good the sisters achieved. He also ignores their determination, their independence of mind and their selfless dedication to the various causes they supported.

An aristocratic outlook

Yeats, it is important to note, was a great believer in the ascendancy or old Protestant aristocracy. He believed that society should be organised in the traditional way, with the wealthy aristocrats in their mansions ruling over the peasants that worked happily in the fields. (We see this in 'Under Ben Bulben' with its peasantry and 'hard-riding country gentlemen'). Yeats valued the aristocratic lifestyle because it was highly civilised, ceremonial and orderly. He valued mansions like Lissadell not only because they were places of beauty and learning but also because they produced people who had goodness, innocence and dignity.

By the time Yeats wrote this poem, however, the ascendancy were no more. Their power waned throughout the nineteenth century and all but disappeared in the new Catholic Ireland that emerged after independence from Britain in 1923. Yeats laments the fact that rich culture and ceremonial lifestyle of the ascendancy has disappeared. (A similar lament is evident in 'The Second Coming', where he complains that 'Everywhere the ceremony of innocence is drowned). He longs to destroy time itself in a great 'conflagration' so that the clock can be turned back and the glory and achievement of this Anglo-Irish class to be restored.

Swift's Epitaph

LINE BY LINE

Jonathan Swift (1667–1745) was a writer, a Protestant clergyman, and, eventually, Dean of St Patrick's Cathedral in Dublin. Swift was born in Dublin but his parents were English. Following his education at Trinity College, he spent a lot of time in England, where he moved in the world of the upper classes. He settled permanently in Dublin in 1714. Like Yeats, Swift had a complex relationship with Ireland. He claimed to hate the country, but devoted a lot of his writing to defending Ireland. In particular he defended the Irish economy, which was being unfairly exploited by the London government. He was also extremely generous to Dublin's poor, to whom he contributed one third of his own small income.

Swift is famous for *Gulliver's Travels* but he was also a poet and one of the greatest prose satirists in the English language. His other well-known works are *The Drapier Letters* and *A Modest Proposal*, where he argues (ironically) that it would make good economic sense for the children of the poor Irish to be raised on farms for consumption on the dinner table of their English masters. Swift implies that this is no more justifiable than the economic system that allowed England to exploit Irish labour and trade.

This poem is Yeats' tribute to Swift. In his middle age Yeats began to regard Swift as one of his most important literary predecessors. There were several reasons for this. Firstly, Yeats was disillusioned with the Catholic middle classes (see 'September 1913') and he identified Swift as a leading example of an alternative Protestant, aristocratic Ireland. Secondly, he saw in Swift the same love/hate relationship he himself experienced with Ireland, and with the Irish people. Finally, he not only admired Swift's skill as a writer, but the courage and tenacity with which his writing opposed greed, stupidity and exploitation. Swift is buried in Saint Patrick's Cathedral, where his epitaph is in Latin. Yeats' poem loosely translates the inscription into English.

The opening line tells us Swift has gone to his rest and reward in the next life, after the struggles of this earthly existence. There, in the next world, he will be relieved from the righteous anger, the 'savage indignation' that prompted him to consistently speak out against the ills of society. His frustration and anger will no longer torment him, will no longer cause his heart to suffer ('lacerate his breast').

In lines four and five Yeats addresses the reader directly, who he describes as 'world-besotted traveller'. We are 'world-besotted' because we are obsessed with the things of this life, for example money, sex, and success. The word 'traveller' reminds us that we are not here forever. It reminds us that we are on a journey through life, a journey that will end when we, like Swift, have sailed into our rest

Yeats concludes this short poem with a challenge to the reader, to us world-besotted travellers. He challenges us to imitate Swift: 'Imitate him if you dare ... he/Served human liberty'. Yeats implies that serving human liberty, as Swift did in his writings, is a risky business. Serving the cause of liberty, Yeats seems to suggest, may bring you only anger, frustration, ingratitude, and the misunderstanding of the public. It will probably leave you with a lacerated breast.

An Acre of Grass

LINE BY LINE

The opening stanza presents a sparse scene. The passing years have whittled the poet's life down until only few details remain. The 'Picture and book' of the first line might refer to the memories the poet is left with. Time and death have removed so much from his world. He is left with an 'acre of grass'. The land he has is no longer for building or planting. It is for 'air and exercise', a prescription for the poet now that his body is weakening. The last two lines of the first stanza are symbolic of the poet's circumstances. It is 'Midnight', the end of the day. There is no more time left, he is 'at life's end'. The house described is just like his own body. It is 'old' and 'nothing stirs'. The 'mouse' represents the meek capacity that remains.

The poet's 'temptation is quiet'. He no longer has the desires and needs of his younger years. It is likely that Yeats is especially referring to sexual temptation. This is no longer a factor in his life. The great concern of the poet is given in lines 9 to 12. With so little time left he cannot wait for casual and undisciplined thought to 'make the truth known'. What the poet desires to know of life will not be given to him by 'loose imagination'. Nor will he access this truth by contemplating the banal details of day-to-day life. Yeats describes the workings of the mind metaphorically as a 'mill' which mechanically processes the unexceptional 'rag and bone' the day delivers. If the poet is going to make headway in his pursuit of truth, something more urgent and drastic is necessary.

Yeats makes an appeal at the beginning of the third stanza. Speaking perhaps to some divine entity, Yeats asks that he be granted 'an old man's frenzy'. Contrary to most who are content to see out their final years with a sound mind and all their faculties intact, the poet wishes to go mad. Such a madness might permit him to see things the rational mind cannot comprehend. Reason imposes shackles on the mind. Yeats wants to be freed of this rigid and orderly thought. Perhaps if the mind is free of rationality it can discover and comprehend the greater truths which otherwise remain hidden.

Whereas in line 13 the poet asks that something intervene and make him mad in his later years, the following lines propose that he must consciously reconstruct or redefine himself if he is to be capable of knowing the truth. He mentions 'Timon' and 'Lear', both Shakespearian characters who rage against old age. Inspiration for change can, therefore, be discovered in great works of art.

He considers modelling himself on 'that William Blake'. Blake, the English poet and artist, believed in the power of the imagination to seek out and discover truth. He famously claimed that if the doors of perception were cleansed everything would appear to man as it is, infinite. Yeats seeks something akin to this, the ability to comprehend the infinite, the ultimate truth which underlies mortal life. According to the poet, Blake had to 'beat upon the wall/ Till Truth obeyed his call'. It seems that it takes some great and frustrating effort to achieve access (rather than copious ingestion of LSD, the preferred method of those in the Sixties who rediscovered Blake's maxim. The American band 'The Doors' subsequently took their name from the quote.).

The necessity to remake the self in order to achieve understanding is most likely derived from the German philosopher Friedrich Nietzsche, with whose work Yeats was quite familiar. Nietzsche believed that it was important to adopt a number of perspectives when seeking to understand something. There is no direct route to knowledge (Nietzsche did not believe that any ultimate truth could be known), but if any satisfactory degree of understanding is to be achieved, a subject should be approached from a variety of angles. Remaking the self, redefining who you are, allows you to see the world in a different way. Yeats believed that this action was both possible and necessary.

The last stanza considers 'A mind Michel Angelo knew'. Michelangelo, the genius of the Renaissance and famous in particular for his statue of David and his painting of the roof of the Sistine Chapel, was much admired by Yeats. The poet obviously believes that Michelangelo possessed the ability to see past the ordinary, to access greater truths. The 'clouds' that are

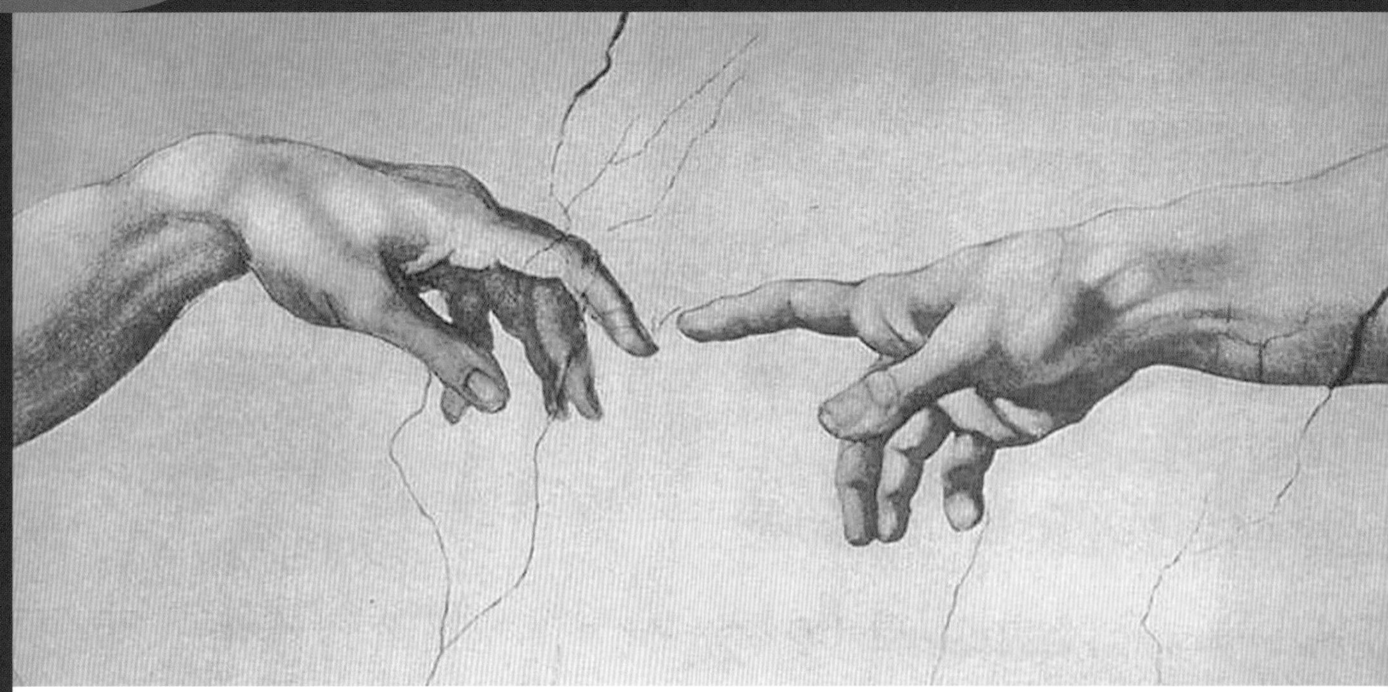

pierced in line 20 are likely a metaphor for that which separates Yeats from the truth he desires.

There is a renewal of spirit and energy in the last two stanzas of the poem. In stark contrast with the lifeless details of the first stanza, the fourth stanza is lively and there is an element of fight apparent in the poet's intentions. He speaks of piercing the clouds and shaking 'the dead in their shrouds'. The poet refuses to be the quiet and dignified old man, serenely seeing out his last years in dignified reserve. Such an existence is fruitless. In the short space left him he desires a 'frenzy' which might permit him to see beyond the normal 'rag and bone'.

from 'Under Ben Bulben'

INTRODUCTION

In 1938 Yeats was seventy-three and understood that he did not have long to live. With such poems as 'Easter 1916' and 'In Memory of Eva Gore-Booth and Con Markiewicz' Yeats had proved himself a great elegist. In the final months of his life he wrote one last elegy, his own. 'Under Ben Bulben' is a richly complex poem that references the central tenets of Yeats' intricate artistic creed. He sweeps through history and reminds us of its cyclical nature with the rise and fall of religions (see 'The Second Coming'). He speaks of the legendary figures from Irish mythology and the early pagan Irish men and women whose tales and beliefs informed his own philosophy and life's work. He assesses death and concludes that it is no big deal, that the soul lives on in many forms and that 'A brief parting from those dear/ Is the worst man has to fear'.

The two sections of the poem that are on the course are the final sections. In the first (Section V) Yeats addresses the poets who will write after he has gone.

LINE BY LINE

PART 5

In this part of 'Under Ben Bulben' Yeats addresses future Irish poets and offers them advice. 'Learn your trade', he tells them. A 'trade' is a job that requires manual skill and special training. The serious poet must understand that poetry is not something to be casually dabbled in; it requires dedication and skill. Considering poetry a 'trade' means that it is a way of life and the poet has a functional and necessary place in society along with other tradesmen. Just as with other trades anyone who undertakes to write poetry must understand how things are done. Yeats strongly believed that order and symmetry were essential to art from its very inception. In the fourth section of the poem he states that 'Measurement began our might/ Forms a stark Egyptian thought'. Great works of art from the time of the Egyptians have followed certain symmetrical rules. Poets ought to familiarise themselves with the forms of the past and understand the significance of balance and order. Poetry, it seems, is not to be a lawless endeavour open to anyone who cares to put pen to paper. It has an important purpose along with the other arts. The import of art can clearly be seen in the poem 'Sailing to Byzantium'. Great works of art, 'Monuments of unageing intellect' represent and celebrate the soul. The poet and the artist 'Bring the soul of man to God' Yeats tells us in Section IV of 'Under Ben Bulben'.

Not only does Yeats think of poetry as something requiring hard work and skill, he also believes that the poet should deal with specific subjects. Future Irish poets should write about 'whatever is well made'. This is a further expression of his belief in the virtue of 'Measurement' or symmetry. Poets should write about things, perhaps great works of art that possess the sort of balance that Yeats so admired – Michelangelo's painting of the Sistine Chapel was one such work. However, we might also presume from the lines that follow that the poet is speaking about certain people who are 'well made'. It is, however, an unusual term to use for people. Yet the description of the 'sort now growing up' being 'All out of shape' suggests that might be referring to people when he advises poets to write about 'whatever is well made'.

If we understand 'whatever is well-made' to mean individuals who are 'well made' then it seems that modern Irish poets will have to look to the past if they are to find any eligible subjects for their poems. Yeats swiftly sweeps aside the possibility of anyone of substance existing in contemporary Ireland. Those 'now growing up' should be scorned. Lines 4 to 7 offer a devastating assessment of the Irish population. Without exception he considers the Irish to be 'All out of shape from toe to top'. And not only does the line state that everybody is 'out of shape' but that every part of everybody is in bad shape.

Yeats is not referring to the modern rise in obesity. However, the line does seem to be about the actual physical appearance of the population and is in keeping with the poet's appreciation of beauty. He placed a very high value on beauty and celebrated its presence in those close to him, mourning its demise at the hands of time. In the poem 'In Memory of Eva Gore-Booth and Con Markiewicz' the word 'beautiful' recurs throughout constantly bringing the reader's attention back to what the poet perceives as the women's finest quality, their physical beauty. Line 4 thus seems to suggest that such beauty is no longer to be found in Ireland.

The fifth line of the poem further criticises the Irish of modern times. Yeats says that their 'hearts and heads' are 'unremembering'. By this he might mean that the Irish no longer remember or hold dear the great heroes of the past. These would be people like Wolfe Tone and Robert Emmet, those that he mentions in September 1913. Yet he might now also include people like Pádraig Pearse and Thomas MacDonagh in this illustrious list considering the belief expressed in 'Easter 1916' that such men as these had 'resigned' their parts in the 'comedy' that was Irish life. Yeats believed that the remembrance of great men was essential for the possibility of greatness recurring in modern times. Only by understanding the heroes of the past and by attempting to ___ them could we ensure the continuing existence of greatness. Line 5 suggests that people in modern Ireland no longer have any knowledge or understanding of past greatness. They are consumed by their own petty interests and have no time for the great events of the past.

Line 6 provides a particularly devastating description of those now 'growing up'. They are, each and every one, 'Base-born products of base beds'. People nowadays are made up of 'base' material. The word 'base', often used to refer to non-precious metals, has in the past been associated with people of low social class. Yet the poet uses it in the sense that it means immoral and unprincipled. Yeats repeats the word twice in the fifth line. The Irish of modern times because they have no understanding of greatness are shallow and ignoble ('base-born') and they are this way precisely because of the previous generation's lack of nobility or integrity. They are the 'products of base beds'. The word 'beds' suggests flowerbeds. So the modern Irish population have sprung up from unhealthily shallow or inferior 'beds' or parentage.

Yeats insists that such people now inhabiting the country should be scorned by modern poets. In their place he suggests a list of people they ought to consider in their place. Write about the 'peasantry', he says. These are given pride of place at the top of the list. Yeats doesn't ever say why the 'peasantry', or any of those he mentions for that matter, are so worthy of consideration. What is apparent from those he mentions is a regard for clear class structure. The Irish peasants of centuries past were much admired by Yeats because they preserved the myths and legends he so cherished. But the hard-working peasant also importantly facilitated the privileged lifestyle of those he mentions next, the 'Hard-riding country gentlemen'.

Yeats was anything but impressed with the middle class mentality that held sway in the twentieth century. In 'September 1913' he speaks bitterly of the middle class preoccupation with money and their blind allegiance to the dictates of the Catholic Church. What he perceived was a high level of mediocrity, a country in which conformity was valued over exception. What Yeats really appreciated was the class structures that existed in previous centuries when rich landowners lived on great sprawling estates worked by families of peasants. In such a world of clear class division a clear understanding of place and purpose was maintained. The peasants worked the land and maintained a rich folk culture that kept alive a strong tradition of myth and legend. On the other hand there were the rich aristocrats who had the leisure and the money to be grand patrons of the art. They invested in buildings and works of magnificence. They were well disposed towards pampering poets if they so wished, giving them the time and space to compose their works. Coole Park was such a place for Yeats and Lady Gregory, its owner, was a good friend and benefactor. However, once this class order began to disappear at the end of the nineteenth century and the new middle classes began to rise, Yeats felt that an ideal form of society was being replaced by a society of little value and worth. The loss of the peasantry meant the loss of a great Irish tradition, along with its language, stories and songs. The loss of the aristocracy meant the loss of patronage, of grandeur and class. Yeats calls on Irish poets to look back upon these kinds of people and celebrate them in poems.

Whereas Yeats was critical of the Catholic Church and those it influenced he had a different view of the 'monks' that lived in Ireland hundreds of years ago. He calls on Irish poets to 'sing' the 'holiness of monks', those austere, devoted men who were responsible for such fine manuscripts as The Book of Kells. And then there is the jovial drunkard with his bawdy humour. Porter is a dark brown bitter beer popular in Ireland up to the twentieth century. The characters that Yeats lists in lines 7 to 10 are what we might call a 'romantic' bunch. They hark back to times past, to times the poet thought ideal. These are robust, colourful characters, each having their own defined place and purpose in an ordered society. Yeats intends them to be contrasted with the 'sort now growing up', the unromantic middle-classes, where everybody conforms to be alike.

The poet finally calls to mind the 'lords and ladies' who were 'beaten into clay' over the course of 'seven heroic centuries'. Yeats is alluding here to the Irish landowners, the original aristocracy, who throughout the course of many centuries were beaten off their land by invaders. He is especially referring here to the Cromwellian plantations of the seventeenth century when the English drove the Irish landowners from their land and 'planted' English settlers in their place. Yeats calls on poets to look back upon these 'heroic' centuries of conflict when the Irish struggled to fight their oppressors and produced great men like Wolfe Tone. Only by contemplating the greatness of the past can we hope to bring about greatness in the future. Yeats saw modern Ireland as a mediocre place where no exceptional men or women lived. If the coming poets are to understand what greatness is and thereby inspire something 'heroic' in the modern population they should forget contemporary Ireland and 'Cast [their minds] on other days'. Theirs is an important role in this regard. Yeats suggests that only if the poets in coming times look to the past and keep alive the spirit of greatness that thrived in Ireland throughout so much of its history can the Irish continue to be 'indomitable', i.e., impossible to defeat.

SECTION 6

Ben Bulben, which Yeats so often climbed as a young boy when holidaying in Sligo and which he mentions at the beginning of 'Under Ben Bulben,' provides the point to which the poet's life and work finally return. This cyclic movement is important to Yeats. The final section of the poem can be seen as rounding off his life, bringing it to its meaningful conclusion. The tone and focus is distinctly different from that of the previous section. The lines are spoken in a detached voice, dispassionately stating the location of the poet's grave and the lines of his epitaph. There is a matter-of-factness to them, a lack of sentimentality that is in keeping with the poet's lack of concern about death. He coolly mentions the 'churchyard' where 'Yeats is laid'. It seems a particularly appropriate place for him to be laid to rest considering the family connection. 'An ancestor was rector there/ Long years ago'. This is a reference to his great-grandfather.

Lines 20 and 21 introduce the conventional Christian symbols of church and cross. However Yeats is by no means suggesting that his will be a conventional Christian ceremony. 'No marble, no conventional phrase' will mark the spot where he rests. He is referring here to the headstone that marks his grave. It will not be like the traditional headstones that contain standard religious sentiments. Yeats' headstone instead shall be of 'limestone quarried near the spot'. And 'By his command these words are cut:

Cast a cold eye
On life, on death.
Horseman, pass by!'

It is interesting that Yeats uses the word 'command'. The word implies importance and power. There might be a link between his choice of wording and certain lines from Shelley's sonnet 'Ozymandias', a poem in which a traveller comes across the remains of a statue of a powerful ruler whilst travelling in the desert. Though only sand remains of the ruler's once great empire, the statue bears the imprint of his personality. Shelley describes the 'cold command' of the statue's face and it interesting how both words occur in the final lines of Yeats' poem. Those who read the poet's epitaph are asked to 'Cast a cold eye/ On life, on death'.

When Yeats says 'Cast a cold eye/ On life, on death' it should not be interpreted in a negative manner. By 'cold' the poet more likely means dispassionate and measured. When considering life and death it is important that we should do so in a balanced, discerning way. A 'cold eye' is capable of acknowledging the natural and the supernatural, the mortal and immortal. Someone properly attuned will not seek to emulate one realm above the other or lose sight of the greater picture by becoming obsessed with a single purpose. Yeats saw how too many people he knew sacrificed their lives for a political cause. They became incapable of detaching themselves from their one goal. As such they became incapable of taking a measured view of life.

The 'Horseman' mentioned in the last line might be some ghostly rider derived from ancient Irish myth, one of the horsemen of the Sidhe or of Finn. He once wrote that the gods of ancient Ireland still ride the country as of old and Ben Bulben was a place long associated with such figures. Alternatively the 'Horseman' might be one of the 'Hard-riding country gentlemen', a member of the aristocracy that Yeats so admired. Of course Yeats may well be referring to both. 'Swear by those horsemen', he wrote in the first part of 'Under Ben Bulben', ... 'Completeness of their passions won;/ Now they ride the wintry dawn/ Where Ben Bulben sets the scene'. The poem has come back around to where it began. Only now the poet lies in the ground beneath the mountain he loved. But he does not ask that we stand and mourn his passing, only that we heed his message.

Politics

Politics' was written in May 1938, just eight months before the poet's death. Yeats positioned it as the last poem in his last book of poetry, and in his Collected Poems.

LINE BY LINE

The poet is in the middle of a conversation about the important matters of the day. The discussion focuses on the political situation in Italy, Russia and Spain. In 1938, when Yeats wrote the poem, the situation in each of these countries was very grave as Europe was sliding toward World War Two. Yet the poet cannot focus or 'fix his attention' on these urgent matters. He is distracted by the beauty of a girl who's 'standing there':

How can I, that girl standing there
My attention fix
On Roman or on Russian
Or on Spanish politics?

Yeats is in conversation with two wise, well-informed people. A well-travelled man who 'knows / What he talks about' and a learned politician. They discuss rumours of approaching war ('war's alarms'). The poet realises that these are knowledgeable men whose opinions are to be respected. He accepts that their predictions of approaching war are probably accurate: 'And maybe what they say is true/Of war and war's alarms'

However, Yeats cannot concentrate on the serious and urgent matters they discuss. His thoughts are continually drawn to the beauty of the young girl. He longs to be young once more, so that he could be her lover: 'But would that I were young again/And held her in my arms'.

THEMES

A longing for youth

Like many of Yeats' poems 'Politics' laments the tragedy of old age. The poet is entranced by a beautiful woman but knows he's now to old to ever win her affections. There is real emotion in the poem's final lines, when he wishes that he could somehow be young again and hold her in his arms. The tragic reality, of course, is that is there is no turning back the clock of old age. The poet's desire for youth, and for this beautiful girl, must remain forever thwarted. 'Politics', then, like 'Sailing to Byzantium' and an 'Acre of Grass' movingly depicts the restrictions and frustrations that come with growing older.

Public and private

'Politics' was inspired by an article by Archibald Macleish that criticised Yeats for failing to comment on political issues in his work. Macleish suggested that Yeats was too concerned with 'private' themes, such as love and old age, and didn't write enough about the key 'public' questions of the day such as the impending war in Europe. The poem contrasts a public catastrophe with private suffering. The public catastrophe is that of the impending war. The private suffering is that of the poet, as he endures the anguish of old age and the frustration of thwarted desire.

The poem suggests that this private tragedy is of more significance to Yeats as an artist than the public tragedy of war. He is unable to shift his attention from the beauty of the girl to important political matters. The poem seems to answer Macleish by suggesting that poets are not obliged to write about 'public' matters of national importance. Instead, they should be free to deal with 'private' matters that will eventually affect us all, such as the delight and torture of romance and the decay and indignity of old age

Therefore, although 'Politics' is a relatively simple poem, it raises a number of important questions. Is it self-centred of Yeats as a writer to award more significance to his private anguish than to the looming disaster of war? Is it wrong for the poet or artist to focus on his or her personal relationships and problems when there is so much evil and suffering in the world? On the other hand, however, it is possible to regard Yeats' involvement with themes of the heart as not arising from self-obsession, but from a desire to write about universal human experiences.

YEATS AT A GLANCE

OLD AGE AND DEATH

- In 'Politics' the poet is overcome by the beauty of a girl 'standing there' and longs to be young again.
- In 'The Wild Swans' the poet suddenly realises how age has crept up on him. Standing before a pool in which the apparently timeless swans glide, the poet feels that he no longer threads with the light step of youth.
- In 'Sailing to Byzantium' Yeats considers how his aged body is decrepit, little more than a 'tattered coat upon a stick'. He contrasts his own decaying body with the eternal durability of art.
- In a similar fashion 'An Acre of Grass' contrasts how an artists body grows weaker with age but his mind remains as sharp as ever.
- In 'In Memory of Eva Gore Booth' Yeats laments how old age transformed two beautiful young girls into gaunt and weary old women.
- In 'Under Ben Bulben' the poet describes how he wishes to be buried and remembered after his death.
- In 'An Irish Airman' death is presented as a welcome prospect, a release from the pointless-ness of life.

WAR AND POLITICS

- In 'September 1913' Yeats celebrates the heroes of the past and laments how their legacy has been betrayed by the people of today'
- In 'Easter 1916' Yeats is troubled by the fact that men and women he knew sacrificed their lives for a cause. He realises that he was wrong to think dismiss them as cowardly and ridiculous.
- In 'The Second Coming' he is haunted by the bloodshed and political chaos that seems to be everywhere evident in the world. He laments the fact that evil triumphs while good men do nothing.
- In 'The Stare's Nest' Yeats is troubled by the fanaticism that causes unquestioning devotion to political beliefs.
- In 'Politics', on the other hand, he is distracted from this kind of political concern by a beautiful woman.
- In 'Memory of Eva Gore Booth' the poet presents politics as something that leaves people tired and drained, a pursuit that is unsuitable for certain classes of people.

SAMPLE ANSWERS

EAVAN BOLAND

Write a personal response to the poetry of Eavan Boland.

Introduction

Of all the poets on the Leaving Cert Boland is the one who has most to say about the war, violence and mayhem that has marked the beginning of the twenty-first century. Much of her work is influenced by her desire to confront history in all its misery and darkness: 'out of myth into history I move'. Her work deals compassionately with history's victims, both from the nineteenth-century and from the recent past, while reserving a special place for the sufferings of women. Her poetry, therefore, is particularly suited to the time of global violence in which we live now. Yet she is also a poet of hope, and her work holds out the possibility that history's myriad victims may not have suffered entirely in vain.

History and compassion

One of the things I like most about Boland's poetry is its deep sense of humanity and compassion. Again and again she writes about history's victims. Her work stands as a memorial to those forgotten people who suffered and died because of war, disease and man's inhumanity to his fellow man. Boland's intense sensitivity to the 'evil that men do' is evident in 'The War Horse'. The sight of the horse that has wandered from the 'tinker camp on the Enniskerry road' fills her with dread as her blood becomes 'still / with atavism', and the horse is transformed into a symbol of the violence that filled the world in general and Northern Ireland in particular. The beast 'stumbles on like a rumour of war' through her neighbourhood, reminding her of the 'screamless dead' of Irish history, the forgotten victims of that 'cause ruined before, a world betrayed'.

Ireland's troubled past is also remembered in 'The Famine Road', where Boland remembers the victims of the Great Famine who found work and a little money building roads 'from nowhere, going nowhere'. I liked the way this poem brought the plight of the Famine victims graphically to life. They are presented almost as zombies, as 'Sick' and 'directionless' beings on the verge of cannibalism: 'cunning as housewives, each eyed – / as if at a corner butcher – the other's buttock'. Particularly moving was the account of the worker who becomes sick with a contagious disease. The other workers avoid this 'typhoid pariah' and will not even pray with this poor man as he suffers his death throes. Similarly, in 'Outside History' Boland faces up to the reality that history is a bloody business. With a memorable use of hyperbole she declares that there are as many of its victims buried in the earth as there are stars in the night sky: 'those fields, / those rivers, those roads clotted as / firmaments with the dead'.

'Child of Our Time' is another poem where Boland's immense compassion is evident. Here, she laments the death of a young boy who was killed in the Dublin bombings of 1974. This child should be hearing fairy stories and learning the 'names for the animals you took to bed'. Instead, he has had his maimed body removed from the ruins of a bombed building. What I found almost unbearably moving about this poem was that it forced us to acknowledge the true price of war. It backs the reader into a corner where he or she must realise that war is not a Hollywood movie or video game but a serious business that has 'robbed the cradle' of many a child throughout the world. The poem suggests that 'idle talk' about patriotism, honour and freedom is not worth the life of a single child. This is a poem I would love George Bush to read, as well as all the other world leaders who take their people to war for no good reason.

Women as victims

Yet Boland's compassion is not simply reserved for the victims of major events such as famine and war. I also admired her because she is acutely conscious of the fact that for centuries women have been routinely victimised by a male-dominated society. We get a sense of this awareness in 'The Famine Road', which presents the tragic case of a woman who is unable to have children: 'Barren, never to know the load / of his child in you'. Somehow, however, her situation is made worse by the unsympathetic attitude of the male doctor who brings her this bad news: 'take it well woman, grow / your garden, keep house, good-bye.'

'The Shadow Doll' also presents women as victims of a male-dominated society. Marriage, in this poem, is a tool whereby women are oppressed and controlled by men. In this instance, Boland's compassion is directed toward a young nineteenth-century bride-to-be who seems terrified at the prospect of her upcoming wedding. Boland also depicts the confusion and uncertainty she felt on the night before her own wedding, describing herself as being 'astray among the cards and wedding gifts'. The poem presents marriage as a trap for women, a restrictive force that leaves them 'Under glass, under wraps'. Marriage, the poem implies, transforms women into dolls to be admired and adorned, making them little more than the play-things of their husbands.

A sense of hope?

Yet one of the things that most attracted me to Boland's work is that it is not all doom and gloom. While the poems confront suffering head on, they also offer hope. In 'Child of Our Time', for instance, Boland suggests that we might learn from the death of the young child: 'We ... must learn from you dead'. The child's death must spur us on to abandon the suspicion and hatred of the past, and find some way of living together in harmony and peace. We must give up the deadly 'idle talk' that leads to murder and mayhem, and replace it with 'a new language' of peace. In 'Outside History', too, Boland suggests that it may be possible to do something for the victims of history, to become 'part of that ordeal' which they suffered. She suggests that it may be possible to somehow comfort these victims, to 'kneel beside them, whisper in their ear'.

Ultimately, however, the hope in Boland's poetry is outweighed by the despair. As a logical person, Boland is forced to conclude that there is of course nothing we can do for those who have suffered in the past: 'And we are too late. We are always too late'. While we might long for 'a new language' to prevent such atrocities occurring in the future, it is far from clear what this new language might be.

Conclusion

To me, Boland's poetry represents a fearless confrontation with much of what is wrong with today's world. She is fully willing to acknowledge the suffering and evil that chokes the globe in this day and age. Yet in an important sense, her work represents a triumph over this evil. While we might be 'always too late' to save the victims of history, we are certainly not too late to remember and pay homage to what they endured. By doing so, we might ensure that their suffering was not completely in vain. The poems themselves, therefore, represent a kind of triumph over this forgetfulness, for as long as there are eyes to read, history's victims will survive in Boland's poetry.

T.S. ELIOT

Write about the feelings that T.S. Eliot's poetry creates in you and the aspects of his poetry (content and/or style) that help create those feelings. Support your points by reference to the poetry by T.S. Eliot that you have read.

Reading the poetry of T.S. Eliot left me with mixed feelings. I found the poems very interesting, and though they were difficult at times, I felt rewarded by the challenges they presented. What I loved most about Eliot's poetry was the insight it gave me into other people's lives. In poems such as 'The Love Song of J. Alfred Prufrock', 'Preludes' and 'A Game of Chess', Eliot captures so perfectly the insecurity and despair that people often feel. These poems also show how shallow and artificial society and people can be, thereby forcing the reader to consider and evaluate the world in which they live. I was equally fascinated by 'The Journey of the Magi', a poem that humanises the experiences of the Magi and allows us to sympathise with their uncertainty and doubt as they travelled to witness the birth of Christ. The structure and style of Eliot's poetry was also refreshing and stimulating. 'A Game of Chess', for example, uses a variety of styles to effectively convey different atmospheres and moods. I also loved the way the language of 'Prufrock' illustrates the chaos and complexities of the mind, the stream of consciousness. 'Preludes', too, with its movement between locations and sharp attention to the small details, really captures the mood and atmosphere of the city. However, while I found Eliot's explorations of human doubt and despair and his critique of artificiality to be very thought-provoking and interesting, I felt at times that his work was just simply too bleak. The depiction in 'Preludes' of life in a modern city is unrelentingly grim, and his account of Christianity in 'East Coker' is disturbing and sombre. Eliot's world-view seems entirely negative. His poetry does not allow for hope and happiness.

'The Love Song of J. Alfred Prufrock' is a fascinating study of one man's psychological despair and struggle to act. Composed as a monologue, the poem allows the reader access to another's mind and to see the world through their eyes. The result is intriguing. We witness Prufrock's insecurities: 'They will say: "How his hair is growing thin!"' We are privy to his fears and doubts: 'Should I, after tea and cakes and ices,/ Have the strength to force the moment to its crisis?' At times, Prufrock is filled with self-loathing: 'I should have been a pair of ragged claws/ Scuttling across the floors of silent seas'. 'The Journey of the Magi' offers us a similar insight into human doubt and uncertainty. The magus who speaks in the poem admits that his journey was 'hard', and that they had 'voices singing in [their] ears, saying/ That this was all folly'. Though 'Preludes' does not give us access to a particular person's thoughts, it does convey a sense of the despair that inhabitants of the city feel. Eliot succinctly captures the tortured night that one woman must endure: 'You dozed, and watched the night revealing/ The thousand sordid images/ Of which your soul was constituted'.

'A Game of Chess' illustrates the despair that people can often experience in a relationship. That two people living so close together could become so alienated and lost to one another is a terrible thing. I really felt that Eliot's poem captures the painful isolation and anguish of the characters so perfectly:

'What are you thinking of? What thinking? What?
I never know what you are thinking. Think.'

I think we are in rats' alley
Where the dead men lost their bones.

Reading 'A Game of Chess' made me think about how empty a materialistic life can be. The poem paints a picture of the hollow, artificial world that the characters inhabit. Though they are surrounded by an abundance of art and fancy furnishings, their world is decadent. The artworks that adorn the wall are described as 'withered stumps of time'. Their senses are 'drowned' by 'strange synthetic perfumes'. Their lives have lost all meaning and they don't know what to do: 'What shall we ever do?' Prufrock's world is similarly shallow and meaningless. He wastes his days sipping tea from porcelain cups and doing nothing of any significance. His life has become a tedious routine: 'For I have known them all already, known them all – / Have known the evenings, mornings, afternoons,/ I have measured out my life with coffee spoons'. He speaks of the 'butt-ends' of his 'days and ways' and says that his life is ultimately 'no great matter'. He realises that the world he lives in is superficial, being well aware of the need to 'prepare a face to meet the faces that you meet'.

Both 'Prufrock' and 'A Game of Chess' use very interesting language and styles to convey different moods and settings. The opening section of 'A Game of Chess' is extremely poetic, featuring a great deal of assonance, alliteration and rich, sumptuous imagery. The 'conversation' between the lady and her partner employs a more fragmentary and repetitive style. The jumpy, jagged sentences suggest the couples' disturbed and agitated mental states. The poem's conclusion involves another stylistic shift. The last forty lines are spoken by a woman who uses the everyday speech of the working classes complete with grammatical errors (she says 'them pills' instead of 'those pills'). Her words come across as genuinely conversational, as if we were overhearing her talking to her friends in the pub. 'Prufrock' is also written in a very interesting manner. There seems to be no logic to the structure of the poem, and it surprised and confused me when I read it for the first time. However, as I became more familiar with the poem I began to appreciate how the structure of 'Prufrock' mirrors the movements of the mind. The shifts and jumps that occur in the poem made the character of Prufrock all the more fascinating and real to me.

'Preludes', however, made me feel a terrible sense of despair. The city that the poem describes is incredibly grim. Everything seems to be dirty and broken. The world that Eliot describes is downtrodden and depressing. The rain beats down on 'broken blinds' and the streets are covered in 'grimy scraps/ Of withered leaves'. Those who live in the city lead terribly unhealthy lives. Eliot describes the monotonous routines of the morning:

The morning comes to consciousness
Of faint stale smells of beer
From the sawdust-trampled street
With all its muddy feet that press
To early coffee-stands.

The poem suggests that modern city life is a soulless, dehumanising affair. It is entirely bleak. When the speaker of the poem entertains the possibility of 'some infinitely gentle' God existing behind such a world, he is moved to scorn such a suggestion: 'Wipe your hand across your mouth, and laugh'. Though I felt that Eliot captured the sense of despair that city life can sometimes bring very well, I found the poem to be too bleak. The message seems unrelentingly grim. Everything that exists seems tarnished and ugly. There is no allowance made for beauty or hope. This sense of bleakness is brought to the extreme in 'East Coker' where Eliot seems to revel in painting as grim a picture of our human condition as possible. By the time I had come to the final stanza – where Eliot insists that 'The dripping blood' is 'our only drink' and 'The bloody flesh our only food' – I felt that the poet was no longer describing my world. Poems such as 'Prufrock' and 'A Game of Chess' deal with despair and suffering but they did this in the context of human lives that I could relate to. 'East Coker' contains a religious message that I just cannot stomach.

In conclusion, I want to say that I found reading Eliot's poetry fascinating and insightful. What I loved most about the poems was the insight it gave me into other people's lives. In poems such as 'The Love Song of J. Alfred Prufrock', 'Preludes' and 'A Game of Chess', Eliot captures so perfectly the insecurity and despair that people often feel. These poems also show how shallow and artificial society and people can be, thereby forcing the reader to consider and evaluate the world in which they live. However, I felt that Eliot is just too bleak in his outlook. His poems fail to consider the possibility of hope, beauty or happiness.

PATRICK KAVANAGH

What poems would you include in a book titled* The Essential Kavanagh*? Give reasons for your choice.

I think any book called *Essential Kavanagh* would have to include the following poems: 'A Christmas Childhood','Advent','Canal Bank Walk','The Hospital', 'Lines Written on a Seat on the Grand Canal, Dublin'. For in these works we see the essential features of Kavanagh's poetry: his love of the everyday, his celebration of childhood, and his humour.

Perhaps more than anything, Patrick Kavanagh is a poet of the everyday. What appeals to me, and to many other readers of his work, is the way in which he makes the ordinary seem extraordinary. In 'Advent', he restores our sense of the 'newness' that exists in everyday, boring things if we look at them in the right way: 'the newness that was in every stale thing'. A poem like 'Advent' manages to make the stale things around seem fresh again – even dull things like 'the tedious talking of an old fool'. His work, as he puts it in 'Canal Bank Walk,' manages to 'wallow in the habitual, the banal' as he is thrilled or 'enraptured' by the everyday sights and sounds of the canal.

In these five poems Kavanagh celebrates the dullest and most ordinary things imaginable, things most of us would never look twice at, never mind celebrate in a poem. In 'The Hospital', for instance, he celebrates the 'functional ward / Of a chest hospital'. He says how he 'fell in love' with this dreary building and came to cherish its 'square cubicles in a row'. For him, the hospital's 'gravelled yard' became a place of 'inexhaustible adventure'. 'Lines Written on a Seat on the Grand Canal, Dublin' also celebrates things we would normally describe as dull and industrial. A barge ferrying goods from Athy to Dublin is depicted as carrying a mystical cargo of 'mythologies'.

'Advent' and 'A Christmas Childhood' deal with the 'habitual and banal' in a more rural context, singling out for celebration 'bog-holes, cart tracks, old stables' and the 'tracks of cattle to a drinking-place'. Similarly, 'Canal Bank Walk' celebrates something as simple as a patch of grass, which in the poet's eyes becomes 'fabulous'. Having read these poems, we find ourselves slowing down and taking notice of the things around us – ordinary and simple things that we are all too often in too much of a rush to take in properly.

A number of these poems deal with childhood – another of Kavanagh's essential themes. In Kavanagh's work, childhood is presented as a magical time, a time when everything in the world is filled with wonder. We see this in 'Advent', which refers to the newness that was in every stale thing / When we looked at it as children'. 'A Christmas Childhood' makes a similar point, describing how to a child even something as mundane as frosty potato-pits can seem wonderful: 'How wonderful that was, how wonderful!' It movingly depicts a Christmas morning from Kavanagh's childhood, on which the 'child poet' looks out from the doorway of his family's house and is filled with wonder at the sights and sounds of the surrounding countryside:

In silver the wonder of a Christmas townland
The winking glitter of frosty dawn

Yet these poems also deal with another of Kavanagh's essential themes: the disappearance of this childhood wonder over time as we grow older. To an innocent child, the world seems filled with wonder. Yet as we grow older, 'knowledge' robs us of this childhood innocence, and the world no longer seems such a wondrous place. We see this in 'Advent', where he declares that the 'knowledge' we gain growing up makes the world seem dull and stale:

We have tested and tasted too much, lover –
Through a chink too wide there comes in no wonder

A similar point is made in 'A Christmas Childhood' ,where 'knowledge' of the world makes the poet's childhood innocence and wonder disappear. He is cast out of the 'gay / Garden that was childhood's', just as Adam was cast out of the Garden of Eden. Kavanagh's poetry expresses his desire to rid himself of this grown-up 'knowledge' and to return to a state of childhood innocence. We see this especially in 'Advent', where he declares that 'We have thrown into the dust-bin the clay-minted wages / Of pleasure, knowledge and the conscious hour'. It is also evident in 'Canal Bank Walk', where he expresses his desire to be as he was 'before he grew'.

While these are serious themes, it would be a mistake

to regard Kavanagh as an overly serious poet. One of the things that I and many others really enjoy about his work is his sense of humour, the light-hearted and amusing way in which he deals with deep and weighty topics. This 'lightness of touch' is another essential feature of Kavanagh's work, and one that can be seen in the five poems I have selected.

His humour is especially evident in his use of hyperbole in 'Lines Written on a Seat on the Grand Canal, Dublin'. The sound of the canal's locks opening is compared to the Niagara falls: 'Where by a lock niagorously roars /The falls'. (This line also features a witty neologism, a common feature of Kavanagh's later work.) There is also something humorously hyperbolic about his declaration that everyone who visits the canal bank will find themselves unable to speak in normal prose. Every sentence they utter will be poetic: 'No one will speak in prose / Who finds his way to these Parnassian islands'.

A similar hyperbole is evident when he compares the canal bank to Parnassus, in Greek mythology the home of the muses, and when he describes a patch of grass as 'fabulous' ('Canal Bank Walk'). There is also something light-hearted about his description of the hospital ward as 'an art lover's woe', and the wonderful metaphor he uses to describe the wind in 'Canal Bank Walk'. The breeze, he says, is like a 'third party' intruding on a 'couple kissing on an old seat'.

In conclusion, these five poems show Kavanagh at his best. In them, he deals with the major issues that obsessed him throughout his writing life, but does so with a characteristic lightness of touch. In this small selection of his fine poems, we see Kavanagh record, as he puts it himself, 'love's mystery without claptrap'.

JOHN KEATS

Write an essay on the poetry of John Keats outlining the reasons why it appealed to you.

The poetry of John Keats appealed to this reader for a number of reasons. First of all there is his exquisite descriptions of the natural world. In poems such as 'To Autumn', 'To One Who Has Been Long in City Pent' and 'Ode to a Nightingale', Keats reveals his enormous love of nature, and shows how the natural world can provide a refuge from the trials and tribulations of everyday life and a consolation in times of hardship. What also appealed to me was the sense I got from reading the poems of Keats' own struggles, the hopes, joys and fears that preoccupied him during his life. Poems such as 'On First Looking Into Chapman's Homer', 'When I Have Fears that I May Cease to Be' and 'Ode to a Nightingale' are concerned with themes that are timeless. Through these poems, Keats explores issues of art, time and despair that are of no less significance today than the time in which they were composed. Finally, there is the language. No other poet on the Leaving Cert course came close to the beauty of his lines, the sustained brilliance of his compositions. In this essay I want to look a little closer at the reasons I have just mentioned, and hopefully show why Keats not only appealed to me but why he ought to appeal to anyone who loves great poetry.

The poetry of John Keats contains many wonderful descriptions of nature. To him, the natural world was a thing of infinite wonder and beauty. 'To Autumn' is one of the greatest nature poems. In three stanzas, Keats captures the very essence and beauty of this time of year. Moving from the early phase of the season when everything is ripening and blossoming, through the harvest, to the season's demise, Keats offers the reader a series of rich images that so beautifully encapsulate autumn. Through sumptuous lines of poetry, Keats describes how the season and the sun 'load and bless/ With fruit the vines that round the thatch-eves run', and 'bend with apples the moss'd cottage-trees'. It is the plaintive, melancholic images of the season's end, however, that I found particularly moving and memorable. Without becoming maudlin, the poet describes the season's end, the 'soft-dying day', 'the stubble-plains with rosy hue', the 'willful choir' of gnats that 'mourn/ Among the river sallows, bourne aloft/ Or sinking as the light wind lives or dies'.

In 'To One Who Has Been Long in City Pent' Keats shows how great it can be to get out of the city into the open expanse of the country and appreciate the serenity and wonder of the natural world. "Tis very sweet', he tells us, 'to look into the fair/ And open face of heaven, – to breathe a prayer/ Full in the smile of the blue firmament'. Who can argue with him, even in this modern age of computers and digital technology, that the greatest pleasure is not to be found out in 'some pleasant lair/ Of wavy grass' where we might escape with a 'gentle tale of love and languishment'. In 'Ode to a Nightingale' the poet again reveals the joys of nature, albeit in a less light-hearted manner. Even in a time of great melancholy, however, the poet's spirits are raised immeasurably by the sweet song of the nightingale and the sensual pleasures to be discovered in the flowers and trees that surround ('the coming musk-rose, full of dewy wine'). He tells the bird how he is 'too happy in thine happiness, – / That thou, light-winged Dryad of the trees,/ in some melodious plot/ Of beechen green, and shadows numberless,/ Singest of summer in full-throated ease'.

As much as it might be a wonderful poem about the pleasures of the natural world, 'Ode to a Nightingale' also reveals the rich and complex thoughts that preoccupy the poet, his great longings and his worries. On this summer's eve, the poet's heart is heavy and sad. He claims to be 'half in love with easeful Death', and he longs to 'fade away into the forest dim' with the nightingale. The world to him seems a painful place. Keats speaks of the 'weariness, the fever, and the fret/ Here, where men sit and hear each other groan'. Yet his soul is lifted by thoughts of beauty and art, thoughts of escape into imagination, flight 'on the viewless wings of Poesy'. The poem captures so exquisitely the pains and sorrows of life whilst also revealing the soul of one who still believes in the power of beauty and art. From the beginning, it was poetry and the imagination that inspired Keats. In 'On First Looking Into Chapman's Homer' he describes the incredible joy of discovering a translation of the great poet's work, how he 'felt like some watcher of the skies/ When a new planet swims into his ken'.

In 'When I Have Fears that I May Cease to Be' Keats again addresses issues that are relevant to all who live. He speaks of his great fear of the possibility that he may not achieve his potential; to write all the great poems that he knows he is capable of before he dies:

'When I have fears that I may cease to be/ Before my pen has glean'd my teeming brain'. The poem is a perfect reminder of the instruction to 'seize the day' and 'make hay whilst the sun shines'. Yet Keats is not so self-obsessed that he thinks it is a matter of worldly importance that he achieves his dreams (though we might disagree). By the close of the sonnet, he puts his life in perspective. Standing alone along the shore, he contemplates the vastness of the universe and acknowledges that he is of little significance in the grand scheme of things: 'then on the shore/ Of the wide world I stand alone, and think/ Till love and fame to nothingness do sink'.

In all four poems I have mentioned, there can be found lines of the greatest beauty. And this is the chief reason why any poet appeals to us. His ideas might interest us and we might sympathise with his feelings, but if the poem lacks any discernible poetic quality, it is hardly worth the paper it is written on. With Keats, we might fairly say that few can near him at his very best. Take the lines I alluded to in my discussion of 'To Autumn': 'While barred clouds bloom the soft-dying day,/ And touch the stubble-plains with rosy hue'. As a depiction of an autumn evening it is exquisite. The alliteration of the '*b*'s and '*d*'s in the first line, coupled with the long, plaintive, assonance of the '*o*'s and the sweet succession of soft '*s*' sounds, makes it a most pleasurable line to read. The image of the bare fields softly touched with the 'rosy hue' of the setting sun captures perfectly the end of the day and the season's demise. There are countless such examples of brilliance to be found in Keats, the description of the night in 'Ode to a Nightingale' ('tender is the night,/ And haply the Queen-Moon is on her throne,/ Cluster'd around by all her starry Fays') being just one more. Studying Keats gave me many reasons to appreciate him and just as many to go on appreciating him.

MICHAEL LONGLEY

Write an essay saying why you like or do not like the poetry of Michael Longley.

When I was first introduced to Longley's poetry I found it quite off-putting because of the extreme violence it contained. I am not the type of person who enjoys horror movies or action films so I wasn't taken with poems such as 'Wounds', which depicts a man getting gunned down in front of his family 'Before they could turn the television down / Or tidy away the supper dishes'. However, as I read over the poems in class, I grew to like them more. Longley's war poems may be violent but they do not glorify violence or depict violence for its own sake. I like the way his work unflinchingly faces up to reality and depicts man's inhumanity to man. I also felt that his poems performed an important task in remembering the victims of forgotten conflicts. I also enjoyed the way the poems show how violence simply begets more violence in an evermore bitter cycle – surely a lesson worth taking from any writer! Yet it is also important to note that Longley's war poetry is not all 'doom and gloom'. His poems suggest that reconciliation is possible, that peace can break through the cycles of violence.

Perhaps the most unflinching portrayal of violence in Longley's work is to be found in 'Wreaths'. The depiction of violence in this poem is so effective because it is so simple. Longley uses a flat conversational tone to tell us what happened, unburdened by metaphor or poetic language: 'He was preparing an Ulster fry for breakfast / When someone walked in and shot him'. The murder of the greengrocer, too, is recounted with brutal simplicity: 'he died / Serving even the death-dealers'. In 'Wounds', the murder of the bus conductor is also described in an almost shockingly casual tone. The bus conductor, we're told, is murdered by a 'shivering boy' who simply 'wandered in'. 'Self-heal', though it is not strictly speaking a war poem, also contains a brutally effective depiction of violence. The boy's punishment for putting his hand between the girl's legs is a terrible one. He is 'tethered' in a hayfield for a week and 'flogged with a blackthorn' everyday. The power of Longley's depiction of violence comes from the fact that he doesn't beat around the bush or mince his words. His plainspoken war poems tell it like it is, facing up to these brutal acts in all their evil.

A powerful aspect of Longley's poetry is the way it remembers the victims of armed conflicts. The title 'Wreaths', therefore, is particularly appropriate. Longley's war poems are like wreaths at a funeral ceremony, tokens of remembrance for those who have departed. 'Wreaths' goes out of its way to provide details about the victims of the Troubles. The civil servant, we're told, was well read and could play the piano. The greengrocer ran 'a good shop' and the linen workers are remembered by the personal items that fall from their pockets: 'Wallets, small change, dentures'. The victims of the First World War, too, are remembered. Longley remembers the bravery of the 'Ulster Division at the Somme' who were 'wilder than Gurkhas' in battle. Longley's poems are an attempt to restore some dignity to these long dead soldiers, much as the 'London-Scottish padre' did when he resettled the kilts of the dead soldiers so that their buttocks would not be exposed in death. The victims of violence, Longley's work reminds us, are not just statistics but individuals.

The victim of violence who Longley commemorates most of all is his own father. Though Longley's father did not die in battle, he endured some horrific experiences. 'Last Requests', for instance, details how Longley's father was almost 'buried alive' in a crater with an 'unexploded shell'. These experiences clearly left the father psychologically damaged. Longley describes how his father walked 'Over a landscape of dead buttocks' for forty years. The lead left in his body from bullet wounds also contributed to the cancer that finally killed him fifty years after the war had ended: 'lead traces flaring till they hurt'. It is unsurprising, therefore, that Longley commemorates his father as if he were a victim of war. In 'Wounds' he imagines himself burying murdered British soldiers in the grave beside his father's. In 'Wreaths' he imagines burying his father 'once again' with the paraphernalia from the murdered linen workers. Finally, in 'Last Requests', the poet longs to give his dying father a Woodbine cigarette, 'the last request / of many soldiers in your company'.

By linking his father's experiences in the First World War to the contemporary troubles in Northern Ireland, Longley seems to suggest that both of these very different conflicts have the same root cause: man's inhumanity to man. His poems seem to argue that an instinct for violence is and always has been at the heart of man. The sectarian slogans shouted at the Somme by the Ulster Regiment stem from the same bitter instincts that lead to the murder of the linen workers in contemporary Northern Ireland. 'Self-heal', also, shows how violence always seems to beget more violence. The boy responds to his brutal punishment by stoning a ram to death.

Yet Longley's work is not entirely pessimistic. It also suggests that there might be a 'way out' of these cycles of violence. In 'Ceasefire', for instance, he shows how Achilles and Priam, two deadly foes, share a moment of peace: 'When they had eaten together, it pleased them both / To stare at each other's beauty'. Yet peace often comes at a terrible price. Like Priam with Achilles, we must be prepared to do the unthinkable and forgive our worst enemies as well as asking them for forgiveness: 'I get down on my knees and do what must be done / And kiss Achilles' hand, the killer of my son'. Perhaps my greatest reason for liking Longley's poetry, then, is that he is ultimately a poet not only of hope but of a brutally realistic hope that takes into account the violent impulses at the heart of human nature.

DEREK WALCOTT

Write a personal response to the poetry of Derek Walcott.

Of all the poets on the Leaving Cert course, Derek Walcott, in my opinion, is the one who has most to say about the 'big issues', about life, the universe and everything. I would recommend his poetry to anyone who has lost someone close to them, or to anyone who finds themselves wondering about man's place in the universe. There are three aspects of Walcott's work in particular that appeal to me: his approach to the notion of endings, his poems about lost love, and his poems about bereavement. I'm not saying that Derek Walcott has the answers to all the questions that surround these issues; just that he asks them in a very beautiful and enlightening way.

One aspect of Walcott's poetry that really hit home with me was his focus on the way everything in this world is moving slowly but surely toward its end. 'Endings', for instance, depicts how things 'do not explode, / they fail, they fade'. Everything, the poem maintains, is disappearing, but too quietly for us to notice. Things fade away as gently and subtly 'as the sunlight fades from the flesh / as the foam drains quick in the sand'. We no more notice most things disappearing than we do the water draining into the sand at the beach. 'For Adrian' makes a similar point. In that poem, Adrian's spirit attempts to point out to his family that even the most sturdy objects that surround us are being slowly eroded: 'Look, and you will see that the furniture is fading, / that a wardrobe is as unsubstantial as a sunset'. Our bodies, too, are dissolving. They are so fragile that to Adrian they are almost transparent: 'I can see through you, the tissue of your leaves, / the light behind your veins'. Because Adrian has passed on, he has gained an awareness of the way in which everything is slowly fading away. As Walcott so memorably puts it, he has 'entered a wisdom, not a silence'. For those of us still alive it is more difficult to have this awareness. Yet reading the poetry of Derek Walcott is one way to be reminded of the fragility and preciousness of all things. His work reminds us to enjoy what we have while it lasts.

For me, one of the finest aspects of Walcott's work is his depiction of lost love. I was particularly taken with 'Summer Elegies'. This poem movingly describes a loving relationship between the poet and Cynthia, his former partner. The poem is almost erotic in its depiction of the poet undressing this beautiful woman: 'her unhooked halter slithered / from sunburnt shoulders'.

I also liked the humour in Walcott's description of the dove that 'gurgled astonished Ooos' while it watched the couple's lovemaking. I also enjoyed the depiction of romance in 'To Norline', where the poet remembers the nights he spent lying beside this woman he once loved. As Walcott so memorably puts it: 'a coffee mug warming his palm / as my body once cupped yours'.

Yet what most struck me about Walcott's love poetry is that it is almost always a depiction of lost love. Cynthia from 'Summer Elegies' is no longer with the poet. He is now alone on the beach where they once made the 'changing shapes of love'. To the poet, the world seems emptier now that she has departed: 'All the beach chairs are full / but the beach is emptier'.

'To Norline', too, is filled with a melancholy longing for a love that has been and will never be again, for this woman the poet's body 'once cupped'. The poem paints a sad portrait of the poet walking along an empty beach remembering his lost love. He seems certain that 'someone else' instead of him will soon be enjoying Norline's affections. Walcott's poetry, then, is keenly aware of the fact that love inevitably fades away. As he puts it in 'Endings', 'love's lightning flash/ has no thunderous end'. Love, like everything else, fades away quietly, without us even noticing: 'it dies with the sound / of flowers fading'. We can no more notice love fading away than we can hear a flower withering. All in all, then, I would recommend the poetry of Derek Walcott to anyone who has had their 'heart broken'. This is writing that would provide real solace and comfort for anyone whose relationship has just ended.

Bereavement is one of Walcott's most recurring themes and he deals with it magnificently. I like the way Walcott does not flinch from portraying the true horror of bereavement. In 'For Adrian', for instance, Adrian's family are depicted howling like statues as they mourn the death of this little boy. Adrian's sister Gem is depicted 'sitting in a corner of her pain'. Even more moving is the depiction of loss in 'The Young Wife'. This poem is about a man whose wife has just died from cancer. He must mourn her quietly so as not to upset their children: 'the muffled sobbing / the children must not hear'. The house he lives in is haunted by memories of his departed partner. There are certain drawers in the house which he 'dare not open' because the objects they contain would remind him too painfully of her.

Yet Walcott's poems about death also contain hope. In 'For Adrian' the spirit or soul of the little boy continues to exist after death. His spirit, the poem suggests, has become one with the universe: 'I am part of the muscle / of a galloping lion, or a bird keeping low over /dark canes'. Adrian's spirit is not gone but has become part of the plants, birds and animals of the natural world. 'The Young Wife', too, contains a ray of hope. The wife may have been claimed by cancer at a tragically young age but she somehow lives on in her children. When her husband sees their children laugh, he is reminded so strongly of her that she may as well be in the room: 'They startle you when they laugh. / She sits there smiling'.

'A Letter from Brooklyn' is another poem that offers hope to the bereaved. Mabel Rawlins, a friend of the family, writes to the poet about his dead father. She is convinced that this man, who died twenty-eight years ago, is at God's side in Heaven: 'he was called home, / And is, I am sure, doing greater work'. Mabel's unquestioning faith helps to overcome the poet's own doubts about the existence of God, and 'restores' his belief in an afterlife: 'I believe. / I believe it all, and for no man's death I grieve'. Just as I would recommend Walcott's poetry to anyone who has had their heart broken, so too I would recommend it to anyone who has been bereaved. Walcott's poetry presents us with a full picture of the sorrow and pain of bereavement. Yet it also suggests that maybe, just maybe, there is hope.

W.B. YEATS

Why I like or do not like the poetry of W.B. Yeats

There are two main reasons why the poetry of W.B. Yeats never appealed to me on a personal level: his focus on old age and his negative view of ordinary Irish. In this essay, I will discuss each of these reasons for disliking this poet's work.

Yeats' poetry is overwhelmingly concerned with old age and with the process of ageing. We see this in 'The Wild Swans at Coole' where the poet contemplates the swans floating upon the lake in Coole Park:

Upon the brimming water among the stones
Are nine and fifty swans

To the poet, it seems as if the swans have not aged or changed in the nineteen years since he first visited this place. They seem 'Unwearied still'. As he gazes at these seemingly unchanging creatures, he is struck by the fact that he has aged himself, that he no longer walks with the 'lighter tread' of youth.

It could be argued that a similar moment of realisation occurs in 'Politics', where the poet is mesmerised by the sight of a beautiful girl who is standing there. The poet wishes he could somehow be young again so that he could be this woman's lover: 'O that I were young again / And held her in my arms'. A similar point is made in 'Sailing to Byzantium' where the old poet laments the fact that he has become excluded from the joys of love and sex. The world of physical passion and joyous reproduction is, he declares, 'no country for old men'.

'Sailing to Byzantium' also depicts the physical decay that accompanies old age. The aged poet describes himself as a 'paltry thing / A tattered coat upon a stick'. A similar note is struck by the poem 'In Memory of Eva Gore-Booth and Con Markiewicz' which laments the fact that old age has transformed the Gore-Booth sisters. They are no longer 'two girls in silk kimonos, both / beautiful one a gazelle' but have become worn and withered with the passing years. They end up 'withered old and skeleton gaunt'. 'An Acre of Grass' also deals with ageing and physical decline as the poet mourns the fact that his 'strength of body goes' as he approaches 'life's end'.

It is fair to say then that in poem after poem, Yeats tackles the regrets and difficulties of growing older. I am sure his portrayal of these issues is accurate, and that many people, especially older people, will find these poems moving. To me, however, this relentless focus on old age is more or less totally irrelevant and even a little depressing. Like most seventeen-year-olds, I do not obsess about my decaying 'with every tatter in its mortal dress'. The regretful realisation of an old man that he is no longer attractive to young women is something I have great difficulty connecting with. Yeats may feel nostalgic because the 'nineteenth autumn has come upon' him since he first visited Coole Park. But I haven't experienced 'nineteen autumns' in my whole life! I think, therefore, that I will be forgiven if I say that this aspect of Yeats' poetry leaves me cold and uninterested. Perhaps my opinion of these poems will change when I myself am older.

Another aspect of Yeats' poetry I dislike his is snobbish contempt for what might be described as the plain and ordinary people of Ireland. We see this in 'Under Ben Bulben' where he longs for an Ireland that resembles a medieval fantasy more than a modern twentieth-century nation:

Sing the peasantry and then
Hard riding country gentlemen
The holiness of monks and after
Porter drinkers randy laughter

Yeats wants Ireland to be a country run by landlords who reside in mansions like Lissadell, as described in 'In Memory of Eva Gore-Booth and Con Markiewicz'. These gentlemen – presumably from Yeats' own protestant Ascendancy class – would ride thorough the fields supervising the jolly peasants working there. This, it seems, is the romantic Ireland whose loss Yeats laments in 'September 1913'. I wonder, however, if such an Ireland ever really existed or if it is just a Yeatsian fantasy.

There is no place in Yeats' fantasy Ireland for 'normal' modern people who work in shops and businesses. These are the 'sort now growing up / All out of shape from toe to top' and must be treated with contempt.

A similar contempt for ordinary people is evident in 'September 1913' where Yeats absolutely cuts loose in a vitriolic attack on the middle-class Catholics of

Dublin. These middle-class people have lost their way. He depicts them as mean and tight-fisted bigots who 'fumble in a greasy till' for a few pennies. He also criticises their religious devotion, which he regards as somewhat hypocritical and superficial. The Catholic middle classes, he declares, pray more out of fear than genuine spiritual devotion. They add 'prayer to shivering prayer'.

Yet we might ask if Yeats' venomous attack is really merited. The people he attacks are ordinary businessman and shopkeepers trying to make their way in the world. Their only 'crime' was to refuse to sponsor Yeats' pet project, a gallery for the paintings donated to the state by Hugh Lane. A similar contempt for the ordinary people of Ireland is evident in 'Easter 1916' where Yeats can barely hide his scorn for the ordinary workers who organised and led the Rising. For years he mocked these patriots, regarding them as foolish and confused:

And thought before I had done
Of a mocking tale or a gibe
To please a companion
Around the fire at a club

This image, of Yeats and his well-heeled companions snickering at Patrick Pearse behind his back, is one that really turns me off his work. There is a real sense here that Yeats looks down on these patriots because they are from a lower social class than him. They come from the same Catholic middle class he attacked in 'September 1913', with their offices and shops and 'grey / Eighteenth century houses'. They are not the Protestant 'Lords and Ladies gay' from whom Yeats would expect heroism. It must be admitted, however, that at least Yeats has the grace to change his mind about the 1916 leaders. He comes to accept that they have been 'transformed utterly' by their heroic revolt.

In conclusion, I hope that I have demonstrated my dislike for the poetry of Yeats, while a personal response to the poems I've studied is reasonable and logical. I believe it is difficult – if not impossible – for someone of my age and background to love the work of this arrogant, death-obsessed poet.